A Journey Through the Kingdom of Oude

Copyright © 2008 BiblioBazaar
All rights reserved

Original copyright: 1858

WILLIAM SLEEMAN
Resident at the Court of Lucknow

A Journey Through the Kingdom of Oude

IN 1849-1850

BY DIRECTION OF THE RIGHT HON.
THE EARL OF DALHOUSIE,
GOVERNOR-GENERAL.

WITH PRIVATE CORRESPONDENCE
RELATIVE TO THE ANNEXATION OF
OUDE TO BRITISH INDIA, &C.

IN TWO VOLUMES

A Journey Through the Kingdom of Oude

CONTENTS

VOLUME I

PREFACE	11
BIOGRAPHICAL SKETCH OF MAJOR-GENERAL SIR W. H. SLEEMAN. K.C.B.	13
INTRODUCTION.	19
PRIVATE CORRESPONDENCE	24

DIARY OF A TOUR THROUGH OUDE

CHAPTER I.	81
CHAPTER II.	119
CHAPTER III.	180
CHAPTER IV.	223
CHAPTER V.	262
CHAPTER VI.	307

VOLUME II

DIARY A TOUR THROUGH OUDE

CHAPTER I.	361
CHAPTER II.	399
CHAPTER III.	433
CHAPTER IV.	483

CHAPTER V.	535
CHAPTER VI.	600
PRIVATE CORRESPONDENCE	633

VOLUME I

PREFACE

My object in writing this DIARY OF A TOUR THROUGH OUDE was to prepare, for submission to the Government of India, as fair and full a picture of the real state of the country, condition, and feeling of the people of all classes, and character of the Government under which they at present live, as the opportunities which the tour afforded me might enable me to draw.

The DIARY must, for the present, be considered as an official document, which may be perused, but cannot be published, wholly or in part, without the sanction of Government previously obtained.*

Lucknow, 1852.

* This permission was accorded by the Honourable Court of Directors in December last.

BIOGRAPHICAL SKETCH OF
MAJOR-GENERAL SIR W. H. SLEEMAN. K.C.B.

This distinguished officer, whose career in India extended over a period of forty years, and whose services were highly appreciated by three Governors-General—Viscount Hardinge, the Earl of Ellenborough, and the Marquess of Dalhousie—evinced by their appointing him to the most difficult and delicate duties—was the son of Philip and Mary Sleeman, and was born at Stratton, Cornwall, 8th August, 1788. In early years he evinced a predilection for the military profession; and at the age of twenty-one (October, 1809), through the good offices of the late Lord De Dunstanville, he was appointed an Infantry Cadet in the Bengal army. Thither he proceeded as soon as possible, and was promoted successively to the rank of Ensign, 23rd September, 1810; Lieutenant, 16th December, 1814; Brevet-Captain, 24th April, 1824; Captain, 23rd September, 1826; Major, 1st February, 1837; Lieutenant-Colonel, 26th May, 1843; Colonel, 24th November, 1853; and obtained the rank of Major-General 28th November, 1854.

Early in his career he served in the Nepaulese war. The value of his talents soon became known, and in 1816, when it was considered necessary to investigate a claim to property as prize-money arising out of that war, Lieutenant Sleeman was selected to inquire into it. The report was accordingly made by him in February 1817, which was designated by the Government as "able, impartial, and satisfactory."

In 1820 he was appointed junior Assistant to the Agent of the Governor-General at Saugur, and remained in the Civil Department in the Saugur and Nerbudda territories, with the exception of absence on sick certificate, for nearly a quarter of a century. Here he manifested that, if he had been efficient in an inferior position, he was also an able administrator in a superior post. He distinguished himself so much by his activity in the suppression of the horrible practice of Thuggism, then so prevalent, that, in 1835, he was employed exclusively in the Thuggee Department; his appointment in the Saugur and Nerbudda districts being kept open, and his promotion going on. The very valuable Papers upon Thuggism submitted to the Governor-General were chiefly drawn up by Sir William Sleeman, and the department specially commissioned for this important purpose was not only organised but worked by him. In consequence of ill-health, however, at the end of 1836, he was compelled to resign this appointment; but on his return to duty in February 1839, he was nominated to the combined offices of Commissioner for the Suppression of Thuggee and Dacoity.

In 1842 he was employed on a special mission in Bundelcund, to inquire into the causes of the recent disturbances there, and he remained in that district, with additional duties, as Resident at Gwalior, from 1844 until 1849, when he was removed to the highly important office of Resident at the Court of Lucknow. Colonel Sleeman held his office at Gwalior in very critical times, which resulted in hostilities and the battle of Maharajpore. But for a noble and unselfish act he would have received this promotion at an earlier period. The circumstance was this: Colonel Low, the Resident at that time, hearing that his father was dangerously ill, tendered his resignation to Lord Auckland, who immediately offered the appointment to Colonel Sleeman. No sooner had this occurred, however, than Colonel Low wrote to his Lordship that, since he had resigned, the house of Gaunter and Co., of Calcutta, in which his brother was a partner, had failed, and, in consequence, every farthing he had saved had been swept away. Under this painful contingency be begged to place himself in his Lordship's hands. This letter was sent by Lord Auckland to Colonel Sleeman, who immediately wrote to Colonel Low, begging that he would retain his situation at Lucknow. This generous conduct of

Colonel Sleeman was duly appreciated; and Lord Auckland, on leaving India, recommended him to the particular notice of his successor. Lord Ellenborough, who immediately appointed Colonel Sleeman to Jhansi with an additional 1000*l.* a-year to his income.

Colonel Sleeman held the appointment of Resident at Lucknow from the year 1849 until 1856. During this period his letters and diary show his unwearied efforts to arrive at the best information on all points with regard to Oude. These will enable the reader to form a just, opinion on the highly-important subject of the annexation of this kingdom to British India. The statements of Colonel Sleeman bear inward evidence of his great administrative talents, his high and honourable character, and of his unceasing endeavours to promote the best interests of the King of Oude, so that his kingdom might have been preserved to him. Colonel Sleeman's views were directly opposed to annexation, as his letters clearly show.

His long and arduous career was now, however, fast drawing to a close. So early as the summer of 1854 it became evident that the health of General Sleeman was breaking up, and in the August of that year he was attacked by alarming illness. "Forty-six years of incessant labour," observes a writer at this date, "have had their influence even on his powerful frame: he has received one of those terrible warnings believed to indicate the approach of paralysis. With General Sleeman will depart the last hope of any improvement in the condition of the unhappy country of Oude. Though belonging to the elder class of Indian officials, he has never been Hindooized. He fully appreciated the evils of a native throne: he has sternly, and even haughtily, pointed out to the King the miseries caused by his incapacity, and has frequently extorted from his fears the mercy which it was vain to hope from his humanity."

Later in the year. General Sleeman went to the hills, in the hope of recruiting his wasted health by change of air and scene; but the expectation proved vain, and he was compelled to take passage for England. But it was now too late: notwithstanding the best medical aid, he gradually sank, and, after a long illness, died on his passage from Calcutta, on the 10th February, 1856, at the age of sixty-seven.

His Indian career was, indeed, long and honourable his labours most meritorious. He was one of those superior men which the Indian service is constantly producing, who have rendered the name of Englishman respected throughout the vast empire of British India, and whose memory will endure so long as British power shall remain in the East.

It is well known that Lord Dalhousie, on his relinquishing the Indian Government, recommended General Sleeman and two other distinguished officers in civil employment for some mark of the royal favour, and he was accordingly nominated K.C.B., 4th February, 1856; of which honour his Lordship apprised him in a highly gratifying letter.

But, however high the reputation of an officer placed in such circumstances—and none stood higher than Sir William Sleeman, not only in the estimation of the Governor-General and the Honourable Company, but also in the opinion of the inhabitants of India, where he had served with great ability for forty years, and won the respect and love particularly of the natives, who always regarded him as their friend, and by whom his equity was profoundly appreciated—it was to be anticipated, as a matter of course, that his words and actions would be distorted and misrepresented by a Court so atrociously infamous. This, no doubt, he was prepared to expect, The King, or rather the creatures who surrounded him, would at all cost endeavour to prevent any investigation into their gross malpractices, and seek to slander the man they were unable to remove.

The annexation of Oude to the British dominions followed, but not as a consequence of Sir W. Sleeman's report. No greater injustice can be done than to assert that he advised such a course. His letters prove exactly the reverse. He distinctly states, in his correspondence with the Governor-General, Lord Dalhousie, that the annexation of Oude would cost the British power more than the value of ten such kingdoms, and would inevitably lead to a mutiny of the Sepoys. He constantly maintains the advisability of frontier kingdoms under native sovereigns, that the people themselves might observe the contrast, to the advantage of the Honourable Company, of the wise and equitable administration of its rule compared with the oppressive and cruel despotism of their own princes. Sir William Sleeman had profoundly studied the Indian character in its different races, and was deservedly much beloved by them for his earnest desire to promote their welfare, and for the effectual manner in which, on all occasions in his power, and these were frequent, he redressed the evils complained of, and extended the *Ægis* of British power over the afflicted and oppressed.

INTRODUCTION.

THE following Narrative of a "Pilgrimage" through the kingdom of Oude was written by the late Major-General Sir William Sleeman in 1851 (while a Resident at the Court of Lucknow), at the request of the Governor-General the Marquess of Dalhousie, in order to acquaint the Honourable Company with the actual condition of that kingdom, and with the view of pointing out the best measures to be suggested to the King for the improvement and amelioration of the country and people.

So early as October, 1847, the King of Oude had been informed by the Governor-General, that if his system of rule were not materially amended (for it was disgraceful and dangerous to any neighbouring power to permit its continuance in its present condition) before two years had expired, the British Government would find it necessary to take steps for such purpose in his name. Accordingly on the 16th September, 1848, the Governor-General addressed the following letter to Sir William Sleeman, commissioning him to make a personal visit to all parts of the kingdom:—

"*Government House, Sept.* 16, 1848.

"MY DEAR COLONEL SLEEMAN,—It was a matter of regret to me that I had not anticipated your desire to succeed Colonel Sutherland in Rajpootana before I made arrangements which prevented my offering that appointment to you. I now regret it no longer, since the course of events has put it in my power to propose an arrangement which will, I apprehend, be more agreeable to you, and which will make your services more *actively* beneficial to the State.

"Colonel Richmond has intimated his intention of immediately resigning the Residency at Lucknow. The communication made by the Governor-General to the King of Oude, in October, 1847, gave His Majesty to understand that if the condition of Government was not very materially amended before two years had expired, the management for his behoof would be taken into the hands of the British Government.

"There seems little reason to expect or to hope that in October, 1849, any amendment whatever will have been effected. The reconstruction of the internal administration of a great, rich, and oppressed country, is a noble as well as an arduous task for the officer to whom the duty is intrusted, and the Government have recourse to one of the best of its servants for that purpose.

"The high reputation you have earned, your experience of civil administration, your knowledge of the people, and the qualifications you possess as a public man, have led me to submit your name to the Council of India as an officer to whom I could commit this important charge with entire confidence that its duties would be well performed. I do myself, therefore, the honour of proposing to you to accept the office of Resident at Lucknow, with especial reference to the great changes which, in all probability, will take place. Retaining your superintendency of Thuggee affairs, it will be manifestly necessary that you should be relieved from the duty of the trials of Thugs usually condemned at Lucknow.

"In the hope that you will not withhold from the Government your services in the capacity I have named, and in the further hope of finding an opportunity of personally making your acquaintance,

> "I have the honour to be,
> "Dear Colonel Sleeman,
> "Very faithfully yours,
> "DALHOUSIE."

"To Colonel Sleeman, &c., &c."

Immediately on receipt of this despatch, Sir William proceeded to make the necessary inquiry. Doubtless the King (instigated by his Ministers and favourites, who dreaded the exposure of all their infamous proceedings) would have prevented this investigation, which, he was aware, would furnish evidence of gross mal-administration, cruelty, and oppression almost unparalleled; but Sir William Sleeman was too well acquainted with the character of the people of the East to be moved either by cajolery or menaces from the important duty which had devolved upon him.

Sir William Sleeman's position as Resident enabled him to ascertain thoroughly the real state of Oude; and the great respect with which he was universally received manifests the high opinion entertained of him personally by all ranks. The details he has given of the prevailing anarchy and lawlessness throughout the kingdom, would scarcely be believed were they not vouched for by an officer of established reputation and integrity. Firmness united to amenity of manner were indeed the characteristics of Sir William in his important and delicate office at such a Court—a Court where the King, deputing the conduct of business to Ministers influenced by the basest motives, and who constantly sacrificed justice to bribery and low intrigues, gave himself up to the effeminate indulgence of his harem, and the society of eunuchs and fiddlers. His Majesty appears to have been governed by favourites of the hour selected through utter caprice, and to have permitted, if he did not order, such atrocious cruelties and oppression as rendered the kingdom of Oude a disgrace to the British rule in India, and called for strong interference, on the score of humanity alone, as well as with the hope of compelling amendment.

The letter addressed by Lord Dalhousie to Sir William Sleeman expresses the desire of the Governor-General that he should endeavour to inform himself of the actual state of Oude, and render his Narrative a guide to the Honourable Company in its Report to the Court of Directors. The details furnish but too faithful a picture of the miserable condition of the people, equally oppressed by the exactions of the King's army and collectors, and by the gangs of robbers and lawless chieftains who infest the whole territory, rendering tenure so doubtful that no good dwellings could be erected, and land only partially cultivated; whilst the numberless cruelties and atrocious murders surpass belief. Shut up in his harem, the voice of justice seldom reached the ear of the monarch, and when it did, was scarcely heeded. The Resident, it will be seen, was beset during his journey with petitions for redress so numerous, that, anxious as he was to do everything in his power to mitigate the horrors he witnessed, he frequently gives vent to the pain he experienced at finding relief impracticable.

The Narrative contains an unvarnished but unexaggerated picture of the actual state of Oude, with many remedial suggestions; but direct annexation formed no part of the policy which Sir William Sleeman recommended. To this measure he was strenuously opposed, as is distinctly proved by his letters appended to the Journal. At the same time, he repeatedly affirms the total unfitness of the King to govern. These opinions are still further corroborated by the following letter from his private correspondence, 1854-5, written when Resident at Lucknow, and published in the *Times* in November last:—

> "The system of annexation, pursued by a party in this country, and favoured by Lord Dalhousie and his Council, has, in my opinion, and in that of a large number of the ablest men in India, a downward tendency—a tendency to crush all the higher and middle classes connected with the land. These classes it should be our object to create and foster, that we might in the end inspire them with a feeling of interest in the stability of our rule. *We shall find a few years hence the tables turned against us.* In fact, the aggressive and absorbing policy, which has done so much mischief of late in India, is beginning to create feelings of alarm in the native mind; and it is when the popular mind becomes agitated by such alarms that fanatics will always be found ready to step into Paradise over the bodies of the most prominent of those from whom injury is

apprehended. I shall have nothing new to do at Lucknow. Lord Dalhousie and I have different views, I fear. If he wishes anything done that I do not think right and honest, I resign, and leave it to be done by others. I desire a strict adherence to solemn engagements, whether made with white faces or black. We have no right to annex or confiscate Oude; but we have a right, under the treaty of 1837, to take the management of it, but not to appropriate its revenues to ourselves. We can do this with honour to our Government and benefit to the people. To confiscate would be dishonest and dishonourable. To annex would be to give the people a government almost as bad as their own, if we put our screw upon them. My position here has been and is disagreeable and unsatisfactory: we have a fool of a king, a knave of a minister, and both are under the influence of one of the cleverest, most intriguing, and most unscrupulous villains in India."

Major Bird, in his pamphlet "Dacoitee in Excelsis," while endeavouring to establish a case for the King of Oude, has assumed that Sir William Sleeman was an instrument in the hands of Lord Dalhousie, to carry out his purpose of annexing Oude to British India. The letters, now first printed, entirely refute this hasty and erroneous statement. Major Bird has, in fact, withdrawn it himself in a lecture delivered by him at Southampton on Tuesday, the 16th of February, 1858.

It will be seen that Sir W. Sleeman's "Diary" commences on December 1, 1849. To preserve chronological order, the letters written before that date are prefixed; those which refer to a later period are added at the end of the narrative.

PRIVATE CORRESPONDENCE

PRECEDING THE JOURNEY THROUGH THE KINGDOM OF OUDE.

Camp, 20th February, 1848.

My Dear Sir,

I thank you for your letter of the 10th instant, and am of opinion that you may be able to make good use of Bhurut Sing under judicious management, and strict surveillance; but you do not mention who and what he is—whether he is a prisoner under sentence, or a free agent, or of what caste and profession. Some men make these offers in order to have opportunities of escape, while engaged in the pretended search after associates in crime; others to extort money from those whom they may denounce, or have the authority and means to arrest. He should be made to state distinctly the evidence he has against persons, and the way he got it; and all should be recorded against the names of the persons in a Register. Major Riddell is well acquainted with our mode of proceedings in all such cases, and I recommend you to put yourself in communication, as soon as possible, with him, and Mr. Dampier, the Superintendent of Police, who fortunately takes the greatest possible interest in all such matters. I have no supervision whatever over the officers of the department employed in Bengal; all rests entirely with Mr. Dampier. You might write to him at once, and tell him that you are preparing such a Register as I suggest; and if he is satisfied with the evidence, he will authorise the arrest of all or part, and well reward Bhurut Sing for his services.

Believe me, my dear Sir,
With best wishes for your success,
Yours sincerely,
(Signed) W. H. SLEEMAN.

To Capt. J. Innes,
Barrackpoor.

* * * * *

Camp, 20th February, 1848.
My Dear Colonel Sutherland,

There are at Jubulpore a good many of the Bagree decoits, who have been sentenced as approvers, by the Courts of Punchaet, in Rajpootana, to imprisonment for very short periods. Unless they are ordered to be retained when these periods expire, on a requisition of security for their future good behaviour, they will make off, and assuredly return to their hereditary trade. The ordinary pay of the grades open to them in our police and other establishments, will not satisfy them when they find that we have no hold upon them, and they become more and more troublesome as the time for their enlargement approaches.

I send you copies of the letters from Government of the 27th June, 1839, from which you will see that it was intended that all professional decoits who gave us their services on a promise of conditional pardon, should have a sentence of imprisonment for life recorded against them, the execution of which was to be suspended during their good behaviour, and eventually altogether remitted in cases where they might be deemed to have merited, by a course of true and faithful services, such an indulgence. In all other parts, as well as in our own provinces as in native states, such sentences, have been recorded against these men, and they have cheerfully submitted to them, under the assurance that they and their children would be provided with the means of earning an honest livelihood; but in Rajpootana it has been otherwise.

By Act 24, of 1843, all such professional gang-robbers are declared liable to a sentence, on conviction, of imprisonment for life; and everywhere else a sentence of imprisonment for life has been passed upon all persons convicted of being gang-robbers by profession. This is indispensably necessary for the entire suppression of the system which Government has in view. Do you not think that in your Courts the final sentence might be left to the European functionaries, and the verdict only left to the Punchaets? The greater part of those already convicted in these Courts will have to be released soon, and all who are so will certainly return to their trade; and the system will continue in spite of all our efforts to put it down. I have just been at Jubulpore, and the bearing of the Bagree decoits, sent from Ajmeer by Buch, is quite different from that of those who have had a sentence of imprisonment for life passed against them in other quarters, and is very injurious to them, for they get so bad a name that no one will venture to give them service of any kind. Do, I pray you, think of a remedy for the future. The only one that strikes me is that above suggested, of leaving the final sentence to the European officers.

I need not say that I was delighted at your getting the great Douger Sing by the means you had yourself proposed for the pursuit—sending an officer with authority to disregard boundaries.

Yours sincerely,
(Signed) W. S. SLEEMAN
To Col. Sutherland.

* * * * *

Jhansee, 4th March, 1848.

My Lord,

I had the gratification to receive your Lordship's letter of the 7th of January last, at Nursingpore, in the valley of the Nerbudda, where I commenced my Civil career more than a quarter of a century before, and where, of all places, I should have wished to receive so gracious a testimonial from such high authority. I should have earlier expressed by grateful acknowledgments, and prepared the narrative so frequently called for, but I was then engaged in preparing a Report on Gang-robbery in India, and wished first to make a little more progress, that I might be able to speak more confidently of its ultimate completion and submission to Government. In a less perfect form this Report was, at the earnest recommendation of the then Lieut.-Governor N.W.P., the Honourable T. Robertson, and with the sanction of the Governor-General Lord Auckland, sent to the Government press so long back as 1842, but his Lordship appeared to me to think that the printing had better be deferred till more progress had been made in the work of putting down the odious system of crime which the Report exposed, and I withdrew it from the press with little hope of ever again having any leisure to devote to it, or finding any other person able and willing to undertake its completion.

During the last rains, however, I began again to arrange the confused mass of papers which I found lying in a box; but in October I was interrupted by a severe attack of fever, and unable to do anything but the current duties of my office till I commenced my tour through the Saugor territories, in November. I have since nearly completed the work, and hope to be able to submit it to Government before the end of this month in a form worthy of its acceptation.

I am afraid that the narrative of my humble services will be found much longer than it ought to be, but I have written it hastily that it might go by this mail, and it is the first attempt I have ever thought of making at such a narrative, for I have gone on quietly "through evil and through good report," doing, to the best of my ability, the duties which it has pleased the Government of India, from time to time, to confide to me, in the manner which appeared to me most conformable to its wishes and its honour, satisfied and grateful for the trust and confidence which enabled me to do so much good for the people, and to secure so much of their attachment and gratitude to their rulers.

Permit me to subscribe myself, with great respect,

Your Lordship's faithful and obedient humble servant,

(Signed) W. H. SLEEMAN.

To Lieut.-General the Right Hon.
Henry Viscount Hardinge,
&c. &c. &c.

* * * * *

Jhansee, 4th March, 1848.

Dear Sir,

Lord Hardinge, in a letter dated the 7th of January last, requested me to make out a narrative of my humble services in India, and to send it under cover to you, as he expected to embark on the 15th, before he could receive it in Calcutta. I take the liberty to send my reply with the narrative, open, and to request that you will do me the favour to have them sealed and forwarded to his Lordship.

Believe me, dear Sir,
Yours very faithfully,
(Signed) W. H. SLEEMAN.

To J. Cosmo Melvill,
Secretary to the East India Company,
India House, London.

* * * * *

Jhansee, 28th March, 1848.

My Dear Elliot,

The Court of Directors complain that decoit prisoners are not tried as soon as they are caught, but they know little of the difficulties that the officers under me find in getting them tried, for political officers have, in truth, had little encouragement to undertake such duties, and it is only a few choice spirits that have entered upon the duty *con amore*. General Nott prided, himself upon doing nothing whatever while he was at Lucknow; General Pollock did all he could, but it was not much; and Colonel Richmond does nothing. There the Buduk decoits, Thugs, and poisoners, remain without sentences, and will do so till Richmond goes, unless you give him a fillip. If you tell him to apply for an assistant to aid him in the conduct of the trials, and tell him to nominate his own, he may go to work, and I earnestly pray you to do something, or the Oude Turae will become what it had for ages been before we cleaned it out. Davidson was prevented from doing anything by technical difficulties, so that out of *four Residents we have not got four days' work*.

You will soon get my Report, and it will be worth having, and the last I shall make on crime in India.

If Hercules had not had better instruments he could not so easily have cleared out his stable; but he had no "Honourable Court" to find fault with his mode of doing the thing, I conclude. The fact is, however, that our prisoners are pretty well tried before they get into quod. Mr. Bird will be delighted at the manner in which he is introduced in my first chapter, and many another good officer well pleased.

Yours sincerely,
(Signed) W. H. SLEEMAN.

To H. M. Elliot, Esq.,
Secretary to the Government of India, Calcutta.

* * * * *

Jhansee, 29th March, 1848.

My Dear Maddock,

I hope you will not disapprove of the resolution to which I have come of resigning the charge of the Saugor territories, now that tranquillity has been restored,—the best possible feelings among the people prevail, and the object you had in view in recommending Lord Ellenborough to confide that charge to me has been effected,—or of the manner in which I have tendered my resignation. Were I longer to retain the charge, I should be subjected to humiliations which the exigencies of the public service do not require that I should at this time of life submit to, and I shall have enough of labour and anxiety in the charge that will still remain to me. If an opening for Sir R. Shakespear could be found, his salary might be saved by my residence being transferred to Gwalior. If either Hamilton or I were to be removed to some other post, it would be well to reduce Gwalior and Indore to political agencies, under the supervision of an agent, as in Rajpootana, with Bundelcund added to his charge. The latter of these two measures has, you know, been under consideration, and was, I think, proposed by Sutherland when you were at Gwalior with Lord Auckland. Had the Lieutenant-Governor known more of the Saugor territories when he wrote the paper on which Government is now acting, he would not, I think, have described the state of things as he has done, or urged the introduction of the system which must end in minutely subdividing all leases, and in having all questions regarding land tenures removed into the civil Courts, as in the provinces. It is the old thing, "nothing like leather." I shall not weary you by anything more on this subject. I hope a good man will be selected for the charge. The selection of Mr. M. Smith as successor to Mr. Brown was a good one. My letter will go off to-day, and be, I trust, well received. I am grieved that Clerk has been obliged to quit his post; he has been throughout his career an ornament to your service, but his friends seem all along to have apprehended that he could not long stand the climate of Bombay. I am anxious to learn how long you are to remain in Council.

Yours very sincerely,
(Signed) W. H. SLEEMAN.

To the Hon. Sir T. H. Maddock,
&c. &c. &c.

* * * * *

Jhansee, 2nd April, 1848.
My dear Elliot,

Till I this morning got the public letter, which will go off to-day, I never heard one word about Shakespear's intention or wish to go to the hills, and only thirteen days remain. The orders of Government as to his *locum tenens* cannot reach me by the 15th, when he is to leave, and I shall have to put in some one to take charge, as there is a treasury under his management.

If Government wish to take Major Stevens from the Byza Bae, and give him some other employment, he might be sent to act for Captain Ross; but I know nothing of his fitness for such an office.

I believe you know Captain Ross, and I need say nothing more than what I have said in my public letter. If he be sent to Gwalior, I hope a good officer may be sent to act for him in Thalone, for the duties are very heavy and responsible. Blake will do very well, and so would his second in command, Captain Erskine, of the 73rd, who is an excellent civil officer. I must pray you to let me have the orders of Government on the subject as soon as possible.

Yours sincerely,
(Signed) W. H. SLEEMAN.

P.S.—I should consider Major Stevens an able man for a civil charge, but have never seen him.

(Signed) W. H. S.

To H. M. Elliot, Esq.,
&c. &c.

* * * * *

Jhansee, 6th May, 1848.

My Dear Maddock,

Your kind letter of the 21st ultimo had prepared me for the public one of the 28th, which I got yesterday from Elliot, and I wrote off at once, to say simply that I should be glad to suspend or to withdraw the application contained in my letter of the 29th of March, as might appear best to Government; and that I should not have made it at all, had I apprehended that a compliance with it would have been attended with any inconvenience.

With the knowledge I have acquired of the duties of the several officers, and the entire command of my time here at a quiet place, and long-established methodical habits, I can get through the work very well, though it becomes trying sometimes. Arrears I never allow to accumulate, and regular hours, and exercise, and sparing diet, with water beverage, keep me always in condition for office work. I often wish that you could have half the command of your hours, mode of living, and movements, that I have. However, they will soon be much more free than mine. I am very glad that you have the one year more for a wind up; and hope that good fortune will attend you to the last. You say nothing, however, about your foot. The papers and letters from home have just come in. I hear that Lord John is very unwell, and will not be able to stand the work many months more, and that Sir R. Peel is obliged to be *cupped* once a-week, and could not possibly take office. Who is to take helm in the troubled ocean, no one knows. I am glad that Metternich has been kicked out, for he and Louis Philippe are the men that have put in peril the peace and institutions of all Europe. I only wish that the middle class was as strong in France as it is in England; it is no doubt infinitely stronger than it was; while the lower order is better than that of England, I believe, for such occasions. They have good men now in the provisional Government—so they had in 1788; and, like them, the present men will probably be swept away by the mob. They are not, however, likely to be embarrassed by other nations, since the days of Pitt and George III. are passed away, and so are the feudal times when the barons could get up civil wars for their own selfish purposes. There are no characters sufficiently prominent to get up a civil war, but the enormous size of the army is enough to create feelings of disquiet. It is, however, officered from the middle classes, who have property at stake, and must be more or less interested in the preservation of order.

The Government has no money to send to Algiers, and must reduce its strength there, so that Egypt is in no danger at present; were it so, we should be called upon to defend it from India, and could well do so. It is evident that the whole French nation was alienated from Louis Philippe, and prepared to cast off him and all his family, though, as you say, I do not believe that there was anywhere any design to oust him and put down monarchy. Had he thrown off Guizot a little sooner, and left some able military leaders free to act, the *émeute* would have been put down; but those who could have acted did not feel free to do so: they did not feel sure of the king, while they were sure of the odium of the people. I am not at all sorry for the change. I am persuaded that it will work good for Europe; but still its peace and best institutions are in peril at present. We are in no danger here, because people do not understand such things; and because England is in a prouder position than ever, and will, I trust, retain it.

Lord Grey seems an able man at home, but he is, I believe, hot-headed, and Lord Stanley is ten times worse; he would soon have up the barricades in London. Lord Clarendon seems a safe guide, but *Peel* is the man for the time, if he has the stamina. Lord Palmerston has conducted the duties of his office with admirable tact of late; and much of the good feeling that prevails in Europe towards England at present seems to arise from it. Amelie begs to be most kindly remembered; she is here with her little boy—two girls at Munsoorie, and two girls and a boy at home.

Yours very sincerely,
(Signed) W. H. SLEEMAN.
To the Hon. Sir T. H. Maddock,
&c. &c. &c.

* * * * *

Jhansee, 14th May, 1848.

My Dear Weston,

I have been directed by Government to name an officer whom I may consider competent to superintend the suppression of Thuggee in the Punjaub, where a new class has been discovered, and some progress has been made in finding and arresting them. I have, in reply, mentioned that I should have Captain Williams, of the 29th, and Captain Chambers, of the 21st; but their services might not be considered available, since the prescribed number of captains are already absent from their regiments, and, in consequence, I have you. I know not whether you will like the duties; if not, pray tell me as soon as possible.

The salary is 700 rupees a-month, with office-rent 40, and establishments 152. The duties are interesting and important; and so good a foundation has been laid by Larkins and the other local authorities, and all are so anxious to have the evil put down, that you will have the most cordial support and co-operation of all, and the fairest prospect of success. But you will have to apply yourself steadily to work, and if you have not *passed*, you should do so as soon as possible. I do not see P. opposite your name, and Government may possibly object on this ground. Let all this be *entre nous* for the present.

If you undertake the duties, you will have to go to Lodheeana, seeing Major Graham at Agra, on the way, to get a little insight into the work.

Yours sincerely,
(Signed) W. H. SLEEMAN.

P.S.—You will be in the most interesting scene in India, and need be under no apprehension about the permanency of the appointment.

To Lieut. Weston,
&c. &c.

* * * * *

Jhansee, 18th May, 1848.

My Dear Maddock,

Things are not going on so well as could be wished in the Punjaub; and it appears to me that we have been there committing an error of the same kind that we committed in Afghanistan—that is, taking upon ourselves the most odious part of the executive administration. In such a situation this should have been avoided, if possible. There is a kind of chivalry in this—if there is anything odious to be done, or repugnant to the feelings of the people, a young Englishman thinks he must do it himself, lest he should be thought disposed to shift off a painful burthen upon others; and he thinks it unbecoming of us to pay any regard to popular feeling. Of course, also, the officers of the Sikh State are glad to get rid of such burthens while they see English gentlemen ready to carry them. Now, it strikes me that we might, with a little tact, have altered all this, and retained the good feelings of the people, by throwing the executive upon the officers of the Sikh State, and remaining ourselves in the dignified position of Appellate Courts for the redress of grievances inflicted by these officers in neglect of duty or abuse of authority. Our duty would have been to guide, control, and check, and the head of all might have been like the sovereigns of England—known only by his acts of grace.

By keeping in this dignified position we should not only have retained the good feelings of the people, but we should have been teaching the Sikh officers their administrative duties till the time comes for making over the country; and the chief and Court would have found the task, made over to them under such a system, more easy to sustain. In Afghanistan we did the reverse of all this, and became intolerably odious to the mass of the people; for they saw that everything that was harsh was done by us, and the officers of the King were disposed to confirm and increase this impression because they were not employed. The people of the Punjaub are not such fanatics, and they are more divided in creed and caste, while they see no ranges of snowy mountains, barren rocks, and difficult passes between us and our reinforcements and resources; but it seems clear that there is a good deal of excitement and bad feeling growing up amongst them that may be very mischievous. All the newspapers, English and native, make the administration appear to be altogether English—it is Captain This, Mr. That, who do, or are expected to do, everything; and all over the country the native chiefs will think, that the leaving the country to the management of the Sirdars was a mere mockery and delusion.

We should keep our hands as much as possible out of the harsh and dirty part of the executive work, that the European officers may be looked up to with respect as the effectual check upon the native administrators; always prepared to check any disposition on their part to neglect their duty or abuse their power, and thereby bring their Government into disrepute. Of course, the outrage at Mooltan must be avenged, and our authority there established; but, when this is done, Currie should be advised to avoid the rock upon which our friend Macnaghten was wrecked. We are too impatient to jump down the throats of those who venture to look us in the face, and to force upon them our modes of doing the work of the country, and to superintend the doing it ourselves in all its details, or having it done by creatures of our own, commonly ten times more odious to the people than we are ourselves.

It is unfortunate that this outrage, and the excitement to which it has given rise, should have come so quickly upon Lord Hardinge's assurances at the London feast, and amidst the turmoil of popular movements at home. It has its use in showing us the necessity of being always prepared.

Baba Bulwunt Row tells me that he has got a letter from you in the form of Khureela, and claims one from me on that ground. Shall I comply? We have avoided this hitherto, as the Pundits put him up to claim everything that the Bae's family had, not even omitting the Thalone principality; and hints have been dropped of a mission to England, if the money could be got. I wish to subdue these pretensions for his own sake, that he may not be entirely ruined by temptations to expensive displays. He has now got the entire management of his own affairs, and is a sensible, well-disposed lad. He was never recognised as the Bae's successor by Government or the Agent, nor was he written to on the Bae's death. Cunput Row Bhaca was the person addressed in the letter of condolence. His son has run through all he has or can borrow, and is in a bad way. Moresor Row has the reputation of being very rich, though he pleads poverty always. The whole of the Saugor territories, save Mundla, have benefited by two very fine seasons, with great demand for land produce, and the people are happy. I have asked for reductions in Mundla, to save the little of tillage and population that has been left. The whole revenue is a mere trifle in such a jungle as you know it to be, and when once the people go off, there is no getting them back. Deer destroy the crops upon the few fields left, tigers come to eat the deer, and malaria follows, to sweep off the remaining few families.

I must not prose any longer at present. Amelia often talks of you, and begs to be kindly remembered.

Ever yours sincerely,
(Signed) W. H. SLEEMAN.

To the Hon. Sir T. H. Maddock,
&c. &c. &c.

* * * * *

Jhansee, 28th May, 1848.
My Dear Maddock,

I yesterday sent off by Dawk Bangy an elaborate Report on Dacoits by hereditary profession, and on the measures adopted by the Government of India for their suppression, and hope it will reach Calcutta before the rains set in heavily. Government may be justly proud of the good which it shows to have been effected for the people of India in the course of a brief period; and I am glad that you have for this period been a member of it. There is much in the Report to interest the general reader, but much of what is inserted would, of course, have been left out by any one who had to consult the wishes of such readers only.

At this time last year I had not the slightest hope of ever being able to lay such a Report before Government; for I never expected to find leisure in my present office, and could not carry the requisite records with me, if driven away by sickness, to where I might find it. The papers lay mouldering in an old box, to which I had consigned them in 1840, when I withdrew them from the press, under the impression that Lord Auckland thought that the exposition of the terrible evil ought not to appear till more progress had been made in its suppression; as G. Thompson and other itinerant orators would be glad to get hold of them to abuse the Government. The Report is infinitely more interesting and complete than it could have been then, and may bid defiance to all such orators.

If printed, it will take from 400 to 450 pages, such as those of the late Report on the Indian Penal Code, and be a neat and useful volume for reference. I began it in the rains last year, but was stopped short by a fever, and unable to continue it till I set out on my tour. Three-fourths of it was written in the intervals between the morning's march and breakfast-time during my tour through the Saugor territories.

The tables of dacoitees ascertained to have been committed by the dacoits described, and of the conditionally pardoned offenders, will follow, and be found useful for reference, but should not, perhaps, be in the same volume with the text of the Report; of that, however, I leave Government to judge. I thank God that I have been able to place before it so complete and authentic a record of what has been done to carry out its views.

Ever most sincerely yours,
(Signed) W. H. SLEEMAN.
To the Hon. Sir T. H. Maddock,
&c. &c. &c.

* * * * *

Jhansee, 15th August, 1848.

My Lord,

As it is possible that the letter which I addressed to your Lordship on the 6th of March last, and sent open to Mr. Melvill, the Secretary at the India House, may have miscarried; I write to mention that I sent it, lest it might be supposed that I was insensible of the kindness which induced your Lordship to write to me before leaving India. The work which made me delay so long to reply to that letter is now being printed in Calcutta, under the authority of Government; and, as it contains much that is curious and entertaining, and honourable to our rule in India, I trust at no distant day to have the honour of presenting a copy to your Lordship.

Amidst events of such absorbing interest as are now taking place every day in Europe, India cannot continue long to engage much of your thoughts; for, with the exception of the little outbreak at Mooltan, tranquillity prevails, and is likely to do so for some time. There has been delay in putting down the Mooltan rebels, but the next mail will, I hope, take home news of the work having been effectually done. This delay seems to have arisen from a notion that troops ought not to be employed in the hot winds and rains; but when occasion requires they can be employed at all times, and the people of India require to be assured that they can be so. It has not, I think, been found that troops actually employed in the hot winds and rains lose more men than in cantonments, at least native troops.

It was, I think, your Lordship's intention that, in the Lahore state, we should guide, direct, and supervise the administration, but not take all the executive upon ourselves, to the exclusion of all the old native aristocracy, as we had done in Afghanistan. This policy has not, I am afraid, been adhered to sufficiently; and we have, probably, less of the sympathy and cordial good-will of the higher and middle classes than we should otherwise have had. But I am too far from the scene to be a fair judge in such matters.

The policy of interposing Hindoo native states between us and the beggarly fanatical countries to the north-west no wise man can, I think, doubt; for, however averse our Government may be to encroach and creep on, it would be drawn on by the intermeddling dispositions and vainglory of local authorities; and every step would be ruinous, and lead to another still more ruinous. With the Hindoo principalities on our border we shall do very well, and trust that we shall long be able to maintain them in the state required for their own interests and ours.

I wish England would put forth its energies to raise the colony of New Zealand, the queen of the Pacific Ocean; for the relations between that island and India must some day become very intimate, and the sooner it begins the better. I am very glad to find by the last mail that the French have put their affairs into better hands—those of practical men, instead of visionaries.

Believe me, with great respect,
Your Lordship's obedient, humble servant,
(Signed) W. H. SLEEMAN.

To Lieut.-General the Right Hon.
Henry Viscount Hardinge, G.C.B.,
&c. &c. &c.

* * * * *

Jhansee, 22nd August 1848.
My Dear Sir Erskine,

I thank you for kindly sending me a copy of your Address to the Native Youth at Bombay and their Parents, and should have done so earlier, but it has been in circulation among many of my friends who feel interested in the subject. Whatever may be thought of the question as to where we should begin, all concur in acknowledging the truth of your conclusions as to the value and use of the knowledge we wish to impart, and in admiring the language and sentiment of your Address.

There are some passages of great beauty, which I wish all persons could read and remember; and I do not recollect ever having seen one that has pleased me more, for its truths and elegance, than that beginning, "But if a manufacturing population." That which begins with—"The views, young men, as to the true object and ends to be attained," is no less truthful and excellent.

It is unfortunate that the education which we have to supplant in India is so blended with the religion of the people, as far as Hindoos are concerned, that we cannot make progress without exciting alarm. Had a nation, endowed with all the knowledge we have, come into Europe in the days of Galileo and Copernicus, and attempted to impart it to the mass of the people, or to the higher classes only, the same alarm would have been raised, or nearly the same. We must be content with small, or slow progress; but there are certain branches of knowledge, highly useful to the people, that are finding their way among them from our metropolitan establishments, and working good.

I might better have said, that had we come into Greece when Homer was the Bible of the people, with all our astronomy, chemistry, and physical science generally, and our literature, blended as it is with our religion, we should have found our Greek fellow-subjects as untractable as the Hindoos or Parsees. The fact is, that every Hindoo, educated through our language in our literature and science, must be more or less wretched in domestic life, for he cannot feel or think with his family, or bring them to feel or think with him. The knowledge which he has acquired satisfies him that the faith to which they adhere, and which guides them in all their duties, ceremonies, acts, and habits, is monstrous and absurd; but he can never hope to impart to them this knowledge, or to alienate them from that faith; nor does he himself feel any confidence in any other creed: he feels that he is an isolated being, who can exchange thoughts and feelings unreservedly with no one. I have seen many estimable Hindoos in this state, with minds highly gifted and cultivated, and with abilities for anything. For such men we cannot create communities, nor can they create them for themselves: they can enjoy their books and conversation with men who understand and enjoy them like themselves; but how few are the men of this class with whom they can ever hope to associate on easy terms! It is not so with Mahommedans. All the literature and science in the world has no more effect on their faith than on ours; and their families apprehend no alienation in any member who may choose to indulge in them; and they indulge in them little, merely because they do not find that they conduce to secure them employment and bread.

I think it would be useful if we could get rid of the terms *education*, *civilization*, &c., and substitute that of *knowledge*. It would obviate much controversy, for the greater part of our disputes arise from the vagueness of the terms we use. All would agree that certain branches of knowledge are useful to certain classes, and that certain modes are the best for imparting them. The subject is deeply interesting and important; but I must not indulge further.

Believe me, My Dear Sir Erskine,
With great respect,
Yours very faithfully,
(Signed) W. H. SLEEMAN.

To Sir Erskine Perry,
Chief Justice, Bombay.

* * * * *

Jhansee, 24th September, 1848.

My Lord,

I feel grateful for the offer contained in your Lordship's letter of the 16th instant, and no less so for the gracious manner in which it has been conveyed, and beg to say that I shall be glad to avail myself of it, and be prepared to proceed to take charge as soon as I am directed to do so, as I have no arrears in any of my offices to detain me, and can make them over to any one at the shortest notice, with the assurance that he will find nothing in them to perplex or embarrass him.

I shall do my best to carry out your Lordship's views in the new charge; and though I am not so strong as I could wish, I may, with prudence, hope to have health for a few years to sustain me in duties of so much interest.

I hope your Lordship will pardon my taking advantage of the present occasion to say a few words on the state of affairs in the north-west, which are now of such absorbing interest. I have been for some time impressed with the belief that the system of administration in the Punjaub has created doubts as to the ultimate intention of our Government with regard to the restoration of the country to the native ruler when he comes of age. The native aristocracy of the country seem to have satisfied themselves that our object has been to retain the country, and that this could be prevented only by timely resistance. The sending European officers to relieve the chief of Mooltan, and to take possession of the country and fort, seems to have removed the last lingering doubt upon this point; and Molraj seems to have been satisfied that in destroying them he should be acting according to the wishes of all his class, and all that portion of the population who might aspire to employment under a native rule. This was precisely the impression created by precisely the same means in Afghanistan; and I believe that the notion now generally prevalent is, that our professed intentions of delivering over the country to its native ruler were not honest, and that we should have appropriated the country to ourselves could we have done so.

There are two classes of native Governments in India. In one the military establishments are all national, and depend entirely upon the existence of native rule. They are officered by the aristocracy of the country, chiefly landed, who know that they are not fitted for either civil or military office under our system, and must be reduced to beggary or insignificance should our rule be substituted for that of their native chief. In the other, all the establishments are foreign, like our own. The Seiks were not altogether of the first class, like those of Rajpootana and Bundelcund, but they were so for the most part; and when they saw all offices of trust by degrees being filled by Captain This and Mr. That, they gave up all hopes of ever having their share in the administration.

Satisfied that this was our error in Afghanistan, in carrying out the views of Lord Ellenborough in the Gwalior State, I did everything in my power to avoid it, and have entirely succeeded, I believe; but it has not been done without great difficulty. I considered Lord Hardinge's measures good, as they interposed Hindoo States between us and a beggarly and fanatical country, which it must be ruinous to our finances to retain, and into which we could not avoid making encroachments, however anxious the Government might be to avoid it, if our borders joined. But I supposed that we should be content with guiding, controlling, and supervising the native administration, and not take all the executive upon ourselves to the almost entire exclusion of the native aristocracy. I had another reason for believing that Lord Hardinge's measures were wise and prudent. While we have a large portion of the country under native rulers, their administration will contrast with ours greatly to our advantage in the estimation of the people; and we may be sure that, though some may be against us, many will be for us. If we succeed in sweeping them all away, or absorbing them, we shall be at the mercy of our native army, and they will see it; and accidents may possibly occur to unite them, or a great portion of them, in some desperate act. The thing is possible, though improbable; and the best provision against it seems to me to be the maintenance of native rulers, whose confidence and affection can be engaged, and administrations improved under judicious management.

The industrial classes in the Punjaub would, no doubt, prefer our rule to that of the Seiks; but that portion who depend upon public employment under Government for their subsistence is large in the Punjaub, and they would nearly all prefer a native rule. They have evidently persuaded themselves that our intention is to substitute our own rule; and it is now, I fear, too late to remove the impression. If your Lordship is driven to annexation, you must be in great force; and a disposition must be shown on the part of the local authorities to give the educated aristocracy of the country a liberal share in the administration.

One of the greatest dangers to be apprehended in India is, I believe, the disposition on the part of the dominant class to appoint to all offices members of their own class, to the exclusion of the educated natives. This has been nobly resisted hitherto; but where every subaltern thinks himself in a condition to take a wife, and the land opens no prospect to his children but in the public service, the competition will become too great.

I trust that your Lordship will pardon my having written so much, and believe me, with great respect, your Lordship's obedient humble servant,

(Signed) W. H. SLEEMAN.

P.S.—The Commander-in-Chief has asked me, through the Quartermaster-General, whether any corps can be spared from Bundelcund. I shall say that we can spare two regiments—one from Nagode, whose place can be supplied by a wing of the regiment at Nowgow, and one from Jhansee, whose place can be supplied from the Gwalior Contingent, if your Lordship sees no objection, as a temporary arrangement.

(Signed) W. H. SLEEMAN.

To the Right Hon.
the Earl of Dalhousie,
&c. &c. &c.

* * * * *

Lucknow, 30th January, 1849.

My Dear Elliot,

A salute of twenty-one guns had been fired here by the King for the sadly dear victory over Shere Sing, and another has been fired to-day for the fall of Mooltan. The King continues very ill, but no danger seems to be apprehended. The disease is accompanied by very untoward secondary symptoms, which are likely ultimately to destroy him, and render his life miserable while it lasts. How much of these symptoms he derives from his birth, and how much from his own excesses, is uncertain.

The impression regarding the minister, mentioned in my last note, was from a talk with him while he was, it seems, under the influence of fever. In later conversations he has been more lucid; but he is a third-rate man, and quite unequal to the burthen that the favour of the King has placed upon him. That favour will, however, be but of short duration, for the King is said to have expressed great distrust in his capacity to do any of the things he promised, more especially to collect the immense arrears of revenue now due.

I am preparing tables of the revenue and expenditure, and of the machinery in all branches, and hope soon to submit a clearer view of the state of things than Government is in the habit of getting on such occasions; but I have to wade through vast volumes of correspondence to ascertain what has been said and done in the questions that will come under consideration, to conduct current duties, and to become acquainted with the people in my new field, European and native.

I want to ask you whether I could, with any prospect of success just now, propose a plan which I have much at heart in the Thuggee and Dacoity Department. The Lieutenant-Governor, I feel assured, will advocate it. Major Graham is about to obtain his regimental majority, with a certain prospect of soon obtaining the command of his regiment, which will give him twelve hundred a-month. I am anxious to retain him; for his services have been, and would continue to be, of vast importance to the North-West Provinces. I should like to propose that he be made superintendent of Thuggee and Dacoity in those provinces upon a salary of, say eleven hundred rupees a-month. I would at the same time propose that the Shahjehanpoor office, lately under Major Ludlow, be done up, and the duties confided to the assistant-magistrate, with a small establishment, he to receive an extra salary, say, one hundred rupees a-month. The same with regard to the Azimghur office, now under Captain Ward, who could be sent to Rajpootana. Elliot is not suited well to the work, according to those who have seen most of him and of it; and you might be able to put him to some other for which he is fitted. Should you think it desirable to retain him in Rajpootana, Captain Ward may for the present remain where he is; and the saving from the Shahjehanpoor office will more than cover the increase for Major Graham. Pray let me know as soon as you can whether such a proposal would be likely to be well received. Graham's services have been and will be most valuable to all the local authorities at and under Agra.

I suppose the fate of the Punjaub is sealed, for though the Governor-General might wish to spare it, the home authorities and the home people will hardly brook the prospect or the chance of another struggle of the same kind, particularly if the Afghans have really joined the Seiks under Chutter Sing. The tendency to annexation, already strong at home, will become still stronger when the news of our late losses arrive. They indicate a stronger assurance of national sympathy on the part of the chiefs and troops opposed to us than was generally calculated upon. The fall of Mooltan will have relieved the Governor-General's mind from much of the anxiety caused by the inartistic management of the Commander-in-Chief.

Yours sincerely,
(Signed) W. H. SLEEMAN.

To H. M. Elliot, Esq.,
&c. &c.

* * * * *

Lucknow, 7th March, 1849.

My Dear Elliott,

I may mention what has been the state of feeling at Lucknow regarding the state of affairs in the Punjaub, though it has become of less interest to the Governor-General now that so decided a victory has crowned his efforts. During the whole contest the Government five per cent. notes have been every day sold in my office at par, and I question whether this can be said of the offices in Calcutta. One day during the races, on the

King's firing a salute for victory, the European gentlemen talked about it at the stand with many of the first of the native aristocracy. They said that the Seiks could not fight as they were fighting unless there had been some general feeling of distrust as to our ultimate intentions with regard to the Punjaub which united them together; and that this feeling must be as strong with the Durbar and those who did not fight as with those who did. I was not present, as I did not attend the races; but I found the same opinion prevailing among all with whom I conversed. But all seemed to be perfectly satisfied as to the utter hopelessness of the struggle, as evinced by the great barometer of the Government paper.

I suppose Dost Mahomed's force in Peshawur will have proceeded in all haste to the Khyber on hearing of the defeat of their friends, and that General Gilbert's fine division will find none of them to contend with; and that Gholab Sing will be glad of an occasion to display his zeal by keeping Shore Sing and his father out of the hills.

The river Indus will, I suppose, hardly be considered so safe a boundary as the hills; for if any danger is to be apprehended from the west, it would not be safe to leave the enemy so fine a field to organize their forces upon after emerging from the difficult passes. Well organized upon that field, a force could cross the river anywhere in the cold and hot seasons; and the revenue of that field would aid in keeping up a force that might in the day of need be used against us. It was a great error committed by Lord Hastings in allowing the Nepaulese the fertile portion of the Jurac, which then yielded only two lacs of rupees, but now yields thirteen, and will, ere long, yield twenty. Without this their military force would have been altogether insignificant; but it is not so now.

Yours sincerely,
(Signed) W. H. SLEEMAN.

To H. M. Elliot, Esq.,
&c. &c.

* * * * *

Lucknow, 20th March, 1849.

My Dear Elliot,

The King continues much the same as when I last wrote. Under skilful treatment he might soon get well; but the prescriptions of his best native physicians are little attended to, and he has not yet consented to consult an European doctor. He could not have a better doctor than Leekie, and the natives have great confidence in him; but his Majesty has not expressed any wish to see or consult him. If he did so, the chances are one hundred to one against his taking his medicine.

I do not like to write a public letter on the subject, but am anxious to know the Governor-General's wishes as to whether any new engagements should be entered into in case of the King's decease, and with whom.

The instructions contained in your letter of the 16th August, 1847, referred to in my last, will be carried out; but the Governor-General may wish to have the new arrangements recorded in a former treaty, the heads of the royal family consenting thereto, as at Gwalior, when the regency was appointed. I have no copy of the treaty made at Lahore, where the regency was appointed.

I should think it desirable to give the members of the regency each distinct duties, so that he may feel responsible for them, and take a pride in doing them well. One should be at the head of the Revenue Department, and another at the head of the Judicial and Police, each having a deputy; and the Resident, as president, should have a deputy. These would be sufficient for a regency, and could form a court, or council, to deliberate and decide about measures of legislation and administration.

The mother of the King would be the best person to consult upon the nomination of the members in the first instance; but neither she nor any other female of the royal family should have any share in the administration.

All important measures adopted by the Council should be submitted for the consideration of the Governor-General; and no member of the Council should be removed without his Lordship's consent. No important measure adopted by the Council, and sanctioned by the Governor-General, should at any future time be liable to be abolished or altered without the sanction of our Government previously obtained through the Resident.

On the heir-apparent attaining his majority, every member of the regency who has discharged his duties faithfully should have for life a pension equal to half the salary enjoyed by him while in office, and be guaranteed in the enjoyment of this half by the British Government.

The measures thus adopted during the minority would form a code for future guidance, and tend at least to give the thing which Oude most wants—stability to good sales, and to the machinery by which they are to be enforced.

The King's brother—a very excellent man, who was Commander-in-Chief during his father's life-time, but is now nothing—might also be consulted with the mother of the King in the nomination of the regency, and made a party with her to the new treaty.

These are all the points which appear to me at present to call for instructions.

The harvests promise to be abundant, but the collections come in slowly, and the establishments are all greatly in arrear. I don't like to write publicly on these subjects, because it is almost impossible here to prevent what is so written from getting to the Court; but the Governor-General's instructions were sent to me in that form without the same risk.

(Signed) W. H. SLEEMAN.

To H. M. Elliot, Esq.,
&c. &c.

* * * * *

Lucknow, 23rd March, 1849.

My Dear Elliot,

It will perhaps be well to add to the regency, in case of the King's death, a controller of the household, making three members of equal grade, and to have no deputy for the Resident, or President of the Regency. It may also be well to add the mother of the heir apparent to the persons to be consulted in the selection of the members of the regency, though she is a person of no mark or influence in either public or private affairs at present.

The mother of the present King, his brother, the mother of the heir-apparent, and the young heir-apparent himself will be enough to have a voice in the selection.

I conclude that it will be the Governor-General's wish that the heir-apparent should be placed on the throne immediately after the death of his father, for the slightest hesitation or delay in this matter would be mischievous in such a place as Lucknow. As soon as this is done, I can proceed to consult about the nomination of the regency. The members will, of course, be chosen from among the highest and most able members of the aristocracy present at the capital, and they can be installed in office the day they are chosen. I do not apprehend any confusion or disturbance; but measures must be adopted immediately to pay up arrears due to the establishments, and dismiss all that are useless.

The, King is not worse—on the contrary, he is said to be better; but the hot season may be too much for him. His present state, with a minister weak in body and not very strong in mind, is very unsatisfactory. Fortunately the harvest is unusually fine.

Yours sincerely,
(Signed) W. H. SLEEMAN.

To H. M. Elliot, Esq.,
&c. &c.

* * * * *

Lucknow, 8th May, 1849.

My Lord,

Dr. Bell, has relieved Dr. Leekie from his charge, and I am glad that so able and experienced a medical officer has been appointed to it by your Lordship, for he will have the means of doing much good here if he can secure the confidence and esteem of his native patients. The way has been well paved for him by Dr. Leekie, who, in professional ability, large experience, and perfect frankness of character, is one of the first men I have met; and I regret exceedingly that the King has never manifested any wish to consult him or any other European physician.

Being anxious that both Dr. Leekie and Dr. Bell should have an opportunity of seeing the King, and forming some opinion as to his state of health, I proposed that his Majesty should receive them at the same time with Captain Bird on his taking leave previous to his departure for Simla. As it is usual for the residency surgeon to wait on his Majesty when he first enters on his charge and when he quits it, I knew that such a proposal would not give rise to any feelings of doubt or uneasiness, and he at once expressed his wish to see them. Yesterday, about noon, all three went to the palace, and sat for some time in conversation with the King. They found him much better in bodily health than they expected, and in the course of conversation, found no signs of any confusion of ideas, and are of opinion that in the hands of a skilful European physician he would soon be quite well. His Majesty is hypochondriac, and frequently under the influence of the absurd delusions common to such persons; but he is quite sane during long intervals, and on all subjects not connected with such delusions.

When in health, the King never paid much attention to business, and his illness is, therefore, less felt than it would have been in the conduct of affairs; but it is nevertheless felt, and that in a very vital part—the collection of the revenue. The expenses of Government are about one hundred

(100) lacs a-year; and the collections this year have not amounted to more than sixty (60), owing to this illness, and to a deficiency in the autumn harvests. All establishments are greatly in arrears in consequence; and the King has been obliged to make some heavy drafts upon the reserved fund left him by his father. I only wish none had been made for a less legitimate purpose. The parasites, by whom he has surrounded himself exclusively, have, it is said, been drawing upon it still more largely during the King's illness, under the apprehension of a speedy dissolution. The minister is a weak man, who stands somewhat in awe of these musicians and eunuchs, who have no fear of anybody but the Resident, whom it is, of course, their interest to keep as much as possible in the dark. As soon as his Majesty gets stronger, I shall see him more frequently than I have yet done, and be better able to judge of what prospect of amendment there may be while he reigns. If he ever conversed with his male relations, or any of the gentlemen at the capital worthy of his confidence, I should have more hope than I now have.

>With great respect I remain
>Your Lordship's obedient humble servant,
>(Signed) W. H. SLEEMAN.

>To the Right Hon.
>The Earl of Dalhousie, K.T.,
>Governor-General of India.

* * * * *

Lucknow, 11th June, 1849.

My Dear Elliot,

It will be desirable to have at least the wing of a regiment sent as soon as possible to Jhansee. Bukhut Sing, who was allowed to escape after having been surrendered to Ellis at Kyrma, has been since allowed to get too much a-head. He is aided by the Khereecha people openly; and secretly, I fear, by some of the Powar Thakoors of Gigree under the rose. There are four small fortified places between thirty and forty miles west of Jhansee, and not far from the Sinde, held by Powar Thakoors, who are a shade higher in caste than the Bondeylas; and, in consequence, all the principal chiefs take their daughters in marriage. They are needy, and as proud as Lucifer, and will always eke out their means by robbery if they can. The Jhansee chief cannot keep them in order without our aid. While I was there, they did not venture to rob after the surrender of the Jylpoor man in September, 1844; and the Hareecha and Hyrwa people ventured only to send a few highwaymen into the Gwalior state west of the Sinde river.

The Powar places I mean are Jignee, Odgow, and Belchree. There was a fourth near them just as bad, called Nowneer; but the Thakoors of that place are all well disposed towards the Jbansee chief, and are obedient. All are in the Jhansee state. If the marauders are pressed with energy and sagacity, they will be soon put down; and you may rely upon the native chiefs not supporting them, though, from their marriage connection, they may afford them an asylum secretly when fugitives.

Who the Gwalior men are that are plundering I know not; but they are men of no note, and, if pressed skilfully and rigorously in time, will soon be put down. The chiefs may all be relied upon, I believe. They are mere gangs of robbers; and you know how easily a fanatic or successful robber may collect a body for plunder in any part of India, where the danger of pursuit is small. Had they been dealt with properly at first, they would never have got a-head so far: time has been lost, and they will now give trouble, particularly at such a season. The evil will be confined to the tract west of Jhansee occupied by these Powars. The chiefs are to the east, north, and south of Jhansee; and the marauders would be allowed to enter their estates. The Governor-General need not feel uneasy about them. The Nurwar chief was always needy, and disposed to keep and shelter robbers. His few villages were resumed on his death last year, and his widows pensioned; but some of his relations are, I conclude, among the marauders. There is a wild tract west of the Sinde in the Gwalior territory, to which the marauders will fly when hard pressed in the Jhansee state.

Yours sincerely,
(Signed) W. H. SLEEMAN.

To H. M. Elliot, Esq.,
&c. &c.

* * * * *

Lucknow, 18th June, 1849.

My Dear Elliot,

I was writing the last sentence of a long Report on Oude affairs when your note came in. There are some parts that will amuse, some that will interest, and the whole gives, I believe, a fair exposition of the evils, with a suggestion for the best remedy that I can think of. It is the formation of a Board, consisting of a President and two members nominated by the King, subject to the confirmation of the Governor-General, and not to be dismissed without his Lordship's previous sanction. This Board to make the settlement of the revenue proposed when Lord Hardinge was here, and to have the carrying it out.

This Board will be a substitute for the Regency, but not so good. The King is well in body; and, unless he will abdicate, we cannot get the minority for the Regency. I think, upon the whole, the Governor-General will think the Report worth reading, and the remedy worth considering. It will bring little additional trouble on Government, but a good deal on the Resident, who will require to have had much administrative experience.

Things are coming fast to the crisis, in which I must be called upon to advise and act, a thing which the fiddlers and eunuchs dread. I can't trust the Report in the office, and the hand may not be so legible as I could wish.

The Court is very averse to the appointment of a successor to Wilcox; and it is with reluctance they have kept on the native officers who go on with the work. I told them either to keep them on or to pension them. I don't think a successor should be urged upon them in the present state of beggary to which they are reduced. Nobody sees any use in it, while there are a vast number of useful things neglected for want of funds; as to the instruments, the Court care nothing about them, knowing nothing of their value; and would, no doubt, be glad to give them to any establishment requiring them.

The minister, singers, and eunuchs are all now sworn to be united; but this cannot last many days. The "pressure from without," in the clamour for pay, will soon upset the minister; but they will find it difficult to get another to undertake the burthen of forty or fifty lacs of balance, and a score of fiddlers and eunuchs as privy councillors. Something must be done to *unthrone* these wretches, or things will be worse and worse. The best remedy that occurs to me is to interpose an authority which they dare not question, and the King cannot stultify; and if the King objects, to tell him that he must abdicate in favour of his son. This, of all courses, will be the best, and give no trouble; things would go on like "marriage bells," without any trouble whatever to the Governor-General and your *secretariat*.

I am glad that the Punjaub Board goes on well. It is a scene of great importance and interest. The only way to get the confidence and affection of men is to show that we confide in them; and I don't think we need fear Seik soldiers while we treat them, and govern the country well.

We were very anxious about Mrs. Elliot for many days, for the accounts from Simla were bad; but she is now, I am told, quite restored. I have suffered much less than I expected: I recovered much sooner. The doctors tell me that I should have had no right to expect an earlier recovery had I been twenty years younger.

Yours sincerely,
(Signed) W. H. SLEEMAN.

To H. M. Elliot, Esq.,
&c. &c.

* * * * *

Lucknow, 24th July, 1849.

My Lord,

I have to-day written to Lord Fitzroy Somerset to request that he will do me the favour to have the name of my only son placed, if possible, upon his Grace the Commander-in-Chief's list of candidates for commissions in Her Majesty's Dragoons. He was sixteen years of age on the 6th of January last, and is now prosecuting his studies under the care of Mr. C. J. Yeatman, Westow Hill, Norwood, Surrey, five miles from London.

He is an amiable and gentlemanly lad, and will, I trust, be able to qualify himself to pass the examination required; and my agents in London will be prepared to lodge the money for his commission when available. He is my eldest child, and will have to take care of four sisters when I am taken from them, as I must be ere long; and I am anxious to place him in the position from which he can do so with most advantage. I could wish to have had him placed in the Bengal Civil Service. But I have no personal friend in the direction, and no good that I may have had an opportunity of doing for the people and government of India can be urged as a claim to any employment for my child.

Having carried out your Lordship's policy successfully over a large and interesting portion of India, and to the advantage, I believe, of many millions of people, you will not, I think, be offended at my soliciting your Lordship's protection for my only son. He will stand in need of it, since I know no other that I can solicit for him; and though my name might be of some use to him in India, it can be of none in England. With a view to his taking care of his sisters, I could wish him to be in a regiment not likely to come to India. General Thackwell tells me that the regiments most likely to come to India soon are the 6th Dragoons, 9th Hussars, and 12th Lancers. Perhaps your Lordship might be willing to speak to Lord F. Somerset, or even to his Grace the Duke himself, in favour of my son, who will be proud at any time when commanded to attend your Lordship. I have the misfortune to have been with some of the most inefficient sovereigns that ever sat upon a throne, with deficient harvests last year, and a threat of still more deficient ones this year; and with a Government so occupied with the new acquisitions of the Punjaub as to be averse to interfere much with the management of any other portion of the country.

I remain, your lordship's most obedient, humble servant,

W. H. SLEEMAN.

To the Right Hon. Gen. Viscount Hardinge, G.C.B., &c. &c.&c.

* * * * *

Lucknow, 24th July, 1849.

My Lord,

May I, request that your Lordship will do me the favour to have the name of my only son, Henry Arthur Sleeman, placed upon his Grace the Commander-in-Chief's list of candidates for a commission in one of her Majesty's Dragoon regiments?

He was sixteen years of age on the 6th of January last; and he is now prosecuting his studies under the care of Mr. C. J. Yeatman, at Westow Hill, in Surrey, five miles from London, who will be instructed to have him prepared for the examination he will have to undergo. My agents, Messrs. Denny, Clark, and Co., Austin Friars, London, will be prepared to lodge the money, and to forward to me any letters with which they may be honoured by your Lordship. My rank is that of Lieut.-Colonel in the Honourable East India Company's service, and present situation, that of Resident at the Court of his Majesty the King of Oude.

I have the honour to be,
    Your Lordship's obedient, humble servant,
        W. H. SLEEMAN.

To Lieut.-General Lord Fitzroy Somerset, G.C.B.,
Military Secretary to his Grace the Commander-in-Chief,
Horse Guards, London.

* * * * *

Lucknow, August 1849.
My Lord,

1. I will answer your Lordship's queries in the order in which they are made.

2. The King, as I shall show in my next official report, is utterly unfit to have anything to do with the administration, since he has never taken, or shown any disposition to take any heed of what is done or suffered in the country. My letters have made no impression whatever upon him. He spends all his time with the singers and the females they provide to amuse him, and is for seven and eight hours together living in the house of the chief singer, Rajee-od Dowla—a fellow who was only lately beating a drum to a party of dancing-girls, on some four rupees a-month. These singers are all Domes, the lowest of the low castes of India, and they and the eunuchs are now the virtual sovereigns of the country, and must be so as long as the King retains any power. The minister depends entirely upon them, and between them and a few others about Court everything that the King has to dispose of is sold.

3. To secure any reform in the administration, it will be necessary to require the King to delegate all the powers of sovereignty to the Board.

This he can do, retaining the name of Sovereign and control of his household; or abdicating in favour of his son the heir apparent, to whom the Board would be a regency till he comes of age. If the alternative be given him, and he choose the former, it should be on the condition, that if his favourites continue to embarrass the Government, he will be required to submit to the latter. Oude is now, in fact, without a Government: the minister sees the King for a few minutes once a week or fortnight, and generally at the house of the singer above named. The King sees nobody else save the singers and eunuchs, and does not even pretend to know anything or care anything about public affairs. His sons have been put under their care, and will be brought up in the same manner. He has become utterly despised and detested by his people for his apathy amidst so much suffering, and will not have the sympathy of any one, save such as have been growing rich by abusing his power.

4. The members of such a Board as I propose, invested with full powers, and secured in office under our guarantee during good conduct, would go fearlessly to work; they would divide the labour; one would have the settlement of the land-revenue, with the charge of the police; the second would have the judicial Courts; and if the Board be a regency during the minority, the control of the household; the third would have the army. Each would have the nomination of the officers of his department, subject to the confirmation of the whole Board, and the dismissal would depend upon the sanction of the whole or two-thirds, as might be found expedient. If the sanction of all three be required. Court influence may secure one vote, and impunity to great offenders. Neither of the three would be liable to be deprived of his office, except with the consent, or on the requisition of the Governor-General; and this privilege they would value too highly to risk it by neglect or misconduct. The King's brother—a most worthy and respectable, though not able man—might be a member, if agreeable to the King.

5. The abuses they would have to remedy are all perfectly well understood, and the measures required to remedy them are all simple and

obvious: a settlement would be made with the landholders, based upon past avowed collections; they would be delighted to bind themselves to pay such an assessment, as they would escape from the more than one-third more, which they have now to pay, in one form or another, to contractors and Court favourites; the large landholders, who are for the most part now in open resistance to the Government, would rejoice at the prospect of securing their estates to their posterity, without the necessity of continually fighting for them.

6. The army would soon become efficient: at present every man purchases his place in it from the minister and the singers and eunuchs, and he loses it as soon as he becomes disabled from wounds or sickness. The only exceptions are the four regiments under Captain Burlow, Captain Bunbury, Captain Magness, and Soba Sing, lately Captain Buckley's; in these, all that are disabled from wounds or sickness are kept on the strength of the corps, and each corps has with it a large invalid establishment of this kind unrecognized by the Government. They could not get their men to fight, without it. These regiments are put up at auction every season, and often several times during one season; the contractor who bids highest gets the services of the best for the season or the occasion; the purchase-money is divided between the minister and the Court favourites, singers, &c. These are really efficient corps, and the others might soon be made the same. The men are as fine-looking and brave as those of our, regular infantry, for Oude teems with such men, who have from their boyhood been fighting against contractors under the heads of their clan or families.

7. The rest are for the most part commanded by boys, or Court favourites, who seldom see them, keep about two-thirds of what are borne on the rolls and paid for, and take about one-third of the pay of what remain for themselves. The singer, Rajee-od Dowla, the prime favourite above named, has two regiments thus treated, and of course altogether inefficient, ragged, hungry, and discontented. It will be easy to remedy all this, get excellent men, and inspire them with excellent spirit

by instituting a modified pension establishment for men disabled in the discharge of their duties, and providing for their regular pay and efficient command.

8. This would prevent the necessity of employing British troops, except on rare and great occasions; the settlement of the land-revenue, and knowledge that they would be employed if required, would keep the great landholders in obedience. It would be well to have back the corps of infantry and two guns that were taken away from Pertanghurh, in Oude, in 1835. This is all the addition that would be required to secure an efficient Government; and the scale to which our troops in Oude had been reduced up to that time (1835) was generally considered the lowest compatible with our engagements. A regiment of cavalry had been borrowed from Pertanghurh for the Nepaul and Mahratta wars in 1814 and 1817; it was finally withdrawn in 1823.

9. The judicial Courts would be well conducted while the presiding officers felt secure in their tenure of office, which they would do when their dismissal depended upon proof of guilt or incompetency sufficient to satisfy a Board guaranteed by our Government.

10. The police would soon become efficient under the supervision and control of respectable revenue-officers, having the same feeling of security in their tenure of office. All the revenue-officers would, of course, be servants of Government instead of contractors. There would be grades answering to our commissioners of divisions, say four; 2nd, to our collectors of revenue, say twenty-eight; 3rd, deputy-collectors, say twenty-eight; all under the Board, and guided by the member intrusted with that branch of the administration: all would be responsible for the police over their respective jurisdictions.

11. Oude ought to be, and would soon be, under such a system, a garden; the soil is the finest in India, so are the men; and there is no want of an educated class for civil office: on the contrary, they abound almost as much as the class of soldiers. From the numerous rivers which flow through the country the water is everywhere near the surface, and the

peasantry would manure and irrigate every field, if they could do so in peace and security, with a fair prospect of being permitted to reap the fruits. The terrible corruption of the Court is the great impediment to all this good: the savings would more than pay all the increased outlay required for rendering establishments efficient in all branches, while the treasury would receive at least one-third more than the expenditure; that is, 1,50,00,000 Rs., or one crore and a half.

12. From the time the treaty of 1801 was made, up to within the last few years, the term "internal enemies" was interpreted to mean the great landholders who might be in resistance to the Government, and this interpretation was always acted upon; the only difficulty was in ascertaining whether the resistance was or was not, under the circumstances, justifiable. While employed in Oude with my regiment, and on the staff in 1818 and 1819, I saw much of the correspondence between the Resident and Commandant; many letters from the Resident, Colonel Baillie, mentioning how bitterly Saadulullee, with whom that treaty was made, had complained, that after the sacrifice of half his kingdom for the aid of British troops in keeping down these powerful and refractory landholders, he could not obtain their assistance without being subject to such humiliating remonstrances as he got from officers commanding stations whenever he asked for it. Aid was often given, and forts innumerable were reduced from time to time, but the privilege of building them up again was purchased from the same or another contractor next season.

13. At this time I have calls for at least two battalions and a train of artillery, from about six quarters, to enforce orders on these landholders. Captain Hearsey has had men of his Frontier Police killed and wounded by them on the western border, and declares that nothing can be done to secure offenders, refugees from our districts, with a less force. Captain Orr has had several men wounded, and prisoners taken from him, by the same class on the eastern border, and declares to the same effect. Sixteen sepoys of our army, 59th N. I., on their way home on furlough were

attacked and two of them killed, three weeks ago, by a third Zumeendar, at Peernugger, his own estate, within ten miles of the Setapore Cantonments, where we have a regiment. Captain Barlow's regiment and artillery, and another, with all Captain Hearsey's Frontier Police, are in pursuit of him. Four others have committed similar outrages on our officers and sepoys and their families, and the Government declares its utter inability to enforce obedience or grant any redress, without a larger force than they have to send. Great numbers of the same class are plundering and burning villages, and robbing and murdering on the highway, and laughing at the impotency of the sovereign. It was certainly for aid in coercing these "internal enemies" that the Sovereign of Oude ceded his territories to us, and for no other, and that aid may be afforded at little cost, and to the great benefit of all under the system I have submitted for your Lordship's consideration. It will be very rarely required, and when called for, a mere demonstration will, in three cases out of four, be sufficient to effect the object.

14, After a time, or when the heir-apparent comes of age, the duties of the guaranteed members of the Board may safely be united to a supervision over the settlement made with the principal landholders, whose obedience our Government may consider itself bound to aid in enforcing; all the rest may be left to a competent sovereign; and there will be nothing in the system opposed to native usages, feelings, and institutions, to prevent its being adhered to. I should mention, that many of these landholders have each armed and disciplined bodies of two thousand foot and five hundred horse; and, what is worse, the command of as many as they like of "Passies," armed with bows and arrows. These Passies are reckless thieves and robbers of the lowest class, whose only professions are thieving and acting as Chowkedars, or village police. They are at the service of every refractory Zumeendar, for what they can get in booty in his depredations. The disorders in Oude have greatly increased this class, and they are now roughly estimated at a hundred thousand families; these are the men from whom travellers on the road suffer most.

15. A second Assistant would be required for a time to enable the Resident to shift off the daily detail of the treasury, which has become the largest in India,—I believe, beyond those at the three Presidencies.

A good English copyist, capable of mapping, will be required in the Resident's office at 150, and two Persian writers 100; total 250. These are the only additions which appear to me to be required.

16. I annex a list of the regiments now in the King's service, Telungas, or regulars, and Nujeebs, or irregulars; and with my next official report I will submit a list of all the establishments, civil and military.

17. The King's habits will not alter; he was allowed by his father to associate, as at present, with these singers from his boyhood, and he cannot endure the society of other persons. His determination to live exclusively in their society, and to hear and see nothing of what his officers do or his people suffer, he no longer makes any attempt to conceal. It would be idle to hope for anything from him but a resignation of power into more competent hands; whatever he retains he will assuredly give to his singers and eunuchs, or allow them to take. No man can take charge of any office without anticipating the income by large gratuities to them, and the average gratuity which a contractor for a year, of a district yielding three lacs of rupees a-year, is made to pay, before he leaves the capital to enter upon his charge, is estimated to be fifty thousand rupees: this he exacts from the landholders as the first payment, for which they receive no credit in the public account. All other offices are paid for in the same way.

18. The King would change his minister to-morrow if the singers were to propose it; and they would propose it if they could get better terms or perquisites under any other. No minister could hold office a week without their acquiescence. Under such circumstances a change of ministers would be of little advantage to the country.

19. The King will yield to the measure proposed only under the assurance, that if he did not, the Governor-General would be reduced to the necessity of having recourse to that which Lord Hardinge threatened

in the 10th, 11th, and 12th paragraphs of his letter of October, 1847, and the Court of Directors, on the representation of Lord William Bentinck, sanctioned in 1831. The Court was at that time so strongly impressed with the conviction that the threat would be carried into execution, that they prevailed upon the President to undertake a mission to the Home Government, with a view to enlarge the President's powers of interference, in order to save them from the alternative. This led to Mr. Maddock's removal from the Presidency; all subsequent correspondence has tended to keep up the apprehension that the threatened measure would be had recourse to, and to stimulate sovereigns and ministers to exertion till the present reign. The present King has, from the time he ascended the throne, manifested a determination to take no share whatever in the conduct of affairs; to spend the whole of his time among singers and eunuchs, and the women whom they provide for his amusement; and carefully to exclude from access, all who suffer from the maladministration of his servants, or who could and would tell him what was done by the one and suffered by the other.

20. But it is not his minister and favourites alone who take advantage of this state of things to enrich themselves; corruption runs through all the public offices, and Maharaja Balkishen, the Dewan, or *Chancellor of the Exchequer*, is notoriously among the most corrupt of all, taking a large portion of the heavy balances due by contractors to get the rest remitted or misrepresented. There is no Court in the capital, criminal, civil, or fiscal, in which the cases are not tampered with by Court favourites, and divided according to their wishes, unless the President has occasion to interfere in behalf of guaranteed pensioners, or officers and sepoys of our army. On his appearance they commonly skulk away, like jackals from a dead carcase when the tiger appears; but the cases in which he can interfere are comparatively very few, and it is with the greatest delay and difficulty that he can get such cases decided at all. A more lamentable state of affairs it is difficult to conceive.

With great respect, I remain,
    Your Lordship's obedient humble servant,
        (Signed) W. H. SLEEMAN.

> To the Most Noble
> the Marquis of Dalhousie, K.T.,
> &c. &c. &c.

P.S.—I find that the King's brother is altogether incompetent for anything like business or responsibility. The minister has not one single quality that a minister ought to have; and the King cannot be considered to be in a sound state of mind.

(Signed) W. H. SLEEMAN.

Annexures.

1. Extracts, pars. 9 to 14 of Lord Hardinge's Memorial.
2. Statement of British troops in Oude in Jan. 1835 and 1849.
3. Table of the King of Oude's troops of all kinds.

* * * * *

Lucknow, 6th September, 1849.

My Lord,

I take the liberty to enclose, for your Lordship's perusal, a more full and correct Table of the troops and police in Oude than that which I submitted with my last letter, as also a Table of all the other branches of expenditure—save those of buildings, charities, presents, &c., which are ever varying.

It may be estimated that two-thirds of the numbers in the corps of Telungas and Nujeebs paid for are kept up; and that one-half of what are kept up are efficient, all having to purchase their places, and those most unfit being disposed to pay highest.

Further: one-half of what are kept up are supposed to be always absent; and when they are so, they receive one-half of their pay, and the other half is divided between the commandant and the paymaster. These two are supposed to take, on one pretence or other, one third of the pay of those who are actually present. The corps of Telungas commanded by Captains Barlow, Bunbury, and Magness are exceptions; but the pay department is not under their control, and they are obliged to acquiesce in abuses that impair the efficiency their corps.

After reducing one-third-of these corps, and rendering the remaining two-thirds efficient, the force would be sufficient for all purposes, and we may well dispense with the corps of regular infantry which in my last letter I proposed to restore to Oude. It will, however, be desirable to have a good and experienced infantry officer as inspector, to see that the measures adopted for reform are effectually carried out. An artillery officer as inspector will also be desirable, as it will be necessary to have that branch of the force in the best possible order, when Oude has to depend chiefly on its own resources. A few European officers, too, for commandants of corps and seconds in command will be desirable—such as have been employed with native corps as sergeant-majors or quartermaster-sergeants, and have obtained distinctions for good conduct.

I should propose six primary stations as seats for the principal Revenue and Judicial Courts, and the headquarters of the best corps with cavalry and artillery; thirty second and third rate stations for the subordinate Courts and detachments of troops and police. All to be chosen, with reference to position in districts under jurisdiction, and to salubrity of climate. At all these Stations suitable buildings would be provided; and as all would be commenced upon simultaneously, all would soon be ready.

Your Lordship will observe the small item put down for the judicial establishments all over Oude. Such as are really kept up are worthless, and are altogether without the confidence of the people. The savings in the other branches of the expenditure will more than cover all the outlay required for good ones.

The King continues to show the same aversion to hear anything about public affairs, or to converse with any but the singers, eunuchs, and females. At the great festival of the Eed, on the first appearance of the present moon, he went out in procession, but deputed his heir-apparent to receive the compliments in Durbar. He does not suffer bodily pain, but is said to have long fits of moping and melancholy, and he is manifestly hypochondriac. He squanders the state jewels among the singers and eunuchs, who send them out of the country as fast as they can. The members of his family who have its interests most at heart, are becoming anxious for some change; and by the time the two years expire, it will not, perhaps, be difficult to induce him to put his affairs into other hands. He would change his minister on the slightest hint from me; but it would be of no use: the successor, pretending to carry on the Government under the King's orders, would be little better than the present minister is, and things would continue to be just as bad as they now are: they certainly could not be worse.

The Board, composed of the first members of the Lucknow aristocracy, would be, I think, both popular and efficient; and with the aid of a few of the ablest of the native judicial and revenue officers of our own districts, invited to Oude by the prospect of higher pay and security in the tenure of office, would soon have at work a machinery capable of securing to all their rights, and enforcing from all their duties in every part of this, at present, distracted country. We should soon have good roads throughout the kingdom; and both they and the rivers would soon be as secure as in our own provinces. I think, too, that I might venture to promise that all would be effected without violence or disturbance; all would see that everything was done for the benefit of an oppressed people, and in good faith towards the reigning family.

With great respect, I remain your Lordship's obedient, humble servant.

(Signed) W. H. SLEEMAN.

To the Most Noble
the Marquis of Dalhousie, K.T.,
&c &c. &c.

P.S.—I may mention that the King is now engaged in turning into verse a long prose history called Hydree. About ten days ago all the poets in Lucknow were assembled at the palace to hear his Majesty read his poem. They sat with him, listening to his poem and reading their own from nine at night till three in the morning. One of the poets, the eldest son of a late minister, Mohamid-od Dowla, Aga Meer, told me that the versification was exceedingly good for a King. These are, I think, the only men, save the minister, the eunuchs, and the singers who have had the honour of conversing with his Majesty since I came here in January last.

W. H. S.

* * * * *

Lucknow, 23rd September, 1849.

My Dear Elliot,

I conclude that no further Tables will be required from me on Oude statistics for the present. Should they be so, pray let me know, and they shall be sent. I thought at first that it would be thought bad taste in me to refer to the domestic troubles of the King, but it is necessary to show the state to which his Majesty is reduced in his palace. The facts mentioned are known and talked of all over Lucknow and Oude generally, and tend more than greater things to bring his conduct and character into contempt.

The time was certainly never so favourable to propose an arrangement that shall secure a lasting and substantial reform, and render Oude what it ought to be—a garden. The King is in constant dread of poison, and would do anything to get relieved from that dread, and all further importunity on the state of the country. His chief wife would poison him to bring on the throne her son, and restore to her her paramour, who is now at Cawnpoor, waiting for such a change. Her uncle, the minister, would, the King thinks, be glad to see him poisoned, in the hope of having to conduct affairs during the minority. He is afraid to admonish his other wife for her infidelities with the chief favourite and singer, lest she should poison him to go off with her paramour to Rampoor, whither he has sent the immense wealth that the King has lavished upon him.

The whole family are most anxious that the King should resign the reins into abler hands, and would, I feel assured, hail the arrangement I have proposed as a blessing to them and the country. All seems ripe for the change, and I hope the Governor-General will consent to its being proposed soon. Any change in the ministry would now be an obstacle to the arrangement, and such a change might happen any morning. At the head of the Board, or Regency, I should put Mohsin-od Dowla, grandson of Ghazee-od Deen, the first King, and son-in-law of Moohummed Alee Shah, the third King. His only son has been lately united in marriage to the King's daughter. He is looked up to as the first man in Oude for character, and the most able member of the royal family. He is forty-five years of age. I should probably put two of the King's uncles in as the other members, Azeemoshan and Mirza Khorum Buksh, whose names you will find in the short appended list of those who have received no stipends since the present King ascended the throne. These princes cannot visit, the Resident except when they accompany the King himself, so that I have never seen the two last that I recollect, and only once conversed with the first. But their characters stand very high. They are never admitted to the King, nor have they seen him for more than a year, I believe.

The King will probably object to members of his family forming the Board, but I dare say I shall be able to persuade him of the advantage of it. Such a Board, so constituted, would be a pledge to all India of the honesty of our intentions, and secure to us the cordial good-will of all who are interested in the welfare of the family and the good government of the country.

I should persuade the members to draw from the *élite* of their own creed in our service to aid in forming and carrying out the new system in their several departments. We can give them excellent men in the revenue and judicial branches, who will be glad to come when assured that they will not be removed so long as they do their duty ably and honestly, and will get pensions if their services are dispensed with after a time. This is all I shall say at present.

Yours sincerely,
(Signed) W. H. SLEEMAN.

To Sir H. M. Elliot, K.C.B.,
&c. &c.

* * * * *

Lucknow.

My Lord,

My Official Report went off on the 25th instant, and will have been submitted, for your Lordship's consideration. It contains, I believe, a faithful description of the abuses that exist and require remedy, and of the obstacles which will be opposed to their removal. But it does not tell all that might be told of the King himself, who has become an object of odium and contempt to all but those few despicable persons with whom he associates exclusively. He eats, drinks, sleeps, and converses with the singers and eunuchs and females alone, and the only female who has any influence over him is the sister of the chief singer, Rusee-od Dowlah, whom he calls his own sister. No member of the royal family or aristocracy of Oude is ever admitted to speak to or see his Majesty, and these contemptible singers are admitted to more equality and familiarity than his own brothers or sons ever were; they go out, too, with greater pomp than they or any of the royal family can; and are ordered to be received with more honours as they pass through the different palaces. The profligacy that exists within the palace passes all belief, and these things excite more disgust among the aristocracy of the capital than all the misrule and malversation that arise from the King's apathy and incapacity.

Should your Lordship resolve upon interposing effectually to remedy these disorders, I think it will be necessary to have at Lucknow, for at least the first few months, a corps of irregular cavalry. We have no cavalry in Oude, and none of the King's can be depended upon. The first thing necessary will be the disbanding of the African, or Hubshee corps, of three hundred men. They are commanded by one of the eunuchs, and a fellow fit for any dark purpose. They were formed into a corps, I believe, because no man's life was safe in Lucknow while they were loose upon society.

I think the King will consent without much difficulty or reluctance to delegate his powers to a Regency, but I am somewhat afraid that he will object to its being composed of members of his own family. The Sovereign has always been opposed to employing any of his own relatives in office. I shall, I dare say, be able to get over this difficulty, and it will be desirable to employ the best members of the family in order to show the people of Oude, and of India generally, that the object of our Government is an honest and benevolent one.

A corps of irregular cavalry might be sent to Lucknow from Goruckpoor, and its place there supplied for a season by a wing from the corps at Legolee. There is little occasion for the services of cavalry at either of these places at present. Without any cavalry of our own here, and with this corps of African assassins at Lucknow at the beck of the singers, eunuchs, and their creature, the minister, neither the Resident nor any of the Regency would be safe. The treasury and crown jewels would be open to any one who would make away with them. If, therefore, your Lordship should determine upon offering the king the alternative proposed, no time should be lost in ordering the irregular corps from Goruckpoor to Lucknow, to be held at the Resident's disposal. Its presence will be required only for a few months.

I have mentioned, in my private letter to Sir H. M. Elliot, three persons of high character for the Regency. Two of them are brothers of the King's father. The third, and best, may be considered as in all respects the first man in Oude. Mohsin-od Dowlah is the grandson of the King, Ghasee-od Deen; his wife, and the mother of his only son, is the sister of the King's father, and his only son has been lately united in marriage to the present King's daughter. He and his wife have large hereditary incomes, under the guarantee of our Government, and his character for good sense, prudence, and integrity stands higher, I believe, than that of any other man in Oude.

All three belong to the number of the royal family who never visit the Resident except in company with the King, and I have, in consequence, never spoken to Mohsin-od Dowlah but once, and never seen either of the other two whom I have named, Azeemoshan and Khorum Bukeh, the King's uncles. The characters of all three are very high, and in general esteem.

Things are coming to a very critical state. There is no money to pay any one in the treasury, and the greater part of what comes in is taken for private purposes, by those who are in power. All see that there must soon be a great change, and are anxious "to make hay while the sun shines." The troops are everywhere in a state bordering on mutiny, but more particularly in and about the capital, because they cannot indemnify themselves by the plunder of the people as those in the distant districts do.

Fortunately the rains have this season been very favourable for tillage, and the crops may be good if we can preserve them by, some timely arrangement.

With great respect I remain,
  Your Lordship's obedient, humble servant,
    (Signed) W. H. SLEEMAN.

To the Most Noble
The Marquis of Dalhousie.

P.S.—I find that the irregular corps of cavalry has been moved from Goruckpoor to Sultanpoor Benares, and that Lagolee and Goruckpoor have now only one corps between them.

The Sultanpoor Benares corps might well spare a wing for Lucknow, and so might the corps at Bareilly spare one.

(Signed) W. H. SLEEMAN.

* * * * *

Lucknow, 11th October, 1849.

My Dear Elliot,

Here is a little item of palace news, communicated by one of the poets who has to assist his Majesty in selecting his verses, and who knows a good deal about what is going on among the favourites. Perhaps you may recollect him, Ameen-od Doulah, the eldest son of the late Aga Meer.

There is not a greater knave than Walee Alee in India, I believe. That his Majesty will consent to what the Governor-General may authorise us to propose I have no doubt, for he and his family are by this time satisfied that we shall propose nothing but what is good for them and the people of Oude.

But the King is no longer in a sound state of mind, and will say and do whatever the most plausible of the bad speakers may recommend. When I see him, I must have his signature before respectable witnesses to all his answers to distinct propositions, and act upon them at once, as far as I may be authorised by the Governor-General, or nothing will be done. It would not do for me to commune with him about affairs till I get instructions from you, as he would be sure to tell the singers, eunuchs, and minister all that has been said the moment I left him.

He has never been a cruel or badly-disposed man, but his mind, naturally weak, has entirely given way, and is now as helpless as that of an infant. Every hour's delay will add to our difficulties, and I wait most anxiously for orders. I am prepared with the new arrangements, and feel sure that the system will work well, and have the Governor-General's approval. I can explain it in a few words, and show the details in a small Table all ready for transmission when called for.

We shall have the royal family, the court, and people with us, with the exception of the minister and the favourites, who are in league with him, and those who share in the fruits of their corruption. Fifteen lacs are spoken of as the means ready to get either me out of the way or put a stop to all attempts of improvement for the present. I have in my public letter mentioned seven lacs as the average annual perquisites of the minister—they are at present at least twelve.

Yours sincerely,
(Signed) W. H. SLEEMAN.

To Sir H. M. Elliot, K.C.B.,
&c. &c.

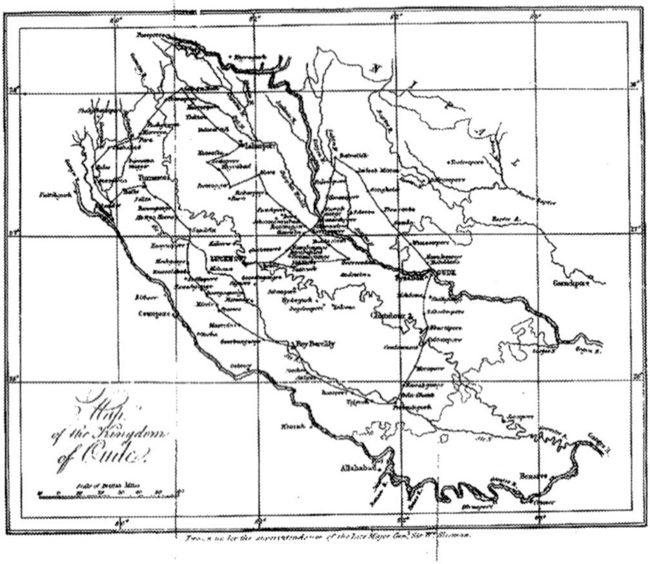
Map
of the Kingdom
of Oude
LUCKNOW
OUDE
Roy Bareilly
Allahabad
Benares
Goruckpore

DIARY OF A TOUR THROUGH OUDE

CHAPTER I.

Departure from Lucknow—Gholam Hazrut—Attack on the late Prime Minister, Ameen-od-Dowla—A similar attack on the sons of a former Prime Minister, Agar Meer—Gunga Sing and Kulunder Buksh—Gorbuksh Sing, of Bhitolee—Gonda Bahraetch district—Rughbur Sing—Prethee Put, of Paska—King of Oude and King of the Fairies—Surafraz mahal.

December 1, 1849.—I left Lucknow to proceed on a tour through Oude, to see the state of the country and the condition of the people. My wish to do so I communicated to Government, on the 29th of March last, and its sanction was conveyed to me, in a letter from the Secretary, dated the 7th of April. On the 16th of November I reported to Government my intention to proceed, under this sanction, on the 1st of December, and on the 19th I sent the same intimation to the King. On the 28th, as soon as the ceremonies of the Mohurrum terminated, His Majesty expressed a wish to see me on the following day; and on the 29th I went at 9 A.M., accompanied by Captain Bird, the first Assistant, and Lieutenant Weston, the Superintendant of the Frontier Police, and took leave of the King, with mutual expression of good-will. The minister, Alee Nakee Khan, was present. On the 30th I made over charge of the Treasury to Captain Bird, who has the charge of the department of the Sipahees' Petitions and the Fyzabad Guaranteed Pensions; and, taking with me all the office establishments not required in these three departments, proceeded, under the usual salute, to Chenahut, eight miles.*

* My escort consisted, of two companies of sipahees, from the 10th Regiment Native Infantry, and my party of Captain Hardwick, lieutenant Weston, and Lieutenant and Mrs. Willows and my wife and children, with occasional visitors from Lucknow and elsewhere.

The Minister, Dewan and Deputy Minister, Ghoolam Ruza, came out the first stage with me, and our friend Moonuwur-od Dowla, drove out to see us in the evening.

December 2, 1849.—We proceeded to Nawabgunge, the minister riding out with me, for some miles, to take leave, as I sat in my tonjohn. At sunrise I ventured, for the first time since I broke my left thigh-bone on the 4th April, to mount an elephant, the better to see the country. The land, on both sides of the road, well cultivated, and studded with groves of mango and other trees, and very fertile.

The two purgunnas of Nawabgunge and Sidhore are under the charge of Aga Ahmud, the Amil, who has under him two naibs or deputies, Ghoolam Abbas and Mahummud Ameer. All three are obliged to connive at the iniquities of a Landholder, Ghoolam Huzrut, who resides on his small estate of Jhareeapoora, which he is augmenting, in a manner too common in Oude, by seizing on the estates of his weaker neighbours. He wanted to increase the number of his followers, and on the 10th of November 1849, he sent some men to aid the prisoners in the great jail at Lucknow to break out. Five of them were killed in the attempt, seven were wounded, and twenty-five were retaken, but forty-five escaped, and among them Fuzl Allee, one of the four assassins, who, in April 1847, cut down the late minister, Ameen-od Dowla, in the midst of his followers, in one of the principal streets of Lucknow, through which the road, leading from the city to Cawnpore, now passes. One of the four, Tuffuzzul Hoseyn, was killed in attempting to escape on the 8th August 1849, and one, Alee Mahomed, was killed in this last attempt. The third, Fuzl Allee, with some of the most atrocious and desperate of his companions, is now with this Ghoolam Huzrut, disturbing the peace of the country. The leader in this attempt was Ghoolam Hyder Khan, who is still in jail at Lucknow.

On my remarking to the King's wakeel that these ruffians had all high-sounding names, he said, "They are really all men of high lineage; and men of that class, who become ruffians, are always sure to be of the worst description." "As horses of the best blood, when they do become vicious, are the most incorrigible, I suppose?" "Nothing can be more true, sir," rejoined the wakeel. An account of the attack made by the above-named ruffians on the minister, may be here given as both interesting and instructive, or at least as illustrative of the state of society and government in Oude.

At five in the morning of the 8th of April 1847, the minister, Ameen-od Dowlah, left his house in a buggy to visit the King. Of his armed attendants he had only three or four with him. He had not gone far when four armed assassins placed themselves in front of his buggy and ordered him to stop. One of them, Tuffuzzul Hoseyn, seized the horse; by the bridle, and told the minister, that he must give him the arrears of pay due before he could go on. The other three, Fuzl Allee, Allee Mahomed, and Hyder Khan, came up and stood on the right side of the buggy. One of the minister's servants, named Hollas, tried to prevent their coming near, but was fired upon by Allee Mahomed. He missed him, but Fuzl Allee discharged his blunderbuss at him, and he fell; but in falling, he wounded Hyder Khan slightly with his sword. Hyder Khan then threw away his fire-arms and sprang into the buggy with his naked dagger in his right hand and the minister in his left. The minister seized him round the waist, forced him back out of the buggy on the left, and fell upon him. Tuffuzzul Hoseyn then quitted his hold of the horse and rushed to his comrade's assistance, but the minister still holding Hyder Khan in his right hand, seized Tuffuzzul Hoseyn with his left. Syud Aman Allee, another personal servant of the minister, was cut down by Fuzl Allee, in attempting to aid his master, and a third personal servant, Shah Meer, was severely wounded by Allee Mahomed, and stood at a distance of twenty paces, calling for help. Fuzl Allee now made two cuts with his sword on the right shoulder and arm of the minister, below the elbow, and he quitted his hold on the two assassins and fell. The four assassins now grasped their victim, and told him that they would do him no farther harm if no rescue were attempted. As they saw the rest of the minister's armed attendants and a crowd approach, Fuzl Allee and Hyder Khan, with their blunderbusses loaded and cocked, stood one at each end of an open space of about sixty yards, and threatened to shoot the first man who should venture to approach nearer. The crowd and attendants of the minister were kept back, and no one ventured to enter this space, in the centre of which the minister lay, grasped by Tuffuzzul Hoseyn and Allee Mahomed, who held their naked daggers at his breast. The minister called out to his attendants and the crowd to keep back. He was then allowed to rise and walk to a small raised terrace on the side of the street, where he lay down on his back, being unable any longer to sit or stand from the loss of blood. Tuffuzzul Hoseyn and Allee Mahomed knelt over him, holding the points of their daggers at his breast, and swearing that they would plunge them to his heart if he attempted to move, or any one presumed to enter the open space to rescue him. Hollas and Syud Aman Allee lay bleeding at the spot where they fell. Hollas died that day, and Syud Aman Allee a few days after, of lock-jaw.

As soon as the attack on the minister was made, information of it was sent off to the Resident, Colonel Richmond, who wrote to request the Brigadier Commanding the Troops in Oude, to send him, as soon as possible, a regiment of infantry with two guns, from the Cantonments, which are three miles and a-half distant from the Residency, on the opposite side from the scene of the attack, to prevent any tumult that the loose characters of the city might attempt to raise on the occasion, and repaired himself to the spot attended by the Assistant, Captain Bird, and a small guard of sipahees. They reached the open spot, in the centre of which the minister lay, about a quarter of an hour after he fell. He found the street, in which the attack took place, crowded with people up to the place where the two sentries, Fuzl Allee and Hyder Khan, stood at each end of the open space, in the centre of which the minister lay, with the daggers of the two other assassins pressing upon his breast. On reaching one end of the open space, the Resident directed Captain Bird to advance to the spot where the minister lay. The assassin who guarded that end at first threatened to shoot him, but no sooner recognized him than he let him pass on unattended. He asked the two men, who knelt over the minister, what they meant by this assault. They told him, that good men were no longer employed in the King's service, and that they were, in consequence, without the means of subsistence; and had been compelled to resort to this mode of obtaining them; that they required fifty thousand rupees from the minister, with a written assurance from the British Resident, that they should be escorted in safety across the Ganges into the British territory with this sum.

The Resident peremptorily refused to enter into any written agreement with them, and told them, through the Assistant, that if they presumed to put the minister to death, or to offer him any further violence, they should be all four immediately shot down and cut to pieces; but, if they did him no further harm, their lives should, be spared; and, to prevent their being killed as soon as they quitted their hold, that he would take them all with him to the Residency, and neither imprison them himself, nor have them made over as prisoners to the Oude Government; but that he declined being a party to any arrangement that the minister might wish to make of paying money for his life.

They continued resolutely to threaten instant death to the minister should any one but the Resident or his Assistant presume to enter the open space in which he lay. Many thousands of reckless and desperate characters filled the street, ready to commence a tumult, for the plunder of the city, the moment that the minister or the assassins should be killed, while the relations and dependents of the minister, with loud cries, offered lacs of rupees to the assassins if they spared his life, so as to encourage them to hold out. They at last collected and brought to the spot, on three or four elephants, the fifty thousand rupees demanded by the assassins, and offered them to his assailants apparently with his concurrence; and the four ruffians, having assented to the terms offered by the Resident, permitted Doctor Login, the Residency Surgeon, to approach the prostrate minister and dress his wounds. One of the assassins, however, continued to kneel by his side with his naked dagger resting on his breast till he saw the other three seated upon the elephants, on which the money was placed, with the understanding, that the guard of sipahees, which the Resident had brought with him, should escort them to the Residency, and that Captain Bird, the Assistant, should accompany them. The fourth man then quitted his hold on the minister, who had become very faint, and climbed upon Captain Bird's elephant and took seat behind him. Captain Bird, however, made him get off, and mount another elephant with his companions. The crowd shouted *shah bash, shah bash!*—well done, well done! and they attempted to scatter some of the money from the elephants among them, but were prevented by Captain Bird, who dreaded the consequences in such a tumult. They were all four taken to the Residency under the guard of sipahees, and accommodated in one of the lower rooms of the office; and a guard was placed over the money with orders to keep back the crowd of spectators, which was very great. Three of the four ruffians had been wounded by the minister's attendants before they could secure his person, and their wounds were now dressed by Doctor Login.

It was now ten o'clock, and at twelve the Resident had an interview with the King, who had become much alarmed, not only for the safety of the minister, but for that of the city, threatened by the thousands of bad characters, anxious for an occasion of pillage; and he expressed an anxious wish that the assassins should be made over to him for trial. But the Resident pleaded the solemn promise which he had made, and his Majesty admitted the necessity of the promise under the circumstances, and that of keeping it; but said that he would have the whole affair carefully investigated. As soon as the Resident left him, he sent a company of sipahees with fetters to the Residency to receive charge of the prisoners, but the Resident would not give them up. The King then wrote a letter to the Resident with his own hand, requesting that the prisoners might be surrendered to him. The Resident, in his reply to His Majesty's, letter, told him, that he could not so far violate the promise he had given, but that he would send them to answer any other charges that might be brought against them, in any open and impartial Court that might be appointed to try them; and if they should be found guilty of other crimes, His Majesty might order any sentence passed upon them, short of death, to be carried into execution.

Charges of many successful attempts of the same kind, and many atrocious murders perpetrated by the ruffians, in distant districts of Oude, were preferred against them; and they were prevailed upon to give up their arms, and to submit to a fair and open trial, on the other charges preferred against them, on condition that they should neither be put to death nor in any way maimed, or put in fetters, or subjected to ill-treatment before trial and conviction. The Resident offered them the alternative of doing this or leaving the Residency, after he had read to them the King's letter, and told them, that his promise extended only to saving their lives and escorting them to the Residency; and, that he would not be answerable for their lives beyond the court-yard of the Residency, if they refused the conditions now offered. They knew that their lives would not be safe for a moment after they got beyond the court-yard, and submitted. Their arms and the fifty thousand rupees were sent to the King. At four in the afternoon, the four prisoners were made over to the King's wakeel, on a solemn promise given under the express sanction of his Majesty, of safe conduct through the streets, of freedom from fetters, or any kind of ill-treatment before conviction, and of fair and open trial.

But they had not gone two paces from the Residency court-yard, when they were set upon by the very people sent by the King to take care of them on the way; the King's wakeel having got into his palkee and gone on before them towards the palace. They were beaten with whips, sticks, and the hilts of swords, till one of the four fell down insensible, and the other three were reduced to a pitiable condition. The Resident took measures to protect them from further violence, recalled the wakeel; and, after admonishing him for his dishonourable conduct, had the prisoners taken unfettered to a convenient house near the prison. The wounded minister wrote to the King, earnestly praying that the prisoners might not suffer any kind of ill-treatment before conviction, after a fair and impartial trial. The Resident reported to Government all that had occurred, and stated, that he should see that the promises made to the prisoners were fulfilled, that, should they be convicted before the Court appointed to conduct the trial, of other crimes perpetrated before this assault on the minister, they would be subject to such punishment as the Mahommedan law prescribed for such crimes. Three of them, Tuffuzzul Hoseyn, Hyder Khan, and Fuzl Allee, were convicted, on their own confessions, and the testimony of their own relations, of many cold blooded murders, and successful attempts to extort money from respectable and wealthy persons in different parts of Oude, similar to this on the minister, and all four were sentenced to imprisonment for life. The Government of India had insisted on their not being executed or mutilated. Fuzl Allee, as above stated, broke jail, and is still at large at his old trade, and Hyder Khan is still in prison at Lucknow.

These ruffians appear to have been encouraged, in this assault upon the minister, for the purpose of extorting money, by a similar but more successful attempt made in the year 1824, by a party headed by a person named Syud Mahomed Eesa Meean, *alias* Eesa Meean.

This person came to Lucknow with a letter of recommendation from Captain Gough. He delivered it in person to the Resident, but was never after seen or heard of by him till this affair occurred. He became a kind of saint, or *apostle*, at Lucknow; and Fakeer Mahomed Khan Rusaldar, who commanded a corps of Cavalry, and had much influence over the minister, Aga Meer, became one of his *disciples*, and prevailed upon the minister to entertain him as a mosahib, or aide-de-camp. He soon became a favourite with Aga Meer, and formed a liaison with a dancing-girl, named Beeba Jan. His conduct towards her soon became too violent and overbearing, and she sought shelter with the Khasmahal, or chief consort, of the minister, who promised her protection, and detained her in her apartments. Eesa Meean appealed to the minister, and demanded her surrender. The minister told him that she was mistress of her own actions, as she had never gone through the ceremonies of permanent marriage, or *nikkah*, nor even those of a temporary one, *motah*; and most be considered as altogether free to choose her own lovers or mode of life.

He then appealed to Moulavee Karamut Allee, the tutor of Aga Meer's children, but was told, that he could not interfere, as the female was a mere acquaintance of his, and bound to him by no legal ties whatever; and must, therefore, be considered as free to reside where and with whom she chose. Eesa Meean then took his resolution, and prevailed upon some fifteen of the loose and desperate characters who always swarm at Lucknow, to aid him in carrying it out. On the 2nd of June 1824, Karamut Allee, the tutor, was bathing, and Aga Meer's two eldest sons, Aga Allee, aged eleven, and Nizam-od Dowlah, aged six years were reading their lessons in the school-room, under the deputy-tutor, Moulavee Ameen Allee. It was early in the morning, but the minister had gone out to wait upon the King. Eesa Meean entered the school-room, and approached the children with the usual courtesy and compliments, followed by six armed men, and one table attendant, or khidmutgar.

The two boys were sitting beside each other, the eldest, Aga Allee, on the left, and the youngest, Nizam-od Dowla, on the right. Eesa Meean sat down on the left side of the eldest, and congratulated both on the rapid progress they were making in their studies. Three of his followers, while he was doing this, placed themselves on the left of the eldest, and the other three on the right of the youngest. On a concerted signal all drew forth and cocked their pistols, and placed themselves at the only three doors that opened from the school-room, two at each, while at a signal made by the khidmutgar, eight more men came in armed in the same manner. Two of them with naked daggers in their right hands seized the two boys with their left, and threatened them with instant death if they attempted to more or call for help. The other six threatened to kill any one who should attempt to force his way into the apartment. The khidmutgar, in the mean time, seized and brought into the room two large gharahs or pitchers of drinking water, that stood outside, as the weather was very hot, and the party would require it They were afraid that poison might be put into the water if left outside after they had commenced the assault. Eesa Meean then declared, that he had been driven to this violent act by the detention of his girl by the Khasmahal, and must have her instantly surrendered, or they would put the boys to death. Hearing the noise from his bathing-room, their tutor, Karamut Allee, rushed into the room with nothing on his person but his waist-band, and began to admonish the ruffians. Seeing him unarmed, and respecting his peaceful character, they let him pass in and vociferate, but paid no regard to what he said.

The alarm had spread through the house and town, and many of the chief officers of the Court were permitted to enter the room unarmed. Roshun-od Dowlah, Sobhan Allee Khan, Fakeer Mahomed Khan, Nuzee Allee Khan, (the Khasmahul's son-in-law,) and others of equal rank, all in loud terms admonished the assailants, and demanded the surrender of the children, but all were alike unheeded. The chief merchant of Lucknow, Sa Gobind Lal, came in; and thinking that all affairs could and ought to be settled in a business-like way, told the chief officers to fix the sum to be given, and he would at once pledge himself to the payment. All agreed to this, and Sobhan Allee Khan, the Chief Secretary of the minister, set to work and drew up a long and eloquent paper of conditions. On his beginning to read it, one of the ruffians, who had one eye, rushed in, snatched it from his hand, tore it to pieces, and threw the fragments into his chief's, Eesa Meean's, face, saying, "that this fellow would write them all out of their lives, as he was writing the people of Oude every day out of their properties; that if they must die, it should not be by pen and paper, but by swords and daggers in a fair fight; that all their lives had been staked, and all should die or live together." He was overpowered by the others, and other papers were drawn up by the ready writer and consummate knave Sobhan Allee, but the one-eyed man contrived to get hold of all, one after the other, and tear them up.

The minister was with the King when he first heard of the affair, and he went off forthwith to the Resident, Mr. Ricketts, to say, that his Majesty had in vain endeavoured to rescue the boys through his principal civil officers, and had sent all his available troops, but in vain; and now earnestly entreated the British Resident to interpose and save their lives. The Resident consented to do so, on condition that any arrangement he might find it necessary to make should be binding on his Majesty and the minister. Aga Meer returned to the King with this message, and his Majesty agreed to this condition. The Resident then sent his head moonshie, Gholam Hossein, to promise Eesa Meean, that the woman should be restored to him, and any grievance he might have to complain of should be redressed, and his party all saved, if he gave up the children. But he and his followers now demanded a large sum of money, and declared, that they would murder the boys unless it was given and secured to them, with a pledge for personal security to the whole party.

The minister, on hearing this, came to the Resident, and implored him to adopt some measures to save the lives of the children. The Resident had been for three weeks confined to his couch from illness, but he sent his Assistant, Captain Lockett, with full powers to make any arrangement, and pledge himself to any engagements, which might appear to him to be necessary, to save the lives of the boys. He went, and being unarmed, was permitted to enter the room. He asked for Eesa Meean, whom he had never before seen, when one of the party that knelt over the boys rose, and saluting him, said, "I am Eesa Meean." Captain Lockett told him that he wanted to speak to him in private, when Eesa Meean pointed to a door leading into a side room, into which they retired. Eesa Meean offered Captain Lockett a chair, and at his request sat down by his side. He then entered into a long story of grievances, which Captain Lockett considered to be frivolous, and said, "that the minister had injured his prospects in many ways, and at last disgraced him in the eyes of all people at Lucknow, by conniving at the elopement of the dancing-girl that he was a soldier and regardless of life under such disgrace, and prepared to abide by the result of his present attempt to secure redress, whatever it might be; that his terms were the payment down of five lacs of rupees, the restoration of his dancing-girl, and the security of his own person and property, with permission to go where he pleased, unmolested." Captain Lockett reminded him quietly of what he had just said: "that he was a soldier, and anxious only for the recovery of his lost honour; that now, to demand, money, was to show to the world that wounded honour was urged as a mere pretext, and the seizure of the boys a means adopted for the sole purpose of extorting money; that he could not condescend to hold further converse with him if he persisted in such preposterous demands; that he might murder the children as they seemed to be in his power, but if he did so, he and his party would be all instantly put to death, as the house was surrounded by thousands of the King's soldiers, ready to fall upon them at the slightest signal." He then recommended him to release the boys forthwith before the excitement without became more strong, and accompany him to the Residency, where his real Wrongs would be inquired into and redressed.

Eesa Meean then rose and said: "Money is not my object. I despise it. I regard nothing but the preservation of my honour, and agree to what you propose; but I have several companions here who require to be consulted: let me speak to them." He then went into the large room. His companions all made objections of one kind or another, and what they all agreed to one moment was rejected the next. They vociferated loudly, and disputed violently with each other, and with all around them, and at times appeared desperate and determined to sacrifice the boys, and sell their own lives as dearly as possible. Eesa Meean himself seemed to be the most violent and boisterous of all, and had his hand frequently on the hilt of his sword when he disputed with the King's officers, whom he abused in the grossest possible terms. They did more harm than good by their want of temper and patience, but above all by their utter want of character, since no one could place the slightest reliance on the word of any one of them in such a trying moment. They seemed to have no control over their feelings, and to think that they could do all that was required by harsh language and loud bawling.

Captain Lockett at last persuaded them to leave the whole affair in his hands; and had they done so at first, he would have settled the matter, he thought, in half the time. They had been discussing matters in this angry manner for four hours and a half, without making the slightest impression on the ruffians; but when all became silent, Captain Lockett prevailed on them to release the boys on the conditions agreed to between him and Eesa Meean, and recorded on paper. In this paper it was declared—"That Syud Mahomed Eesa Khan, together with the woman, Beeba Jan, shall be allowed to go where he liked, with security to his life and honour, and with all the property and effects he might have, whether he got it from the King of Oude or from his minister; and that no one, either in the Honourable Company's or in the King of Oude's dominions, shall offer him any molestation; that no obstruction shall be thrown in his way by the officers of the British Government in the countries of any of the Rajahs at whose courts there may be a British Resident; and further, that no molestation shall be offered to him in the British territories in consequence of the disturbance which took place at Bareilly in 1816.

"(Signed) A. LOCKETT, *Assistant Resident.*"

After this paper had been signed by Captain Lockett, the two boys were set at liberty, and sent off in palanqeens to their mother under a guard. The minister had, in the morning, promised to give the assailants twenty thousand rupees, and they arrived before the discussions closed, and were placed on the floor of the school-room.

The girl, Beeba Jan, was now brought into the room, and made over to Eesa Meean. When first brought before him, she thought she was to be sacrificed to save the lives of the boys, and was in a state of great agitation. She implored Captain Lockett to save her life; but, to the great surprise of all present, Eesa Meean took up one of the bags of money, containing one thousand rupees, and, with a smile, put it into her arms, and told her that she was now at liberty to return to her home or go where she pleased. The joy expressed by the girl and by all who witnessed this scene was very great; for they had all considered him to be a mere ruffian, incapable of anything like a generous action.

It had been arranged that Eesa Meean, with all his party, should go with Captain Lockett to the Residency; but when the time came, and the excitement had passed away in the apartment, he began to be alarmed, and told Captain Lockett that he felt sure he should be murdered on the road. He wanted to go with Captain Lockett on the same elephant, but to this Captain Lockett would not consent, as it would compromise his dignity, to sit on the same elephant with so atrocious a character. There was no palanqeen available for him, and he would not allow Captain Lockett to enter his, declaring that if he did so, he, Eesa Meean, would be instantly cut down by the King's people. Captain Lockett was, therefore, obliged to walk with him from the minister's house at Dowlut Poora to the Residency, a distance of a mile, in the heat of the day, and the hottest month in the year, followed by the King's troops, and an immense multitude from the city. About four o'clock Captain Lockett reached the Residency, and made over Eesa Meean and his sixteen followers to the Resident, who ratified the written engagement, and sent the party to the cantonments, three miles distant from the city, to Brigadier-General Price, who commanded the troops in Oude, to be taken care of for a few days till arrangements could be made for their safe conduct to Cawnpore, within the British territory. Their arms were taken from them, to be sent to the magistrate at Cawnpore, for delivery to them when they might be released. On the morning of the 3rd the King came to the Resident to thank him for what he had done, and express the sense he entertained of the judicious conduct of his Assistant during the whole of this trying scene; and to request that he might be permitted to go to the palace to receive some mark of distinction which his Majesty wished to confer upon him. Captain Lockett went with the minister, and was received with marked distinction; and thirteen trays of shawls and other articles were presented to him. Captain Lockett selected one pair, which he accepted, and placed, as usual, in the Resident's Toshuk-khana.

When he signed the paper he remarked the omission of all mention of Eesa Meean's associates in that document, but did not consider it to be his duty to point out the oversight, lest it might increase the excitement, and prolong the angry discussions. In his report of the circumstances to the Resident, however, he mentioned it to him, and told him that the omission clearly arose from an oversight, and unless his associates received the same indulgence as the principal, Eesa Meean himself, their exclusion from the benefits of the engagement might be attributed to decoit or artifice on his part. The Resident concurred in this opinion, and in his report of the following day to Government, he recommended that they should all be considered as included in the engagement.

Government, in its reply of the 25th of June 1824, consents to this construction of the written engagement, but notices a no less important oversight on the part of the Resident and his Assistant, in the free pardon given to Eesa Meean, for the share he had taken in the Bareilly insurrection, which had caused the loss of so many lives in April 1816. Government infers, that they could, neither of them have been aware, that this ruffian was the original instigator and most active leader in that formidable insurrection; that it was chiefly, if not entirely, owing to his endeavours to inflame the popular phrenzy, and to collect partizans from the neighbouring towns, that the efforts of the local authorities, to quell or avert the rising storm, failed wholly of success; that he stood charged as a principal in the murder of Mr. Leycester's son, and that, on these grounds, he was expressly excluded from the general amnesty, declared after the successful suppression of the rebellion, and a reward of two thousand rupees offered for his arrest; that this written pledge had involved Government in the dilemma of either cancelling a public act of the British Resident, or pardoning and setting at large, within its territory, a proclaimed outlaw, and notorious rebel and most dangerous incendiary; and that it felt bound in duty to guard the public peace from the hazard of further interruption, through the violence or intrigue of so desperate and atrocious an offender; and to annul that part of the engagement which absolves Eesa Meean from his guilt in the Bareilly insurrection, since the Resident and his Assistant went beyond their powers in pledging their Government to such a condition. Government directed, that he and his associates should be safely escorted over the border into the British territory, and that he should not be brought to trial before a Judicial Court, with a view to his being capitally punished for his crimes at Bareilly, but be confined, as a state prisoner, in the fortress of Allahabad. The Government, in strong but dignified terms, expresses its surprise and displeasure at his having been placed in so confidential a position, and permitted to bask in the sunshine of ministerial favour, when active search was being made for him all over India; for the King and his minister must have been both aware of the part he had taken in the Bareilly insurrection, since the King himself alludes to it in a letter submitted by the Resident to Government on the 8th of June 1824.

The Resident and his Assistant, in letters dated 15th of July, declare that they were altogether unacquainted with the part which Eesa Meean had taken in the Bareilly rebellion in 1816, the Resident being at that time at the Cape of Good Hope, and his Assistant in England. Eesa Meean was confined, as directed, in the fort of Allahabad; but soon afterwards released on the occasion of the Governor-General's visit to that place. He returned again to Lucknow in the year 1828, soon after Aga Meer had been removed from his office of minister. As soon as it was discovered that he was in the city, he was seized and sent across the Ganges; and is said to have been killed in Malwa or Goozerat, in a similar attempt upon some native chief or his minister.

The two boys are still living, the eldest, Aga Allee, or Ameen-od Dowla, at Lucknow, and Nizam-od Dowla, the youngest, at Cawnpore; both drawing large hereditary pensions, under the guarantee of the British Government. This is not the Ameen-od Dowla who was attacked in the streets, as above described, in the year 1847.

About two years ago this Ghoolam Huzrut took by violence possession of the small estate of Golha, now in the Sibhore purgunnah; and turned out the proprietor, Bhowannee Sing, a Rathore Rajpoot, whose ancestors had held it for several centuries. The poor man was re-established in it by the succeeding contractor, Girdhara Sing; but on his losing his contract, Ghoolam Huzret, on the 23rd of September last, again attacked Bhowanne Sing at midnight, at the head of a gang of ruffians; and after killing five of his relatives and servants, and burning down his houses, turned him and his family out, and secured possession of the village, which he still holds. The King's officers were too weak to protect the poor man, and have hitherto acquiesced in the usurpation of the village. Ghoolam Huzrut has removed all the autumn crops to his own village; and cut down and taken away sixty mango-trees planted by Bhowannee Sing's ancestors. Miherban Sing, the son of the sufferer, is a sipahee in the 63rd Regiment Native Infantry, and he presented a petition through the Resident in behalf of his father. Other petitions have been since presented, and the Court has been strongly urged to afford redress. Ghoolam Huzrut has two forts, to which he retires when pursued, one at *Para*, and one at *Sarai*, and a good many powerful landholders always ready to support him against the government, on condition of being supported by him when necessary.

On crossing the river Ghagra, I directed Captain Bunbury, (who commands a regiment in the King of Oude's service with six guns, and was to have accompanied me, and left the main body of his regiment with his guns under his second in command, Captain Hearsey, at Nawabgunge,) to surprise and capture Ghoolam Huzrut, if possible, by a sudden march. He had left his fort of Para, on my passing within a few miles of it, knowing that the minister had been with me, and thinking that he might have requested my aid for the purpose. Captain Bunbury joined his main body unperceived, made a forced march during the night, and reached the fort of Para at daybreak in the morning, without giving alarm to any one on the road. In this surprise he was aided by Khoda Buksh, of Dadra, a very respectable and excellent landholder, who had suffered from Ghoolam Huzrut's depredations.

He had returned to his fort with all his family on my passing, and it contained but few soldiers, with a vast number of women and children. He saw that it would be of no use to resist, and surrendered his fort and person to Captain Bunbury, who sent him a prisoner to Lucknow, under charge of two Companies, commanded by Captain Hearsey. He is under trial, but he has so many influential friends about the Court, with whom he has shared his plunder, that his ultimate punishment is doubtful. Captain Bunbury was praised for his skill and gallantry, and was honoured with a title by the king.

December 3, 1849.—Kinalee, ten miles over a plain, highly cultivated and well studded with groves, but we could see neither town, village, nor hamlet on the road. A poor Brahmin, Gunga Sing, came along the road with me, to seek redress for injuries sustained. His grandfather was in the service of our Government, and killed under Lord Lake, at the first siege of Bhurtpore in 1804. With the little he left, the family had set up as agricultural capitalists in the village of Poorwa Pundit, on the estate of Kulunder Buksh, of Bhitwal. Here they prospered. The estate was, as a matter of favour to Kulunder Buksh, transferred from the jurisdiction of the contractor to that of the Hozoor Tehseel.* Kulunder Buksh either could not, or would not, pay the Government demand; and he employed two of his relatives, Godree and Hoseyn Buksh, to plunder in the estate and the neighbourhood, to reduce Government to his own terms. These two persons, with two hundred armed men, attacked the village in the night; and, after plundering the house of this Brahmin, Gunga Sing, they seized his wife, who was then pregnant, and made her point out a hidden treasure of one hundred and seven gold mohurs, and two hundred and seventy-seven rupees. She had been wounded in several places before she did this, and when she could point out no more, one of the two brothers cut her down with his sword, and killed her. In all the Brahmin lost two thousand seven hundred and fifty-five rupees' worth of property; and, on the ground of his grandfather having been killed in the Honourable Company's service, has been ever since urging the Resident to interpose with the Oude government in his behalf.

* The term "Hozoor Tehseel" signifies the collections of the revenue made by the governor himself whether of a district or a kingdom. The estates of all landholders who pay their land-revenues direct to the governor, or to the deputy employed under him to receive such revenues and manage such estates, are said to be in the "Hozoor Tehseel." The local authorities of the districts on which such estates are situated have nothing whatever to do with them.

The estate of Bhitwal has been retransferred to the jurisdiction of the Amil of Byswara, who has restored it to Kulunder Buksh; and his two relatives, Godree and Hoseyn Buksh, are thriving on the booty acquired, and are in high favour with the local authorities. I have requested that measures may be adopted to punish them for the robbery and the cruel murder of the poor woman; but have little hope that they will be so. *No government in India is now more weak for purposes of good than that of Oude.*

This village of Kinalee is now in the estate of Ramnuggur Dhumeereea, held by Gorbuksh, a large landholder, who has a strong fort, Bhitolee, at the point of the Delta, formed by the Chouka and Ghagra rivers, which here unite. He has taken refuge with some four thousand armed followers in this fort, under the apprehension of being made to pay the full amount of the Government demand, and called to account for the rescue of some atrocious offenders from Captain Hearsey, of the Frontier Police, by whom they had been secured. Gorbuksh used to pay two hundred thousand rupees a-year for many years for this estate, without murmur or difficulty; but for the last three years he has not paid the rate, to which he has got it reduced, of one hundred and fifty thousand. Out of his rents and the revenues due to Government he keeps up a large body of armed followers, to intimidate the Government, and seize upon the estates of his weaker neighbours, many of which he has lately appropriated by fraud, violence, and collusion. An attempt was this year made to put the estate under the management of Government officers; but he was too strong for the Government, which was obliged to temporise, and at last to yield. He is said to exact from the landholders the sum of two hundred and fifty thousand rupees a-year. He holds also the estate of Bhitolee, at the apex of the delta of the Ghagra and Chouka rivers, in which the fort of Bhitolee is situated. The Government demand on this estate is fifty thousand (50,000) rupees a-year. His son, Surubjeet Sing, is engaged in plunder, and, it is said, with his father's connivance and encouragement, though he pretends to be acting in disobedience of his orders. The object is, to augment their estate, and intimidate the Government and its officers by gangs of ruffians, whom they can maintain only by plunder and malversation. The greater part of the lands, comprised in this estate of Ramnuggur Dhumeereea, of which Rajah Gorbuksh is now the local governor, are hereditary possessions which have been held by his family for many generations. A part has been recently seized from weaker neighbours, and added to them. The rest are merely under him as the governor or public officer, intrusted with the collection of the revenue and the management of the police.

December 4, 1849.—Gunesh Gunge, *alias* Byram-ghat, on the right bank of the river Ghagra, distance about twelve miles. The country well cultivated, and studded with good groves of mango and other trees. We passed through and close to several villages, whose houses are nothing but mud walls, without a thatched or tiled roof to one in twenty. The people say there is no security in them from the King's troops and the passies, a large class of men in Oude, who are village watchmen but inveterate thieves and robbers, when not employed as such. All refractory landholders hire a body of passies to fight for them, as they pay themselves out of the plunder, and cost little to their employers. They are all armed with bows and arrows, and are very formidable at night. They and their refractory employers keep the country in a perpetual state of disorder; and, though they do not prevent the cultivation of the land, they prevent the village and hamlets from being occupied by anybody who has anything to lose, and no strong local ties to restrain him.

The town of Ramnuggur, in which Gorbuksh resides occasionally, is on the road some five miles from the river. It has a good many houses, but all are of the same wretched description; mud walls, with invisible coverings or no coverings at all; no signs of domestic peace or happiness; but nothing can exceed the richness and variety of the crops in and around Ramnuggur. It is a fine garden, and would soon be beautiful, were life and property better secured, and some signs of domestic comfort created. The ruined state of the houses in this town and in the villages along the road, is, in part, owing to the system which requires all the King's troops to forage for themselves on the march, and the contractors, and other collectors of revenue, to be continually on the move, and to take all their troops with them. The troops required in the provinces should be cantoned in five or six places most convenient, with regard, to the districts to be controlled, and most healthy for the people; and provided with what they require, as ours are, and sent out to assist the revenue collectors and magistrates only when their services are indispensably necessary. Some Chundele Rajpoot landholders came to me yesterday to say, that Ghoolam Huzrut, with his bands of armed ruffians, seemed determined to seize upon all the estates of his weaker Hindoo neighbours, and they would soon lose theirs, unless the British Government interposed to protect them. Gorbuksh has not ventured to come, as he was ordered, to pay his respects to the Resident; but has shut himself up in his fort at Bhitolee, about six miles up the river from our camp. The Chouka is a small river which there flows into the Ghagra.

He is said to have four or five thousand men with him; and several guns mounted in his fort. The ferry over the Ghagra is close to our tents, and called Byram-ghat.

December 5, 1849.—Crossed the river Ghagra, in boats, and encamped at Nawabgunge, on the left bank, where we were met by one of the collectors of the Gonda Bahraetch district. He complained of the difficulties experienced in realizing the just demands of the exchequer, from the number and power of the tallookdars of the district, who had forts and bands of armed followers, too strong for the King's officers. There were, he said, in the small purgunnah of Gouras—

1.—Pretheeput Sing, of Paska, who has a strong fort called Dhunolee, on the right bank of the Ghagra, opposite to Paska and Bumhoree, two strongholds, which he has on the left bank of that river, and he is always ready to resist the Government.
2.—Murtonjee Buksh, of Shahpoor, who is always ready to do the same; and a great ruffian.
3.—Shere Bahader Sing, of Kuneear.*
4.—Maheput Sing, of Dhunawa.*
5.—Surnam Sing, of Arta.*
6.—Maheput Sing, of Paruspoor.*

* All four are at present on good terms with the Government and its local authorities.

They have each a fort, or stronghold, mounting five or six guns, and trained bands of armed and brave men of five or six hundred, which they augment, as occasion requires, by Gohars, or auxiliary bands from their friends.

Hurdut Sing, of Bondee, *alias* Bumnootee, held an estate for which he paid one hundred and eighty-two thousand (1,82,000) rupees a year to Government; but he was driven, out of it in 1846-47, by Rughbur Sing, the contractor, who, by rapacity and outrage, drove off the greater part of the cultivators, and so desolated the estate that it could not now be made to yield thirty thousand (30,000) rupees a-year. The Raja has ever since resided with a few followers in an island in the Ghagra. He has never openly resisted or defied the Government, but is said to be sullen, and a bad paymaster. He still holds the estate in its desolate condition.

The people of Nawabgunge drink the water of wells, close to the bank of the river, and often the water of the river itself, and say that they never suffer from it; but that a good many people in several villages, along the same bank, have the goitre to a very distressing degree.

December 6, 1849.—Halted at Byram-ghat, in order to enable all our people and things to come up. One of our elephants nearly lost his life yesterday in the quick-sands of the river. Capt. Weston rode out yesterday close to Bhitolee, the little fort of Rajah Gorbuksh Sing, who came out in a litter and told him, that he would come to me to-day at noon, and clear himself of the charges brought against him of rescuing and harbouring robbers, and refusing to pay the Government demand. He had been suffering severely from fever for fifteen days.

Karamut Allee complains that his father, Busharut Allee, had been driven out from the purgunnahs of Nawabgunge and Sidhore, by Ghoolum Huzrut and his associates, who had several times attacked and plundered the town of Nawabgunge, our second stage, and a great many other villages around, from which they had driven off all the cultivators and stock, in order to appropriate them to themselves, and augment their landed estates; that they had cut down all the groves of mango-trees planted by the rightful proprietors and their ancestors, in order to remove all local ties; and murdered or maimed all cultivators who presumed to till any of the lands without their permission, that Busharut Allee had held the contract for the land revenue of the purgunnah for twenty years, and paid punctually one hundred and thirty-five thousand (1,35,000) rupees a-year to the treasury, till about four years ago, when Ghoolam Huzrut commenced this system of spoliation and seizure, since which time the purgunnah had been declining, and could not now yield seventy thousand (70,000) rupees to the treasury; that his family had held many villages in hereditary right for many generations, within the purgunnah, but that all had, been or were being seized by this lawless freebooter and his associates.

Seeta Ram, a Brahmin zumeendar of Kowaree, in purgunnah Satrick, complains, that he has been driven out of his hereditary estate by Ghoolam Imam, the zumeendar of Jaggour, and his associate, Ghoolam Huzrut; that his house had been levelled with the ground, and all the trees, planted by his family, have been cut down and burned; that he has been plundered of all he had by them, and is utterly ruined. Many other landholders complain in the same manner of having been robbed by this gang, and deprived of their estates; and still more come in to pray for protection, as the same fate threatens all the smaller proprietors, under a government so weak, and so indifferent to the sufferings of its subjects.

The Nazim of Khyrabad, who is now here engaged in the siege of Bhitolee, has nominally three thousand four hundred fighting men with him; but he cannot muster seventeen hundred. He has with him only the seconds in command of corps, who are men of no authority or influence, the commandants being at Court, and the mere creatures of the singers and eunuchs, and other favourites about the palace. They always reside at and about Court, and keep up only half the number of men and officers, for whom they draw pay. All his applications to the minister to have more soldiers sent out to complete the corps, or permission to raise men in their places, remain unanswered and disregarded. The Nazim of Bharaetch has nominally four thousand fighting men; but he cannot muster two thousand, and the greater part of them are good for nothing. The great landholders despise them, but respect the Komutee corps, under Captains Barlow, Bunbury, and Magness, which is complete, and composed of strong and brave men. The despicable state to which the Court favourites have reduced the King's troops, with the exception of these three corps, is lamentable. They are under no discipline, and are formidable only to the peasantry and smaller landholders and proprietors, whose houses they everywhere deprive of their coverings, as they deprive their cattle of their fodder.

December 7, 1849.—Hissampoor, 12 miles north-east, over a plain of fine soil, more scantily tilled than any we saw on the other side of the Ghagra, but well studded with groves and fine single trees, and with excellent crops on the lands actually under tillage. One cause assigned for so much fine land lying waste is, that the Rajpoot tallookdars, above named, of the Chehdewara, have been long engaged in plundering the Syud proprietors of the soil, and seizing upon their lands, in the same manner as the Mahomedan ruffians, on the other side of the river, have been engaged in plundering the small Rajpoot proprietors, and seizing upon their lands. Four of them are now quiet; but two, Prethee Put and Mirtonjee, are always in rebellion. Lately, while the Chuckladar was absent, employed against Jote Sing, of Churda, in the Turae, these two men took a large train of followers, with some guns, attacked the two villages of Aelee and Pursolee, in the estate of Deeksa, in Gonda, killed six persons, plundered all the houses of the inhabitants, and destroyed all their crops, merely because the landholders of these two villages would not settle a boundary dispute in the way 'they proposed'. The lands of the Hissampoor purgunnah were held in property by the members of a family of Syuds, and had been so for many generations; but neighbouring Rajpoot tallookdars have plundered them of all they had, and seized upon their lands by violence, fraud, or collusion, with public officers. Some they have seized and imprisoned, with torture of one kind or another, till they signed deeds of sale, *Bynamahs*; others they have murdered with all their families, to get secure possession of their lands; others they have despoiled by offering the local authorities a higher rate of revenue for their lands than they could possibly pay.

The Nazim has eighteen guns, and ten auxiliary ones sent out on emergency—not one-quarter are in a state for service; and for these he has not half the draft-bullocks required, and they are too weak for use; and of ammunition or *stores* he has hardly any at all.

Rajah Gorbuksh Sing came yesterday, at sunset, to pay his respects, and promised to pay to the Oude Government all that is justly demandable from him. Written engagements to this effect were drawn up, and signed by both the "high contracting parties." Having come in on a pledge of personal security, he was, of course, permitted to return from my camp to his own stronghold in safety. In that place he has collected all the loose characters and unemployed soldiers he could gather together, and all that his friends and associates could lend him, to resist the Amil; and to maintain such a host, he will have to pay much more than was required punctually to fulfil his engagements to the State. He calculates, however, that, by yielding to the Government, he would entail upon himself a perpetual burthen at an enhanced rate, while, by the temporary expenditure of a few thousands in this way, he may still further reduce the rate he has hitherto paid.

The contract for Gonda and Bahraetch was held by Rughbur Sing, one of the sons of Dursun Sing, for the years 1846 and 1847 A.D., and the district of Sultanpoor was held by his brother, Maun Sing, for 1845-46 and 1847 A.D. Rughbur Sing in 1846-47 is supposed to have seized and sold or destroyed no less than 25,000 plough-bullocks in Bhumnootee, the estate of Rajah Hurdut Sing, alone. The estate of Hurhurpoor had, up to that time, long paid Government sixty thousand (60,000) rupees a-year, but last year it would not yield five thousand (5,000) rupees, from the ravages of this man, Rughbur Sing. The estate of Rehwa, held by Jeswunt Sing, tallookdar, had paid regularly fifty-five thousand (55,000) rupees a-year; but it was so desolated by Rughbur Sing, that it cannot now yield eleven thousand (11,000) rupees. This estate adjoins Bhumnootee, Rajah Hurdut Sing's, which, as above stated, regularly paid one hundred and eighty-two thousand (182,000) rupees; it cannot now pay thirty thousand (30,000) rupees. Such are the effects of the oppression of this bad man for so brief a period.

Some tallookdars live within the borders of our district of Goruckpoor, while their lands lie in Oude. By this means they evade the payment of their land revenues, and with impunity commit atrocious acts of murder and plunder in Oude. These men maim or murder all who presume to cultivate on the lands which they have deserted, without their permission, or to pay rents to any but themselves; and the King of Oude's officers dare not follow them, and are altogether helpless. Only two months ago, Mohibollah, a zumeendar of Kuttera, was invited by Hoseyn Buksh Khan, one of these tallookdars, to his house, in the Goruckpoor district, to negotiate for the ransom of one of his cultivators, a weaver by caste, whom he had seized and taken away. As he was returning in the evening, he was waylaid by Hoseyn Buksh Khan, as soon as he had recrossed the Oude borders, and murdered with one of his attendants, who had been sent with him by the Oude Amil. Such atrocities are committed by these refractory tallookdars every day, while they are protected within our bordering districts. Their lands must lie waste or be tilled by men who pay all the rent to them, while they pay nothing to the Oude Government. The Oude Government has no hope of prosecuting these men to conviction in our Judicial Courts for specific crimes, which they are known every day to commit, and glory in committing. In no part of India is there such glaring abuse of the privileges of sanctuary as in some of our districts bordering on Oude; while the Oude Frontier Police, maintained by the King, at the cost of about one hundred thousand (100,000) rupees a-year, and placed under our control, prevents any similar abuse on the part of the Oude people and local authorities. Some remedy for this intolerable evil should be devised. At present the magistrates of all our conterminous districts require, or expect, that their charges against any offender in Oude, who has committed a crime in their districts, shall be held to be sufficient for their arrest; but some of them, on the other band, require that nothing less than some unattainable judicial proof, on the part of the officers of the Oude Government, shall be held to be sufficient to justify the arrest of any Oude offender who takes refuge in our districts. They hold, that the sole object of the Oude authorities is to get revenue defaulters into their power, and that the charges against them for heinous crimes are invented solely for that purpose. No doubt this is often the object, and that other charges are sometimes invented, for the sole purpose of securing the arrest and surrender of revenue defaulters; but the Oude revenue defaulters who take refuge in our districts are for the most part, the tallookdars, or great landholders, who, either before or after they do so, invariably fight with the Oude authorities, and murder and plunder indiscriminately, in order to reduce them to their own terms.

The Honourable the Court of Directors justly require that requisition for the surrender of offenders by and from British officers and Native States, shall be limited to persons charged with having committed heinous crimes within their respective territories; and that the obligation to surrender such offenders shall be strictly reciprocal, unless, in any special case, there be very strong reason for a departure from the rule.* But some magistrates of districts disregard altogether applications made to them by the sovereign of Oude, through the British Resident, for the arrest of subjects of Oude who have committed the most atrocious robberies and murders in the Oude territory in open day, and in the sight of hundreds; and allow refugees from Oude to collect and keep up gangs of robbers within their own districts, and rob and murder within the Oude territory. Happily such Magistrates are rare. Government, in a letter dated the 25th February, 1848, state—"that it is the duty of the magistrates of our districts bordering on Oude to adopt vigorous measures for preventing the assembling or entertaining of followers by any party, for the purpose of committing acts of violence on the Oude side of the frontier."

* See their letter to the Government of India, 27th May 1835.

December 8, 1849.—Pukharpoor, a distance of fourteen miles, over a fine plain of good soil, scantily tilled. For some miles the road lay through Rajah Hurdut Sing's estate of Bumnootee, which was, with the rest of the district of Bahraetch and Gonda, plundered by Rughbur Sing, during the two years that he held the contract. We passed through no village or hamlet, but saw some at a distance from the road, with their dwellings of naked mud walls, the abodes of fear and wretchedness; but the plain is well studded with groves and fine single trees, and the crops are good where there are any on the ground. Under good management, the country would be exceedingly beautiful, and was so until within the last four years.

In the evening I had a long talk with the people of the village, who had assembled round our tents. Many of them had the goitre; but they told me, that in this and all the villages within twenty miles the disease had, of late years, diminished; that hardly one-quarter of the number that used to suffer from it had now the disease; that the quality of the water must have improved, though they knew not why, as they still drank from the same wells. These wells must penetrate into some bed of mineral or other substance, which produces this disease of the glands, and may in time exhaust it. But it is probable, that the number who suffer from this disease has diminished merely with the rest of the population, and that the proportion which the goitered bear to the ungoitered may be still the same. They told me that they had been plundered of all their stock and moveable property by the terrible scourge, Rughber Sing, during his reign of two years, and could not hope to recover from their present state of poverty for many more; that their lands were scantily tilled, and the crops had so failed for many years, since this miscreant's rule, that the district which used to supply Lucknow with grain was obliged to draw grain from it, and even from Cawnpore. This is true, and grain has in consequence been increasing in price ever since we left Lucknow. It is now here almost double the price that it is at Lucknow, while it is usually twice as cheap here.

December 9, 1849.—Bahraetch, ten miles north-east. We encamped on a fine sward, on the left bank of the Surjoo river, a beautiful clear stream. The cultivation very scanty, but the soil good, with water everywhere, within a few feet of the surface. Groves and single trees less numerous; and of villages and hamlets we saw none. Under good government, the whole country might, in a few years, be made a beautiful garden.

The river Surjoo is like a winding stream in a park; and its banks might, everywhere, be cultivated to the water's edge. No ravines, jungle, or steep embankments. It is lamentable to see so fine a country in so wretched a state.

The Turae forest begins a few miles to the north of Bahraetch, and some of the great baronial landholders have their residence and strongholds within it. The Rajah of Toolseepoor is one of them. He is a kind-hearted old man, and a good landlord and subject; but he has lately been driven out by his young and reprobate son, at the instigation and encouragement of a Court favourite. The Rajah had discharged an agent, employed by him at Court for advocating the cause of his son while in rebellion against his father. The agent then made common cause with the son, and secured the interest of two powerful men at Court, Balkrishen Dewan and Gholam Ruza, the deputy minister, who has charge of the estates in the Hozoor Tehsel. The jurisdiction over the estate had been transferred from the local authorities to the Hozoor Tehsel; and, by orders from Court, the father's friends, the Bulrampoor and other Rajahs of the clan, were prevented from continuing the aid they had afforded to support the father's authority. The father unwilling to have the estate devastated by a contest with the band of ruffians whom his son had collected, retired, and allowed him to take possession. The son seized upon all the property the father had left, and now employs it in maintaining this band and rewarding the services of Court favourites. The Nazim of the district is not permitted to interfere, to restore rights or preserve order in the estate, nor would he, perhaps, do either, if so permitted, for he has been brought up in a bad school, and is not a good man. The pretext at Court is, that the father is deranged; but, though not wise, he is learned, and no man can be more sober than he is, or better disposed towards his sovereign and tenants. That he is capable of managing his estate, is shown by the excellent condition in which he left it.

Prethee Put, of Paska, is not worse than many of the tallookdars of Oude, who now disturb the peace of the country; and I give a brief sketch of his history, as a specimen of the sufferings inflicted on the people by the wild licence which such landholders enjoy under the weak, profligate, and apathetic government of Oude.

Keerut Sing, the tallookdar of Paska, on the left bank of the Ghagra, between Fyzabad and Byram-ghaut, was one of the Chehdwara landholders, and had five sons, the eldest Dirgpaul Sing, and the second Prethee Put, the hero of this brief history. Before his death, Keerut Sing made over the management of his estate to his eldest son and heir; but gave to his second son a portion of land out of it, for his own subsistence and that of his family. The father and eldest son continued to reside together in the fort of Dhunolee, situated on the right bank of the Ghagra, opposite Paska. Prethee Put took up his residence in his portion of the estate at Bumhoree, collected a gang of the greatest ruffians in the country, and commenced his trade, and that of so many of his class, as an indiscriminate plunderer. Keerut Sing and his eldest son, Dirgpaul, continued to pay the Government demand punctually, to obey the local authorities, and manage the estate with prudence.

Prethee Put, in 1836, attacked and took a despatch of treasure, consisting of twenty-six thousand rupees, on its way to Lucknow, from the Nazim of Bahraetch. In 1840 he attacked and took another of eighty-five thousand rupees, on its way to Lucknow from the same place. With these sums, and the booty which he acquired from the plunder of villages and travellers, he augmented his gang, built a fort at Bumhoree, and extended his depredations. In January 1842, his father, who had been long ill, died. The local authorities demanded five thousand rupees from the eldest son, Dirgpaul Sing, on his accession. He promised to pay, and sent his eldest son, Dan Bahader Sing, a lad of eighteen, as a hostage for the payment to the Nazim. Soon after, Prethee Pat attacked the fort of Dhunolee, in which his elder brother resided with his family, killed fifty-six persons, and made Dirgpaul, his wife, and three other sons prisoners. Dirgpaul's sister tried to conceal her brother under some clothes; but, under a solemn oath from Prethee Put, that no personal violence should be offered to him, he was permitted to take him. His wife and three sons were sent off to be confined under the charge of Byjonauth Bhilwar, zumeendar of Kholee, in the estate of Sarafraz Ahmud, one of his associates in crime, on the left bank of the Goomtee river.

Three days after, finding that no kind of torture or intimidation could make his elder brother sign a formal resignation of his right to the estate in his favour, he took him into the middle of the river Ghagra, cut off his head with his own hands, and threw the body into the stream. Deeming this violation of his pledge a dishonourable act his friend, Byjonauth, from whom he had demanded the widow and her three sons, released them all, to seek protection elsewhere, as he was not strong enough to resist Prethee Put himself. They found shelter with some friends of the family in another district, and Wajid Allee Khan, the Nazim of Bahraetch, in the beginning of November 1843, went with the best force he could muster, drove Prethee Pat out of Dhunolee and Paska, and put Dan Bahader Sing, the eldest son of Dirgpaul, and rightful heir, into possession. In the latter end of the same month, however, he was attacked by his uncle, Prethee Put, and driven out with the loss of ten men. He again applied for aid to the Nazim; but, thinking it more profitable to support the stronger party, he took a bribe of ten thousand rupees from Prethee Put, and recognized him as the rightful heir of his murdered brother. Dan Bahader collected a small party of fifteen men, and took possession of a small stronghold in the jungle of the Shapoor estate, belonging to Murtonjee, another of the Chehdwara tallookdars, where he was again attacked by his uncle in March 1844, and driven out with the loss of four out of his fifteen men. Soon after Prethee Put attacked and took another despatch of treasure, on its way to Lucknow from Bahraetch, consisting of eighteen thousand rupees. Soon after, in June, the Nazim, Ehsan Allee, sent a force with Dan Bahader, and re-established him in possession of the estate of Paska; but Ehsan Allee was soon after superseded in the contract by Rughbur Sing, who adopted the cause of the strongest, and restored Prethee Put, who continued to hold the estate for 1845.

In April 1847, Mahommed Hossein, one of the Tusseeldars under Rughbur Sing, seized and confined Prethee Put, once more put Dan Bahader in possession of the estate, and sent his uncle to Rughbur Sing. In November 1847, Incha Sing superseded his nephew, Rughbur Sing; and, thinking Prethee Put's the more profitable cause to adopt, he turned out Dan Bahader, and restored Prethee Put to the possession of the Paska estate, which he has held ever since. He has continued to pursue his system of indiscriminate plunder and defiance of the Government authorities, and has seized upon the estates of several of his weaker neighbours.

In 1848, he attacked and plundered the village of Sahooreea, belonging to Sarafraz Allee, Chowdheree of Radowlee, and this year he has done the same to the village of Semree, belonging to Rajah Bukhtawar Sing. He carried off fifty-two persons from this village of Semree, and confined them for two months, flogging and burning them with red-hot ramrods, till they paid the ransom of five thousand rupees required. He has this year plundered another village, belonging to the same person, called Nowtee, and its dependent hamlet of Hurhurpoora. He has also this year attacked, plundered, and burnt to the ground the villages of Tirkolee, in the Radowlee purgunnah, and Aelee Pursolee, in Bahraetch. The attack on Tirkolee took place in September last, and five of the inhabitants were killed; and in the attack on Aelee Pursolee, six of the zumeendars were killed in defending themselves. In this attack he was joined by the gang under Murtonjee. He also plundered and confined a merchant of Gowaris till he paid a ransom of seven hundred rupees; and about twenty-five days ago he attacked and plundered two persons from Esanugur, on their way to Ojodheea, on pilgrimage, and kept them confined and tortured till they paid a ransom of five hundred rupees.

Prethee Put has, as before stated, in collusion with local authorities, and by violence, seized upon a great portion of the lands of Hissampoor, and ruined and turned out the Syud proprietors, by whose families they had been held for many generations. He is bound to pay twenty thousand rupees a year; but has not, for many years, paid more than seven thousand.

Mahommed Hossein, the present Nazim of the Gonda Bahraetch districts, describes the capture of Prethee Put by himself, as follows:— "In 1846, the purgunnahs of Gowaris and Hissampoor were reduced to a state of great disorder by the depredations of Prethee Put, and the roads leading through them were shut up. He had seized Syud Allee Asgar, the tallookdar of Aleenughur, in the Hissampoor purgunnah, taken possession of his estate, and driven out, or utterly ruined, all the landholders and cultivators. He tried, by all kinds of torture, to make Allee Asgar sign, in his favour, a deed of sale; but his family found means to complain to the Durbar, and Rughbur Sing, the Nazim, was ordered to seize him and rescue his prisoner. I was sent to manage the two purgunnahs, seize the offender, and rescue Allee Asgar. When I approached the fort of Bumhoree, where he kept his prisoner confined, Prethee Put put him in strong irons, left him in that fort, and, with his followers, passed over the Ghagra, in boats, to his stronger fort of Dhunolee, on the right bank. I took possession of Bumhoree without much resistance, rescued the prisoner, and restored him to the possession of his estate, and put all the rest of the lands held by Prethee Put under the management of Government officers. Two months after, seeing my force much reduced by these arrangements, he came at the head of a band of seventeen hundred men to attack me in the village of Dhooree Gunge. The place was not defended by any wall, but we made the best of it, drove him back, and killed or wounded about fifty of his men, with the loss on our side, in killed or wounded, of about twenty-three.

"I kept Prethee Put confined for two months, when Rughbur Sing sent for him, on pretence that he wished to send him to Lucknow. He kept him till the end of the year, when he was superseded in the contract by his uncle, Incha Sing, who released Prethee Put at the intercession of Maun Sing, the brother of Rughbur Sing, who expected to make a good deal out of him." Prethee Put, of Paska, was attacked on the morning of the 26th of March, 1850, in his fort of Dhunolee, by a force under the command of Captains Weston, Thompson, Magness, and Orr; and, on their approach, he vacated the fort, separated himself from his gang, and took shelter in the house of a Brahmin. He was then traced by a party from Captain Magness's corps; and, as he refused to surrender, he was cut down and killed. His clan, the Kulhunsies, refused to take the body for interment. The head had been cut off to be sent to Lucknow as a trophy, but Captain Weston opposed this, and it was replaced on the body, which was sewn up in a winding-sheet and taken into the river Ghagra by some sipahees, as the best kind of interment for a Hindoo chief of his rank. The persons employed in the ceremony were Hindoos, who knew nothing of Prethee Put's history; but it was afterwards found that the place where the body was committed to the stream was that on which he had killed his eldest brother, and thrown his body into the river from his boat. This was a remarkable coincidence, and tended to impress upon the minds of the people around a notion that his death was effected by divine interposition. All, except his followers, were rejoiced at the death of so atrocious a character. Dan Bahader, the eldest son of the brother he had murdered, being poor and unable to pay the usual fees and gratuities to the minister and court favourites, was not, however, permitted to take possession of his patrimonial estate, and he died in December, 1850, in poverty and despair. Dhunolee and Bhumoree have been levelled with the ground.

December 9, 1849.—In the news-writer's report of the 3rd December, 1849, it is stated—"that Ashfakos Sultan, Omrow Begum, one of the King's wives, reported to his Majesty, that a man named Sadik Allee had come to Lucknow while the King was suffering from palpitations of the heart, and, in the disguise of a Durveish, hired a house in Muftee Gunge, and taken up his residence in it. He there gave himself out as one of the Kings of the Fairies (*Amil-i-Jinnut*); and the fakeer, to whom his Majesty's confidential servants, the singers, had taken him to be cured of his disease, was no other than this Sadik Allee. The King, on hearing this, sent for Sadik Allee, who was seized and brought before him on the 2nd December. He confessed the imposture, but pleaded that he had practised it merely to obtain some money, and that the singers were associated with him in all that he did. The King soothed his apprehensions, and conferred upon him a dress of honour, consisting of a doshala and roomul, and then made him over to the custody of Ashfak-os Sultan. At night the King sent for the minister, and, summoning Sadik Allee, bid him dress himself exactly as he was dressed on the night he visited him, and prepare a room in the palace exactly in the same manner as he had prepared his own to receive his Majesty on that night. He chose a small room in the palace, and under the ceiling he suspended a second ceiling, so that no one could perceive how it was fixed on, and placed himself between the two. When all was ready the King went to the apartment with the minister, accompanied by Ruzee-od Dowlah, the head singer. When the door of the apartment was closed, they first heard a frightful voice, without being able to perceive whence it came. Neither the minister nor the King could perceive the slightest opening or fissure in the ceiling. They then came out and closed the door, but immediately heard from within the peaceful salutation of 'salaam aleekom,' and the man appeared within as King of the Fairies, and presented his Majesty with some jewels and other offerings. All was here enacted precisely as it had been acted on the occasion of the King's visit to Muftee Gunge. Turning an angry look upon Ruzee-od Dowlah, the King said, 'All the evil that I have so often heard of you, men of Rampoor, I have now with my own eyes seen realized;' and, turning to the minister, he said, 'How often have these men spoken evil of you before me!' Ruzee-od Dowlah then said, 'If your Majesty thinks me guilty, I pray you to punish me as may seem to you proper; but I entreat you not to make me over to the minister.' The King, without deigning any reply, summoned Hajee Shureef, and told him to place mounted sentries of his own corps of cavalry over the door of Saadut Allee Khan's mausoleum, in which these singers resided, and infantry sentries in the apartments with them, with strict orders that no one should be permitted to go out without, being first strictly searched. The sister of Ruzee-od Dowla could nowhere be found, and was supposed to have made her escape."

The King had several interviews of this kind with his Majesty, the King of the Fairies, who described the symptoms from which he suffered, and prescribed the remedies, which consisted chiefly of rich offerings to the Fairies, who were to relieve him. He frequently received letters from the Fairy King to the same effect, written in an imperious style, suited to the occasion. The farce was carried on for several months, and the King at different times is supposed to have given the Fairy King some two lacs of rupees, which he shared liberally with the singers.

I had heard of the affair of the Durveish from the minister, through his wakeel, and from Captain Bird, the first Assistant, in a letter. I requested that he would ask for an audience, and congratulate his Majesty on the discovery of the imposture, and offer any assistance that he might require in the banishment of the impostors. He was received by the King in the afternoon of the 6th. He expressed his regret that the King should have been put to so much trouble by the bad conduct of those who had received from him all that a king could give-wealth, titles, and intimate companionship; hinted at the advantage taken of this by Ruzee-od Dowlah, in his criminal intercourse with one of his Sultanas, Surafraz Muhal; and earnestly prayed him to put an end to the misery and disgrace which these men had brought and were still bringing on himself, his house, and his country. The King promised to have Ruzee-od Dowlah, his sister, and Kotub-od Dowlah, banished across the Ganges; but stated, that he could do nothing against Sadik Allee, however richly he deserved punishment, since he had pledged his royal word to him, on his disclosing all he knew about the imposition. The King asked captain Bird, whether he thought that he had felt no sorrow at parting with Surafraz Muhal, with whom he had lived so intimately for nine years; that he had, he said, cast her off as a duty, and did Captain Bird think that he would spare the men who had so grossly deceived him, caused so much confusion in his kingdom, and ill-feeling towards him, on the part of the British Government and its representative? His Majesty added, "I cherished low-bred men, and they have given me the low-bred man's reward, had I made friends of men of birth and character it would have been otherwise;" and concluded by saying, that he could not touch the money he had given to these fellows, because people would say that he had got rid of them merely to recover what he had bestowed upon them.*

* When he afterwards confined and banished them in June and July 1850, he took back from them all that they had retained; but they had sent to their families and friends, property to the value of many lacs of rupees.

The King, in the latter end of November, divorced Surafraz Muhal, and sent her across the Ganges, to go on a pilgrimage to Mecca. She had long been cohabiting with the chief singer, Gholam Ruza, and was known to be a very profligate woman. She is said to have given his Majesty to understand that she would not consent to remain in the palace with him without the privilege of choosing her own lovers, a privilege which she had freely enjoyed before she came into it, and could not possibly forego.

CHAPTER II.

Bahraetch—Shrine of Syud Salar—King of the Fairies and the Fiddlers—Management of Bahraetch district for forty-three years—Murder of Amur Sing, by Hakeem Mehndee—Nefarious transfer of *khalsa* lands to Tallookdars, by local officers—Rajah Dursun Sing—His aggression on the Nepaul Territory—Consequences—Intelligence Department—How formed, managed, and abused—Rughbur Sing's management of Gonda and Bahraetch for 1846-47—Its fiscal effects—A gang-robber caught and hung by Brahmin villagers—Murder of Syampooree Gosaen—Ramdut Pandee—Fairies and Fiddlers—Ramdut Pandee, the Banker—the Rajahs of Toolseepoor and Bulrampoor—Murder of Mr. Ravenscroft, of the Bengal Civil Service, at Bhinga, in 1823.

Bahraetch is celebrated for the shrine of Syud Salar, a *martyr*, who is supposed to have been killed here in the beginning of the eleventh century, when fighting against the Hindoos, under the auspices of Mahmood Shah, of Ghuznee, his mother's brother. Strange to say, Hindoos as well as Mahommedans make offerings to this shrine, and implore the favours of this military ruffian, whose only recorded merit consists of having destroyed a great many Hindoos in a wanton and unprovoked invasion of their territory. They say, that he did what he did against Hindoos in the conscientious discharge of his duties, and could not have done it without God's permission—that God must then have been angry with them for their transgressions, and used this man, and all the other Mahommedan invaders of their country, as instruments of his vengeance, and means to bring about his purposes: that is, the thinking portion of the Hindoos say this. The mass think that the old man must still have a good deal of interest in heaven, which he may be induced to exercise in their favour, by suitable offerings and personal applications to his shrine.

The minister reports to the Resident on the 9th, that the King had relented, and wished to retain the singer, Ruzee-od Dowlah, and his sister, and Kotub Allee, at Lucknow, with orders never to approach the presence. Captain Bird, in a letter, confirms this report.

December 11, 1849.—Left Bahraetch and came south-east to Imaleea, on the road to Gonda, over a plain in the Pyagpoor estate, almost entirely waste. Few groves or single trees to be seen; scarcely a field tilled or house occupied; all the work of the same atrocious governor, Rughbur Sing. No oppressor ever wrote a more legible hand.

The brief history of the management of this district for the last forty-three years, is as follows. The district consisted in 1807, of

	Khalsa Lands	Present Khalsa Lands
Bahraetch.....................	2,50,000	4,000
Hissampoor...............	2,00,000	40,000
Hurhurpoor................	1,25,000	10,000
Buhareegunge	1,50,000	15,000
	7,25,000	69,000

The contract was held by Balkidass Kanoongoe, for five years, from 1807 to 1811, when he died, and was succeeded in the contract by his son, Amur Sing, who held it till 1816. In the end of that year, or early in 1817, Amur Sing was seized, put into confinement, and murdered by Hakeem Mehndee, who held the contract for 1817 and 1818. In the year 1816, Hakeem Mehndee, who held the contract for the Mahomdee district, at four lacs of rupees a-year, and that for Khyrabad at five, heard of the great wealth of Amur Sing, and the fine state to which he and his father had brought the district by good management; and offered the Oude government one lac of rupees a-year more than he paid for the contract for the ensuing year. Hakeem Mehndee resided chiefly at the capital of Lucknow, on the pretence of indisposition, while his brother, Hadee Allee Khan, managed the two districts for him. He had acquired a great reputation by his judicious management of these two districts, and become a favourite with the King, by the still more skilful management of a few male and female favourites about his Majesty's person. The minister, Aga Meer, was jealous of his growing fame and favour, and persuaded the King to accept the offer, in the hope that he would go himself to his new charge, in order to make the most of it. As soon as he heard of his appointment to the charge of Bahraetch, Hakeem Mehndee set out with the best body of troops he could collect, and sent on orders for Amur Sing to come out and meet him. He declined to do so until he got the pledge of Hadee Allee Khan, the Hakeem's brother, for his personal security. This mortified the Hakeem, and tended to confirm him in the resolution to make away with Amur Sing, and appropriate his wealth. Both Hakeem Mehndee and his brother are said to have sworn on their Koran that no violence whatever should be offered to or restraint put upon him; and, relying on these oaths and pledges, Amur Sing met them on their approach to Bahraetch.

After discussing affairs and adjusting accounts for some months at Bahraetch, the Hakeem, by his courteous manners and praises of his excellent management, put Amur Sing off his guard. When sitting with him one evening in his tents, around which he had placed a select body of guards, he left him on the pretext of a sudden call, and Amur Sing was seized, bound, and confined. Meer Hyder and Baboo Beg, Mogul troopers, were placed in command of the guards over him, with orders to get him assassinated as soon as possible. Sentries were, at the same time, placed over his family and wealth. At midnight he was soon after strangled by these two men and their attendants. Baboo Beg was a very stout, powerful man; and he attempted to strangle him with his own hands, while his companions held him down; but Amur Sing managed to scream out for help, and, in attempting to close his mouth with his left hand, one of his fingers got between Amur Sing's teeth, and he bit off the first joint, and kept it in his mouth. His companions finished the work; and Baboo Beg went off to get his fingers dressed without telling any one what had happened. In the morning Hakeem Mehndee gave out, that Amur Sing had poisoned himself, made the body over to his family, and sent off a report of his death to the minister, expressing his regret at Amur Sing's having put an end to his existence by poisoning, to avoid giving an account of his stewardship. The property which Hakeem Mehndee seized and appropriated, is said to have amounted, in all, to between fifteen and twenty lacs of rupees!

Amur Sing's family, in performing the funeral ceremonies, had to open his mouth, to put in the usual small bit of gold, Ganges water, and leaf of the toolsee-tree; and, to their horror, they there found the first joint of a man's finger. This confirmed all their suspicions, that he had been murdered during the night, and they sent off the joint of the finger to the minister, demanding vengeance on the murderer. Aga Meer was delighted at this proof of his rival's guilt, and would have had him seized and tried for the murder forthwith, but Hakeem Mehndee gave two lacs of rupees, out of the wealth he had acquired from the murder, to Rae Doulut Rae, Meer Neeaz Hoseyn, Munshee Musaod, Sobhan Allee Khan, and others, in the minister's confidence; and they persuaded him, that he had better wait for a season, till he could charge him with the more serious offence of defalcations in the revenue, when he might crush him with the weight of manifold transgressions.

They communicated what they had done to Hakeem Mehnde, who, by degrees, sent off all his disposable wealth to Shabjehanpoor and Futtehghur, in British territory. In April 1818, the Governor-General the Marquess of Hastings passed through the Khyrabad and Bahraetch districts, attended by Hakeem Mehndee, on a sporting excursion, after the Mahratta war; and the satisfaction which he expressed to the King with the Hakeem's conduct during that excursion, added greatly to the minister's hatred and alarm. He persuaded his Majesty to demand from Hakeem Mehndee an increase of five lacs of rupees upon nine lacs a-year, which he already paid for Mahomdee and Khyrabad; and resolved to have him tried for the murder of Amur Sing, as soon as he could get him into his power. Hakeem Mehndee knew all this from the friends he had made at Court, refused to keep the contract at the increased rate, and, on pretence of settling his accounts, went first to Seetapoor from Bahraetch, and thence over the border to Shahjehanpoor, with all his family, and such of the property as he had not till then been able to send off. The family never recovered any of the property he had taken from Amur Sing, nor was any one of the murderers ever punished, or called to account for the crime.

On the departure of Hakeem Mehndee, Hadee Allee Khan (not the brother of Hakeem Mehndee, but a member of the old official aristocracy of Oude) got the contract of the district of Bahraetch with that of Gonda, which had been held in Jageer by and for the widow of Shoja-od Dowlah, the mother of Asuf-od Dowlah, commonly known by the name of the Buhoo Begum, of Fyzabad, where she resided. Hadee Allee Khan held the contract of these two districts for nine years, up to 1827. He was succeeded by Walaeut Allee Khan, who held the contract for only half of the year 1828, when he was superseded by Mehndoo Khan, who held it for two years and a half, to the end of 1830, when Hadee Allee Khan again got the contract, and he held it till he died in 1833. He was succeeded by his nephew, Imdad Allee Khan, who held the contract till 1835.

Rajah Dursun Sing superseded him in 1836, and was the next year superseded by the widow of Hadee Allee, named "Wajee-on-Nissa Begum," who held the contract for one year and a half to 1838. For the remainder of 1838, the contract was held by Fida Allee Khan and Ram Row Pandee jointly; and for 1839, by Sunker Sahae Partuk. For 1840, it was held by Sooraj-od Dowlah, and for 1841 and up to September 1843, Rajah Dursun Sing held it again. For 1844 and 1845, Ehsan Allee and Wajid Allee held it. For 1846 and 1847, Rughbur Sing, one of the three sons of Rajah Dursun Sing, held it. For 1848, it was held by Incha Sing, brother of Dursun Sing; and for 1849, it has been held by Mahummud Hasun. The Gonda district consisted of the purgunnahs of Gonda and Nawabgunge, and a number of tallooks, or baronial estates.

Under the paternal government of Balukram and his son, Amur Sing, hereditary canoongoes of the district, life and property were secure, the assessment moderate, and the country and people prosperous. It was a rule, strictly adhered to, under the reign of Saadut Allee Khan, from 1797 to 1814, never under any circumstances to permit the transfer of *khalsa* or allodial lands (that is, lands held immediately under the Crown) to tallookdars or baronial proprietors, who paid a quit-rent to Government, and managed their estates with their own fiscal officers, and military and police establishments. Those who resided in or saw the district at that time, describe it as a magnificent garden; and some few signs of that flourishing state are still to be seen amidst its present general desolation.

The adjoining district of Gonda became no less flourishing under the fostering care of the Buhoo Begum, of Fyzabad, who held it in Jageer till her death, which took place 18th December, 1815. Relying upon the pledge of the British Government, under the treaty of 1801, to protect him against all foreign and domestic enemies, and to put down for him all attempts at insurrection and rebellion by means of its own troops, without any call for further pecuniary aid, Saadut Allee disbanded more than half his army, and reduced the cost, while he improved the efficiency of the other half, to bring his expenditure within his income, now so much diminished by the cession of the best half of his dominions to the British Government. He assessed, or altogether resumed, all the rent-free lands in his reserved half of the territory; and made all the officers of his two lavish and thoughtless predecessors,* disgorge a portion of the wealth which they had accumulated by the abuse of their confidence;

and, at the same time, laboured assiduously to keep within bounds the powers and possessions of his landed aristocracy.

*   Asuf-od Dowlah and Wuzeer Allee.

Hakeem Mehndee exacted from the landholders of Bahraetch two annas in the rupee, or one-eighth, more than the rate they had hitherto paid; and his successor, Hadee Allee, exacted an increase of two annas in the rupee, upon the Hakeem's rate. It was difficult to make the landholders and cultivators pay this rate, and a good deal of their stock was sold off for arrears; and much land fell out of cultivation in consequence. To facilitate the collection of this exorbitant rate, and at the same time to reduce the cost of collection, he disregarded systematically the salutary rule of Saadut Allee Khan, who had died in 1814, and been succeeded by his do-nothing and see-nothing son, Ghazee-od Deen Hyder; and transferred the khalsa estates of all defaulters to the neighbouring tallookdars, who pledged themselves to liquidate the balances due, and pay the Government demand punctually in future. This arrangement enabled him to reduce his fiscal, military, and police establishments a good deal for the time, and his tenure of office was too insecure to admit of his bestowing much thought on the future.

As soon as these tallookdars got possession of khalsa villages, they plundered them of all they could find of stock and other property; and, with all possible diligence, reduced to beggary all the holders and cultivators who had any claim to a right of property in the lands, in order to prevent their ever being again in a condition to urge such claims in the only way in which they can be successfully urged in Oude—cut down all the trees planted by them or their ancestors, and destroyed all the good houses they had built, that they might have no local ties to link their affections to the soil. As the local officers of the Oude government became weak, by the gradual withdrawal of British troops, from aiding in the collection of revenue and the suppression of rebellion and disorder, and by the deterioration in the character of the Oude troops raised to supply their places, the tallookdars became stronger and stronger. They withheld more and more of the revenue due to Government, and expended the money in building forts and strongholds, casting or purchasing cannon, and maintaining large armed bands of followers. All that they withheld from the public treasury was laid out in providing the means for resisting the officers of Government; and, in time, it became a point of honour to pay nothing to the sovereign without first fighting with his officers.

Hadee Allee Khan's successors continued the system of transferring khalsa lands to tallookdars, as the cheapest and most effectual mode of collecting the revenue for their brief period of authority. The tallookdars, whose estates were augmented by such transfers, in the Gonda Bahraetch district, are Ekona, Pyagpoor, Churda, Nanpoora, Gungwal, Bhinga, Bondee, Ruhooa, and the six divisions of the Gooras, or Chehdwara estate. The hereditary possessions of the tallookdars, and, indeed, all the lands in the permanent possession of which they feel secure, are commonly very well cultivated; but those which they acquire by fraud, violence, or collusion, are not so, till, by long suffering and "hope deferred," the old proprietors have been effectually crushed or driven out of the country. The old proprietors of the lands so transferred to the tallookdars of the Gonda Baraetch districts from time to time had, under a series of weak governors, been so crushed or driven out before 1842, and their lands had, for the most part, been brought under good tillage.

The King of Oude, in a letter, dated the 31st of August 1823, tells the Resident, "that the villages and estates of the large refractory tallookdars are as flourishing and populous as they can possibly be; and there are many estates among them which yield more than two and three times the amount at which they have been assessed; and even if troops should be stationed there, to prevent the cultivation of the land till the balances are liquidated, the tallookdars immediately come forward to give battle; and, in spite of everything, cultivate the lands of their estates, so that their profits from the land are even greater than those of the Government." This picture is a very fair one, and as applicable to the state of Oude now as in 1823.

But if a weak man, by favour, fraud, or collusion, gets possession of a small estate, as he often does, the consequences are more serious than where the strong man gets it. The ousted proprietors fight "to the death" to recover possession; and the new man forms a gang of the most atrocious ruffians he can collect, to defend his possession. He cannot afford to pay them, and permits them to subsist on plunder. In the contest the estate itself and many around it become waste, and the fellow who has usurped it, often—nolens-volens—becomes a systematic leader of banditti; and converts the deserted villages into strongholds and dens of robbers. I shall have occasion to describe many instances of this kind as I proceed in my Diary.

Dursung Sing was strong both in troops and Court favour, and he systematically plundered and kept down the great landholders throughout the districts under his charge, but protected the cultivators, and even the smaller land proprietors, whose estates could not be conveniently added to his own. When the Court found the barons in any district grow refractory, under weak governors, they gave the contract of it to Dursun Sing, as the only officer who could plunder and reduce them to order. During the short time that he held the districts of Gonda and Bahraetch in 1836, he did little mischief. He merely ascertained the character and substance of the great landholders, exacted from the weaker all that they could pay, and "bided his time." When he resumed the charge in 1842, the greater landholders had become strong and substantial; and he was commanded by the Durbar to coerce and make them pay all the arrears of revenue due, or pretended to be due, by them.

Nothing loth, he proceeded to seize and plunder them all, one after the other, and put their estates under the management of his own officers. The young Rajah of Bulrampoor had gone into the Goruckpoor district, to visit his friend, the Rajah of Basee, Mahpaul Sing, when Dursun Sing marched suddenly to his capital at the head of a large force. The garrison of the small stronghold was taken by surprise; and, in the absence of their chief, soon induced to surrender, on a promise of leave to depart with all their property. They passed over into a small island in the river, which flows close by; and as soon as Dursun Sing saw them collected together in that small space, he opened his guns and musketry upon them, and killed between one and two hundred. The rest fled, and he took possession of all their property, amounting to about two hundred thousand rupees. The Rajah was reduced to great distress; but his personal friend, Matabur Sing, the minister of Nepaul, aided him with loans of money; and gave him a garden to reside in, about five hundred yards from the village of Maharaj Gunge, in the Nepaul territory, fifty-four miles from Bulrampoor, where Dursun Sing remained encamped with his large force.

The Rajah had filled this garden with small huts for the accommodation of his family and followers during the season of the rains, and surrounded it with a deep ditch, knowing the unscrupulous and enterprising character of his enemy. In September 1843, Dursun Sing, having had the position and all the road leading to it well reconnoitred, marched one evening, at the head of a compact body of his own followers, and reached the Rajah's position at daybreak the next morning. The garden was taken by a rush; but the Rajah made his escape with the loss of thirty men killed and wounded. Dursun Sing's party took all the property the Rajah and his followers left behind them in their flight, and plundered the small village of Maharaj Gunge; but in their retreat they were sorely pressed by a sturdy landholder of the neighbourhood, who had become attached to his young sporting companion, the Rajah, and whose feeling of patriotism had been grievously outraged by this impudent invasion of his sovereign's territory; and they had five sipahees and one trooper killed. The Bulrampoor Rajah had been plundered in the same treacherous manner in 1839, by the Nazim, Sunkersahae and Ghalib Jung, his deputy or *collector*. He had invited them to a feast, and they brought an armed force and surrounded and plundered his house and capital. He escaped with his mother into British territory; and tells me, that he was a lad at the time, and had great difficulty in making his mother fly with him, and leave all her wardrobe behind her.

The Court of Nepaul complained of this aggression on their territory, and demanded reparation. The Governor-General Lord Ellenborough called upon the Oude government, in dignified terms, to make prompt and ample atonement to that of Nepaul. "Promptness," said his Lordship, "in repairing an injury, however unintentionally committed is as conducive to the honour of a sovereign, as promptness in demanding reparation where an injury has been sustained." The Nepaul Court required, that Dursun Sing should be seized and sent to Nepaul, to make an apology in person to the sovereign of that state; should be deprived of all his offices, with an assurance, on the part of Oude, that he should never be again employed in any office under that government; and, that the amount of injury sustained by the subjects of Nepaul should be settled by arbitrators sent to the place on the part of both States, and paid by the Oude government. The Governor-General did not insist upon Oude's complying with the first of these requirements; but Dursun Sing was dismissed from all employments, arbitrators were sent to the place, and the Oude government paid the nine hundred and fourteen rupees, which they decided to be due to the subjects of Nepaul.

Dursun Sing at first fled in alarm into the British territory, as the Nepaul government assembled a large force on the border, and appeared to threaten Oude with invasion; while the Governor-General held in readiness a large British force to oppose them; and he knew not what the Oude government, in its alarm, might do to the servant who had wantonly involved it in so serious a scrape. His brother, Bukhtawar Sing, the old courtier, knew that they had enemies, or interested persons at Court, who would take advantage of the occasion to exasperate the King, and persuade him to plunder them of all they had, and confiscate their estates, unless Dursun Sing appeared and pacified the King by his submission, and aided him in a judicious distribution of the ready money at their command; and he prevailed upon him to hasten to Court, and throw himself at his Majesty's feet.

He came, acknowledged that he had been precipitate in his over-zeal for his Majesty's service; but pleaded, in excuse, that the young Rajah of Bulrampore had been guilty of great contumacy, and owed a large balance to the Exchequer, which he had been peremptorily commanded to recover; and declared himself ready to suffer any punishment, and make any reparation or atonement that his master, the King, might deem proper. The British and Nepaul governments had expressed themselves satisfied; but other parties had become deeply interested in the dispute. The King, with many good qualities, was a very parsimonious man, who prided himself upon adding something every month to his reserved treasury; and he thought, that advantage should be taken of the occasion, to get a large sum out of so wealthy a family. Three of his wives, Hoseynee Khanum, Mosahil Khanum, and Sakeena Khanum, had at the time great influence over his Majesty, and they wished to take advantage of the occasion, not only to screw out of the family a large sum for the King and themselves, but to confiscate the estates, and distribute them among their male relations. The minister, Menowur-od Dowlah, the nephew and heir of Hakeem Mehndee, who has been and will be often mentioned in this Diary, thought that, after paying a large sum to gratify his Majesty's ruling passion, and enable him to make handsome presents to the three favourites, Dursun Sing ought to be released and restored to office, for he was the only man then in Oude capable of controlling the refractory and turbulent territorial barons; and if he were crushed altogether for subduing one of them, the rest would all become unmanageable, and pay no revenue whatever to the Exchequer. He, therefore, recommended the King to take from the two brothers the sum of twenty-five lacs of rupees, leave them the estates, and restore Dursun Sing to all his charges, as soon as it could be done without any risk of giving umbrage to the British Government.

The King thought the minister's advice judicious, and consented; but the ladies called him a fool, and told him, that the brothers had more than that sum in stores of seed-grain alone, and ought to be made to pay at least fifty lacs, while the brothers pleaded poverty, and declared that they could only pay nineteen. The minister urged the King, to take even this sum, give two lacs to the three females, and send seventeen to the reserved treasury; and called upon the Chancellor of the Exchequer to give in his accounts of the actual balance due by the two brothers, on their several contracts, for the last twenty-five years. He, being on good terms with the minister, and anxious to meet his wishes, found a balance of only one lac and thirty-two thousand due by Dursun Sing, and one of only fifteen lacs due by his brother, Bukhtawar Sing, in whose name the contracts had always been taken up to 1842. The King, sorely pressed by the females, resolved to banish Dursun Sing, and confiscate all his large estates; but the British Resident interposed, and urged, that Dursun Sing should be leniently dealt with, since he had made all the reparation and atonement required. The King told him, that Dursun Sing was a notorious and terrible tyrant, and had fearfully oppressed his poor subjects, and robbed them by fraud, violence, and collusion, of lands yielding a rent-roll of many lacs of rupees a-year; and, that unless he were punished severely for all these numerous atrocities, his other servants would follow his example, and his poor subjects be everywhere ruined!

The Resident admitted the truth of all these charges; but urged, in reply, that the Oude government had, in spite of all these atrocities, without any admonition, continued to employ him with unlimited power in the charge of many of its finest districts, for twenty-five or thirty years; and, that it would now be hard to banish him, and confiscate all his fine estates, when his Majesty had so lately offered, not only to leave them all untouched, but to restore him to all his charges, on the payment of a fine of twenty-five lacs. The King was perplexed in his desire to please the Resident, meet the wishes of his three ladies, and add a good round sum to his reserved treasury; and at last closed all discussions by making Dursun Sing pay the one lac and thirty-two thousand rupees, found to be due by him, and sending him into banishment; holding Bukhtawar Sing responsible for the fifteen lacs due by him, and seizing upon his estates, and putting them under the management of Hoseyn Allee, the father of Hoseynee Khanum, the most influential of the three favourites, till the whole should be paid. She satisfied herself that she should be able to make the banishment of the man and the confiscation of the estate perpetual; and, before he set out, she secured the transfer of the strong fort of Shahgunge, with all its artillery and military stores, from Dursun Sing's to the King's troops. Dursun Sing went into banishment on the 17th of March 1844; but before he set out he addressed a remonstrance to the British Resident, stating—"that he had paid all that had been found to be due by him to the Exchequer, and made every atonement required for the offence charged against him; but had, nevertheless, been ordered into banishment—had all his charges taken from him, and his lands, houses, gardens, &c., worth fifty lacs, taken from him, and made over to strangers and Court favourites."

Hoseyn Allee had promised to pay to the Exchequer one lac of rupees a-year for these estates more than Dursun Sing had paid. He had paid annually for the Mehdona estates two lacs and eight thousand two hundred and seventy-six; and for the Asrewa estates, in the same district of Sultanpoor, one lac thirty-one thousand and eighty-nine-total, three lacs and thirty-nine thousand three hundred and sixty-five; and they probably yielded to him an annual rent of nearly double that sum, or at least five lacs of rupees. Hoseyn Allee, however, found it impossible to fulfil his pledges. The landholders and cultivators would not be persuaded that the sovereign of Oude could long dispense with the services of such a man as Dursun Sing, or bring him back without restoring to him his landed possessions; or that he would, when he returned, give them credit for any payments which they might presume to make to any other master during his absence. They, therefore, refused to pay any rent for the past season, and threatened to abandon their lands before the tillage for the next season should commence, if any attempt were made to coerce them. All the great revenue contractors and other governors of districts declared their inability to coerce the territorial barons into paying anything, since they had lost the advantage of the prestige of his great name; and the minister found that he must either resign his office or prevail upon his sovereign to recall him. The King, finding that he must either draw upon his reserved treasury or leave all his establishments unpaid under such a falling off in the revenue, yielded to his minister's earnest recommendation, and in May 1844, consented to recall Dursun Sing from our district of Goruckpoor, in which he had resided during his banishment.

On the 10th of that month he was taken by the minister to pay his respects to his Majesty, who, on the 30th, conferred upon him additional honours and titles, and appointed him Inspector-general of all his dominions, with orders "to make a settlement of the land revenue at an increased rate; to cut down all the jungles, and bring all the waste lands into tillage; to seize all refractory barons, destroy all their forts, and seize and send into store all the cannon mounted upon them; to put down all disturbances, protect all high roads, punish all refractory and evil-minded persons; to enforce the payment of all just demands of his sovereign upon landholders of all degrees and denominations; to invite back all who had been driven off by oppression, and re-establish them on their estates, or punish them if they refused to return; to ascertain the value of all estates transferred from the jurisdiction of the local authorities to the 'Hozoor Tehsel,' without due inquiry; and report, for the consideration of his Majesty and his minister, any *nankar* or rent-free lands, assigned, of late years, by Amils and other governors of districts; to enforce the payment of all recoverable balances, due on account of past years; to muster the troops, and report, through the commander-in-chief, all officers and soldiers borne on the muster-rolls, and paid from the treasury, but in reality dead, absent without leave, or unfit for further service;" in short, to reform all abuses, and make the government of the country what the King and his minister thought it ought to be. Dursun Sing assured them that he would do his best to effect all the objects they had in view; and, after recovering possession of his estates, and conciliating, by suitable gratuities, all the reigning favourites at Court, he went to work heartily at his Herculean task after his wonted way. But he, soon after, became ill, and retired to his residence at Fyzabad, where he died on the 20th of August, 1844, leaving his elder brother, Bukhtawar Sing—my Quartermaster-general—at Court; and his three sons, Ramadeen, Rughbur Sing, and Mann Sing, to fight among themselves for his landed possessions and immense accumulated wealth.

The minister was a man of good intentions; and, having inherited an immense fortune from his uncle, Hakeem Mehndee, he cared little about money; but he was an indolent man, and indulged much in opiates, and his object was to reform the administration at the least possible cost of time and trouble to himself. He had, he thought, found the man who could efficiently supervise and control the administration in all its branches; and he invested him with plenary powers to do so. Of the duty, on his part and that of his master; efficiently to supervise and control the exercise of these plenary powers on the part of the man of their choice, in order to prevent their being abused to the injury of the state and the people; or of the necessity of taking from Court favourites the nomination of officers to the charge of all districts and all fiscal and judicial Courts, and to the command of all corps and establishments, in order to render them efficient and honest, and prevent justice from being perverted, and the revenues of the state from being absorbed on their way to the treasury, they took no heed. Court favourites retained their powers, and the King and his minister relied entirely, as heretofore, upon the reports of the news-writers, who attend officially upon all officers in charge of districts, fiscal and judicial Courts, corps and establishments of all kinds, for the facts of all cases on which they might have to pass orders; and remained as ignorant as their predecessors of the real state of the administration and the real sufferings of the people, if not of the real losses to the Exchequer.

The news department is under a Superintendent-general, who has sometimes contracted for it, as for the revenues of a district, but more commonly holds it in *amanee*, as a manager. When he contracts for it he pays a certain sum to the public treasury, over and above what he pays to the influential officers and Court favourites in gratuities. When he holds it in *amanee*, he pays only gratuities, and the public treasury gets nothing. His payments amount to about the same in either case. He nominates his subordinates, and appoints them to their several offices, taking from each a present gratuity and a pledge for such monthly payments as he thinks the post will enable him to make. They receive from four to fifteen rupees a-month each, and have each to pay to their President, for distribution among his patrons or patronesses at Court from one hundred to five hundred rupees a-month in ordinary times. Those to whom they are accredited have to pay them, under ordinary circumstances, certain sums monthly, to prevent their inventing or exaggerating cases of abuse of power or neglect of duty on their part; but when they happen to be really guilty of great acts of atrocity, or great neglect of duty, they are required to pay extraordinary sums, not only to the news-writers, who are especially accredited to them, but to all others who happen to be in the neighbourhood at the time. There are six hundred and sixty news-writers of this kind employed by the King, and paid monthly three thousand one hundred and ninety-four rupees, or, on an average, between four and five rupees a-month each; and the sums paid by them to their President for distribution among influential officers and Court favourites averages above one hundred and fifty thousand rupees a-year. Many, whose avowed salary is from four to ten rupees a-month, receive each, from the persons to whom they are accredited, more than five hundred, three-fourths of which they must send for distribution among Court favourites, or they could not retain their places a week, nor could their President retain his. Such are the reporters of the circumstances in all the cases on which the sovereign and his ministers have to pass orders every day in Oude. Some of those who derive part of their incomes from this source are "persons behind the throne, who are greater than the throne itself." The mother of the heir-apparent gets twelve thousand rupees a-year from it.

But their exactions are not confined to government officers of all grades and denominations; they are extended to contractors of all kinds and denominations, to him who contracts for the supply of the public cattle with grain, as well as to him who contracts for the revenue and undivided government of whole provinces; and, indeed, to every person who has anything to do under, or anything to apprehend from, government and its officers and favourites; and, in such a country, who has not? The European magistrate of one of our neighbouring districts one day, before the Oude Frontier Police was raised, entered the Oude territory at the head of his police in pursuit of some robbers, who had found an asylum in one of the King's villages. In the attempt to secure them some lives were lost; and, apprehensive of the consequences, he sent for the official news-writer, and *gratified* him in the usual way. No report of the circumstances was made to the Oude Durbar; and neither the King, the Resident, nor the British Government ever heard anything about it. Of the practical working of the system, many illustrations will be found in this Diary.

The Akbar, or Intelligence Department, had been farmed out for some years, at the rate of between one and two lacs of rupees a-year, when, at the recommendation of the Resident, the King expressed his willingness to abolish the farm, and intrust the superintendence to *men of character and ability*, to be paid by Government. This resolution was communicated to Government by the Resident on the 24th of April, 1839; and on the 6th of May the Resident was instructed to communicate to his Majesty the satisfaction which the Governor-General derived on hearing that he had consented to abolish this farm, which had produced *so large a revenue to the state*. This was considered by the Resident to be a great boon obtained for the people of Oude, as the farmers of the department consented to pay a large revenue, only on condition that they should be considered as the only legitimate reporters of events—the only recognised *masters in the Oude Chancery*; and, as the Resident observed, "they choked up all the channels the people had of access to their sovereign;" but they have choked them up just as much since the abolition of the farm, and have had to pay just as much as before.

A brief sketch of the proceedings of Rughbur Sing, the son of Dursun Sing, in his government of these districts of Gonda and Baraetch, for the years 1846 and 1847, may here be given as further illustration of the Oude government and its administration, in this part of the country at least. It had not suffered very much under his uncle's brief reign in 1842 and 1843, and the governors who followed him, up to 1846, were too weak to coerce the Tallookdars, or do much injury to their estates. Rughbur Sing had a large body of the King's troops to aid him in enforcing from them the payment of the current revenue and balances, real or pretended, for past years; and a large body of armed retainers of his own to assist him in his contest with his brothers for the possessions of the Mehdona and Asrewa estates, which had been going on ever since the death of their father.

I have stated that Rughbur Sing held in contract the districts of Gonda and Bahraetch for the years 1846 and 1847, and shown to what a state of wretchedness he managed to reduce them in that brief period. In 1849, some months after I took charge of my office, I deputed a European gentleman of high character, Captain Orr, of the Oude Frontier Police, to pass through these districts, and inquire into and report upon the charges of oppression brought against him by the people, as his agents were diligently employed at Lucknow in distributing money among the most influential persons about the Court, and a disposition to restore him to power had become manifest. He had purchased large estates in our districts of Benares and Goruckpoor, where he now resided for greater security, while he had five thousand armed men, employed under other agents, in fighting with his brother, Maun Sing, for the possession of the *bynamah* estates, above described, in the Sultanpoor district. In this contest a great many lives were lost, and the peace of the country was long and much disturbed, but, after driving all his brother's forces and agents out of the district. Maun Sing retained quiet possession of the estates. This contest would, however, have been again renewed, and the same desolating disorders would have again prevailed, could Rughbur Sing's agents at the capital, by a judicious distribution of the money at their disposal, have induced the Court to restore him to the government of these or any other districts in Oude.

On the 23rd of July 1849, Captain Orr sent in his report, giving a brief outline of such of the atrocities committed by Rughbur Sing and his agents in these districts as he was able, during his tour, to establish upon unquestionable evidence; but they made but a small portion of the whole, as the people in general still apprehended that he would be restored to power by Court favour, and wreak his vengeance upon all who presumed to give evidence against him; while many of the most respectable families in the districts were ashamed to place on record the suffering and dishonour inflicted on their female members; and still more had been reduced by them to utter destitution, and driven in despair into other districts. To use his own words—"The once flourishing districts of Gonda and Bahraetch, so noted for fertility and beauty, are now, for the greater part, uncultivated; villages completely deserted in the midst of lands devoid of all tillage everywhere meet the eye; and from Fyzabad to Bahraetch I passed through these districts, a distance of eighty miles, over plains which had been fertile and well cultivated, till Rughbur Sing got charge, but now lay entirely waste, a scene for two years of great misery ending in desolation."

Rajah Hurdut Sahae, the proprietor of the Bondee estate, was the head of one of the oldest Rajpoot families in Oude. Having placed the most notorious knaves in the country as revenue collectors over all the subdivisions of his two districts, Rajah Rughbur Sing, in 1846, demanded from Hurdut Sahae an increase of five thousand rupees upon the assessment of the preceding year. The Rajah pleaded the badness of preceding seasons, and consequent poverty of his tenants and cultivators; but at last he consented to pay the increase, and on solemn pledges of personal security he collected all his tenants, to take upon themselves the responsibility of making good this demand. To this they all agreed; but they had no sooner done so, than Rughbur Sing's agent, Prag Pursaud, demanded a gratuity of seven thousand rupees for himself, over and above the increase of five thousand upon the demand of the preceding year. The Rajah would not agree to pay the seven thousand, but went off to request some capitalists to furnish securities for the punctual payment of the rent.

The agent sent off secretly to Rughbur Sing to say, that unless he came at the head of his forces he saw no chance of getting the revenues from the Rajah or his tenants, who were all assembled and might be secured if he could contrive to surprise them. Rughbur Sing came with a large force at night, surrounded his agent's camp, where the tenants and the Rajah's officers were all assembled, and seized them. He then sent out parties of soldiers of from one hundred to two hundred each, to plunder all the towns and villages on the estate, and seize all the respectable residents they could find. They plundered the town of Bondee, and pulled down all the houses of the Rajah, and those of his relatives and dependents; and, after plundering all the other towns and villages in the neighbourhood, they brought in one thousand captives of both sexes and all ages, who were subjected to all manner of torture till they paid the ransom demanded, or gave written pledges to pay. Five thousand head of cattle were, at the same time, brought in and distributed as booty.

The Rajah made his escape, but his agents were put to the same tortures as his tenants. Rughbur Sing, among other things, commanded them to sign a declaration, to the effect that his predecessor and enemy, Wajid Allee Khan, had received from them the sum of thirty thousand rupees more than he had credited to his government, but this they all refused to do. Rughbur Sing remained at Bondee for six weeks, superintending personally all these atrocities; and then went off, leaving, as his agent, Kurum Hoseyn. He continued the tortures upon the tenants and officers of the Rajah, and the captives collected in his camp. He rubbed the beards of the men with moist gunpowder; and, as soon as it became dry in the sun, he set fire to it. Other tortures, too cruel and indecent to be named, were inflicted upon four servants of the Rajah, Kunjun Sing, Bustee Ram, Admadnt Pandee, and Bhugwant Rae, and upon others, who were likely to be able to borrow or beg anything for their ransom.

Finding that the tenants did not return, and that the estate was likely to be altogether deserted, unless the Rajah returned, Kurum Hoseyn was instructed by Rughbur Sing to invite him back on any terms. The poor Rajah, having nothing in the jungles to which he had fled to subsist upon, ventured back on the solemn pledge of personal security given by Pudum Sing, a respectable capitalist, whom the collector had induced, by solemn oaths on the holy Koran, to become a mediator; and, as a token of reconciliation and future friendship, the Rajah and collector changed turbans. They remained together for five months on the best possible terms, and the Rajah's tenants returned to their homes and fields. All having been thus lulled into security, Rughbur Sing suddenly sent another agent, Maharaj Sing, to supersede Kurum Hoseyn, and seize the Rajah and his confidential manager, Benee Ram Sookul. They, however, went off to Balalpoor, forty miles distant from Bondee, and kept aloof from the new collector, till he prevailed upon all the officers, commanding corps and detachments under him, to enter into solemn written pledges of personal security. The Rajah had been long suffering from ague and fever, and had become very feeble in mind and body. He remained at Balalpoor; but, under the assurance of these pledges from military officers of rank and influence, Benee Ram and other confidential officers of the Rajah came to his camp, and entered upon the adjustment of their accounts.

When he found them sufficiently off their guard, Maharaj Sing, while sitting one evening with Benee Ram, who was a stout, powerful man, asked him to show him the handsome dagger which he always wore in his waistband. He did so, and as soon as he got it in his hand, the collector gave the concerted signal to Roshun Allee, one of the officers present, and his armed attendants, to seize him. As he rose to leave the tent he was cut down from behind by Mattadeen, khasburdar; and the rest fell upon him and cut him to pieces in presence of the greater part of the officers who had given the solemn pledges for his personal security. Not one of them interposed to save him. Doulut Rae, another confidential servant of the Rajah, however, effected his escape, and ran to the Rajah, who prepared to defend himself at Balalpoor, where Maharaj Sing tried, in vain, to persuade his troops' to attack him. For two months the towns and villages were deserted, but the crops were on the ground, and guarded by the Passee bowmen, who are usually hired for the purpose.

Beharee Lal, the principal agent of Rughbur Sing in these districts, now wrote a letter of condolence to the Rajah, on the death of his faithful servant, Benee Ram—told him that he had dismissed from all employ the villain Maharaj Sing, and appointed to his place Kurum Hoseyn, who would make all reparation and redress all wrongs. This letter he sent by a very plausible man, Omed Rae, the collector of the Rahooa estate. Kurum Hoseyn resumed charge of his office, and went unattended to the Rajah, with whom he remained some days feasting, and swearing on the Koran, that all had been without his connivance or knowledge, and that he had come back with a full determination to see justice done to his friend, the Rajah, and his landholders and cultivators in everything. Having thus soothed the poor old Rajahs apprehensions, he prevailed on him to go back with him to Bondee, where he behaved for some time with so much seeming frankness and cordiality, and swore so solemnly on the Koran to respect the persons of all men who should come to him on business, that the Rajah's tenants and agents lost all their fears, and again came freely to his camp. The Rajah now invited all his tenants as before, to enter into engagements to pay their rents to officers appointed by the collector as jumogdars; and the people had hopes of being permitted to gather their harvests in peace. Kurum Hoseyn now suggested to Beharee Lal, to come suddenly with the largest force he could collect, and seize the many respectable men who had assembled-at his invitation.

He made a forced march daring the night, appeared suddenly at Bondee with a large force, and seized all who were there assembled, save the Rajah and his family, who escaped to the jungles. Detachments of from one hundred to two hundred were sent out as before, to plunder the country, and seize all from whom anything could be extorted. All the towns and villages on the estate were plundered of everything that could be found, and fifteen hundred men, and about five hundred women and children, were brought in prisoners, with no less than eighty thousand animals of all kinds. There were twenty-five thousand head of cattle; and horses, mares, sheep, goats, ponies, &c., made up the rest. All with the men, women, and children were driven off, pell-mell, a distance of twenty miles to Busuntpoor, in the Hurhurpoor district, where Beharee Lal's headquarter had been fixed. For three days heavy rain continued to fall. Pregnant women were beaten on by the troops with bludgeons and the butt-ends of muskets and matchlocks. Many of them gave premature birth to children and died on the road; and many children were trodden to death by the animals on the road, which was crowded for more than ten miles.

Rughbur Sing and his agents, Beharee Lal, Kurum Hoseyn, Maharaj Sing, Prag Sing, and others, selected several thousand of the finest cattle, and sent them to their homes; and the rest were left to the officers and soldiers of the force to be disposed of; and, for all this enormous number of animals, worth at least one hundred thousand rupees, the small sum of one hundred and thirty rupees was credited in the Nazim's accounts to the Rajah's estate. At Busuntpoor the force was divided into two parties, for the purpose of torturing the surviving prisoners till they consented to sign bonds, for the payment of such sums as might be demanded from them. Beharee Lal presided over the first party, in which they were tortured from day-break till noon. They were tied up and flogged, had red-hot ramrods thrust into their flesh, their tongues were pulled out with hot pincers and pierced through; and, when all would not do, they were taken to Kurum Hoseyn, who presided at the other party, to be tortured again till the evening. He sat with a savage delight, to witness this brutal scene and invent new kinds of torture. No less than seventy men, besides women and children, perished at Busuntpoor from torture and starvation; and their bodies were left to rot in the mud, and their friends were afraid to approach them. Bustee's body was stolen at night by his son, and Guyadut's was sold to his family by the soldiers.

Among the persons of respectability who died under the tortures, several are named below.* Buldee Sing, the husband of the Rajah's sister, took poison and died; and Ramdeen, a Brahmin of great respectability, stabbed himself to death, to avoid further torture and dishonour. For two months did these atrocities continue at Busuntpoor; and during that time the prisoners got no food from the servants of Government. All that they got was sent to them by their friends, or by the charitable peasantry of the country around; and when sweetmeats were sent to them as food, which the most scrupulous could eat from any hand, the soldiers often snatched them from them and ate them themselves, or took them to their officers. The women and children were all stripped of their clothes, and many died from cold and want of sustenance. It was during the months of September and October that these atrocities were perpetrated. The heavy rain had inundated the country, and the poor prisoners were obliged to lie naked and unsheltered on the damp ground.

* 1. Byjonauth, the Rajah's accountant.
   2. Gijraj Sing, Rajpoot.
   3. Sheopersaud.
   4. Rampersaud.
   5. Jhow Lal.
   6. Guyadut.
   7. Duyram.
   8. Budaree Chobee.
   9. Mungul Sing, Rajpoot.
  10. Seodeen Sing, ditto.
  11. Akber Sing.
  12. Bustee, a farmer.

Apreel Sing, a respectable Jagheerdar of Bondee, was tortured till he consented to sell his two daughters, and pay the money; and a great many respectable females, who were taken from Bondee to Busuntpoor, have never been heard of since. Whether they perished or were sold their friends have never been able to discover. The sipahees and other persons, employed to torture, got money from their victims or their friends, who ventured to approach, or from the pitying peasantry around; and all laughed and joked at the screams of the sufferers. Several times, during the two months, Rughbur Sing paid off heavy arrears, due to his personal servants, by drafts on his agents for prisoners, to be placed at the disposal of the payee, ten and twenty at a time. It is worthy of remark, that an old Subadar of one of our regiments of Native Infantry, who was then at home in furlough, happened to pass Busuntpoor with his family, on his way to Guya, on a pilgrimage. He and his family had saved what was to them a large sum, to be spent in offerings, for the safe passage of his deceased relatives through purgatory. On witnessing the sufferings of the poor prisoners at Busuntpoor, he and his family offered all they had for a certain number of women and children, who were made over to them. He took them to their homes, and returned to his own, saying, that he hoped God would forgive them for the sake of the relief which they had afforded to sufferers.

In the latter end of October, Beharee Lal took off all the force that could be spared, to attack the Rajah of Bhinga, and plunder his estate in the same manner; and Kurum Hoseyn took another to plunder Koelee, Murdunpoor, Budrolee, and some other villages of the Bondee estate, which had suffered least in the last attack. He collected two thousand plough-bullocks, and sold them for little to Nuzur Allee and Sufder Allee, who commanded detachments under him. He soon after made an attack upon Sookha and other villages, in the vicinity of Busuntpoor, and collected between twenty and thirty thousand head of cattle; but, on his way back, he was attacked by a party of twenty brave men (under a landholder named Nabee Buksh, whom he wished to seize), and driven back to his camp at Busuntpoor, with the loss of all his booty. He attempted no more enterprises after this check. The tortures ceased, and ten days after he ran off, on hearing that Rughbur Sing had been deprived of his charge by orders from Lucknow. At this time one hundred and fifty prisoners remained at Busuntpoor, and they were released by Incha Sing, the successor and uncle of Rughbur Sing.

The Akhbar Naveeses, so far from admonishing the perpetrators of these atrocities, were some of them among the most active promoters of them. Jorakhun, the news-writer at Bondee, got one anna for every prisoner brought in; and from two to three rupees for every prisoner released. He got every day subsistence for ten men from Kurum Hoseyn. All the news-writers in the neighbourhood got a share of the booty in bullocks, cows, and other animals. Two chuprassies are said to have come from Government, and remained at Busuntpoor for nearly the whole two months, while these tortures were being inflicted, without making any report of them. When the order for dismissing Rughbur Sing came from the Durbar, Maharaj Sing went off, saying, that he would soon smother all complaints, in the usual way, at Lucknow.

In September 1847, Rughbur Sing's agents, with a considerable force, encamped at Parbatee-tolah, in the Gonda district, and made a sudden attack upon the fine town of Khurgoopoor. After plundering the town, the troops seized forty of the most respectable merchants and shopkeepers of the place, and made them over to Rughbur Sing's agents, at the rate agreed upon, of so much a head, as the perquisites of the soldiers; and these agents confined and tortured them till they each paid the ransom demanded, and rated according to their supposed means. The troops did the same by Bisumberpoor, Bellehree Pundit, Pyaree, Peepree, and many other towns and villages in the same district of Gonda. A trooper and his son, who tried to save the honour of their family, by defending the entrance to their house, were cut down and killed at Khurgapoor; and in Bisumberpoor one of the soldiers, with his sword, cut off the arm of a respectable old woman, in order the more easily to get her gold bracelets.

The poor woman died a few hours afterwards. The only relative of the poor old woman who could have assisted her was seized, with forty other respectable persons, and taken off to the camp at Parbatee-tola, where they were all tortured till they paid the ransom demanded, and a gratuity, in addition, to the soldiers who had seized them. One of the persons died under the tortures inflicted upon him.

In the Gungwal district similar atrocities were committed by Rughbur Sing's agents and their soldiers. These agents were Gouree Shunkur and Seorutun Sing. The district formed the estate of Rajah Sreeput Sing, who resided with his family in the fort of Gungwal. The former Nazim, Suraj-od Dowlah, had attacked this fort on some frivolous pretence; and, having taken it by surprise, sacked the place and plundered the Rajah and his family of all they had. The Rajah died soon after of mortification, at the dishonour he and his family had suffered, and was succeeded by his son, Seetul Persaud Sing, the present Rajah, who was now plundered again, and driven an exile into the Nepaul hills. The estate was now taken possession of by the agents, Goureeshunker and Seorutun Sing. Seorutun Sing seized a Brahmin who was travelling with his wife and brother, and, on the pretence that he must be a relation of the fugitive Rajah, had him murdered, and his head struck off on the spot. The wife took the head of her murdered husband in her arms, wrapped it up in cloth, and, attended by his brother, walked with it a distance of fifty miles to Ajoodheea, where Rughbur Sing was then engaged in religious ceremonies. The poor woman placed the head before him, and demanded justice on her husband's murderers. He coolly ordered the head to be thrown into the river, and the woman and her brother-in-law to be driven from his presence. Many other respectable persons were seized and tortured on similar pretext of being related to, or having served or assisted, the fugitive Rajah. Moistened gunpowder was smeared thickly over the beards of the men, and when dry set fire to; and any friend or relatives who presumed to show signs of pity was seized and tortured, till he or she paid a ransom. All the people in the country around, who had moveable property of any kind, were plundered by these two atrocious agents, and tortured till they paid all that they could beg and borrow. Many respectable families were dishonoured in the persons of wives, sisters, or daughters, and almost all the towns and villages around became deserted.

In Rajah Nirput Sing's estate of Pyagpoor, the same atrocities were committed. Rajah Rughbur Sing seized upon this estate as soon as he entered upon his charge in 1846, and put it under the management of his own agents; and, after extorting from the tenants more than was justly due, according to engagement, he attacked the Rajah's house by surprise, and plundered it of property to the value of fifteen thousand rupees. The Rajah, however, contrived to make his escape with his family. He had nothing with him to subsist upon, and in 1847 he was invited back on solemn pledges of personal security; and, from great distress, was induced again to undertake the management of his own estate, at an exorbitant rate of assessment.

In spite of this engagement, Goureeshunker, when the tenants had become lulled into security by the hope of remaining under their own chief, suddenly, with his troops, seized upon all he could catch, plundered their houses, and tortured them till they paid all that they could prevail upon their relatives and friends to lend them. Eighteen hundred of their plough-bullocks were seized and sold by him, together with many of their wives and daughters. While under torture, Seetaram, a respectable Brahmin, of Kandookoeea, put an end to his existence, to avoid further sufferings and dishonour. Sucheet, another respectable Brahmin, of Pagaree, did the same by opening a vein in his thigh. A cloth steeped in oil was bound round the hands of those who appeared able, but unwilling, to pay ransoms, and set fire to, so as to burn like a torch. In these tortures, Lala Beharee Lal, Rughbur Sing's deputy, was the chief agent. "I found," says Captain Orr, "the estate of Pyagpoor in a desolate condition; village after village presenting nothing but bare walls—the finest arable lands lying waste, and no sign of cultivation was anywhere to be seen. Even the present Nazim, Mahommed Hussan, after conciliating and inviting in the Rajah on further solemn assurances of personal security, seized him and all his family, and kept them confined in prison for several months, till they paid him an exorbitant ransom. The poorer classes told me, that it was impossible for them to plough their fields, since all their ploughbullocks had been seized and sold by the Nazim's agents. Great numbers in this and the adjoining estates have subsisted entirely upon wild fruits, and some species of aquatic plants, since they were ruined by these atrocities."

This picture is not at all overdrawn. In passing through the estate, and communing with the few wretched people who remain, I find all that Captain Orr stated in his report to be strictly correct.

In the Hurhurpoor district similar atrocities were committed by Rughbur Sing and his agents. He confided the management to his agent, Goureeshunker. In 1846 he made his settlement of the land revenue, at an exorbitant rate, with the tallookdar, Chinghy Sing; and, in the following year, he extorted from him an increase to this rate of twenty-five thousand rupees. He was, in consequence, obliged to fly; but he was soon invited back on the usual solemn assurances for his personal security, and induced to take on himself the management of the estate. But he was no sooner settled in his house than he was again attacked at night and plundered. One of his attendants was killed, and another wounded; and all the respectable tenants and servants who had ventured to assemble around him on his return were seized and tortured till they paid ransoms. No less than two thousand and five hundred bullocks from this estate were seized and sold, or starved to death. A great many women were seized and tortured till they paid ransoms like the men; and many of them have never since been seen or heard of. Some perished in confinement of hunger and cold, having been stripped of their clothes, and exposed at night to the open air on the damp ground, while others threw themselves into wells and destroyed themselves after their release, rather than return to their families after the exposure and dishonour they had suffered.

In the Bahraetch district, the same atrocities were practised by Rughbur Sing and his agents. Here also Goureeshunker was the chief agent employed, but the few people who remained were so terrified, that Captain Orr could get but little detailed information of particular cases. The present Nazim had been one of Rughbur Sing's agents in all these atrocities, and the people apprehended that he was in office merely as his "locum tenens;" and that Rughbur Sing would soon purchase his restoration to power, as he boasted that he should. The estate of the Rajah of Bumunee Paer was plundered in the same manner; and Rughbur Sing's agents seized, drove off, and sold two thousand bullocks, and cut down and sold or destroyed five hundred and five mhowa-trees, which had, for generations, formed the strongest local ties of the cultivators, and their best dependence in seasons of drought.

In the Churda estate, in the Tarae forest, the same sufferings were inflicted on the people by the same agents, Goureeshunker and Beharee Lal. They seized Mudar Buksh, the manager, and made him over to Moonshee Kurum Hoseyn, who had him beaten to death. The estate of the Rajah of Bhinga was treated in the same way. Beharee Lal attacked the town with a large force, plundered all the houses in it, and all the people of their clothes and ornaments. They seized all the plough-bullocks and other cattle, and had them driven off and sold. The women were all seized and driven off in crowds to the camp of Rughbur Sing at Parbatee-tolah. Many of them who were far gone in pregnancy perished on the road, from fatigue and harsh treatment The estate of the Rajah of Ruhooa was treated in the same manner; and the Rajah, to avoid torture and disgrace, fled with his family to the jungles. In July 1846, being in great distress, he was induced to come back on the most solemn assurances from Rughbur Sing of personal security for himself, family, and attendants. He left the Rajah his *nankar* lands for his subsistence, pledging himself to exact no rents or revenues from them; but put the estate under the management of his own agents, Lala Omed Rae and others. He at the same time pledged himself not to exact from any of the poor Rajah's tenants higher rates than those stipulated for in the engagements then made. But he immediately after saddled the Rajah with the payment of five hundred armed men, on the pretence that they were necessary to protect him, and aid him in the management of these *nankar* lands. In May 1847, when the harvests had been gathered, and he had exacted from the tenants and cultivators the rates stipulated, Goureeshunker was put into the management. He seized all the tenants and cultivators by a sudden and simultaneous attack upon their several villages, and extorted from them a payment of fifty thousand rupees more. Not satisfied with this, Goureeshunker seized the Rajah's chief manager, Mungul Pershad, tied him up to a tree, and had him beaten to death. Many of the Rajah's tenants and servants were beaten to death in the same manner; and no less than forty villages were attacked and plundered. A good many respectable females were seized and compelled to make up the ransoms of their husbands and fathers who were under torture. Many of the females who had been seized perished from the cruel treatment and from want of food. Two thousand head of cattle, chiefly plough-bullocks, were seized and sold from this estate.

I have passed through all the districts here named, save two, Churda and Bhinga, and I can say, that everything I saw and heard tended to confirm the truth of what has here been told. Rughbur Sing and the agents employed by him were, by all I saw, considered more as terrible demons who delighted in blood and murder than as men endowed with any feelings of sympathy for their fellow-creatures; and the government, which employed such men in the management of districts with uncontrolled power, seemed to be utterly detested and abhorred.

It will naturally be asked, whether the circumstances described were ever reported to the Oude Government or to the British Resident; and whether they did anything to punish the guilty and afford redress and relief to the sufferers. The following are the reports which were made to the Oude Durbar by the news-writers, employed in the several districts, and communicated to the Resident and his Assistant, by the Residency news-writer, in his daily reports, which are read out to them every morning.

July 10, 1847.—Report from Bondee states, that Rajaram, Rughbur Sing's collector of Mirzapoor and other villages in that estate, had attacked and plundered Mirzapoor, and carried off sixty head of cattle.

August 12, 1847.—Report from Bondee states, that the estates of Bondee and Tiperha, which yielded one hundred and fifty thousand rupees a-year, had become so desolated by the oppression of Beharee Lal and Kurum Hoseyn, the agents of Rughbur Sing, that they could not possibly yield anything for the ensuing year; that Kurum Hoseyn had seized all the cattle and other property of the peasantry, sold them and appropriated the money to his own use, and had so beaten the landholders and cultivators, that many of them had died. Order by the Durbar, that these two agents be deterred from such acts of oppression, fined five thousand rupees, and made to release the remaining prisoners, and restore the property taken. Nothing whatever was done!

August 14, 1847.—Report from Bondee states, that although the landholders and cultivators of this estate had paid all that was due, according to engagements, Beharee Lal and Kurum Hoseyn were having them flogged and tortured every day to extort more; selling off all their stock and other property, and selecting all the good bullocks and cows and sending them to their own houses. Order by the Durbar, that the minister punish the oppressors, and cause their property to be given back to the oppressed. The minister ordered his deputy, Ramchurn, to see this done. He did nothing whatever!

September 6, 1847.—Report from Gonda states, that all the lands from Bondee and Pyagpoor had been left waste from the oppression of Rughbur Sing. Order by the Durbar, that the minister hasten to get the lands tilled, as the season was passing away. Nothing whatever was done!

September 24, 1847.—Report from the same place states, that Rughbur Sing had seized no less than eighteen thousand bullocks, from the villages of the Bondee estate, collected them at Neemapoor, and ordered his agents to get them all sold off as fast as possible; and that the cultivators could till none of the lands in consequence. Order by the Durbar, that the minister put a stop to all this oppression. Nothing whatever was done!

September 24, 1847.—Report from the same place states, that Kurum Hoseyn had seized Ahlad Sing, the malgoozar of Hurkapoor in Bondee, and had red-hot ramrods thrust into his flesh, on account of a balance due, and then had him put upon an ass and paraded through the streets. Order by the Durbar, that the minister see to this. Nothing whatever was done!

August 2, 1847.—Report from Gonda states, that the troops under Beharee Lal were robbing all the females of the country of their ornaments; and that Beharee Lal neither did nor said anything to prevent them. Order by the Durbar, that Rughbur Sing be directed to restrain his soldiers and restore the ornaments. Nothing whatever was done!

September 6, 1847—Report from the same place states, that Luchman Naraen, malgoozar of Bhurduree in Gonda, had paid all the rents due, according to his engagements; that Beharee Lal had, nevertheless, sent a force of three hundred men, who attacked his house, plundered it of all that it contained, and took off five thousand seven hundred and thirty-one maunds of stored grain. Order by the Durbar, that the minister punish and restrain the oppressors, and cause all the property to be restored. Nothing whatever was done in the matter!

October 2, 1847.—Report from Gonda states, that Jafir Allee and Hemraj Sing, Rughbur Sing's agents, had, with a body of sixteen hundred troops, attacked the town of Khurgapoor in Gonda, plundered it, and attacked and plundered five villages in the vicinity, and seized Sudasook and thirty other merchants and shopkeepers of Khurgapoor, Chungul Sing, the farmer of that place, Kaleechurn, a writer, and Benee, the agent of the Gonda Rajah, and no less than one hundred landholders and cultivators. Order by the Durbar: Let the minister seize all the offenders, and release and satisfy all the sufferers. Nothing whatever was done in the matter.

October 5, 1847.—Report from Gonda states, that Rughbur Sing's troops had seized and brought off from Gonda to Nawabgunge, two hundred men and women, and shut up the road where they were confined, that no one might pass near them—that three or four of the women were pregnant, and near their confinement, and suffered much from harsh treatment and want of food. Order by the Durbar: Let the minister grant redress, and send a suzawal to see that the sufferers are released. A suzawal was sent, it appears, but he remained a quiet spectator of the atrocities, having received something for doing so.

September 1, 1847.—Report from Hissampoor states, that Byjonauth Sing, agent of Rughbur Sing, in Hissampoor, had seized all the plough-bullocks and cows he could find, sent the best to his own home, and made the rest over to Wazeer Allee, Canongoe, to be sold. Order by the Durbar, that Rughbur Sing be directed to restore all that has been taken, and collect the revenue with more moderation. Nothing whatever was done.

September 11, 1847.—Report from Bahraetch states, that the estate of Aleenugger in Hissampoor, which yielded eighteen thousand rupees a-year, had become so deserted from the oppressions of Rughbur Sing, that it could no longer yield anything. Order by the Durbar, that Rughbar Sing be directed to restore the tillage, or hold himself responsible for the King's revenue!

July 28, 1847.—Report from Gonda states, that Goureeshunker, the collector of Gungwal and Pyagpoor, had, by order of Beharee Lal, attacked the village of Ruhooa, and seized and carried off sixty-four cultivators, and confined them in his camp. No order whatever was passed by the Durbar.

September 7, 1847.—From Nawabgunge in Gonda reports, that Beharee Lal's soldiers were then engaged in sacking that town, and carrying off the property. Order by the Durbar. Let the minister see that the property be restored and wrongs redressed. Nothing whatever was done.

September 18, 1847.—Report from Bahraetch states, that Cheyn Sing, the tallookdar of Bahmanee Paer, had fled into the British territory, but returned to his fort; that Beharee Lal heard of his return and sent two thousand men to seize him; that the tallookdar had only sixty men, but held out for three hours, killed ten of the King's soldiers, and then evacuated the fort and fled; that Beharee Lal's soldiers had collected two thousand bullocks from the estate, and brought them all off to his camp. Order by the Durbar, that the minister give stringent orders in this case. Nothing whatever was done.

October 2, 1847.—Report from Seerora states, that Mahommed Hussan (the present Nazim), one of Rughbur Sing's collectors, with one thousand horse and foot and one gun, had come to the hamlet of Sondun Lal, and the village of Seerora, attacked and plundered these places, and seized and taken off one hundred men and women, and two hundred bullocks, killed two hundred Rajpoots in a fight, and then gone back to his camp at Bahoreegunge. Order by the Durbar, that the minister seize and send the oppressors to Lucknow, and restore the property to its proper owners. The minister did nothing of the kind; and soon after made this oppressor the governor of these districts.

September 20, 1847.—Report from Radowlee states, that armed men belonging to Kurum Hoseyn, escorting one thousand selected bullocks, sent by Rughbar Sing, had come to Radowlee, on their way to his fort of Shahgunge. Order by the Durbar: Let the minister see to this affair. Nothing was done.

On the 28th September 1847 an order was addressed by the Durbar to Rughbur Sing, that his agent, Kurum Hoseyn, appeared to have attacked the house of Seodeen, though he had paid all that was due by him to the State, according to his engagements, and plundered it of property to the value of eighteen thousand rupees, and seized and confined all his relations—that he must cause all the property to be restored, and obtain acquittances from the sufferers. Rughbur Sing took no notice whatever of this order.

On the 2nd of October 1847, the Resident, Colonel Richmond, wrote to the King, acquainting him, that he had heard, that Rughbur Sing had seized and sold all the ploughs and bullocks in the Bahraetch district, and, seized and sold also five hundred men, women, and children of the landholders and cultivators; that he regrets all this and prays that his Majesty will cause inquiries to be made; and, should the charges prove true, cause the articles taken, or their value, to be restored, and the men, women, and children to be released. On the 25th of October 1847, the Resident again addressed the King, stating, that he had heard, that, on the 2nd of October, Jafir Allee and Maharaj Sing, agents of Rughbur Sing, with eleven hundred soldiers, had attacked and plundered the town of Khurgapoor and five villages in its neighbourhood, and seized and taken off Ramdeen Sudasook, and thirty merchants, shopkeepers and other respectable persons, also Junglee, the farmer of that town, Kaleechurn Mutsudee, Dabey Pershad, the Rajah's manager, and one hundred landholders and cultivators; and praying that orders be given for inquiry and redress. Nothing whatever was done; but on the 30th of October, the King replied to these letters, and to one written to him by the Resident on the 31st of August 1847, transmitting a list of unanswered letters. His Majesty stated, that he had sent orders to Rughbur Sing and to his brother Maun Sing, in all the cases referred to by the Resident; but that they were contumacious servants, as he had before described them to the Resident to be; and had taken no notice whatever of his orders!

August 20, 1846.—Report from Bahraetch states, that Goureeshunkur, the agent of Rughbur Sing, in Bahraetch, had taken four persons from among the many whom he had in confinement on account of balances, had them suspended to trees, and cruelly flogged, and then had their hands wrapped up in thick cloth, steeped in oil, and set fire to till they burned like torches; and that he sat listening to their screams and cries for mercy with indifference. Order by the King: Let the minister, Ameen-od Dowlah, be furnished with a copy of this report, and let him send out three troopers, as suzawuls, to bring in Goureeshunkur and the four men whose hands had been burnt, and let him employ Mekhlis Hoseyn, to inquire into the affair, and report the result. Nothing was done.

On the 29th of August, the Resident, Mr. Davidson, addressed a letter to the King stating, that he had before represented the cruelties which Rughbur Sing was inflicting upon the people of his district, but had heard of no redress having been afforded in any case; that he had received another report on the same subject, and now forwards it to show what atrocities his agent, Goureeshunkur, was committing in Bahraetch; that in no other country could the servants of the sovereign commit such cruel outrages upon his subjects; that he had been wrapping up the bodies of the King's subjects in oilcloths, and setting, fire to them as to torches; that he could not do all this without the knowledge and sanction of his master, Rughbur Sing; and the Resident prays, that he may be punished, and that his punishment may be intimated to him, the Resident. Nothing was ever done, nor was any answer given to this letter, till it was, on the 30th of August 1847, acknowledged with the many others contained in the list sent to the King, in his letter of the 31st August 1847, by the then Resident, Colonel Richmond.

No report appears to have reached either the Durbar or the Resident, of the atrocious proceedings of Rughbur Sing's agents at Busuntpoor, where so many persons perished from torture, starvation, and exposure; nor was any notice taken of them till I took charge of my office in January 1849. Incha Sing had offered for the contract of the two districts four lacs less than Rughbur Sing had pledged himself to pay, and obtained it, and quietly superseded his nephew, with whom he was on cordial good terms. Rughbur Sing went into the British territory, to evade all demands for balances, and reside for an interval, with the full assurance that he would be able to purchase a restoration to favour and power in Oude, unless the Resident should think it worth while to oppose him, which my predecessor did not.* I had his agents arrested, and charges sent in against them, with all the proofs accumulated, by Captain Orr; but they all soon purchased their way out, and no one was punished. At my suggestion the King proclaimed Rughbur Sing as an outlaw, and offered three thousand rupees for his arrest, if he did not appear within three months. He never appeared, but continued to carry on his negociations for restoration to power at Lucknow, through the very agents whom he had employed in the scenes above described, Beharee Lal, Goureeshunker, Kurum Hoseyn, Maharaj Sing, &c.

* Incha Sing absconded before the end of the season, and has never returned to Oude. Mahommed Hussan got the contract on a reduction of two hundred and thirty-one thousand rupees, below the rates which Incha Sing bound himself to pay. But in 1850, he consented to an increase of three hundred and ninety-nine thousand, with, I believe, the deliberate intention to raise the funds for the payment by the murder of Ramdut Pandee, and the confiscation of his estate.

Amjud Allee Shah, who was something of a man of business, died 13th February 1847, and was succeeded by his eldest son, the present King, who knows nothing of, and cares nothing whatever about, business. His minister, Ameen-od Dowlah, who had some character of his own, was removed some three or four months after, and succeeded by the present minister, Allee Nakee Khan, who has none.

The following table of the actual payments into the treasury, from these two districts of Gonda-Bahraetch, for four years from 1845, will serve to show the fiscal effects of such atrocities as were permitted to be perpetrated in them for a brief period of two years:—

For 1845, under Wajid Allee	11,65,132	5	3
For 1846, under Rughbur Sing	14,01,623	7	6
For 1847, under ditto	10,27,898	4	6
For 1848, under Incha Sing	6,05,492	0	3

But what table can show the sufferings of the people, and the feelings of hatred and abhorrence of the Government and its officers, to which they gave rise! Not one of the agents, employed in the atrocities above described, was ever punished. The people see that all the members of the Government are accessaries, either before or after the fact, in all these dreadful cruelties and outrages, and, that the more of them a public officer commits, the more secure is he of protection and favour at Court. Their hatred and abhorrence of the individual, in consequence, extend to and embrace the whole of the Government, and would extend also to the British Government, by whom that of Oude is supported, did they not see how earnestly the British Resident strives to alleviate their sufferings, and make the Oude sovereign and minister do their duty towards them; and how much all British officers sympathise with their sufferings as they pass through the country.*

* Beharee Lal is now (June 1851) employed in a confidential situation, in the office of the deputy minister. Goureeshunker is a Tusseeldar, or native collector, in the same district of Bahraetch, under the new contractor, Mann Sing. Moonshee Kurum Hoseyn holds a similar office in some other district. Maharaj Sing, and the rest, all hold, I believe, situations of equal emolument and respectability.

Almost all the khalsa lands of the Hissampoor purgunnah belonged to the different branches of a very ancient and respectable family of Syuds. Their lands have, as already stated, been almost all transferred to powerful tallookdars, and absorbed by them in their estates, by the usual process. It is said, and I believe truly, that Hadee Allee Khan tried to induce the head of the Syud family to take his daughter in marriage for his eldest son, as he was also a Syud, (lineal descendant of the prophet.) The old Syud was too proud to consent to this; and he and all his relations and connection were ruined in consequence. The son, to whom Hadee Allee wished to unite his daughter, still lives on his lands, but in poverty and fear. The people say that family pride is more inveterate among the aristocracy of the country than that of the city; and had the old man lived at Lucknow, he would probably have given his son, and saved his family and estate.

Captain Hardwick, while out shooting on the 10th, saw a dead man hanging by the heels in a mango-tree, close to the road. He was one of a gang of notorious robbers who had attacked a neighbouring village belonging to some Brahmins. They killed two, and caught a third member of the gang, and hung him up by the heels to die. He was the brother-in-law of the leader of the gang, Nunda Pandee. There he still hangs, and the greater part of my camp took a look at him in passing.

Tallookdars of Bahraetch—Government Land Revenue according to the Estimate of this Year.

Names of Villages	Government Demand	Present Condition
Bandee	65,000	Almost waste
Ruhooa	20,000	Ditto
Nanpara	1,50,000	Falling off
Gungwal	26,000	Much out of tillage
Pyagpoor	59,000	Ditto
Ekona	1,80,000	Ditto
Bulrampoor	1,50,000	Well tilled
Toolseepoor	1,05,000	Ditto
Atrola	80,000	Much out of tillage
Munkapoor	35,000	Ditto
Bahmanee Paer	12,000	Ditto
Gowras alias Chehdwara		
Paruspoor	14,000	Well tilled
Aruta	18,000	Ditto
Shahpoor	30,000	Ditto
Dhunawa	42,000	Ditto
Paska	20,000	Ditto
Kumeear	48,000	Ditto
Churda	62,000	Falling off
Gonda Pergunnah.		
Desumberpoor	95,000	Rajah Davey Buksh, in good order.
Bhinga	64,000	Recovering.
Akkerpoor	46,015	In good order under Ramdut Pandee.
Sagha Chunda	1,20,729	Ramdut Pandee, in good order.
Birwa	24,000	A little out of tillage.

December 12, 1849.—Gungwal, thirteen miles. The road lay through the estate of Pyagpoor to within a mile of Gungwal. Little cultivation was to be seen the whole way, and what we could see was bad. Little variety of crops, and the tillage slovenly, and without manure or irrigation. The tallookdar was ruined by Rughbur Sing, and is not on terms with the present Nazim, and he did not appear. The estate of Gungwal is not better cultivated than that of Pyagpoor; nor better peopled—both may be considered as mere wastes, and their assessments as merely nominal.

The tallookdar did not appear. Both were ruined by the rapacious Nazim and his atrocious agents, Goureeshunker, Beharee Lal, Kurum Hoseyn, and others.

The Rajah of Toolseepoor, Dirgraj Sing, has an only son, Sahibjee, now 17 years of age. The Rajah's old servants, thinking they could make more out of the boy than out of the prudent father, first incited him to go off, with all the property he could collect, to Goruckpoor, where he spent it in ten months of revelry. The father invited him back two mouths ago, on condition that he should come alone. When he got within six miles of Toolseepoor, however, the father found, that three thousand armed followers had there been assembled by his agents, to aid him in seizing upon him and the estate. Fearing that his estate might be desolated, and he himself confined, and perhaps put to death, the Rajah ran off to his friend, the Rajah of Bulrampore, for protection.

December 13, 1849.—Purenda, eleven miles. The first half of the way, through the lands of Gungwal, showed few signs of tillage or population; the latter half through, those of Purenda and other villages of Gonda, held by Ramdut Pandee, showed more of both. Some nice villages on each side, at a small distance, and some fine groves of mango-trees. On the road this morning, Omrow Pooree, a non-commissioned officer of the Gwalior Contingent, whose family resided in a neighbouring village, came up to me as I passed along, and prayed me to have the murderer of his father seized and punished. He described the circumstances of the case, and on reaching camp, I requested Captain Weston to take the depositions of the witnesses, and adopt measures for the arrest of the offenders. Syampooree was the name of the father of the complainant. He resided in a small hamlet, near the road, called after himself, as the founder, "Syampooree ka Poorwa," or Syampooree's Hamlet. He had four sons, all fine, stout men. The eldest, Omrow Pooree, a corporal in the Gwalior Contingent, Bhurut Pooree, a private in Captain Barlow's regiment, Ramchurun and Ramadeen, the two youngest, still at home, assisting their father in the management of their little estate, which the family had held for many generations. One day in the beginning of December 1848, a short, thick-set man passed through the hamlet, accosted Syampooree and his two sons, as they sat at the door, and asked for some tobacco, and entered into conversation with them. He pretended that his cart had been seized by the Nazim's soldiers; and, after chatting with them for a short time, departed.

The second morning after this, before daylight, Ramadeen, the youngest son, was warming himself at a fire on a small terrace in front of the door, when he saw a party of armed men approaching. He called out, and asked who they were and what they wanted. They told him that they were Government servants, had traced a thief to the village, and come to seize him. Four of the party, who carried torches, now approached the fire and lighted them. Syampooree and his other son, Ramchurun, hearing the noise, came out, and placed themselves by the side of Ramadeen. By the light of the torches they now recognised the short, thick-set man with whom they had been talking two days before, at the head of a gang of fifteen men, carrying fire-arms with matches lighted, and five more armed with swords and shields. The short, thick-set man was Nunda Pandee, the most notorious robber in the district. He ordered his gang to search the house: on the father and sons remonstrating, he drew his sword and cut down Ramchurun. The father and Ramadeen having left their swords in the house, rushed back to secure them; but Nunda Pandee, calling out to one of his followers, Bhowaneedeen, to despatch the son, overtook the father, and at one cut severed his right arm from his body. He inflicted several other cuts upon him before the old man could secure his sword with his left arm. Having got it, he placed the scabbard under his foot, drew forth the blade, and cut Nunda Pandee across his sword-arm which placed him *hors-de-combat*; and rushing out among the assailants, he cut down two more, when he was shot dead by a third and noted robber, Goberae. Bhowaneedeen and others of the gang had cut down Ramadeen, and inflicted several wounds upon him as he lay on the ground. The gang then plundered the house, and made off with property to the value of one thousand and fifty rupees, leaving the father and both sons on the ground. The brave old father died soon after daybreak; but before he expired he named his assailants.

The two youngest sons were too severely wounded to admit of their pursuing the murderers of their father, but their brother, Bhurut Pooree, obtaining leave of absence, returned home, and traced the leader of the gang, Nunda Pandee, to the house of one of his relatives in the village of Kurroura, in Pyagpoor, where he had had his wound sewn up and dressed, and lay concealed. The family then tried, in vain, to get redress from all the local authorities, none of whom considered it to be their duty to look after murderers and robbers of this kind. Captain Weston succeeded in arresting this atrocious gang-leader, Nunda Pandee, who described to him minutely many of the numerous enterprises of this kind in which he had been engaged, and seemed to glory in his profession. He mentioned that the man whom he had seen suspended in the tree was his brother-in-law; that he had had two other members of his gang killed by the villagers on that occasion, but had succeeded in carrying off their bodies; that Goberae, Bhowaneedeen, and the rest of his followers were still at large and prosecuting their trade. Nunda Pandee was by the Resident made over for trial and punishment to the Durbar; and Goberae and Bhowaneedeen have since been arrested and made over also. They both acknowledged that they murdered the Gosaen in the manner above described, May 1851. The Mahommedan law-officer before whom the case was tried declared, that he could not, according to law, admit as valid the evidence of the wife and two sons of the murdered Gosaen, because they were relatives and prosecutors; and, as the robbers denied before him that they were the murderers, he could not, or pretended he could not, legally sentence them to punishment The King was, in consequence, obliged to take them from his Court, and get them sentenced to perpetual imprisonment by another Court, not trammelled by the same law of evidence. This difficulty arises from *blood* having its *price* in money in the country where the law was made, or the *Deeut*; any person who had a right to share in this *Deeut*, or price of blood, was therefore held to be an invalid or incompetent witness to the fact.

On the road from Bahraetch to Gungwal we saw very few groves or fine single trees on either side. The water is close to the surface, and the soil good, but for the most part flooded during the rains, and fit only for rice-cultivation. To fit it for the culture of other autumn crops would require a great outlay in drainage; and this no one will incur without better security for the returns than the present government can afford. Ramdut Pandee is the greatest agricultural capitalist in these parts.

On the 8th of December it had become known all over the city of Lucknow, that the King had promised Captain Bird that he would banish Gholam Ruza and his sister, and Kotub Allee, across the Ganges; and it was entered in the news-writer's report, though Captain Bird had spoken of it to no one. He was asked by the minister whether he would excuse the King for not keeping his word so far, and said he could not. He demanded an audience of the King, who tried to avoid a meeting by pleading indisposition; but the first Assistant, being very urgent, he was admitted. He found the King in a small inner room lying on a cot covered with a ruzae or quilt.

There were closed doors on the side of the room where the cot stood, and Captain Bird perceived that persons were behind listening to the conversation. On the minister advancing to meet him at the door. Captain Bird declined taking his proffered hand, and in a loud voice declared—"that he believed that he was mixed up with the fiddlers, and was afraid of their being removed, or he would have carried his Majesty's order for their dismissal into effect." He then advanced to the King, shook him by the hand, apologized for intruding upon him after his excuse of illness, and stated—"that his own character was at stake, and he had been obliged to take this step to save it, and requested that the minister might be told to retire during the conversation, as he had already shown his partiality for the characters whom his Majesty had stigmatized as low, intriguing, and untrustworthy—as ruiners of his good name and his kingdom, and the cause of ill-feeling between the British Government and himself. The King expressed a wish that the minister might remain, that he might have an opportunity to listen to what Captain Bird had to state, as it appeared to be against him. Captain Bird replied, that he had no complaint to make against the minister; that his object in coming was, to claim the fulfilment of the promise which his Majesty had so solemnly made to him, to dismiss Gholam Ruza and his sister, and Kotub Allee, and send them across the Ganges; that he was induced to demand this audience by the minister's visit of the preceding evening, to ask him to excuse his Majesty's fulfilling the promise which he had made; and by the written report given to him that morning by the news-writer, stating, that his Majesty had changed his mind, and pardoned the parties."

The King declared that he had never given Captain Bird any such promise. Captain Bird then repeated to his Majesty the conversation which had taken place on that occasion. The King seemed to be staggered; but the minister came to his aid, and said—"that his Majesty had ascertained from Sadik Allee himself, that Gholam Ruza was not an accomplice in that affair." Captain Bird replied—"that the King had told him, that the deception had been so fully proved, that they were speechless; and that his Majesty had spit in their faces." The King said "not in Gholam Ruza's. His sister and Kotub Allee are alone guilty." Captain Bird urged, that all were alike guilty, and he besought the King to fulfil his promise, saying,—"that his, Captain Bird's, name was at stake; that if the parties were not removed, the whole city would say, that the King had bribed him, and bought off his promise." The King replied, "This is all nonsense; do you wish me to swear that Gholam Ruza is innocent, and that I never gave the promise you mention?" and, calling the minister, he placed his right hand on his head, and said,—"I swear, as if this was my son's head, and by God, that I believe Gholam Ruza to be entirely innocent; and that I never promised to turn him out, or to send him across the Ganges." Captain Bird then heard a movement of feet in the next room behind the closed doors. He was horrified; but returning to the charge, said, "Your

Majesty has, at any rate, acknowledged the guilt of Gholam Ruza's sister, and that of Khotub Allee; pray fulfil your promise on the guilty." The King said—"When absent from my sight, they are as far off as across one hundred rivers. I know they are intriguers, and shall keep my eyes upon them." Captain Bird said—"I have reported the circumstances of the case thus far to the Resident. Your Majesty has made me a participator in the breaking of your word. I have told Colonel Sleeman you would turn these men out." The King said—"This case has reference only to my house—it has no connection with the Government; but if you wish to use force, take me also by the beard, and pull me from my throne!" Captain Bird said—"I pray your Majesty to recollect how often, when force might have been used, under your own sign-manual and seal, on these fiddlers interfering in State affairs, the Resident has hesitated to put your written permission for their removal into force; and now who can be your friend, or save you from any danger, which may hereafter threaten your life or your well-being? I must, of course, report all to the Resident." The minister now said—"Yes, report to the Resident that the King has changed his mind, broken his word, and will not fulfil his promise; and ask for permission to employ direct force for the removal of these men: see if he will give permission." Captain Bird replied, "that any orders he received from the Resident would certainly be carried, into effect; but if his Majesty's own acknowledgment of the deceitfulness of these men, and their intriguing rascality were not sufficient to induce him to remove them—if the King set so little value on his promise—a promise now known to the whole city, and which he must in self-defence now speak openly of, he foresaw the speedy downfall of the kingdom. Who, he asked, will subject themselves to be deceived in an endeavour to prop it up by the removal of those who were living on its heart's blood, or be made liars by reporting promises never to be fulfilled?" Thus ended this interview.

The next day Sadik Allee had a dress of honour conferred upon him, and an increase of one hundred rupees a-month made to his salary; and

Gholam Ruza, and his relative the fiddler, Anees-od Dowla, were seated behind his Majesty in his carriage-and-four, and paraded through the city, as in full possession of his favour. After the King had alighted from the carriage at the palace, the coachman drove the two singers to their apartments in the Mukbura, seated as before in the khuwas, or hind seat. [On the 25th of May 1850, the King caused the chief singer, Gholam Ruza, his father, Nathoo, his sister, and her husband, Dummun Khan, Gholam Hyder Khan, Kotub Allee, his brother, Sahib Allee, and the females of his family, in all fourteen persons, to be seized and confined in prison. On the 2nd of June, all but Gholam Ruza and Dummun Khan were transported across the Ganges into British territory; and, on the 23rd of July, these two men were transported in the same manner. The immediate cause of the King's anger was the discovery that his divorced and banished wife, Surafrazmahal, had actually come back, and remained concealed for seven days and seven nights in the palace, in the apartments of the chief singer, Gholam Ruza. They were all made to disgorge the Company's notes and jewels found upon them, but the King visited Gholam Ruza the day before his departure, and treated him with great kindness, and seemed very sorry to part with him.]

On the 10th, I had written to Captain Bird to mention the distinction which he appeared to have overlooked in his zeal to get the fiddlers removed. The offence with which these persons stood charged in this case was a personal affront to the King, or an affront to his understanding, and not any interference with the administration of the Government; and the first Assistant was requested by the Resident to wait upon his Majesty, merely with a view to encourage him in his laudable resolution to banish them, and to offer his aid in doing so should his Majesty manifest any wish to have it; and not to demand their punishment on the part of the British Government. In the one case, if the King promised to punish the offenders and relented and forgave them, we could only regret his weakness; but in the other, if he promised to punish them and failed to do so, we should consider it due to the character of our Government to insist upon the fulfilment of his promise. On the evening of the 11th I got the above report of his interview with the King from Captain Bird; and, on the 12th, I wrote to tell him, that I considered him to have acted very indiscreetly; that he had brought this vexation and mortification upon himself by his overweening confidence in his personal influence over the King; that he ought to have waited for instructions from me, or at least for a reply from me to his letter, regarding the former interview at Court; that I could not now give him the support he required, as I could neither demand that his requisitions should be complied with, nor tell the King that I approved of them that he had been authorized by me to act on his own discretion in any case of great emergency, but this could not be considered of such a character, for no evil or inconvenience was to be apprehended from a day or two's delay, since the question really was, whether his Majesty should have a dozen fiddlers or only ten.

In the beginning of September 1850, the King became enamoured of one of his mother's waiting-maids, and demanded her in marriage. See was his mother's favourite bedfellow, and she would not part with her. The King became angry, and to soothe him his mother told him that it was purely out of regard for him and his children that she refused to part with this young woman; that she had a "*sampun*," or the coiled figure of a snake in the hair on the back of her neck. No man, will purchase a horse with such a mark, or believe that any family can be safe in which a horse or mare with such a mark is kept. His mother told him, that if he cohabited with a woman having such a mark, he and all his children must perish. The King said that he might probably have, among his many wives, some with marks of this kind; and that this might account for his frequent attacks of palpitation of the heart. "No doubt," said the old Queen Dowager; "we have long thought so; but your Majesty gets into such a towering passion when we venture to speak of your wives, that we have been afraid to give expression to our thoughts and fears." "Perhaps," said the King, "I may owe to this the death, lately, of my poor son, the heir-apparent." "We have long thought so," replied his mother. The chief eunuch, Busheer, was forthwith ordered to inspect the back of the necks of all save that of the chief consort, the mother of the late and present heir-apparent. He reported that he had found the *fatal mark* upon the necks of no less than eight of the King's wives, Nishat-mahal, Koorshed-mahal, Sooleeman-mahal, Huzrut-mahal, Dara Begum, Buree Begum, Chotee Begum, and Huzrut Begum. The chief priest was summoned, and the divorce, from the whole eight, pronounced forthwith; and the ladies were ordered to depart with all that they had saved while in the palace. Some of their friends suggested to his Majesty, that Mahommedans were but unskilful judges in such matters, and that a Court of Brahmins should be assembled, as they had whole volumes devoted exclusively to this science. The most learned were accordingly collected, and they declared that though there were marks resembling in some degree the *sampun*, it was of no importance; and the evil it threatened might be averted by singeing the head of the snake with a hot iron. The ladies were very indignant, and six of them insisted upon leaving the palace, in virtue of the divorce. Two only consented to remain, the Buree Begum and Chota Begum.

December 14, 1849.—Came on twelve miles to Gonda. The country well studded with groves and fine single trees; the soil naturally fertile, and water near the surface. Cultivation good about Gonda, and about some of the villages along the road it is not bad; but there is nowhere any sugar-cane to be seen beyond a small garden patch. The country is so wretchedly stocked with cattle that little manure is available for tillage.

The Bulrampore Rajah, a lively, sensible, and active young man, joined me this morning, and rode along by the side of my elephant, with the capitalist, Ramdut Pandee, the Nazim, Mahommed Hussan, and old Bukhtawar Sing, the brother of the late Dursun Sing, whom I have often mentioned in this Diary. Rajah Bukhtawar Sing is the King's Mohtamin, or Quartermaster-General of the Resident's' camp. The Rajah of Toolseepore also, who has been ousted by his son from his estate, joined me last night; but he was not well enough to ride with me. Dogs, hawks, and panthers attend for sport, but they afford little or no amusement. Hawking is a very dull and very cruel sport. A person must become insensible to the sufferings of the most beautiful and most inoffensive of the brute creation before he can feel any enjoyment in it. The cruelty lies chiefly in the mode of feeding the hawks. I have ordered all these hunting animals to return to Lucknow.

Although the personal character of the Toolseepoor Rajah is not respected, that of his son is much worse; and the Bulrampoor Rajah and other large landholders in the neighbourhood would unite and restore him to the possession of his estate, but the Nazim is held responsible for their not moving in the matter, in order that the influential persons about the Court may have the plucking of it at their leisure. The better to insure this, two companies of one of the King's regiments have been lately sent out with two guns, to see that the son is not molested in the possession. The father was restored to his estate in 1850, and the son fled again to the Goruckpoor district. He became reconciled to his father some months after, through the mediation of the magistrate, Mr. Chester, and returned to Toolseepoor. The father and son, however, distrusted each other too much to live long together on amicable terms, and the son has gone off again to Goruckpoor.

The Toolseepoor estate extends along from east to west for about one hundred miles, in a belt of from nine to twelve miles wide, upon the southern border of that part of the Oude Tarae forest which we took from Nepaul in 1815, and made over to the Oude Government by the treaty of the 11th May 1816, in lieu of the one crore of rupees which our Government borrowed from Oude for the conduct of that war. The rent-roll of Toolseepoor is now from two to three lacs of rupees a-year; but it pays to the Oude Government a revenue of only one lac and five thousand, over and above gratuities to influential officers. The estate comprises that of Bankee, which was held by a Rajah Kunsa. Dan Bahader, the father of the present Rajah of Toolseepoor, attacked him one night in 1832, put him and some two hundred and fifty of his followers and family to death, and absorbed the estate. Mahngoo, the brother of Kunsa, escaped and sought redress from the Oude Durbar; but he had no money and could get no redress; and, in despair, he went off to seek employment in Nepaul, and died soon after. Dan Bahader, enriched by the pillage of Bankee, came to Lucknow, and purchased permission to incorporate Bankee with his old estate of Toolseepoor.

Khyreeghur and Kunchunpoor, on the western border of that forest, were made over by us to Oude at the same time, as part of the cession. They had been ceded to our Government by the treaty of 1801, at an estimated value of two hundred and ten thousand, but, up to 1816, they had never yielded to us fifty thousand rupees a-year. They had, however, formerly yielded from two to three lacs of rupees a-year to the Oude Government, and under good management may do so again; but, at present, Oude draws from them a revenue of only sixteen thousand, and that with difficulty. The rent-roll, however, exceeds two hundred thousand, and may, in a few years, amount to double that sum, as population and tillage are rapidly extending.

The holders of Khyreegur and Kunchunpoor are always in a state of resistance against the Oude Government, and cannot be coerced into the payment of more than their sixteen thousand rupees a-year; and hundreds of lives have been sacrificed in the collection of this sum. The climate is so bad that no people from the open country can venture into it for more than four months in the year—from the beginning of December to the end of March. The Oude Government occasionally sends in a body of troops to enforce the payment of an increased demand during these four months. The landholders and cultivators retire before them, and they are sure to be driven out by the pestilence, with great loss of life, in a few months; and the landholders refuse to pay anything for some years after, on the ground that all their harvests were destroyed by the troops. The rest of the Tarae lands ceded had little of tillage or population at that time, and no government could be less calculated than that of Oude to make the most of its capabilities. It had, therefore, in a fiscal point of view, but a poor equivalent for its crore of rupees; but it gained a great political advantage in confining the Nepaulese to the hills on its border. Before this arrangement took place there used to be frequent disputes, and occasionally serious collisions between the local authorities about boundaries, which were apt to excite the angry feelings of the sovereigns of both States, and to render the interposition of the paramount power indispensable.

It was at Bhinga, on the left bank of the Rabtee River, in the Gonda district, and eight miles north-east from Bulrampoor, that Mr. George Ravenscroft, of the Bengal Civil Service, was murdered on the night of the 6th May, 1823. He had been the collector of the land revenue of the Cawnpore district for many years; but, having taken from the treasury a very large sum of money, and spent it in lavish hospitality and unsuccessful speculations, he absconded with his wife and child, and found an asylum with the Rajah of Bhinga, on the border of the Oude Tarae, where he intended to establish himself as an indigo planter. Strict search was being made for him throughout India by the British Government, and his residence at Bhinga was concealed from the Oude Government by the local authorities. The Rajah made over to him a portion of land for tillage, and a suitable place in a mango grove, about a mile from his fort, to build a house upon. He built one after the Hindoostanee fashion, with bamboos and grass from the adjoining jungle. It consisted of a sitting-room, bed-room, and bathing-room, all in a line, and forming one side of a quadrangle, and facing inside, with only one small door on the outside, opening into the bathing-room. The other three sides of the quadrangle consisted of stables, servants' houses, and out-offices, all facing inside, and without any entrances on the outside, save on the front side, facing the dwelling-house, where there was a large entrance.

PLAN OF MR. RAVENSCROFT'S HOUSE.

```
+----------------+  +-----------+  +----------+
| Sitting Room.  |  | Bed Room. | | Bathing  |
|                |  |           | | Room.    |
+----------------+  +-----------+  +----------+
|   |                                        |
|   |         +---+                          |
|   |         |   |                          |
|   |         |___|                          |
|   |          Cot                           |
|   |                                        |
| O |                                     S  |
| u |                                     t  |
| t |                                     a  |
|   |                                     b  |
| O_|                                     l__|
| f |                                     e  |
| f |                                     s  |
| i |                                        |
| c |                                        |
| e |                                        |
| s |                                        |
|   |                                        |
|___|                                     ___|
|   |                                        |
|   |     Entrance                           |
|   |___      ___      ___                   |
|         |  |                               |
|         |  |                               |
|_____|  |_____|
```

The Rajah, Seo Sing, was a worthy old man. He had four sons, Surubjeet Sing, the eldest, Omrow Sing, Kaleepurkas Sing, and Jypurkas Sing. The eldest was then married, and about the age of twenty-five; the other three were still boys. The old man left the management of the estate to the eldest son, a morose person, who led a secluded life, and was never seen out of the female apartments, save twice a-year, on the festival of the hooley and the anniversary of his marriage. Mr. Ravenscroft had never seen or held any communion with him, save through his father, brothers, or servants; but he was in the habit of daily seeing and conversing with the father and his other sons on the most friendly terms. The eldest son became alarmed when he saw Mr. Ravenscroft begin to plant indigo, and prepare to construct vats for the manufacture; and apprehended that he would go on encroaching till he took the whole estate from him, unless he was made away with. He therefore hired a gang of Bhuduk dacoits from the neighbouring forest of the Oude Tarae to put him to death, after he had been four months at Bhinga. During this time Mrs. Ravenscroft had gone on one occasion to Cawnpoor, and on another to Secrora, on business.

Bhinga lies fifty miles north-east from Secrora, where the 20th Regiment of Native Infantry, under the command of Colonel Patton, was then cantoned. On the 6th of May 1823, Ensign Platt, of that corps, had come out to see him. In the evening, the old Rajah and his second and third sons came to visit Mr. Ravenscroft as usual, and they sat conversing with the family on the most friendly terms till nine o'clock, when they took leave, and Mrs. Ravenscroft, with her child and two female attendants, retired to the sleeping-room in the house. Ensign Platt went to his small sleeping-tent outside the quadrangle, under a mango-tree. This tent was just large enough to admit his small cot, and a few block-tin travelling-boxes, which he piled away inside, to the right and left of his bed. Mr. Ravenscroft slept on a cot in the open air, in the quadrangle, a few paces from the door leading to Mrs. Ravenscroft's sleeping-apartment. He that night left his arms in the sitting-room, and Ensign Platt had none with him. Mr. Ravenscroft was the handsomest and most athletic European gentleman then in India, and one of the most expert in the use of the sword and shield.

His servants had been accustomed to stand sentry, by turns, at the entrance of the quadrangle, and it was his groom Munsa's turn to take the first watch that night. He was to have been relieved by the chowkeedar, Bhowaneedeen; but, in the middle of his watch, he roused the chowkeedar, and told him that he had been taken suddenly ill, and must go to his house for relief. The chowkeedar told him that he might go at once, and he would get up and take his place immediately; but he lay down and soon fell asleep again.

About eleven o'clock the whole quadrangle was filled by a gang of about sixty dacoits, who set their torches in a blaze, and began to attack Mr. Ravenscroft with their spears. He sprang up, and called loudly for his sword and shield, but there was no one to bring them. He received several spears through his body as he made for the door of Mrs. Ravenscroft's apartment, calling out to her in English to fly and save herself and child, and defending himself as well as he could with his naked arms. Mosahib, a servant who slept by his cot, got to Mrs. Ravenscroft's room and assisted her to escape, with her child and two female attendants, through the bathing-room to the outside. A party had been placed to stab Ensign Platt with their long spears through the sides of his small tent; but they passed through and through the block-tin boxes, and roused without hurting him. He rushed out and attempted to defend himself by seizing the spears of his assailants; but he received several of them through his arms. He made for the entrance to the quadrangle, and there, by the blaze of the torches, saw Mr. Ravenscroft still endeavouring to defend himself, but covered with blood, which was streaming from his wounds and mouth.

On seeing Ensign Platt at the entrance, he staggered towards him, but the dacoits made a rush at Ensign Platt with their spears at the same time. He saved himself by springing over a thick and thorny hedge on one side of the quadrangle, and ran round behind to the small door leading into the bathing-room, which he reached in time to assist Mrs. Ravenscroft to escape, as the dacoits were forcing their way through the screen into her bed-room from the sitting-room. As soon as he saw her under the shade of the trees, beyond the blaze of the torches, he left her and her child, and the two female attendants, to the care of Mosahib, and went round to the entrance in search of her husband. He had got to a tree, outside the entrance, into which Deena, Ensign Platt's servant, had climbed to save himself as soon as he saw his master attacked, and was leaning against it; but, on seeing Ensign Platt, he again staggered towards him, saying faintly bus, bus—enough, enough. These were the last words he was heard to utter, and must have referred to the escape of his wife and child, of which he had become conscious. By this time the gang had made off with the little booty they found. On attacking Mr. Ravenscroft at first, some of them were heard to say, "You have run from Cawnpoor to come and seize upon the estate of Bhinga, but we will settle you." Mrs. Ravenscroft, her infant, and female attendants, remained concealed under the shade of the trees, and her husband was now taken to her with eighteen spear wounds through his body. The Rajah and his two young sons soon after made their appearance, and in the evening the survivors were all taken by the old man to a spacious building, close outside the fort, where they received every possible attention; but the eldest son never made his appearance. Out of the twenty-nine men who composed the party when the attack commenced, seven had been killed and eighteen wounded. Mr. Ravenscroft died during the night of the 7th, after great suffering. He retained his consciousness till near the last; but the blood continued to flow from his mouth, and he could articulate nothing. On the morning of the 8th, he was buried in the grove, and Ensign Platt read the funeral service over his grave. Mrs. Ravenscroft and her child were taken to Colonel Patton, at Secrora, and soon after sent by him to Lucknow.

On the 10th, he reported the circumstances of this murder to the Resident, Mr. Ricketts; and sent him the narratives of Mosahib and Deena; and his report, with translations of these narratives, was submitted by the Resident to Government on the 12th of that month. But in these narratives no mention whatever was made of a British officer having been present at the murder and the burial of Mr. Ravenscroft. This suppression arose, no doubt, from the apprehension that Government might be displeased to find that the military authorities at Secrora had become aware of Mr. Ravenscroft's residence at Bhinga without reporting the circumstance to Government; and still more so to find, that he had been there visited by a British officer, when search was being made for him throughout India.

In acknowledging the receipt of the Resident's letter on the 23rd of May, the Secretary, Mr. George Swinton, observes, that the Governor-General in Council concludes, that he shall receive a more full and satisfactory report on the subject from Colonel Patton than that to which his letter had given cover, since he considered that report to be very imperfect; that one of the narrators, Mosahib, states, that he himself conducted Mrs. Ravenscroft and her child to a neighbouring village, and yet he brought no message whatever from that lady to Colonel Patton at Secrora; that none of the wounded people or servants of the deceased, except Deena, appear to have found their way to Sacrora, though four days had elapsed from the date of the murder to that of the despatch of the report; that the body seemed to have been hastily interred by the people of the village, without any notice having been sent to the officer commanding the troops at Secrora; that such an atrocious outrage as that described in these narratives, on the person of a subject and servant of the British Government, demanded the exertion of every effort to ascertain the real facts of the case by local inquiry; yet it did not appear that any person had been despatched to the spot to verify the evidence of the two men examined by Colonel Patton, or to clear up the doubts to which all these circumstances must naturally have given rise; nor did it appear that the defects in Colonel Patton's report had occurred to the Resident, or that he had directed any further inquiry to be made.

The Resident was, therefore, directed to instruct Colonel Patton, to depute one or more officers to the place where the murder was said to be perpetrated, with orders to hold an inquiry on the spot in communication with the King of Oude's officers, to take the evidence of the wounded men, and that of any other persons who might have been witnesses to any part of the transaction, and to the burial of Mr. Ravenscroft; and to examine the grave in which the body of the deceased was said to have been deposited; and further, to call upon Colonel Patton to state whether any information had previously reached Secrora of Mr. Ravenscroft's actually residing at Bhinga, or at any other place within the dominions of the King of Oude. "His Lordship in Council was," Mr. Swinton says, "satisfied, from the known humanity of Colonel Patton's character, that every possible aid and comfort had been extended to Mrs. Ravenscroft and her child; and the information which that lady and her attendants must have it in their power to give, could not fail to place the whole affair in its proper light." Extracts from this letter were sent by the Resident to Colonel Patton, on the 2nd of June, with a request that he would adopt immediate measures to carry the orders of Government into effect; and reply to the question whether any information of Mr. Ravenscroft's residing at Bhinga had previously reached him.

A committee of British officers was assembled at Bhinga on the 11th June, and their proceedings were transmitted to the Resident on the 18th of that month; but the committee, for some reasons stated in the report, did not examine "the grave in which the body of the deceased was said to have been deposited." Though in this committee Ensign Platt stated that he was present when the murder was perpetrated; that he attended the deceased till he died the next night, and performed the funeral ceremonies over the body on the morning of the 8th; still he seemed to narrate the circumstances of the event with some reserve, while there was a good deal of discrepancy in the evidence of the other eye-witnesses, as recorded in the report, seemingly from the dread of compromising Ensign Platt.

The Resident did not, therefore, think that Government would be satisfied with the result of this inquiry; and, on the 20th of June he directed Colonel Patton to reassemble the committee at Bhinga, and require it to hold an inquest on the body, and take the depositions of all the witnesses on oath. On the same day the Resident reported to Government what he had done. The second committee proceeded to Bhinga, and, on the 13th of July, Colonel Patton transmitted its report to the Resident, who submitted it to Government on the 17th of that month. The committee had taken the evidence of the witnesses on oath, and held an inquest on the body; but, in doing so, it had been necessary to dig through the tomb which Mrs. Ravenscroft had, in the interval, caused to be erected over the remains of her husband; and, at the suggestion of Colonel Patton, this tomb was rebuilt and improved at the cost of Government, who were perfectly satisfied with the result.

But in its reply, dated the 31st July, Government very justly remarks, that all the unnecessary trouble which had attended this investigation, as well as the very painful step of having the body disinterred, which the Resident found himself compelled to adopt in obedience to its orders, arose from a want of those obvious precautions in the first instance which ought to have suggested themselves to Colonel Patton. Had he made the requisite inquiries at Secrora, he must have learnt that an English officer belonging to his own regiment, who had been present at the interment, had been wounded when Mr. Ravenscroft was murdered, and, for a time, rendered unfit for duty. The facts since deposed to on oath by Ensign Platt might have been elicited, and his testimony, if necessary, might have been confirmed by the evidence of the widow of the deceased; and had such conclusive evidence been submitted to Government in the first instance, the doubts excited by the extraordinary circumstances of the whole affair would never have existed. When ordered on the inquiry to Bhinga, had Ensign Platt at once declared at Secrora that he could there afford all the information required as to the fact of the murder and interment of the body, the necessity of further inquiry on the spot would have been obviated. He had apparently been deterred from doing this by the apprehension of compromising both himself and his commanding officer. Colonel Patton had no knowledge of Mr. Ravenscroft being at Bhinga, though he had heard a rumour of his being somewhere in the Oude territory; and, in his application for a few days' leave, Ensign Platt made no mention of him or of his intention to visit him. This is stated in a subsequent letter from Colonel Patton to the Resident, dated 27th of August 1823.

The opinion that the Rajah had nothing whatever to do with the murder, and that the gang was secretly hired for the purpose by his eldest son, Surubjeet, has been confirmed by time, and is now universal among the people of these parts. He died soon after of dropsy, and the people believe that the disease was caused by the crime. He left an only son, Krishun Dutt Sing. The Rajah, Seo Sing, survived his eldest son some years; and, on his death, he was succeeded by Krishun Dutt Sing, who now leads precisely the same secluded life that his father led, and leaves the management of the Bhinga estate entirely to his only surviving uncle, Kaleepurkas Sing, the youngest of the two boys who visited Mr. Ravenscroft on the evening of the murder. The other three sons of the old Rajah are dead. The actual perpetrators of the murder were never punished or discovered. Mrs. Ravenscroft afterwards became united in marriage to the Resident at the time, Mr. Mordaunt Ricketts, and still lives. Her child, a boy, was drowned at the Lucknow Residency some time after his mother's marriage with the Resident. He had been shut up by his mother in a bathing-room for some fault; and, looking into a bathing-tub at his image in the water, he lost his balance, fell in, and was drowned. When the servants went to let him out they found him quite dead.

CHAPTER III.

Legendary tale of breach of Faith—Kulhuns tribe of Rajpoots—Murder of the Banker, Ramdut Pandee, by the Nazim of Bahraetch—Recrossing the Ghagra river—Sultanpoor district, State of Commandants of troops become sureties for the payment of land revenue—Estate of Muneearpoor and the Lady Sogura—Murder of Hurpaul Sing, Gurgbunsee, of Kupragow—Family of Rajahs Bukhtawar and Dursun Sing—Their bynama Lands—Law of Primogeniture—Its object and effect—Rajah Ghalib Jung—Good effects of protection to Tenantry—Disputes about Boundaries—Our army a safety-valve for Oude—Rapid decay of Landed Aristocracy in our Territories—Local ties in groves, wells, &c.

December 15, 1849.-Wuzeergunge. On the way this morning, we passed Koorassa, which is said once to have been the capital of a formidable Rajah, the head of the Kulhuns tribe of Rajpoots. The villages which we see along the road seem better, and better peopled and provided with cattle. The soil not naturally very fertile, but yields fine returns under good culture, manure, and irrigation. Water everywhere very near the surface. The place is called after the then Nawab Wuzeer, Asuf-od Dowlah, who built a country-seat here with all appurtenances of mosque, courts, dwelling-houses, &c., on the verge of a fine lake, formed in the old bed of the Ghagra river, with tillage and verdure extending down to the water's edge. The garden-wall, which surrounds a large space of ground, well provided with fruit and ornamental trees, is built of burnt bricks, and still entire. The late minister, Ameen-od

Dowlah, persuaded his master, Amjad Allee Shah, to give this garden and the lands around, with which it had been endowed, to his moonshee, Baker Allee Khan, who now resides at Fyzabad, and subsists upon the rents which he derives from them, and which are said to be about twelve hundred rupees a-year.

The Bulrampoor Rajah, Ramdut Pandee, the banker, and Rajah Bukhtawar Sing, rode with me this morning. The Rajah of Bulrampoor is an intelligent and pleasing young man. He was a child when Mr. Ravenscroft was killed, but said he had heard, that the Bhinga chief had suffered for the share which he had had in the murder; his body swelled, and he died within a month or two. "If men's bodies swelled for murder, my friend," I said, "we should have no end of swelled bodies in Oude, and among the rest, that of Prethee Put's, of Paska." "Their bodies all swell, sooner, or later," said old Bukhtawar Sing, "when they commit such atrocious crimes, and Prethee Puts will begin to swell when he finds that you are inquiring into his." "I am afraid, my friends, that the propensity to commit them has become inveterate. One man hears that another has obtained lands or wealth by the murder of his father or brother, and does not rest till he has attempted to get the same by the murder of his, for he sees no man punished for such crimes." "It is not all nor many of our clan" (Rajpoots), said the Rajah of Bulrampoor, "that can or will do this: we never unite our sons or daughters in marriage with the family of one who is so stained with crimes. Prethee Put and all who do as he has done, must seek an union with families of inferior caste." I asked him whether the people, in the Tarae forest, were still afraid to point out tigers to sportsmen. "I was lately out with a party after a tiger," he said, "which had killed a cowherd, but his companions refused to point out any trace of him, saying, that their relatives' spirit must be now riding upon his head, to guide him from all danger, and we should have no chance of shooting him. We did shoot him, however," said the Rajah, exultingly, "and they were all, afterwards, very glad of it. The tigers in the Tarae do not often kill men, sir, for they find plenty of deer and cattle to eat."—"Can you tell me, Rajah Sahib," said I, "why it is that among the Arabs, the lion is called 'the father of cultivation,' 'abol hurs, or abo haris.'" "No," replied the Rajah; "it is an odd name for a beast that feeds on nothing but the flesh of deer, cattle, and men." "It is, I suppose, Rajah Sahib," I remarked, "because he feeds upon the deer, which are the greatest enemies of their young crops."

The Rajahs of Toolseepoor and Bulrampoor, and all the merchants and respectable landholders in these parts assure me, that all the large colonies of Bhuduks, or gang robbers by hereditary profession, who had, for so many generations, up to A.D. 1840, been located in the Oude Terae forest, have entirely disappeared under the operation of the "Special Police," of the Thuggee and Dacoitee Department, aided and supported by the Oude Government; and that not one family of them can now be found anywhere in Oude. They have not been driven out as formerly, to return as soon as the temporary pressure ceased, but hunted down and punished, or made to blend with the rest of society in service or at honest labour.

December 16, 1849.—Nawabgunge, eight miles, over a plain of the same good soil, but not much better cultivated. The people tell me, that garden tillage is now almost unknown in these districts; first, because kachies or gardeners (here called moraes) having been robbed, ruined, and driven into exile by Rughbur Sing, cannot be induced to return to and reside in places, where they would have so little chance of reaping the fruits of their labour; and, secondly, because there are no people left who can afford to purchase their garden produce. They tell me also, that the best classes of ordinary cultivators, the Koormies and Lodhees, have been almost all driven out of the district from the same cause. The facts are manifest—there are no gardeners, and but few Koormies and Lodhees left; and there is, in consequence, little good tillage of any kind, and still less of garden cultivation.

The Rajah of Bulrampoor and Ramdut Pandee, the banker, rode with me, and related the popular tradition regarding the head of the Kulhuns family of Rajpoots, Achul Sing, who, about a century and a quarter ago, reigned over the district intervening between Gonda and Wuzeer Gunge, and resided at his capital of Koorassa. The Rajah had a dispute with one of his landholders, whom he could not get into his power. He requested Rutun Pandee, the banker, to mediate a reconciliation, and invite the landholder to an amicable adjustment of accounts, on a pledge of personal security. The banker consented, but made the Rajah swear by the River Sarjoo, which flowed near the town, that he should be received with courtesy, and escorted back safely. The landholder relied on the banker's pledge and came; but the Rajah no sooner got him into his power, than he caused him to be put to death. The banker could not consent to live under the dishonour of a violated pledge; and, abstaining from food, died in twenty-one days, invoking the vengeance of the River Sarjoo, on the head of the perfidious Prince. In his last hours the banker was visited by one of the Rajah's wives, who was then pregnant, and implored him to desist from his purpose in mercy to the child in her womb; but she was told by the dying man, that he could not consent to survive the dishonour brought upon him by her perjured husband; and that she had better quit the place and save herself and child, since the incensed river Sarjoo would certainly not spare any one who remained with the Rajah. She did so. The banker died, and his death was followed by a sudden rise of the river and tempest. The town was submerged, and the Rajah with all who remained with him perished. The ruins of the old town are said to be occasionally still visible, though at a great depth under the water in the old bed of the Sarjoo, which forms a fine lake, near the present village of Koorassa, midway between Gonda and Wuzeer Gunge.

The pregnant wife fled, and gave birth to a son, whose descendant is now the head of the Kulhuns Rajpoots, and the Rajah of Bahmanee Paer, a district on the eastern border of Oude towards Goruckpoor. But, it is a remarkable fact, that the male descendants have been all blind from their birth, or, at least, the reigning portion of them, and the present Rajah is said to have two blind sons. This is popularly considered to be one of the effects of the Rajah's violated pledge to the banker. A handmaid of the Rajah, Achul Sing, is said to have fled at the same time, and given birth to a son, from whom are descended the Kulhuns tallookdars of the Chehdwara, or Gowaris district, already noticed. The descendants of Rutun Pandee are said still to hold rent-free lands, under Achul Sing's descendant, in Bahmanee Paer; and the Pandee is worshipped throughout the districts as a saint or martyr. He has a shrine in every village, at which offerings are made on all occasions of marriage, and blessings invoked for the bride and bridegroom, from the spirit of one who set so much value on his plighted faith while on earth. The two branches of the Kulhuns family above mentioned, propitiate the spirit of the deceased Pandee by offerings; but there is a branch of the same family at Mohlee, in the Goruckpoor district, who do not. Though Hindoos, they adopt some Mussulman customs, and make offerings to the old Mussulman saint, at Bahraetch, in order to counteract the influence of the Pandee's spirit.

Such popular traditions, arising from singular coincidences of circumstances, have often a salutary effect on society, and seem to be created by its wants and wishes; but rivers have, of late years, become so much less prompt in the vindication of their honour, that little reliance is placed, upon the oaths taken in their names by the Prince, his officers or his landowners in Oude.

Nawabgunge, Munkapoor, and Bahmanee transferred to the British Government, with the other lands, under the treaty of 1801; and retransferred to Oude, by the treaty of the 11th of May 1816, in exchange for Handeea, alias Kewae, a slip of land extending along the left bank of the Ganges, between Allahabad and Benares.

	Rent Roll.	Kankur.	Govt. demand
Nawabgunge, Wuzeergunge, Mahadewa	1,08,000	32,000	76,000
Munkapoor	40,000	12,000	28,000
Bahmanee Paer	12,000	3,000	9,000

The landholders and cultivators complain sadly of the change of sovereigns; and the tillage and population have greatly diminished under the Oude Government since 1816, but more especially, since the monster, Rughbur Sing got the government. Here Ramdut Pandee, the Rajah of Bulrampoor, and the Nazim of the district, have taken leave of me, this being my last stage in their district. Ramdut Pandee holds two estates in this district, for which he pays an annual revenue to Government of 1,66,744 13 3.* He holds, at the same time, a small estate in our district of Goruckpoor, where he resides and keeps his family, till he obtains solemn written pledges, confirmed on oath, for their security, not only from the local authority of the day, but from all the commandants of corps and establishments, comprising the military force employed under him. These pledges include all his clients, who may have occasion to visit or travel with him, as the Rajah of Bulrampoor is now doing. These pledges require to be renewed on every change in the local authorities and in the military officers employed under them. He is one of the most substantial and respectable of the agricultural capitalists of Oude, and the highest of his rank and class in this district. He every year stands security for the punctual payment of the revenues due, according to existing engagements, by the principal landholders of the district, to the extent of from six to eight lacs of rupees; and for this he gets a certain per centage, varying with the character and capability of the landholders. Some are of doubtful ability, others of doubtful character, and he rates his risks and per centage accordingly. He does much good, and is more generally esteemed than any other man in the district; but he has, no doubt, enlarged his own landed possessions occasionally, by taking advantage of the necessities of his clients, and his influence over the local authorities of government The lands he does get, however, he improves by protecting and aiding his tenants, and inviting and fostering a better class of cultivators, He is looked up to with respect and confidence by almost all the large landholders of the district, for his pledge for the punctual payment of the revenues saves their estates from the terrible effects of a visit from the Nazim and his disorderly and licentious troops; and this pledge they can always obtain, when necessary, by a fair assurance of adherence to their engagements.

* The estate of Ramdut Pandee, for this year, 1849, comprises
    Sirgha, Chunda, &c.   1,20,729   11   0
    Akberpoor, &c.   46,015   2   3
         Total   1,66,744   13   3

On the 8th of November 1850, Ramdut Pandee lent the Nazim eighty thousand rupees on his bond, after paying all that was due to the State for the season, by him and all his clients, and on the 16th of that month he went to Gonda, where the Nazim, Mahommed Hussan, was encamped with his force, to take leave preparatory to his going to bathe at Ajoodheea, on the last day of the month of Kartick, as was his invariable custom. He was accompanied by the Rajah of Bulrampoor, and they encamped separately in two mango-groves near to each other, and about a mile and a half from the Nazim's camp. About nine at night the Nazim sent two messengers, with silver sticks, to invite and escort them to his tent. They set out immediately, leaving all their armed followers in their camps, and taking only a few personal attendants and palankeen bearers. No person is permitted to take arms into the Nazim's tent; nor does any landholder or merchant of Oude enter his tent without the pledges for personal security above mentioned. Ramdut Pandee and the Rajah entered with only a few personal servants, leaving all their other attendants outside the outer curtain. This curtain surrounded the tent at a distance of only a few yards from it, and the tent was pitched in the centre. They were received with all due ceremony, and in the same friendly manner as usual. The Rajah had no business to talk about, while the Nazim and banker had; and, after a short conversation, he took leave to return to his tents and break his fast, which he had kept that day for some religious purpose. He left in the tent the Nazim, his deputy, Jafir Allee, and his nephew and son-in-law, Allee Hoseyn, sitting together on the carpet, on the right, all armed, and Ramdut sitting unarmed, on the left, with a Brahmin lad, Jowahir, standing at the door, with the banker's paundan and a handkerchief. Kurunjoo, a second person, with the banker's shoes, and a third attendant of his standing outside the tent door.

The Nazim and Ramdut talked for some time together, seemingly on the most friendly and cordial terms; but the Nazim, at last, asked him for a further loan of money, and further securities for landholders of doubtful character, before he went to bathe. The banker told him, that he could lend him no more money till he came back from bathing, as he had lent him eighty thousand rupees only eight days before; and, that he could not increase his pledges of security without further consultation with the landholders, as he had not yet recovered more than four out of the seven lacs of rupees which he had been obliged to advance to the Treasury, on the securities given for them during the last year. He then took leave and rose to depart. The Nazim turned and made some sign to his deputy, Jafir Allee, who rose, presented his gun and shot Ramdut through the right side close under the arm-pit. Exclaiming "Ram! Ram!"—God! God!— the banker fell; and the Nazim, seizing and drawing the sword which lay on the carpet before him, cut the falling banker across the forehead. His nephew and deputy drew theirs; and together they inflicted no less than twenty-two cuts upon the body of Ramdut.

The banker's three attendants, seeing their master thus shot down and hacked to pieces, called out for help; but one of the three ruffians cut Jowahir, the Brahmin lad, across the shoulder, with his sword, and all ran off and sought shelter across the border in the British territory. The Nazim and his attendants then buried the body hastily near the tent, and ordered the troops and artillery to advance towards and fire into the two camps. They did so, and the Bulrampoor Rajah had only just reached his tents when the shot came pouring in upon them from the Nazim's guns. He galloped off as fast as he could towards the British border, about twenty miles distant, attended only by a few mounted followers, some of whom he sent off to Bulrampoor, to bring his family as fast as possible across the border to him. The rest he ordered to follow him. His followers and those of the murdered banker fled before the Nazim's forces, which had been concentrated for this atrocious purpose, and both their camps were plundered. Before the Rajah fled, however, the murdered banker's son-in-law, who had been left in the camp, ran to him with a small casket, containing Ramdut's seals, the bond for the eighty thousand rupees, and the written pledges given by the Nazim and commanding officers of corps, for the banker's and the Rajah's personal security. He mounted him upon one of his horses, and took both him and the casket off to the British territory.

It was now about midnight, and the Nazim took his forces to the towns and villages upon the banker's estate, in which his family and relatives resided, and in which he kept the greater part of his moveable property. He sacked and plundered them all without regard to the connection or relationship of the inhabitants with the murdered banker. The property taken from the inhabitants of these towns and villages is estimated at from ten to twelve lacs of rupees. As many as could escape fled for shelter across the border, into the British territory. The banker's brother, Kishen Dutt, who resided in the British territory, came over, collected all he could of his brother's followers, attacked the Amil's forces, killed and wounded some forty or fifty of his men, and captured two of his guns. The body of the banker was discovered two days after, and disinterred by his family and friends, who counted the twenty-two wounds that had been inflicted upon it by the three assassins, and had it burned with due ceremonies.

The Nazim's agent at Court, on the 18th of November, submitted to the minister his master's report of this affair, in which it was stated, that the banker was a defaulter on account of his own estate, and those of the other landholders for whom he had given security—that he, the Nazim, had earnestly urged him to some adjustment of his accounts, but all in vain—that the banker had disregarded all his demands and remonstrances, and had with him five hundred armed followers, one of whom had fired his pistol at him, the Nazim, and killed one of his men—that they had all then joined in an attack upon the Nazim and his men, and that, in defending themselves, they had killed the banker. On the 19th, another report, dated the 16th, reached the minister from the Nazim's camp, stating, that the banker had come to his tent at ten at night, with his armed followers, and had an interview [with] him—that as the banker rose to depart, the Nazim told him that he must not go without some settlement of his accounts; and a dispute followed, in which the banker was killed, and two of the Nazim's followers were severely wounded-that so great was the confusion that the Durbar news-reporters could not approach to get information.

On the 20th, a third report reached the minister, stating, that the Rajah of Bulrampoor had come with the banker to visit the Nazim, but had taken leave and departed before the collision took place—that the Nazim urged the necessity of an immediate settlement of accounts, but the banker refused to make any, grossly abused the Nazim, and, at last, presented his pistol and fired at him; and thereby wounded two of his people—that he was, in consequence, killed by the Nazim's people, who joined the banker's own people in the plunder of his camp.

On receiving this last report, the minister, by order of his Majesty, presented to the agent of the Nazim a dress of honour of fourteen pieces, such as is given to the highest officers for the most important services; and ordered him to send it to his master, to mark the sense his sovereign entertained of his gallant conduct and valuable services, in crushing so great a rebel and oppressor, and to assure him of a long-continued tenure of office.

By the interposition of the British Resident and the aid of the magistrate of Goruckpoor, Mr. Chester, the real truth was elicited, the Nazim was dismissed from office, and committed for trial, before the highest judicial Court at Lucknow. He at first ran off to Goruckpoor, taking with him, besides his own, two elephants belonging to the Rajah of Gonda, with property on them to the value of fifty thousand rupees, which he overtook in his flight. The Rajah had sent off these elephants with his valuables, on hearing of the assassination of the banker, thinking that the Nazim would secure impunity for this murder, as Hakeem Mehndee had for that of Amur Sing, and be tempted to extend his operations. Finding the district of Goruckpoor unsafe, the Nazim came back and surrendered himself at Lucknow. Jafir Allee was afterwards seized in Lucknow. There is, however, no chance of either being punished, since many influential persons about the Court have shared in the booty, and become accessaries interested in their escape. Moreover, the Nazim is a Mahommedan, a Syud, and a Sheeah. No Sheeah could be sentenced to death, for the murder, even of a Soonnee, at Lucknow, much less for that of a Hindoo. If a Hindoo murders a Hindoo, and consents to become a Mussulman, he cannot be so sentenced; and if he consents to become so after sentence has been passed, it cannot be carried into execution. Such is the law, and such the every-day practice.

The elephants were recovered and restored through the interposition of the Resident, but none of the property of the Rajah or the banker has been recovered. May 18, 1851.—The family of the banker has obtained a renewal of the lease of their, two estates, on agreeing to pay an increase of forty thousand rupees a-year.

Sirgha Chunda	1,20,729	11	0			
Increase	30,000	0				
				1,50,729	11	0
Akberpoor	46,015	2	3			
Increase	10,000	0	0			
				56,015	2	3
Total annual demand	2,06,744	13	3			

They bold the Nazim's bond for the eighty thousand rupees, borrowed only eight days before his murder.

December 17, 1849.—Five miles to the left bank of the Ghagra, whence crossed over to Fyzabad, on platformed boats, prepared for the purpose by the Oude authorities. Our tents are in one of the large mango-groves, which are numerous on the right bank of the river, but scanty on the opposite bank. From the time we crossed this river at Byram-ghaut on the 5th, till we recrossed it this morning, we were moving in the jurisdiction of the Nazim of the Gonda and Bahraetch district. After recrossing the Ghagra we came within that of the Nazim of Sultanpoor, Aga Allee, who was appointed to it this year, not as a contractor, but manager, under the Durbar. The districts under contractors are called ijara, or farmed districts; those under the management of non-contracting servants of Government are called amanee, or districts under the amanut, or trust of Government officers. The morning was fine, the sky clear, and the ground covered with hoar frost. It was, pleasing to see so large a camp, passing without noise, inconvenience, or disorder of any kind in so large a river.

The platformed boats were numerous, and so were the pier-heads prepared on both sides, for the convenience of embarking and landing. Carriages, horses, palankeens, camels and troops, all passed without the slightest difficulty. The elephants were preparing to cross, some in boats and some by swimming, as might seem to them best. Some refuse to swim, and others to enter boats, and some refuse to do either; but the fault is generally with their drivers. On the present occasion, two or three remained behind, one plunged into the stream from his boat, in the middle of the river, with his driver on his back, and both disappeared for a time, but neither was hurt. Those that remained on the left bank, got tired of their solitude, and were at last coaxed over, either in boats or in the water.

The Sarjoo rejoins the Ghagra a little above Fyzabad, and the united stream takes the old name of the Sarjoo. This is the name the river bears, till it emerges from the Tarae forest, when the large body takes that of the Ghagra, and the small stream, which it throws off, or which perhaps flows in the old bed, retains that of the Sarjoo. The large branch absorbs the Kooreeala, Chouka, and other small streams, on its way to rejoin the smaller. Some distance below Fyzabad, the river takes the name of Dewa; and uniting, afterwards, with the Gunduck, flows into the Ganges. Fyzabad is three miles above Ajoodheea, on the same bank of the river. It was founded by the first rulers of the reigning family, and called for some time Bungalow, from a bungalow which they built on the verge of the stream. Asuf-od Dowlah disliked living near his mother, after he came to the throne, and he settled at Lucknow, then a small village on the right bank of the Goomtee river. This village, in the course of eighty years, grown into a city, containing nearly a million of souls. Fyzabad has declined almost in the same proportion.

The Nazim has six regiments, and part of a seventh, on duty under him, making, nominally, six thousand fighting men, but that he cannot, he tells me, muster two thousand; and out of the two thousand, not five hundred would, he says be ready to fight on emergency. All the commandants of corps reside at Court, knowing nothing whatever of their duties, and never seeing their regiments. They are mere children, or Court favourites, worse than children. He has, nominally, forty-two guns, of various calibre; but he, with great difficulty, collected bullocks enough to draw the three small guns he brought with him from Sultanpoor, to salute the Resident, on his entering his district. I looked at them in the evening. They were seventy-four in number, but none of them were in a serviceable condition, and the greater part were small, merely skin and bone. He was obliged to purchase powder in the bazaar for the salutes; and said, that when he entered his charge two months ago, the usual salute of seven guns, for himself, could not be fired for want of powder, and he was obliged to send to the bazaar to purchase what was required. The bazaar-powder used by the Oude troops is about one-third of the strength of the powder used by our troops. His authority is despised by all the tallookdars of the district, many of whom refuse to pay any rent, defy the Government, and plunder the country, as all their rents are insufficient to pay the armed bands which they keep up. All his numerous applications to Court, for more and better troops and establishments, are disregarded, and he is helpless. He cannot collect the revenue, or coerce the refractory landholders and robbers, who prey upon the country.*

* The Nazim for 1850-51, got both Captain Magness's and Captain Banbury's regiments.

He says that the two companies and two guns, which were sent out at the Resident's urgent recommendation, to take possession of Shahgunge, and prevent the two brothers, Maun Sing and Rughbur Sing, from disturbing the peace of the country, in their contests with each other, joined Maun Sing, as partisan; to oppose his brother; and that Maun Sing has taken for himself all the bynamah lands, from which his brother, Rughbur Sing, has been ousted, under the favour of the minister. He tells me also, that Beebee Sogura, the lady who holds the estate of Muneearpoor, and pays fifty thousand rupees a-year to the Government, was seized by Wajid Allee, his predecessor, before he made over charge of the district to him, and made over to a body of troops, on condition, that she should enter into engagement to pay to them the ten months' arrears of pay due to them, out of the rents of the ensuing year; and that they should give him receipts for the full amount of these arrears of pay at once, to be forwarded to the Durbar, that he might get credit for the amount in his accounts for last year—that she has paid them fifteen thousand rupees, but can collect no more from her tenants, as the crops are all being cut or destroyed by the troops, and she is in close confinement, and treated with cruel indignity. The rent-roll of her estate is, it is said, equal to one hundred thousand rupees a year.

This was a common practice among governors of districts at the close of last year; and thus they got credit, on account, for large sums, pretended to have been paid out of the revenues of last year; but, in reality, to be paid out of the revenues of the ensuing year. But the collections are left to be made by the troops, for whose arrears of pay the revenue has been assigned, and they generally destroy or extort double what they are entitled to from their unhappy debtors. This practice of assigning revenues due, or to be due, by landholders, for the arrears of pay due to the troops, is the source of much evil; and is had recourse to only when contractors and other collectors of revenue are unable to enforce payment in any other way; or require to make it appear that they have collected more than they really have; and to saddle the revenue of the ensuing year with the burthens properly incident upon those of the past. The commandant of the troops commonly takes possession of the lands, upon the rents, or revenues, of which the payments have been assigned, and appropriates the whole produce to himself and his soldiers, without regard to the rights of landholders, farmers, cultivators, capitalists, or any other class of persons, who may have invested their capital and labour in the lands, or depend upon the crops for their subsistence. The troops, too, are rendered unfit for service by such arrangements, since all their time is taken up in the more congenial duty of looking after the estate, till they have desolated it. The officers and soldiers are converted into manorial under-stewards of the worst possible description. They are available for no other duty till they have paid themselves all that may have been due or may become due to them during the time of their stay, and credit to Government but a small portion of what they exact from the landholders and cultivators, or consume or destroy as food, fodder, and fuel.

This system, injurious alike to the sovereign, the troops, and the people, is becoming every season more and more common in Oude; and must, in a few years, embrace nearly the whole of the land-revenue of the country. It is denominated kubz, or contract, and is of two kinds, the "lakulame kubz," or pledge to collect and pay a certain sum, for which the estate is held to be liable; and "wuslee kubz," or pledge to pay to the collector or troops the precise sum which the commandant may be able to collect from the estate put under him. In the first, the commandant who takes the kubz must pay to the Government collector or the troops the full sum for which the estate is held to be liable, whether he be able to collect it or not, and his kubz is valid at the Treasury, as so much money paid to the troops. In the second, it is valid only as a pledge, to collect as much as he can, and to pay what he collects to the Government collector, or the troops he commands. The collector, however, commonly understands that he has shifted off the burthen of payment to the troops—to the extent of the sum named—from his own shoulders to those of the commandant of the troops; and the troops understand, that unless they collect this sum they will never get it, or be obliged to screw it out of their commandant; and they go to the work con amore. If they can't collect it from the sale of all the crops of the season, they seize and sell all the stock and property of all kinds to be found on the estate; and if this will not suffice, they will not scruple to seize and sell the women and children. The collector, whose tenure of office seldom extends beyond the season, cares little as to the mode as long as he gets the money, and feels quite sure that the sovereign and his Court will care just as little, and ask no questions, should the troops sell every living thing to be found on the estate.

The history, for the last few years, of the estate of Muneearpoor, involves that of the estate of Kupragow and Seheepoor, held by the family of the late Hurpaul Sing, and may be interesting as illustrative of the state of society in Oude. Hurpaul Sing's family is shown in the accompanying note.*

* Purotee Sing had two sons, Gunga Persaud and Nihal Sing. Gunga Persaud had one son, Seosewak, who had three sons, Seoumber Sing, Hobdar Sing, and Hurpaul Sing. Seoumber Sing had one son, Ramsurroop Sing, the present head of the family, who holds the fort and estate of Kupradehee. Hobdar Sing had one son, who died young. Hurpaul Sing died young, Nihal Sing had no son, but left a widow, who holds his share of one-half of the estate, and resides at Seheepoor.

In the year A.D. 1821, after the death of Purotee Sing, his second son, Nihal Sing, held one-half of the estate, and resided in Seheepoor, and the family of his eldest son, Gunga Persaud, held the other half, and resided in Kupragow. The whole paid a revenue to Government of between six and seven hundred rupees a-year, and yielded a rent-roll of something more than double that sum. The neighbouring estate of Muneearpoor, yielding a rent-roll of about three hundred and fifty thousand rupees a-year, was held by Roshun Zuman Khan, in whose family it had been for many generations. He had an only brother, Busawan Khan, who died, leaving a widow, Bussoo, and a daughter, the Beebee, or Lady, Sogura. Roshun Zuman Khan also died, leaving a widow Rahamanee, who succeeded to the estate, but soon died, and left it to the Lady Sogura and her mother. They made Nihal Sing, Gurgbunsee, of Seheepoor, manager of their affairs. From the time that he entered upon the management, Nihil Sing began to increase the number of his followers from his own clan, the Gurgbunsies; and, having now become powerful enough, he turned out his mistress, and took possession of her estate, in collusion with the local authorities.

Rajah Dursun Sing, who then, 1836, held the contract for the district, wished to take advantage of the occasion, to seize upon the estate for himself, and a quarrel, in consequence, took place between him and Nihal Sing. Unable, as a public servant of the State, to lead his own troops against him, Dursun Sing instigated Baboo Bureear Sing, of Bhetee, a powerful tallookdar, to attack Nihal Sing at night, with all the armed followers he could muster, and, in the fight, Nihal Sing was killed. Hurpaul Sing, his nephew, applied for aid to the Durbar, and Seodeen Sing was sent, with a considerable force, to aid him against Bureear Sing. When they were ready for the attack, Dursun Sing sent a reinforcement of troops, secretly, to Bureear Sing, which so frightened Seodeen Sing, that he retired from the conflict.

The Gurgbunsee family had, however, by this time added a great part of the Muneearpoor estate to their own, and many other estates belonging to their weaker neighbours; and, by the plunder of villages, and robbery on the highways, become very powerful. Dursun Sing was superseded in the contract, in 1837, by the widow of Hadee Allee Khan; and Hurpaul recovered possession of the Muneearpoor estate, which he still held in the name of the Lady Sogura. In 1843, she managed to get the estate transferred from the jurisdiction of the contractor for Sultanpoor, to that of the Hozoor Tehseel, and held it till 1845, when Maun Sing, who had succeeded to the contract for the district, on the death of his father, Dursun Sing, in 1844, managed through his uncle, Bukhtawar Sing, to get the estate restored to his jurisdiction. Knowing that his object was to absorb her estate, as he and his father had done so many others, she went off to Lucknow to seek protection; but Maun Sing seized upon all her nankar and seer lands, and put the estate under the management of his own officers. The Lady Sogura, unable to get any one to plead her cause at Court, in opposition to the powerful influence, of Bukhtawur Sing, returned to Muneearpoor. Maun Sing, after he had collected the greater part of the revenue for 1846, made over the estate to Hurpaul and Seoumber Sing, who put the lady into confinement, and plundered her of all she had left.

Feeling now secure in the possession of the Muneearpoor estate, Hurpaul and Seoumber Sing left a small guard to secure the lady, and went off, with the rest of their forces, to seize upon the estate of Birsingpoor, in the purgunnah of Dehra, belonging to the widow of Mahdoo Sing, the tallookdar. She summoned to her aid Roostum Sa and other Rajkomar landholders, friends of her late husband. A fight ensued, in which Seoumber Sing and his brother, Hobdar Sing were killed. Hurpaul Sing fled and returned to his fort of Kupragow. The Lady Sogura escaped, and presented herself again to the Court of Lucknow, under better auspices; and orders were sent to Maun Sing, and all the military authorities, to restore her to the possession of her estate, and seize or destroy Hurpaul Sing. In alarm Hurpaul Sing then released the mother of the Lady Sogura, and prepared to fly.

Maun Sing sent confidential persons to him to say, that he had been ordered by the Court of Lucknow to confer upon him a dress of honour or condolence, on the death of his two lamented brothers, and should do so in person the next day. Hurpaul Sing was considered one of the bravest men in Oude, but he was then sick on his bed, and unable to move. He received the message without suspicion, being anxious for some small interval of repose; and willing to believe that common interests and pursuits had united him and Maun Sing in something like bonds of friendship.

Maun Sing came in the afternoon, and rested under a banyan-tree, which stood opposite the gateway of the fort. He apologized for not entering the fort, on the ground, that it might lead to some collision between their followers, or that his friend might not wish any of the King's servants, who attended with the dress of honour, to enter his fortress. Hurpaul Sing left all his followers inside the gate, and was brought out to Maun Sing in a litter, unable to sit up without support. The two friends embraced and conversed together with seeming cordiality till long after sunset, when Maun Sing, after investing his friend with the dress of honour, took leave and mounted his horse. This was the concerted signal for his followers to despatch his sick friend, Hurpaul. As he cantered off, at the sound of his kettle-drum and the other instruments of music, used by the Nazims of districts, his armed followers, who had by degrees gathered round the tree, without awakening any suspicion, seized the sick man, dragged him on the ground, a distance of about thirty paces, and then put him to death. He was first shot through the chest, and then stabbed with spears, cut to pieces with swords, and left on the ground. They were fired upon from the fort, while engaged in this foul murder, but all escaped unhurt. Maun Sing had sworn by the holy Ganges, and still more holy head of Mahadeo, that his friend should suffer no personal hurt in this interview; and the credulous and no less cruel and rapacious Gurgbunsies were lulled into security. The three persons who murdered Hurpaul, were Nujeeb Khan, who has left Mann Sing's service, Benee

Sing, who still serves him, and Jeskurun Sing, who has since died. Sadik Hoseyn and many others aided them in dragging their victim to the place where he was murdered, but the wounds which killed him were inflicted by the above-named persons.

The family fled, the fort was seized and plundered of all that could be found, and the estate seized and put under the management of Government officers. Maun Sing had collected half the revenues of 1847, when he was superseded in the contract by Wajid Allee Khan, who re-established the Lady Sogura in the possession of all that remained of her estate. He, at the same time, reinstated the family of Hurpaul Sing, in the possession of their now large estate—that is, the widow of Nihal Sing, to Seheepoor, comprising one-half; and Ramsurroop Sing, the son of Seoumber Sing, to Kupragow, comprising the other half.* The rent-roll of the whole is now estimated at 1,29,000 a-year; and the nankar, or recognized allowance for the holders, is 73,000, leaving the Government demand at 56,000, of which they hardly ever pay one-half, or one-quarter, being inveterate robbers and rebels. Wajid Allee Khan had been commissioned, by the Durbar, to restore the Lady Sogura to her patrimonial estate, and he brought her with him from Lucknow for the purpose; but he soon after made over a part of the estate to his friend, Bakir Allee, of Esoulee, and another part to Ramsurroop, the son of Seoumber Sing, for a suitable consideration, and left only one-half to the Lady Sogura. This she at first refused to take, but he promised to restore the whole the next year, when he saw she was resolved to return again to her friends at Lucknow, and she consented to take the offered half on condition of a large remission of the Government demand upon it. When the season of collections came, however, he would make no remission for the half he had permitted her to retain, or give her any share in the perquisites of the half he had made over to others; nor would he give her credit for any portion of the collections, which had been anticipated by Maun Sing. He made her pledge the whole rents of her estate to Hoseyn Allee Khan, the commandant of a squadron of cavalry, on detached duty, under him. Unable to conduct the management under all these outrages and exactions, she begged to have the estate put under Government officers. Her friends at Court got an order issued for her being restored to the possession of the whole estate, having credit for the whole amount collected by Maun Sing, and a remission in the revenue equal to all that Government allowed to the proprietors of such estates.

> * In May 1851, the Nazim besieged Ramsurroop, in Kupragow, with a very large force, including Bunbury's and Magness's Regiments and Artillery. After the loss of many lives from fighting, and more from cholera, on both sides, Ramsurroop marched out with all his garrison and guns at night, and passed, unmolested, through that part of the line where the non-fighting corps were posted.

Wajid Allee Khan disregarded the order, and made over or sold Naraenpoor and other villages belonging to the estate, to Rughbur Sing, the atrocious brother of Maun Sing, who sent his myrmidons to take possession. They killed the Lady Sogura's two agents in the management, plundered her of all she had of property, and all the rents which she had up to that time collected, for payment to Government; and took possession of Naraenpoor and the other villages, sold to their master by Wajid Allee. Wajid Allee soon after came with a large force, seized the lady and carried her off to his camp, put all her officers and attendants into confinement, and refused all access to her. When she became ill, and appeared likely to sink under the treatment she received, he made her enter into written engagements to pay to the troops, in liquidation of their arrears of pay, all that he pretended that she owed to the State. He prevailed upon Ghuffoor Beg, who commanded the artillery, to take these her pledges, and give him, Wajid Allee, corresponding receipts for the amount, for transmission to the Treasury; and then made her over a prisoner to him. Ghuffoor Beg took possession of the lady and the estate, kept her in close confinement, and employed his artillery-men in making the collections in their own way, by appropriating all the harvests to themselves.

Wajid Allee was superseded in October 1849, by Aga Allee, who, on entering on his charge, directed that martial-law should cease in Muneearpoor; but Ghuffoor Beg and his artillery-men were too strong for the governor, and refused to give up the possession of so nice an estate. When I approached the estate in my tour, Ghuffoor Beg took the lady off to Chundoly, where she was treated with all manner of indignity and cruelty by the artillery. The estate was going to utter ruin under their ignorant and reckless management, and the Nazim, Aga Allee, prayed me to interpose and save it, and protect the poor Lady Sogura. I represented the hardship of the case to the Durbar, but with little hope of any success, under the present government, who say, that if the troops are not allowed to pay themselves in this way, they shall have to pay them all the arrears for which the estate is pledged, not one rupee of which is reduced by the collections they make. If they were to hold the estate for twenty years, they would not allow it to appear that any portion of the arrears had been paid off. The estate is a noble one, and, in spite of all the usurpations and disorders from which it has lately suffered, was capable last year of yielding to Government a revenue of fifty thousand rupees a-year, after providing liberally for all the requirements of the poor Lady Sogura and her family, or a rent-roll of one hundred thousand rupees a-year.

December 19, 1849.—Shahgunge, distance twelve miles. This town is surrounded by a mud wall, forty feet thick, and a ditch three miles round, built thirty years ago, and now much out of repair. It belongs to the family of Rajah Bukhtawar Sing. The wall, thirty feet high, was built of the mud taken from the ditch, in which there is now some six or seven feet of water. The wall has twenty-four bastions for guns, but there is no platform, or road for guns, round it on the inside. A number of respectable merchants and tradesmen reside in this town, where they are better protected than in any other town in Oude. It contains a population of between twenty and thirty thousand persons. They put thatch over the mud walls during the rains to preserve them. The fortifications and dwelling-houses together are said to have cost the family above ten lacs of rupees. There are some fourteen old guns in the fort. Though it would be difficult to shell a garrison out of a fort of this extent, it would not be difficult to take it. No garrison, sufficient to defend all parts of so extended a wall, could be maintained by the holder; and it would be easy to fill the ditch and scale the walls. Besides, the family is so very unpopular among the military classes around, whose lands they have seized upon, that thousands would come to the aid of any government force brought to crush them, and overwhelm the garrison. They keep their position only by the purchase of Court favour, and have the respect and attachment of only the better sort of cultivators, who are not of the military classes, and could be of little use to them in a collision with their sovereign. The family by which it is held has long been very influential at Court, where it has been represented by Bukhtawar Sing, whose brother, Dursun Sing, was the most powerful subject that Oude has had since the time of Almas Allee Khan. They live, however, in the midst of hundreds of sturdy Rajpoots, whom they have deprived of their lands, and who would, as I have said, rise against them were they to be at any time opposed to the Government The country over which we have passed this morning is well studded with groves, and well cultivated; and the peasantry seemed contented and prosperous. The greater part of the road lay through the lands acquired, as already described, by this family. Though they have acquired the property in the land by abuse of authority, collusion and violence, from its rightful owners, they keep their faith with the cultivators, effectually protect them from thieves, robbers, the violence of their neighbours, and, above all, from the ravages of the King's troops; and they encourage the settlement of the better or more skilful and industrious classes of cultivators in their villages, such as Kachies, Koormies, and Lodhies. They came out from numerous villages, and in considerable bodies, to salute me, and expressed themselves well satisfied with their condition, and the security they enjoyed under their present landholders. We came through the village of Puleea, and Rajah Bukhtawar Sing seemed to have great pleasure in showing me the house in which he was born, seventy-five years ago, under a fine tamarind-tree that is still in vigour. The history of this family is that of many others in the Oude territory.

The father of Bukhtawar Sing, Porunder, was the son of Mungul, a Brahmin, who resided in Bhojpoor, on the right bank of the Ganges, a little below Buxar. The son, Porunder, was united in marriage to the daughter of Sudhae Misser, a respectable Brahmin, who resided in Puleea, and held a share of the lands. He persuaded his son-in-law to take up his residence in the same village. Prouder had five sons born to him in this village:—1. Rajah Bukhtawar Sing, my Quartermaster-General. 2. Pursun Sing, died without issue. 3. Rajah Dursun Sing, died 1844, leaving three sons. 4. Incha Sing lives, and has two sons. 5. Davey Sing died, leaving two sons.

The eldest son was a trooper in the Honourable Company's 8th Regiment of Light Cavalry; and while still a very young man, and home on furlough, he attracted the attention of Saadnt Allee Khan, the sovereign of Oude, whom he attended on a sporting excursion. He was very tall, and exceedingly handsome; and, on one occasion, saved his sovereign's life from the sword of an assassin. He became one of Saadut Alee's favourite orderlies, and rose to the command of a squadron. In a fine picture of Saadut Allee and his Court on the occasion of a Durbar, at which the Resident, Colonel Scott, and his suite were present, Bukhtawar Sing is represented in the dress he wore as an orderly cavalry officer. This picture is still preserved at Lucknow. His brothers, Dursun, Incha, and Davey Sing became, one after the other, orderlies in the same manner, under the influence of Bukhtawar Sing, during the reign of Saadnt Allee, and his son, Ghazee-od Deen. Dursan Sing got the command of a regiment of Nujeebs in 1814, and Incha Sing and Davey Sing rose in favour and rank, both civil and military.

Bhudursa and five other villages were held in proprietary right by the members of a family of Syuds. They enjoyed Bhudursa rent free, and still hold it; but the other five villages (Kyl, Mahdono, Tindooa, Teroo, and Pursun) were bestowed, in jagheer, upon another Syud, a Court favourite, Khoda Buksh, in 1814. He fell into disfavour in 1816, and all these and other villages were let, in 1817, to Dursun Sing, in farm, at 60,000 rupees a-year. The bestowal of an estate in jagheer, or farm, ought not to interfere with the rights of the proprietors of the lands comprised in it, as the sovereign transfers merely his own territorial rights, not theirs; but Dursun Sing, before the year 1820, had, by rack-renting, lending on mortgage, and other fraudulent or violent means, deprived all the Syud proprietors of their lands in the other five villages. They were, however, still left in possession of Bhudursa. He pursued the same system, as far as possible, in the other districts, which were, from time to time, placed under him, as contractor for the revenue. He held the contract for Sultanpoor and other districts, altogether yielding fifty-nine lacs of rupees a-year, in 1827; and it was then that he first bethought himself of securing his family permanently in the possession of the lands he had seized, or might seize upon, by bynamahs, or deeds of sale, from the old proprietors.

He imposed upon the lands he coveted, rates which he knew they could never pay; took all the property of the proprietors for rent, or for the wages of the mounted and foot soldiers, whom he placed over them, or quartered upon their villages, to enforce his demands; seized any neighbouring banker or capitalist whom he could lay hold of, and by confinement and harsh treatment, made him stand security for the suffering proprietors, for sums they never owed; and when these proprietors were made to appear to be irretrievably involved in debt to the State and to individuals, and had no hope of release from prison by any other means, they consented to sign the bynamahs, or sale deeds for lands, which their families had possessed for centuries. Those of the capitalists who had no friends at Court were made to pay the money, for which they had been forced to pledge themselves; and those who had such friends, got the sums which they had engaged to pay, represented as irrecoverable balances due by proprietors, and struck off. The proprietors themselves, plundered of all they had in the world, and without any hope of redress, left the country, or took service under our Government, or that of Oude, or descended to the rank of day-labourers or cultivators in other estates.*

---

* Estates held by the family under bynamahs or sale deeds:

1. Puchumrath	1,13,000
2. Howelee	45,000
3. Mogulsee, including Hindoo Sing's estate of Shapoor, obtained by fraud and violence	28,000
4. Bhurteepoor and Laltapoor	30,000
5. Rudowlee	12,000
Turolee in Huldeemow	17,000
6. Bahraetch in Sagonputtee	4,000
7. Gosaengunge	3,000
Total Company's Rupees	2,52,000

Dursun Sing's contracts, for the land revenue, of districts, amounted from 1827 to 1830, to 59,00,000 rupees a year. From 1830 to 1836, to 58,00,000. In 1836 to 46,100,000. In 1837 to 47,00,000. He continued to hold the whole or greater part of these districts up to September 1843.

There were four brothers, the sons of a Canoongo, of Fyzabad; first, Birj Lal; second, Lala; third, Humeer Sing, a corporal in one of our Regiments of Native Infantry; fourth, Hunooman Persaud; fifth, Gunga Persaud. The family held-eight villages, in hereditary right, with a rent-roll of 6,000, of which they paid 3,000 to Government, and took 3,000 for themselves. While Dursun Sing was dying, in 1844, his eldest son, Ramadeen, tried to get possession of this estate. He seized and confined, in the usual way, Gunga Persaud, the Canoongo, and kept him with harsh treatment, for 1844; and when his brother the corporal complained, in the usual way, through the Resident, Gunga Persaud was released, and he attended the Residents Court, as his brother's attorney, till 1847, when the family recovered possession of the estate. But in 1846, when Dursun Sing's son saw that the case was going against him, he made their local agent, Davey Persaud, plunder all the eight villages of all the stock in cattle, grain, &c., that they contained, and all the people, of whatever property they possessed.

Dursun Sing's family now pay to the Oude Government, a revenue of 1,88,000 rupees a-year, for their bynamah estates, which were acquired by them in the manner described. The rent-roll, recognized in the Exchequer, is 2,56,000; and the nankar 68,000; but the real rent-roll is much greater-perhaps double. The village of Tendooa, in Mehdona, belonged, in hereditary right, to Soorujbulee Sing and Rugonauth Sing, Rajpoots, whom the family of Dursun Sing wished to coerce, in the usual mode, into signing a bynamah, or deed of sale. They refused, and some of the family are said to have been in confinement in consequence, since the year A.D. 1844. When Gunga Persaud, the Canoongo, was confined by Dursun Sing's family, on account of his own estate, they extorted from him, on the pretence of his being security for the punctual payment of what might be demanded from these two men, Soorujbulee' and Rugonauth, the sum of 4,000 rupees. One of the eight villages, held by the Canoongoes, named Aboo Surae, Ghalib Jung, alias Dursun Sing, another Court favourite, is now trying to take by violence, for himself, following the practice of his namesake. He has possessed himself of many by the same means, keeping the troops he commands upon them at exercise and target-practice, till he drives both cultivators and proprietors out, or shoots them.

This Rajah, Ghalib Jung, is now a great favourite with the minister, and no man manifests a stronger disposition to make his influence subservient to his own interest and that of his family. By fraud and violence, and collusion with the officers who have charge of districts and require his aid at Court, he seizes upon the best lands of his weaker neighbours, in the same manner as his namesake, Rajah Dursun Sing, used to do; and of the money which he receives for contracts of various kinds, he appropriates by far the greater part to himself. He is often sent out, with a considerable force, to adjust disputes between landholders and local authorities, and he decides in favour of the party most able and willing to pay, under the assurance that, if called to account, he will be able to clear himself, by giving a share of what he gets to those who send and support him. He commands a large body of mounted and foot police, and he is often ordered to go and send detachments in pursuit of daring offenders, particularly those who have given offence to the British authorities. In such cases he generally succeeds in arresting and bringing in some of the offenders; but he as often seizes the landholders and others who may have given them shelter, intentionally or otherwise; and, after extorting from them as much as they can be made to pay, lets them go. He is not, of course, very particular as to the quantity or quality of the evidence forthcoming to prove that a person able to pay has intentionally screened the offenders from justice.

Rajah Ghalib Jung was the superintendent of the City Police, and commandant of a Brigade of Infantry, and a prime favourite of the King, Nuseer-od Deen Hyder, for two years, up to November 1835. He had many other employments, was always in attendance upon the King, and was much liked by him, because he saw his orders carried into immediate effect, without any regard to the rank or sufferings of the persons whom they were to affect. For these two years he was one of the most intimate companions of his sovereign, in his festivities and most private debaucheries. He became cordially detested throughout the city for his reckless severity, and still more throughout the Court, for the fearless manner in which he spoke to the King of the malversation and peculations of the minister and all the Court favourites who were not in his interest. He thwarted the imbecile old minister, Roshun-od Dowlah, in everything; and never lost an opportunity of turning him into ridicule, and showing his contempt for him.

The King had become very fond of a smart young lad, by name Duljeet, who had been brought up from his infancy by the minister, but now served the King as his most confidential personal attendant. He was paid handsomely by the minister for all the services he rendered him, and deeply interested in keeping him in power and unfettered, and he watched eagerly for an opportunity to remove the man who thwarted him. Mucka, the King's head tailor, was equally anxious, for his own interests, to get rid of the favourite, and so was Gunga Khowas, a boatman, another personal servant and favourite of the King. These three men soon interested in their cause some of the most influential ladies of the palace, and all sought with avidity the opportunity to effect their object. Ghalib Jung was the person, or one of the persons, through whom the King invited females, noted for either their beauty or their accomplishments, and he was told to bring a celebrated dancing-girl, named Mogaree. She did not appear, and the King became impatient, and at last asked Dhuneea Mehree the reason. She had often been employed in a similar office, and was jealous of Ghalib Jung's rivalry. She told his Majesty, that he had obstructed his pleasures on this as on many other occasions, and taken the lady into his own keeping. All the other favourites told him the same thing, and it is generally believed that the charge was true; indeed the girl herself afterwards confessed it. The King, however, "bided his time," in the hope of finding some other ground of revenging himself upon the favourite, without the necessity of making him appear in public as his rival.

On the 7th of October, 1835, the King was conversing with Ghalib Jung, in one of his private apartments, on affairs of state. Several crowns stood on the table for the King's inspection. They had been prepared under Mucka, the tailor's, inspection, from materials purchased by him. He always charged the King ten times the price of the articles which he was ordered to provide, and Ghalib Jung thought the occasion favourable to expose his misconduct to his master. He took up one of the crowns, put his left hand into it, and, turning it round on his finger, pointed out the flimsy nature of the materials with which it had been made. His left finger slipped through the silk on the crown, whether accidentally, or designedly, to prove the flimsy nature of the silk and exasperate the King, is not known; but on seeing the finger pass through the crown, his Majesty left the room without saying a word. Soon after several attendants came in, surrounded Ghalib Jung, and commanded him to remain till further orders. In this state they remained for about two hours, when other attendants came in, struck off his turban on the floor, and had it kicked out of the room by sweepers.

They then dragged out Ghalib Jung, and thrust him into prison. The next day heavy iron fetters were put upon his legs, and upon those of three of his principal followers, who were imprisoned along with him; and his mother, father, wife, and daughters were made prisoners in their own houses; and all the property of the family that could be found was confiscated. On the third day, while still in irons, Ghalib Jung and his three followers were tied up and flogged severely, to make them point out any hidden treasure that they might have. That night the King got drunk, and, before many persons, ordered the minister to have Ghalib Jung's right hand and nose cut off forthwith. The minister, who prayed forgiveness and forbearance, was abused and again commanded, but again entreated his Majesty to pause, and prayed for a private audience. It was granted, and the minister told his Majesty that the British Government would probably interpose if the order were carried into effect.

The King then retired to rest, but the next morning had Ghalib Jung and his three followers again tied up and flogged. Six or seven days after, all Ghalib Jung's attendants were taken from him, and no person was permitted to enter the room where he lay in irons, and he could in consequence get neither food nor drink of any kind. On the 19th of October, the King ordered all the females of Ghalib Jung's family to be brought on foot from their houses to the palace by force, and publicly declared that they should all on the next day have their hair shaved off, be stripped naked, and in that state turned out into the street. After giving these orders, the King went to bed, and the females were all brought, as ordered, to the palace; but the sympathies of the King's own servants were excited by the sufferings of these unoffending females, and they disobeyed the order for their being made to walk on foot through the streets, and brought them in covered litters.

The Resident, apprehending that these poor females might be further disgraced, and Ghalib Jung starved to death, determined to interpose, and demanded an interview, while the King was still in bed. The King was sorely vexed, and sent the minister to the Resident to request that he would not give himself the trouble to come, if his object was to relieve Ghalib Jung's family, as he would forthwith order the females to be taken to their homes. The minister had not been to the Resident for ten or twelve days, or from the first or second day after the fall of the favourite. He prayed that the Resident would not speak harshly to the King on the subject of the treatment Ghalib Jung and his family had received, lest he, the minister, should himself suffer. The Resident insisted upon an audience. He found the King sullen and doggedly silent. The minister was present, and spoke for his master. He denied, what was known to be true, that the prisoner had been kept for two days and two nights' without food or drink; but admitted that he had been tied up and flogged severely, and that the females of his family were still there, but he promised to send them back. He said that it was necessary to confiscate the property of the prisoner, since he owed large sums to the State. The females were all sent back to their homes, and Ghalib Jung was permitted, to have four of his own servants in attendance upon him.

The Resident reported all these things to Government, who entirely approved of his proceedings; and desired that he would tell his Majesty that such savage and atrocious proceedings would ruin his reputation, and, if persisted in, bring on consequences most injurious to himself. When the Resident, at the audience above described, remonstrated with the King for not calling upon his officers periodically to render their accounts, instead of letting them run on for indefinite periods, and then confining them and confiscating their property, he replied—"What you state is most true, and you may be assured that I will in future make every one account to me every three months for the money he has received, and never again show favour to any one."

Rajah Dursun Sing, the great revenue contractor, and at that time the most powerful of the King's subjects beyond the precincts of the Court, had, like the minister himself, been often thwarted by Ghalib Jung when in power; and, after the interposition of the Resident, he applied to have him put into his power. The King and minister were pleased at the thought of making their victim suffer beyond the immediate supervision of a vigilant Resident, and the minister made him over to the Rajah for a consideration, it is said, of three lacs of rupees; and at the same time assured the Resident that this was the only safe way to rescue him from the further vengeance of an exasperated King; that Rajah Dursun Sing was a friend of his, and would provide him and his family and attendants with ample accommodation and comfort. The Rajah had him put into an iron cage, and sent to his fort at Shahgunge, where, report says, he had snakes and scorpions put into the cage to torment and destroy him, but that Ghalib Jung had "a charmed life," and escaped their poison. The object is said to have been to torment and destroy him without leaving upon his body any marks of violence.

On the death of Nuseer-od Deen Hyder, Ghalib Jung was released from confinement, on the payment, it is said, of four lacs of rupees, in Government securities, and a promise of three lacs more if restored to office. He went to reside at Cawnpore, in British territory; but, on the dismissal of the minister, Roshun-od Dowlah, three months after, and the appointment of Hakeem Mehndee to his place, Ghalib Jung was restored to his place. The promise of the three lacs was communicated to the new King, Mahommed Allee Shah, by Roshun-od Dowlah himself, while in confinement; and it is said that Ghalib Jung paid one-half, or one hundred and fifty thousand.

Ghalib Jung had, in many other ways, abused the privileges of intimate companionship which he enjoyed with his master, as better servants under better and more guarded masters will do; and the King, having discovered this, had for some time resolved to take advantage of the first fair occasion to discharge him. The people of Lucknow liked their King, with all his faults—and they were many—and hated the favourite as much for the injury which he did to his master's reputation, as for the insults and injuries inflicted by him on themselves. But when the unoffending females of the favourite were dragged from their privacy to the palace, to be disgraced, the feelings of the whole city were shocked, and expressed in tones which alarmed the minister as much as the Resident's interposition alarmed the King. They had no sympathy for the fallen favourite, but a very deep one for the ladies and children of his family, who could have no share in his guilt, whatever it might be.

Ghalib Jung was raised, from a very humble grade, by Ghazee-od Deen Hyder, and about the year 1825 he had become as great a favourite with him as he afterwards became with his son, Nuseer-od Deen Hyder, and he abused his master's favour in the same manner. The minister, Aga Meer, finding his interference and vulgar insolence intolerable, took advantage one day of the King's anger against him, had him degraded, seized, and sent off forthwith to one of his creatures, Taj-od Deen Hoseyn, then in charge of the Sultanpoor district, where he was soon reduced almost to death's door by harsh treatment and want of food, and made to disgorge all the wealth he had accumulated. Four years after the death of Ghazee-od Deen and the accession of his son, Nuseer-od Deen, Ghalib Jung was, in the year 1831, again appointed to a place of trust at Court by the minister, Hakeem Mehndee, who managed to keep him in order during the two years that he held the reins of government.*

*   Ghalib Jung died on the 1st of May 1851, at Lucknow, aged about 80 years.

December 20, 1849.—Saleepoor, ten miles. The country, on both sides of the road, well studded with trees, hamlets, and villages, and well cultivated and peopled. The landholders and peasantry seem all happy and secure under their present masters, the brother and son of the late Dursun Sing. They are protected by them from thieves and robbers, the attacks of refractory barons, and, above all, from the ravages of the King's troops; and the whole face of the country, at this season, is like that of a rich garden. The whole is under cultivation, and covered with the greatest possible variety of crops. The people showed us, as we passed, six kinds of sugar-cane, and told us that they had many more, one soil agreeing best with one kind, another with another. The main fault in the cultivation of sugar-cane is here, as in every other part of India that I have seen, the want of room and the disregard of cleanliness. They crowd the cane too much, and never remove the decayed leaves, and sufficient air is never admitted.

Bukhtawar Sing has always been considered as the head of the family to whom Shahgunge belongs, but he has always remained at Court, and left the local management of the estate and the government of the districts, placed under their charge in contract or in trust, to his brothers and nephews. Bukhtawar Sing has no child of his own, but he has adopted Maun Sing, the youngest son of his brother, Dursun Sing, and he leaves all local duties and responsibilities to him. He is a small, slight man, but shrewd, active, and energetic, and as unscrupulous as a man can be. Indeed old Bukhtawar Sing himself is the only member of the family that was ever troubled with scruples of any kind whatever; for he is the only one whose boyhood was not passed in the society of men in the every-day habit of committing with impunity all kinds of cruelties, atrocities, and outrages. There is, perhaps, no school in the world better adapted for training thoroughbred ruffians (men without any scruple of conscience, sense of honour, or feeling of humanity) than the camp of a revenue-contractor in Oude. It has been the same for the last thirty years that I have known it, and must continue to be the same as long as we maintain, in absolute sway over the people, a sovereign who never bestows a thought upon them, has no feeling in common with them, and can never be persuaded that his high office imposes upon him the obligation to labour to promote their good, or even to protect them against the outrage and oppression of his own soldiers and civil officers. All Rajah Bukhtawar Sing's brothers and nephews were bred up in such camps, and are thorough-bred ruffians.

They have got the lands which they hold by much fraud and violence no doubt, but they have done much good to them. They have invited and established in comfort great numbers of the best classes of cultivators from other districts, in which they had ceased to feel secure, and they have protected and encouraged those whom they found on the land. To establish a new cultivator of the better class, they require to give him about twenty-five rupees for a pair of bullocks; for subsistence for himself and family till his crops ripen, thirty-six more, for a house, wells, &c., thirty more, or about ninety rupees, which he pays back with or without interest by degrees. Every village and hamlet is now surrounded by fine garden cultivation, conducted by the cultivators of the gardener caste, whom the family has thus established.

The greatest benefit conferred upon the lands which they hold has been in the suppression of the fearful contests which used to be perpetual between the small proprietors of the military classes, among whom the lands had become minutely subdivided by the law of inheritance, about boundaries and rights to water for irrigation. Many persons used to be killed every year in these contests, and their widows and orphans had to be maintained by the survivors. Now no such dispute leads to any serious conflict. They are all settled at once by arbitrators, who are guided in their decisions by the accounts of the Putwaries of villages and Canoongoes of districts. These men have the detailed accounts of every tenement for the last hundred years; and, with their assistance, village traditions, and the advice of their elders, all such boundary disputes and misunderstandings about rights to water are quickly and amicably adjusted; and the landlords are strong, and able to enforce whatever decision is pronounced. They are wealthy, and pay the Government demand punctually, and have influence at Court to prevent any attempt at oppression on the part of Government officers on themselves or their tenants. Not a thief or a robber can live or depredate among their tenants. The hamlets are, in consequence, numerous and peopled by peasantry, who seem to live without fear. They adhere strictly to the terms of their engagements with their tenants of all grades; and their tenants all pay their rents punctually, unless calamities of season deprive them of the means, when due consideration is made by landlords, who live among them, and know what they suffer and require.

The climate must be good, for the people are strong and well-made, and without any appearance of disease. Hardly a beggar of any kind is to be seen along the road. The residence of religious mendicants seems to be especially discouraged, and we see no others. It is very pleasing to pass over such lands after going through such districts as Bahraetch and Gonda, where the signs of the effects of bad air and water upon men, women, and children are so sad and numerous; and those of the abuse of power and the neglect of duty on the part of the Government and its officers are still more so.

Last evening I sent for the two men above named, who had been confined for six or seven years, and were said to have been so because they would not sign the bynamahs required from them by Mann Sing: their names are Soorujbulee Sing and Rugonath Sing. They came with the King's wakeel, accompanied by their cousin, Hunooman Sing, on whose charge they were declared to have been confined. I found that the village of Tendooa had been held by their family, in proprietary right, for many generations, and that they were Chouhan Rajpoots by caste. When Dursun Sing was securing to himself the lands of the district, those of Tendooa were held in three equal shares by Soorujbulee and his brothers, Narind and Rugonath; Hunooman Sing, their cousin; and Seoruttun, their cousin.

Maun Sing took advantage of a desperate quarrel between them, and secured Soorujbulee and Rugonath. Narind escaped and joined a refractory tallookdar, and Seoruttun and Hunooman did the same. Hunooman Sing was, however, invited back, and intrusted, by Maun Sing, with the management of the whole estate, on favourable terms. In revenge for his giving in to the terms of Maun Sing, and serving him, the absconded co-sharers attacked his house several times, killed three of his brothers, and many other persons of his family, and robbed him of almost all he had. This was four years ago. He complained, and the two brothers were kept more strictly confined than ever, to save him and the village. Hunooman Sing looked upon the two prisoners as the murderers of his brothers, though they were in confinement when they were killed, and had been so for more than two years, and was very violent against them in my presence. They were no less violent against him, as the cause of their continued confinement They protested to me, that they had no communication whatever with Seoruttun or Narind Sing, but thought it very likely, that they really did lead the gangs in the attacks upon the village, to recover their rights. They offered to give security for their future good behaviour if released; but declared, that they would rather die than consent to sign a bynamah, or deed of sale, or any relinquishment whatever of their hereditary rights as landholders.

Bukhtawar and Maun Sing said,—"That the people of the village would not be safe, for a moment, if these two brothers were released, which they would be, on the first occasion of thanksgiving, if sent to Lucknow; that people who ventured to seize a thief or robber in Oude must keep him, if they wished to save themselves from his future depredations, as the Government authorities would have nothing to do with them."

I ordered the King's wakeel to take these two brothers to the Chuckladar, and request him to see them released on their furnishing sufficient security for their future good behaviour, which they promised to produce.* They were all fine-looking men, with limbs that would do honour to any climate in the world. These are the families from which our native regiments are recruited; and hardly a young recruit offers himself for enlistment, on whose body marks will not be found of wounds received in these contests, between landlords themselves, and between them and the officers and troops of the sovereign. I have never seen enmity more strong and deadly than that exhibited by contending co-sharers and landholders of all kinds in Oude. The Rajah of Bulrampoor mentioned a curious instance of this spirit in a village, now called the Kolowar village, in the Gonda district, held in copartnership by a family of the Buchulgotee tribe of Rajpoots. One of them said he should plant sugar-cane in one of his fields. All consented to this. But when he pointed out the place where he should have his mill, the community became divided. A contest ensued, in which all the able-bodied men were killed, though not single cane had been planted. The widows and children survived, and still hold the village, but have been so subdued by poverty that they are the quietest village community in the district. The village from that time has gone by the name of Kolowar village, from Koloo, the sugar-mill, though no sugar-mill was ever worked in the village, he believed. He says, the villagers cherish the recollection of this fight; and get very angry when their neighbours twit them with the folly of it.

* They were released, and have been ever since at large on security. One of them visited me in April 1851, and said, that as a point of honour, they should abstain from joining in the fight for their rights, but felt it very hard to be bound to do so.

In our own districts in Upper India, they often kill each other in such contests; but more frequently ruin each other in litigation in our Civil Courts, to the benefit of the native attorneys and law-officers, who fatten on the misery they create or produce. In Oude they always decide such questions by recourse to arms, and the loss of life is no doubt fearful. Still the people generally, or a great part of them, would prefer to reside in Oude, under all the risks to which these contests expose them, than in our own districts, under the evils the people are exposed to from the uncertainties of our law, the multiplicity and formality of our Courts, the pride and negligence of those who preside over them, and the corruption and insolence of those who must be employed to prosecute or defend a cause in them, and enforce the fulfilment of a decree when passed.

The members of the landed aristocracy of Oude always speak with respect of the administration in our territories, but generally end with remarking on the cost and uncertainty of the law in civil cases, and the gradual decay, under its operation, of all the ancient families. A less and less proportion of the annual produce of their lands is left to them in our periodical settlements of the land revenue, while family pride makes them expend the same sums in the marriage of their children, in religious and other festivals, personal servants, and hereditary retainers. They fall into balance, incur heavy debts, and estate after estate is put up to auction, and the proprietors are reduced to poverty. They say, that four times more of these families have gone to decay in the half of the territory made over to us in 1801, than in the half reserved by the Oude sovereign; and this is, I fear, true. They named the families—I cannot remember them.

In Oude, the law of primogeniture prevails among all the tallookdars, or principal landholders; and, to a certain extent, among the middle class of landholders, of the Rajpoot or any other military class. If one co-sharer of this class has several sons, his eldest often inherits all the share he leaves, with all the obligations incident upon it, of maintaining the rest of the family.

The brothers of Soorujbulee, above named, do not pretend to have any right of inheritance in the share of the lands he holds; but they have a prescriptive right to support from him, for themselves and families, when they require it. This rule of primogeniture is, however, often broken through during the lifetime of the father, who, having more of natural affection than family pride, divides the lands between his sons. After his death they submit to this division, and take their respective shares, to descend to their children, by the law of primogeniture, or be again subdivided as may seem to them best; or they fight it out among themselves, till the strongest gets all. Among landholders of the smallest class, whether Hindoos or Mahommedans, the lands are subdivided according to the ordinary law of inheritance.

Our army and other public establishments form a great "safety-valve" for Oude, and save it from a vast deal of fighting for shares in land, and the disorders that always attend it. Younger brothers enlist in our regiments, or find employment in our civil establishments, and leave their wives and children under the protection of the elder brother, who manages the family estate for the common good. They send the greater part of their pay to him for their subsistence, and feel assured that he will see that they are provided for, should they lose their lives in our service. From the single district of Byswara in Oude, sixteen thousand men were, it is said, found to be so serving in our army and other establishments; and from Bunoda, which adjoins it to the east, fifteen thousand, on an inquiry ordered to be made by Ghazee-od Deen Hyder some twenty-five years ago.

The family of Dursun Sing, like good landholders in all parts of Oude, assigned small patches of land to substantial cultivators, merchants, shopkeepers, and others, whom it is useful to retain in their estates, for the purpose of planting small groves of mango and other trees, as local ties. They prepare the well and plant the trees, and then make over the land to a gardener or other good cultivator, to be tilled for his own profit, on condition that he water the trees, and take care to preserve them from frost during the cold season, and from rats, white ants, and other enemies; and form terraces round them, where the water lies much on the surface during the rains, so that it may not reach and injure the bark. The land yields crops till the trees grow large and cover it with their shade, by which time they are independent of irrigation, and begin to bear fruit. The crops do not thrive under the shade of the trees, and the lands they cover cease to be of any value for tillage. The stems and foliage of the trees, no doubt, deprive the crops of the moisture, carbonic gas and ammonia, they require from the atmosphere. They are, generally, watered from six to ten years. These groves form a valuable local tie for the cultivators and other useful tenants. No man dare to molest them or their descendants, in the possession of their well and grove, without incurring, at least, the odium of society; and, according to their notion, the anger of their gods.

The cultivators always point out to them, in asserting their rights to the lands they hold; and reside and cultivate in the village, under circumstances that would drive them away, had they no such ties to retain them. They feel a-great pride in them; and all good landlords feel the same in having their villages filled with tenants who have such ties.

December 21, 1849.—Bhurteepoor, ten miles, almost all the way through the estate of Maun Sing. No lands could be better cultivated than they are all the way, or better studded with groves and beautiful single trees. The villages and hamlets along the road are numerous, and filled with cultivators of the gardener and other good classes, who seem happy and contented. The season has been favourable, and the crops are all fine, and of great variety. Sugar-cane abounds, but no mills are, as yet, at work. We passed through, and by three or four villages, that have been lately taken from Maun Sing, and made over to farmers by the local authorities, under instructions from Court; but they are not so well cultivated, as those which he retains. The cultivators and inhabitants generally do not appear to enjoy the same protection or security in the engagements they make. The soil is everywhere good, the water near the surface, and the climate excellent. The soil is here called doomuteea, and adapted to all kinds of tillage.

I should mention, with regard to the subdivision of landed property, that the Rajahs and tallookdars, among whom the law of primogeniture prevails, consider their estates as principalities, or reeasuts. When any Rajah, or tallookdar, during his lifetime, assigns portions of the land to his sons, brothers, or other members of the family, they are separated from the reeasut, or principality, and are subdivided as they descend from generation to generation, by the ordinary Hindoo or Mahommedan law of inheritance. This is the case with portions of the estate of the

Rajah of Korwar, in the Sultanpoor district, one of the oldest Hindoo principalities in Oude, which are now held by his cousins, nephews, &c., near this place, Bhurteepoor.*

* Sunkur Sing, of Korwar, had four sons: first, Dooneeaput died without issue; second, Sookraj Sing, whose grandson, Madhoo Persaud, is now the Rajah; third, Bureear Sing, who got from his brother lands yielding forty thousand rupees a-year out of the principality. They are now held by his son, Jydut; fourth, Znbar Sing, who got from his brother lands yielding nineteen thousand rupees a-year, which are now held by his son, Moheser Persaud. Sunkir Sing was the second brother, but his elder brother died without issue.

Dooneeaput succeeded to the reeasut on the death of his uncle, the Rajah, who died without issue; and he bestowed portions of the estate on his brothers, Burear and Zubur Sing, which their descendants enjoy, but which do not go to the eldest son, by the law of primogeniture. He was succeeded by his brother, Sookraj, whose grandson, Madhoo Persaud, now reigns as Rajah, and has the undivided possession of the lands belonging to this branch. All the descendants of his grandfather, Sookraj, and their widows and orphans, have a right to protection and support from him, and to nothing more. Jydut, who now holds the lands, yielding forty thousand rupees a-year, called upon me, this morning, and gave me this history of his family. The Rajah himself is in camp, and came to visit me this afternoon.

It is interesting and pleasing to see a large, well-controlled camp, moving in a long line through a narrow road or pathway, over plains, covered with so rich a variety of crops, and studded with such magnificent evergreen trees. The solitary mango-tree, in a field of corn, seems to exult in its position-to grow taller and spread wider its branches and rich foliage, in situations where they can be seen to so much advantage. The peepul and bargut trees, which, when entire, are still more ornamental, are everywhere torn to pieces and disfigured by the camels and elephants, buffaloes and bullocks, that feed upon their foliage and tender branches.

There are a great many mhowa, tamarind, and other fine trees, upon which they do not feed, to assist the mango in giving beauty to the landscape.

The Korwar Rajah, Madhoo Persaud, a young man of about twenty-two years of age, came in the evening, and confirmed what his relative, Jydut, had told me of the rule which required that his lands should remain undivided with his eldest son, while those which are held by Jydut, and his other relatives, should be subdivided among all the sons of the holder. This rule is more necessary in Oude than elsewhere, to preserve a family and its estate from the grasp of its neighbours and Government officers. When there happens to be no heir left to the portion of the estate which has been cut off, it is re-annexed to the estate; and the head of the family frequently anticipates the event, by murdering or imprisoning the heir or incumbent, and seizing upon the lands. Another Rajah, of the same name, Mahdoo Persaud, of Amethee, in Salone, has lately seized upon the estate of Shahgur, worth twenty thousand rupees a-year, which had been cut off from the Amethee estate, and enjoyed by a collateral branch of the family for several generations. He holds the proprietor, Bulwunt Sing, in prison, in irons, and would soon make away with him were the Oude Government to think it worth while to inquire after him. He has seized upon another portion, Ramgur, held by another branch of the family, worth six thousand rupees a-year, and crushed all the proprietors. This is the way in which estates, once broken up, are reconsolidated in Oude, under energetic and unscrupulous men. Of course when they think it worth while to do so, they purchase the collusion of the local authorities of the day, by promising to pay the revenues, which the old proprietors paid during their tenure of office. The other barons do not interfere, unless they happen to be connected by marriage with the ousted proprietors, or otherwise specially bound, by interest and honour, to defend them against the grasp of the head of their family. Many struggles of this kind are taking place every season in Oude.

CHAPTER IV.

Recross the Goomtee river—Sultanpoor Cantonments—Number of persons begging redress of wrongs, and difficulty of obtaining it in Oude—Apathy of the Sovereign—Incompetence and unfitness of his Officers—Sultanpoor, healthy and well suited for Troops—Chandour, twelve miles distant, no less so—lands of their weaker neighbours absorbed by the family of Rajah Dursun Sing, by fraud, violence, and collusion; but greatly improved—Difficulty attending attempt to restore old Proprietors—Same absorptions have been going on in all parts of Oude—and the same difficulty to be everywhere encountered—Soils in the district, mutteear, doomutteea, bhoor, oosur—Risk at which lands are tilled under Landlords opposed to their Government—Climate of Oude more invigorating than that of Malwa—Captain Magness's Regiment—Repair of artillery guns—Supply of grain to its bullocks—Civil establishment of the Nazim—Wolves—Dread of killing them among Hindoos—Children preserved by them in their dens, and nurtured.

December 22, 1849.—Sultanpoor, eight miles. Recrossed the Goomtee river, close under the Cantonments, over a bridge of boats prepared for the purpose, and encamped on the parade-ground. The country over which we came was fertile and well cultivated. For some days we have seen and heard a good many religions mendicants, both Mahommedans and Hindoos, but still very few lame, blind, and otherwise helpless persons, asking charity. The most numerous and distressing class of beggars that importune me, are those who beg redress for their wrongs, and a remedy for their grievances,—"their name, indeed, is Legion," and their wrongs and grievances are altogether without remedy, under the present government and inveterately vicious system of administration. It is painful to listen to all these complaints, and to have to refer the sufferers for redress to authorities who want both the power and the will to afford it; especially when one knows that a remedy for almost every evil is hoped for from a visit such as the poor people are now receiving from the Resident. He is expected "to wipe the tears from off all faces;" and feels that he can wipe them from hardly any. The reckless disregard shown by the depredators of all classes and degrees to the sufferings of their victims, whatever be the cause of discontent or object of pursuit, is lamentable. I have every day scores of petitions delivered to me "with quivering lip and tearful eye," by persons who have been plundered of all they possessed, had their dearest relatives murdered or tortured to death, and their habitations burnt to the ground, by gangs of ruffians, under landlords of high birth and pretensions, whom they had never wronged or offended; some, merely because they happened to have property, which the ruffians wished to take—others, because they presumed to live and labour upon lands which they coveted, or deserted, and wished to have left waste. In these attacks, neither age, nor sex, nor condition are spared. The greater part of the leaders of these gangs of ruffians are Rajpoot landholders, boasting descent from the sun and moon, or from the demigods, who figure in the Hindoo religious fictions of the Poorans. There are, however, a great many Mahommedans at the head of similar gangs. A landholder of whatever degree, who is opposed to his government from whatever cause, considers himself in a state of war', and he considers a state of war to authorize his doing all those things which he is forbidden to do in a state of peace.

Unless the sufferer happens to be a native officer or sipahee of our army, who enjoys the privilege of urging his claims through the Resident, it is a cruel mockery to refer him for redress to any existing local authority. One not only feels that it is so, but sees, that the sufferer thinks that he must know it to be so. No such authority considers it to be any part of his duty to arrest evil-doers, and inquire into and redress wrongs suffered by individuals, or families, or village communities. Should he arrest such people, he would have to subsist and accommodate them at his own cost, or to send them to Lucknow, with the assurance that they would in a few days or a few weeks purchase their way out again, in spite of the clearest proofs of the murders, robberies, torturings, dishonourings, house-burning, &c., which they have committed. No sentence, which any one local authority could pass on such offenders, would be recognised by any other authority in the State, as valid or sufficient to justify him in receiving and holding them in confinement for a single day. The local authorities, therefore, either leave the wrong-doers unmolested, with the understanding that they are to abstain from doing any such wrong within their jurisdictions as may endanger or impede the collection of revenues during their period of office, or release them with that understanding after they have squeezed all they can out of them. The wrong-doers can so abstain, and still be able to murder, rob, torture, dishonour, and burn, upon a pretty large scale; and where they are so numerous, and so ready to unite for purposes "offensive and defensive," and the local authorities so generally connive at or quietly acquiesce all their misdeeds, any attempt on the part of an honest or overzealous individual to put them down would be sure to result in his speedy and utter ruin!

To refer such sufferers to the authorities at Lucknow would be a still more cruel mockery. The present sovereign never hears a complaint or reads a petition or report of any kind. He is entirely taken up in the pursuit of his personal gratifications. He has no desire to be thought to take any interest whatever in public affairs; and is altogether regardless of the duties and responsibilities of his high office. He lives, exclusively, in the society of fiddlers, eunuchs, and women: he has done so since his childhood, and is likely to do so to the last. His disrelish for any other society has become inveterate: he cannot keep awake in any other. In spite of average natural capacity, and more than average facility in the cultivation of light literature, or at least "de faire des petits vers de sa focon," his understanding has become so emasculated, that he is altogether unfit for the conduct of his domestic, much less his public, affairs. He sees occasionally his prime minister, who takes care to persuade him that he does all that a King ought to do; and nothing whatever of any other minister. He holds no communication whatever with brothers, uncles, cousins, or any of the native gentlemen at Lucknow, or the landed or official aristocracy of the country. He sometimes admits a few poets or poetasters to hear and praise his verses, and commands the unwilling attendance of some of his relations, to witness and applaud the acting of some of his own silly comedies, on the penalty of forfeiting their stipends; but any one who presumes to approach him, even in his rides or drives, with a petition for justice, is instantly clapped into prison, or otherwise severely punished.

His father and grandfather, while on the throne, used to see the members of the royal family and aristocracy of the city in Durbar once a-day, or three or four times a-week, and have all petitions and reports read over in their own presence. They dictated the orders, and their seal was affixed to them in their own presence, bearing the inscription molahiza shud, "it has been seen." The seal was then replaced in the casket, which was kept by one confidential servant, Muzd-od Dowlah, while the key was confided to another. Documents were thus read and orders passed upon them twice a-day-once in the morning, and once again in the evening; and, on such occasions, all heads of departments were present. The present King continued this system for a short time, but he soon got tired of it, and made over seal and all to the minister, to do what he liked with them; and discontinued altogether the short Durbar, or levees, which his father, grandfather, and all former sovereigns had held—before they entered on the business of the day—with the heads of departments and secretaries, and at which all the members of the royal family and aristocracy of the city attended, to pay their respects to their sovereign; and soon ceased altogether to see the heads of departments and secretaries, to hear orders read, and to ask questions about state affairs.

The minister has become by degrees almost as inaccessible as his sovereign, to all but his deputies, heads of departments, secretaries, and Court favourites, whom it is his interest to conciliate. Though the minister has his own confidential deputies and secretaries, the same heads of departments are in office as under the present King's father and grandfather; and, though no longer permitted to attend upon or see the King, they are still supposed to submit to the minister, for orders, all reports from local authorities, intelligence-writers, &c., and all petitions from sufferers; but, in reality, he sees and hears read very few, and passes orders upon still less. Any head of a department, deputy, secretary, or favourite, may receive petitions, to be submitted to the minister for orders; but it is the special duty of no one to receive them, nor is any one held responsible for submitting them for orders. Those only who are in the special confidence of the minister, or of those about Court, from whom he has something to hope or something to fear, venture to receive and submit petitions; and they drive a profitable trade in doing so. A large portion of those submitted are thrown aside, without any orders at all; a portion have orders so written as to show that they are never intended to be carried into effect; a third portion receive orders that are really intended to be acted upon. But they are taken to one of the minister's deputies, with whose views or interests some of them may not square well; and he may detain them for weeks, months, or years, till the petitioners are worn out with "hope deferred," or utterly ruined, in vain efforts to purchase the attention they require. Nothing is more common than for a peremptory order to be passed for the immediate payment of the arrears of pension due to a stipendiary member of the royal family, and for the payment to be deferred for eight, ten, and twelve months, till he or she consents to give from ten to twenty per cent., according to his or her necessities, to the deputy, who has to see the order carried out. A sufferer often, instead of getting his petition smuggled on to the minister in the mode above described, bribes a news-writer to insert his case in his report, to be submitted through the head of the department.

At present the head of the intelligence department assumes the same latitude, in submitting reports for orders to the minister, that his subordinates in distant districts assume in framing and sending them to him; that is, he submits only such as may suit his views and interests to submit! Where grave charges are sent to him against substantial men, or men high in office, he comes to an understanding with their representatives in Lucknow, and submits the report to the minister only as a dernière resort, when such representatives cannot be brought to submit to his terms. If found out, at any time, and threatened, he has his feed patrons or patronesses "behind the throne, and greater than the throne itself," to protect him.

The unmeaning orders passed by the minister on reports and petitions are commonly that so and so is to inquire into the matter complained of; to see that the offenders are seized and punished; that the stolen property and usurped lands be restored; that razeenamas, or acquittances, be sent in by the friends of persons who have been murdered by the King's officers; that the men, women, and children, confined and tortured by King's officers, or by robbers and ruffians, be set at liberty and satisfied; the said so and so being the infant commander-in-chief, the King's chamberlain, footman, coachman, chief fiddler, eunuch, barber, or person uppermost in his thoughts at the time. Similar orders are passed in his name by his deputies, secretaries, and favourites upon all the other numerous petitions and reports, which he sends to them unperused. Not, perhaps, upon one in five does the minister himself pass any order; and of the orders passed by him, not one in five, perhaps, is intended to be taken notice of. His deputies and favourites carry on a profitable trade in all such reports and petitions: they extort money alike from the wrong-doer and the wrong-sufferer; and from all local authorities, or their representatives, for all neglect of duty or abuses, of authority charged against them.

As to any investigation into the real merits of any case described in these reports from the news-writers and local authorities, no such thing has been heard of for several reigns. The real merits of all such cases are, however, well and generally known to the people of the districts in which they occur, and freely discussed by them with suitable remarks on the "darkness which prevails under the lamp of royalty;" and no less suitable execrations against the intolerable system which deprives the King of all feeling of interest in the well-being of his subjects, all sense of duty towards them, all feeling of responsibility to any higher power for the manner in which he discharges his high trust over the millions committed to his care.

As I have said, the King never sees any petition or report: he hardly ever sees even official notes addressed to him by the British Resident, and the replies to almost all are written without his knowledge.* The minister never puts either his seal or signature to any order that passes, or any document whatsoever, with his own hand: he merely puts in the date, as the 1st, 5th, or 10th; the month, year, and the order itself are inserted by the deputies, secretaries, or favourites, to whom the duty is confided. The reports and petitions submitted for orders often accumulate so fast in times of great festivity or ceremony, that the minister has them tied up in bundles, without any orders whatever having been passed on them, and sent to his deputies for such as they may think proper to pass, merely inserting his figure 1, 5, or 10, to indicate the date, on the outermost document of each bundle. If any orders are inserted by his deputies on the rest, they have only to insert the same date. There is nothing but the figure to attest the authenticity of the order; and it would be often impossible for the minister himself to say whether the figure was inserted by himself or by any other person. These deputies are the men who adjust all the nuzuranas, or unauthorized gratuities, to be paid to the minister.

* On the 17th of October, 1850, Hassan Khan, one of the khowas, or pages, whose special duty it is to deliver all papers to the King, fell under his Majesty's displeasure, and his house was seized and searched. Several of the Resident's official notes were found unopened among his papers. They had been sent to the palace as emergent many months before, but never shown to the King. Such official notes from the Resident are hardly every shown to the King, nor is he consulted about the orders to be passed upon them.

They share largely in all that he gets; and take a great deal, for which they render him no account. Knowing all that he takes, and ought not to take, he dares not punish them for their transgressions; and knowing this, sufferers are afraid to complain against them. In ordinary times, or under ordinary sovereigns, the sums paid by revenue authorities in nazuranas, or gratuities, before they were permitted to enter on their charges, amounted to, perhaps, ten or fifteen per cent.: under the present sovereign they amount, I believe, to more than twenty-five per cent. upon the revenue they are to collect. Of these the minister and his deputies take the largest part. A portion is paid in advance, and good bonds are taken for the rest, to be paid within the year. Of the money collected, more than twenty-five per cent., on an average, is appropriated by those intrusted with the disbursements, and by their patrons and patronesses. The sovereign gets, perhaps, three-fourths of what is collected; and of what is collected, perhaps two-thirds, on an average, reaches its legitimate destination; so that one-half of the revenues of Oude may be considered as taken by officers and Court favourites in unauthorized gratuities and perquisites. The pay of the troops and establishments, on duty with the revenue collectors, is deducted by them, and the surplus only is sent to the Treasury at Lucknow. In his accounts he receives credit for all sums paid to the troops and establishments on duty under him. Though the artillery-bullocks get none of the grain, for which he pays and charges Government, a greater portion of the whole of what he pays and charges in his accounts reaches its legitimate destination, perhaps, than of the whole of what is paid from the Treasury at the capital. On an average, however, I do not think that more than two-thirds of what is paid and charged to Government reaches that destination.

I may instance the two regiments, under Thakur Sing, Tirbaydee; which are always on duty at the palace. It is known that the officers and sipahees of those regiments do not get more than one-half of the pay which is issued for them every month from the Treasury; the other half is absorbed by the commandant and his patrons at Court. On everything sold in the palace, the vender is obliged to add one-third to the price, to be paid to the person through whom it is passed in. Without this, nothing can be sold in the palace by European or native. Not a single animal in the King's establishments gets one-third of the food allowed for it, and charged for; not a building is erected or repaired at less than three times the actual outlay, two-thirds at least of the money charged going to the superintendent and his patrons.

December 23, 1849.—Halted at Sultanpoor, which is one of the healthiest stations in India, on the right bank of the Goomtee river, upon a dry soil, among deep ravines, which drain off the water rapidly. The bungalows are on the verge, looking down into the river, upon the level patches of land, dividing the ravines. The water in the wells is some fifty feet below the surface, on a level with the stream below. There are no groves within a mile of the cantonments; and no lakes, marshes, or jungles within a great many; and the single trees in and near the cantonments are few. The gardens are small and few; and the water is sparingly used in irrigating them, as the expense of drawing it is very great.

There is another good site for a cantonment at Chandour, some twelve miles up the river, on the opposite bank, and looking down upon the stream, from the verge, in the same manner. Chandour was chosen for his cantonments by Rajah Dursun Sing when he had the contract for the district; and it would be the best place for the head-quarters of any establishments, that any new arrangements might require for the administration of the Sultanpoor and surrounding districts. Secrora would be the best position for the head-quarters of those required for the administration of the Gonda-Bahraetch, and other surrounding districts. It is central, and has always been considered one of the healthiest places in Oude. It was long a cantonment for one of our regiments of infantry and some guns, which were, in 1835, withdrawn, and sent to increase the force at Lucknow, from two to three regiments of infantry. The regiment and guns at Sultanpoor were taken away in 1837. Secrora was, for some years after our regiment and guns had been withdrawn, occupied by a regiment and guns under Captain Barlow, one of the King of Oude's officers; but it is now altogether deserted. Sultanpoor has been, ever since 1837, occupied by one of the two regiments of Oude local Infantry, without any guns or cavalry of any kind. There was also a regiment of our regular infantry at Pertabghur, three marches from Sultanpoor, on the road to Allahabad, with a regiment of our light cavalry. The latter was withdrawn in 1815 for the Nepaul war, and employed again under us during the Mahratta war in 1817 and 1818. It was sent back again in 1820; but soon after, in 1821, withdrawn altogether, and we have since had no cavalry of any kind in Oude. Seetapoor was also occupied by one of our regular regiments of infantry and some guns till 1837, when they were withdrawn, and their place supplied by the second regiment of Oude Local Infantry. Our Government now pays the two regiments of Oude Local Infantry stationed at Sultanpoor and Seetapoor; but the places of those stationed at Secrora and Pertabghur have never been supplied. One additional regiment of infantry is kept at Lucknow, so that our force in Oude has only been diminished by one regiment of infantry, one of cavalry, and eight guns, with a company and half of artillery. To do our duty honestly by Oude, we ought to restore the regiment of infantry; and in the place of the corps of light, send one of irregular cavalry. We ought also to restore the company and half of artillery and eight guns which have been withdrawn. We draw annually from the lands ceded to as in 1801, for the protection which we promised to the King and his people from "all internal and external enemies," no less than two crores and twelve lacs of rupees, or two millions sterling a-year; while the Oude Government draws from the half of its territories which it reserved only one-half that sum, or one crore of rupees.

Maun Sing is to leave my camp to-day, and return to Shahgunge. Of the fraud and violence, abuse of power, and collusion with local authorities, by which he and his father seized upon the lands of so many hundreds of old proprietors, there can be no doubt; but to attempt to make the family restore them now, under such a government, would create great disorder, drive off all the better classes of cultivators, and desolate the face of the country, which they have rendered so beautiful by an efficient system of administration. Many of the most powerful of the landed aristocracy of Oude have acquired, or augmented, their estates in the same manner and within the same time; and the same difficulty would attend the attempt to restore the old proprietors in all parts. A strong and honest government might overcome all these difficulties, and restore to every rightful proprietor the land unjustly taken from him, within a limited period; but it should not attempt to enforce any adjustment of the accounts of receipts and disbursements for the intervening period. The old proprietor would receive back his land in an improved condition, and the usurper might fairly be considered to have reimbursed himself for all his outlay. The old proprietor should be required to pledge himself to respect the rights of all new tenants.

December 24, 1849.—Meranpoor, twelve miles. Soil between this and Sultanpoor neither so fertile nor so well cultivated, as we found it on the other side of the Goomtee river, though it is of the same denomination—generally doomut, but here and there mutear. The term mutear embraces all good argillaceous earth, from the light brown to the black, humic or ulmic deposit, found in the beds of tanks and lakes in Oude. The natives of Oude call the black soil of Malwa and southern India, and Bundlekund, muteear. This black soil has in its exhausted state abundance of silicates, sulphates, phosphates, and carbonates of alumina, potassa, lime, &c., and of organic acids, combined with the same unorganic substances, to attract and fix ammonia, and collect and store up moisture, and is exceedingly fertile and strong.

Both saltpetre and common salt are made by lixiviation from some of the poor oosur soils; but, from the most barren in Oude, carbonates of soda, used in making glass and soap, are taken. The earth is collected from the surface of the most barren spots and formed into small, shallow, round tanks, a yard in diameter. Water is then poured in, and the tank filled to the surface, with an additional supply of the earth, and smoothed over. This tank is then left exposed to the sun for two days, during the hottest and driest months of the year. March, April, and May, and part of June, when the crust, formed on the surface, is taken off. The process is repeated once; but in the second operation the tank is formed around and below by the debris of the first tank, which is filled to the surface, after the water has been poured in, with the first crust obtained. The second crust is called the reha, which is carbonate or bicarbonate of soda. This is formed into small cakes, which are baked to redness in an oven, or crucible, to expel the moisture and carbonic acid which it contains. They are then powdered to fine dust, which is placed in another crucible, and fused to liquid glass, the reha containing in itself sufficient silica to form the coarse glass used in making bracelets, &c.

A superabundance of nitrates seem also to impair or destroy fertility in the soil, and they may arise from the decomposition of animal or vegetable matter, in a soil containing a superabundance of porous lime. The atmospheric air and water, contained in the moist and porous soil, are decomposed. The hydrogen of the water combines with the nitrogen of the air, and that given off by the decomposing organic bodies, and forms ammonia. The nitrogen of the ammonia then takes up the oxygen of the air and water, and becoming nitric acid, forms nitrates with the lime, potash, soda, &c., contained in the soil. Without any superabundance of lime in the soil, however, the same effects may be produced, when there is a deficiency of decaying vegetable and animal matter, as the oxygen of the decomposed air and water, having no organic substances to unite with, may combine with the nitrogen of the ammonia, and form nitric acid; which, uniting with the lime, potash, soda, &c., may form the superabounding nitrates destructive of fertility.

This superabundance of reha, or carbonate of soda, which renders so much of the surface barren, must, I conclude, arise from deposits of common salt, or chloride of sodium. The water, as it percolates through these deposits towards the surface, becomes saturated with their alkaline salts; and, as it reaches the surface and becomes evaporated in the pure state, it leaves them behind at or near the surface. On its way to the surface, or at the surface, the chloride of sodium becomes decomposed by contact with carbonates of ammonia and potassa—sulphuric and nitric acids. In a soil well supplied with decaying animal or vegetable matter, these carbonates or sulphates of soda, as they rise to the surface, might be formed into nutriment for plants, and taken up by their roots; or in one well flooded occasionally with fresh water, any superabundance of the salts or their bases might be taken up in solution and carried off. The people say, that the soil in which these carbonates of soda (reha) abound, are more unmanageable than those in which nitrates abound: they tell me that, with flooding, irrigating, manuring, and well ploughing, they can manage to get crops from all but the soils in which this reha abounds.

The process above described, by which the bracelet makers extract the carbonates of soda and potash from the earth of the small, shallow tanks, is precisely the same as that by which they are brought from the deep bed of earth below and deposited on or near the surface. In both processes, the water which brings them near the surface goes off into the atmosphere in a pure state, and leaves the salts behind. To make soap from the reha, they must first remove the silex which it contains.

There are no rocks in Oude, and the only form in which lime is found for building purposes and road-pavements is that of kunkur, which is a carbonate of lime containing silica, and oxide of iron. In proportion as it contains the last, the kunkur is more or less red. That which contains none is of a dirty-white. It is found in many parts of India in thin layers, or amorphous masses, formed by compression, upon a stiff clay substratum; but in Oude I have seen it only in nodules, usually formed on nuclei of flint or other hard substances. The kingdom of Oude must have once been the bed, or part of the bed, of a large lake, formed by the diluvial detritus of the hills of the Himmalaya chain, and, as limestone abounds in that chain, the bed contains abundance of lime, which is taken up by the water that percolates through it from the rivers and from the rains and floods above. The lime thus taken up and held in solution with carbonic add gas, is deposited around the small fragments of flint or other hard substances which the waters find in their way. Where the floods which cover the surface during the rains come in rivers, flowing from the Himmalaya or other hills abounding in limestone rocks, they of course contain lime and carbonic-acid gas, which add to the kunkur nodules formed in the bed below; but in Oude the rivers seldom overflow to any extent, and the kunkur is, I believe, formed chiefly from the lime already existing in the bed.

Doctor O'Shaughnessy, the most eminent chemist now in India, tells me that there are two marked varieties of kunkur in India—the red and the white; that the red differs from the white solely in containing a larger proportion of peroxide of iron; that the white consists of carbonate of lime, silica, alumina, and sometimes magnesia and protoxide of iron. He states that he considers the kunkur to be deposited by calcareous waters, abounding in infusorial animalculæ; that the waters of the annual inundation are rich in lime, and that all the facts that have come under his observation appear to him to indicate that this is the source of the kunkur deposit, which is seen in a different form in the Italian travertine, and the crescent nodules of the Isle of Sheppey and of Bologne.

Doctor O'Shaughnessy further states, that the reha earth, which I sent to him from Oude, is identical with the sujjee muttee of Bengal, and contains carbonate of soda and sulphate of soda as its essential characteristic ingredients, with silicious clay and oxide of iron. But in Oude, the term "sujjee" is given to the carbonate and sulphate of soda which remains after the silex has been removed from the reha. The reha is fused into glass after the carbonic acid and moisture have been expelled by heat, and the sujjee is formed into soap, by the addition of lime, fat, and linseed oil, in the following proportions, I am told:—6 sujjee, 4 lime, 2½ fat, and 1½ ulsee oil.

The sujjee is formed from the reha by filtration. A tank is formed on a terrace of cement. In a hole at one corner is a small tube. Rows of bricks are put down from one end to the other, with intervals between for the liquor to flow through to the tube. On these rows a layer of stout reeds is first placed, and over them another layer composed of the leaves of these reeds. On this bed the coarse reha earth is placed without being refined by the process described in the text above. Some coarse common salt (kharee nimuck) is mixed up with the reha. The tank is then filled with water, which filters slowly through the earth and passes out through the tube into pans, whence it is taken to another tank upon a wider terrace of cement, where it evaporates and leaves the sujjee deposited. The second tank is commonly made close under the first, and the liquor flows into it through the tube, rendering pans unnecessary. It is only in the hot months of March, April, May, and part of June, till the rains begin to fall, that the reha and sujjee are formed. During the other nine months, the Looneas, who provide them, turn their hands to something else. The reha, deprived of its carbonic acid and moisture by heat, is fused into glass. Deprived of silex by this process of filtration, it is formed into sujjee, from which the soap is made.

On this process of filtration. Doctor O'Shaughnessy observes:—"I do not clearly understand the use of the common salt, used in the extraction of soda, in the process you described. But many of the empirical practices of the natives prove, on investigation, to square with the most scientific precepts. For example, their proportions in the manufacture of corrosive sublimate are precisely identical with those which the atomic theory leads the European chemist to follow. The filtering apparatus which you describe is really admirable, and I doubt much whether the best practical chemist could devise any simpler or cheaper way of arriving at the object in view."

The country is well provided with mango and other fine trees, single, and in clusters and groves; but the tillage is slovenly and scanty, strongly indicative of want of security to life, property, and industry. No symptom of the residence of gardeners and other cultivators of the better classes, or irrigation, or the use of manure in tillage.

December 25, 1849.—Nawabgunge, eleven miles. The soil good, as indicated by the growth of fine trees on each side of the road as far as we could see over the level plain, and by the few fields of corn in sight; but the cultivation is deficient and slovenly. A great part of the road lay through the estate of Mundone, held by Davey Persaud, the tallookdar; and the few peasants who stood by the side of the road to watch their fields as we passed, and see the cavalcade, told me that the deficient tillage and population arose from his being in opposition to Government and diligently employed in plundering the country generally, and his own estates in particular, to reduce the local authorities to his own terms. The Government demand upon him is twenty thousand rupees. He paid little last year, and has paid still less during the present year, on the ground that his estate yields nothing. This is a common and generally successful practice among tallookdars, who take to fighting against the Government whether their cause be just or unjust. These peasants and cultivators told us that they had taken to the jungles for shelter, after the last harvest, till the season for sowing again commenced; remained in the fields, still houseless, during the night, worked in their fields in fear of their lives during the day; and apprehended that they should have to take to the jungles again as soon as their crops were gathered, if they were even permitted to gather them. They attributed as much blame to their landlord as to the Nazim, Wajid Allee Khan. He, however, bears a very bad character, and is said to have designedly thrown a good deal of the districts under his charge out of tillage in the hope that no other person would venture to take the contract for it in that condition, and that he should, in consequence, be invited to retain it on more favourable terms. He was twelve lacs of rupees in balance when superseded at the end of the year, in September last, by the present governor, Aga Allee, who manages the same districts on a salary of two thousand rupees a-month, without any contract for the revenues, but with the understanding that he is to collect, or at least to pay, a certain sum.

The late contractor will no doubt relieve himself from the burthen of this balance in the usual way. He will be imprisoned for a time till he pays, or enters into engagements to pay, to the minister and the influential men at Court, as much as they think he can be made to pay, in bribes, and some half of that sum into the Treasury, and have all the rest struck out of the accounts as irrecoverable—perhaps two lacs in bribes, and one to the Treasury may secure him an acquittance, and a fair chance of employment hereafter. His real name is Wajid Allee; but as that is the name of the King, he is commonly called Ahmud Allee, that the royal ears may not take offence.

December 26, 1849.—Pertabghur, distance eight miles. In the course of fourteen years, almost all signs of one of the most healthful and most agreeable cantonments of the Bengal army have been effaced. Fine crops of corn now cover what were the parades for cavalry, infantry, and artillery, and the gardens and compounds of officers' bungalows. The grounds, which were once occupied by the old cantonments, are now let out to cultivators, immediately under Government, and they are well cultivated; but the tillage of the rest of the country we have this morning passed over is scanty and slovenly. The Rajah of Pertabghur has, for some time, been on bad terms with the contractors, greatly in arrears, and commonly in opposition to the Government, having his band of armed followers in the jungles, and doing nothing but mischief. This is the case with most of the tallookdars of the country over which I have passed. Not one in five, or I may say one in ten, attends the viceroys, because it would not be safe to do so; or pays the demands of Government punctually, because there is no certainty in them.

I passed down the line of Captain Magness's corps, which is at present stationed at Pertabghur. It is as well-dressed, and as fine a looking corps as any infantry regiment in our own native army, and has always shown itself as good on service. It has eight guns attached to it, well provided and served. The artillery-men, drivers, &c., are as well dressed and as fit for their duties as our own. Stores and ammunition are abundant, but the powder is execrable. Captain Magness is a good officer. The guns are six 6-pounders, drawn by bullocks; and two gallopers of very small calibre, drawn by horses. They are not adapted for the duties they have to perform, which is chiefly against mud-forts and strongholds; and four 9-pounders, two howitzers, and two mortars would be better. They are, however, well manned and provided with bullocks, ammunition and stores. The finest young men in Oude are glad to take service under Captain Magness; and the standard height of his men is at present five feet ten inches. He has some few men, good for nothing, called sufarishies, whom he is obliged to keep in on account of the persons by whom they are recommended, eunuchs, fiddlers, and Court favourites, of all kinds. In no country are there a body of finer looking recruits than Captain Magness now has at drill. All of the first families in the country, and of unquestionable courage and fidelity to their salt. He has four hundred Cavalry, of what is called the body guard, men well dressed, and of fine appearance. These Cavalry are, however, likely soon to be taken from him, and made over to some good-for-nothing Court favourite.* He has about seven hundred men present with his Infantry corps. His adjutant, Yosuf Khan, speaks English well, and has travelled a good deal in England, Europe generally, and Palestine. He is a sensible, unprejudiced man, and good soldier. Captain Magness attends the Nazim of the district; but, unfortunately, like all the commandants of corps and public servants of the State, he is obliged to forage for fodder and fuel. A foraging party is sent out every day, be where they will, to take these things gratis, wherever they can find them most conveniently. Bhoosa, grass and wood are the things which they are authorized to take, without payment, wherever they can find them; but they, of course, take a good many other things. The Government allows nothing to any of its troops or establishments, for these things, except when they are in Lucknow. The consequence is, that there is hardly a good cover to any man's house, or sufficient fodder for the cattle of any village, during the hot season and rains.

* They were soon after taken from Captain Magness and given to Mr. Johannes; and soon after taken from him, and made over to an eunuch, who turned out all the good men, to sell their places to men good for nothing. They mutinied; but the King and minister supported the eunuch, and the greater part of the men were discharged and their officers ruined.

December 27, 1849—Halted at Pertabghur. I had a visit from many of the persons who were in my service, when I was here with my regiment thirty years ago, as watchmen, gardeners, &c. They continue to hold and till the lands, which they or their fathers then tilled; and the change in them is not so great as that which has taken place within the same time among my old native friends, who survive in the Saugor and Nerbudda districts, where the air is less dry, and the climate less congenial to the human frame. The natives say that the air and water of Malwa may produce as good trees and crops as those of Oude, but can never produce such good soldiers. This, I believe, is quite true. The Sultanpoor district is included in the Banoda division of Oude; and the people speak of the water of this division for tempering soldiers, as we talk of the water of Damascus, for tempering sword blades. They certainly never seem so happy as when they are fighting in earnest with swords, spears, and matchlocks. The water of the Byswara division is considered to be very little inferior to that of Banoda, and we get our sipahees from these two divisions almost exclusively.

Captain Magness's corps is, at present, attached to the Nazim of this district, with its guns, and squadron of horse, as an auxiliary force. Over and above this force, he has nine regiments of Nujeebs, detachments of other Corps, Artillery, Pioneers, &c., amounting, in all, according to the musters and pay-drafts, to seven thousand seven hundred and seventy-eight men, for whom thirty-seven thousand seven hundred and ninety-three rupees a-month are drawn. Of these, fifteen hundred are dead or have deserted, or are absent on leave without pay. Their pay is all appropriated by the commandants of corps or Court favourites. Fifteen hundred more are in attendance on the commandants of corps, who reside at the capital, and their friends or other influential persons about the Court, or engaged in their own trades or affairs, having been put into the corps by influential persons at Court, to draw pay, but do no duty. Of the remaining four thousand seven hundred and seventy-eight, one-third, or one thousand five hundred and ninety-two, are what is called sufarishies, or men who are unfit for duty, and have been put in by influential persons at Court, to appear at muster and draw pay. Of the remaining three thousand one hundred and eighty-six present, there would be no chance of getting more than two-thirds, or two thousand one hundred and twenty-four men to fight on emergency—indeed, the Nazim would think himself exceedingly lucky if he could get one-third to do so.

Of the forty-two guns, thirteen are utterly useless on the ground; and out of the remaining twenty-nine, there are draft bullocks for only five. But there are no stores or ammunition for any of them; and the Nazim is obliged to purchase what powder and ball he may require in the bazaars. None of the gun-carriages have been repaired for the last twenty years, and the strongest of them would go to pieces after a few rounds. Very few of them would stand one round with good powder. Five hundred rupees are allowed for fitting up the carriage and tumbril of each gun, after certain intervals of from five to ten years; and this sum has, no doubt, been drawn over and over for these guns, during the twenty years, within which they have had no repairs whatever. If the local governor is permitted to draw this sum, he is sure never to expend one farthing of it on the gun. If the person in charge of the ordnance at Lucknow draws it, the guns and tumbrils are sent in to him, and returned with, at least, a coating of paint and putty, but seldom with anything else. The two persons in charge of the two large parks at Lucknow, from which the guns are furnished, Anjum-od Dowlah, and Ances-od Dowlah, a fiddler, draw the money for the corn allowed for the draft bullocks, at the rate of three pounds per diem for each, and distribute, or pretend to distribute it through the agents of the grain-dealers, with whom they contract for the supply; and the district officers, under whom these draft bullocks are employed, are never permitted to interfere. They have nothing to do but pay for the grain allowed; and the agents, employed to feed the bullocks, do nothing but appropriate the money for themselves and their employers. Not a grain of corn do the bullocks ever get.

The Nazim has charge of the districts of Sultanpoor, Haldeemow, Pertabghur, Jugdeespoor, and that part of Fyzabad which is not included in the estate of Bukhtawar Sing, yielding, altogether, about ten and a half lacs of rupees to Government. He exercises entire fiscal, judicial, magisterial and police authority over all these districts. To aid him in all these duties, he has four deputies—one in each district—upon salaries of one hundred and fifty rupees each a-month, with certain fees and perquisites. To inquire into particular cases, over all these districts, he employs a special deputy, paid out of his own salary. All the accountants and other writers, employed under him, are appointed by the deputies and favourites of the minister; and, considering themselves as their creatures, they pay little regard to their immediate master, the Nazim. But over and above these men, from whom he does get some service, he has to pay a good many, from whom he can get none. He is, before he enters upon his charge, obliged to insert, in his list of civil functionaries, to be paid monthly, out of the revenues, a number of writers and officers, of all descriptions, recommended to him by these deputies and other influential persons at Court. Of these men he never sees or knows anything. They are the children, servants, creatures, or dependents of the persons who recommend them, and draw their pay. These are called civil sufarishies, and cost the State much more than the military sufarishies, already mentioned—perhaps not less than six thousand rupees a-month in this division alone.

The Nazim is permitted to levy for incidental expenses, only ten per cent. over and above the Government demand; and required to send one-half of this sum to Court, for distribution. He is ostensibly required to limit himself to this sum, and to abstain from taking the gratuities, usually exacted by the revenue contractors, for distribution among ministers and other influential persons at Court. Were he to do so, they would all be so strongly opposed to the amanee, or trust system of management, and have it in their power so much to thwart him, in all his measures and arrangements, that he could never possibly get on with his duties; and the disputes between them generally results in a compromise. He takes, in gratuities, something less than his contracting predecessors took, and shares, what he takes, liberally, with those whose assistance he requires at Court. These gratuities, or nuzuranas, never appeared, in the public accounts; and were a governor, under the amanee system, to demand the full rates paid to contractors, the more powerful landholders would refer him to these public accounts, and refuse to pay till he could assure them of the same equivalents in nanker and other things, which they were in the habit of receiving from contractors. These, as a mere trust manager, he may not be able to give; and he consents to take something less. The landholders know that where the object is to exact the means to gratify influential persons about Court, the Nazim would be likely to get good military support, if driven to extremity, and consent to pay the greater part of what is demanded. When the trust manager, by his liberal remittances to Court patrons, gets all the troops he requires, he exacts the full gratuities, and still higher and more numerous if strong enough. The corps under Captains Magness, Bunbury, Barlow, and Subha Sing, are called komukee, or auxiliary regiments; and they are every season, and sometimes often in the same season, sold to the highest bidder as a perquisite by the minister. The services of Captain Magness and Captain Bunbury's corps were purchased in this way for 1850 and 1851, by Aga Allee, the Nazim of Sultanpoor, and he has made the most of them. No contractor ever exacted higher nazuranas or gratuities than he has, by

Of these he has, generally, from fifty to sixty employed, on salaries varying from fifteen to thirty rupees a-month each. The Tehseeldar is employed here, as elsewhere, in the collection of the land revenue, in the usual way; but the Jumogdar is an officer unknown in our territories. Some are appointed direct from Court, and some by the Nazims and Amils of districts. When a landholder has to pay his revenue direct to Government (as all do, who are included in what is called the Hozoor Tehseel), and he neglects to do so punctually, a Jumogdar is appointed. The landholder assembles his tenants, and they enter into pledges to pay direct to the Jumogdar the rents due by them to the landholder, under existing engagements, up to a certain time. This may be the whole, or less than the whole, amount due to Government by the landholder. If any of them fail to pay what they promise to the Jumogdar, the landholder is bound to make good the deficiency at the end of the year. He also binds himself to pay to Government whatever may be due over and above what the tenants pledge themselves to pay to the Jumogdar. This transfer of responsibility, from the landholder to his tenants, is called "Jumog Lagana," or transfer of the jumma. The assembly of the tenants, for the purpose of such-adjustment, is called zunjeer bundee, or linking together. The adjustment thus made is called the bilabundee. The salary of the Jumogdar is paid by the landholder, who distributes the burthen of the payment upon his tenants, at a per centage rate. The Jumogdar takes written engagements from the tenants; and they are bound not to pay anything to the landholder till they have paid him (the Jumogdar) all that they are, by these engagements, bound to pay him. He does all he can to make them pay punctually; but he is not, properly, held responsible for any defalcation. Such responsibility rests with the landlords. Where much difficulty is expected from the refractory character of the landholder, the officer commanding the whole, or some part of the troops in the district, is often appointed the Jumogdar; and the amount which the tenants pledge themselves to pay to him is debited to him, in the pay of the troops, under his command.

their aid, this season, though he still holds the district as a trust manager. Ten, twenty, or thirty thousand rupees are paid for the use of one of these regiments, according to the exigency of the occasion, or the time for which it may be required.

The system of government under which Oude suffers during the reign of the best king is a fearful one; and what must it be under a sovereign, so indifferent as the present is, to the sufferings of his people, to his own permanent interests, and to the duties and responsibilities of his high station? Seeing that our Government attached much importance to the change, from the contract to the trust system of management, the present minister is putting a large portion of the country under that system in the hope of blinding us. But there is virtually little or no change in the administration of such districts; the person who has the charge of a district under it is obliged to pay the same gratuities to public officers and court favourites, and he exacts the same, or nearly the same from the landholders; he is under no more check than the contractor, and the officers and troops under him, abuse their authority in the same manner, and commit the same outrages upon the suffering people. Security to life and property is disregarded in the same manner; he confines himself as exclusively to the duties of collecting revenue, and is as regardless of security to life and property, and of fidelity to his engagements, as the landholders in his jurisdiction. The trust management of a district differs from that of the contractors, only as the wusoolee kubaz differs from the lakulamee; though he does not enter into a formal contract to pay a certain sum, he is always expected to pay such a sum, and if he does not, he is obliged to wipe off the balance in the same way, and is kept in gaol till he does so, in the same way. Indeed, I believe, the people would commonly rather be under a contractor, than a trust manager under the Oude Government; and this was the opinion of Colonel Low, who, of all my predecessors, certainly knew most about the real state of Oude.

The Nazim of Sultanpoor has authority to entertain such Tehseeldars and Jumogdars as he may require, for the collection of the revenue.

The Jumogdars, who are appointed by the Nazims and Amils, act in the same manner with regard to the landlords and tenants, to whom they are accredited, and are paid in the same manner. There may be one, or there may be one hundred, Jumogdars in a district, according to the necessity for their employment, in the collection of the revenue. They are generally men of character, influence, and resolution; and often useful to both, or all three parties; but when they are officers commanding troops, they are often very burthensome to landlords and tenants. The Jumogdar has only to receive the sums due, according to existing engagements between the parties, and to see that no portion of them is paid to any other person. He has nothing to do with apportioning the demand, or making the engagements between tenants and landlords, or landlords and Government officers.

The Canoongoes and Chowdheries in Oude are commonly called Seghadars, and their duties are the same here as everywhere else in India.

December 28, 1849.—Twelve miles to Hundore, over a country more undulating and better cultivated than any we have seen since we recrossed the Goomtee river at Sultanpoor. It all belongs to the Rajah of Pertabghur, Shumshere Babadur, a Somebunsee, who resides at Dewlee, some six miles from Pertabghur. His family is one of the oldest and most respectable in Oude; but his capital of Pertabghur, where he used to reside till lately, is one of the most beggarly. He seems to have concentrated there all the beggars in the country, and there is not a house of any respectable to be seen. The soil, all the way, has been what they call the doomut, or doomuteea, which is well adapted to all kinds of tillage, but naturally less strong than muteear or argillaceous earth, and yields scanty crops, where it is not well watered and manured.

The Rajah came to my camp in the afternoon, and attended me on his elephant in the evening when I went round the town, and to his old mud fort, now in ruins, within which is the old residence of the family. He does not pay his revenue punctually, nor is he often prepared to attend the viceroy when required; and it was thought that he would not come to me. Finding that the Korwar and other Rajahs and large landholders, who had been long on similar terms with the local authorities, had come in, paid their respects, and been left free, he also ventured to my camp. For the last thirty years the mutual confidence which once subsisted between the Government authorities and the great landholders of these districts has been declining, and it ceased altogether under the last viceroy, Wajid Allee Khan, who appears to have been a man without any feeling of humanity or sense of honour. No man ever knew what he would be called upon to pay to Government in the districts under him; and almost all the respectable landholders prepared to defend what they had by force of arms; deserted their homes, and took to the jungles with as many followers as they could collect and subsist, as soon as he entered on his charge. The atrocities charged against him, and upon the best possible evidence, are numerous and great.

The country we have passed through to-day is well studded with fine trees, among which the mhowa abounds more than usual. The parasite plant, called the bandha, or Indian mistletoe, ornaments the finest mhowa and mango trees. It is said to be a disease, which appears as the tree grows old, and destroys it if not cut away. The people, who feel much regard for their trees, cut these parasite plants away; and there is no prejudice against removing them among Hindoos, though they dare not cut away a peepul-tree which is destroying their wells, houses, temples, or tombs; nor do they, with some exceptions, dare to destroy a wolf, though he may have eaten their own children, or actually have one of them in his mouth. In all parts of India, Hindoos have a notion that the family of a man who kills a wolf, or even wounds it, goes soon to utter ruin; and so also the village within the boundaries of which a wolf has been killed or wounded. They have no objection to their being killed by other people away from the villages; on the contrary, are very glad to have them so destroyed, as long as their blood does not drop on their premises. Some Rajpoot families in Oude, where so many children are devoured by wolves, are getting over this prejudice. The bandha is very ornamental to the fine mhowa and mango trees, to the branches of which it hangs suspended in graceful festoons, with a great variety of colours and tints, from deep scarlet and green to light-red and yellow.

Wolves are numerous in the neighbourhood of Sultanpoor, and, indeed, all along the banks of the Goomtee river, among the ravines that intersect them; and a great many children are carried off by them from towns, villages, and camps. It is exceedingly difficult to catch them, and hardly any of the Hindoo population, save those of the very lowest class who live a vagrant life, and bivouac in the jungles, or in the suburbs of towns and villages, will attempt to catch or kill them. All other Hindoos have a superstitious dread of destroying or even injuring them; and a village community within the boundary of whose lands a drop of wolf's blood has fallen believes itself doomed to destruction. The class of little vagrant communities above mentioned, who have no superstitious dread of destroying any living thing, eat jackalls and all kinds of reptiles, and catch all kinds of animals, either to feed upon themselves, or to sell them to those who wish to keep or hunt them.

But it is remarkable, that they very seldom catch wolves, though they know all their dens, and could easily dig them out as they dig out other animals. This is supposed to arise from the profit which they make by the gold and silver bracelets, necklaces and other ornaments worn by the children whom the wolves carry to their dens and devour, and are left at the entrance of their dens. A party of these men lately brought to our camp alive a very large hyæna, which was let loose and hunted down by the European officers and the clerks of my office. One of the officers asked them whether this was not the reason why they did not bring wolves to camp, to be hunted down in the same way, since officers would give more for brutes that ate children, than for such as fed only on dogs or carrion. They dared not deny, though they were ashamed or afraid to acknowledge, that it was. I have myself no doubt that this is the reason, and that they do make a good deal in this way from the children's ornaments, which they find at the entrance of wolves' dens. In every part of India, a great number of children are every day murdered for the sake of their ornaments, and the fearful examples that come daily to the knowledge of parents, and the injunctions of the civil authorities are unavailing against this desire to see their young children decked out in gold and silver ornaments.

There is now at Sultanpoor a boy who was found alive in a wolf's den, near Chandour, about ten miles from Sultanpoor, about two years and a half ago. A trooper, sent by the native governor of the district to Chandour, to demand payment of some revenue, was passing along the bank of the river near Chandour about noon, when he saw a large female wolf leave her den, followed by three whelps and a little boy. The boy went on all fours, and seemed to be on the best possible terms with the old dam and the three whelps, and the mother seemed to guard all four with equal care. They all went down to the river and drank without perceiving the trooper, who sat upon his horse watching them. As soon as they were about to turn back, the trooper pushed on to cut off and secure the boy; but he ran as fast as the whelps could, and kept up with the old one. The ground was uneven, and the trooper's horse could not overtake them. They all entered the den, and the trooper assembled some people from Chandour with pickaxes, and dug into the den. When they had dug in about six or eight feet, the old wolf bolted with her three whelps and the boy. The trooper mounted and pursued, followed by the fleetest young men of the party; and as the ground over which they had to fly was more even, he headed them, and turned the whelps and boy back upon the men on foot, who secured the boy, and let the old dam and her three cubs go on their way.

They took the boy to the village, but had to tie him, for he was very restive, and struggled hard to rush into every hole or den they came near. They tried to make him speak, but could get nothing from him but an angry growl or snarl. He was kept for several days at the village, and a large crowd assembled every day to see him. When a grown-up person came near him, he became alarmed, and tried to steal away; but when a child came near him, he rushed at it, with a fierce snarl like that of a dog, and tried to bite it. When any cooked meat was put before him, he rejected it in disgust; but when any raw meat was offered, he seized it with avidity, put it on the ground under his paws, like a dog, and ate it with evident pleasure. He would not let any one come near him while he was eating, but he made no objection to a dog coming and sharing his food with him. The trooper remained with him four or five days, and then returned to the governor, leaving the boy in charge of the Rajah of Hasunpoor. He related all that he had seen, and the boy was soon after sent to the European officer commanding the First Regiment of Oude Local Infantry at Sultanpoor, Captain Nicholetts, by order of the Rajah of Hasunpoor, who was at Chandour, and saw the boy when the trooper first brought him to that village. This account is taken from the Rajah's own report of what had taken place.

Captain Nicholetts made him over to the charge of his servants, who take great care of him, but can never get him to speak a word. He is very inoffensive, except when teased, Captain Nicholetts says, and will then growl surlily at the person who teases him. He had come to eat anything that is thrown to him, but always prefers raw flesh, which he devours most greedily. He will drink a whole pitcher of butter-milk when put before him, without seeming to draw breath. He can never be induced to keep on any kind of clothing, even in the coldest weather. A quilt stuffed with cotton was given to him when it became very cold this season, but he tore it to pieces, and ate a portion of it, cotton and all, with his bread every day. He is very fond of bones, particularly uncooked ones, which he masticates apparently with as much ease as meat. He has eaten half a lamb at a time without any apparent effort, and is very fond of taking up earth and small stones and eating them. His features are coarse, and his countenance repulsive; and he is very filthy in his habits. He continues to be fond of dogs and jackals, and all other small four-footed animals that come near him; and always allows them to feed with him if he happens to be eating when they approach.

Captain Nicholetts, in letters dated the 14th and 19th of September, 1850, told me that the boy died in the latter end of August, and that he was never known to laugh or smile. He understood little of what was said to him, and seemed to take no notice of what was going on around him. He formed no attachment for any one, nor did he seem to care for any one. He never played with any of the children around him, or seemed anxious to do so. When not hungry he used to sit petting and stroking a pareear or vagrant dog, which he used to permit to feed out of the same dish with him. A short time before his death Captain Nicholetts shot this dog, as he used to eat the greater part of the food given to the boy, who seemed in consequence to be getting thin. The boy did not seem to care in the least for the death of the dog. The parents recognised the boy when he was first found, Captain Nicholetts believes; but when they found him to be so stupid and insensible, they left him to subsist upon charity. They have now left Hasunpoor, and the age of the boy when carried off cannot be ascertained; but he was to all appearance about nine or ten years of age when found, and he lived about three years afterwards. He used signs when he wanted anything, and very few of them except when hungry, and he then pointed to his mouth. When his food was placed at some distance from him, he would run to it on all fours like any four-footed animal; but at other times he would walk upright occasionally. He shunned human beings of all kinds, and would never willingly remain near one. To cold, heat, and rain he appeared to be indifferent; and he seemed to care for nothing but eating. He was very quiet, and required no kind of restraint after being brought to Captain Nicholetts. He had lived with Captain Nicholetts' servants about two years, and was never heard to speak till within a few minutes of his death, when he put his hands to his head, and said "it ached," and asked for water: he drank it, and died.

At Chupra, twenty miles east from Sultanpoor, lived a cultivator with his wife and son, who was then three years of age. In March, 1843, the man went to cut his crop of wheat and pulse, and the woman took her basket and went with him to glean, leading her son by the arm. The boy had lately recovered from a severe scald on the left knee, which he got in the cold weather, from tumbling into the fire, at which he had been warming himself while his parents were at work. As the father was reaping and the mother gleaning, the boy sat upon the grass. A wolf rushed upon him suddenly from behind a bush, caught him up by the loins, and made off with him towards the ravines. The father was at a distance at the time, but the mother followed, screaming as loud an she could for assistance. The people of the village ran to her aid, but they soon lost sight of the wolf and his prey.

She heard nothing more of her boy for six years, and had in that interval lost her husband. At the end of that time, two sipahees came, in the month of February, 1849, from the town of Singramow, which is ten miles from Chupra, on the bank of the Khobae rivulet. While they sat on the border of the jungle, which extended down to the stream, watching for hogs, which commonly come down to drink at that time in the morning, they saw there three wolf cubs and a boy come out from the jungle, and go down together to the stream to drink. The sipahees watched them till they had drank, and were about to return, when they rushed towards them. All four ran towards a den in the ravines. The sipahees followed as fast as they could; but the three cubs had got in before the sipahees could come up with them, and the boy was half way in when one of the sipahees caught him by the hind leg, and drew him back. He seemed very angry and ferocious, bit at them, and seized in his teeth the barrel of one of their guns, which they put forward to keep him off, and shook it. They however secured him, brought him home, and kept him for twenty days. They could for that time make him eat nothing but raw flesh, and they fed him upon hares and birds. They found it difficult to provide him with sufficient food, and took him to the bazaar in the village of Koeleepoor; and there let him go to be fed by the charitable people of the place till he might be recognised and claimed by his parents. One market-day a man from the village of Chupra happened to see him in the bazaar, and on his return mentioned the circumstance to his neighbours. The poor cultivator's widow, on hearing this, asked him to describe the boy more minutely, when she found that the boy had the mark of a scald on the left knee, and three marks of the teeth of an animal on each side of his loins. The widow told him that her boy when taken off had lately recovered from a scald on the left knee, and was seized by the loins when the wolf took him off, and that the boy he had seen must be her lost child.

She went off forthwith to the Koelee bazaar, and, in addition to the two marks above described, discovered a third mark on his thigh, with which her child was born. She took him home to her village, where he was recognised by all her neighbours. She kept him for two months, and all the sporting landholders in the neighbourhood sent her game for him to feed upon. He continued to dip his face in the water to drink, but he sucked in the water, and did not lap it up like a dog or wolf. His body continued to smell offensively. When the mother went to her work, the boy always ran into the jungle, and she could never get him to speak. He followed his mother for what he could get to eat, but showed no particular affection for her; and she could never bring herself to feel much for him; and after two months, finding him of no use to her, and despairing of even making anything of him, she left him to the common charity of the village. He soon after learnt to eat bread when it was given him, and ate whatever else he could get during the day, but always went off to the jungle at night. He used to mutter something, but could never be got to articulate any word distinctly. The front of his knees and elbows had become hardened from going on all fours with the wolves. If any clothes are put on him, he takes them off, and commonly tears them to pieces in doing so. He still prefers raw flesh to cooked, and feeds on carrion whenever he can get it. The boys of the village are in the habit of amusing themselves by catching frogs and throwing them to him; and he catches and eats them. When a bullock dies, and the skin is removed, he goes and eats it like a village dog. The boy is still in the village, and this is the description given of him by the mother herself, who still lives at Chupra. She has never experienced any return of affection for him, nor has he shown any such feeling for her. Her story is confirmed by all her neighbours, and by the head landholders, cultivators, and shopkeepers of the village.*

* In November, 1850, Captain Nicholetts, on leaving the cantonments of Sultanpoor, where he commanded, ordered this boy to be sent in to me with his mother, but he got alarmed on the way and ran to a jungle. He will no doubt find his way back soon if he lives.

The Rajah of Hasunpoor Bundooa mentions, as a fact within his own knowledge, besides the others, for the truth of which he vouches, that, in the year 1843, a lad came to the town of Hasunpoor, who had evidently been brought up by wolves. He seemed to be twelve years of age when he saw him—was very dark, and ate flesh, whether cooked or uncooked. He had short hair all over his body when he first came, but having, for a time, as the Rajah states, eaten salt with his food, like other human beings, the hair by degrees disappeared. He could walk, like other men, on his legs, but could never be taught to speak. He would utter sounds like wild animals, and could be made to understand signs very well. He used to sit at a bunneea's shop in the bazaar, but was at last recognised by his parents, and taken off. What became of him afterwards he knows not. The Rajah's statement regarding this lad is confirmed by all the people of the town, but none of them know what afterwards became of him.

About the year 1843, a shepherd of the village of Ghutkoree, twelve miles west from the cantonments of Sultanpoor, saw a boy trotting along upon all fours, by the side of a wolf, one morning, as he was out with his flock. With great difficulty he caught the boy, who ran very fast, and brought him home. He fed him for some time, and tried to make him speak, and associate with men or boys, but he failed. He continued to be alarmed at the sight of men, but was brought to Colonel Gray, who commanded the first Oude Local Infantry, at Sultanpoor. He and Mrs. Gray, and all the officers in cantonments, saw him often, and kept him for several days. But he soon after ran off into the jungle, while the shepherd was asleep. The shepherd, afterwards, went to reside in another village, and I could not ascertain whether he recovered the boy or not.

Zoolfukar Khan, a respectable landholder of Bankeepoor, in the estate of Hasunpoor, ten miles east from the Sultahpoor cantonments, mentions that about eight or nine years ago a trooper came to the town, with a lad of about nine or ten years of age, whom he had rescued from wolves among the ravines on the road; that he knew not what to do with him, and left him to the common charity of the village; that he ate everything offered to him, including bread, but before taking it he carefully smelt at it, and always preferred undressed meat to everything else; that he walked on his legs like other people when he saw him, though there were evident signs on his knees and elbows of his having gone, very long, on all fours; and when asked to run on all fours he used to do so, and went so fast that no one could overtake him; how long he had been with the trooper, or how long it took him to learn to walk on his legs, he knows not. He could not talk, or utter any very articulate sounds. He understood signs, and heard exceedingly well, and would assist the cultivators in turning trespassing cattle out of their fields, when told by signs to do so. Boodhoo, a Brahmin cultivator of the village, took care of him, and he remained with him for three months, when he was claimed and taken off by his father, a shepherd, who said that the boy was six years old when the wolf took him off at night some four years before; he did not like to leave Boodhoo, the Brahmin, and the father was obliged to drag him away. What became of him afterwards he never heard. The lad had no hair upon his body, nor had he any dislike to wear clothes, while he saw him. This statement was confirmed by the people of the village.

About seven years ago a trooper belonging to the King, and in attendance on Rajah Hurdut Sing of Bondee, alias Bumnotee, on the left bank of the Ghagra river, in the Bahraetch district, was passing near a small stream which flows into that river, when he saw two wolf cubs and a boy drinking in the stream. He had a man with him on foot, and they managed to seize the boy, who appeared to be about ten years of age. He took him up on the pummel of his saddle, but he was so wild and fierce that he tore the trooper's clothes and bit him severely in several places, though he had tied his hands together. He brought him to Bondee, where the Rajah had him tied up in his artillery gun-shed, and gave him raw-flesh to eat: but he several times cut his ropes and ran off; and after three months the Rajah got tired of him, and let him go. He was then taken by a Cashmeeree mimic, or comedian (bhand), who fed and took care of him for six weeks*; but at the end of that time he also got tired of him (for his habits were filthy), and let him go to wander about the Bondee bazaar. He one day ran off with a joint of meat from a butcher's shop, and soon after upset some things in the shop of a bunneeah, who let fly an arrow at him. The arrow penetrated the boy's thigh. At this time Sanaollah, a Cashmere merchant of Lucknow, was at Bondee, selling some shawl goods to the Rajah, on the occasion of his brother's marriage. He had many servants with him, and among them Janoo, a khidmutgar lad, and an old sipahee, named Ramzan Khan. Janoo took compassion upon the poor boy, extracted the arrow from his thigh, had his wound dressed, and prepared a bed for him under the mango-tree, where he himself lodged, but kept him tied to a tent-pin. He would at that time eat nothing but raw flesh. To wean him from this, Janoo, with the consent of his master, gave him rice and pulse to eat. He rejected them for several days, and ate nothing; but Janoo persevered, and by degrees made him eat the balls which he prepared for him: he was fourteen or fifteen days in bringing him to do this. The odour from his body was very offensive, and Janoo had him rubbed with mustard-seed soaked in water, after the oil had been taken from it (khullee), in the hope of removing this smell. He continued this for some months, and fed him upon rice, pulse, and flour bread, but the odour did not leave him. He had hardened marks upon his knees and elbows, from having gone on all fours. In about six weeks after he had been tied up under the tree, with a good deal of beating, and rubbing of his joints with oil, he was made to stand and walk upon his legs like other human beings. He was never heard to utter more than one articulate sound, and that was "Aboodeea," the name of the little daughter of the Cashmeer mimic, who had treated him with kindness, and for whom he had shown some kind of attachment. In about four months he began to understand and obey signs. He was by them made to prepare the hookah, put lighted charcoal upon the tobacco, and bring it to Janoo, or present it to whomsoever he pointed out.

One night while the boy was lying under the tree, near Janoo, Janoo saw two wolves come up stealthily, and smell at the boy. They then touched him, and he got up; and, instead of being frightened, the boy put his hands upon their heads, and they began to play with him. They capered around him, and he threw straw and leaves at them. Janoo tried to drive them off but he could not, and became much alarmed; and he called out to the sentry over the guns, Meer Akbur Allee, and told him that the wolves were going to eat the boy. He replied, "Come away and leave him, or they will eat you also;" but when he saw them begin to play together, his fears subsided and he kept quiet. Gaining confidence by degrees, he drove them away; but, after going a little distance, they returned, and began to play again with the boy. At last he succeeded in driving them off altogether. The night after three wolves came, and the boy and they played together. A few nights after four wolves came, but at no time did more than four come. They came four or five times, and Janoo had no longer any fear of them; and he thinks that the first two that came must have been the two cubs with which the boy was first found, and that they were prevented from seizing him by recognising the smell. They licked his face with their tongues as he put his hands on their heads.

Soon after his master, Sanaollah, returned to Lucknow, and threatened Janoo to turn him out of his service unless he let go the boy. He persisted in taking the boy with him, and his master relented. He had a string tied to his arm, and led him along by it, and put a bundle of clothes on his head. As they passed a jungle the boy would throw down the bundle and try to run into the jungle, but on being beaten, he would put up his hands in supplication, take up the bundle and go on; but he seemed soon to forget the beating, and did the same thing at almost every jungle they came through. By degrees he became quite docile. Janoo was one day, about three months after their return to Lucknow, sent away by his master for a day or two on some business, and before his return the boy had ran off, and he could never find him again. About two months after the boy had gone, a woman, of the weaver caste, came with a letter from a relation of the Rajah, Hurdut Sing, to Sanaollah, stating that she resided in the village of Chureyrakotra, on his estate, and had had her son, then about four years of age, taken from her, about five or six years before, by a wolf; and, from the description which she gave of him, he, the Rajah's relation, thought he must be the boy whom his servant, Janoo, took away with him. She said that her boy had two marks upon him, one on the chest of a boil, and one of something else on the forehead; and as these marks corresponded precisely with those found upon the boy, neither she nor they had any doubt that he was her lost son. She remained for four months with the merchant Sanaollah, and Janoo, his kidmutghur, at Lucknow; but the boy could not be found, and she returned home, praying that information might be sent to her should he be discovered. Sanaollah, Janoo, and Ramzan Khan, are still at Lucknow, and before me have all three declared all the circumstances here stated to be strictly true. The boy was altogether about five months with Sanaollah and his servants, from the time they got him; and he had been taken about four months and a half before. The wolf must have had several litters of whelps during the six or seven years that the boy was with her. Janoo further adds, that he, after a month or two, ventured to try a waist-band upon the boy, but he often tore it off in distress or anger. After he had become reconciled to this, in about two months, he ventured to put on upon him a vest and a pair of trousers. He had great difficulty in making him keep them on, with threats and occasional beatings. He would disencumber himself of them whenever left alone, but put them on again in alarm when discovered; and to the last often injured or destroyed them by rubbing them against trees or posts, like a beast, when any part of his body itched. This habit he could never break him of.

Rajah Hurdut Sewae, who is now in Lucknow on business, tells me (28th January, 1851) that the sowar brought the boy to Bondee, and there kept him for a short time, as long as he remained; but as soon as he went off, the boy came to him, and he kept him for three months; that he appeared to him to be twelve years of age; that he ate raw meat as long as he remained with him, with evident pleasure, whenever it was offered to him, but would not touch the bread and other dressed food put before him; that he went on all fours, but would stand and go awkwardly on two legs when threatened or made to do so; that he seemed to understand signs, but could not understand or utter a word; that he seldom attempted to bite any one, nor did he tear the clothes that he put upon him; that Sanaollah, the Cashmeeree merchant, used at that time to come to him often with shawls for sale, and must have taken the boy away with him, but he does not recollect having given the boy to him. He says that he never himself sent any letter to Sanaollah with the mother of the boy, but his brother or some other relation of his may have written one for her.

It is remarkable that I can discover no well-established instance of a man who had been nurtured in a wolf's den having been found. There is, at Lucknow, an old man who was found in the Oude Tarae, when a lad, by the hut of an old hermit who had died. He is supposed to have been taken from wolves by this old hermit. The trooper who found him brought him to the King some forty years ago, and he has been ever since supported by the King comfortably. He is still called the "wild man of the woods." He was one day sent to me at my request, and I talked with him. His features indicate him to be of the Tharoo tribe, who are found only in that forest. He is very inoffensive, but speaks little, and that little imperfectly; and he is still impatient of intercourse with his fellow-men, particularly with such as are disposed to tease him with questions. I asked him whether he had any recollection of having been with wolves. He said "the wolf died long before the hermit;" but he seemed to recollect nothing more, and there is no mark on his knees or elbows to indicate that he ever went on all fours. That he was found as a wild boy in the forest there can be no doubt; but I do not feel at all sure that he ever lived with wolves. From what I have seen and heard I should doubt whether any boy who had been many years with wolves, up to the age of eight or ten, could ever attain the average intellect of man. I have never heard of a man who had been spared and nurtured by wolves having been found; and, as many boys have been recovered from wolves after they had been many years with them, we must conclude that after a time they either die from living exclusively on animal food, before they attain the age of manhood, or are destroyed by the wolves themselves, or other beasts of prey, in the jungles, from whom they are unable to escape, like the wolves themselves, from want of the same speed. The wolf or wolves, by whom they have been spared and nurtured, must die or be destroyed in a few years, and other wolves may kill and eat them. Tigers generally feed for two or three days upon the bullock they kill, and remain all the time, when not feeding, concealed in the vicinity. If they found such a boy feeding upon their prey they would certainly kill him, and most likely eat him. If such a boy passed such a dead body he would certainly feed upon it. Tigers often spring upon and kill dogs and wolves thus found feeding upon their prey. They could more 'easily kill boys, and would certainly be more disposed to eat them. If the dead body of such a boy were found anywhere in the jungles, or on the plains, it would excite little interest, where dead bodies are so often found exposed, and so soon eaten by dogs, jackals, vultures, &c., and would scarcely ever lead to any particular inquiry.

CHAPTER V.

Salone district—Rajah Lal Hunmunt Sing of Dharoopoor—Soil of Oude—Relative fertility of the mutteear and doomutteea—Either may become oosur, or barren, from neglect, and is reclaimed, when it does so, with difficulty—Shah Puna Ata, a holy man in charge of an eleemosynary endowment at Salone—Effects of his curses—Invasion of British Boundary—Military Force with the Nazim—State and character of this Force—Rae Bareilly in the Byswara district—Bandha, or Misletoe—Rana Benee Madhoo, of Shunkerpoor—Law of Primogeniture—Title of Rana contested between Benee Madhoo and Rogonath Sing—Bridge and avenue at Rae Bareilly—Eligible place for cantonment and civil establishments—State of the Artillery—Sobha Sing's regiment—Foraging System—Peasantry follow the fortunes of their refractory Landlords—No provision for the king's soldiers, disabled in action, or for the families of those who are killed—Our sipahees, a privileged class, very troublesome in the Byswara and Banoda districts—Goorbukshgunge—Man destroyed by an Elephant—Danger to which keepers of such animals are exposed—Bys Rajpoots composed of two great families, Sybunsies and Nyhassas—Their continual contests for landed possessions—Futteh Bahader—Rogonath Sing—Mahibollah the robber and estate of Balla—Notion that Tillockchundee Bys Rajpoots never suffer from the bite of a snake—Infanticide—Paucity of comfortable dwelling-houses—The cause—Agricultural capitalists—Ornaments and apparel of the females of the Bys clan—Late Nazim Hamid Allee—His father-in-law Fuzl Allee—First loan from Oude to our Government—Native gentlemen with independent incomes cannot reside in the country—Crowd the city, and tend to alienate the Court from the people.

December 29, 1849.—Ten miles to Rampoor. Midway we passed over the border of the Sultanpoor district into that of Salone, whose Amil, Hoseyn Buksh, there met us with his cortège. Rampoor is the Residence of Rajah Hunmunt Sing, the tallookdar of the two estates of Dharoopoor and Kalakunkur, which extend down to and for some miles along the left bank of the river Ganges. There is a fort in each of these estates, and he formerly resided in that of Dharoopoor, four miles from our present encampment. That of Kalakunkur is on the bank of the Ganges. The lands along, on both sides the road, over which we are come, are scantily cultivated, but well studded with good trees, where the soil is good for them. A good deal of it is, however, the poor oosur soil, the rest muteear, of various degrees of fertility. The territory of Oude, as I have said above, must once have formed part of the bed of a lake,* which contained a vast fund of soluble salts. Through this bed, as the waters flowed off, the rivers from the northern range of hills, which had before fed the lake, cut their way to join the larger stream of the Ganges; and the smaller streams, which have their sources in the dense forest of the Tarae, which now extends along the southern border of that range, have since cut their way through this bed in the same manner to the larger rivers. The waters from these rivers percolate through the bed; and, as they rise to the surface, by the laws of capillary attraction, they carry with them these salts in solution. As they reach the surface in dry weather, they give off by evaporation pure water; and the salts, which they held in solution, remain behind in the upper surface. The capillary action goes on; and as the pure water is taken off in the atmosphere in vapour, other water impregnated with more salts comes up to supply its place; and the salts near the surface either accumulate or are supplied to the roots of the plants, shrubs, or trees, which require them.

*   Caused, possibly, by the Vendeya range once extending E. N. E. up to the Himmalaya chain, which runs E. S. E. It now extends up only to the right bank of the Ganges, at Chunar and Mirzapoor.

Rain-water,* which contains no such salts, falls after the dry season is over, and washes out of the upper surface a portion of the salts, which have thus been brought up from below and accumulated, and either takes them off in floods or carries them down again to the beds below. Some of these salts, or their bases, may become superabundant, and render the lands oosur or unfit for ordinary tillage. There may be a superabundance of those which are not required, or cannot be taken up by the plants, actually on the surface, or there may be a superabundance of the whole, from the plants and rain-water being insufficient to take away such as require to be removed. These salts are here, as elsewhere, of great variety; nitrates of ammonia, which, combining with the inorganic substances—magnesia, lime, soda, potash, alumina, and oxide of iron—form double salts, and become soluble in water, and fit food for plants. Or there may be a deficiency of vegetable mould (humus) or manure to supply, with the aid of carbonic acid, air, water, and ammonia, the organic acids required to adapt the inorganic substances to the use of plants.

*   Rain-water contains small quantities of carbonic acid, ammonia, atmospheric air, and vegetable or animal matter.

All are, in due proportion, more or less conducive to the growth and perfection of the plants, which men and animals require from the soil: some plants require more of the one, and some more of another; and some find a superabundance of what they need, where others find a deficiency, or none at all. The muteear seems to differ from the doomuteea soil, in containing a greater portion of those elements which constitute what are called good clay soils. The inorganic portions of these elements—silicates, carbonates, sulphates, phosphates, and chlorides of lime, potash, magnesia, alumina, soda, oxides of iron and manganese—it derives from the detritus of the granite, gneiss, mica, and chlorite slate, limestone and sandstone rocks, in which the Himmalaya chain of mountains so much abounds; and the organic elements—humates, almates, geates, apoerenates, and crenates—it derives from the mould, formed from the decay of animal and vegetable matter. It is more hydroscopic, or capable of absorbing and retaining moisture, and fixing ammonia than the doomuteea. It is of a darker colour, and forms more into clods to retain moisture. I may here mention that the Himmalaya chain does not abound in volcanic rocks, like the chains of Central and Southern India; and that the soils, which are formed from its detritus, contain, in consequence, less phosphoric acid, and is less adapted to the growth of that numerous class of plants which cannot live without phosphates. The volcanic rocks form a plateaux upon the sandstone, of almost all the hills of Central and Southern India; and the soil, which is formed from their detritus, is exceedingly fertile, when well combined, as it commonly is, with the salts and double salts formed by the union of the organic acids with the inorganic bases of alkalies, earths, and oxides which have become soluble, and been brought to the surface from below by capillary attraction. I may also mention, that the basaltic plateaux upon the sandstone rocks of Central and Southern India are often surmounted with a deposit, more or less deep, of laterite, or indurated iron clay, the detritus of which tends to promote fertility in the soil. I have never myself seen any other deposit than this iron clay or laterite above the basaltic plateaux. I believe that this laterite is never found, in any part of the Himmalaya chain. I have never seen it there, nor have I ever heard of any one having seen it there. In Bundelkund and other parts of Central and Southern India, the basaltic plateaux are sometimes found deposing immediately upon beds of granite.

The doomuteea is of a light-brown colour, soon powders into fine dust, and requires much more outlay in manure and labour than the muteear. The oosur soil appears to be formed out of both, by a superabundance of one or other of the salts or their bases, which are brought to the surface from the beds below, and not carried off or taken back into these beds. It is known that salts of ammonia are injurious to plants, unless combined with organic acids, supplied to the soil by decayed vegetable or animal matter. This matter is necessary to combine with, and fix the ammonia in the soil, and give it out to plants as they require it.

It is possible that nitrates may superabound in the soil from the oxydizement of the nitrogen of a superfluity of ammonia. The people say that all land may become oosur from neglect; and when oosur can never be made to bear crops, after it has been left long fallow, till it has been flooded with rain-water for two or three seasons, by means of artificial embankments, and then well watered, manured, and ploughed. When well tilled in this way, all but the very worst kinds of oosur are said to bear tolerable crops. In the midst of a plain of barren oosur land, which has hardly a tree, shrub, or blade of grass, we find small oases, or patches of low land, in which accumulated rain-water lies for several months every year, covered with stout grasses of different kinds, a sure indication of ability to bear good crops, under good tillage. From very bad oosur lands, common salt or saltpetre, or both, are taken by digging out and washing the earth, and then removing the water by evaporation. The clods in the muteear soil not only retain moisture, and give it out slowly as required by the crops, but they give shelter and coolness to the young and tender shoots of grain and pulse. Of course trees, shrubs, and plants, of all kind in Oude, as elsewhere, derive carbonic acid gas and ammonia from the atmosphere, and decompose them, for their own use, in the same manner.

In treating of the advantages of greater facilities for irrigation in India, I do not recollect ever having seen any mention made of that of penetrating by wells into the deep deposits below of the soluble salts, or their bases, and bringing them to the surface in the water, for the supply of the plants, shrubs, and trees we require. People talk of digging for valuable metals, and thereby "developing resources;" but never talk of digging for the more valuable solutions of soluble salts, to be combined with the organic acids already existing in the soil, or provided by man in manures—and with the carbonic acid, ammonia, and water from the atmosphere—to supply him with a never-ending succession of harvests. The practical agriculturists of Oude, however, say, that brackish water in irrigation is only useful to tobacco and shama; and where the salts which produce it superabound, rain-water tanks and fresh-water rivers and canals would, no doubt, be much better than wells for irrigation. All these waters contain carbonic acid gas, atmospheric air, and solutions of salts, which form food for plants, or become so when combined with the organic acids, supplied by the decayed animal and vegetable matter in the soil.

Soils which contain salts, which readily give off their water of crystallization and effloresce, sooner become barren than those which contain salts that attract moisture from the air, and deliquesce, as chlorides of calcium and magnesia, carbonates and acetates of potassa, alumina, &c. Canals flowing over these deep dry beds, through which little water from the springs below ever percolates to the surface, are not only of great advantage for irrigating the crops on the surface, but for supplying water as they flow along, to penetrate through these deep dry beds; and, as they rise to the surface by capillary attraction, carrying along with them the soluble salts which they pick up on their way. In Oude, as in all the districts that extend along to the north of the Ganges, and south of the Himmalaya chain, easterly winds prevail, and bring up moisture from the sea of the Bay of Bengal. All these districts are, at the same time, abundantly studded with groves of fine trees and jungle, that attract this moisture to the earth in rain and dew. Through Goozerat, Malwa, Berar, and Bundelkund, and all the districts bordering the Nerbudda river, from its mouth to its sources, westerly winds prevail, and bring up moisture from the Gulf of Cambay; and these districts are all well studded with groves, &c., and single trees, which act in the same manner, in attracting the moisture from the atmosphere to the earth, in rain and dew. In Rajpootana and Sinde no prevailing wind, I believe, comes from any sea nearer than the Atlantic ocean; and there are but few trees to attract to the earth the little moisture that the atmosphere contains. The rain that falls over these countries is not, I believe, equal to more than one-third of what falls over the districts, supplied from the Bay of Bengal, or to one-fourth of what falls in those supplied from the Gulf of Cambay. Our own districts of the N. W. Provinces, which intervene between those north of the Ganges and Rajpootana, have the advantage of rivers and canals; but their atmosphere is not so well supplied with moisture from the sea, nor are they so well studded as they ought to be with trees. The Punjab has still greater advantages from numerous rivers, flowing from the Himmalaya chain, and is, like Egypt, in some measure independent of moisture from the atmosphere as far as tillage is concerned; but both would, no doubt, be benefited by a greater abundance of trees. They not only tend to convey to and retain moisture in the soil, and to purify the air for man, by giving out oxygen and absorbing carbonic acid gas, but they are fertilizing media, through which the atmosphere conveys to the soil most of the carbon, and much of the ammonia, without which no soil can be fertile. It is, I believe, generally admitted that trees derive most of their carbon from the air through their leaves, and most of their ammonia from the soil through their roots; and that when the trees, shrubs, and plants, which form our coal-measures, adorned the surface of the globe, the atmosphere must have contained a greater portion of carbonic acid gas than at present. They decompose the gases, use the carbon, and give back the oxygen to the atmosphere.

December 30, 1849.—Ten miles to Salone, over a pretty country, well studded with fine trees and well tilled, except in large patches of oosur land, which occur on both sides of the road. The soil, doomuteea, with a few short intervals of muteear. The Rajah of Pertabghur, and other great landholders of the Sultanpoor division, who had been for some days travelling with me, and the Nazim and his officers, took leave yesterday. The Nazim, Aga Allee, is a man of great experience in the convenances of court and city life, and of some in revenue management, having long had charge of the estates comprised in the "Hozoor Tehseel," while he resided at Lucknow. He has good sense and an excellent temper, and his manners and deportment are courteous and gentlemanly. The Rajah of Pertabghur is a very stout and fat man, of average understanding. The rightful heir to the principality was Seorutun Sing, whom I have mentioned in my Rambles and Recollections, as a gallant young landholder, fighting for his right to the succession, while I was cantoned at Pertabghur in 1818. He continued to fight, but in vain, as the revenue contractors were too strong for him. Gholam Hoseyn, the then Nazim, kept him down while he lived, and Dursun Sing got him into his power by fraud, and confined him for three years in gaol.

He died soon after his release, leaving one son. Rajah Dheer Sing,* who still lives upon the portion of land which his father inherited. He has taken up the contest for the right bequeathed to him by his father; and his uncle, Golab Sing, the younger brother of Seorutun, a brave, shrewd, and energetic man, has been for some days importuning me for assistance. The nearest relations of the family told me yesterday, that they were coerced by the Government authorities into recognising the adoption of the present Rajah, though it was contrary to all Hindoo law and usage. Hindoos, they said, never marry into the same gote or family, and they never ought to adopt one of the relations of their wives, or a son of a sister, or any descendant in the female line, while there is one of the male line existing. Seoruttun Sing was the next heir in the male line; but the Rajah, having married a young girl in his old age, adopted as his heir to the principality her nearest relative, the present Rajah, who is of a different gote. The desire to keep the land in the same family has given rise to singular laws and usages in all nations in the early stages of civilization, when industry is confined almost exclusively to agriculture, and land is almost the only property valued. Among the people of the Himmalaya hills, as in all Sogdiana, it gave rise to polyandry; and, among the Israelites and Mahommedans, to the marriage of many brothers in succession to the same woman.

* Rajah Deer Sing died in April 1851, leaving a very young son under the guardianship of his uncle, Golab Sing.

The Rajah of Dharoopoor, who resides at Rampoor, our last halting-place, holds, as above stated, a tract of land along the left bank of the Ganges, called the Kalakunkur, in which he has lately built a mud-fort of reputed strength. He is a very sensible and active man of pleasing manners. He has two grown-up sons, who were introduced to me by him yesterday. The Government authorities complain of his want of punctuality in the payment of his revenue; and he complains, with much more justice, of the uncertainty in the rate of the demand on the part of Government and its officers or Court favourites, and in the character of the viceroys sent to rule over them; but, above all, of the impossibility of getting a hearing at Court when they are wronged and oppressed by bad viceroys. He went twice himself to Lucknow, to complain of grievous wrongs suffered by him and his tenants from an oppressive viceroy; but, though he had some good friends at Court, and among them Rajah Bukhtawar Sing, he was obliged to return without finding access to the sovereign or his minister, or any one in authority over the viceroy. He told me that all large landholders, who had any regard for their character, or desire to retain their estates, and protect their tenants, were obliged to arm and take to their strongholds or jungles as their only resource, when bad viceroys were sent—that if they could be assured that fair demands only would be made, and that they would have access to authority, when they required to defend themselves from false charges, and to complain of the wrong doings of viceroys and their agents, none of them would be found in resistance against the Government, since all were anxious to bequeath to their children a good name, as well as a good estate. He promised punctual payment of his revenues to Government, and strict obedience in all things, provided that the contractor did not enhance his demand upon him, as he now seemed disposed to do, in the shape of gratuities to himself and Court favourites. "To be safe in Oude" he said, "it is necessary to be strong, and prepared always to use your strength in resisting outrage and oppression, on the part of the King's officers."

At Salone resides a holy Mahommedan, Shah Puna Ata, who is looked up to with great reverence by both Mahommedans and Hindoos, for the sanctity of his character, and that of his ancestors, who sat upon the same religions throne, for throne his simple mattress is considered to be. From the time that the heir is called to the throne, he never leaves his house, but stays at home to receive homage, and distribute blessings and food to needy travellers of all religions. He gets from the King of Oude twelve villages, rent free, in perpetuity; and they are said to yield him twenty-five thousand rupees a-year, with which he provides for his family, and for needy travellers and pilgrims. This eleemosynary endowment was granted, about sixty years ago, by the then sovereign, Asuf-od Dowlah. The lands had belonged to a family of Kumpureea Rajpoots, who were ousted for contumacy or rebellion, I believe. He was plundered of all he had, to the amount of some twenty thousand rupees, in 1834, during the reign of Nuseer-on Deen Hyder, by Ehsan Hoseyn, the Nazim of Byswara and Salone, one of the sons of Sobhan Allee Khan, the then virtual minister; but some fifteen days after, he attacked the tallookdar of Bhuderee, and lost his place in consequence. The popular belief is, that he became insane in consequence of the holy man's curses, and that his whole family became ruined from the same cause.

Bhuderee, which lies a few miles to the south of Salone, was then held by two gallant Rajpoot brothers, Jugmohun Sing and Bishonath Sing, the sons of Zalim Sing. In the month of October, A.D. 1832, Dhokul Sing got the contract of the district, and demanded from Bhuderee an increase of ten thousand rupees in its revenue. They refused to pay this increase. At the established rate they had always paid the Government demand punctually, and been good subjects and excellent landlords. Dhokul Sing was superseded by Ehsan Hoseyn, in March 1833; and he insisted upon having the increase of ten thousand. They refused to pay, and Ehsan Hoseyn besieged and attacked their fort in September. After defending themselves resolutely for five days, Bishonath Sing consented to visit Ehsan Hoseyn, in his camp, on a solemn assurance of personal security; but he no sooner came to his tent than he was seized and taken to Rae Bareilly, the headquarters, a prisoner, in the suite of the Nazim. He there remained confined, in irons, under charge of a wing of a regiment, commanded by Mozim Khan, till February 1834, when he effected his escape, and went back to Bhuderee. In March, a large force was collected, with an immense train of artillery, to aid the Nazim, and he again laid siege to the fort. Having sent off their families before the siege began, and seeing, in the course of a few days, that they could not long hold out against so large a force, the two brothers buried eight out of their ten guns, left the fort at midnight with the other two, cut their way through the besiegers, and passed over a plain six miles to Ramchora, on the left bank of the Ganges, and within the British territory, followed by the whole of the Nazim's force.

A brisk cannonade was kept up, on both sides, the whole way, and a great many lives were lost The two brothers thought they should be safe at Ramchora, under the protection of the British Government; but the Nazim's force surrounded the place, and kept up a fire upon it. The brothers contrived, however, to send over the Ganges the greater part of their followers, under the protection of their two guns, and the few men retained to defend and serve them. Jugmohun Sing at last consented to accept the pledge of personal security tendered by Rajah Seodeen Sing, the commander-in-chief of the attacking forces; but while he and his brother were on their way to the camp, with a few armed attendants, the soldiers of the Nazim, by whom they were escorted, attempted to seize and disarm them. They resisted and defended themselves. Others came to their rescue, and the firing recommenced. Jugmohun Sing, and his brother, Bishonath Sing and all their remaining followers were killed. The two brothers lost about one hundred and fifty men, and the Nazim about sixty, in killed. The heads of the two brothers were taken off, forthwith, and sent to the King. Three villages in the British territory were plundered by the Oude troops on this occasion. This violation of our territory the King of Oude was called upon to punish; and Ehsan Hoseyn was deprived of his charge, and heavily fined, to pay compensation to our injured subjects.

Roshun-od Dowlah, the minister, was entirely in the hands of Sobhan Allee Khan; and, as long as he retained office, the family suffered no other punishment. When he, Roshun-od Dowlah, was afterwards deprived of office, he went to Cawnpore to reside, and Sobhan Allee and all his family were obliged to follow his fortunes. On his dismissal from office, Roshun-od Dowlah was put into gaol, and not released till he paid twenty-two lacs of rupees into the Treasury. He had given eight lacs, in our Government promissory notes, to his wife, and three to his son, and he took some lacs with him to Cawnpore, all made during the five years he held office. Sobhan Allee Khan, his deputy, was made to pay into the Treasury seven lacs, and five in gratuities—all made during the same five years. Sobhan Allee died last year on a pilgrimage to Mecca, with the character of one of the ablest and least scrupulous of men; and his sons continue to reside at Cawnpore and Allahabad, with the character of having all the bad, without any of the good, qualities of their father. The widow of Jugmohun manages the estate; but she has adopted the nearest heir to her husband, the present Rajah of Bhuderee, a fine, handsome, and amiable youth, of sixteen years of age, who is now learning Persian. He was one of the many chiefs who took leave of me yesterday, and the most prepossessing of all. His adoptive mother, however, absorbs the estates of her weaker neighbours, by fraud, violence, and collusion, like other landholders, and the dispossessed become leaders of gang robbers as in other parts.

The Shah receives something from the local authorities, and contributions from Mahommedan Princes, in remote parts of India, such as Bhopal, Seronge, &c. Altogether his income is said to amount to about fifty thousand rupees a-year. He has letters from Governors-General of India, Lieutenant-Governors of the North-Western Provinces and their Secretaries; and from Residents at the Court of Lucknow, all of a complimentary character. He has lately declared his eldest son to be his heir to the throne, and is said to have already put him upon it. I received from him the usual letter of compliments and welcome, with a present of a tame antelope, and some fruit and sugar; and I wrote him a reply in the usual terms. His name is Shah Puna Ata, and his character is held in high esteem by all classes of the people, of whatever creed, caste, or grade.

The Bhuderee family give their daughters in marriage to the Bugheela Rajahs of Rewa and the Powar Rajahs of Ocheyra, who are considered to be a shade higher in caste than they are among the Rajpoots. Not long ago they gave one hundred thousand rupees, with one daughter, to the only son of the Rewa Rajah, as the only condition on which he would take her. Golab Sing, the brother of Seoruttun Sing, of Pertabghur, by caste a Sombunsee, is said to have given lately fifty thousand rupees, with another daughter, to the same person. Rajah Hunmunt Sing, of Dharoopoor, who is by caste a Beseyn Rajpoot, the year before last went to Rewa, accompanied by some fifty Brahmins, to propose an union between his daughter and the same son of the Rewa Rajah. A large sum was demanded, but he pleaded poverty, and at last got the Rajah to consent to take fifty thousand rupees down, and seventy-five thousand at the last ceremony of the barat, or fetching home of the bride. When all had been prepared for this last ceremony, the Rajah of Rewa pleaded the heat of the weather, and his son would not come to complete it, and take away his bride. Hunmunt Sing collected one hundred resolute Brahmins, and proceeded with them to Rewa, where they sat dhurna at the Rajah's door, without tasting food, and declared that they would all die there unless the marriage were completed.

The Rajah did all he could, or could make his people do, to get rid of them; but at last, afraid that some of the Brahmins would really die, he consented that his son should go and fetch his bride, if Hunmunt Sing would pay down twenty-five thousand rupees more, to defray the cost of the procession, in addition to the seventy-five thousand. He did so, and his daughter was taken off in due form. He has another daughter to dispose of in the same way. The Rewa Rajah has thus taken five or six wives for his son, from families a shade lower in caste; but the whole that he has got with them will not be enough to pay one of the Rajpoot families, a shade higher in caste than he is, in Rajpootana, to take one daughter from him. It costs him ten or twelve lacs of rupees to induce the Rajah of Oudeepoor, Joudhpoor, or Jypoor, to take away, as his bride, a daughter of Rewa. All is a matter of bargain and sale. Those who have money must pay, in proportion to their means, to marry their daughters into families a shade higher in caste or dignity, or to get daughters from them when such families are reduced to the necessity of selling their daughters to families of a lower grade.

Among Brahmins it is the same. Take, for example, the Kunojee Brahmins, among whom there are several shades of caste. The member of a family a shade higher will not give his son in marriage to a daughter of a family a shade lower, without receiving a sum in proportion to its means; nor will he give a daughter in marriage to such a family till he is so exalted as to be able to disregard the feelings of his clan, or reduced to such a degree of poverty as shall seem to his clan sufficient to justify it. This bargain and sale of sons and daughters prevails, more or less, throughout all Hindoo society, and is not, even now, altogether unknown among Christian nations. In Oude, this has led to the stealing of young girls from our own districts. Some men and women from our districts make a trade of it. They pretend to be of Rajpoot caste, and inveigle away girls from their parents, to be united in marriage to Rajpoots in Oude. They pretend to have brought them with the consent of their parents, of the same or higher caste, in our territories, and make large sums by the trade.

December 31, 1849.—Eight miles to Sotee, over a country well studded with trees, and generally well cultivated. The soil is, all the way, doomuteea. The road, the greater part of the way, lies in the purgunnah of Nyn, held by Jugunnath Sing, a Kumpureea Rajpoot, and his nephew, and the collateral branches of their family. They have a belt of jungle, extending for some twelve miles along the right bank of the Saee river, and on the right side of the road, and within from two to six miles from it—in some parts nearer, and in others more remote. Wild hogs, deer, neelgae, and wild cattle abound in this jungle, and do great injury to the crops in its vicinity. The peasantry can kill and eat the hogs and deer, but dare not kill or wound the wild cattle or neelgae. The wild cattle are said to be from a stock which strayed or were let loose in this jungle some centuries ago. They are described as fat, while the crops are on the ground, and well formed—some black, some red, some white, and some mixed—and to be as wild and active as the deer of the same jungle. They are sometimes caught by being driven into the Saee river; but the young ones are said to refuse all food, and die soon, if not released. Hindoos soon release them, from the religious dread that they may die in confinement. The old ones sometimes live, and are considered valuable. They are said to be finer in form than the tame cattle of the country; and from July to March, when grass abounds, and the country around is covered successively with autumn and spring crops, more fat and sleek.

The soil is good and strong, and the jungle which covers it very thick. It is preserved by a family of Kumpureea Rajpoots, whose whole possessions, in 1814, consisted of nine villages. By degrees they have driven out or murdered all the other proprietors, and they now hold no less than one hundred and fifty, for which they pay little or no revenue to Government. The rents are employed in keeping up large bands of armed followers and building strongholds, from which they infest the surrounding country. The family has become divided into five branches, each branch having a fort or stronghold in the Nyn jungle, and becoming by degrees subdivided into smaller branches, who will thrive and become formidable in proportion as the Government becomes weak. Each branch acts independently in its depredations and usurpations from weaker neighbours but all unite when attacked or threatened by the Government.

Rajah Dursun Sing held the district of Salone from 1827 to 1836, and during this time he made several successful attacks upon the Kumpureea Rajpoots of the Nyn jungle; and during his occasional temporary residence he had a great deal of the jungle around his force cut down, but he made no permanent arrangement for subduing them. In 1837, the government of this district was transferred to Kondon Lal Partak, who established a garrison in the centre of the jungle, had much of it cut down, and kept the Kumpureea barons effectually in check. He died in 1838, and Rajahs Dursun Sing and Buktawar Sing again got the government, and continued the partaks system for the next five years, up to 1843. They lost the government for 1844 and 1845, but their successors followed the same system, to keep the Kumpureeas in order. Bukhtawar Sing got the government again for 1846 and 1847, and persevered in this system; but in 1848 the government was made over to Hamid Allee, a weak and inexperienced man. His deputy, Nourouz Allee, withdrew the garrison, and left the jungle to the Kumpureeas, who, in return, assigned to him three or four of their villages, rent free, in perpetuity, which in Oude means as long as the grantee may have the power or influence to be useful to the granters, or to retain the grants. Since that time the Kumpureeas have recovered all the lands they had lost, restored all the jungle that had been cut down, and they are now more powerful than ever. They have strengthened their old forts and built some new, and added greatly to the number of their armed followers, so that the governor of the district dares not do anything to coerce them into the payment of the just demands of Government, or to check their usurpations and outrages.*

* This Nourouz Allee was, 1851, the agent of the Kumpureea barons of this jungle, at the Durbar, where he has made, in the usual way, many influential friends, in collusion with whom he has seized upon many estates in the vicinity of the jungle, and had them made over to these formidable barons.

The present Nazim has with him two Nujeeb Regiments, one of nine hundred and fifty-five, and the other of eight hundred and thirty men; a squadron of horse and fourteen guns. The two corps are virtually commanded by fiddlers and eunuchs at Court. Of the men borne on the muster rolls and paid, not one-half are present; of the number present, not one-half are fit for the duties of soldiers; and of those fit for such duties, not one-half would perform them. They get nominally four rupees a-month, liable to numerous deductions, and they are obliged to provide their own clothing, arms, accoutrements, and ammunition, except on occasions of actual fighting, when they are entitled to powder and ball from the Government officer under whom they are employed. He purchases powder in the bazaars, or has it sent to him from Lucknow; and, in either case, it is not more than one-third of the strength used by our troops. It is made in villages and supplied to contractors, whose only object is to get the article at the cheapest possible rate; and that supplied to the most petted corps is altogether unfit for service.

The arms with which they are expected to provide themselves are a matchlock and sword. They are often ten or twelve months in arrears, and obliged to borrow money for their own subsistence and that of their families, at twenty-four per cent. interest. If they are disabled, they have little chance of ever recovering the arrears of pay due to them; and if they are killed, their families have still less. Even the arms and accoutrements which they have purchased with their own money are commonly seized by the officers of Government, and sold for the benefit of the State. Under all these disadvantages, the Nazim tells me that he thinks it very doubtful whether any of the men of the two corps would fight at all on emergency. The cavalry are still worse off, for they have to subsist their horses, and if any man's horse should be disabled or killed, he would be at once dismissed with just as little chance of recovering the arrears of pay due to him. Of the fourteen guns, two only are in a state fit for service. Bullocks are provided for six out of fourteen, but they are hardly able to stand from want of food, much less to draw heavy guns. I looked at them, and found that they had had no grain for many years, and very little grass or chaff, since none is allowed by Government for their use, and little can be got by forage, or plunder, which is the same thing. One seer and half of grain, or three pounds a-day for each bullock, is allowed and paid for by Government, but the bullocks never get any of it. Of the six best guns, for which he has draft bullocks, the carriage of one went to pieces on the road yesterday, and that of another went to pieces this-morning in my camp, in firing the salute, and both guns now lie useless on the ground. He has one mortar, but only two shells for it; and he has neither powder nor ball for any of the guns. He was obliged to purchase in the bazaar the powder required for the salute for the Resident.

The Nazim tells me, that he has entertained at his own cost two thousand Nujeebs or Seobundies, on the same conditions as those on which the others serve in the two Regiments, on duty under him—that is, they are to get four rupees a-month each, and furnish themselves with food, clothing, a matchlock, sword, accoutrements, and ammunition, except on occasions of actual fighting, when he is to provide them with powder and ball from the bazaar. The minister, he tells me, promised to send him another Nujeeb corps—the Futteh Jung—from Khyrabad; but he has heard so bad an account of its discipline, that he might as well be without it. All the great landholders see the helpless state of the Nazim, and not only withhold from him the just dues of Government, but seize upon and appropriate with impunity the estates of the small proprietors in their neighbourhood.

January 1, 1850.—Fourteen miles to Rae Bareilly, over a plain with more than usual undulation, and the same doomuteea light soil, tolerably cultivated, and well studded with trees of the finest kind. The festoons of the bandha hang gracefully from the branches, with their light green and yellow leaves, and scarlet flowers, in the dark green foliage of the mango and mhowa trees in great abundance. I saw them in no other, but they are sometimes said to be found in the banyan, peepul, and other trees, with large leaves, though not in the tamarind, babul, and other trees, with small leaves. I examined those on the mango and mhowa trees, and they are the same in leaf and flower, and are said to be the same in whatever tree found. Rae Bareilly is in the estate of Shunkurpoor, belonging to

Rana Benee Madho, a large landholder. He resides at Shunkurpoor, ten miles from this, and is strong, and not very scrupulous in the acquisition, by fraud, violence, and collusion, of the lands of the small proprietors in the neighbourhood. I asked Rajah Hunmunt Sing, of Dharoopoor, as he was riding by my side, this morning, whether he was not a man of bad character. He said, "No, by no means; he is a man of great possessions, credit, and influence, and of good repute." "But does he not rob smaller proprietors of their hereditary lands?" "If," replied the Rajah, "you estimate men's character in Oude on this principle, you will find hardly any landholder of any rank with a good one, for they have all been long doing the same thing—all have been augmenting their own estates by absorbing those of smaller proprietors, by what you will call fraud, violence, and collusion, but they are not thought the worse of for this by the Government or its officers." Nothing could be more true. Men who augment their estates in this way, purchase the acquiescence of temporary local officers, either by gratuities, or promises of aid, in putting down other powerful and refractory landholders; or they purchase the patronage of Court favourites, who get their estates transferred to the "Hozoor Tehseel," and their transgressions overlooked. Those who augment their resources in this way, employ them in maintaining armed bands, building forts, and purchasing cannon, to secure themselves in the possession, and to resist the Government and its officers, who might otherwise make them pay in some proportion to their usurpations.

Benee Madho called upon me after breakfast, and gave me the little of his history that I desired to hear. He is of the Byans Rajpoot clan, and his ancestors have been settled in Oude for about twenty-five generations, as landholders of different grades. The tallook or estate now belongs to him, and is considered to be a principality, to descend entire by the law of primogeniture, to the nearest male heir, unless the lands become divided during his life-time among his sons. Such a division has already taken place, as will be seen by the annexed note :*

* Abdool-Sing, the tallookdar of Shunkurpoor, had three sons; first, Doorga Buksh, to whom he gave three shares; second, Chundha Buksh, to whom he gave two shares; third, Bhowanee Buksh, to whom he gave one and half share. The three shares of Doorga Buksh descended to his son, Sheopersaud, who died without issue. Chunda Buksh left two sons, Ramnaraen and Gor Buksh, Ramnaraen inherited the three shares of Sheopersaud, as well as the two shares of his father. He had three sons, Rana Benee Madho, Nirput Sing, and Jogray Sing; Benee Madho inherited the three shares, and one of the other two was given to Nirput Sing, and the other to Jogray Sing. Gorbuksh Sing left one son, Sheopersaud, who gets the one and half share of Bhowanee Buksh, whose son, Joorawun, died without issue. Benee Madho is now the head of the family; and he has more than quadrupled his three shares by absorptions, made in the way above mentioned.

The three and half shares held by his brothers and cousins are liable to subdivision by the Hindoo law of inheritance, or the custom of his family and clan; but his own share must descend undivided, unless he divides it during his lifetime, or his heirs divide it during theirs, and consent to descend in the scale of landholders. He says that, during the five years that Fakeer Mahommed Khan was Nazim, a quarrel subsisted between him and the tallookdar of Khujoor Gow, Rugonath Sing, his neighbour; that Sahib Rae, the deputy of Fakeer Mahommed, who was himself no man of business, adopted the cause of his enemy, and persuaded his master to attack and rob him of all he had, turn him out of his estate, and make it over to Rugonath Sing. He went to Lucknow for redress, and remained there urging his claims for fourteen months, when he got an order from the minister, Ameen-od Dowlah, for the estate being restored to him and transferred to the Hozoor Tehseel. He recovered his possessions, and the transfer was made; and he has ever since lived in peace. He might have added that he has been, at the same time, diligently employed in usurping the possessions of his weaker neighbours.*

* Benee Madho and Rugonath Sing have since quarrelled about the title of Rana. Benee Madho assumed the title, and Rugonath wished to do the same, but Benee Madho thought this would derogate from his dignity. They had some fighting, but Rugonath at last gave in, and Benee Madho purchased, from the Court a recognition of his exclusive right to the title, which is a new one in Oude. They had each a force of five thousand brave men, besides numerous auxiliaries.

On our road, two miles from Rae Bareilly, we passed over a bridge on the Saee river, built by Reotee Ram, the deputy of the celebrated eunuch, Almas Allee Khan, some sixty or seventy years ago. He at the same time planted an avenue of fine trees from Salone to Rae Bareilly, twenty miles; and from Rae Bareilly to Dalamow, on the Ganges, south, a distance of fourteen miles more. Many of the trees are still standing and very fine; but the greater part have been cut down during the contests that have taken place between the Government officers and the landholders, or between the landholders themselves. The troops in attendance upon local government authorities have, perhaps, been the greatest enemies to this avenue, for they spare nothing of value, either in exchange or esteem, that they have the power to take. The Government and its officers feel no interest in such things, and the family of the planter has no longer the means to protect the trees or repair the works.

Rae Bareilly is the head-quarters of the local authorities in the Byswara district, and is considered to be one of the most healthy places in Oude. It is near the bank of the small river Saee, in a fine, open plain of light soil, and must be dry at all seasons, as the drainage is good; and there are no jheels or jungles near. It would be an excellent cantonment for a large force, and position for large civil establishments. The town is a melancholy ruin, and the people tell me that whatever landholder in the district quarrels with the local authorities is sure, as his first enterprise, to sack Rae Bareilly, as there is no danger in doing it. The inhabitants live so far from each other, and are separated by such heaps of ruins and deep water-courses, that they can make no resistance. The high walls and buildings, all of burnt brick, erected in the time of Shahjehan, are all gone to ruin. The plain, around the town, is open, level, well cultivated, and beautifully studded with trees. There is a fine tank of puckah masonry to the north-west of the town, built by the same Reotee Ram, and repaired by some member of his family, who holds and keeps in good order the pretty garden around it. The best place for a cantonment, courts, &c., is the plain which separates the town from the river Saee to the south-east: they should extend along from the town to the bridge over the Saee river. The water of this river is said to be excellent, though not quite equal to that of the Ganges. There is good water in most of the wells, but in some it is said to be brackish. The bridge requires repair.

January 2, 1850.—We halted at Rae Bareilly, and I inspected the bullocks belonging to the guns of Sobha Sing's regiment and some guns belonging to the Nazim. The bullocks have been starved, are hardly able to walk, and quite unfit for any work. Some of the carriages of the guns are broken down, and those that are still entire are so rotten that they could not bear a march. This regiment of Sobha Sing's was as good as any of those commanded by Captains Magness, Bunbury, and Barlow, while commanded by the late Captain Buckley;* and the native officers and sipahees trained under him are all still excellent, but they are not well provided. Like the others, this regiment was to have had guns permanently attached to it, but the want of Court influence has prevented this. They now have them only when sent on service from one or other of the batteries at Lucknow, and the consequence is that they are good for nothing. Sobha Sing is at Court, in attendance on the minister; and his adjutant, Bhopaul Sing, a near relative of the Rajah of Mynpooree, commands: he seems to be a good soldier, and an honest and respectable man.

* Captain Buckley was the son of Colonel Buckley, of the Honourable Company's service, a good soldier and faithful servant of the Oude Government. His mother, widow, and son, were left destitute; but on my earnest recommendation, the King granted the lad a pension of fifty rupees a-month.

The Nazim has with him this one Komukee, or auxiliary regiment, and half of three regiments of Nujeebs, amounting, according to the pay abstracts and muster-rolls, to fifteen hundred men. He has one hundred cavalry and seven guns, of which one only is fit for use, and for that one he has neither stores nor ammunition. He was obliged to purchase in the bazaar the powder and cloth required to make up the cartridges for a salute for the Resident. Of the fifteen hundred Nujeebs not two-thirds are present, and of these hardly one-half are efficient: they are paid, armed, clothed, and provided like the corps of Nujeebs placed under the other local officers. The tallookdars of the districts have not as yet presented themselves to the Nazim, but they have sent their agents, and, with few exceptions, shown a disposition to pay their revenues. The chief landholder in the district is Rambuksh, of Dondeea Kherah, a town, with a fort, on the bank of the river Ganges. He holds five of the purgunnahs as hereditary possessions:—1, Bhugwuntnuggur; 2, Dondeea Kherah; 3, Mugraen; 4, Punheen; 5, Ghutumpoor. The present Nazim has put all five under the management of Government officers, as the only safe way to get the revenues, as Rambuksh is a bad paymaster. Had he not been so, as well to his own retainer as to the King's officers, the Nazim would not have been able to do this. It is remarked as a singular fact among Rajpoot landholders that Rambuksh wants courage himself, and is too niggardly to induce others to fight for him with spirit. The last Nazim, Hamid Allee, a weak and inexperienced man, dared not venture upon such a measure to enforce payment of balances.*

* Rambuksh recovered the management of his estate, and had it transferred to the Hozoor Tehseel: but he failed in the payment of the expected gratuities; and in April, 1851, he was attacked by a large force, and driven across the Ganges, into British territory. He had gone off on the pretence of a visit to some shrine, and his followers would not fight. The fort was destroyed, and estate confiscated. He is still, January, 1851, negotiating for the purchase of both, and will succeed, as he has plenty of money at command. The King's troops employed committed all manner of atrocities upon the poor peasantry: many men were murdered, many women threw themselves down in wells, after they had been dishonoured; and all were indiscriminately plundered.

He married the daughter of Fuzl Allee, the prime minister for fifteen months, during which time he made a fortune of some thirty or thirty-five lacs of rupees, twelve of which Hamid Allee's wife got. He was persuaded by Gholam Allee, his deputy, and others, that he might aspire to be prime minister at Lucknow if he took a few districts in farm, to establish his character and influence. In the farm of these districts he has sunk his own fortune and that of his wife, and is still held to be a defaulter to the amount of some eighteen lacs, and is now in gaol. This balance he will wipe off in time in the usual manner: he will beg and borrow to pay a small sum to the Treasury, and four times the amount in gratuities to the minister, and other persons, male and female, of influence at Court. The rest will be struck off as irrecoverable, and he will be released. He was a man respected at Delhi, as well on account of his good character as on that of his wealth; but he is here only pitied as an ambitious fool.

The wakeel, on the part of the King, with the Resident, has been uniting his efforts to those of Hoseyn Buksh,* the present Nazim of Salone, to prevail upon Rajah Hunmunt Sing, the tallookdar of Dharoopoor, to consent to pay an addition of ten or fifteen thousand rupees to the present demand of one hundred and sixteen thousand rupees a-year for his estate. He sturdily refused, under the assurance of the good offices of Rajah Bukhtawar Sing, who has hitherto supported him. Among other things urged by him to account for his inability to pay is the obligation he is under to liquidate, by annual instalments, a balance due to Bukhtawar Sing; himself, when he held the contract of the district many years ago. Bukhtawar Sing acknowledges the receipt of the instalments, and declares that they are justly due; but these payments are, in reality, nothing more than gratuities, paid for his continued good offices with the minister and Dewan.

*   Hoseyn Buksh was killed in March following, by the followers of a female landholder, whom he was trying to coerce into payment. He was killed by a cannon shot through the chest, while engaged in the siege of Shahmow, held by Golab Kour, the widow of Rajah Dirguj Sing, who had succeeded to the estate, and would not or could not pay her revenue.

A few days before, Hoseyn Buksh attached the crops of another tallookdar, Seodut Sing, of Dhunawan, who would pay no revenue. A body of the King's cavalry was sent to guard the crops, but the tallookdar drove them off, and killed one and wounded another. Hoseyn Buksh then sent a regiment, the Futtehaesh, a corps of his own Seobundies, and six guns, to coerce the tallookdar. Two guns were mounted on one battery, under the Futtehaesh regiment, and four on another, under the Seobundies. A crowd of armed peasants attacked the battery with the two guns, drove back the regiment, captured the guns, and fired upon the soldiers as they fled. They then attacked the battery with the four guns, and the Seobundies fled, taking their guns with them for four miles. In their flight they had three men killed, and twelve wounded. Hoseyn Buksh, on hearing this, sent his whole force, under his brother, Allee Buksh, to avenge the insult. Seodut, thinking he could not prudently hold out any longer, evacuated his fort during the night, and retired, and Hoseyn Buksh took possession of the fort, and recovered his two guns. His successor restored both Seodut and the widow, Golab Kour, to their estates, on their own terms, after trying in vain to arrest them.]

While Dursun Sing, and his brother, Bukhtawar, held the contract of Salone, the estate was put under management, and yielded one hundred and seventy-four thousand rupees a-year, out of which they allowed a deduction, on account of nankar, or subsistence, of some twenty thousand. The Rajah and Bukhtawar Sing urge that this was, for the most part, paid out of the property left by Byree Saul, to whom Himmut Sing succeeded; and that the estate can now be made to yield only one hundred and sixteen thousand, from which is to be deducted a nankar of forty thousand. They offer him a deduction of this forty thousand, out of a rent-roll rated at one hundred and thirty thousand; and threaten him with the vengeance of his Majesty if he refuses. He looks at their military force and smiles. The agents of all the tallookdars, who are in attendance on the Nazim, do the same. They know that they are strong, and see that the Government is weak, and they cease to respect its rights and orders.

They see at the same time that the Government and its officers regard less the rights than the strength of the landholders; and, from fear, favour the strong while they oppress and crush the weak.*

* Rajah Hunmunt Sing afterwards brought the contractor to consent to take the same rate as had been paid to his predecessor; but he was obliged to pay above six thousand rupees in gratuities.

January 3, 1850.—Gorbuksh Gunge, alias Onae, fourteen miles. The soil of the country over which we came is chiefly a light doomuteea; but there is a good deal of what they call bhoor, or soil in which sand superabounds. The greater part belongs to the estate of Benee Madho, and is admirably cultivated, and covered with a great variety of crops. The country is better peopled than any other part that we have seen since we recrossed the Goomtee. We passed through several villages, the people of which seemed very happy. But their habitations had the same wretched appearance—naked mud walls, with invisible mud coverings. The people told me that they could not venture to use thatched or tiled roofs, for the King's troops, on duty with the local authorities, always took them away, when they had any. They were, they said, well secured from all other enemies by their landlord. Bhopaul Sing, acting commandant of Sobha Sing's Regiment, riding with me, said,-"Nothing can be more true than what the people tell you, sir; but the Koomukee Regiments, of which mine is one, have tents provided for them, which none of the Nujeeb and other corps have, and in consequence, these corps never take the choppers of the peasantry for their accommodations. The peasantry, however, always suffer more or less even from the Koomukee corps, sir, for they have to forage for straw, wood, fuel, bhoosa, &c., like the rest, and to take it wherever they can find it. When we have occasion to attack, or lay siege to a stronghold, all the roofs, doors, and windows of the people are, of course, taken to form scaling-ladders, batteries, &c.; and it is lamentable, sir, to see the desolation created around, after even a very short siege."

Rajah Hunmunt Sing and Benee Madho were riding with me, and when we had passed through a large crowd of seemingly happy peasantry in one village, I asked Benee Madho (whose tenants they were), whether they would all have to follow his fortunes if he happened to take up arms against the Government.

"Assuredly," said he, "they would all be bound in honour to follow me, or to desert their lands at least."

"And if they did not, I suppose you would deem it a point of honour to plunder them?"

"That he assuredly would," said Rajah Hunmunt Sing; "and make them the first victims."

"And if any of them fell fighting on his side, would he think it a point of honour to-provide for their families?"

"That we all do," said he; "they are always provided for, and taken the greatest possible care of."

"And if any one is killed in fighting for the King?"

They did not reply to this question, but the adjutant, Bhopaul Sing, said,—"his family would be left to shift for themselves,—no one asks a question about them."

"This," observed Rajah Bukhtawar Sing, "is one of the great sources of the evil that exists in Oude. How can men be expected to expose their lives when they know that no care will be taken of their families if they are killed or disabled?"

It is the rule to give a disabled man one month's pay and dismiss him; and to give the family of any one killed in the service two months' pay. But, though the King is charged for this, it is seldom that the wounded man, or the family of the killed, get any portion of it. On the contrary, the arrears of pay due-which are at all times great—are never paid to the disabled sipahee, or the family of the sipahee killed. If issued from the Treasury, they are appropriated by the commandants and their friends at Court; and the arms and accoutrements, which the deceased has purchased with his own money, are commonly sold for the benefit of the State or its officers.

They mentioned, that the family of the person who planted a mango-tree, or grove, continued to hold it as their exclusive property in perpetuity; but, that the person who held the mhowa trees, was commonly expected to pay to the landlord, where there was one, and to the Government officers, where there was not, a duty amounting to from four annas to two rupees a-year for each tree, according to its fruitfulness—that the proprietor often sold the fruit of one tree for twenty rupees the season. The fruit of one mango-tree has, indeed, often been sold for a hundred rupees the season, where the mangoes are of a quality much esteemed, and numerous. The groves and fine solitary trees, on the lands we have to-day passed through, are more numerous than usual; and the country being undulating and well cultivated, the scenery is beautiful; but, as everywhere else, it is devoid of all architectural beauty in works of ornament or utility—not even a comfortable habitation is anywhere to be seen. The great landholders live at a distance from the road, and in forts or strongholds. These are generally surrounded by fences of living bamboos, which are carefully kept up as the best possible defence against attacks. The forts are all of mud, and when the walls are exposed to view they look ugly. The houses of the peasants in the villages are, for the most part, covered with mud, from which the water is carried off, by tubes of wood or baked clay, about two feet long. There are parapets around the roof a foot or two high, so that it cannot be seen, and a village appears to be a mass of dead mud walls, which have been robbed of their thatched or tiled roofs. Most of the tubes used for carrying off the water from the roofs, are the simple branches of the palm-tree, without their leaves.

Among the peasantry we saw a great many sipahees, from our Native Infantry Regiments, who have come home on furlough to their families. From the estate of Rajah Hunmunt Sing, in the Banoda district, there are one thousand sipahees in our service. From that of Benee Madho, in the Byswara district, there are still more. They told us that they and their families were very happy, and they seemed to be so; but Hunmunt Sing said, they were a privileged class, who gave much trouble and annoyance, and were often the terror of their non-privileged neighbours and co-sharers in the land. Benee Madho, as I have stated above, sometimes makes use of his wealth, power, and influence, to rob his weaker neighbours of their estates. The lands on which we are encamped he got two years ago from their proprietor, Futteh Bahader, by foreclosing a mortgage, in which he and others had involved him. The gunge or bazaar, close to our tents, was established by Gorbuksh, the uncle of Futteh Bahader, and became a thriving emporium under his fostering care; but it has gone to utter ruin under his nephew, and heir, and the mortgagee. The lands around, however, could never have been better cultivated than they are; nor the cultivators better protected or encouraged. It rained slightly before sunset yesterday, and heavily between three and four this morning; but not so as to prevent our marching.

This morning, a male elephant belonging to Benee Madho killed one of his attendants near to our camp. He had three attendants, the driver and two subordinates. The driver remained in camp, while the two attendants took the elephant to a field of sugar-cane, to bring home a supply of the cane for his fodder for the day. A third subordinate had gone on to cut the cane and bind it into bundles. One of the two was on the neck of the elephant, and another walking by the side, holding one of the elephant's teeth in his left hand all the way to the field, and he seemed very quiet. The third attendant brought the bundles, and the second handed them up to the first on the back to be stowed away. When they had got up about a dozen, the elephant made a rush at the third attendant, who was bringing the bundles, threw him to the ground with his foot, knelt down upon him, and crushed him to death with his front. The second attendant ran off as soon as he saw the elephant make a rush at the third; and the first fell off under the bundles of sugar-cane, as soon as the elephant knelt down to crush the third to death. When the elephant rose from the poor man, he did not molest, or manifest any wish to molest either of the other two, but stood still, watching the dead body. The first, seeing this, ventured to walk up to him, to take him by the ear and ask him what he meant. At first he seemed surly, and shoved the man off, and he became alarmed, and retired a few paces; but seeing the elephant show no further signs of anger, he again walked up, and took him by the ear familiarly. Had he ran or shown any signs of fear, the elephant would, he thought, have killed him also, for he had killed three men in the service of his former proprietor, and was now in his annual fit of madness, or must. Holding the elephant by the ear, he led him to the first tree, and placed himself on the opposite side to see whether the animal had become quite sober. Seeing that he had, he again approached, and put upon his two forelegs the chain fetters, which they always have with them, suspended to some part of the body of elephants in this state. He could not venture to command the elephant to kneel down in the usual way, that he might get upon his neck; and, ascending the tree, he let himself down from one of the branches upon his back, where he sat. He then made the animal walk on in fetters, towards camp, and on the way, met the mahout, or driver, to whom the second attendant had reported the accident. The driver came up, and, after the usual volume of abuse on the elephant, his mother, father, and sundry female relations, he ordered the attendant to make him sit down that he might get on his neck. He did so in fear and trembling, and the driver got on his neck, while the attendant sat on his back, and the elephant took them to Benee Madho's village, close to my camp, where he was fastened in chains to a tree, to remain for some months on reduced allowances, till he should get over his madness. The body of the poor man was burnt with the usual ceremonies, and the first attendant told me, that his family would be provided for by Benee Madho, as a matter of course.

I asked him how he or any other person could be found to attend a beast of that kind? Pointing to his stomach, he said—"We poor people are obliged to risk our lives for this, in all manner of ways; to attend elephants has been always my profession, and there is no other open to me; and we make up our minds to do whatever our duties require from us, and trust to Providence." He told me that when the elephant shoved him off, he thought that in his anger he might have forgotten him, and called out as loud as he could,—"What, have you forgotten a service of six years, and do you intend to kill the man who has fed you so long?" That the beast seemed to recollect his voice and services, and became, at once, quiet and docile—"that had he not so called out, and reminded the animal of his long services, he thought he should have been killed; that the driver came, armed with a spear, and showed himself more angry than afraid, as the safest plan in such cases."

Dangerous as the calling of the elephant-driver is, that of the snake-keepers, in the King's service, seems still greater. He has two or three very expert men of this kind, whose duty it is to bring him the snakes, when disposed to look at them, and see the effects of their poison on animals. They handle the most venomous, with apparently as much carelessness as other men handle fighting-cocks or quail. When bitten, as they sometimes are, they instantly cut into the part, and suck out the poison, or get their companions to suck it out when they can't reach the part with their own mouths. But they depend chiefly upon their wonderful dexterity in warding off the stoops or blows of the snakes, as they twist them round their necks and limbs with seeming carelessness. While they are doing so, the eye of the spectator can hardly detect the stoops of the one and the guards of the other. After playing in this way with the most venomous snakes, they apply them to the animals. Elephants have died from their bites in a few hours—smaller animals sooner. I have never, myself, seen the experiments, but any one may see them at the palace. Elephants and the larger animals are too expensive to be often experimented on.

January 4, 1850.—Halted at the village of Onae, alias Gorbuksh Gunge. It lost the name of Onae, after the proprietor, Gorbuksh, who had built the Gunge, and made it a great emporium of trade in corn, cotton cloth, &c.; but is recovering it again, now that the Gunge has become a ruin, and the family of the builder has been dispossessed of the lands. I rode out in the morning to look at the neighbouring village of Doolarae-ka Gurhee, or the fort of Doolarae, and have some talk with the peasantry, who are Bys Rajpoots, of one of the most ancient Rajpoot families in Oude. They told me,—"That their tribe was composed of two great families, Nyhussas and Synbunsies—that the acknowledged head of the Synbunsies was, at present, Rugonath Sing, of Kojurgow, and that Hindpaul, tallookdar of Korree Sudowlee, was the head of the Nyhussas; that Baboo Rambuksh, tallookdar of Dhondeea Kheera, had the title of Row, and Dirg Bijee Sing, tallookdar of Morarmow, that of Rajah—that is, he was the acknowledged Rajah of the clan, and Baboo Rambuksh, the Row, an inferior grade—that these families had been always fighting with each other, for the possession of each others lands, from the time their ancestors came into Oude, a thousand years ago, except when they were united in resistance against the common enemy, the governor or ruler of the country—that one family got weak by the subdivision of the lands, among many sons or brothers, or by extravagance, or misfortune, while another became powerful, by keeping the lands undivided, and by parsimony and prudence; and the strong increased their possessions by seizing upon the lands of the weak, by violence, fraud or collusion with the local authorities—that the same thing had been going on among them for a thousand years, with some brief intervals, during which the rulers of Oude managed, by oppression, to unite them all against themselves, or by prudence, to keep them all to their respective rights and duties—that Doolarae, who gave his name to the village, by building the fort, was of the Nyhussa family, and left two sons, and only two villages, Gurhee and Agoree, out of a very large estate, the rest having been lost in the contests with the other families of the tribe—that these two had become minutely subdivided among their descendants: and Bhugwan Das, Synbunsee of Simree, four years ago, seized upon the Gurhee, in collusion with the local authorities; that Thakoor Buksh Nyhussa, talookdar of Rahwa seized upon Agoree in the same way that the local authorities designedly assessed these villages at a higher rate than they could be made to pay, and then, for a bribe, transferred them to the powerful tallookdars, on account of default."

Gorbuksh Sing, Synbunsee, died some twenty years ago, leaving an estate, reduced from a greater number to ninety-three villages. His nephew, Futteh Bahader, a child, was adopted by his widow, who continued to manage the whole till she died, four years after. The heir was still a boy; and Rugonath Sing, of Kojurgow, the head of the Synbunsee family, took advantage of his youth, seized upon the whole ninety-three villages, and turned him out to beg subsistence among his relatives. In this he, Rugonath Sing, was, as usual, acting in collusion with the local authorities of the Government. He continued to possess the estate for ten years, but to reside in his fort of Hajeepoor. Koelee Sing, a Guhlote, by caste, and a zumeendar of Bheeturgow, and its eight dependent villages, which formed part of the estate of Futteh Bahader, went to Court at Lucknow, and represented, that Rugonath Sing had no right whatever to the lands he held, and the Court had better make them over to him and the other zumeendars, if they did not like to restore them to their rightful heir. Bheeturgow and its dependent eight villages, were made over to him; and ten sipahees, from Captain Hyder Hearsey's Regiment, were sent to establish and support him in possession. Rugonath attacked them, killed two of the sipahees, and drove out Koelee Sing. He repaired to Court; and Mahomed Khan was sent out, as Special Commissioner, with orders to punish Rugonath Sing. He and Captain Hearsey attacked him in his fort of Hajeepoor, drove him out, and restored Futteh Bahader, to twenty-four villages; and re-established Koelee Sing, in Bheeturgow, and the eight villages dependent upon it. Futteh Bahader was poor, and was obliged to tender the security of Benee Madho, the wealthy tallookdar of this place, for the punctual payment of the revenue. The year before last, when a balance of revenue became due, he, the deputy, in collusion with Gholam Allee, seized upon all the twenty-four villages.

Futteh Bahader went to seek redress at Lucknow, but had no money to pay his way at Court, while Benee Madho had abundance, and used it freely, to secure the possession of so fine an addition to his estate. Futteh Bahader, as his last resource, got his uncle, Bustee Sing, of the 3rd Cavalry, whom he called his father,* to present a petition for redress to the Resident, in April 1849. Gholam Allee was ordered to release Futteh Bahader, whom Benee Madho had confined, and send him to Lucknow. The order was not obeyed, and it was repeated in December without effect; but his uncle's agent, Gorbuksh, was diligent at the Residency, and the case was made over for investigation and decision to the Ameen, Mahomed Hyat. Finding Futteh Bahader still in confinement, with sundry members of his family, when I came here yesterday, I ordered him to be made over to the King's wakeel, in attendance upon me, to be sent to the Court, to prosecute his claim, and produce proofs of his right. Of his right there can be no question, and the property of which he was robbed, in taking possession, and the rents since received, if duly accounted for, would more than cover any balance due by Futteh Bahader. When he gave the security of Benee Madho, for the payment of the revenue, he gave, at the same time, what is called the Jumog of his villages to him; that is, bound his tenants to pay to him their rents at the rate they were pledged to pay to him; and the question pending is, simply, what is fairly due to Benee Madho, over and above what he may have collected from them. Benee Madho had before, by the usual process of violence, fraud, and collusion, taken eighteen of the ninety-three villages, and got one for a servant; and all the rest had, by the same process, got into the possession of others; and Futteh Bahader had not an acre left when his uncle interposed his good offices with the Resident.** The dogs of the village of Doolarae-kee Gurhee followed us towards camp, and were troublesome to the horses and my elephant. I asked the principal zumeendar why they were kept. He said they amused the children of the village, who took them out after the hares, and by their aid and that of the sticks with which they armed themselves, they got a good many; that all they got for food was the last mouthful of every man's dinner, which no man was sordid enough to grudge them—that when they wished to describe a very sordid man, they said—"he would not even throw his last mouthful (koura) to a dog!"

* He called Bustee Sing his father, as sipahees can seek redress through the Resident, for wrongs suffered by no others than their mothers, fathers, their children, and themselves.

** A punchaet was assembled at Lucknow, to decide the suit between Benee Madho and Futteh Bahader, at the instance of the Resident: and they awarded to Benee Madho a balance due on account of thirty thousand rupees, which Futteh Bahader has to pay before he can recover possession of his estate.

January 5, 1851.—Halted at Onae, in consequence of continued rain, which incommodes us, but delights the landholders and cultivators, whose crops will greatly benefit by it. The halting of so large a camp inconveniences them, however, much more than us; for they are called upon to supply us with wood, grass, and straw, for which they receive little or no payment; for the Kings people will not let us pay for these things, and pay too little themselves. Those who attend us do not plunder along the road; but the followers of the local authorities, who attend us, through their respective jurisdictions, do so; and sundry fields of fine carrots and other vegetables disappear, as under a flight of locusts along the road. The camp-followers assist them, and as our train extends from the ground we leave to that to which we are going, for twelve or fourteen miles, it is impossible, altogether, to prevent such injuries from so undisciplined a band. The people, however, say, they suffer much less than they would from one-fourth of the number under a contractor marching without an European superior, and I give compensation in flagrant cases. Captain Weston acts as our Provost Marshal. He leaves the ground an hour or two after I do, and seizes and severely punishes any one found trespassing.

In my ride this morning I found that Nyhussa and Synbunsee are two villages distant about ten miles from our camp, to the south-east—that all the Byses, who give the name of Byswara to this large district, are called Tilokchundees, from Tilokchund, the founder of the family in Oude. He had two sons, Hurhur Deo and Prethee Chund. Hurhur Deo had two sons, one of whom, Kurun Rae, established himself in Nyhussa, and the other, Khem Kurun, in Synbunsee. Their descendants have taken their titles from their respective villages. Prethee Chund's descendants established themselves in other parts, and the descendants of both bear the appellation of Tilokchundee Byses. The Rajahs and Rows are of the same family, and are so called from their ancestors having, at some time, had the title of Rajah and Row conferred upon them.

Rajah Seodursun Sing, of Simrotee, who resides in the village of Chundapoor upon his estate, four miles east of Bulla, has been with me for the last five days. He is a strong man, and has been refractory occasionally; but at present he pays his revenue punctually, and keeps his estate in good order. He rendered good service yesterday in the way in which all of his class might, by good management, be made to aid the government of Oude. A ruffian, by name Mohiboollah, who had been a trooper in the King of Oude's service, contrived to get the lease of the estate of Bulla, which is about twenty miles north-east from our camp; and turning out all the old landholders and cultivators, he there raised a gang of robbers, to plunder his neighbours and travellers. He had been only two months in possession, when he attacked the house of an old invalid subadar-major of the Honourable Company's service, (fifty-seventh Native Infantry,) on the 21st of December, 1849, robbed him of all he had, and confined him and all his family, till he promised, under good security, to pay, within twenty days, a ransom of one thousand two hundred rupees more. He had demanded a good deal more, but hearing that the Resident's camp was approaching, he consented to take this sum four days ago, and released all his prisoners. The subadar presented a petition to me, and, after taking the depositions of the old zumeendars and other witnesses, I requested the king's wakeel, to send off a company of Soubha Sing's Regiment, to arrest him and his gang.

They went off from Rae Bareilly on the night of the 1st instant; but, finding that the subadar-major and his family had been released the day before, and that the village was full of armed men, ready to resist, they returned on the evening of the 2nd. On the 3rd, the whole regiment, with its artillery, and three hundred auxiliaries, under Rajah Seodursun Sing, left my camp, at Onae, at midnight, and before daylight surrounded the village. There were about one hundred and fifty armed men in it; and, after a little bravado, they all surrendered, and were brought to me. Mohiboollah had, however, gone off, on the pretence of collecting his rents, two days before; but his father and brother were among the prisoners. All who were recognised as having been engaged in the robbery, were sent off prisoners to Lucknow, and the rest were disarmed and released.

Among those detained were some notorious robbers, and the gang would soon have become very formidable but for the accident of my passing near. He had got the lease of the estate through the influence of Akber-od Dowlah, one of the Court favourites, for the sole purpose of converting it into a den of robbers; and, the better to secure this object, he had got it transferred from the jurisdiction of the Nazim to the Hozoor Tehseel, over the manager of which the Court favourite had paramount influence. He was to share with his client the fruits of his depredations, and, in return, to secure him impunity for his crimes. Many of his retainers were among the prisoners brought in to me, having been present at the distribution of the large booty acquired from the old subadar, some thirty or forty thousand rupees. The subadar had resided upon the estate of Seodursun Sing; but having, seven years ago complained through the Resident of over-exactions for the small patch of land he held, and got back the grain which had been attacked for the rent, he was obliged to give it up and reside in the hamlet he afterwards occupied near Bulla, whose zumeendars assured him of protection.* He had a large family, and a great deal of property in money and other valuables concealed under ground. Mohiboollah first seized and sent off the subadar, and then had ramrods made red-hot and applied to the bodies of the children till the females gave him all their ornaments, and pointed out to him all the hidden treasures: they were then all taken to Bulla and confined till the subadar had pledged himself to pay the ransom demanded.

* The greater part of this property is understood to have been confided, in trust, to the old subadar, by some other minion of the Court, and the chief object of the gang was to get hold of it; as their patron, Akber-od Dowlah, had become aware that his fellow-minion had intrusted his wealth to the old subadar, after he had taken up his residence near Bulla. The estate was made over, in farm, to Benee Madho, as the best man to cope with Mohiboollah, should he return and form a new gang.

I requested the King to take the estate from this ruffian and restore it to its old proprietors, whose family had held it for several centuries, or bestow it in lease to some other strong and deserving person.

The Tilokchundee Byses take the daughters of other Rajpoots, who are a shade lower in caste, in marriage for their sons, but do not give their daughters in marriage to them in return. They have a singular notion that no snake ever has destroyed or ever can destroy one of the family, and seem to take no precautions against its bite. If bitten by a snake they do not attempt any remedy, nor could Benee Madho recollect any instance of a Tilokchundee Bysee having died from a bite. He tells me that some families in every Rajpoot tribe in Oude destroy their female infants to avoid the cost of marrying them, though the King prohibited infanticide and suttee in the year 1833. That infanticide does still prevail among almost all the Rajpoot tribes in Oude is unquestionable.

January 6, 1850.—Yesterday evening we moved to Omrowa West, [Transcriber's note: this appears to be a misspelling for Morowa West] a distance of twelve miles, over a plain of bad oosur soil, scantily cultivated near the road. To the left and right of the road, at a little distance, there are some fine villages, thickly peopled, and situated in fine and well-cultivated soil. The country is well wooded, except in the worst parts of the soil, where trees do not thrive. We saw a great deal of sugar-cane in the distance and a few pawn-gardens. The population of the villages came to the high road to see us pass; and among them were a great many native officers and sipahees of our Regiments, who are at their homes on furlough, Government having given a very large portion of the native army the indulgence of furlough during the present cold season. They all seemed happy; but, to my discomfort, a vast number take advantage of this furlough and my movements to urge their claims against the Government, its officers, and subjects. Nothing can be more wretched than the appearance of the buildings in which the people of all grades live in these villages—mud walls without any appearance of coverings, and doors and windows worse than I have seen in any other part of India. Better would not be safe against the King's troops, and these would certainly not be safe against a slight storm; a good shower and a smart breeze would level the whole of the villages with the ground in a few hours. "But," said the people, "the mud would remain, and we could soon raise up the houses again without the aid of masons, carpenters, or blacksmiths." It is enough that they are used to them.

Morowa is a large town, well situated and surrounded with groves of the finest trees in great variety; and, to the surprise of the officers with me, they saw a respectable house of burnt brick. It belongs to the most substantial banker and agricultural capitalist in these parts, Chundun Lal. These capitalists and their families are, generally, more safe than others, as their aid is necessary to the Government and its officers, and no less so to the landholders, cultivators, and people of all classes. Their wealth consists in their credit in different parts of India; and he who has most of it may have little at his house to tempt the robber, while the Government officers stand generally too much in daily need of his services and mediation to molest him. A pledge made by these officers to landholders and cultivators, or to these officers by such persons, is seldom considered safe or binding till the respectable banker or capitalist has ratified it by his mediation, to which all refer with confidence.

He understands the characters and means of all, and will not venture to ratify any pledge till he is assured of both the disposition and ability of the party to fulfil it. Chundun Lal is one of the most respectable of this class in Oude. He resides at this place, Morowa, but has a good landed estate in our territories, and banking establishments at Cawnpoor and many other of our large stations. He is a very sensible, well-informed man, but not altogether free from the ailing of his class—a disposition to abuse the confidence of the Government officers; and, in collusion with them, to augment his possessions in land at the cost of his weaker neighbours.

I am told here that the Tilokchund Byses, when bitten by a snake, do sometimes condescend to apply a remedy. They have a vessel full of water suspended above the head of the sufferer, with a small tube at the bottom, from which water is poured gently on the head as long as he can bear it. The vent is then stopped till the patient is equal to bear more; and this is repeated four or five times till the sufferer recovers. I have not yet heard of any one dying under the operation, or from the bite of a snake. I find no one that has ever heard of a member of this family dying of the bite of a snake. One of the Rajahs of this family, who called on me to-day, declared that no member of his family had ever been known to die of such a bite, and he could account for it only "from their being descended from Salbahun, the rival and conqueror of Bickermajeet, of Ojein."

This Salbahun* is said to have been a lineal descendant of the sake-god! He told me that the females of this family could never wear cotton cloth of any colour but plain white; that when they could not afford to wear silk or satin they never wore anything but the piece of white cotton cloth which formed, in one, the waistband, petticoat, and mantle, or robe (the dhootee and loongree), without hemming or needlework of any kind whatever. Those who can afford to wear silk or satin wear the petticoat and robe, or mantle of that material, and of any colour. On their ankles they can wear nothing but silver, and above the ankles, nothing but gold; and if not, nothing, not even silver, except on the feet and ankles. No Hindoo of respectability, however high or wealthy, can wear anything more valuable than silver below the waist. The Tilokchundee Byses can never condescend to hold the plough; and if obliged to serve, they enlist in the army or other public establishments of the Oude or other States.

* Salbahun must have been one of the leaders of the Scythian armies, who conquered India in the reign of Vickramadittea.

The late governor of this district, Hamid Allee Khan, is now, as I have already stated, in prison, as a great defaulter, at Lucknow. He was a weak and inexperienced man, and guided entirely by his deputies, Nourooz Allee and Gholam Allee. Calamities of season and other causes prevented his collecting one-quarter of the revenue which he had engaged in his contract to pay. Gholam Allee persuaded the officers commanding regiments under him to pledge themselves for the personal security of some of the tallookdars whom he invited in to discuss the claims of Government, and their ability to meet them. Four of them came— Hindooput, of Sudowlee, who called on me this morning; Rugonath Sing, of Khojurgow; Rajah Dirg Bijee Sing, of Morarmow; and Bhoop Sing, of Pahor. They were all seized and put into confinement as soon as they appeared, by the officers who had pledged themselves for their personal safety; and Gholam Allee went off to Lucknow to boast of his prowess in seizing them. There he was called upon to pay the balance due, and seeing no disposition to listen to any excuse on the ground of calamity of season, he determined to escape across the Ganges. He wrote to Hamid Allee to suggest that he should do the same, and meet him at Horha, on the bank of the Ganges, on a certain night.

Hamid Allee sent his family across the Ganges, and prepared to meet Gholam Allee at the appointed place; but the commandants of corps, who suspected his intentions, and had not received from him any pay for their regiments for many months, seized him, and sent him a prisoner to Lucknow. Gholam Allee, however, effected his escape across the Ganges, and is now at Delhi. The story of his having run away with three lacs of Hamid Allee's money is represented here as a fiction, as the escape had been concerted between them, and they had sent across the Ganges all that they could send with that view. This may or may not be the real state of the case. Hamid Allee, as I have above stated, married a daughter of Fuzl Allee. Fuzl Allee's aunt, Fyz-on Nissa, had been a great favourite with the Padshad Begum, the wife of the King, Ghazee-od Deen, and adoptive mother of his successor, Nuseer-od Deen Hyder, who ascended the throne in 1827. She had been banished from Oude by Ghazee-od Deen, but on his death she returned secretly to Lucknow; and, in December of that year, her nephew, Fuzl Allee, who had been banished with her, returned also, and on the 31st of that month he was appointed prime minister, in succession to Aga Meer. Hakeem Mehndee had been invited from Futtehghur to fill the office, and had come so far as Cawnpoor, when Fyz-on Nissa carried the day with the Queen Dowager, and he was ordered back. In November, 1828, the King, at his mother's request, gave him the sum of 21,85,722 1 11, the residue of the principal of the pension of Shums-od Dowlah, the King's uncle, who had died. The whole principal amounted to 33,33,333 5 4, but part had been appropriated as a fund to provide for some members of the King's family.

In February, 1829, Fuzl Allee resigned the office of prime minister, and was protected by the Government of India, on the recommendation of the Resident, and saved, from the necessity of refunding to the State any of the wealth (some thirty-five lacs of rupees) which he had acquired during his brief period of office. This was all left to his three daughters and their husbands on his death, which took place soon after. He was succeeded in office by Hakeem Mehndee. Shums-od Dowlah's pension of 16,666 10 6 a-month, was paid out of the interest, at 6 per cent., of the loan of one crore, eight lacs, and fifty thousand rupees, obtained from the sovereign of Oude (Ghazee-od Deen Hyder, who succeeded his father on the 11th of July, 1814,) by Lord Hastings, in October, 1814, for the Nepaul war. All the interest (six lacs and fifty-one thousand) was, in the same manner, distributed in stipends to different members of the family, and the principal has been paid back as the incumbents have died off. Some few still survive.*

* The ground, on the north-west side of Morowa, would be good for a cantonment, as the soil is sandy, and the plain well drained. Water must lie during the rains on all the other sides, and the soil has more clay in it.

January 7, 1850.—To Mirree, twelve miles, over a plain of light doomuteea soil, sufficiently cultivated, and well studded with trees. We passed Runjeet-ka Poorwa half-way—once a large and populous town, but now a small one. The fog was, however, too thick to admit of my seeing it. From this place to Lucknow, thirty miles, Seetlah Buksh, a deputy of Almas Allee Khan's, planted an avenue of the finest kind of trees. We had to pass through a mile of it, and the trees are in the highest perfection, and complete on both sides. I am told that there are, however, many considerable intervals in which they have been destroyed. The trees must have been planted about sixty years ago.

I may here remark that no native gentleman from Lucknow, save such as hold office in districts, and are surrounded by troops, can with safety reside in the country. He would be either suspected and destroyed by the great landholders around him, or suspected and ruined by the Court. Under a better system of government, a great many of these native gentlemen, who enjoy hereditary incomes, under the guarantee of the British Government, would build houses in distant districts, take lands, and reside on them with their families, wholly or occasionally, and Oude [would] soon be covered with handsome gentlemen's seats, at once ornamental and useful. They would tend to give useful employment to the people, and become bonds of union between the governing and the governed. Under such an improved system, our guarantees would be of immense advantage to the whole country of Oude, in diffusing wealth, protection, education, intelligence, good feeling, and useful and ornamental, works. At present, these guarantees are not so. They have concentrated at the capital all who subsist upon them, and surrounded the Sovereign and his Court with an overgrown aristocracy, which tends to alienate him more and more from his people. The people derive no benefit from, and have no feeling or interest in common with, this city aristocracy, which tends more and more to hide their Sovereign from their view, and to render him less and less sensible of his duties and high responsibilities; and what would be a blessing under a good, becomes an evil under a bad system, such as that which has prevailed since those guarantees began.

In this overgrown city there is a perpetual turmoil of processions, illuminations, and festivities. The Sovereign spends all that he can get in them, and has not the slightest wish to perpetuate his name by the construction of any useful or ornamental work beyond its suburbs. All the members of his family and of the city aristocracy follow his example, and spend their means in the same way. Indifferent to the feelings and opinions of the landed aristocracy and people of the country, with whom they have no sympathy, they spend all that they can spare for the public in gratifying the vitiated tastes of the overgrown metropolis. Hardly any work calculated to benefit or gratify the people of the country is formed or thought of by the members of the royal family or aristocracy of Lucknow; and the only one formed by the Sovereign for many years is, I believe, the metalled road leading from Lucknow to Cawnpoor, on the Ganges.

One good these guarantees certainly have effected—they have tended greatly to inspire the people of the city with respect for the British Government, by whom the incomes of so large and influential a portion of the community and their dependents are secured. That respect extends to its public officers and to Europeans generally; and in the most crowded streets of Lucknow they are received with deference, courtesy, and kindness, while in those of Hydrabad, their lives, I believe, are never safe without an escort from the Resident.

The people of the country respect the British Government, its officers, and Europeans generally, from other causes. Though the Resident has not been able to secure any very substantial or permanent reform in the administration, still he has often interposed with effect, in individual cases, to relieve suffering and secure redress for grievous wrongs. The people of the country see that he never interposes, except for such purposes, and their only regret is that he interposes so seldom, and that his efforts, when he does so, should be so often frustrated or disregarded. In the remotest village or jungle in Oude, as in the most crowded streets of the capital, an European gentleman is sure to be treated with affectionate respect; and the humblest European is as sure to receive protection and kindness, unless be forfeits all claim to it by his misconduct.

The more sober-minded Mahommedans of Lucknow and elsewhere are much scandalized at the habit which has grown up among them, in the cities of India, of commemorating every event, whether of sadness or of joy, by brilliant illuminations and splendid processions, to amuse the idle populations of such cities. It is, they say, a reprehensible departure from the spirit of their creed, and from the simple tastes of the early Mahommedans, who laid out their superfluities in the construction of great and durable works of ornament and utility. Certainly no event can be more sorrowful among Mahommedans than that which is commemorated in the mohurrum by illuminations and processions with the Tazeeas; and yet no illuminations are more brilliant, and no processions more noisy, costly, and splendid. It is worthy of remark, that Hindoo princes in Central and Southern India, even of the Brahmin caste, commemorate this event in the same way; and in no part of India are these illuminations and processions more brilliant and costly. Their object is solely to amuse the population of their capitals, and to gratify the Mahommedan women whom they have under their protection, and their children, who must all be Mahommedans.

CHAPTER VI.

Nawabgunge, midway between Cawnpoor and Lucknow—Oosur soils how produced—Visit from the prime minister—Rambuksh, of Dhodeeakhera—Hunmunt Sing, of Dharoopoor—Agricultural capitalists. Sipahees and native offices of our army—Their furlough, and petitions—Requirements of Oude to secure good government. The King's reserved treasury—Charity distributed through the Mojtahid, or chief justice—Infanticide—Loan of elephants, horses, and draft bullocks by Oude to Lord Lake in 1804—Clothing for the troops—The Akbery regiment—Its clothing, &c.,—Trespasses of a great man's camp in Oude—Russoolabad and Sufeepoor districts—Buksh Allee, the dome—Budreenath, the contractor for Sufeepoor—Meeangunge—Division of the Oude Territory in 1801, in equal shares between Oude and the British Governments—Almas Allee Khan—His good government—The passes of Oude—Thieves by hereditary profession, and village watchmen—Rapacity of the King's troops—Total absence of all sympathy between the governing and governed—Measures necessary to render the Oude troops efficient and less mischievous to the people—Sheikh Hushmut Allee, of Sundeela.

January 8, 1850.—Nawabgunge, eleven miles over a plain, the soil of which, near the road, is generally very poor oosur. No fruit or ornamental trees, few shrubs, and very little grass. Here and there, however, even near the road, may be seen a small patch of land, from which a crop of rice has been taken this season; and the country is well cultivated all along, up to within half a mile of the road, on both tides [sides]. Nawabgunge is situated on the new metalled road, fifty miles long, between Lucknow and Cawnpoor, and about midway between the two places.* It was built by the late minister, Nawab Ameen-od Dowlah, while in office, for the accommodation of travellers, and is named after him. It is kept up at his expense for the same purpose now that he has descended to private life. There is a small house for the accommodation of European gentlemen and ladies, as well as a double range of buildings, between which the road passes, for ordinary travellers, and for shopkeepers to supply them.

* The term Gunge, signifies a range of buildings at a place of traffic, for the accommodation of merchants, and all persons engaged in the purchase and sale of goods and for that of their goods and of the shopkeepers who supply them.

Some people told me, that even the worst of this oosur soil might be made to produce fair crops under good tillage; while others denied the possibility, though all were farmers or landholders. All, however, agreed that any but the worst might be made so by good tillage—that is, by flooding the land by means of artificial embankments, for two or three rainy seasons, and then cross-ploughing, manuring, and irrigating it well. All say that the soil hereabouts is liable to become oosur, if left fallow and neglected for a few years. The oosur, certainly, seems to prevail most near the high roads, where the peasantry have been most exposed to the rapacity of the King's troops; and this tends to confirm the notion that tillage is necessary in certain soils to check the tendency of the carbonates or nitrates, or their alkaline bases, to superabundance. The abundance of the chloride of sodium in the soil, from which the superabounding carbonates of soda are formed, seems to indicate, unequivocally, that the bed from which they are brought to the surface by capillary attraction must at some time have been covered by salt water.

The soil of Scind, which was at one time covered by the sea, seems to suffer still more generally from the same superabundance of the carbonates of soda, formed from the chlorides of sodium, and brought to the surface in the same manner. But in Scind the evil is greater and more general from the smaller quantity of rain that falls. Egypt would, no doubt, suffer still more from the same cause, inasmuch as it has still less rain than Scind, but for the annual overflowing of the Nile. The greater part of the deserts which now disfigure the face of the globe in hot climates arise chiefly from the same causes, and they may become covered by tillage and population as man becomes wiser, more social, and more humane.

January 9, 1850.—Halted at Nawabgunge. A vast deal of grain of all sorts has for the last two years passed from Cawnpoor to Lucknow for sale. The usual current of grain is from the northern and eastern districts of Oude towards Cawnpoor; but for these two years it has been from Cawnpoor to these districts. This is owing to two bad seasons in Oude generally, and much oppression in the northern and eastern districts, in particular, and the advantage which the navigation of the Ganges affords to the towns on its banks on such occasions. The metalled road from Cawnpoor to Lucknow is covered almost with carts and vehicles of all kinds. Guards have been established upon it for the protection of travellers, and life and property are now secure upon it, which they had not been for many years up to the latter end of 1849. This road has lately been completed under the superintendence of Lient. G. Sim of the engineers, and cost above two lacs of rupees.

The minister came out with a very large cortège yesterday to see and talk with me, and is to stay here to-day. I met him this morning on his way out to shoot in the lake; and it was amusing to see his enormous train contrasted with my small one. I told him, to the amusement of all around, that an English gentleman would rather get no air or shooting at all than seek them in such a crowd. The minister was last night to have received the Rajahs and other great landholders, who had come to my camp, but they told me this morning that they had some of them waited all night in vain for an audience; that the money demanded by his followers, of various sorts and grades, for such a privilege was much more than they could pay; that to see and talk with a prime minister of Oude was one of the most difficult and expensive of things. Rajah Hunmunt Sing, of Dharoopoor, told me that he feared his only alternative now was a very hard one, either to be utterly ruined by the contractor of Salone, or to take to his jungles and strongholds and fight against his Sovereign.*

> * The Rajah was too formidable to be treated lightly, and the Amil was obliged to give in, and consent to take from him what he had paid to his predecessor; but to effect this, the Rajah was, afterwards obliged to go to Lucknow, and pay largely in gratuities.

Rajah Rambuksh, of Dondhea Kheera, is in the same predicament. He tells me, that a great part of his estate has been taken from him by Chundun Lal, of Morowa, the banker already mentioned, in collusion with the Nazim, Kotab-od Deen, who depends so much on him as the only capitalist in his district; that he is obliged to conciliate him by acquiescing in the spoliation of others; that he has already taken much of his lands by fraud and collusion, and wishes to take the whole in the same way; that this banker now holds lands in the district yielding above two lacs of rupees a-year, can do what he pleases, and is every day aggrandizing himself and family by the ruin of others. There is some truth in what Rambuksh states, though he exaggerates a little the wrong which he himself suffers; and it is lamentable that all power and influence in Oude, of whatever kind or however acquired, should be so sure to be abused, to the prejudice of both sovereign and people. When these great capitalists become landholders, as almost all do, they are apt to do much mischief in the districts where their influence lies, for the Government officers can do little in the collection of the revenue without their aid; and as the collection of revenue is the only part of their duty to which they attach much importance, they are ready to acquiesce in any wrong that they may commit in order to conciliate them. The Nazim of Byswara, Kotab-od Deen, is an old and infirm man, and very much dependent upon Chundun Lal, who, in collusion with him, has certainly deprived many of their hereditary possessions in the usual way in order to aggrandize his own family. He has, at the same time, purchased a great deal of land at auction in the Honourable Company's districts where he has dealings, keeps the greater part of his wealth, and is prepared to locate his family when the danger of retaining any of either in Oude becomes pressing. The risk is always great; but they bind the local authorities, civil and military, by solemn oaths and written pledges, for the security of their own persons and property, and those of their families and clients.

January 10, 1850.—At Nawabgunge, detained by rain, which fell heavily yesterday, with much thunder and lightning, and has continued to fall all night. It is painful and humiliating to pass through this part of Oude, where the families of so many thousands of our sipahees reside, particularly at this time when so large a portion of them are at their homes on furlough. The Punjab war having closed, all the corps engaged in it have this year been sent off to quiet stations in our old provinces, and their places supplied by others which have taken no share in that or any other war of late. As a measure of economy, and with a view to indulge the native officers and sipahees of the corps engaged in that war, Government has this season given a long furlough to all the native army of Bengal. Some three hundred and fifty native officers and sipahees from each regiment are, or are to be, absent on leave this season. This saves to Government a very large sum in the extra allowance which is granted to native officers and sipahees, during their march from one station to another, and in the deductions which are made from the pay and allowances of those who go on furlough. During furlough, subadars receive 52 rupees a-month instead of 67; jemadars 17, instead of 24; havildars 9, instead of 14; naicks 7, instead of 12; and sipahees 5-8, instead of 7.

These native officers and sipahees, with all their gallantry on service and fidelity to their salt, are the most importunate of suitors, and certainly among the most untruthful and unscrupulous in stating the circumstances of their claims, or the grounds of their complaints. They crowd around me morning and evening when I venture outside my tent, and keep me employed all day in reading their petitions. They cannot or will not understand that the Resident is, or ought to be, only the channel through which their claims are sent for adjustment through the Court to the Oude tribunals and local authorities; and that the investigation and decision must, or ought to, rest with them. They expect that he will at once himself investigate and decide their claims, or have them investigated and decided forthwith by the local authorities of the district through which he is passing; and it is in vain to tell them that the "law's delay" is as often and as justly complained of in our own territory as in Oude, whatever may be the state of its uncertainty.

The wrongs of which they complain are of course such as all men of their class in Oude are liable to suffer; but no other men in Oude are so prone to exaggerate the circumstances attending them, to bring forward prominently all that is favourable to their own side, and keep back all that is otherwise, and to conceal the difficulties which must attend the search after the truth, and those still greater which must attend the enforcement of an award when made. Their claims are often upon men who have well-garrisoned forts and large bands of armed followers, who laugh at the King's officers and troops, and could not be coerced into obedience without the aid of a large and well-appointed British force. For the immediate employment of such a force they will not fail to urge the Resident, though they have, to the commanding officer of their company and regiment represented the debtor or offender as a man of no mark, ready to do whatever the Resident or the Oude authorities may be pleased to order. On one occasion no less than thirty lives were lost in attempting to enforce an award in favour of a sipahee of our army.

I have had several visits from my old friend Sheikh Mahboob Allee, the subadar-major, who is mentioned in my Essay on Military Discipline. He is now an invalid pensioner in Oude, and in addition to the lands which his family held before his transfer to the invalids, he has lately acquired possession of a nice village, which he claimed in the usual way through the Resident. He told me that he had possession, but that he found it very difficult to keep cultivators upon it.

"And why is this, my old friend?" I asked. "Cultivators are abundant in Oude, and glad always to till lands on which they are protected and encouraged by moderate rents and a little occasional aid in seed, grain, and stock, and you are now in circumstances to afford them both."

"True, sir," said the old subadar, "but the great refractory landholder, my neighbour, has a large force, and he threatens to bring it down upon me, and my cultivators are afraid that they and their families will all be cut up some dark night if they stay with me."

"But what has your great neighbour to do with your village? Why do you not make friends with him?"

"Make friends with him, sir!" replied the subadar; "the thing is impossible."

"And why, subadar sahib?"

"Sir, it was from him that the village was taken by the orders of the Durbar, through the interposition of the Resident, to be made over to me, and he vows that he will take it back, whatever number of lives it may cost him to do so."

"And how long may he and his family have held it?"

"Only thirty or thirty-five years, sir."

"And neither you nor your family have ever held possession of it for that time?"

"Never, sir; but we always hoped that the favour of the British Government would some day get it for us."

"And in urging your claim to the village, did you ever tell the Resident that you had been so long out of possession?"

"No, sir, we said nothing about time"

"You know, subadar sahib, that in all countries a limit is prescribed in such cases, and at the Residency that limit is six years; and had the Resident known that your claim was of so old a date he would never have interposed in your favour, more especially when his doing so involved the risk of the loss of so many lives, first in obtaining possession for you, and then keeping you in it." Cases of this kind are very numerous.

The estate of Rampoor which we lately passed through belonged to the grandfather of Rajah Hunmunt Sing. His eldest son, Sungram Sing, died without issue, and the estate devolved on his second son, Bhow Sing, the father of Rajah Hunmunt Sing. The third brother separated from the family stock during the life of his father, and got, as his share, Sursae, Kuttra Bulleepoor, and other villages. He had five sons: first, Lokee Sing; second, Dirguj Sing; third, Hul Sing; fourth, Dill Sing; and fifth, Bul Sing, and the estate was, on his death, subdivided among them. Kuttra Bulleepoor devolved on Lokee Sing, the eldest, who died without issue; and the village was subdivided among his four brothers or their descendants. But Davey Buksh, the grandson, by adoption of the second brother, Dirguj Sing, unknown to the others, assigned, in lieu of a debt, the whole village to a Brahmin named Bhyroo Tewaree, who forthwith got it transferred to Hozoor Tehseel, through Matadeen, a havildar of the 5th Troop, 7th-Regiment of Cavalry, who, in an application to the Resident, pretended that the estate was his own. It is now beyond the jurisdiction of the local authorities, who could ascertain the truth; and all the rightful co-sharers have been ever since trying in vain to recover their rights. The Bramin [Brahmin] and the Havildar, with Sookhal a trooper in the same regiment, now divide the profits between them, and laugh at the impotent efforts of the old proprietors to get redress. Gholam Jeelanee, a shopkeeper of Lucknow, seeing the profits derived by sipahees, from the abuse of this privilege, purchased a cavalry uniform—jacket, cap, pantaloon, boots, shoes, and sword—and on the pretence of being an invalid trooper of ours, got the signature of the brigadier commanding the troops in Oude to his numerous petitions, which were sent for adjustment to the Durbar through the Resident. He followed this trade profitably for fifteen years. At last he got possession of a landed estate, to which he had no claim of right. Soon after he sent a petition to say that the dispossessed proprietor had killed four of his relations and turned him out. This led to a more strict inquiry, when all came out. In quoting this case to the Resident, in a letter dated the 16th of June 1836, the

King of Oude observes: "If a person known to thousands in the city of Lucknow is able, for fifteen years, to carry on such a trade successfully, how much more easy must it be for people in the country, not known to any in the city, to carry it on!"

The Resident communicated to the King of Oude the resolution of the Honourable the Court of Directors to relieve him from the payment of the sixteen lacs of rupees a-year for the auxiliary force; and on the 29th of July 1839, he reported to Government the great gratification which his Majesty had manifested and expressed at this opportune relief. But his gratification at this communication was hardly so great as that which he had manifested on the 14th of December 1837, when told by the Resident that the British Government would not insist upon giving to the subjects of Oude who might enlist into that force the privilege of forwarding complaints about their village affairs and disputes, through their military superiors and the Resident; and it appeared to the Resident, "that this one act of liberality and justice on the part of the British Government had done more to reconcile the King of Oude to the late treaty, in which the Oude auxiliary force had originated, than all that he had said to him during the last three months as to the prospective advantages which that treaty would secure to him and his posterity." The King observed: "This kindness on the part of the British Government has relieved my mind from a load of disagreeable thoughts." The prime minister, Hakeem Mehndee, who was present, replied: "All will now go on smoothly. When the men have to complain to their own Government, they will seldom complain without just cause, being aware that a false story will soon be detected by the native local authorities, though it could not be so by European officers at a distance from the villages; and that in all cases of real grievances their claims will soon be fairly and speedily adjusted. If," added he, "the sipahees of this force had been so placed that they could have enlisted their officers on their side in making complaints, while such officers could know nothing whatever of the circumstances beyond what the sipahees themselves told them, false and groundless complaints would have become endless, and the vexations thereby caused to Government and their neighbours would have become intolerable. These troops," said he, "will now be real soldiers; but if the privileges enjoyed by the Honourable Company's sipahees had been conferred upon the seven regiments composing this force, with the relations and pretended relations of the sipahees, it would have converted into corrupt traders in village disputes sixteen or seventeen thousand of the King's subjects, settled in the heart of the country, privileged to make false accusations of all kinds, and believed by the people to be supported in these falsehoods by the British Government." Both the King and the minister requested the Resident earnestly and repeatedly to express to the Governor-General their most sincere thanks for having complied with his Majesty's solicitations on this point.*

* See King of Oude's letter to the Governor-General, dated 5th October, 1837, and Residents letters of the 7th idem and 14th December, 1837.

This privilege which the native officers and sipahees of our native army enjoy of petitioning for redress of grievances, through the Resident, has now been extended to all the regular, irregular, and local corps of the three Presidencies—that is, to all corps paid by the British Government, and to all native officers and sipahees of contingent corps employed in and paid by native States, who were drafted into them from the regular corps of our army up to a certain time; and the number cannot be less than fifty or sixty thousand. But European civil and political functionaries, in our own provinces and other native States, have almost all some men from Oude in their offices or establishments, whose claims and complaints they send for adjustment to the Resident; and it is difficult for him to satisfy them, that he is not bound to take them up in the same manner as he takes up those of the native officers and sipahees of our native army; and he is often induced to yield to their importunity, and thereby to furnish grounds for further applications of the same sort. This privilege is not recognized or named in any treaty, or other engagement with the

Sovereign of Oude; nor does any one now know its origin, for it cannot be found in any document recorded in the Resident's office.

If the Resident happens to be an impatient, overbearing man, he will often frighten the Durbar and its Courts, or local officers, into a hasty decision, by which the rights of others are sacrificed for the native officers and sipahees; and if he be at the same time an unscrupulous man, he will sometimes direct that the sipahee shall be put in possession of what he claims in order to relieve himself from his importunity, or that of his commanding officer, without taking the trouble to inform himself of the grounds on which the claim is founded. Of all such errors there are unhappily too many instances recorded in the Resident's office. This privilege is in the hands of the Resident an instrument of torture, which it is his duty to apply every day to the Oude Durbar. He may put on a screw more or a screw less, according to his temper or his views, or the importunity of officers commanding corps or companies, and native officers and sipahees in person, which never cease to oppress him more or less.

The most numerous class of complaints and the most troublesome is that against the Government of Oude or its officers and landholders, for enhanced demands of rents; and whenever these officers or landholders are made to reduce these demands in favour of the privileged sipahees, they invariably distribute the burthen in an increased rate upon their neighbours.

Officers who have to pass through Oude in their travels or sporting excursions have of late years generally complained that they receive less civility from villages in which our invalid or furlough sipahees are located than from any others; and that if they are anywhere treated with actual disrespect, such sipahees are generally found to be either the perpetrators or instigators. This complaint is not, I fear, altogether unfounded; and may arise from the diminished attachment felt by the sipahees for their European officers in our army, and partly from the privilege of urging their claims through the Resident, enjoyed by native officers and sipahees, now ceasing on their being transferred to the invalid establishment.

But the privilege itself is calculated to create feelings of dissatisfaction with their European officers, among the honest and hard-working part of our native army. Such men petition only when they have just cause; and not one in five of them can obtain what they demand, and believe to be their just right, under an administration like that of Oude, whatever efforts the Resident may make to obtain it for them; and where one is satisfied, four become discontented; while the dishonest and idle portion of their brother soldiers, who have no real wrongs to complain of, and feign them only to get leave of absence, throw all the burthen of their duties upon them. Others again, by fraud and collusion with those whose influence they require to urge their claims, often obtain more than they have any right to; and their unmerited success tends to increase the dissatisfaction felt by the honest, and more scrupulous portion of the native officers and sipahees who have failed to obtain anything.

Government will not do away with the privilege without first ascertaining the views and wishes of the military authorities. They are not favourable to the abolition, for though the honest and hard-working sipahees may say that it is of no use to them, the idle and unscrupulous, who consider it as a lottery in which they may sometimes draw a prize, or a means of getting leave of absence when they are not entitled to it, will tell them that the fidelity of the whole native army depends upon its being maintained and extended. I am of opinion, after much consideration, and a good deal of experience in the political working of the system, that the abolition of the privilege would be of great advantage to the native army; and it would certainly relieve the European officers from much importunity and annoyance which they now suffer from its enforcement. It is not uncommon for a sipahee of a regiment in Bombay to obtain leave of absence for several times over for ten months at a time, on the pretence of having a case pending in Oude. When his leave is about to expire, he presents a petition to the Resident, who obtains for him from the Court an order for the local authorities to settle his claim. This order is sent to the officer commanding his regiment. The man then makes up a piteous story of his having spent the whole ten months in prosecuting his claim in vain, when, in reality, he has been enjoying himself at home, and had no claim whatever to settle. The next year, or the year after, he gets another ten months' leave, for the same purpose, and when it is about to expire, he presents himself to the Resident, and declares that the local authorities have been changed, and the new officers pay no regard to the King's orders. New orders are then got for the new officers, and sent to his regiment, and the same game is played over again.

Native officers and sipahees, in the privilege of presenting petitions through the Resident, are now restricted to their own claims and those of their wives, fathers, mothers, sons, and daughters. They cannot petition through the Resident for the redress of wrongs suffered, or pretended to have been suffered, by any other relations. In consequence, it has become a common custom with them to lend or sell their names to more remote relations, or to persons not related to them at all. The petition is made out in their own name, and the real sufferer or pretended sufferer, who is to prosecute the claim, is named as the mookteear or attorney. A great many bad characters have in this way deprived men of lands which their ancestors had held in undisputed right of property for many generations or centuries; for the Court, to save themselves from the importunity of the Residency, has often given orders for the claimant being put in possession of the lands without due inquiry or any inquiry at all. The sipahees are, in consequence, much dreaded by the people among whom they reside; for there really is no class of men from whom it is more difficult to get the truth in any case. They have no fear of punishment, because all charges against them for fraud, falsehood, or violation of the rules laid down by Government have to be submitted either to a court-martial, composed of native officers, or to the Governor-General. Both involve endless trouble, and it would, I fear, be impossible to get a conviction before a court-martial so composed. No Resident will ever submit to a Governor-

General the scores of flagrant cases that every month come before him; still less will he worry unoffending and suffering people by causing them to be summoned to give evidence before a military court.

In a recent instance (July 1851), a sipahee in a regiment stationed at Lucknow was charged before a court-martial with three abuses of the privilege. He required no less than seventy-four witnesses to be summoned in his defence. The Court had to wait till what could be got out of the seventy-four appeared, and the man became an object of sympathy, because he was kept so long in arrest. He named the first Assistant to the Resident, who has charge of the Sipahee Petition Department, as a witness; and he was not, in consequence, permitted to attend the Court on the part of the Resident, who preferred the charges, though he was never called or examined by the Court on the part of the defence. The naming him, and the summoning of so many witnesses were mere ruses on the part of the sipahee to escape. No person on the part of the Resident was allowed to attend the Court and see that his witnesses were examined; nor had he any means of knowing whether they were or not. He had reason to believe that the most important were not. The sipahee was of course acquitted, as sipahees charged with such abuses of the privilege always will be. This man's regiment was at Lucknow, and near the place where the cause of action arose, his own village, and the Resident's office. How much more difficult would it be to get a conviction against a sipahee whose regiment happens to be many hundred miles off!

The transfer of their lands from the jurisdiction of the local authorities to that of the Hozoor Tehseel is often the cause of much suffering to their copartners and neighbours. Their co-sharers in the land often find much inconvenience from it, and apprehend that, sooner or later, the influence of the sipahee will enable him to add their shares to his own. The village so transferred, being removed from the observation and responsibility of the local authorities, often becomes a safe refuge for the bad characters of the district, who thence depredate upon the country around with impunity. Claims to villages, to which the claimant had really no right whatever, have been successfully prosecuted by or through sipahees, for the sole purpose of having them transferred to the Hozoor Tehseel, and made dens of thieves and highway robbers. The person in charge of the Hozool Tehseel villages has generally a good deal of influence at Court, and this he lends to such claimants, for a consideration, without fear or scruple, as he feels assured that he shall be able to counteract any representations on the part of the local authorities of the evils suffered from the holders and occupants of such villages. He never pretends to be able to watch over or control the conduct of the holders and occupiers of the villages under his charge, situated, as they mostly are, in remote districts. The transfer of such villages can be justified only in districts that are held in contract, and even in them it might be easy to provide effectually for the protection of the holders from over-exactions on the part of the contractors.

This privilege is attended with infinite difficulty and perplexity to the Resident and Government; and is at the same time exceedingly odious to the people and Government of Oude. Officers commanding regiments and companies have much trouble with such petitions. Able to hear only one side of any question, they think that the evils suffered by the sipahees are much greater and more numerous than they really are, and grant leave to enable them to prosecute their claims to redress more often than is necessary. Men who want leave, when they are not otherwise entitled to it, feign wrongs which they never suffered, or greatly exaggerate such as may really have been inflicted on them in order to obtain it; or, as I have stated, lend their names to others and ask leave to prosecute claims with which they have really nothing whatever to do. The sipahees and native officers of our army are little better with than they would be without the privilege; and a great many enlist or remain in the service solely with the view of better prosecuting their claims, and resign or desert as soon as they have effected their purpose, or find that the privilege is no longer necessary. They make a convenience in this way of our service, and are the most useless soldiers in our ranks. I am persuaded that we should have from Oude just as many and as good recruits for our army without as with this privilege.

The regiments of the Gwalior Contingent get just as good recruits from Oude as those of the Line, though they do not enjoy the privilege. I believe that those corps which did not enjoy the privilege till within the last two years got just as good recruits from Oude as they now do, since it has been extended to them. Till 1848 the privilege was limited to the native officers and soldiers of our regular army, and to such as had been drafted from our regular army into local corps up to a certain date; but in July of that year the privilege was extended to all corps, regular and irregular, attached to the Bengal, Madras, and Bombay Presidencies, which are paid by the British Government. The feelings and opinions of the Oude Government had not been consulted in the origin of this privilege, nor were they now consulted in the extension given to it.

Officers commanding regiments and companies complain that the sipahees and native officers never get redress, whatever trouble they take to obtain it for them; and, I believe, they hardly ever hear a sipahee or native officer acknowledge that he has had redress. A sipahee one day came to the first Assistant, Captain Shakespear, clamouring for justice, and declared that not the slightest notice had been taken of his petition by the Oude Government or its local authorities. On being questioned, he admitted that no less than forty persons had been seized and were in prison on his requisition; but he would not admit that this was any proof of the slightest notice having been taken of his complaint. All are worried, and but few benefited by the privilege, and the advantage of it to the army never can counterbalance all the disadvantages. Invalid pensioners do not now enjoy the privilege, but are left to prefer their claims direct to the King's Courts, like others of the King's subjects, on the ground that they cannot—like sipahees still serving—plead distance from their homes; but a large proportion of the sipahees still serving who have, or pretend to have, claims, obtain leave of absence from their regiments to prosecute them in person.

The objection once raised by Lord William Bentinck against our employing troops in support of the Government of Oude against refractory landholders, is equally valid against our advocacy of the claims of sipahees to lands. "If," said his Lordship, "British troops be lent to enforce submission, it seems impossible to avoid becoming parties to the terms of submission and guarantees of their observance afterwards on both sides; in which case we should become mixed up in every detail of the administration." If the sipahee does not pay punctually the assessment upon the lands which he has obtained through the Resident, the Oude Government calls upon the Resident to enforce payment; and if the Oude Government ventures to add a rupee to the rate demanded for the year, or for any one year, the sipahee, through the commandant of his corps, and, perhaps, the Commander-in-Chief and Governor-General, calls upon the Resident to have the rate reduced, or to explain the grounds upon which it has been made; or if the sipahee has a dispute with his numerous co-sharers, the Resident is called upon to settle it. If the King's troops have trespassed, if the crops have suffered from calamities of season or marauders, or the village has been robbed, the sipahee refuses to pay, and demands a remission of the Government demand; and if he does not get it, appeals in the same manner to the Resident. If a sipahee be arrested or detained for defalcation, a demand comes for his immediate release; and if his crops or stock be distrained for balance, or lands attached, the Resident is called upon to ascertain and explain the reason why, and obtain redress. All such distraint is represented as open robbery and pillage.

It is not at all uncommon for a sipahee to obtain leave of absence from his regiment three or four times to enable him to prosecute the same case in person at Lucknow, though he might prosecute it just as well through an attorney. He often enjoys himself at his home while his attorney prosecutes his claim, if he really has any, at Lucknow. The commanding officers of his regiment and company of course believe all he says regarding the pressing necessity for his presence at Lucknow; and few of them know that the cases are derided in the King's Courts, and that the Resident could not possibly decide them himself if he had five times the establishment he has and full powers to do so. If the Resident finds that a sipahee has lent his name to another, and reports his conduct, he makes out a plausible tale, which his commanding officer believes to be true; the Commander-in-Chief is referred to; the case is submitted to the Governor-General, and sometimes to the Court of Directors, and a voluminous correspondence follows, till the Resident grows weary, and the sipahee escapes with impunity. In the mean time, troops of witnesses have been worried to show that the sipahee has no connection whatever with the estate, or thing claimed in his name, or with the family to whom his name was lent. Many a man has, in this way, as above stated, been robbed of an estate which his family had held for many generations; and many a village which had been occupied by an honest and industrious peasantry has been turned into a den of robbers. In flagrant cases of false claims, the Resident may get the attorney, employed by the sipahee in prosecuting it, punished by the Durbar, but he can rarely hope to get the sipahee himself punished.

In a case that occurred shortly before I took charge, a sipahee complained that a tallookdar had removed him, or his friends, from their village by over exactions, demanding two thousand eight hundred rupees a-year instead of eight hundred. An ameen was sent out to the district to settle the affair. Having some influence at Court, he got the sipahee put into possession, at the rate of eight hundred, and obtained from him a pledge to pay to him, the ameen, a large portion of the two thousand profit! The tallookdar, being a powerful man, made the contractor reduce his demand upon his estate, of which the village was a part, in proportion; and the contractor made the Government give him credit for the whole two thousand eight hundred, which the estate was well able to pay, in any other hands, and ought to have paid. The holder continued, I believe, to pay the ameen, who continued to give him the benefit of his influence at Court. Cases of this kind are not uncommon. The Resident is expected by commandants of corps and companies to secure every native officer and sipahee in the possession of his estate at a fixed rate, in perpetuity; and as many of their relations and friends as may contrive to have their claims presented through the Resident in their names. He is expected to adjust all disputes that may arise between them and their co-sharers and neighbours; or between them and their landholders and Government officers; to examine all their complicated accounts of collections and balances, fair payments, and secret gratuities.

Sipahees commonly enter the service under false names, and give false names to their relatives and places of abodes, in order that they may not be traced if they desert; or that the truth may not be discovered if they pretend to be of higher caste than they really are, or otherwise offend. When they find, in the prosecution of their claims through the Resident, that this is discovered, they find an alias for each name, whether of person, place, or thing: the troubles and perplexities which arise from this privilege are endless.

The Court of Directors, in a despatch dated the 4th March, 1840, remarking on a report dated the 29th November, 1838, from the Resident, Colonel Low, relating to abuses arising from the interference of the Resident in respect to complaints preferred by subjects of Oude serving in our army, observes, "that these abuses appear to be even more flagrant than the Court had previously believed them to be, and no time ought to be lost in applying an effectual remedy: cases are not wanting in which complaints and claims, that are utterly groundless, meet with complete success, the officers of the Oude Government finding it less troublesome to comply with the unjust demand than to investigate the case in such a manner as to satisfy the Resident; and the Oude Government, for the purpose of getting rid of importunity, reduces the assessment on the lands of these favoured individuals, making up the loss by increased exactions from their neighbours." The Court orders the immediate abolition of the privilege in the case of invalided and pensioned sipahees, and directs that those still serving in our army be no longer allowed to complain in respect of all their relatives, real or pretended, but only in cases in which they themselves, their parents, wives, or children are actually interested. "All unfounded complaints, and all false allegations made in order to render complaints cognizable, ought to be, when discovered, punishable by our own military authorities, who ought not to be remiss in inflicting such punishment when justly incurred." "Under the restrictions which we have enjoined," continues the Court, "the trial may once more be made whether this privilege is compatible with good government in Oude, and with the rightful authority of the King of Oude and his officers. Should the abuses which have prevailed still continue under the altered system, the whole subject must be again taken into consideration, and the Resident is to be required to submit a report on the operation of the privilege after the expiration of one year."

How the rule with regard to relationship is evaded has been already stated, and among the numerous instances of this evasion that have been discovered every year since this order of the Honourable Court was passed, the offence has never been punished by any military authority in one. The Resident has no hope, nor the sipahee any fear, that such an offence will ever be punished by a court-martial; and the former feels averse to trespass on the time and attention of the Governor-General and the Commander-in-Chief with such references. He hardly ever submits them till the necessity is forced upon him by references made to the Commander-in-Chief, by officers commanding regiments, in behalf of offenders in whose veracity they are disposed to place too much confidence.

In one of the cases quoted by Colonel Low in his letter of the 29th November, 1838, Reotee Barn, a sipahee, claimed a village, which was awarded to him by the Court, without due inquiry, to avoid further importunity. The owner in possession would not give it up. A large force was sent to enforce the award; lives were lost; the real owner was seized and thrown into gaol, and there died. Reotee Ram had no right whatever to the village, and he could not retain possession among such a sturdy peasantry. His commanding officer again appealed to the Commander-in-Chief, and the case was referred to the Governor-General and to the Honourable the Court of Directors, and a voluminous correspondence took place. It was afterwards fully proved, that the sipahee, Reotee Ram, had never had the slightest ground of claim to the village; and had been induced to set up one solely at the instigation of an interested attorney with whom he was to share the profits.

In another case quoted by Colonel Low in that letter, a pay havildar of the 58th Regiment complained, jointly with his brother Cheyda, through the Commander-in-Chief, to the Governor-General, in June 1831, stating, that Rajah Prethee Put had murdered two of his relations, plundered his house, burnt his title-deeds, cut down five of his mango-groves, seized seventy-three beegahs of land belonging to him, of hereditary right, turned all his family out of the village, including the widows of the two murdered men, and still held in confinement his relative Teekaram, a sipahee of the Bombay army. On investigation before the Assistant Resident, Captain Shakespear, the havildar and Cheyda admitted-first, that Teekaram had rejoined his regiment before they complained; second, that of the two murdered men, one had been killed fifty-five years before, and the other twenty years, and that both had fallen in affrays between landholders, in which many lives had been lost on both sides; third, that he had never himself held the lands, and that his father had been forty years before deprived of them by the father of Cheyda, who had the best claim to them, and had mortgaged them to a Brahmin, from whom Prethee Put had taken them for defalcation; fourth, that it was not his own claim he was urging, but that of Cheyda, who was not his brother, but the great grandson of his grandfather's brother, and that he had never been in the British service; fifth, that the lands had been taken from his father by Cheyda's father fourteen years before he, the havildar, entered the British service twenty-eight years ago; sixth, that his family had lost nothing in the village, by Prethee Put, and that the persons deprived of their mango-groves were only very distantly related to him.

Fuzl Allee, a notorious knave, having, in collusion with the local authorities of the district, taken from Hufeez-ollah the village of Dewa, which had been held by his family in proprietory right for many generations, and tried to extort from him a written resignation of all his rights to the lands, Hufeez-ollah made his escape, and went to Lucknow to seek redress. During his absence his relations tried to recover possession, and in the contest one of Fuzl Allee's followers was killed. Fuzl Allee then prevailed upon Ihsan Allee, a pay havildar in the 9th Regiment of our Cavalry, who was in no way whatever connected with the parties, and had no claim whatever on the lands, to present a petition to the Resident, charging Hufeez-ollah with having committed a gang-robbery upon his house, and murdered one of his servants. Hufeez-ollah was seized and thrown into prison, and the case was made over for trial to Zakir Allee. No proof whatever having been adduced against him for four months, Zakir Allee declared him innocent, and applied for his release; but before his application reached the Durbar, another petition was presented to the Resident, Colonel Richmond, in the name of the pay havildar; and the Durbar ordered that the case should be made over to the Court of Mahommed Hyat, and that the prisoner should not be released without a settlement and the previous sanction of the Durbar, as the affair related to the English.

The prisoner proved that he was at Lucknow at the time of the affray, and that the lands in dispute had belonged to his family for many generations. No proof whatever was produced against him, but by frequently changing the attorneys of the pay havildar, pretending that he required to attend in person but could not get leave of absence, and other devices, Fuzl Allee contrived to postpone the final decision till the 27th of February, 1849, when Mahommed Hyat acquitted the prisoner, and declared that the pay havildar had in reality no connection whatever either with the parties or with the lands; that his name had been used by Fuzl Allee for his own evil purposes; that he had become very uneasy at the thought of keeping an innocent man so long in prison merely to gratify the malice and evil designs of his enemy; and prayed the Durbar to call upon the prosecutor to prove his charges before the Minister or other high officer within a certain period, or to direct the release of the poor man.

On the 16th of January, 1852, the prisoner sent a petition to the Resident, Colonel Sleeman, to say, that after he had been acquitted by Mahommed Hyat on the 27th of February, 1849, his enemy, Fuzl Allee, had contrived to prevail upon the Durbar to have his case made over to the Court of the Suder-os Sudoor, by whom he had been a third time acquitted; but that the Durbar dared not order his release, as the case was one in which British officers were concerned. He therefore prayed that the Resident would request the King to order his release, on his giving security for his appearance when required, as he had been in prison for more than four years. On the 24th of January, 1852, the Resident requested the King to have the prisoner immediately released. This was the first time that the case came to the notice of Colonel Sleeman, though Hufeez-ollah had been four years in prison, under a fictitious charge from the pay havildar.

January 11, 1850.—At Nawabgunge, detained by rain, which fell heavily all last night, to the great delight of the landed interest, and great discomfort of travellers. Nothing but mud around us—our tents wet through, but standing, and the ground inside of them dry. Fortunately there has been no strong wind with the heavy rain, and we console ourselves with the thought that the small inconvenience which travellers suffer from such rain at this season is trifling, compared with the advantage which millions of our fellow-creatures derive from it. This is what I have heard all native travellers say, however humble or however great— all sympathise with the landed interests in a country where industry is limited almost exclusively to the culture of the soil, and the revenue of the sovereign derived almost exclusively from the land. After such rains the cold increases—the spirits rise—the breezes freshen—the crops look strong—the harvest is retarded—the grain gets more sap and becomes perfect—the cold season is prolonged, as the crops remain longer green, and continue to condense the moisture of the surrounding atmosphere. Without such late rain, the crops ripen prematurely, the grain becomes shrivelled, and defective both in quantity and quality. While the rain lasts, however, a large camp is a wretched scene; for few of the men, women, and children, and still fewer of the animals it contains, can find any shelter at all!

January 12, 1850.-At Nawabgunge, still detained by rain. The Minister had ordered out tents for himself and suite on the 8th, but they had not come up, and I was obliged to lend him one of my best, and some others as they came up, or they would have been altogether without shelter. When he left them on the 10th, his attendants cut and took away almost all the ropes, some of the kanats or outer walls, and some of the carpets. He knew nothing about it, nor will he ever learn anything till told by me. His attendants were plundering in all the surrounding villages while he remained; and my people tried in vain to prevent them, lest they should themselves be taken for the plunderers. Of all this the Minister knew nothing. The attendants on the contractors and other local officers are, if possible, still worse; and throughout the country the King's officers all plunder, or acquiesce in the plunder, utterly regardless of the sufferings of the people and the best interests of their Sovereign. No precaution whatever is taken to prevent this indiscriminate plunder by the followers of the local authorities; nor would any one of them think it worth his while to interpose if he saw the roofs of the houses of a whole village moving off on the heads of his followers to his camp; or a fine crop of sugar-cane, wheat, or vegetables cut down for fodder by them before his face. It is the fashion of the country, and the Government acquiesces in it.

Among the people no man feels mortified, or apprehends that he shall stand the worse in the estimation of the Government or its officers, for being called and proved to be a robber. It is the trade of every considerable landholder in the country occasionally, and that of a great many of them perpetually; the murder of men, women, and children generally attends their depredations. A few days ago, when requested by the King to apply to officers commanding stations, and magistrates of bordering districts, for aid in the arrest of some of the most atrocious of these rebels and robbers, I told his Majesty, that out of consideration for the poor people who suffered, I had made a requisition for that aid for the arrest of three of the worst of them; but that I could make no further requisition until he did something to remove the impression now universal over Oude, that those who protected their peasantry managed their estates well, obeyed the Government in all things, and paid the revenue punctually, were sure to be oppressed, and ultimately ruined by the Government and its officers, while those who did the reverse in all these things were equally sure to be favoured and courted.

As an instance, I mentioned Gholam Huzrut, who never paid his revenues, oppressed his peasantry, murdered his neighbours, and robbed them of their estates, attacked and plundered the towns around with his large band of robbers, and kept the country in a perpetual state of disorder; yet, when seized and sent in a prisoner to Lucknow by Captain Bunbury, he managed to bribe courtiers, and get orders sent out to the local authorities to have his son kept in possession of all his ill-gotten lands, and favoured and protected in all possible ways. I knew that such orders had been obtained by bribery; and the Minister told me, that he had ordered nothing more than that the son should have the little land which had been held of old by the family, and should be required to give up all that he had usurped. I showed him a copy of the order issued by his confidential servant, Abid Allee, to all commanders of troops in the district, which had been obtained for me for the occasion of the Minister's visit to my camp; and he seemed much ashamed to see that his subordinates should so abase the confidence he placed in them. The order was as follows:—

"To the Officers commanding the Forces in the District of Sidhore, Nawabgunge, Dewa, &c.

"By Order of the Minister.—The King's chuprassies have been sent to Para to invite in Bhikaree the son of Gholam Huzrut; and you all are informed that the said Bhikaree is to be honoured and cherished by the favour of the King; and if any of you should presume to prevent his coming in, or molest him in the possession of any of the lands he holds, you will incur the severe displeasure of his Majesty. You are, on no account, to molest or annoy him in any way connected with his affairs.

(Signed) "ABID ALLEE."

The thing necessary in Oude is a system and a machinery that shall inspire all with a feeling-first, of security in their tenure in office so long as the duties of it are performed ably and honestly; second, in their tenure in their lands assessed at moderate rates, as long as the rents and revenues so assessed are fully and punctually paid, and the duties of the holders towards the Government, their tenants, and the public, are faithfully discharged; third, in the safety of life, person, and property on the roads and in the towns, villages, and hamlets scattered over the country. This good can never be effected with the present system and machinery, whatever be the ability and diligence of the King, the Minister, and the Resident; be they of the highest possible order, the good they can effect must be small and temporary; there can be, under such a system, no stability in any rule, no feeling of security in any person or thing!

A tribunal, formed under the guarantee of the British Government, might, possibly—first, form a settlement of the land revenue of the whole country, and effectually enforce from all parties, the fulfilment of the conditions it imposed; second, decide, finally, upon all charges against public officers—protect the able and honest, and punish all those who neglect their duties or abuse their authority; third, reform the military force in all its branches—give it the greatest possible efficiency, compatible with the outlay—concentrate it at five or six stations, and protect the people of the country from its rapacity; fourth, raise and form a police, distinct altogether from this military force, and efficient for all the duties required from it; fifth, create and maintain judicial courts to which all classes might look up with confidence and respect. But to effect all this it would require to transfer at least twenty-five lacs of rupees a-year from the pockets of official absorbants and Court favourites to those of efficient public officers; and, finally, to set aside the present King, Minister, and Commander-in-Chief, and take all the executive upon itself.

The expenditure is now about twenty lacs of rupees a-year above the income, and the excess is paid out of the reserved treasury. This reserved treasury was first established by Saadut Allee Khan in A.D. 1801, when he had serious thoughts of resigning the government of his country into the hands of the Honourable Company, and retiring into private life. Up to this time he used to drink hard, and to indulge in other pleasures, which tended to unfit him for the cares and duties of sovereignty; but, in 1801, he made a solemn vow at the shrine of Huzrut Abbas at Lucknow to cease from all such indulgences, and devote all his time and attention to his public duties. This vow he kept, and no Sovereign of Oude has ever conducted the Government with so much ability as he did for the remaining fourteen years of his life. On his death, which took place on the 12th of July, 1814, he left in this reserved treasury the sum of fourteen crores of rupees, or fourteen millions sterling, with all his establishments paid up, and his just debts liquidated. When he ascended the musnud on the 21st January, 1798, he found nothing in the Treasury, and the public establishments all much in arrears.

Out of this reserved treasure, the zukaat, or two and a-half per cent., is every year paid to the mojtahid for distribution among the poor of the Sheea sect at Lucknow. No person of the Sonnee sect is permitted to partake of this charity. Syuds or lineal descendants of the Prophet are not permitted to take any part of this charity, except for the bonâ fide payment of debt due. The mojtahid is, at the same time, the high priest and the highest judicial functionary in the State. Being a Syud, neither he nor any member of his family can legally take any part of this charity for themselves, except for the bonâ fide purpose of paying debts; but they get over the difficulty by borrowing large sums before the money is given out, and appropriate the greater part of the money to the liquidation of these debts, though they all hold large sums in our Government securities. To his friends at Court he sends a large share, with a request that they will do him the favour to undertake the distribution among the poor of their neighbourhood. To prevent popular clamour, a small portion of the money given out is actually distributed among the poor of the Sheea sect at Lucknow; but that portion is always small.

Saadut Allee's son and successor, Ghazee-od Deen Hyder, spent four crores out of the reserved treasury over and above the whole income of the State; and when he died, on the 20th of October, 1827, he left ten crores of rupees in that treasury. His son and successor, Nusseer-od Deen Hyder, spent nine crores and thirty lacs; and when he died, on the 7th of July, 1837, he left only seventy lacs in the reserved treasury. His successor, Mahommed Allee Shah, died on the 16th of May, 1842, leaving in the reserved treasury thirty-five lacs of rupees, one hundred and twenty-four thousand gold mohurs, and twenty-four lacs in our Government securities—total, seventy-eight lacs and eighty-four thousand rupees. His son and successor, Amjud Allee Shah, died on the 13th of February, 1847, leaving in the reserved treasury ninety-two lacs of rupees, one hundred and twenty-four thousand gold-mohurs, and twenty-four lacs in our Government securities—total, one crore and thirty-six lacs. His son and successor, his present Majesty, Wajid Allee Shah, is spending out of this reserved treasury, over and above the whole income of the country, above twenty lacs of rupees a-year; and the treasury must soon become exhausted. His public establishments, and the stipendiary members of the royal family, are, at the same time, kept greatly in arrears.*

* November 30, 1851.—The gold-mohurs have been all melted down, and the promissory notes of our Government all, save four lacs, given away; and of the rupees, I believe, only three lacs remain; so that the reserved treasury must be entirely exhausted before the end of 1851; while the establishments and stipendiary members of the royal family are in arrears for from one to three years. Fifty lacs of rupees would hardly suffice to pay off these arrears. The troops on detached duty, in the provinces with local officers, are not so much in arrears as those in and about the capital. They are paid out of the revenues as they are collected, and their receipts sent in to the treasury. For some good or pleasing services rendered by him to the minister this year, in the trial of offenders whom that minister wished to screen, three lacs of rupees have been paid to the mojtahid as zukaat for distribution to the poor. This has all been appropriated by the mojtahid, the minister, and Court favourites.

The State, like individuals, is bound to pay this zukaat only when it is free from debts of all kinds. The present King's father was free from debt, and had his establishments always paid up; and he always paid this charity punctually. The present King is not bound to pay it, but the high-priest, minister, and Court favourites are too deeply interested in its payment to permit its discontinuance; and the king, like a mere child in their hands, acquiesces in all they propose. The zukaat has, in consequence, increased as the treasury has become exhausted.]

January 13, 1850.—Russoolabad, twelve miles, over a country better peopled and cultivated than usual, where the soil admits of tillage. There is a good deal that requires drainage, and still more that is too poor to be tilled without great labour and outlay in irrigation, manure, &c. The villages are, however, much nearer to each other than in any other part of the country that we have passed over; and the lands, close around every village, are well cultivated. The landholders and cultivators told me, that the heavy rain we have had has done a vast deal of good to the crops; and, as it has been followed by a clear sky and fine westerly wind, they have no fear of the blight which might have followed had the sky continued cloudy, and the winds easterly. Certainly nothing could look better than the crops of all kinds do now, and the people are busily engaged in ploughing the land for sugar-cane, and for the autumn crops of next season.

I had some talk with the head zumeendar of Naraenpoor about midway. He is of the Ditchit family of Rajpoots, who abound in the district we have now entered. We passed over the boundary of Byswara, about three miles from our last encampment, and beyond that district there are but few Rajpoots of the Bys clan. These Ditchits give their daughters in marriage to the Bys Rajpoots, but cannot get any of theirs in return. Gunga Sing, the zumeendar, with whom I was talking, told me that both the Ditchits and Byses put their infant daughters to death, and that the practice prevailed more or less in all families of these and, he believed, all other clans of Rajpoots in Oude, save the Sengers.* I asked him whether it prevailed in his own family, and he told me that it did, more or less, as in all others. I bade him leave me, as I could not hold converse with a person guilty of such atrocities, and told him that they would be all punished for them in the next world, if not in this.

* The Sengers are almost the only class of Rajpoots in Bundelkund, and Boghilcund, Rewa, and the Saugor territories, who used to put their female infants to death; and here, in Oude, they are almost the only class who do not.

Rajah Bukhtawar Sing, who was on his horse beside my elephant, said, "They are all punished in this world, and will, no doubt, be punished still more in the next. Scarcely any of the heads of these landed aristocracy are the legitimate sons of their predecessors; they are all adopted, or born of women of inferior grade. The heads of families who commit or tolerate such atrocities become leprous, blind, deaf or dumb, or are carried off in early life by some terrible disease. Hardly any of them attain a good old age, nor can they boast of an untainted line of ancestors like other men. If they get sons, they commonly die young. They unite themselves to women of inferior castes for want of daughters in families of their own ranks, and there is hardly a family among these proud Rajpoots unstained by such connections.* Even the reptile Pausies become Rajpoots by giving their daughters to Powars and other Rajpoot families, when by robbery and murder they have acquired wealth and landed property. The sister of Gunga Buksh, of Kasimgunge, was married to the Rajah of Etondeea, a Powar Rajpoot in Mahona; and the present Rajah—Jode Sing—is her son. Gunga Buksh is a Pausee, but the family call themselves Rawats, and are considered to be Rajpoots, since they have acquired landed possessions by the murder and ruin of the old proprietors. They all delight in murder and rapine—the curse of God is upon them, sir, for the murder of their own innocent children!"

*   A great number of girls are purchased and stolen from our territories, brought into Oude, and sold to Rajpoot families, as wives for their sons, on the assurance, that they are of the same or higher caste, and that their parents have been induced to part with them from poverty. A great many of our native officers and sipahees, who marry while home on furlough, and are pressed for time, get such wives. Some of their neighbours are always bribed by the traders in such girls, to pledge themselves for the purity of their blood. If they ever find out the imposition, they say nothing about it.

"When I was sent out to inquire into the case of Brigadier Webber, who had been attacked and robbed while travelling in his palkee, with relays of bearers, from Lucknow to Seetapoor, I entered a house to make some inquiries, and found the mistress weeping. I asked the cause, and she told me that she had had four children, and lost all—that three of them were girls, who had been put to death in infancy, and the last was a fine boy, who had just died! I told her that this was a just punishment from God for the iniquities of her family, and that I would neither wash my hands nor drink water under her roof. I never do under the roof of any family in which such a cruel practice prevails. These Rajpoots are all a bad set, sir. When men murder their own children, how can they scruple to murder other people? The curse of God is upon them, sir.

"In the district of Byswara," he continued, "through which we have just passed, you will find at least fifty thousand men armed to fight against each other, or their government and its officers: in such a space, under the Honourable Company's dominion, you would not find one thousand armed men of the same class. Why is this, but because you do not allow such crimes to be perpetrated? Why do you go on acquiring dominion over one country after another with your handful of European troops and small force of native sipahees, but because God sees that your rule is just, and that you have an earnest desire to benefit the people and improve the countries you take?"

He told me that he had charge of the cattle under Saadut Allee Khan when Lord Lake took the field at the first siege of Bhurtpoor; that his master lent his Lordship five hundred elephants, eight thousand artillery bullocks, and five hundred horses; that two hundred and fifty of the elephants returned; but whether any of the bullocks and horses came back or not he could not say.

The country we came over to-day is well studded with groves and fine single trees, but the soil is generally of the lighter doomuteea kind, which requires much labour and outlay in water and manure. The irrigation is all from wells and pools. In the villages we came through, we saw but few of the sipahees of our army home on furlough; they are chiefly from the Byswara and Bunoda districts. We found our tents pitched upon a high and dry spot, with a tight soil of clay and sand. After the heavy rain we have had, it looked as if no shower had fallen upon it for an age. The mud walls of the houses we saw on the road were naked, as usual. The rapacity of the King's troops is everywhere, directly or indirectly, the cause of this: and till they are better provided and disciplined the houses in the towns and villages can never improve.

The commandant, Imdad Hoseyn, of the Akberee or Telinga Regiment, on duty with the Amil of the Poorwa district, in which our camp was last pitched, followed me a few miles this morning to beg that I would try to prevail upon the Durbar to serve out clothing for his corps. He told me that the last clothing it got from the Government was on the occasion of Lord Hastings' visit to Lucknow, some thirty-three years ago, in 1817; that many orders had been given since that time for new clothing, but there was always some one about Court to counteract them, from malice or selfishness; that his father, Zakir Allee, commanded the corps when it got the last clothing, and he succeeded him many years ago. The Telinga Regiments are provided with arms, accoutrements, and clothing by Government. The sipahees formerly got five rupees a-month, but for only ten months in the year; they now get four rupees and three and a-half annas a-month for all the twelve months. 'He is, he says, obliged to take a great many sufarashies, or men put in by persons of influence at Court, out of favour, or for the purpose of sharing in their pay; and, under the deductions and other disadvantages to which they are liable, he could get no good men to enlist. The corps, in consequence, has a wretched appearance, and certainly could not be made formidable to an enemy. The "Akbery" is one of the Telinga corps of infantry, and was intended to be, in all things, like those of Captains Barlow, Bunbury, and Magness; but Imdad Hoseyn told me that they had a certain weight at Court, which secured for their regiments many advantages necessary to make the corps efficient, while he had none: that they had occasional intercourse with the Resident, and were all at Court for some months in the year to make friends, while he was always detached.

January 14, 1850.—Halted at Russoolabad, for our second set of tents, which did not come up till night, when it was too late to send them on to our next ground. We have two sets of sleeping and dining tents—one to go on and the other to remain during the night—but only one set of office tents. They are struck in the afternoon, when the office duties of the day are over, and are ready by the time we reach our ground the next morning. This is the way in which all public functionaries march in India. Almost all officers who have revenue charges march through the districts under their jurisdiction during the cold season, and so do many political officers who have control over more than one native principality. I have had charges that require such moving ever since the year 1822, or for some twenty-eight years; and with the exception of two intervals of absence on medical certificate in 1826 and 1836, I have been every cold season moving in the way I describe.

No Resident at the Court of Lucknow ever before moved, over the country as I am doing to inquire into the condition of the people, the state of the country, and character of the administration; nor would it be desirable for them to do so unless trained to civil business, and able and disposed to commune freely with the people of all classes. The advantages would hardly counterbalance the disadvantages. When I apologize to the peasantry for the unavoidable trespasses of my camp, they always reply good-humouredly, "The losses we suffer from them are small and temporary, while the good we hope from your visit is great and permanent." Would that I could realize the hopes to which my visit gives rise.

January 15, 1850.—To Meeangunge, five miles, over a plain of good doomuteea soil, well studded with trees; but much of the land lies waste, and many of the villages and hamlets are unoccupied and in ruins. We passed the boundary of the Russoolabad district, about two miles from our last ground, and crossed into that of Meeangunge or Safeepoor. The Russoolabad district was held in contract for some years by one of the greatest knaves in Oude, Buksh Allee, a dome by caste, whose rise to wealth and influence may be described as illustrative of the manners and customs of the Lucknow Court and Government. This man and his deputy, Munsab Allee, reduced a good deal of the land of the district to waste, and depopulated many of its villages and hamlets by over-exactions and by an utter disregard of their engagements with the landholders and cultivators; and they were in league with many atrocious highway robbers, who plundered and murdered so many travellers along the high road leading from Lucknow to Cawnpoor, which runs through the district, that it was deemed unsafe to pass it except in strong bodies.

When I took charge of my office in January last, they used to seize every good-looking girl or young woman, passing the roads with parents and husbands, who were too poor to purchase redress at Court, and make slaves or concubines of them; and, feeling strong in the assurance of protection from the fiddlers in the palace, who are of the same caste—

domes—Buksh Allee defied all authority, and kept those girls and women in his camp and house at Lucknow, while their parents and husbands, for months and years, in vain besought all who were likely to have the least influence or authority to interpose for their release. Some of them came to me soon after I took charge, and, having collected sufficient proof of these atrocities, and of some robberies which he had committed or caused to be committed along the high road, I insisted upon his being deprived of his charges and punished. He remained for many months concealed in the city, but was at last seized by some of the Frontier Police, under the guidance of an excellent officer, Lieutenant Weston, the Superintendent.

I had prevailed on the King to offer two thousand rupees for his apprehension, and the two thousand rupees were distributed among the captors. The girls and young women were released, their parents and husbands compensated for the sufferings they had endured, and many of the persons who had been robbed by him and his deputy had the value of their lost property made good. Great impediments were thrown in the way of all this by people of influence about Court; but they were all surmounted by great skill and energy on the part of Lieutenant Weston and steady perseverance on mine; and Buksh Allee remained in gaol, treated as a common felon, till all was effected. All had, in appearance, been done by the King's officers, but in reality by ours, under his Majesty's sanction, for it was clear that nothing would be done unless we supervised and guided their proceedings. The district is now held in contract by a very respectable man, Mahommed Uskaree, who has taken it for four years.

The district of Safeepoor, in which we are now encamped, has been held in contract for five years by Budreenath, a merchant of Lucknow, who had given security for the former contractor. He could not fulfil his engagements to Government, and the contract was made over to him as surety, on condition that he paid the balance. He has held it ever since, while his younger brother, Kiddernath, has conducted their mercantile affairs at Lucknow. Budreenath has always considered the affair as a mercantile speculation, and thought of nothing but the amount he has to pay to Government and that which he can squeeze out of the landholders and cultivators. He is a bad manager; the lands are badly tilled, and the towns, villages, and hamlets are scantily peopled and most wretched in appearance.

Near the border, we passed one village, Mahommedpoor, entirely in ruins. After some search we found a solitary man of the Pausee tribe, who told us that it had been held for many generations by the family of Rugonath, a Gouree Rajpoot, who paid for it at an uniform rate of six hundred rupees a-year. About three years ago the contractor demanded from him an increased rate, which he could not pay. Being sorely pressed, he fled to the jungles with the few of his clan that he could collect, and ordered all the cultivators to follow his fortunes. They were of a different clan—mostly Bagheelas—and declined the honour. He urged that, if they followed him for a season or two, the village would be left untilled, and yield nothing to the contractor, who would be constrained to restore him to possession at the rate which his ancestors had paid; that his family had nothing else to depend upon, and if they did not desert the land and take to the jungles and plunder with him, he must, of necessity, plunder them. They had never done so, and would not do so now. He attacked and plundered the village three times, killed three men, and drove all the rest to seek shelter and employment in other villages around. Not a soul but himself, our informant, was left, and the lands lay waste. Rogonath Sing rented a little land in the village of Gouree, many miles off, and in another district, still determined to allow no man but himself to hold the village or restore its tillage and population. This, said the Pausee, is the usage of the country, and the only way in which a landholder can honestly or effectually defend himself against the contractor, who would never regard his rights unless he saw that he was prepared to defend them in this way, and determined to involve all under him in his own ruin, depopulate his estate, and lay waste his lands.

Meean Almas, after whom this place, Meeangunge, takes his name, was an eunuch. He had a brother, Rahmut, after whom the town of Rahmutgunge, which we passed some days ago, took its name. Meean Almas was the greatest and best man of any note that Oude has produced. He held for about forty years this and other districts, yielding to the Oude Government an annual revenue of about eighty lacs of rupees. During all this time he kept the people secure in life and property, and as happy as people in such a state of society can be; and the whole country under his charge was, during his life-time, a garden. He lived here in a style of great magnificence, and was often visited by his sovereign, who used occasionally to spend a month at a time with him at Meeangunge. A great portion of the lands held by him were among those made over to the British Government, on the division of the Oude territory, by the treaty of 1801, concluded between Saadut Allee Khan and the then Governor-General Lord Wellesley.

The country was then divided into equal shares, according to the rent-roll at the time. The half made over to the British Government has been ever since yielding more revenue to us, while that retained by the sovereign of Oude has been yielding less and less to him; and ours now yields, in land-revenue, stamp-duty, and the tax on spirits, two crore and twelve lacs a-year, while the reserved half now yields to Oude only about one crore, or one crore and ten lacs. When the cession took place, each half was estimated at one crore and thirty-three lacs. Under good management the Oude share might, in a few years, be made equal to ours, and perhaps better, for the greater part of the lands in our share have been a good deal impoverished by over-cropping, while those of the Oude share have been improved by long fallows. Lands of the same natural quality in Oude, under good tillage, now pay a much higher rate of rent than they do in our half of the estate.

Almas Allee Khan, at the close of his life, was supposed to have accumulated immense wealth; but when he died he was found to have nothing, to the great mortification of his sovereign, who seized upon all.

Large sums of money had been lent by him to the European merchants at Lucknow, as well as to native merchants all over the country. When he found his end approaching, he called for all their bonds and destroyed them. Mr. Ousely and Mr. Paul were said to have at that time owed to him more than three lacs of rupees each. His immense income he had expended in useful works, liberal hospitality, and charity. He systematically kept in check the tallookdars, or great landholders; fostered the smaller, and encouraged and protected the better classes of cultivators, such as Lodhies, Koormies, and Kachies, whom he called and considered his children. His reign over the large extent of country under his jurisdiction is considered to have been its golden age. Many of the districts which he held were among those transferred to the British Government by the treaty of 1801; and they were estimated at the revenue which he had paid for them to the Oude Government. This was much less than any other servant of the Oude Government would have been made to pay for them; and this accounts, in some measure, for the now increased rate they yield to us. Others pledged themselves to pay rates which they never did or could pay; and the nominal rates in the accounts were always greater than the real rates. He never pledged himself to pay higher rates than he could and really did pay.

Now the tallookdars keep the country in a perpetual state of disturbance, and render life, property, and industry everywhere insecure. Whenever they quarrel with each other, or with the local authorities of the Government, from whatever cause, they take to indiscriminate plunder and murder over all lands not held by men of the same class; no road, town, village, or hamlet is secure from their merciless attacks; robbery and murder become their diversion—their sport; and they think no more of taking the lives of men, women, and children who never offended them, than those of deer or wild hogs. They not only rob and murder, but seize, confine, and torture all whom they seize, and suppose to have money or credit, till they ransom themselves with all they have, or can beg or borrow. Hardly a day has passed since I left Lucknow in which I have not had abundant proof of numerous atrocities of this kind committed by landholders within the district through which I was passing, year by year, up to the present day. The same system is followed by landholders of smaller degrees and of this military class—some holders of single villages or co-sharers in a village. This class comprises Rajpoots of all denominations, Mussulmans, and Pausies. Where one co-sharer in a village quarrels with another, or with the Government authorities, on whatever subject, he declares himself in a state of war, and adopts the same system of indiscriminate plunder and reckless murder. He first robs the house and murders all he can of the family of the co-sharer with whom he has quarrelled, or whose tenement he wishes to seize upon; and then gets together all he can of the loose characters around, employs them in indiscriminate plunder, and subsists them upon the booty, without the slightest apprehension that he shall thereby stand less high in the estimation of his neighbours, or that of the officers of Government; on the contrary, he expects, when his pastime is over, to be at least more feared and courted, and more secure in the possession of increased lands, held at lower rates.

All this terrible state of disorder arises from the Government not keeping faith with its subjects, and not making them keep faith with each other. I one day asked Rajah Hunmunt Sing how it was that men guilty of such crimes were tolerated in society, and he answered by quoting the following Hindee couplet:—"Men reverence the man whose heart is wicked, as they adore and make offerings to the evil planet, while they let the good pass unnoticed, or with a simple salute of courtesy."*

* There is another Hindee verse to the same effect. "Man dreads a crooked thing—the demon Rahoo dares not seize the moon till he sees her full." They consider the eclipse to be caused by the demon Rahoo seizing the moon in his mouth.

The contractor for this district, Budreenath, came to call in the afternoon, though he is suffering much from disease. He bears a good character with the Government, because he contrives to pay its demand;

but a very bad one among the people, from whom he extorts the means. He does not adhere to his engagements with the landholders and cultivators, but exacts, when the crops are ripe, a higher rate than they had engaged to pay at the commencement of tillage; and the people suffer not only from what he takes over and above what is due, but from the depredations of those whom such proceedings drive into rebellion. Against such persons he is too weak to protect them; and as soon as the rebels show that they can reduce his income by plundering and murdering the peasantry, and all who have property in the towns and villages, he re-establishes them on their lands on their own terms. He had lately, however, by great good luck, seized two very atrocious characters of this description, who had plundered and burnt down several villages, and murdered some of their inhabitants; and as he knew that they would be released on the first occasion of thanksgiving at Lucknow, having the means to bribe Court favourites, he begged my permission to make them over to Lieutenant Weston, superintendent of the Frontier Police, as robbers by profession. "If they come back, sir, they will murder all who have aided in their capture, or given evidence against them, and no village or road will be safe."

Some shopkeepers in the town complained that the contractor was in the habit of forcing them to stand sureties for the fulfilment, on the part of landholders, of any engagements they might make, to pay him certain sums, or to make over to him certain land produce at the harvest. This, they said, often involved them in heavy losses, as the landholders frequently could not, or would not, do either when the time came, and they were made to pay. This is a frequent practice throughout Oude. Shopkeepers and merchants who have property are often compelled by the contractors and other local officers to give such security for bad or doubtful paymasters with whom they may happen to have had dealings or intercourse, and by this means robbed of all they have. All manner of means are resorted to to compel them: they and their families are seized and confined, and harshly or disgracefully treated, till they consent to sign the security bonds. The plea that the bonds had been forced from them would not avail in any tribunal to which they might appeal: it would be urged against them that the money was for the State; and this would be considered as quite sufficient to justify the Government officer who had robbed them. The brief history which I propose to give of Buksh Allee, the late contractor for the Russoolabad district, is as follows:—

Mokuddera Ouleea, one of the consorts of the King, Nuseer-od Deen Hyder, was the daughter of Mr. George Hopkins Walters, a half-pay officer of one of the regiments of British Dragoons, who came to Lucknow as an adventurer. He there united himself (though not in marriage) to the widow of Mr. Whearty, an English merchant or shopkeeper of that city, who had recently died, leaving this widow, who was the daughter of Mr. Culloden, an English merchant of Lucknow, and one son, now called Ameer Mirza, and one daughter, now called Shurf-on Nissa. By Mr. Walters this widow had one daughter, who afterwards became united to the King in marriage (in 1827), under the title of "Mokuddera Ouleea." Mr. Walters died at Lucknow, and the widow and two daughters went to reside at Cawnpoor. The daughters were good-looking, and the mother was disposed to make the most of their charms, without regard to creed or colour.

Buksh Allee, a dome by caste, who had been by profession a drummer to a party of dancing-girls, served them as a coachman and table attendant. At Cawnpoor he cohabited with Mrs. Walters, and prevailed upon her to take her children back to Lucknow as the best possible market for them, as he had friends at Court who would be able to bring them to the notice of the sovereign. They were shown to the King as soon as he succeeded his father on the throne in 1827. He was captivated with the charms of Miss Walters, though they were not great, demanded her hand from the mother, and was soon after united to her in marriage according to the Mahommedan law. A suitable establishment was provided by the King for her mother, father-in-law, brother, and sister; and as his Majesty considered that the manner in which Buksh Allee and her mother had hitherto lived together was unsuitable to the connection which now subsisted between them, he caused them to be married in due form according to the Mahommedan law. The mother and her three children now changed their creed for that of Islamism, and took Mahommedan names.

By a deed of engagement with the British Government, hearing date the 1st of March 1829, the King contributed to the five per cent loan the sum of sixty-two lacs and forty thousand rupees, the interest of which, at five per cent., our Government pledged itself to pay to the four females.*

* Mulika Zumanee, 10,000; Taj Mahal, 6,000; Mokuddera Ouleea, 6,000; Zeenut-on Nissa, the daughter of Mulika Zumanee, 4,000.

These pensions were to descend in perpetuity to their heirs, if they left any; and if they left none, they were to have the power to bequeath them by will to whomsoever and for what purposes soever they chose, the British Government reserving to itself the power to pay to the heirs the principal from which the pensions arose, instead of continuing the pensions.

The King died in July 1837, and Mokuddera Ouleea went to reside near her mother and Buksh Allee, taking with her great wealth in jewels and other things, which she had accumulated during the King's lifetime. Her sister, Ashrof—alias Shurf-on Nissa—resided in the same house with her mother and Buksh Allee. Mokuddera Ouleea had from the time she became estranged from her husband, the King, led a very profligate life, and she continued to do the same in her widowhood. On the 14th of September 1839, the mother died; and the sister, Shurf-on Nissa, supplied her place, as the wife or concubine of Buksh Allee.

Mokuddera Ouleea became pregnant, and on the 9th of November 1840, she was taken very ill from some violent attempt to produce abortion. She continued insensible and speechless till the evening of the 12th of that month, when she expired. The house which Buksh Allee occupied at that time is within the Residency compound, and had been purchased by Mr. John Culloden, the father of Mrs. Walters, from Mr. George Prendergast on the 22nd of February 1802. Mr. Prendergast purchased the house from Mr. S. M. Taylor, an English merchant at Lucknow, who obtained it from the Nawab Assuf-od Dowlah, as a residence. The Nawab afterwards, on the 5th of January 1797, gave him, through the Resident, Mr. J. Lumsden, permission to sell it to Mr. Prendergast. The remains of Mokuddera Ouleea were interred within the compound of that house, near those of her mother, though the King, Mahommed Allee Shah, wished to have them buried by the side of those of her husband, the late King. The house is still occupied by Shurf-on Nissa, who succeeded to her sister's pension and property, under the sanction of the British Government, and has built, or completed within the enclosure, a handsome mosque and mausoleum.

On the death of Mr. Walters, Mrs. Whearty made application, through the house of Colvin and Co., for the arrears of pension or half-pay due to him up to the time of his death, and for some provision for herself as his widow; but she was told that unless she could produce the usual certificate, or proof of her marriage with him, she could get neither. No proof whatever of the marriage was forthcoming, and the claim was prosecuted no further. Shurf-on Nissa, and her brother and his son, continued to live with Buksh Allee, who, upon the wealth and pension left by Mokuddera Ouleea to her sister, kept up splendid establishments both at Lucknow and Cawnpoor.

At the latter place he associated on terms of great intimacy with the European gentlemen, and is said to have received visits from the Major-General commanding the Division and his lady. With the aid of his wealth and the influence of his brother domes (the singers and fiddlers who surround the throne of his present Majesty), Buksh Allee secured and held for some years the charge of this fertile and populous district of Russoolabad, through which passes the road from Lucknow to Cawnpoor, where, as I have already stated, he kept up bands of myrmidons to rob and murder travellers, and commit all kinds of atrocities. This road became, in consequence, the most unsafe of all the roads in Oude, and hardly a day passed in which murders and robberies were not perpetrated upon it. Proof of his participation in these atrocities having been collected, Buksh Allee was, in October 1849, seized by order of the Resident, tried before the King's Courts, convicted and sentenced to imprisonment, and ordered to restore or make good the property which he was proved to have taken, or caused to be taken, from travellers. His house had become filled with girls of all ages, whom he had taken from poor parents, as they passed over this road, and converted into slaves for his seraglio. They were all restored to their parents, with suitable compensation; and the Cawnpoor road has become the most safe, as well as the best, road in Oude.

On the death of Mokuddera Ouleea, a will was sent to the Resident by her sister, who declared that it had been under her sister's pillow for a year, and that she had taken it out on finding her end approaching, and made it over to her, declaring it to contain her last wishes. By this document pensions were bequeathed to the persons mentioned in the note below* out of one-third, and the other two-thirds were bequeathed to her sister and brother. In submitting this document to Government, the Resident declared that he believed it to be a forgery; and in reply he was instructed to ascertain whether the persons named in the document had any objections to consider Shurf-on Nissa sole heir to her sister's property and pension. Should they have none to urge, he was directed to consider her as sole heir, and the pretended will as of no avail. They all agreed to consider her as sole heir; and the Resident was directed to make over to her the property, and pay to her the pension or the principal from which it arose. The Resident considered the continuance of the pension as the best arrangement for the present, and of this Government approved.

*   Buksh Allee, 1,000 rupees per month; Allee Hoseyn, 75; Sooraj Bhan, 40; Syud Hoseyn, 30; Sheik Hingun, 20; Mirza Allee, 30; Ram Deen, 12; Meea

Sultan, 15; Sudharee, 10; Imam Buksh, 3; Ala Rukhee, 10; Sadoo Begum, 20; Akbar, 15; Mahdee Begum, 30.

Shurf-on Nissa has no recognised children, and her brother and his reputed son are her sole heirs, so that no injury can arise to him from the omission, on the part of Government and the Resident, of all mention of his right as co-sharer in the inheritance. Neither brother nor sister had really any legal right whatever to succeed to this pension, for Mokuddera Ouleea was an illegitimate child, and had no legal heirs according to either English or Mahommedan law. This fact seems to have been concealed from the Resident, for he never mentioned it to Government. It was the dread that this fact would cause the whole pension to be sent to the shrines in Turkish Arabia, that made them forge the will. All readily consented to consider Shurf-on Nissa the heir, when they found that our Government had no objection to consider her as such. The King wished to have the money to lay out on bridges and roads in Oude, and the Resident advocated this wish; but our Government, ignorant of the fact of the illegitimacy of the deceased, and with the guaranteed bequest of the late King before them, could not consent to any such arrangement.

Government has long been strongly and justly opposed to all such guarantees, and the Resident was told on the 14th November 1840, "that the Governor-General in Council could not consent to grant the absolute and unqualified pledge of protection which the King was solicitous of obtaining in favour of four other females; and directed to state to his Majesty that, although in the instances he had cited, such guarantees had certainly been afforded in former times, yet they were always given either under the impression of an overruling necessity, or in consequence of some acknowledged claims, or previously existing engagements, the force of which could not be avoided; that their existence had often operated practically in the most embarrassing manner, while it constituted a standing and perpetual infringement of the rights of the Government of Oude; and that his Lordship in Council was, consequently, decidedly opposed to the continuance of a system so plainly at variance with every just principle of policy." The objections of the British Government to such guarantees are stated in letters dated 18th February, 28th March, 20th May, 3rd October, and 19th December 1839, and 11th May 1848.

In a despatch from the Honourable the Court of Directors, dated 4th March 1840, their just disapprobation of such guarantees is expressed; and reference is made to former strong expressions of disapprobation. In their despatch of the 28th March 1843, the Honourable Court again express their disapprobation of such guarantees; and refer to their letter of the 16th March, in which they gave positive orders that no such engagement should ever be concluded without a previous reference to the Court. The argument that the arrangement did not, in any particular case, add to the number of guaranteed persons, such persons being already under guarantee, did not in the opinion of the Court touch the stronger objection to such a measure, that of the impropriety of our aiding, especially by the grant of peculiar privileges, the appropriation of the resources of the State to the advantage of individuals. The Court expresses a hope that they shall never have occasion to notice any future violation of their orders as respects such engagements.

January 16, 1850.—We were to have gone this morning to Ouras, but were obliged to encamp at Burra, eight miles from Meeangunge, on the left bank of the Saee river, which had been too much increased by the late rains to admit of our baggage and tents passing over immediately on anything but elephants. As we have but few of them, our tents were pitched on this side of the river, that our things might have the whole day before them to pass over on carts and camels, as the river subsided. Ouras is three miles from our camp, and we are to pass through it and go on to Sundeela to-morrow. There is no bridge, and boats are not procurable on this small river, which we have to cross and recross several times.

The country from Meeangunge is scantily cultivated, but well studded with trees, and generally fertile under good tillage. The soil is the light doomuteea, but here and there very sandy and poor, running into what is called bhoor. The villages and hamlets which we could see are few and wretched. We have few native officers and sipahees in our army from the districts we are now in, and I am in consequence less oppressed with complaints from this class of the Oude subjects.

We met, near our tents, a party of soldiers belonging to Rajah Ghalib Jung, a person already mentioned, and at present superintendent of police, along the Cawnpoor road, escorting a band of thieves, who robbed Major Scott some ten months ago on his way, by dawk, from Lucknow, and an European merchant, two months ago, on his way, by dawk, from Cawnpoor to Lucknow. They had been seized in the Sundeela districts, and the greater part of the stolen property found in their houses. They are of the Pausie tribe, and told me that thieving was their hereditary trade, and that they had long followed it on the Cawnpoor road with success. The landholder, who kept them upon his estate and shared in their booty, was also seized, but made over to the revenue contractor, who released him after a few days' imprisonment for a gratuity.

Of these Pausies there are supposed to be about one hundred thousand families in Oude. They are employed as village watchmen, but, with few exceptions, are thieves and robbers by hereditary profession. Many of them adopt poisoning as a trade, and the numbers who did so were rapidly increasing when Captain Hollings, the superintendent of the Oude Frontier Police, arrested a great many of them, and proceeded against them as Thugs by profession, under Act III. of 1848. His measures have been successfully followed up by Captain Weston, his successor, and this crime has been greatly diminished in Oude. It prevails still, however, more or less, in all parts of India.

These Pausies of Oude generally form the worst part of the gangs of refractory tallookdars in their indiscriminate plunder. They use the bow and arrow expertly, and are said to be able to send an arrow through a man at the distance of one hundred yards. There is no species of theft or robbery in which they are not experienced and skilful, and they increase and prosper in proportion as the disorders in the country grow worse.

They serve any refractory landholder, or enterprising gang-robber, without wages, for the sake of the booty to be acquired.

Many of the sipahees of the Mobarick Pultun, on detached duty with the king's wakeel in attendance upon me, were this morning arrested, while taking off the choppers from the houses of villages along the road and around my camp, for fuel and fodder, in what they called the "usual way." The best beams and rafters and the whole of the straw were fast moving off to my camp; and when seized, the sipahees seemed much surprised, and asked me what they were to do, as they had not received any pay for six months, and the Government expected that they would help themselves to straw and timber wherever they could most conveniently find it. All were fined; but the hope to put a stop to this intolerable evil, under the present system, is a vain one. The evil has the acquiescence and encouragement of the Government and its functionaries of all kinds and grades throughout the country. It is distressing to witness every day such melancholy proofs of how much is done that ought not to be done, and how much that ought to be done is left undone, in so fine a country.

A want of sympathy or fellow-feeling between the governing and governed is common in all parts of India, but in no part that I have seen is it so marked as in Oude. The officers of the Government delight in plundering the peasantry, and upon every local Governor who kills a landholder of any mark, rewards and honours are instantly bestowed, without the slightest inquiry as to the cause or mode. They know that no inquiry will be made, and therefore kill them when they can; no matter how, or for what cause. The great landholders would kill the local Governors with just as little scruple, did they not fear that it might make the British Government interpose and aid in the pursuit after them.

January 17, 1850.—Sundeela, about thirteen miles from our last camp, on the bank of the little River Saee, over a plain of good doomuteea soil, very fertile, and well cultivated in the neighbourhood of villages. The greater portion of the plain is, however, uncultivated, though capable of the best tillage, and shows more than the usual signs of maladministration.

In this district there are only three tallookdars, and they do not rob or resist the Government at present. They distrust the Government authorities, however, and never have any personal intercourse with them. The waste is entirely owing to the bad character of the contractors, and the license given to the troops and establishments under them. The district is now held in amanee tenure, and under the management of Hoseyn Buksh, who entered into his charge only six weeks ago. He is without any experience in, or knowledge of, his duties; he has three regiments of Nujeebs on duty under him, and all who are present came out to meet me. Anything more unlike soldiers it would be difficult to conceive. They are feared only by the honest and industrious. Wherever the Amil goes they go with him, and are a terrible scourge to the country—by far the worst that the country suffers under.

The first thing necessary to effect a reform is—to form out of these disorderly and useless bodies a few efficient regiments; do away with the purveyance system, on which, they are now provided with fuel, fodder, carriage, &c.; pay them liberally and punctually; supply them with good clothing, arms, accoutrements, and ammunition; and concentrate them at five or six points in good cantonments, whence they can move quickly to any part where their services may be required. No more than are indispensably required should attend the local authorities in their circuits. All the rest should remain in cantonments till called for on emergency; and when so called for, they should have all the conveyance they require, and the supplies provided for them—the conveyance at fixed rates, and the supplies at the market price, in good bazaars. For police duties and revenue collections there should be a sufficient body of men kept up, and at the disposal of the revenue and police authorities. The military establishments should be under the control of a different authority. But all this would be of no avail unless the corps were under able commanders, relieved from the fear of Court favourites, and under a Commander-in-Chief who understood his duty and had influence enough to secure all that the troops required to render them efficient, and not a child of seven years of age.

Several of the villages of Sundeela are held by Syud zumeendars, who are peaceable and industrious subjects, and were generally better protected than others under the influence of Chowdhere, Sheik Hushmut Allee, of Sundeela, an agricultural capitalist and landholder, whom no local authority could offend with impunity. His proper trade was to aid landholders of high and low degree, by becoming surety for their punctual payment of the Government demand, and advancing the instalments of that demand himself when they had not the means, and thereby saving them from the visits of the local authorities and their rapacious and disorderly troops: but in an evil hour he ventured to extend his protection a little further, and, to save them from the oppressions of an unscrupulous contractor, he undertook to manage the district himself, and make good all the Government demand upon it. He was unable to pay all that he had bound himself to pay. His brother was first seized by the troops and taken to Lucknow. He languished under the discipline to which he was there subjected, and when on the point of death from what his friends call a broken heart, and the Government authorities choleramorbus, he was released. He died immediately after his return home, and Hushmut Allee was then seized and taken to Lucknow, where he is now confined. The people here lament his absence as a great misfortune to the district, as he was the only one among them who ever had authority and influence, united with a fellow-feeling for the people, and a disposition to promote their welfare and happiness.*

*   Hushmut Allee is still in confinement, but under the troops at Sundeela, and not at Lucknow. July 20, 1851.

END OF VOL. 1.

VOLUME II

DIARY A TOUR THROUGH OUDE

CHAPTER I.

Sundeela—The large landholders of the district—Forces with the Amil—Tallookdars, of the district—Ground suited for cantonments and civil offices—Places consecrated to worship—Kutteea Huron—Neem Sarang, traditions regarding—Landholders and peasantry of Sundeela—Banger and Sandee Palee, strong against the Government authorities from their union—Nankar and Seer. Nature and character of—Jungle—Leaves of the peepul, bur, &c., used as fodder—Want of good houses and all kinds of public edifices—Infanticide—Sandee district—Security of tenure in groves—River Gurra—Hafiz Abdulla, the governor—Runjeet Sing, of Kutteearee—Thieves in the Banger district—Infanticide—How to put down the crime—Palee—Richness of the foliage, and carpeting of spring crops—Kunojee Brahmins—Success of the robber's trade in Oude—Shahabad—Timber taken down the little river Gurra to the Ganges, from the Tarae forest—Fanaticism of the Moosulman population of Shahabad; and insolence and impunity with which they oppress the Hindoos of the town.

The baronial proprietors in the Sundeela district are Murdun Sing, of Dhurawun, with a rent-roll of 38,000; Gunga Buksh, of Atwa, with one of 25,000; Chundeeka Buksh, of Birwa, with one of 25,000; and Somere Sing, of Rodamow, with one of 34,000. This is the rent-roll declared and entered in the accounts; but it is much below the real one. The Government officers are afraid to measure their lands, or to make any inquiries on the estates into their value, lest they should turn robbers and plunder the country, as they are always prepared to do. They have always a number of armed and brave retainers, ready to support them in any enterprise, and can always add to their number on emergency. There is never any want of loose characters ready to fight for the sake of plunder alone. A tallookdar, however, when opposed to his government, does not venture to attack another tallookdar or his tenants. He stands too much in need of his aid, or at least of his neutrality and forbearance.

January 18, 1850.—Halted at Sundeela. To the north of the town there is a large uncultivated plain of oosur land, that would answer for cantonments; but the water lies, for some time after rain, in many places. The drainage is defective, but might be made good towards a rivulet to the north and west. There is another open plain to the west of the town, between the suburbs and the small village of Ausoo Serae, where the Trigonometrical Survey has one of its towers. It is about a mile from east to west, and more from north to south, and well adapted for the location of troops and civil establishments. The climate is said to be very good. The town is large and still populous, but the best families seem to be going to decay, or leaving the place. Many educated persons from Sundeela in our civil establishments used to leave their families here; but life and property have become so very insecure, that they now always take them with them to the districts in which they are employed, or send them to others. I observed many good houses of burnt brick and cement, but they are going fast to decay, and are all surrounded by numerous mud-houses without coverings, or with coverings of the same material, which are hidden from view by low parapets. These houses have a wretched appearance.

The Amil has twelve guns with him; but the bullocks are all so much out of condition from want of food that they can scarcely walk; and the Amil was obliged to hire a few plough-bullocks from the cultivators, to draw out two guns to my camp to fire the salute. They get no grain, and there is little or no grass anywhere on the fallow and waste lands, from the want of rain during June, July, and August. The Amil told me, that he had no stores or ammunition for the guns; and that their carriages were all gone, or going, to pieces, and had received no repairs whatever for the last twelve years. I had in the evening a visit from Rajah Murdun Sing, of Dharawun, a stout and fat man, who bears a fair character. He is of the Tilokchundee Bys clan, who cannot intermarry with each other, as they are all of the sama gote or family. It would, according to their notions, be incestuous.

January 19, 1850.—Hutteeah Hurrun, thirteen miles. The plain level as usual, and of the loose doomuteea soil, fertile in natural powers everywhere, and well tilled around the villages, which are more numerous than in any other part that we have passed over. The water is everywhere near the surface, and wells are made at little cost. A well is dug at a cost of from five to ten rupees; and in the muteear, or argillaceous soil, will last for irrigation for forty years. To line it with burnt bricks without cement will cost from one to two hundred rupees; and to add cement will cost a hundred more. Such lining is necessary in light soil, and still more so in sandy or bhoor. They frequently line their wells at little cost with long thick cables, made of straw and twigs, and twisted round the surface inside. The fields are everywhere irrigated from wells or pools, and near villages well manured; and the wheat and other spring crops are excellent. They have been greatly benefited by the late rains, and in no case injured. The ground all the way covered with white hoar frost, and the dews heavy in a cloudless sky. Finer weather I have never known in any quarter of the world.

This place is held sacred from a tradition, that Ram, after his expedition against Cylone, came here to bathe in a small tank near our present camp, in order to wash away the sin of having killed a Brahmin in the person of Rawun, the monster king of that island, who had taken away his wife, Seeta. Till he had done so, he could not venture to revisit his capital, Ajoodheea. There are many legends regarding the origin of the sanctity of this and the many other places around, which pilgrims must visit to complete the pykurma, or holy circuit. The most popular seems to be this.

Twenty-eight thousand sages of great sanctity were deputed, with the god Indur at their head, on a mission to present an address to Brimha, as he reposed upon the mountain Kylas, praying that he would vouchsafe to point out to them the place in Hindoostan most worthy to be consecrated to religious worship. He took a discus from the top-knot on his head, and, whirling it in the air, directed it to proceed in search. After much search it rested at a place near the river Goomtee, which it deemed to be most fitted for the purification of one's faith, and which thenceforth took the name of Neem Sarung, a place of devotion. The twenty-eight thousand sages followed, and were accompanied by Brimha himself, attended by the Deotas, or subordinate gods. He then summoned to the place no less than three crores and half, or thirty millions and half of teeruts, or angels, who preside each over his special place of religions worship. All settled down at places within ten miles of the central point, Neem Sarung; but their departure does not seem to have impaired the sanctity of the places whence they came. The angels, or spirits, who presided over them sent out these offshoots to preside at Neemsar and the consecrated places around it, as trees send off their grafts without impairing their own powers and virtues.

Misrik, a few miles from this, and one of the places thus consecrated, is celebrated as the residence of a very holy sage, named Dudeej. In a great battle between the Deotas and the Giants, the Deotas were defeated. They went to implore the aid of the drowsy god, Brimha, upon his snowy mountain top. He told them to go to Misrik and arm themselves with the bones of the old sage, Dudeej. They found Dudeej alive and in excellent health; but they thought it their duty to explain to him their orders. He told them, that he should be very proud indeed to have his bones used as arms in so holy a cause; but he had unfortunately vowed to bathe at all the sacred shrines in India before he died, and must perform his vow. Grievously perplexed, the Deotas all went and submitted their case to their leader, the god Indur. Indur consulted his chaplain, Brisput, who told him, that there was really no difficulty whatever in the case—that the angels of all the holy shrines in India had been established at and around Neemsar by Brimha himself; and the Deotas had only to take water from all the sacred places over which they presided, and pour it over the old sage, to get both him and themselves out of the dilemma. They did so, and the old sage, expressing himself satisfied, gave up his life. In what mode it was taken no one can tell me. The Deotas armed themselves with his bones, attacked the Giants forthwith, and gained an easy and complete victory. The wisdom of the orders of drowsy old Brimha, in this case, is as little questioned by the Hindoos of the present day as that of the orders of drunken old Jupiter was in the case of Troy, by the ancient Greeks and Romans. Millions, "wise in their generation," have spent their lives in the reverence of both.

There is hardly any sin that the waters of these dirty little ponds are not supposed to be capable of washing away; and, over and above this, they are supposed to improve all the good, and reduce to order all the bad passions and emotions of those who bathe in them, by propitiating the aid of the deity, and those who have influence over him.

A good deal of the land, distant from villages, lies waste, though capable of good tillage; and from the all pervading cause, the want of confidence in the Government and its officers, and of any feeling of security to life, property, and industry. Should this cause be removed, the whole surface of the country would become the beautiful garden which the parts well cultivated and peopled now are. It is all well studded with fine trees—single and in clusters and groves. The soil is good, the water near the surface, and to be obtained in any abundance at little outlay, and the peasantry are industrious, brave, and robust. Nothing is wanted but good and efficient government, which might be easily secured. I found many Kunojee Brahmins in the villages along the road, who tilled their own fields without the aid of ploughmen; and they told me, that when they had no longer the means to hire ploughmen, they were permitted to hold their own ploughs—that is, they were not excommunicated for doing so.

In passing along, with wheat-fields close by on our left, while the sun is a little above the horizon on the right, we see a glory round the shadows of our heads as they extend into the fields. All see these glories around their own heads, but cannot see them around those of their neighbours. They stretch out from the head and shoulders, with gradually-diminished splendour, to some short distance. This beautiful and interesting appearance arises from the leaves and stalks of the wheat being thickly bespangled with dew. The observer's head being in the direct rays of the sun, as they pass over him to that of his shadow in the field, he carries the glory with him. Those before and behind him see the same glory around the shadows of their own heads, but cannot see it round that of the head of any other person before or behind; because he is on one or other side of the direct rays which pass over them. It is best seen when the sky is most clear, and the dew most heavy. It is not seen over bushy crops such as the arahur, nor on the grass plains.

January 20, 1850.—Beneegunge, eight miles, over a slightly-undulating plain of light sandy soil, scantily cultivated, but well studded with fine trees of the best kind. Near villages, where the land is well watered and manured, the crops are fine and well varied. All the pools are full from the late rain, and they are numerous and sufficient to water the whole surface of the country, with a moderate fall of rain in December or January. If they are not available, the water is always very near the surface, and wells can be made for irrigation at a small cost. The many rivers and rivulets which enter Oude from the Himmalaya chain and Tarae forest, and flow gently through the country towards the Ganges, without cutting very deeply into the soil, always keep the water near the surface, and available in all quarters and in any quantity for purposes of irrigation. Never was country more favoured, by nature, or more susceptible of improvement under judicious management. There is really hardly an acre of land that is not capable of good culture, or that need be left waste, except for the sites of towns and villages, and ponds for irrigation, or that would be left waste under good government. The people understand tillage well, and are industrious and robust, capable of any exertion under protection and due encouragement.

The Government has all the revenues to itself, having no public debt and paying no tribute to any one, while the country receives from the British Government alone fifty lacs, or half a million a-year; first, in the incomes of guaranteed pensioners, whose stipends are the interest of loans received by our Government at different times from the sovereigns of Oude, as a provision for their relatives and dependents in perpetuity, and as endowments for their mausoleums and mosques, and other religious and eleemosynary establishments; second, in the interest paid for Government securities held by people residing in Oude; third, in the payment of pensions to the families of men who have been killed in our service, and to invalid native officers and sipahees of our army residing there, fourth, in the savings of others who still serve in our army, while their families reside in Oude; and those of the native officers of our civil establishments, whose families remain at their homes in Oude; fifth, in the interest on a large amount of our Government securities held by people at Lucknow, who draw the interest not from the Resident's Treasury, but from the General Treasury in Calcutta, or the Treasuries of our bordering districts, in order to conceal their wealth from the King and his officers. Over and above all this our Government has to send into Oude, to be expended there, the pay of five regiments of infantry and a company of artillery, which amounts to some six or seven lacs more. Oude has so many places of pilgrimage, that it receives more in the purchase of the food and other necessaries required by the pilgrims, during their transit and residence, than it sends out with pilgrims who visit shrines and holy places in other countries. It requires little from other countries but a few luxuries for the rich—in shawls from Kashmere and the Punjab, silks, satins, broad-cloth, muslins, guns, watches, &c. from England.

A great portion of the salt and saltpetre required is raised within Oude, and so is all the agricultural produce, except in seasons of drought; and the arms required for the troops are manufactured in Oude, with the exception of some few cannon and shells, and the muskets and bayonets for the few disciplined regiments. The royal family and some of the Mahommedan gentlemen at Lucknow send money occasionally to the shrines of Mecca, Medina, Kurbala, and Nujuf Ashruf, in Turkish Arabia; and some Hindoos send some to Benares and other places of worship, to be distributed in charity or laid out in useful works in their name. Some of the large pensions enjoyed by the relatives and dependents of former sovereigns, under the guarantee of our Government, go in perpetuity to the shrines in Turkish Arabia, in default of both will and heir. When Ghazee-od Deen succeeded his father on the musnud in 1814, contrary to his expectation and to his father's wish, he gave the minister about fifty lacs of rupees to be expended in charity at those shrines, and in canals, saraees, and other works of utility. Letters, full of expressions of gratitude and descriptions of these useful works, were often shown to him; but the minister, Aga Meer, is said to have kept the whole fifty lacs to himself, and got all these letters written by his private secretaries. Some few Hindoo and Mahommedan gentlemen, when they have lost their places and favour at the Oude Court, go and reside at Cawnpoor, and some few other places in the British territory for greater security; but generally it may be said, that in spite of all disadvantages Mahommedan gentlemen from Oude, in whatever country they may serve, like to leave their families in Oude, and to return and spend what they acquire among them. They find better society there than in our own territories, or society more to their tastes; better means for educating their sons; more splendid processions, festivals, and other inviting sights, in which they and their families can participate without cost; more consideration for rank and learning, and more attractive places for worship and religious observances. The little town of Karoree, about ten or twelve miles from Lucknow, has, I believe, more educated men, filling high and lucrative offices in our civil establishments, than any other town in India except Calcutta. They owe the greater security which they there enjoy, compared with other small towns in Oude, chiefly to the respect in which they are known to be held by the British Government and its officers, and to the influence of their friends and relatives who hold office about the Court of Lucknow.

January 21, 1849.—Sakin, ten miles north-west. The country well studded with fine trees, and pretty well cultivated, but the soil is light from a superabundance of sand; and the crops are chiefly autumn, except in the immediate vicinity of villages, and cut in December. The surface on which they stood this season appears to be waste, except where the stalks of the jowar and bajara, are left standing for sale and use, as fodder for cattle. These stalks are called kurbee, and form good fodder for elephants, bullocks, &c., during the cold, hot, and rainy season. They are said to keep better when left on the ground, after the heads have been gathered, than when stacked. The sandy soil, in the vicinity of villages, produces fine spring crops of all kinds, wheat, gram, sugarcane, arahur, tobacco, &c., being well manured by drainage from the villages, and by the dung stored and spread over it; and that more distant would produce the same, if manured and irrigated in the same way.

The head men or proprietors of some villages along the road mentioned, "that the fine state in which we saw them was owing to their being strong, and able to resist the Government authorities when disposed, as they generally were, to oppress or rack-rent them; that the landholders owed their strength to their union, for all were bound to turn out and afford aid to their neighbour on hearing the concerted signal of distress; that this league, 'offensive and defensive,' extended all over the Baugur district, into which we entered about midway between this and our last stage; and that we should see how much better it was peopled and cultivated in consequence than the district of Mahomdee, to which we were going; that the strong only could keep anything under the Oude Government; and as they could not be strong without union, all landholders were solemnly pledged to aid each other, to the death, when oppressed or attacked by the local officers." They asked Captain Weston, who was some miles behind me, what was the Resident's object in this tour, whether the Honourable Company's Government was to be introduced into Oude? He told them that the object was solely to see the state of the country and condition of the people, with a view to suggest to the King's Government any measures that might seem calculated to improve both; and asked them whether they wished to come under the British rule? They told him, "that they should like much to have the British rule introduced, if it could be done without worrying them with its complicated laws and formal and distant courts of justice, of which they had heard terrible accounts."

The Nazim of the Tundeeawun or Baugur district met me on his border, and told me, "that he was too weak to enforce the King's orders, or to collect his revenues; that he had with him one efficient company of Captain Bunbury's corps, with one gun in good repair, and provided with draft-bullocks, in good condition; and that this was the only force he could rely upon; while the landholders were strong, and so leagued together for mutual defence, that, at the sound of a matchlock, or any other concerted signal, all the men of a dozen large villages would, in an hour, concentrate upon and defeat the largest force the King's officers could assemble; that they did so almost every year, and often frequently within the same year; that he had nominally eight guns on duty with him, but the carriage of one had already gone to pieces; and those of the rest had been so long without repair that they would go to pieces with very little firing, that the draft-bullocks had not had any grain for many years, and were hardly able to walk; and he was in consequence obliged to hire plough-bullocks, to draw the gun required to salute the Resident; but he had only ten days ago received an order to give them grain himself, charge for it in his accounts, and hold himself responsible for their condition; that they had been so starved, that he was obliged to restrict them to a few ounces a-day at first, or they would have all died from over-eating." This order has arisen from my earnest intercession in favour of the artillery draft-bullocks; but so many are interested in the abuse, that the order will not be long enforced. Though the grain will, as heretofore, be paid for from the Treasury, it will, I hear, be given to the bullocks only while I am out on this tour.

In the evening some cultivators came to complain that they had been robbed of all their bhoosa (chaff) by a sipahee from my camp. I found, on inquiry, that the sipahee belonged to Captain Hearsey's five companies of Frontier Police; that these companies had sixteen four-bullock hackeries attached to them for the carriage of their tents and luggage; and that these hackeries had gone to the village, and taken all that the complainants had laid up for their own cattle for the season; that such hackeries formerly received twenty-seven rupees eight annas a-month each, and their owners were expected to purchase their own fodder; but that this allowance had for some years been cut down to fourteen rupees a-month, and they were told to help themselves to fodder wherever they could find it; that all the hackeries hired by the King and his local officers, for the use of troops, establishments, &c. had been reduced at the same rate, from twenty-seven eight annas a-month to fourteen, and their owners received the same order. All villages near the roads along which the troops and establishments move are plundered of their bhoosa, and all those within ten miles of the place, where they may be detained for a week or fortnight, are plundered in the same way.

The Telinga corps and Frontier Police are alone provided with tents and hackeries by Government. The Nujeeb corps are provided with neither. The Oude Government formerly allowed for each four-bullock hackery thirty rupees a-month, from which two rupees and half were deducted for the perquisites of office. The owners of the hackeries were expected to purchase bhoosa and other fodder for their bullocks at the market price; but they took what they required without payment, in collusion with the officers under whom they were employed, or in spite of them; and the Oude Government in 1845 cut the allowance down to seventeen rupees and half, out of which three rupees and half are cut for perquisites, leaving fourteen rupees for the hackeries: and their owners and drivers have the free privilege of helping themselves to bhoosa and other fodder wherever they can find them. Some fifty or sixty of these hackeries were formerly allowed for each Telinga corps with guns, now only twenty-two are allowed; and when they move they must, like Nujeeb corps, seize what more they require. They are allowed to charge nothing for their extra carriage, and therefore pay nothing.

January 22, 1849.—Tundeeawun, eight miles west. The country level, and something between doomuteen and muteear, very good, and in parts well cultivated, particularly in the vicinity of villages; but a large portion of the surface is covered with jungle, useful only to robbers and refractory landholders, who abound in the purgunnah of Bangur. In this respect it is reputed one of the worst districts in Oude. Within the last few years the King's troops have been frequently beaten and driven out with loss, even when commanded by an European officer. The landholders and armed peasantry of the different villages unite their quotas of auxiliaries, and concentrate upon them on a concerted signal, when they are in pursuit of robbers and rebels. Almost every able-bodied man of every village in Bangur is trained to the use of arms of one kind or another, and none of the King's troops, save those who are disciplined and commanded by European officers, will venture to move against a landholder of this district; and when the local authorities cannot obtain the aid of such troops, they are obliged to conciliate the most powerful and unscrupulous by reductions in the assessment of the lands or additions to their nankar.

To illustrate the spirit and system of union among the chief landholders of the Bangur district, I may here mention a few facts within my own knowledge, and of recent date. Bhugwunt Singh, who held the estate of Etwa Peepureea, had been for some time in rebellion against his sovereign; and he had committed many murders and robberies, and lifted many herds of cattle within our bordering district of Shajehanpoor; and he had given shelter, on his own estate, to a good many atrocious criminals, from that and others of our bordering district. He had, too, aided and screened many gangs of Budhuks, or dacoits by hereditary profession.

The Resident, Colonel Low, in 1841, directed every possible effort to be made for the arrest of this formidable offender, and Captain Hollings, the second in command of the 2nd battalion of Oude local infantry, sent intelligencers to trace him.

They ascertained that he had, with a few followers, taken up a position two hundred yards to the north of the village of Ahroree, in a jungle of palas-trees and brushwood in the Bangur district, about twenty-eight miles to the south-west of Seetapoor, where that battalion was cantoned, and about fourteen miles west from Neemkar. Captain Hollings made his arrangements to surprise this party; and on the evening of the 3rd of July 1841, he marched from Neemkar at the head of three companies of that battalion, and a little before midnight he came within three-quarters of a mile of the rebel's post. After halting his party for a short time, to enable the officers and sipahees to throw off all superfluous clothing and utensils, Captain Hollings moved on to the attack. When the advanced guard reached the outskirts of the robber's position about midnight, they were first challenged and then fired upon by the sentries. The subadar in command of this advance guard fell dead, and a non-commissioned officer and a sipahee severely wounded.

The whole party now fired in upon the gang and rushed on. One of the robbers was shot, and the rest all escaped out on the opposite side of the jungle. The sipahees believing, since the surprise had been complete, that the robbers must have left all their wealth behind them, dispersed, as soon as the firing ceased and the robbers disappeared, to get every man as much as he could. While thus engaged they were surrounded by the Gohar, (or body of auxiliaries which these landholders send to each other's aid on the concerted signal,) and fired in upon from the front, and both right and left flanks. Taken by surprise, they collected together in disorder, while the assailants from the front and sides continued to pour in their fire upon them; and they were obliged to retire in haste and confusion, closely followed by the auxiliaries, who gained confidence, and pressed closer as their number increased by the quotas they received from the villages the detachment had to pass in their retreat.

All efforts on the part of Captain Hollings to preserve order in the ranks were vain. His men returned the fire of their pursuers, but without aim or effect. At the head of the auxiliaries were Punchum Sing, of Ahroree, and Mirza Akbar Beg, of Deureea; and they were fast closing in upon the party, and might have destroyed it, when Girwur Sing, tomandar, came up with a detachment of the Special Police of the Thuggee and Dacoitee Department. At this time the three companies were altogether disorganized and disheartened, as the firing and pursuit had lasted from midnight to daybreak; but on seeing the Special Police come up and join with spirit in the defence, they rallied, and the assailants, thinking the reinforcement more formidable than it really was, lost confidence and held back. Captain Hollings mounted the fresh horse of the tomandar, and led his detachment without further loss or molestation back to Neemkar. His loss had been one subadar, one havildar, and three sipahees killed; one subadar, two havildars, one naik, and fourteen sipahees wounded and missing. Captain Hollings' groom was shot dead, and one of his palankeen-bearers was wounded. His horse, palankeen, desk, clothes, and all the superfluous clothing and utensils, which the sipahees had thrown off preparatory to the attack fell into the hands of the assailants. Attempts were made to take up and carry off the killed and wounded; but the detachment was so sorely pressed that they were obliged to leave both on the ground. The loss would have been much greater than it was, but for the darkness of the night, which prevented the assailants from taking good aim; and the detachment would, in all probability, have been cut to pieces, but for the timely arrival of the Special Police under Girwur Sing.

Such attacks are usually made upon robber bands about the first dawn of day; and this attack at midnight was a great error. Had they not been assailed by the auxiliaries, they could not, in the darkness, have secured one of the gang. It was known, that at the first shot from either the assailing or defending party in that district, all the villages around concentrate their quotas upon the spot, to fight to the death against the King's troops, whatever might be their object; and the detachment ought to have been prepared for such concentration when the firing began, and returned as quickly as possible from the place when they saw that by staying they could not succeed in the object.

Four months after, in November, Punchum Sing, of Ahroree, himself cut off the head of the robber, Bhugwunt Sing, with his own hand, and sent it to the governor, Furreed-od Deen, with an apology for having by mistake attacked Captain Hollings' detachment. The governor sent the head to the King, with a report stating that he had, at the peril of his life, and after immense toil, hunted down and destroyed this formidable rebel; and his Majesty, as a reward for his valuable services, conferred upon Furreed-od Deen a title and a first-rate dress of honour. Soon after, in the same month of July 1841, his Majesty the King of Oude's second regiment of infantry, under the command of a very gallant officer, Captain W. D. Bunbury, was encamped near the village of Belagraon, when information was brought that certain convicts, who had escaped from the gaol at Bareilly, had taken refuge in the village of Parakurown, about fifty miles to the north-west of his camp. Captain Bunbury immediately detached three companies, with two six-pounders, under his brother, Lieutenant A. C. Bunbury, to arrest them. After halting for a short time at Gopamow, to allow his men to take breath, Lieutenant Bunbury pushed on, and reached the place a little before the dawn of day. He demanded the surrender of the outlaws from the chief of the village, named Ajrael Sing, a notoriously bad character, who insolently refused to give them up. A fight commenced, in which one of the convicts, and some others, were killed; but at last Lieutenant Bunbury succeeded in securing Arjael Sing himself, with some few of his followers, and the outlaws.

Hearing the firing of the field-pieces, the surrounding villages concentrated their quotas of auxiliaries upon the place, and attacked Lieutenant Bunbury's detachment on all sides. He had taken possession of the village; but finding it untenable against so large and increasing a body of assailants, he commenced his retreat. He had scarcely reached the outskirts when he found himself surrounded by overwhelming numbers of these auxiliaries, through whom he was obliged to fight his way for a distance of fourteen miles to Pahanee. The armed peasantry of every village, on the right and left of the road as they passed, turned out and joined the pursuers in their attempt to rescue his prisoners. Lieutenant Bunbury's conduct of this retreat was most gallant and judicious; and his men behaved admirably. When the assailants appeared likely to overwhelm him, he abandoned one of his two guns, and hastened on, leaving three men lying under them apparently wounded, and unable to move. On this they pressed on, sword in hand, to despatch the wounded men, and seize the guns. When the assailants were within thirty or forty yards of the gun, they started up, and poured in upon the dense crowd a discharge of grape with deadly effect. A party then doubled back from the main body of the detachment, protected the artillery men in limbering up the gun, and escorting it to the main body, which again resumed its march. This experiment was repeated several times with success as they passed other villages, from which further auxiliaries poured out, till they approached Pahanee, where they found support. In this retreat Lieutenant Bunbury lost sixty men out of his three companies, or about one-third of his number; but he retained all his prisoners. Ajrael Sing soon after died of the wounds he had received in defending the convicts in his village; and the rest of the prisoners were all sent to the Oude Durbar. Lieutenant Bunbury is now in the Honourable Company's Service, and in the 34th Regiment of Bengal Native Infantry.

On the 23rd of January 1849, Captain Hearsey, of the Oude Frontier Police, sent his subadar-major, Ramzan Khan, with a party of one hundred and fifty men of that police, to arrest a notorious robber, Mendae Sing, and other outlaws, from the Shajehanpoor district, who had found an asylum in the village of Sahurwa, in the Mahomdee district, whence they carried on their depredations upon our villages across the border. The party reached Sahurwa the next morning a little before sunrise. The subadar-major having posted his men so as to prevent the escape of the outlaws, demanded their surrender from the village authorities. They were answered by a volley of matchlock-balls; and finding the village too strong to be taken by his small detachment without guns, he withdrew to a more sheltered position to the westward, and detached a havildar with fifty men to take possession of a large gateway to the south of the village. During this movement the villagers continued to fire upon them; and the quotas of auxiliaries from the surrounding villages, roused by the firing, came rushing on from all quarters. Seeing no chance of being able either to take the village or to maintain his position against such numbers, the subadar-major drew off his detachment, and proceeded for support to Pahanee, a distance of twelve miles. He reached that place pursued by the auxiliaries, and with the loss of one havildar and one sipahee killed, and three sipahees very severely wounded. There are numerous instances of this sort in which the King's troops have been attacked and beaten back, and their prisoners rescued by the landholders of Bangur, and the adjoining districts of Mahomdee and Sandee Palee. They are never punished for doing so, as the King is too weak, and the aid of the British troops, for the purpose, has seldom been given.

It would be of advantage to remove the Regiment of Oude Local Infantry from Seetapoor to Tundeeawun, where its presence and services are much more required. The climate is as good, and all that native soldiers require for food and clothing are cheaper. The drainage is good; and to the east of the town there is one of the finest plains for a cantonment that I have ever seen. There are but few wells, but new ones can be made at a trifling cost; and the Oude Government would willingly incur the outlay required for these and for all the public buildings required for the new cantonments, to secure the advantage of such a change. The cost of the public buildings would be only 12,000 rupees; and the same sum would have to be given in compensation for private buildings-total 24,000. The refractory landholders would soon be reduced to order, and prevented from any longer making their villages dens of robbers as they now do; and the jungles around would all soon disappear. These jungles are not thick, or unhealthy, consisting of the small dhak or palas tree, with little or no underwood; and the surface they now occupy would soon be covered with fine spring crops, and studded with happy village communities, were people encouraged by an assurance of protection to settle upon it, and apply their capital and labour to its cultivation. The soil is everywhere of the finest quality, the drainage is good, and there are no jheels. A few ponds yield the water required for the irrigation of the spring crops, during their progress to maturity, from November to March: they are said all to become dry in the hot season. It is, I think, capable of being made the finest part of this fine country of Oude.

It was in contemplation to make the road from Lucknow to Shajehanpoor and Bareilly pass through this place, Tundeeawun, by which some thirty miles of distance would be saved, and a good many small rivers and watercourses avoided. Why this design was given up I know not; but I believe the only objection was the greater insecurity of this line from the bad character of the great landholders of the Bangur and Sandee Palee districts; and the greater number of thieves and robbers who, in consequence, reside in them. There has been but little outlay in works of any kind in the whole line through Seetapore; and when measures have been taken to render this line more secure, a good road will, I hope, be made through Tundeeawun. It was once a populous place, but has been falling off for many years, as the disorders in the district have increased. The Nazim resides here. The last Nazim, Hoseyn Allee, who was removed to Khyrabad, at the end of last year, is said to have given an increase of nankar to the refractory landholders of this district during that year, to the extent of forty thousand rupees a-year, to induce them to pay the Government demand, and desist from plunder. By this means he secured a good reputation at Court, and the charge of a more profitable and less troublesome district; and left the difficult task of resuming this lavish increase of the nankar to his successor, Seonath, the son of Dilla Ram, who held the contract of the district for some twenty years up to the time of his death, which took place last year. Seonath is a highly respectable and amiable man; but he is very delicate in health, and, in consequence, deficient in the vigour and energy required to manage so turbulent a district. He has, however, a deputy in Kidder Nath, a relative, who has all the ability, vigour, and energy required, if well supported and encouraged by the Oude Durbar. He was deputy under Dilla Ram for many years, and the same under Hoseyn Allee last year. He is a man of great intelligence and experience; and one of the best officers of the Oude Government that I have yet seen.

There are two kinds of recognised perquisites which landholders enjoy in Oude and in most other parts of India—the nankar and the seer land. The nankar is a portion of the recognised rent-roll acknowledged by the ruler to be due to the landholder for the risk, cost, and trouble of management, and for his perquisite as hereditary proprietor of the soil when the management is confided to another. It may be ten, twenty, or one hundred percent upon the rent-roll of the estate, which is recognised in the public accounts, as the holder happens to be an object of fear or of favour, or otherwise; and the real rent-roll may be more or less than that which is recognised in the public accounts. The actual rent which the landholder receives may increase with improvements, and he may conceal the improvement from the local authorities, or bribe them to conceal it from Government; or it may diminish from lands falling out of tillage, or becoming impoverished by over-cropping, or from a diminution of demand for land produce; and the landholder may be unable to satisfy the local authorities of the fact, or to prevail upon them to represent the circumstance to Government. The amount of the nankar once recognised remains the same till a new rate is recognised by Government; but when the Government becomes weak, the local authorities assume the right to recognise new rents, to suit their own interest, and pretend that they do so to promote that of their sovereign.

I may instance the Amil of this district last year. He was weak, while the landholders were strong. They refused to pay, on the plea of bad seasons. He could send no money to the Treasury, and was in danger of losing his place. The man who had to pay a revenue of ten thousand could not be induced to pay five: he enjoyed an acknowledged nankar of two thousand upon a recognised rent-roll of twelve thousand; and, to induce him to pay, he gives him an increase to this nankar of one thousand, making the nankar three thousand, and reducing the revenue to nine thousand. Being determined to render the increase to his nankar permanent, whether the Government consents or not, the landholder agrees to pay the ten thousand for the present year. The collector sends the whole or a part of the one thousand as gratuities to influential men at Court, and enters it in the public accounts as irrecoverable balance. The present Amil, finding that the increase to the nankar has not been acknowledged by Government, demands the full ten thousand rupees for the present year. The landholder refuses to pay anything, takes to the jungles, and declares that he will resist till his permanent right to the increase be acknowledged.

The Amil has taken the contract at the rate of last year, as the Government had sanctioned no increase to the nankar, and he pleads in vain for a remission in the rate, which he pledged himself to pay, or an increase of means to enforce payment among so turbulent and refractory a body of landholders. As I have before mentioned, the Oude Government has this season issued an order to all revenue collectors to refuse to recognise any increase to the nankar that has been made since the year A.D. 1814, or Fusilee 1222, when Saadut Allee died, as none has since that year received the sanction of Government, though the nankar has been more than doubled within that period in the manner above described by local authorities. The increase to the nankar, and the alienation in rent-free tenure of lands liable to assessment in 1814 by local authorities and influential persons at Court, are supposed to amount in all Oude to forty lacs of rupees a-year. None of them have been formally recognised by the Court, but a great part of them has been tacitly acquiesced in by the minister and Dewan for the time being.

They cannot enforce the order for reverting to the nankar of 1814, and if they attempt to do so the whole country will be in disorder. Indeed, the minister knows his own weakness too well to think seriously of ever making such an attempt. The seer lands are those which the landholders and their families till themselves, or by means of their servants or hired cultivators. Generally they are not entered at all in the rent-rolls; and when they are entered, it is at less rates than are paid for the other lands. The difference between the no rent, or less rates, and the full rates is part of their perquisites. These lands are generally shared out among the members of the family as hereditary possessions.

January 23, 1850.—Behta, ten miles, over a plain of fine muteear soil. The greater part of the surface is, however, covered by a low palas jungle. The jungle remains, because no one will venture to lay out his capital in rooting up the trees and shrubs, and bringing the land under culture where the fruits of his industry, and his own life and those of his family, would be so very insecure, and because the powerful landholders around require the jungles to run to when in arms against the Government officers, as they commonly are. The land under this jungle is as rich in natural powers as that in tillage; and nothing can be finer than the crops in the cultivated parts, particularly in those immediately around villages. There are numerous large trees in the jungles, but the fine peepul and banyan trees are torn to pieces for the use of the elephants and camels of the establishments of the local officers, and for the cows, bullocks, and buffaloes of the peasantry. The cows and buffaloes are said to give greater quantities of milk when fed on the leaves of these trees than when fed on anything else available in the dry season; but the milk is said to be of inferior quality. All the cultivated and peopled parts are beautifully studded with single trees and groves.

No respectable dwelling-house is anywhere to be seen, and the most substantial landholders live in wretched mud-hovels with invisible covers. I asked the people why, and was told that they were always too insecure to lay out anything in improving their dwelling-houses; and, besides, did not like to have such local ties, where they were so liable to be driven away by the Government officers or by the landholders in arms against them, and their reckless followers. The local officers of Government, of the highest grade, occupy houses of the same wretched description, for none of them can be sure of occupying them a year, or of ever returning to them again when once removed from their present offices; and they know that neither their successors nor any one else will ever purchase or pay rent for them. No mosques, mausoleums, temples, seraees, colleges, courts of justice, or prisons to be seen in any of the towns or villages. There are a few Hindoo shrines at the half-dozen places which popular legends have rendered places of pilgrimage, and a few small tanks and bridges made in olden times by public officers, when they were more secure in their tenure of office than they are now. All the fine buildings raised by former rulers and their officers at the old capital of Fyzabad are going fast to ruin. The old city of Ajoodhea is a ruin, with the exception of a few buildings along the bank of the river raised by wealthy Hindoos in honour of Ram, who once lived and reigned there, and is believed by all Hindoos to have been an incarnation of Vishnoo.

I have often mentioned that the artillery draft-bullocks receive no grain, and are everywhere so poor that they can hardly walk, much less draw heavy guns and tumbrils. The reason is this, the most influential men at Court obtain the charge of feeding the cattle in all the different establishments, and charge for a certain quantity of grain or other food at the market price for each animal. They contract for the supply of the cattle with some grain-merchant of the city, who undertakes to distribute it through his own agents. The contractor for the supply of the artillery draft-bullocks sends an agent with those in attendance upon every collector of the land revenue, and he gives them as little as possible. The contractor, afraid of making an enemy of the influential man at Court, who could if he chose deprive him of his contract or place, never presumes to interfere, and the agent gives the poor bullocks no grain at all. The collector, or officer in charge of the district, is, however, obliged every month to pay the agent of the contractor the full market price of the grain supposed to be consumed—that is, one seer and half a-day by every bullock. The same, or some other influential person at Court, obtains and transfers in the same way the contract for the feeding of the elephants, horses, camels, bullocks, and other animals kept at Lucknow for use or amusement, and none of them are in much better condition than the draft-bullocks of the artillery in the remote districts—all are starved, or nearly starved, and objects of pity. Those who are responsible for their being fed are too strong in Court favour to apprehend any punishment for not feeding them at all.

In my ride this morning I asked the people of the villages through and near which we passed whether infanticide prevailed: they told me that it prevailed amongst almost all the Rajpoot families of any rank in Oude; that very poor families of those classes retained their daughters, because they could get something for them from the families of lower grade, into which they married them; but that those who were too well off in the world to condescend to take money for their daughters from lower grades, and were obliged to incur heavy costs in marrying them into families of the same or higher grade, seldom allowed their infant daughters to live.

"It is strange," I observed, "that men, who have to undergo such heavy penance for killing a cow, even by accident, should have to undergo none for the murder of their own children, nor to incur any odium among the circle of society in which they live—not even among Brahmins and the ministers of their religion."

"They do incur odium, and undergo penance," said Rajah Bukhtawur Sing; "do they not?" said he to some Brahmins standing near. They smiled, but hesitated to reply. "They know they do," said the Rajah, "but are afraid to tell the truth, for they and their families live in villages belonging to these proud Rajpoot landholders, and would be liable to be turned out of house and home were they to tell what they know." One of the Brahmins then said, "All this is true, sir; but after the murder of every infant the family considers itself to be an object of displeasure to the deity, and after the twelfth day they send for the family priest (Prohut), and, by suitable gratuities, obtain absolution. This is necessary, whether the family be rich or poor; but when the absolution is given, nothing more is thought or said about the matter. The Gour and other Rajpoots who can afford to unite their daughters in marriage to the sons of Chouhans, Byses, and other families of higher grade, though they cannot obtain theirs in return for their sons, commit less murders of this kind than others; but all the Rajpoot clans commit more or less of them. Habit has reconciled them to it; but it appears very shocking to us Brahmins and all other classes. They commonly bury the infants alive as soon as possible after their birth. We, sir, are helpless, living as we do among such turbulent and pitiless landholders, and cannot presume to admonish or remonstrate: our lives would not be safe for a moment were we to say anything, or seem to notice such crimes."

I do not think that any landholder of this class, in the Bangur district, would feel much compunction for the commission of any crime that did not involve their expulsion from caste, or degradation in rank. Great crimes do not involve these penalties: they incur them only by small peccadillos, or offences deemed venal among other societies. The Government of Oude, as it is at present constituted, will never be able to put down effectually the great crimes which now stain almost every acre of land in its dominions. It is painful to pass over a country abounding so much in what the evil propensities of our nature incite men to do, when not duly restrained; and so little in what the good prompt us to perform and create, when duly protected and encouraged, under good government.

January 24, 1850.—Sandee, fourteen miles, over a plain of light domuteea soil, which becomes very sandy for the last four or five miles. The crops are scanty upon the more sandy parts, except in the vicinity of villages; but there is a little jungle, and no undue portion of fallow for so light a soil. About five miles from our last ground, we came through the large and populous village of Bawun; about three miles further, through another of nearly the same size, Sungeechamow; and about three miles further on, through one still larger, Admapoor, which is three miles from Sandee. Sandee and Nawabgunge join each other, and are on the bank of the Gurra river, a small stream whose waters are said to be very wholesome. We passed the boundary of the Bangur district, just before we entered the village of Sungeechamow, which lies in that of Sandee.

There is a Hindoo shrine on the right of the road between Sandee and Admapoor, which is said to be considered very sacred, and called Barmawust. It is a mere grove, with a few priests, on the bank of a large lake, which extends close up to Sandee on the south. The river Gurra flows under the town to the north. The place is said to be healthy, but could hardly be so, were this lake to the west or east, instead of the south, whence the wind seldom blows. This lake must give out more or less of malaria, that would be taken over the village, for the greater portion of the year, by the prevailing easterly and westerly winds. I do not think the place so eligible for a cantonment at Tundeeawun, in point either of salubrity, position, or soil.

January 25, 1850.—Halted at Sandee. The lake on the south side, mentioned yesterday, abounds in fish, and is covered with wild fowl; but the fish we got from it yesterday was not good of its kind. I observed very fine groves of mango-trees close to Sandee, planted by merchants and shopkeepers of the place. The oldest are still held by the descendants of those by whom they were first planted, more than a century ago; and no tax whatever is imposed upon the trees of any kind, or upon the lands on which they stand. Many young groves are growing up around, to replace the old ones as they decay; and the greatest possible security is felt in the tenure by which they are held by the planter, or his descendants, though they hold no written lease, or deed of gift; and have neither written law nor court of justice to secure it to them. Groves and solitary mango, semul, tamarind, mhowa and other trees, whose leaves and branches are not required for the food of elephants and camels, are more secure in

Oude than in our own territories; and the country is, in consequence, much better provided with them. While they give beauty to the landscape, they alleviate the effects of droughts to the poorer classes from the fruit they supply; and droughts are less frequently and less severely felt in a country so intersected by fine streams, flowing from the Tarae forest, or down from the perpetual snows of neighbouring hills, and keeping the water always near the surface. These trees tend also to render the air healthy, by giving out oxygen in large quantities during the day, and absorbing carbonic acid gas. The river Gurra enters the Ganges about twelve miles below Sandee. Boats take timber on this stream from the Phillibeet district to Cawnpoor. It passes near the town of Shajehanpoor; and the village of Palee, twenty miles north-west from Sandee, where we shall have to recross it.

January 26, 1850.—Busora, twelve miles north-west from Sandee, over a plain of light sandy soil, or bhoor, with some intervals of oosur. The tillage extends over as much of the surface as it ought in so light a soil; and the district of Sandee Palee generally is said to be well cultivated. It has been under the charge of Hafiz Abdoollah, a very honest and worthy man, for seven years up to his death, which took place in November last. He is said never to have broken faith with a landholder; but he was too weak in means to keep the bad portion under control; and too much occupied in reading or repeating the Koran, which he knew all by heart, as his name imports. His son Ameer Gholam Allee, a lad of only thirteen years of age, has been appointed his successor. He promises to be like his father in honesty and love of the holy book.*

* He has been since removed, and was in prison as a defaulter, July 1851.

About half way we passed the village of Bhanapoor, held by zumeendars of the Dhaukurree Rajpoot clan, who told me, that they gave their daughters in marriage to the Rykwars, but more to the Sombunsie Rajpoots, who abound in the district, and hold the greater part of the lands; that these Sombunsies have absorbed almost all the lands of the other classes by degrees, and are now seizing upon theirs; that the Sombunsies give their daughters in marriage only to the Rathore and Chouhan Rajpoots, few of whom are to be found on the Oude side of the Ganges; and, in consequence, that they take such as they preserve to our districts on the other side of that river, but murder the greater part rather than condescend to marry them to men of the other Rajpoot clans whom they deem to be of inferior grade, or go to the expense of uniting them in marriage to clans of higher or equal grade in Oude. Some Sombunsies, who came out to pay their respects from the next village we passed, told us, that they did not give their daughters even to the Tilokchundee Bys Rajpoots; but in this they did not tell the truth.

At the next village, the largest in the parish, Barone, the chief landholder, Kewul Sing, came out and presented his offering of a fine fighting-ram. He was armed with his bow, and "quiver full of arrows," but told me, that he thought a good gun, with pouch and flask, much better, and he carried the bow and quiver merely because they were lighter. He was surrounded by almost all the people of the town, and told me, that the family held in copartnership fifty-two small villages, immediately around Barone—that this village had been attacked and burnt down by Captain Bunbury and his regiment the year before last, without any other cause that they could understand save that he had recommended him not to encamp in the grove close by. The fact was, that none of the family would pay the Government demand, or obey the old Amil, Hafiz Abdoollah; and it was necessary to make an example. On being asked whether his family and clan, the Sombunsies, preserved or destroyed their daughters, he told me, in the midst of his village community, that he would not deceive me; that they, one and all, destroyed their infant daughters; but that one was, occasionally, allowed to live (ek-adh); that the family was under a taint for twelve days after the murder of an infant, when the family priest (Prohut) was invited and fed in due form; that he then declared the absolution complete, and the taint removed.

The family priest was present, and I asked him what he got on such occasions? He said, that to remove the taint, or grant absolution after the murder of a daughter, he got little or no money; he merely partook of the food prepared for him in due form; but that, on the birth of a son, he got ten rupees from the parents. All the assembled villagers bore testimony to the truth of what the patriarch and the priest told me. They said, that no one would enter a house in which an infant daughter had been destroyed, or eat or drink with any member of the family till the Prohut had granted the absolution, which he did after the expiration of twelve days, as a matter of course, depending as he did upon the goodwill of the landholders, who were all of the same clan, Sombunsies. Few other Brahmins will condescend to eat, drink, or associate with these family and village priests, who take the sins of such murderers upon their own heads.

The old patriarch rode on with me upon his pony, five miles to my tents, as if I should not think the worse of him for having murdered his own daughters, and permitted others to murder theirs. I told him, that I could hold no converse with men who were guilty of such crimes; and that the vengeance of God would crush them all, sooner or latter. For his only excuse he told me, that it was a practice, derived from a long line of ancestors, wiser and better than they were; and that it prevailed in almost every Rajpoot family in the country; that they had, in consequence, become reconciled to it, and knew not how to do without it. Family pride is the cause of this terrible evil!

The estate of Kuteearee, on the left-hand side of the road towards the Ramgunga and Ganges, is held by Runjeet Sing, of the Kuteear Rajpoot clan. His estate yields to him about one hundred and twenty thousand rupees a-year, while he is assessed at only sixteen thousand. While Hakeem Mehndee was in banishment at Futtehgurh, about fifteen years ago, he became intimate with Runjeet Sing, of Kuteearee; and when he afterwards became minister, in 1837, he is said to have obtained for him the King's seal and signature to a perpetual lease at this rate, from which is deducted a nankar of four thousand, leaving an actual demand of only twelve thousand. Were such grants, in perpetuity, respected in Oude, the ministers and their minions would soon sell the whole of his Majesty's dominions, and leave him a beggar. He has not yet been made to pay a higher rate; not, however, out of regard for the King's pledge, but solely out of that for Runjeet's fort of Dhunmutpoor, on the bank of the Ganges, his armed bands, and his seven pieces of cannon. He has been diligently employing all his surplus rents in improving his defensive means; and, besides his fort and guns, is said to have a large body of armed and disciplined men. He has seized upon a great many villages around, belonging to weaker proprietors: and is every year adding to his estate in this way. In this the old Amil, Hafiz Abdoollah, acquiesced, solely because he had not the means nor the energy to prevent it. He got his estate excluded from the jurisdiction of the local authorities, and placed in the Huzoor Tuhseel.

Like others of his class, who reside on the border, he has a village in the British territory to reside in, unmolested, when charged by the Oude authorities with heavy crimes and balances. He had been attacked and driven across the Ganges, in 1837, for contumacy and rebellion; deprived of his estate, and obliged to reside at Futtehgurh, where he first became acquainted with Hakeem Mehndee. The Oude Government has often remonstrated against the protection which this contumacious and atrocious landholder receives from our subjects and authorities.* Crimes in this district are not quite so numerous as in Bangur; but they are of no less atrocious a character. The thieves and robbers of Bangur, when taken and taxed with being so, say, "of course we are robbers—if we were not, how should we have been permitted to reside in Bangur?" All are obliged to fight and plunder with the landholders, or to rob for them on distant roads, and in distant villages.

* See the Resident's letter to Government North-Western Provinces, 3rd August, 1837. The King's letter to the Resident, 7th April, 1837. The same to the same, 19th May, 1837. Depositions and urzies. Runjeet Sing was attacked by the King's troops and driven across the Ganges again in June 1851, and died during the contest, which is being continued by his son. 1851.—W. H. S.

My camp has been robbed several times within the time I have been out, and the property has been traced to villages in the Sundeela and Bangur districts. In the Sundeela district it can be recovered when traced with a small force, and the thieves taken; but in the Bangur district it would require a large military force well commanded, and a large train of artillery to recover the one or seize the other.

A respectable landholder of this place, a Sombunsie, tells me, that the custom of destroying their female infants has prevailed from the time of the first founder of their race; that a rich man has to give food to many Brahmins, to get rid of the stain, on the twelfth or thirteenth day, but that a poor man can get rid of it by presenting a little food in due form to the village priest; that they cannot give their daughters in marriage to any Rajpoot families, save the Rhathores and Chouhans; that the family of their clan who gave a daughter to any other class of Rajpoots, would be excluded from caste immediately and for ever; that those who have property have to give all they have with their daughters to the Chouhans and Rhathores, and reduce themselves to nothing; and can take nothing from them in return, as it is a great stain to take "kuneea dan," or virgin price; from any one; that a Sombunsie may, however, when reduced to great poverty, take the "kuneea dan" from the Chouhans and Rhathores for a virgin daughter without being excommunicated from the clan, but even he could not give a daughter to any other clan of Rajpoots without being excluded for ever from caste; that it was a misfortune no doubt, but it was one that had descended among them from the remotest antiquity, and could not be got rid of; that mothers wept and screamed a good deal when their first female infants were torn from them, but after two or three times giving birth to female infants, they become quiet and reconciled to the usage, and said, "do as you like;" that some poor parents of their clan did certainly give their daughters for large sums to wealthy people of lower Clans, but lost their caste for ever by so doing; that it was the dread of sinking, in substance from the loss of property, and in grade from the loss of caste, that alone led to the murder of female infants; that the dread prevailed more or less in every Rajpoot clan, and led to the same thing, but most in the clan that restricted the giving of daughters in marriage to the smallest number of clans.

The infant is destroyed in the room where it is born, and there buried. The floor is then plastered over with cow-dung, and on the thirteenth day the village or family priest must cook and eat his food in that room. He is provided with wood, ghee, barley, rice, and tillee (sesamum). He boils the rice, barley, and sesamum in a brass vessel, throws the ghee over them when they are dressed, and eats the whole. This is considered as a hom, or burnt-offering, and by eating it in that place the priest is supposed to take the whole hutteea or sin upon himself, and to cleanse the family from it. I am told that they put the milk of the mudar shrub "asclepias gigantea," into the mouth of the infant to destroy it, and cover the mouth with the faeces that first pass from, the infant's bowels. It soon dies; and after the expiation the parents again occupy the room, and there receive the visits of their family and friends, and gossip as usual!

Rajah Bukhtawar Sing tells me, that he has heard the whole process frequently described in this way by the midwives who have attended the birth. These midwives are however generally sent out of the room with the mother when the infant is found to be a girl. In any law for the effectual prevention of this crime, it would be necessary to prescribe a severe punishment for the priest, as an accessary after the fact. The only objection to this is, I think, that it might deprive the Court of the advantage of an important witness when required at the trial of the parents, but when necessary he might be admitted as King's evidence. All the people here that I talk to on the subject, say that the crime has been put down in the greater part of the British territories, and that judicious measures honestly and firmly carried out would put it down in Oude, and do away with the scruples which one clan of Rajpoots have to give their daughters in marriage to another. Unable to murder their daughters, they would be glad to dispose of them in marriage to all clans of Rajpoots. It might be put down in Oude, as it was put down by Mr. Willoughby, of Bombay, in the districts under his charge, by making the abolition one of the conditions on which all persons of the Rajpoot clans hold their lands, and strictly enforcing the observance of that condition. The Government of Oude as now constituted could do nothing whatever towards putting it down in this or any other way.

January 27, 1850.—Palee, eight miles north-west. The road half way from Sandee to Busora, and half way from Busora to Palee, passes over a very light, sandy soil—bhoor. I have already stated that kutcha wells, or wells without burnt brick and cement, will not last in this sandy soil, while it stands more in need of irrigation. The road for the last half way of this morning's stage passes over a good doomuteea soil. The whole country is however well cultivated, and well studded with fine trees; and the approach to Palee is at this season very picturesque. The groves of mango and other fine trees amidst which the town stands, on the right bank of the Gurra river, appear very beautiful as one approaches, particularly now that the surrounding country is covered by so fine a carpet of rich spring crops. The sun's rays, falling upon such rich masses of foliage, produce an infinite variety of form, colour, and tint, on which the eye delights to repose. We intended to have our camp on the other side of the river, but no good ground could be found for it, without injury to the crops, within three miles from Palee, and we must cross it on our way to Shahabad to-morrow.

This small river flows along a little to the right of our march this morning. About half way we passed a very pretty village, held and cultivated by families of Kunojee Brahmins, who condescend to hold and drive their own ploughs. Other families of this class pride themselves upon never condescending to drive their own ploughs, and consider themselves in consequence a shade higher in caste. Other Brahmin families have different shades or degrees of caste, like the Kunojeeas; but I am not aware that any family of any other class of Brahmins condescend to hold their own ploughs. I told them, that "God seemed to favour their exertions, and bless them with prosperity, for I had not seen a neater village or village community." They seemed to be all well pleased with my compliment. At Palee resides Bulbhuder Sing, a notorious robber, who was lately seized and sent as a felon to Lucknow. After six months' confinement he bribed himself out, got possession of the estate which he now holds, and to which he had no right whatever, and had it excluded from the jurisdiction of the local authorities, and transferred to the "Hozoor Tuhseel." He has been ever since diligently employed in converting it into a den of robbers, and in the usual way seizing upon other people's lands, stock, and property of all kinds.

Hundreds in Oude are doing the same thing in the same way. Scores of those who suffer from the depredations of this class of offenders, complain to me every day; but I can neither afford them redress, nor hold out any hope of it from any of the Oude authorities. It is a proverb, "that those who are sentenced to six years' imprisonment in Oude, are released in six months, and those who are sentenced to six months, are released in six years." Great numbers are released every year at Lucknow for thanksgivings, or propitiation. If the King or any member of his family becomes sick, prisoners are released, that they may recover; and when they recover, others are released as a grateful, and, at the same time, profitable acknowledgment, since the Government relieves itself from the cost of keeping them; and its servants appropriate the money paid for their ransom. Those who are in for long periods are, for the most part, great offenders, who are the most able and most willing to pay high for their release; those who are in for short ones are commonly the small ones, who are the least able and least disposed to give anything. The great offenders again are those who are most disposed, and most able, to revenge themselves on such persons as have aided the Government in their arrest or conviction; and they do all they can to murder and rob them and their families and relatives, as soon as they are set at large, in order to deter others from doing the same. This would be a great evil in any country, but is terrible in Oude, where no police is maintained for the protection of life and property. The cases of atrocious murders and robberies which come before me every day, and are acknowledged by the local authorities, and neighbours of the sufferers, to have taken place, are frightful. Such sufferings, for which no redress is to be found, would soon desolate any part of India less favoured by nature.

In the valley of the Nerbudda, for instance, such sufferings would render a district desolate for ages. The people, driven off from an estate, go and settle in another better governed. The grass grows rankly from the richness of the soil, and the humidity of the air, and becomes filled with deer and other animals, that are food for beasts of prey. Tigers, leopards, wolves, wild dogs, &c. follow, to feed upon them; and they render residence and industry unsafe. Malaria follows, and destroys what persons the tigers leave. I have seen extensive tracts of the richest soil and most picturesque scenery, along the banks of the Nerbudda, which had been rendered desolate for ages by the misrule of only a few years. It is the same in the Tarae forest, which separates Oude from Nepaul. But in the rest of Oude, from the Ganges to this belt of forest, no such effects follow misrule, however great and prolonged. Here no grass grows too rankly, few deer fill it, few tigers, leopards, wolves, or wild dogs come in pursuit of them, and no malaria is feared. If a landholder takes to rebellion and plunder, he is followed by all his retainers and clansmen; and their families, and the cultivators of other classes, feeling no longer secure, go and till lands on other estates, till they are invited back. The cowherds and shepherds, who live by the produce of their cattle and sheep, remain and thrive by the abundance of pasture lands, from which the rich spring and harvest crops have disappeared. These cattle and sheep graze over them, and enrich the soil by restoring to it a portion of those elements of fertility, of which a long succession of harvests had robbed it. Over and above what they leave on the grounds, over which they graze, large stores of manure are collected for future use by the herdsmen, who now exclusively occupy the villages. The landholder and his followers, in the meantime, subsist and enrich themselves by the indiscriminate plunder of the surrounding country; and are at last invited back by a weak and wearied Government, to reoccupy the lands, improved by this salutary fallow, at a lower rate of rent, or no rent at all for some years, and a remission of all balances for past years, on account of paemalee, or treading down of crops, during the disorder that has prevailed.

The cultivators return to occupy their old lands, so enriched, at reduced rates of rent; and, in two or three years, these lands become again carpeted with a beautiful variety of spring and autumn crops. The crops, in our districts, on the opposite side of the river Ganges, bear no comparison with those on the Oude side. The lands are all overcropped and under-stocked with cattle and sheep from the want of pasture lands. There is little manure, the water is too far below the surface to admit of sufficient irrigation, without greater outlay than the farmers and cultivators can afford; the rotation of crops is insufficient, and no salutary fallow comes to the relief of the soil, from the labour of men living and working under the efficient protection of a strong and able Government. The difference in the crops is manifest to the beholder, and shown in the rate of rents paid for the lands where the price of land produce is the same in both; the same river conveying the produce of both to and from the same markets.

A Murhutta army, under the Peshwa, Ballajee, invaded the districts, about the source of the Nerbudda river, about one hundred and seven years ago, A.D. 1742. They ravaged these districts as they did all others which they invaded; but they, like the greater part of the Oude Tarae, remain waste; while the others, like the rest of Oude, soon recovered and become prosperous from the circumstances above stated. The soil of some of the districts, about the source of the Nerbudda, then ravaged, is among the finest in the world; but the long grass and rich foliage, by which it is covered, are occupied, like the pampos of South America, almost exclusively by wild cattle, buffaloes, deer, and tigers. The district of Mundula, which intervenes between them and the rich and highly-cultivated district of Jubbulpoor, in the valley of that river, was populous and well cultivated when we took possession of it in the year 1817; but it has become almost as waste under our rule by a more gradual but not less desolating process. Not considering the diminishing markets for land produce, our assessments of the land revenue were too high, and the managing officers never thought the necessity of reduction established, till the villages were partially or wholly deserted. The farmers and cultivators all emigrated, by degrees, into the neighbouring districts of Nagpoor and Rewa, where they had more consideration and lighter assessments, and the markets for land produce were improving. The lands of Mundula became waste, and covered with rank grass filled with deer; tigers followed to feed upon them, and carried off all the poor peasantry, who remained and attempted to cultivate small patches; malaria followed and completed the work.

Like the tharoos of the Oude forest, the Gonds born in this malaria are the only people who can live in it; and the ravages of tigers and endemial disease prevent their numbers from increasing. Those who once emigrate never come back, and population and tillage have been decreasing ever since we took possession, or for thirty-three years. The same process has been going on in other parts of the Nerbudda valley with the same results. In Oude, from the causes above described, lands of the same denomination and kind often yield double the rate of rent that they yield in our own conterminous districts, or districts on the opposite side of the Ganges, and other rivers that separate our territories from those of Oude. Under a tolerable Government, Oude would soon become one of the most beautiful countries in India; but the lands would fall off, in fertility, as ours do from over-cropping, no doubt.

January 28, 1850.—Shahabad, ten miles. We crossed, close under Palee, the little river Gurra, which continued for some miles to flow along, in its winding course, close by on our left. It is here some five or six miles to the south-west of the town. The soil we have come over is chiefly muteear, or the doomuteea, tightened by a mixture of clay, or argillaceous earth. Rich crops of rice are grown on this muteea, which retains its moisture so much better than the looser doomutea soil.

Half-way we came through a neat village, the lands of which are subdivided between the members of a large family of Kunojee Brahmins, who came out to see us pass, and pay their respects. The cultivation was so fine that I hoped they were of the class who condescended to hold their own ploughs. I asked them; and they, with seeming pride, told me that they did not—that they employed servants to hold their ploughs for them. When I told them that this was their misfortune, they seemed much amused, but were all well-behaved and respectful, though they must have thought my notion very odd.

The little Gurra flows from the Oude Tarae forest by the town of Phillibheet, where boats are built, to be taken down to Cawnpoor, on the Ganges, for sale. About four hundred, great and small, are supposed to be taken down the Gurra every year, in the season of the rains. They take down the timber of the Tarae forest, rice, and other things; and all are sold, with their cargoes, at Cawnpoor, or other places on the Ganges. The timbers are floated along on both sides of the boats. Palee is a good place for a cantonment, or seat of public civil establishments, and Shahabad is no less so. The approach to both, from the south-east, is equally beautiful, from the rich crops which cover the ground up to the houses, and the fine groves and majestic single trees which surround them.

Shahabad is a very ancient and large town, occupied chiefly by Pathan Mussulmans, who are a very turbulent and fanatical set of fellows. Subsookh Rae, a Hindoo, and the most respectable merchant in the district, resided here, and for some time consented to officiate, as the deputy of poor old Hafiz Abdoollah, for the management of the town, where his influence was great. He had lent a good deal of money to the heads of some of the Pathan families of the town, but finding few of them disposed to repay, he was last year obliged to refuse further loans. They determined to take advantage of the coming mohurrum festival to revenge the affront as men commonly do who live among such a fanatical community. The tazeeas are commonly taken up, and carried in procession, ten days after the new moon is first seen, at any place where they are made; but in Oude all go by the day in which the moon is seen from the capital of Lucknow. As soon as she is seen at Lucknow, the King issues an order throughout his dominions for the tazeeas to be taken in procession ten days after. The moon was this year, in November, first seen on the 30th of the month at Lucknow; but at Shahabad, where the sky is generally clearer, she had been seen on the 29th. The men to whom Subsookh Rae had refused farther loans determined to take advantage of this incident to wreak their vengeance; and when the deputy promulgated the King's order for the tazeeas to be taken in procession ten days after the 30th, they instigated all the Mahommedans of the town to insist upon taking them out ten days after the 29th, and persuaded them that the order had been fabricated, or altered, by the malice of their Hindoo deputy, to insult their religious feelings. They were taken out accordingly, and having to pass the house of Subsookh Rae, when their excitement, or spirit of religious fervour, had reached the highest pitch, they there put them down, broke open the doors, entered in a crowd, and plundered it of all the property they could find, amounting to above seventy thousand rupees. Subsookh Rae was obliged to get out, with his family, at a back door, and run for his life. He went to Shajehanpoor, in our territory, and put himself under the protection of the magistrate. Not content with all this, they built a small miniature mosque at the door with some loose bricks, so that no one could go either out or in without the risk of knocking it down, or so injuring this mock mosque as to rouse, or enable the evil-minded to rouse, the whole Mahommedan population against the offender. Poor Subsookh Rae has been utterly ruined, and ever since seeking in vain for redress. The Government is neither disposed nor able to afford it, and the poor boy who has now succeeded his learned father in the contract is helpless. The little mock mosque, of uncemented bricks, still stands as a monument of the insolence of the Mahommedan population, and the weakness and apathy of the Oude Government.

CHAPTER II.

Infanticide—Nekomee Rajpoots—Fallows in Oude created by disorders—Their cause and effect—Tillage goes on in the midst of sanguinary conflicts—Runjeet Sing, of Kutteearee—Mahomdee district—White Ants—Traditional decrease in the fertility of the Oude soil—Risks to which cultivators are exposed—Obligations which these risks impose upon them—Infanticide—The Amil of Mahomdee's narrow escape—An infant disinterred and preserved by the father after having been buried alive—Insecurity of life and property—Beauty of the surface of the country, and richness of its foliage—Mahomdee district—State and recent history of—Relative fertility of British and Oude soil—Native notions of our laws and their administration—Of the value of evidence in our Courts—Infanticide—Boys only saved—Girls destroyed in Oude—The priests who give absolution for the crime abhorred by the people of all other classes—Lands in our districts becoming more and more exhausted from over-cropping—Probable consequences to the Government and people of India—Political and social error of considering land private property—Hakeem Mehndee and subsequent managers of Mahomdee—Frauds on the King in charges for the keep of animals—Kunojee Brahmins—Unsuccessful attempt to appropriate the lands of weaker neighbours—Gokurnath, on the border of the Tarae—The sakhoo or saul trees of the forest.

Lalta Sing, of the Nikomee Rajpoot tribe, whom I had lately an opportunity of assisting, for his good services in arresting outlays [outlaws ?] from our territories, has just been to pay his respects. Our next encamping ground is to be on his estate of Kurheya and Para. He tells me that very few families of his tribe now destroy their female infants; that tradition ascribes the origin of this evil to the practice of the Mahommedan emperors of Delhi of demanding daughters in marriage from the Rajpoot princes of the country; that some of them were too proud to comply with the demand, and too weak to resist it in any other way than that of putting all their female infants to death. This is not impossible. He says that he believes the Dhankuries, whom I have described above to be really the only tribe of Rajpoots among whom no family destroys its infant daughters in Oude; that all tribes of Rajpoots get money with the daughters they take from tribes a shade lower in caste, to whom they cannot give theirs in return; and pay money with the daughters they give in marriage to tribes a shade higher, who will not give their daughters to them in return. The native collector of Shahabad, a gentlemanly Mahommedan, came out two miles to pay his respects on my approach, and we met on a large space of land, lying waste, while all around was covered with rich crops. I asked, "Pray why is this land left waste?" "It is, sir, altogether unproductive." "Why is this? It seems to me to be just as good as the rest around, which produces such fine crops." "It is called khubtee—slimy, and is said to be altogether barren." "I assure you, sir," said Rajah Bukhtawar Sing, "that it is good land, and capable of yielding good crops, under good tillage, or it would not produce the fine grass you see upon it. You must not ask men like this about the kinds and qualities of soils for they really know nothing whatever about them: they are city gentlemen's sons, who get into high places, and pass their lives in them without learning anything but how to screw money out of such as we are, who are born upon the soil, and depend upon its produce all our lives for subsistence. Ask him, sir, whether either he or any of his ancestors ever knew anything of the difference between one soil and another."

The collector acknowledged the truth of what the old man said, and told me that he really knew nothing about the matter, and had merely repeated what the people told him. This is true with regard to the greater part of the local revenue officers employed in Oude. "One of these city gentlemen, sir," said. Bukhtawar Sing, "when sent out as a revenue collector, in Saadut Allee's time, was asked by his assistants what they were to do with a crop of sugar-cane which had been attached for balances, and was becoming too ripe, replied, 'Cut it down, to be sure, and have it stacked!' He did not know that sugar-cane must, as soon as cut, be taken to the mill, or it spoils." "I have heard of another," said the old Rusaldar Nubbee Buksh, "who, after he entered upon his charge, asked the people about him to show him the tree on which grew the fine istamalee* rice which they used at Lucknow." "There is no question, sir," said Bukhtawar Sing, "that is too absurd, for these cockney gentlemen to ask when they enter upon such revenue charges as these. They are the aristocracy of towns and cities, who are learned enough in books and court ceremonies and intrigues, but utterly ignorant of country life, rural economy, and agricultural industry."

*   The istamalee rice is rice of fine quality, which has been kept for some years before used. To be good, rice must be kept for some years before used, and that only which has been so kept is called istamalee or useable.

For a cantonment or civil station, the ground to the north of Shahabad, on the left-hand side of the road leading to Mahomdee, seems the best. It is a level plain, of a stiff soil formed of clay and sand, and not very productive.

The country, from Sandee and Shahabad to the rivers Ganges and Ramgunga, is one rich sheet of spring cultivation; and the estate of Kuteearee, above described, is among the richest portions of this sheet. The portions on which the richest crops now stand became waste during the disorders which followed the expulsion of Runjeet Sing, in the usual way, in 1837, and derived the usual benefit from the salutary fallow. A stranger passing through such a sheet of rich cultivation, without communing with the people, would little suspect the fearful crimes that are every year committed upon it, from the weakness and apathy of the Government, and the bad faith and bad character of its officers and chief landholders. The land is tilled in spite of all obstacles, because all depend upon its produce for subsistence; but there is no indication of the beneficial interference of the Government for the protection of life, property, and character, and for the encouragement of industry and the display of its fruits. The land is ploughed, and the seed sown, often by stealth at night, in the immediate vicinity of a sanguinary contest between the Government officers and the landholders. It is only when the latter are defeated, and take to the jungles, or the Honourable Company's districts, and commence their indiscriminate plunder, that the cultivator ceases from his labours, and the lands are left waste.

Runjeet Sing two or three years ago seized upon the village of Mulatoo, in his vicinity, to which he had no claim whatever, and he has forcibly retained it. It had long paid Government ten thousand a-year, but he has consented to pay only one thousand. Lands yielding above nine thousand he has cut off from its rent-roll, and added to those of his hereditary villages on the borders. Last year he seized upon the village of Nudua, with a rent-roll of fourteen hundred rupees, and he holds it with a party of soldiers and two guns. The Amil lately sent out a person with a small force to demand the Government dues; but they were driven back, as he pretends that he got it in mortgage from Dumber Sing, who had taken a short lease of that and other khalsa villages, and absconded as a defaulter; and that he has purchased the lands from the cultivating proprietors, and is, therefore, bound to pay no revenue whatever for them-to the King. All defaulters and offenders who take refuge on his estate he instigates to plunder, and provides with gangs, on condition of getting the greater part of the booty. He thinks that he is sure of shelter in the British territory, should he be driven from Oude; he feels also sure of aid from other large landholders of the same class in the neighbourhood.

January 30, 1850.—Kurheya Para, twelve miles, over a plain of excellent muteear soil, a good deal of which-is covered with jungle. Para is a short distance from Kurheya, and our camp is midway between the two villages. The boundary of the Sandee Palee and Mahomdee districts we crossed about four miles from our present encampment. This district, of Mahomdee was taken in contract by Hakeem Mehndee, at three lacs and eleven thousand rupees a-year, in 1804 A.D., and in a few years he brought it into full tillage, and made it yield above seven lacs. It has been falling off ever since it was taken from him, and now yields only between three and four lacs. The jungle is studded with large peepul-trees, which are all shorn of their small branches and leaves. The landholders and cultivators told me that they were taken off by the cowherds who grazed their buffaloes, bullocks, and cows in these jungles; that they formed their chief and, in the cold season, their best food, as the leaves of the peepul-tree were supposed to give warmth to the stomach, and to increase the quantity of the milk; that the cowherds were required to pay nothing for the privilege of grazing their cattle in these jungles, by the person to whom the lands belonged, because they enriched the soil with their manure, and all held small portions of land under tillage, for which they paid rent; that they had the free use of the peepul-trees in the jungles, but were not permitted to touch those on the cultivated lands and in villages.

White ants are so numerous in the argillaceous muteear soil, in which their food abounds, that it is really dangerous to travel on an elephant, or swiftly on horseback, over a new road cut or enlarged through any portion of it that has remained long untilled. The two fore legs of my elephant went down yesterday morning into a deep pit made by them, but concealed by the new road, which has been made over it for the occasion of my visit near Shahabad, and it was with some difficulty that he extricated them. We have had several accidents of the same kind since we came out. In cutting a new road they cut through large ant-hills, and leave no trace of the edifices or the gulf below them, which the little insects have made in gathering their food and raising their lofty habitation. They are not found in the bhoor or oosur soils, and in comparatively small numbers in the doomuteea or lighter soil, but they abound In the muteear soil in proportion to its richness. Cultivation, where the crops are irrigated, destroys them, and the only danger is in passing over new roads cut through jungle, or lands that have remained long untilled, or along the sides of old pathways, from which these land-marks have been removed in hastily widening them for wheeled carriages.

A Brahmin cultivator, whose cart we had been obliged to press into our own service for this stage, came along with me almost all the way. He said, "The spring crops of this season, sir, are no doubt very fine; but in days of yore, before the curse of Bhurt Jee (the brother of Ram) came upon the landholders and cultivators of Oude, they were much finer; when he set out from his capital of Ajoodheea for the conquest of Cylone, he left the administration to his brother, Bhurt Jee, who made a liberal settlement of the land tax. He put a ghurra or pitcher, with a round bottom, turned upside down, into every half acre (beegha) of the cultivated land, and required the landholder or cultivator to leave upon it, as much of the grain produced as the rounded bottom would retain, which could not be one ten-thousandth part of the produce; he lived economically, and collected at this rate during the many years that his brother was absent. But when his brother returned and approached the boundary of his dominions, he met hosts of landholders and cultivators clamouring against the rapacity and oppression of his brother's administration. The humanity of Ram's disposition was shocked, sir, at all this, and he became angry with his brother before he heard what he had to say. When Bhurt had satisfied his brother that he had not taken from them the thousandth part of what he had a right to take, and Ram had, indeed, taken from them himself, he sighed at the wickedness and ingratitude of the agricultural classes of Oude; and the baneful effects of this sad sigh has been upon us ever since, sir, in spite of all we can do to avert them. In order to have the blessing of God upon our labours, it is necessary for us to fulfil strictly all the responsibilities under which we hold and till the land; first, to pay punctually the just demands of Government; second, all the wages of the labour employed; third, all the charities to the poor; fourth, all the offerings to our respective tutelary gods; fifth, a special offering to Mahabeer, alias Hunooman. These payments and offerings, sir, must all be made before the cultivator can safely take the surplus produce to his store-room for sale and consumption."

Old Bukhtawar Sing, who was riding by my side, said, "A conscientious farmer or cultivator, sir, when he finds that his field yields a great deal more than the usual returns, that is when it yields twenty instead of the usual return of ten, gives the whole in charity, lest evil overtake him from his unusual good luck and inordinate exultation."

I asked the Brahmin cultivator why all these offerings were required to be made by cultivators in particular? He replied, "There is, sir, no species of tillage in which the lives of numerous insects are not sacrificed, and it is to atone for these numerous murders, and the ingratitude to Bhurt, that cultivators, in particular, are required to make so many offerings;" and, he added, "much sin, sir, is no doubt brought upon the land by the murder of so many female infants. I believe, sir, that all the tribes of Rajpoots murder them; and I do not think than one in ten is suffered to live. If the family or village priest did not consent to eat with the parents after the murder, no such murders could take place, sir; for none, even of their nearest relatives, will ever eat with them till the Brahmin has done so."

The bearers of the tonjohn in which I sat, said, "We do not believe, sir, that one girl in twenty among the Rajpoots is preserved. Davey Buksh, the Gonda Rajah, is, we believe, the only one of the Biseyn Rajpoot tribe who preserves his daughters;* his father did the same, and his sister, who was married to the Bhudoreea Rajah of Mynpooree, came to see him lately on the occasion of a pilgrimage to Ajoodheea, on the death of her husband; of the six Kulhuns families of Chehdwara, two only preserve their daughters—Surnam Sing of Arta, and Jeskurn of

Kumeear; but whether their sons or successors in the estates will do the same is uncertain." These bearers are residents of that district.

* There are a great many families of the Biseyn Rajpoots who never destroy their infant daughters.

I may here remark, that oak-trees in the hills of the Himmelah chain are disfigured in the same manner, and for the same purpose, as the peepul and banyan trees are here; their small branches and leaves are torn off to supply fodder for bullocks and other animals. The ilex of the hills has not, however, in its nakedness the majesty of the peepul and banyan of the plains, though neither of them can be said to be "when unadorn'd, adorn'd the most."

January 31, 1850.—Puchgowa, north-east, twelve miles over a plain of doomuteea soil, a good deal of which is out of tillage at present. On the road we came through several neat villages, the best of which was occupied exclusively by the families of the Kunojeea Brahmin proprietors, and the few persons of inferior caste who ploughed their lands for them, as they are a shade too high in caste to admit of their holding their own ploughs. They are, however, very worthy people, and seemed very much pleased at being put so much at their ease in a talk with the great man about their own domestic and rural economy. They told me, that they did not permit Rajpoots to reside in or have anything to do with their village.

"Why?" I asked.—"Because, sir, if they once get a footing among us, they are, sooner or later, sure to turn us all out." "How?"—"They get lands by little and little at lease, soon refuse to pay rent, declare the lands to be their own, collect bad characters for plunder, join the Rajpoots of their own clan in all the villages around in their enterprises, take to the jungles on the first occasion, of a dispute, attack, plunder, and burn the village, murder us and our families, and soon get the estate for themselves, on their own terms from the local authorities, who are wearied out by the loss of revenue arising from their depredations; our safety, sir, depends upon our keeping entirely aloof from them."

Under a government so weak, the only men who prosper seem to be these landholders of the military classes who are strong in their union, clan feeling, courage, and ferocity. The villages here are numerous though not large, and by far the greater part are occupied by Rajpoots of the Nikomee tribe.

The Amil of the Mahomdee district, Krishun Sahae, had come out so far as Para to meet me, and have my camp supplied. He had earned a good reputation as a native collector of long standing in the Shajehanpore district, under Mr. Buller; but being ambitious to rise more rapidly than he could hope to do, under our settled government, he came to Lucknow with a letter of introduction from Mr. Buller to the Resident, Colonel Richmond, paid his court to the Durbur, got appointed Amil of the Mahomdee district, under the amanee system, paid his nazuranas on his investiture, in October last, and entered upon his charge. A few days ago it pleased the minister to appoint to his place Aboo Toorab Khan, the nephew and son-in-law of Moonowur-ood Dowla; and orders were sent out immediately, by a camel-messenger, to the commandants of the corps on duty, with Krishun Sahae, to seize and send him, his family, and all his relations and dependents, with all his property to be found upon them, to Lucknow. The wakeel, whom he kept at Court for such occasions, heard of the order for the supercession and arrest, and forthwith sent off a note to his master by the fastest foot-messenger he could get. The camel-messenger found that the Amil had left Mahomdee, and gone out two stages to Para, to meet the Resident. He waited to deliver his message to the commandants and subordinate civil officers of the district, and see that they secured all the relatives, dependents, and property of the Amil that could be found. The foot-messenger, more wise, went on, and delivered his letter to Krishun Sahae; at Para, on the evening of Tuesday the 29th. He ordered his elephant very quietly, and mounting, told the driver to take him to a village on the road to Shajehanpoor.

On reaching the village about midnight, the driver asked him whither he was going—"I am flying from my enemies," said Krishun Sahae; "and we must make all haste, or we shall be overtaken before we reach the boundary." "But," said the driver, "my house and family are at Lucknow, and the one will be pulled to the ground and the other put into gaol if I fly with you." Krishun Sahae drew out a pistol and threatened to shoot him if he did not drive on as told. They were near a field of sugar-cane, and the driver hedged away towards it, without the Amil's perceiving his intention. When they got near the field the elephant dashed in among the cane to have a feast; and the driver in his seeming effort to bring him out, fell off and disappeared under the high cane. The Amil did all he could to get out his elephant, but the animal felt that he was no longer in danger of severe treatment from above, and had a very comfortable meal before him in the fine ripe cane, and would not move. The poor Amil was obliged to descend, and make all possible haste on foot across the border, attended by one servant who had accompanied him in his flight. The driver ran to the village and got the people to join him in the pursuit of his master, saying that he was making off with a good deal of the King's money. With an elephant load of the King's money in prospect, they made all the haste they could; but the poor Amil got safely over the border into British territory. They found the elephant dining very comfortably on the sugar-cane. After abusing the driver and all his female relations for deluding them with the hope of a rich booty, they permitted him to take the empty elephant to the new Amil at Mahomdee. News of all this reached my camp last night.

I omitted to mention that, at Busora on the 27th, a Rajpoot landholder of the Sombunsie tribe, came to my camp with a petition regarding a mortgage, and mentioned that he had a daughter, now two years of age; that when she was born he was out in his fields, and the females of the family put her into an earthen pot, buried her in the floor of the apartment, where the mother lay, and lit a fire over the grave; that he made all haste home as soon as he heard of the birth of a daughter, removed the fire and earth from the pot, and took out his child. She was still living, but two of her fingers which had not been sufficiently covered were a good deal burnt. He had all possible care taken of her, and she still lives, and both he and his wife are very fond of her. Finding that his tale interested me, he went home for the child; but his village was far off, and he has not been able to overtake me. He had given no orders to have her preserved, as his wife was confined sooner than he expected; but the family took it for granted that she was to be destroyed, and in running home to preserve her he acted on the impulse of the moment. The practice of destroying female infants is so general among this tribe, that a family commonly destroys the daughter as soon as born, when the father is from home, and has given no special orders about it, taking it to be his wish as a matter of course.

Several respectable landholders of the Chouhan, Nikomee, and other tribe of Rajpoots, were talking to me yesterday evening, and as they were connected by marriage with Rajpoot families of the same and higher clans in the British territories, I asked them whether some plan could not be devised to suppress the evil in Oude, as it had been suppressed there; for the disorders which prevailed seemed to me to be only a visitation from above for such an all-pervading sin. They told me that there would be little difficulty in putting down this system under an honest and strong Government that would secure rights, enforce duties, and protect life and property, as in the British territories. Atrocious and cruel as this crime is in Oude, it is hardly more so than that which not long ago prevailed in France and other nations of Europe, of burying their daughters alive in nunneries in order to gratify the same family pride.

It is painful to me to walk out of my tent of an evening, for I have every day large crowds seeking redress for grievous wrongs, for which I see no hope of redress: men and women, who have had their dearest relatives murdered, their houses burnt down, their whole property taken away, their lands seized upon, their crops destroyed by ruffians residing in the same or neighbouring villages, and actually in the camp of the Amil, without the slightest fear of being punished or made to surrender any portion of what they have taken. The Government authorities are too weak, even to enforce the payment of the Government demand, and have not the means to seize or punish offenders of any kind, if they have the inclination. In some districts they not only acquiesce in the depredations of these gangs of robbers, but act in collusion with their leaders, in order to get their aid in punishing defaulters or pretended defaulters, among the landholders. They murder the landholders, and as many as possible of their families, and as a reward for their services the local authorities make over their lands to them at reduced rates.

The Nazim of Sandee Palee told me on taking leave, that he had only two wings of Nujeeb Regiments with him, one of which was fit for some service, and in consequence, spread over the district on detached duties. The other was with him, but out of the five hundred, for which he had to issue monthly pay, he should not be able to get ten men to follow him on any emergency. They are obliged to court and conciliate the strong and reckless who prey upon the weak and industrious; and in consequence become despised and detested by the people. I feel like one moving among a people afflicted with incurable diseases, who crowd around him in hope, and are sent away in despair. I try to make the local authorities exert themselves in behalf of the sufferers; but am told that they have already done their utmost in vain; that if they seize robbers and murderers and send them to Lucknow, they are sure to purchase their enlargement and return to wreak their vengeance on them and on all who have aided them in their arrest and conviction; that if they attempt to seize one of the larger landholders, who refuses to pay the Government demand, seizes upon the lands of his weaker neighbours, and murders and robs them indiscriminately, he removes across the Ganges, into one of the Honourable Company's districts, and thence sends his myrmidons to plunder and lay waste the whole country, till he is invited back by a weak and helpless Government upon his own terms; that formerly British troops were employed in support of the local authorities against offenders of this class; but that of late years all such aid and support have been withdrawn from the Oude Government, while the offenders find all they require from the subjects and police authorities of the bordering British districts.

The country we passed over to-day, between Para and Puchgowa, is a plain, beautifully studded with groves and fine solitary trees, in great perfection. The bandha or mistletoe, upon the mhowa and mango trees, is in full blossom, and adds much to their beauty; the soil is good, and the surface everywhere capable of tillage, with little labour or outlay; for the jungle where it prevails the most is of grass, and the small palas-trees (butea-frondosa) which may be-easily uprooted. The whole surface of Oude is, indeed, like a gentleman's park of the most beautiful description, as far as the surface of the ground and the foliage go. Five years of good Government would make it one of the most beautiful parterres in nature. To plant a large grove, as it ought to be, a Hindoo thinks it necessary to have the following trees:—

The banyan, or burgut; peepul, ficus religiosa; mango; tamarind; jamun, eugenia jambolana; bele, cratoeva marmelos; pakur, ficus venosa; mhowa, bassia latifolia; oula, phyllanthus emblica; goolur, figus glomerata; kytha, feronia elephantum; kuthal, or jack; moulsaree, mimusops elengi; kuchnar, bauhinea variegata; neem, melia azadirachta; bere, fizyphus jujuba; horseradish, sahjuna; sheeshum, dalbergia sisa; toon, adrela toona; and chundun, or sandal.

Where he can get or afford to plant only a small space, he must confine himself to the more sacred and generally useful of these trees; and they are the handsomest in appearance. Nothing can be more beautiful than one of those groves surrounded by fields teeming with rich spring crops, as they are at present; and studded here and there with fine single banyan, peepul, tamarind, mhowa, and cotton trees, which, in such positions, attain their highest perfection, as if anxious to display their greatest beauties, where they can be seen to the most advantage. Each tree has there free space for its roots, which have the advantage of the water supplied to the fields around in irrigation, and a free current of air, whose moisture is condensed upon its leaves and stems by their cooler temperature, while its carbonic acid and ammonia are absorbed and appropriated to their exclusive use. Its branches, uncommoded by the proximity of other trees, spread out freely, and attain their utmost size and beauty.

I may here mention what are the spring crops which now in a luxuriance not known for many years, from fine falls of rain in due season, embellish the surface over which we are passing :—

Spring Crops.—Wheat; barley; gram; arahur, of two kinds (pulse); musoor (pulse); alsee (linseed); surson (a species of fine mustard); moong (pulse); peas, of three kinds; mustard; sugar-cane, of six kinds; koosum (safflower); opium; and palma christi.

February 1, 1850.—Mahomdee, eleven miles, over a level plain of muteear soil of the best quality, well supplied with groves and single trees of the finest kind; but a good deal of the land is out of tillage, and covered with the rank grass, called garur, the roots of which form the fragrant khus, for tatties, in the hot winds; and dhak (butea frondosa) jungle. Several villages, through and near which we passed, belong to Brahmin zumeendars, who were driven away last year by the rapacity of the contractor, Mahomed Hoseyn, a senseless oppressor, who was this year superseded by a very good officer and worthy man, who was driven out with disgrace, as described yesterday, while engaged in inviting back the absconded cultivators to these deserted villages, and providing them with the means of bringing their lands again into tillage. Hoseyn Allee had seized and sold all their plough-bullocks, and other agricultural stock, between the autumn and spring harvests, together with all the spring crops, as they became ripe, to make good the increased rate of revenue demanded; and they were all turned out beggars, to seek subsistence among their relatives and friends, in our bordering district of Shajehanpoor. The rank grass and jungle are full of neelgae and deer of all kinds; and the cowherds, who remain to graze their cattle on the wide plains, left waste, find it very difficult to preserve their small fields of corn from their trespass. They are said to come in herds of hundreds around these fields during the night, and to be frequently followed by tigers, several of which were killed last year, by Captain Hearsey, of the Frontier Police. Waste lands, more distant from the great Tarae forest, are free from tigers.

I had a long talk with the Brahmin communities of two of these villages, who had been lately invited back from the Shajehanpoor district, by Krishun Sahae, and resettled on their lands. They are a mild, sensible, and most respectable body, whom a sensible ruler would do all in his power to protect and encourage; but these are the class; of landholders and cultivators whom the reckless governors of districts, under the Oude Government, most grievously oppress. They told me—"that nothing could be better than the administration of the Shajehanpoor district by the present collector and magistrate, Mr. Buller, whom all classes loved and respected; that the whole surface of the country was under tillage, and the poorest had as much protection as the highest in the land; that the whole district was, indeed, a garden." "But the returns, are they equal to those from your lands in Oude?"—"Nothing like it, sir; they are not half as good; nor can the cultivator afford to pay half the rate that we pay when left to till our lands in peace." "And why is this?"—"Because, sir, ours is sometimes left waste to recover its powers, as you now see all the land around you, while theirs has no rest" "But do they not alternate their crops, to relieve the soil?"—"Yes, sir, but this is not enough: ours receive manure from the herds of cattle and deer that graze upon it while fallow: and we have greater stores of manure than they have, to throw over it when we return and resume our labours. We alternate our crops, at the same time, as much as they do; and plough and cross-plough our lands more." "And where would you rather live—there, protected as the people are from all violence, or here, exposed as you are to all manner of outrage and extortion."—"We would rather live here, sir, if we could; and we were glad to come back." "And why? There the landholders and cultivators are sure that no man will be permitted to exact a higher rate of rent or revenue than that which they voluntarily bind themselves to pay during the period of a long lease; while here you are never sure that the terms of your lease will be respected for a single season."—"That is all true, sir, but we cannot understand the 'aen and kanoon' (the rules and regulations), nor should we ever do so; for we found that our relations, who had been settled there for many generations, were just as ignorant of them as ourselves. Your Courts of justice (adawluts) are the things we most dread, sir; and we are glad to escape from them as soon as we can, in spite of all the evils we are exposed to on our return to the place of our birth. It is not the fault of the European gentlemen who preside over them, for they are anxious to do, and have justice done, to all; but, in spite of all their efforts, the wrong-doer often escapes, and the sufferer is as often punished."

"The truth, sir, is seldom told in these Courts. There they think of nothing but the number of witnesses, as if all were alike; here, sir, we look to the quality. When a man suffers wrong, the wrong-doer is summoned before the elders, or most respectable men of his village or clan; and if he denies the charge and refuses redress, he is told to bathe, put his hand upon the peepul-tree, and declare aloud his innocence. If he refuses, he is commanded to restore what he has taken, or make suitable reparation for the injury he has done; and if he refuses to do this, he is punished by the odium of all, and his life becomes miserable. A man dares not, sir, put his hand upon that sacred tree and deny the truth—the gods sit in it and know all things; and the offender dreads their vengeance. In your adawluts, sir, men do not tell the truth so often as they do among their own tribes, or village communities—they perjure themselves in all manner of ways, without shame or dread; and there are so many men about these Courts, who understand the 'rules and regulations,' and are so much interested in making truth appear to be falsehood, and falsehood truth, that no man feels sure that right will prevail in them in any case. The guilty think they have just as good a chance of escape as the innocent. Our relations and friends told us, that all this confusion of right and wrong, which bewildered them, arose from the multiplicity of the 'rules and regulations,' which threw all the power into the hands of bad men, and left the European gentlemen helpless!"

"But you know that the crime of murdering female infants, which pervades the whole territory of Oude, and brings the curse of God upon it, has been suppressed in the British territory, in spite of these 'aens and kanoons?'"—"True, sir, it has been put down in your bordering districts; but the Rajpoot families who reside in them manage to escape your vigilance, and keep up the evil practice. They intermarry with Rajpoot families in Oude, and the female infants, born of the daughters they give in marriage to Oude families, are destroyed in Oude without fear or concealment; while the daughters they receive in marriage, from Oude families, are sent over the border into Oude, when near their confinement, on the pretence of visiting their relations. If they give birth to boys, they bring them back with them into your districts; but if they give birth to girls, they are destroyed in the same manner, and no questions are ever asked about them." "Do you ever eat or drink with Rajpoot parents who destroy their female infants?"—"Never, sir! we are Brahmins, but we can take water in a brass vessel from the hands of a Rajpoot, and we do so when his family is unstained with this crime; but nothing would ever tempt us to drink water from the hands of one who permitted his daughters to be murdered." "Do you ever eat with the village or family priest who has given absolution to parents who have permitted their daughters to be murdered, by eating in the room where the murder has been perpetrated?"—"Never, sir; we abhor him as a participator in the crime; and nothing would ever induce one of us to eat or associate with him: he takes all the sin upon his own head by doing so, and is considered by us as an outcast from the tribe, and accursed! It is they who keep up this fearful usage. Tigers and wolves cherish their offspring, and are better than these Rajpoots, who out of family or clan pride, destroy theirs. As soon as their wives give birth to sons, they fire off guns, give largely in charity, make offerings to shrines, and rejoice in all manner of ways; but when they give birth to poor girls, they bury them alive without pity, and a dead silence prevails in the house; it is no wonder, sir, that you say that the curse of God is upon the land in which such sins prevail!"

The quality of testimony, no doubt, like that of every other commodity, deteriorates under a system, which renders the good of no more value in exchange than the bad. The formality of our Courts here, as everywhere else, tends to impair, more or less, the quality of what they receive. The simplicity of Courts, composed of little village communities and elders, tends, on the contrary, to improve the quality of the testimony they get; and in India, it is found to be best in the isolated hamlets of hills and forests, where men may be made to do almost anything rather than tell a lie. A Marhatta pandit, in the valley of the Nerbudda, once told me, that it was almost impossible to teach a wild Gond of the hills and jungles the occasional value of a lie! It is the same with the Tharoos and Booksas, who are, almost exclusively the cultivators of the Oude Tarae forest, and with the peasantry of the Himmalaya chain of mountains, before they have come much in contact with people of the plains, and become subject to the jurisdiction of our Courts. These Courts are, everywhere, our weak point in the estimation of our subjects; and they should be, everywhere, simplified to meet the wants and wishes of so simple a people.

That the lands, under the settled Government of the Honourable East India Company, are becoming more and more deteriorated by overcropping is certain; and an Indian statesman will naturally inquire, what will be the probable consequence to the people and the Government? To the people, the consequence must be, a rise in the price of land produce, proportioned to the increased cost of producing and bringing to market what is required for consumption. The price in the market must always be sufficient to cover the cost of producing, and bringing what is required from the poorest and most distant lands to which that market is at any time obliged to have recourse for supply; and as these lands deteriorate in their powers of fertility, recourse must be had to lands more distant, or more cost must be incurred in manure, irrigation, &c., to make these, already had recourse to, to produce the same quantity, or both. The price in the market must rise to meet the increased outlay required, or that outlay will not be made; and the market cannot be supplied.

As men have to pay more for the Land produce they require, they will have less to lay out in other things; and as they cannot do without the land produce, they must be satisfied with less of other things, till their incomes increase to meet the necessity for increased outlay. People will get this increase in proportion as their labour, services, talents, or acquirements are more or less indispensable to the society; and the price of other things will diminish, as the cost of producing and bringing them to market diminishes, with improvements in manufactures, and in the facilities of transport. No very serious injury to the people of our territories is, therefore, to be apprehended from the inevitable deterioration in the natural powers of the soil, under our settled Government, which gives so much security to life, property, and character, and so much encouragement to industry.

The consequence to the Government will be less serious than might at first appear. Under a system of limited settlements of the land-revenue, such as prevail over all our dominions, except in Bengal, the Government is in reality the landlord; and our land-revenue is in reality land-rent.* We alienate a portion of that rent for limited periods in favour of those with whom we make such settlements, and take all the rest ourselves. On an average, perhaps, our Government takes one-sixth of the gross produce of the land; and the persons, with whom the settlements are made, take another sixth. The net rent, which the Government and they divide equally between them, may be taken, on an average, at one-third of the gross produce of the land. The cultivator would, I believe, always be glad to take and cultivate land, on an average, on condition of giving one-third of the gross produce, or the value of one-third, to be divided between the Government and its lessee; and the lessee will always consider himself fortunate if he gets one-half of this third, to cover the risk and cost of management.

* I believe our Government committed a great political and social error, when it declared all the land to be the property of the lessees: and all questions regarding it to be cognizable by Judicial Courts. It

would have been better for the people, as well as the Government, had all such questions been left to the Fiscal and Revenue Courts. There is the same regular series of these Courts, from the Tuhseeldar to the Revenue Sudder Board, as of the Judicial Courts, from the Moonsiff to the Judicial Sudder Board; and they are all composed of the same class of persons, with the same character and motives to honest exertion. Why force men to run the gauntlet through both series? It tends to make the Government to be considered as a rapacious tax-gatherer, instead of a liberal landlord, which it really is; and to foster the growth of a host of native pettifogging attorneys, to devour, like white ants, the substance of the landholders of all classes and grades.

Where the soil of a particular village in a district deteriorates, an immediate reduction in the assessment must be given, or the lands will be deserted. If the Government does not consent to such a reduction, the lessee must sustain the whole burthen, for he cannot shift it off upon the cultivators, without driving them from the lands. The lessee may sustain the whole burthen for one or two years; but if the officers of Government attempt to make him sustain it longer, they drive him after his cultivators, and the land is left waste. I have seen numerous estates of villages and some districts made waste by such attempts in India. I have seen land in such estates, which, when unexhausted, yielded, on an average, twelve returns of the seed, without either manure or irrigation, and paid a rent of twenty shillings an acre, become so exhausted by overcropping in a few years as to yield only three or four returns, and unable to pay four shillings an acre—indeed, unable to pay any rent at all. The cultivator, by degrees, ceases to sow the more exhausting and profitable crops, and is at last obliged to have recourse to manure, or desert his land altogether; but no manure will enable him to get the same quantity of produce as he got before, while what he gets sells at the same rate in the market. He can, therefore, no longer pay the same rate of rent to Government and its lessee. He has got a less quantity of produce, and it has cost him much more to raise it, while it continues to sell at the same price in the market.

But when the lands of a whole country, or a large extent of country, deteriorate in the same manner, and all cultivators are obliged to do the same thing, the price of land produce must rise in the markets, so as to pay the additional costs of supply. All but the poorest and most distant to which these markets must have recourse for supply, at any particular time, will pay rent, and pay it at a rate proportioned to their greater fertility or nearer proximity to the markets. Such Markets must pay for land produce a price sufficient to cover the costs of producing and bringing it from the poorest and most distant lands, to which they are obliged at any particular time to have recourse for supply. All land produce of the same quality must, at the same time and place, sell in the market at the same price; and all that is over and above the cost of producing and bringing it to market will go to the proprietors of the land, that is, to the Government and its lessees. The poorest and most distant land, to which any market may have recourse at any particular time, may pay no rent, because the price is no more than sufficient to pay the cost of producing and bringing their supply to that market; but all that is less poor and distant will pay rent, because the price which their produce brings in that market will be more than sufficient to pay the cost of producing and bringing their supply to that market.

The increase in the price of land produce which must take place, as the lands become generally exhausted by overcropping, will, probably, prevent any great falling off in the money rate of rents and revenues, from the land in our Indian possessions; and with the improvements in manufactures, and in the facilities of transport, which must tend to reduce the price of other articles, that money will purchase more of them in the market; and the establishments which have to be maintained out of these rents and revenues may not become more costly. Government and its lessees may have the same incomes in money, and the greater price, they and their establishments are obliged to pay for land produce may be compensated by the lesser price they will have to pay for other things.

As facilities for irrigation are extended and improved in wells and canals, new elements of fertility will be supplied to the surface, in the soluble salts contained in their waters. The well-waters will bring these salts from great depths, and the canal-waters will collect them as they flow along, or percolate through, the earth; and as they rise, by capillary attraction, they will convey them to the surface, where they are required for tillage. The atmosphere, in water, ammonia, and carbonic-acid gas will continue to supply plants with the oxygen, hydrogen, nitrogen, and carbon which they require from it; and judicious selection and supply of manure will provide the soil with those elements in which it happens to be deficient. Peace, security, instruction, and a due encouragement to industry, will, it may be hoped, secure to the people all that they require from our Government, and to our Government all that it can fairly require from the people.

The soil of Mahomdee is as fine as that of any part of Oude that I have seen; and the soil of Oude, generally, is equal to the best that I have seen in any part of India. It is all of the kinds above described—muteear (argillaceous), doomuteea (light), bhoor (sandy), and oosur (barren), as far as I have seen. In some parts, the muteear is more productive than in others, and the same may be said of all the other denominations of soil. In the poorer parts of the muteear, the stiff clay, devoid of decayed vegetable and animal matter, seems to superabound, as the sand does in the lightest or poorer portions of the soil, called doomuteea, which runs into bhoor. The oosur, or soil rendered unproductive by a superabundance of substances not suitable to the growth of plants, seems to be common to both kinds. In all soils, except the oosur, fine trees grow, and good crops are produced under good tillage; but in the muteear, the outlay to produce them is the least. It is an error to suppose that a soil, even of pure sand, must be absolutely barren. Quartz-sand commonly contains some of the inorganic substances necessary to plants—silica, lime, potash, alumina, oxide of iron, magnesia, &c.—and they are rendered soluble, and fit for the use of plants by atmospheric air and water, impregnated with carbonic-acid gas, as all water is more or less. The only thing required from the hand of man, besides water, to render them cultivable, is vegetable or animal substances, to supply them, as they decay or decompose, with organic acids.

The late Hakeem Mehndee, took the contract of the Mahomdee district, as already stated, in the year A.D. 1804, when it was in its present bad state, at 3,11,000 rupees a-year; and he held it till the year 1819, or for sixteen years. He had been employed in the Azimgurh district, under Boo Allee Hakeem, the contractor; and during the negotiations for the transfer of that district, with the other territories to the British Government, which took place in 1801; he lost his place, and returned to Lucknow, where he paid his court to the then Dewan, or Chancellor of the Exchequer, who offered him the contract of the Mahomdee district, at three lacs and eleven thousand rupees a-year, on condition of his depositing in the Treasury a security bond for thirty-two thousand rupees. There had been a liaison between him and a beautiful dancing-girl, named Peeajoo, who had saved a good deal of money. She advanced the money, and Hakeem Mehndee deposited the bond, and got the contract. The greater part of the district was then, as now, a waste; and did not yield more than enough to cover the Government demand, gratuities to courtiers, and cost of management. The Hakeem remained to support his influence at Court, while his brother, Hadee Allee Khan, resided at Mahomdee, and managed the district. The Hakeem and his fair friend were married, and lived happily together till her death, which took place before that of her husband, while she was on a pilgrimage to Mecca. While she lived, he married no other woman; but on her death he took to himself another, who survived him; but he had no child by either. His vast property was left to Monowur-od Dowlah, the only son of his brother, Hadee Allee Khan, and to his widow and dependents. The district improved rapidly under the care of the two brothers; and, in a few years, yielded them about seven lacs of rupees a-year. The Government demand increased with the rent-roll to the extent of four lacs of rupees a-year. This left a large income for Hakeem Mehndee and his family, who had made the district a garden, and gained the universal respect and affection of the people.

In the year 1807, Hakeem Mehndee added, to the contract of Mahomdee, that of the adjoining district of Khyrabad, at five lacs of rupees a-year, making his contract nine lacs. In 1816, he added the contract for the Bahraetch district, at seven lacs and seventy-five thousand; but he resigned this in 1819, after having held it for two years, with no great credit to himself. In 1819, he lost the contract for Mahomdee and Khyrabad, from the jealousy of the prime minister, Aga Meer. In April 1818, the Governor-General the Marquess of Hastings passed through his district of Khyrabad, on his way to the Tarae forest, on a sporting excursion, after the Marhatta war. Hakeem Mehndee attended him during this excursion, and the Governor-General was so much pleased with his attentions, courteous manners, and sporting propensities, and treated him with so much consideration and kindness, that the minister took the alarm, and determined to get rid of so formidable a rival. He in consequence made the most of the charge preferred against him, of the murder of Amur Sing; and demanded an increase of five lacs of rupees a-year, or fourteen lacs of rupees a-year, instead of nine. This Hakeem Mehndee would not consent to give; and Shekh Imam Buksh was, in 1819, sent to supersede him, as a temporary arrangement.

In 1820, Poorun Dhun, and Govurdhun Dass, merchants of Lucknow, took the contract of the two districts at twelve lacs of rupees a-year, or an increase of three lacs; and from that time, under a system of rack-renting, these districts have been falling off. Mahomdee is now in a worse state than Khyrabad, because it has had the bad luck to get a worse set of contractors. Hakeem Mehndee retired with his family, first to Shajehanpoor, and then to Futtehgurh, on the Ganges, and resided there, with his family, till June 1830, when he was invited back by Nusseer-do Deen Hyder, to assume the office of prime minister. He held the office till August 1832, when he was removed by the intrigues of the Kumboos, Taj-od Deen Hoseyn, and Sobhan Allee Khan, who persuaded the King that he was trying to get him removed from the throne, by reporting to the British Government the murder of some females, which had, it is said, actually taken place in the palace. Hakeem Mehndee was invited from his retirement by Mahomed Allee Shah, and again appointed minister in 1837; but he died three months after, on the 24th of December, 1837.

During the thirty years which have elapsed since Hakeem Mehndee lost the contract of Mahomdee, there have been no less than seventeen governors, fifteen of whom have been contractors; and the district has gradually declined from what it was, when he left it, to what it was when he took it—that is from a rent-roll of seven lacs of rupees a-year, under which all the people were happy and prosperous, to one of three, under which all the people are wretched. The manager, Krishun Sahae, who has been treated as already described, would, in a few years, have made it what it was when the Hakeem left it, had he been made to feel secure in his tenure of office, and properly encouraged and supported. He had, in the three months he had charge, invited back from our bordering districts hundreds of the best classes of landholders and cultivators, who had been driven off by the rapacity of his predecessor, re-established them in their villages and set them to work in good spirit, to restore the lands which had lain waste from the time they deserted them; and induced hundreds to convert to sugar-cane cultivation the lands which they had destined for humbler crops, in the assurance, of the security which they were to enjoy under his rule. The one class tells me, they must suspend all labours upon the waste lands till they can learn the character of his successor; and the other, that they must content themselves with the humbler crops till they can see whether the richer and more costly ones will be safe from his grasp, or that of the agents, whom he may employ to manage the district for him. No man is safe for a moment under such a Government, either in his person, his character, his office, or his possession; and with such a feeling of insecurity among all classes, it is impossible for a country to prosper.*

* Krishun Sahae has been restored, but does not feel secure in his tenure of office.

I may here mention one among the numerous causes of the decline of the district. The contract for it was held for a year and half, in A.D. 1847-48, by Ahmed Allee. Feeling insecure in his tenure of office, he wanted to make as much as possible out of things as they were, and resumed Guhooa, a small rent-free village, yielding four hundred rupees a-year, held by Bahadur Sing, the tallookdar of Peepareea, who resides at Pursur. He had recourse to the usual mode of indiscriminate murder and plunder, to reduce Ahmed Allee to terms. At the same time, he resumed the small village of Kombee, yielding three hundred rupees a-year, held rent-free by Bhoder Sing, tallookdar of Magdapoor, who resided in Koombee; and, in consequence, he united his band of marauders to that of Bahadur Sing; and together they plundered and burnt to the ground some dozen villages, and laid waste the purgunnah of Peepareea, which had yielded to Government twenty-five thousand rupees a-year, and contained the sites of one hundred and eight villages, of which, however, only twenty-five were occupied.

During the greater part of the time that these depredations were going on, the two rebels resided in our bordering district of Shajehanpoor, whence they directed the whole. Urgent remonstrances were addressed to the magistrate of that district, but he required judicial proof of their participation in the crimes, that were committed by their followers, upon the innocent and unoffending peasantry; and no proof that the contractor could furnish being deemed sufficient, he was obliged to consent to restore the rent-free villages. The lands they made waste, still remain so, and pay no revenue to Government.

Saadut Allee Khan (who died in 1814), when sovereign of Oude, was fond of this place, and used to reside here for many months every year. He made a garden, about a mile to the east of the town, upon a fine open plain of good soil, and planted an avenue of fine trees all the way. The trees are now in perfection, but the garden has been neglected; and the bungalow in the centre, in which he resided, is an entire ruin. He kept a large establishment of men and cattle, for which sixty thousand rupees a-year were regularly charged in the accounts of the manager of the district, through his reign and those of Ghazee-od Deen, Nuseer-od Deen Hyder, Mahomed Allee Shah, and Amjud Allee Shah, and the first year of the reign of his present Majesty, Wajid Allee Shah; though, with the exception of two bullocks and two gardeners, the cattle had all disappeared, and the servants been all discharged some thirty years before.

In October last, when six guns were required from the great park of artillery at Lucknow, to be sent out on detached duty with the Gungoor Regiment, an inspection of the draft-bullocks took place, and it was found, that the Court favourite who had charge of the park had made away with no less than one thousand seven hundred and thirty of them, and only twenty could be found to take the guns. He had been charging for the food of these one thousand seven hundred and thirty for a long series of years. On mentioning this fact to a late minister, he told me of two facts within his own knowledge, illustrative of these sort of charges. This same Court favourite, in the reign of Nuseer-od Deen Hyder, in 1835, received charge of sixteen bullocks, of surpassing beauty, which had been presented to the King, and he was allowed to draw, from the Treasury, a rupee a-day, for the food of each bullock.

In the reign of Mahomed Allee Shah, his prudent successor, a muster of all the bullocks was called for, and Ghalib Jung, to whom the muster was intrusted, to spite the favourite, called for these sixteen bullocks. The favourite had disposed of them, though, he continued to draw the allowance; and, to supply their place, he sent to the bazaar and seized sixteen of the bullocks which had that day brought corn to market. They were presented to Ghalib Jung for muster. He pretended to be very angry, declared that it was disgraceful to keep such poor creatures on the King's establishment, and still more so to charge a rupee a-day for the food of each, and ordered them to be sold forthwith by auction. Soon after they had been sold, the poor men to whom they belonged came up to claim them, but could never get either the bullocks or their price, nor could the

425

favourite ever be persuaded to refund any portion of the money he had drawn for the sixteen he had sold.*

* The favourite, in both these cases, was Anjum-od Dowlah.

In the early part of the reign of Ghazee-od Deen Hyder, a fine dog from the Himmalaya Hills was presented to him, and made over to the charge of one of the favourites, who drew a rupee a-day for his food. Soon after his Majesty became ill and very irritable, and one day complained much of this dog's barking. He was told that the only way to silence a dog of this description was to give him a seer of conserve of roses to eat every day, and a bottle of rose-water to drink. His Majesty ordered them to be given forthwith, and his repose was never after disturbed by the dog's barking. A rupee a-day continued to be drawn for these things for the dog for the rest of the long reign of Ghazee-od Deen Hyder, and through that of his successor, Nuseer-od Deen, which lasted for ten years, and ended in 1837, though the animal had died soon after the order for these things was given, or in 1816, and he believed it continued to be drawn up to the present day.

The cantonment at Mahomdee stands between this garden of Saadut Allee's and the town, and this is the best site for any civil or military establishments that may be required at Mahomdee. The Nazims usually reside in the fort in the town.

February 2, 1850.—Halted at Mahomdee. The spring crops around the town are very fine, and the place is considered to be very healthy. There is, however, some peculiarity in the soil, opposed to the growth of the poppy. The cultivators tell me that they have often tried it; that it is stunted in growth, whatever care be taken of it, and yields but little juice, and that of bad quality, though it attains perfection in the Shahabad and other districts around. The doomuteea soil is here esteemed better than the muteear, though it requires more labour in the tillage. It is said that mote and mash, two pulses, do not thrive in the muteear soil so well as in the doomuteea.

February 3, 1850.—Poknapoor, eight miles. We crossed the Goomtee about midway, over a bridge of boats that had been prepared for us. The boats came up the river thus far for timber, and were detained for the occasion. The stream is here narrow, and said to flow from a basin (the phoola talao) in the Tarae forest, some fifty miles to the north, at Madhoo Tanda. There is some tillage on the verge of the stream on the other side; but from the river to our tents, four miles, there is none. The country is level and well studded with groves and fine single trees, bur, peepul, mhowa, mango, &c., but covered with rank grass.

Near the river is a belt of the sakhoo and other forest trees, with underwood, in which tigers lodge and prey upon the deer, which cover the grass plain, and frequently upon the bullocks, which are grazed upon it in great numbers. Several bullocks have been killed and eaten by them within the last few days; and an old fakeer, who has for some months taken up his lodging on this side the river under a peepul-tree, in a straw hut just big enough to hold him, told us that he frequently saw them come down to drink in the stream near his lodging. We saw a great many deer in passing, but no tigers. The soil near the river is sandy, and the ground uneven, but still cultivable; and on this side of the sandy belt it is all level and of the best kind of doomuteea. Our tents are in a fine grove of mango-trees, in the midst of a waste, but level and extensive, plain of this soil, not a rood of which is unfit for the plough or incapable of yielding crops of the finest quality. It is capable of being made, in two or three years, a beautiful garden.

The single trees, which are scattered all over it, have been shorn of their leaves and small branches by the cowherds for their cattle, but they would all soon clothe themselves again under protection. The groves are sufficiently numerous to furnish sites for the villages and hamlets required. All the large sakhoo-trees have been cut down and taken away on the ground we have come over, which is too near the river for them to be permitted to attain full size. Not an acre or a foot of the land is oosur, or unfit for tillage. Poknapoor is in the estate of Etowa, which forms part of the pergunnah of Peepareea, to which Bahadur Sing, the person above described, lays claim. He holds a few villages round his residence at Pursur; but the pergunnah is under the management of a Government officer, under the Amil of Mahomdee. The Rajah, Syud Ashruf Allee Khan, of Mahomdee, claims a kind of suzerainty over all the district, and over this pergunnah of Peepareea among the rest. From all the villages tilled and peopled he is permitted to levy an income for himself at the rate of two rupees a-village. This the people pay with some reluctance, though they recognise his right.

The zumeendars of Poknapoor are Kunojee Brahmins, who tell me that they can do almost everything in husbandry save holding their own ploughs: they can drive their own harrows and carts, reap their own crops, and winnow and tread out their own corn; but if they once condescend to hold their own ploughs they sink in grade, and have to pay twice as much as they now pay for wives for their sons from the same families, and take half of what they now take for their daughters from the same families, into which they now marry them. They have, they say, been settled in these pergunnahs, north-east of the Goomtee River, for fifty-two generations as farmers and cultivators; and their relatives, who still remain at Aslamabad, a village one koss south-east of Mahomdee, which was the first abode of the tribe in Oude, have been settled there for no less than eighty-four generations. They form village communities, dividing the lands among the several members, and paying over and above the Government demand a liberal allowance to the head of the village and of the family settled in it, to maintain his respectability and to cover the risk and cost of management, either in kind, in money, or in an extra share of the land.

The lands of Poknapoor are all divided into two equal shares, one held by Dewan and the other by Ramnath, who were both among the people with whom I conversed. Teekaram, who has a share in Dewan's half, mentioned that about thirteen years ago the Amil, Khwaja Mahmood, wanted to increase the rate of the Government demand on the village from the four hundred, which they had long paid, to four hundred and fifty; that they refused to pay, and Hindoo Sing, the Rajpoot tallookdar of Rehreea, one koss east of Poknapoor, offered to take the lease at four hundred and fifty, and got it. They refused to pay, and he, at the head of his gang of armed followers, attacked, plundered, and burnt down the village, and killed his, Teekaram's, brother Girdharee, with his two sons, and inflicted three severe cuts of a sabre on the right arm of his wife, who is now a widow among them. Hindoo Sing's object was to make this village a permanent addition to his estate; but, to his surprise, the Durbar took serious notice of the outrage, and he fled into the Shajehanpoor district, where he was seized by the magistrate, Mr. Buller, and made over to the Oude authorities for trial. He purchased his escape from them in the usual way; but soon after offered to surrender to the collector, Aboo Torab Khan, on condition of pardon for all past offences.

The collector begged the Brahmins to consent to pardon him for the murders, on condition of getting from Hindoo Sing some fifty beeghas of land, out of his share in Rehreea. They said they would not consent to take five times the quantity of the land among such a turbulent set; but should be glad to get a smaller quantity, rent-free, in their own village, for the widow of Girdharee. The collector gave them twenty-five beeghas, or ten acres, in Poknapoor; and this land Teekaram still holds, and out of the produce supports the poor widow. A razenamah, or pardon, was given by the family, and Hindoo Sing has ever since lived in peace upon his estate, The lease of the village was restored to the Brahmin family, at the reduced rate of two hundred and fifty, but soon after raised to four hundred, and again reduced to two hundred and fifty, after the devastation of Bahadur Sing and Bhoder Sing.

These industrious and unoffending Brahmins say that since these Rajpoot landholders came among them, many generations ago, there has never been any peace in the district, except during the time that Hakeem Mehndee held the contract, when the whole plain that now lies waste became a beautiful chummun (parterre); that since his removal, as before his appointment, all has been confusion; that the Rajpoot landholders are always quarrelling either among themselves or with the local Government authorities; and, whatever be the nature or the cause of quarrel, they always plunder and murder, indiscriminately, the unoffending communities of the villages around, in order to reduce these authorities to their terms; that when these Rajpoot landholders leave them in peace, the contractors seize the opportunity to increase the Government demand, and bring among them the King's troops, who plunder them just as much as the rebel landholders, though they do not often murder them in the same reckless manner. They told me that the hundreds of their relatives who had gone off during the disorders and taken lands, or found employment in our bordering districts, would be glad to return to their own lands, groves, and trees, in Oude, if they saw the slightest chance of protection, and the country would soon become again the beautiful parterre which Hakeem Mehndee left it thirty years ago, instead of the wilderness in which they were now so wretched; that they ventured to cultivate small patches here and there, not far from each other, but were obliged to raise small platforms, upon high poles, in every field, and sit upon them all night, calling out to each other, in a loud voice, to keep up their spirits, and frighten off the deer which swarmed upon the grass plain, and would destroy the whole of the crops in one night, if left unprotected; that they were obliged to collect large piles of wood around each platform, and keep them burning all night, to prevent the tigers from carrying off the men who sat upon them; that their lives were wretched amidst this continual dread of man and beast, but the soil and climate were good, and the trees and groves planted by their forefathers were still standing and dear to them; and they hoped, now that the Resident had come among them, to receive, at no distant day, the protection they required. This alone is required to render this the most beautiful portion of Oude, and Oude the most beautiful portion of India.

February 4, 1850.—Gokurnath, thirteen miles, north-east, over a level plain of the same fine muteear soil, here and there running into doomuteea and bhoor, but in no case into oosur. The first two miles over the grass plain, and the next four through a belt of forest trees, with rank grass and underwood, abounding in game of all kinds, and infested by tigers. Bullocks are often taken by them, but men seldom. The sal (alias sakhoo) trees are here stunted, gnarled, and ugly, while in the Tarae forest they are straight, lofty, and beautiful. The reason is, that beyond the forest their leaves are stripped off and sold for plates. They are carried to distant towns, and stored up for long periods, to form breakfast and dinner plates, and the people in the country use hardly anything else. Plates are formed of them by sewing them together, when required; and they become as pliable as leather, even after being kept for a year or more, by having a little water sprinkled over them. They are long, wide, and tough, and well suited to the purpose. All kinds of food are put upon them, and served up to the family and guests. The cattle do not eat them, as they do leaves of the peepul, bur, neem, &c. The sakhoo, when not preserved, is cut down, when young, for beams, rafters, &c., required in building. In the Tarae forest, the proprietors of the lands on which they stand preserve them till they attain maturity, for sale to the people of the plains; and they are taken down the Ghagra and other rivers that flow through the forest to the Ganges, and vast numbers are sold in the Calcutta market. The fine tall sakhoos in the Tarae forest are called "sayer"; the knotted, stunted, and crooked shakoos, beyond the forest, are called "khohurs." There are but few teak (or sagwun) trees in this part of the Tarae forest. The country is everywhere studded with the same fine groves and single trees, and requires only tillage to become a garden. From the belt of jungle to our camp at Gokurnath, seven miles, the road runs over an open grass plain, with here and there a field of corn. The sites of villages are numerous, but few of them are occupied at present. All are said to have been in a flourishing state, and filled by a happy peasantry, when Hakeem Mehndee lost the government. Since that time these villages and hamlets have diminished by degrees, in proportion as the rapacity of the contractors and the turbulence of the Rajpoot landholders have increased.

The first village we passed through, after emerging from the belt of jungle, was Pureylee, which is held and occupied by a large family of cultivating proprietors of the Koormee caste. Up to the year 1847, it had for many years been in a good condition, and paid a revenue of two thousand rupees a-year to Government. In that year Ahmud Allee, the collector, demanded a thousand more. They could not pay this, and he sold all their bullocks and other stock to make up the demand; the lands became waste as usual; and Lonee Sing, of Mitholee, offered the next contractor one thousand rupees a-year for the lease, and got it. The village has now been permanently absorbed in his estate, in the usual way; and, as the Koormees are a peaceful body, they have quietly acquiesced in the arrangement, and get all the aid they require from their new landlord. Before this time they had held their lands, as proprietors, directly under Government. From allodial* proprietors they are become feudal tenants under a powerful Rajpoot chief.

* By allodial, I mean, lands held in proprietary right, immediately under the crown, but liable to the land-tax.

CHAPTER III.

Lonee Sing, of the Ahbun Rajpoot tribe—Dispute between Rajah Bukhtawar Sing, and a servant of one of his relatives—Cultivation along the border of the Tarae forest—Subdivision of land among the Ahbun families—Rapacity of the king's troops, and establishments of all kinds—Climate near the Tarae—Goitres—Not one-tenth of the cultivable lands cultivated, nor one-tenth of the villages peopled—Criterion of good tillage—Ratoon crops—Manure available—Khyrabad district better peopled and cultivated than that of Mahomdee, but the soil over-cropped—Blight—Rajah Ajeet Sing and his estate of Khymara—Ousted by collusion and bribery—Anrod Sing of Oel, and Lonee Sing—State of Oude forty years ago compared with its present state—The Nazim of the Khyrabad district—Trespasses of his followers—Oel Dhukooa—Khalsa lands absorbed by the Rajpoot barons—Salarpoor—Sheobuksh Sing of Kuteysura—Bhulmunsee, or property-tax—Beautiful groves of Lahurpoor—Residence of the Nazim—Wretched state of the force with the Nazim—Gratuities paid by officers in charge of districts, whether in contract or trust—Rajah Arjun Sing's estate of Dhorehra—Hereditary gang-robbers of the Oude Tarae suppressed—Mutiny of two of the King's regiments at Bhitolee—Their rapacity and oppression—Singers and fiddlers who govern the King—Why the Amils take all their troops with them when they move—Seetapoor, the cantonment of one of the two regiments of Oude Local Infantry—Sipahees not equal to those in Magness's, Barlow's, and Bunbury's, or in our native regiments of the line—Why—The prince Momtaz-od Dowlah—Evil effects of shooting monkeys—Doolaree, alias Mulika Zumanee—Her history, and that of her son and daughter.

Lonee Sing, who visited me yesterday afternoon with a respectable train, has, in this and other ways less creditable, increased his estate of Mitholee from a rent-roll of forty to one of one hundred and fifty thousand rupees a-year, out of which he pays fifty thousand to Government, and he is considered one of its best subjects. He is, as above stated, of the Ahbun Rajpoot clan, and a shrewd and energetic man. The estate was divided into six shares. It had formed one under Rajah Davey Sing, whose only brother, Bhujun Sing, lived united with him, and took what he chose to give him for his own subsistence and that of his family. Davey Sing died without issue, leaving the whole estate to his brother, Bhujun Sing, who had two sons, Dul Sing and Maun Sing, among whom he divided the estate.* Dul Sing had six sons, but Maun Sing had none. He, however, adopted Bhowanee Sing, to whom he left his portion of the estate. Dul Sing's share became subdivided among his six sons; but Khunjun Sing, the son of his eldest son, when he became head of the family, got together a large force, with some guns, and made use of it in the usual way by seizing upon the lands of his weaker neighbours. He attacked his nephew, Bhowanee Sing, and took all his lands; and got, on one pretence or another, the greater part of those of his other relatives.

* Mitholee contains the sites of one thousand four hundred and eighty-six villages, only one-third of which are now occupied.

He died without issue, leaving his possessions and military force to Lonee Sing, his brother, who continued to pursue the same course. In 1847 he, with one thousand armed men and five guns, attacked his cousin, Monnoo Sing, of Mohlee, the head of the family of the fourth son of Dul Sing, killed four and wounded two persons; and, in collusion with the local governor, seized upon all his estate. Redress was sought for in vain; and as I was passing near, Monnoo Sing and his brother Chotee

Sing came to me at Mahomdee to complain. Monnoo Sing remained behind sick at Mahomdee; but Chotee Sing followed me on. He rode on horseback behind my elephant, and I made him give me the history of his family as I went along, and told him to prepare for me a genealogical table, and an account of the mode in which Lonee Sing had usurped the different estates of the other members of the family. This he gave to me on the road between Poknapoor and Gokurnath by one of his belted attendants, who, after handing it up to me on the elephant, ran along under the nose of Rajah Bukhtawur Sing's fine chestnut horse without saying a word.

I asked the Rajah whether he knew Lonee Sing? "Yes," said he; "everybody knows him: he is one of the ablest, best, and most substantial men in Oude; and he keeps his estate in excellent order, and is respected by all people."—"Except his own relations," said the belted attendant; "these he robs of all they have, and nobody interposes to protect them, because he has become wealthy, and they have become poor!" "My good fellow," said the Rajah, "he has only taken what they knew not how to hold, and with the sanction of the King's servants."—"Yes," replied the man, "he has got the sanction of the King's servants, no doubt, and any one who can pay for it may get that now-a-days to rob others of the King's subjects. Has not Lonee Sing robbed all his cousins of their estates, and added them to his own, and thereby got the means of bribing the King's servants to let him do what he likes?" "What," said the Rajah, with some asperity, "should you, a mere soldier, know about State affairs? Do you suppose that all the members of any family can be equal? Must there not be a head to all families to keep the rest in order? Nothing goes on well in families or governments where all are equal, and there is no head to guide; and the head must have the means to guide the rest."—"True," said the belted attendant, "all can't be equal in the rule of States; but in questions of private right, between individuals and subjects, the case is different; and the ruler should give to every one his due, and prevent the strong from robbing the weak. I have five fingers in my hand: they serve me, and I treat them all alike. I do not let one destroy or molest the other." "I tell you," said the Rajah, with increasing asperity, "that there must be heads of families as well as heads of States, or all would be confusion; and Lonee Sing is right in all that he has done. Don't you see what a state his district is in, now that he has taken the management of the whole upon himself? I dare say all the waste that we see around us has arisen from the want of such heads of families."—"You know," said the man, "that this waste has been caused by the oppression of the King's officers, and their disorderly and useless troops, and the strong striving to deprive the weak of their rights."

"You know nothing about these matters," said the Rajah, still more angrily. "The wise and strong are everywhere striving to subdue the weak and ignorant, in order that they may manage what they hold better than they can. Don't you see how the British Government are going on, taking country after country year after year, in order to manage them better than they were managed under others? and don't you see how these countries thrive under their strong and just Government? Do you think that God would permit them to go on as they do unless he thought that it was for the good of the people who come under their rule?" Turning to me, the Rajah continued: "When I was one day riding over the country with Colonel Low, the then Resident, as I now ride with you, sir, he said, with a sigh, 'In this country of Oude what darkness prevails! No one seems to respect the right of another; and every one appears to be grasping at the possessions of his neighbour, without any fear of God or the King'—'True, sir,' said I; 'but do you not see that it is the necessary order of things, and must be ordained by Providence? Is not your Government going on taking country after country, and benefiting all it takes? And will not Providence prosper their undertakings as long as they do so? The moment they come to a stand, all will be confusion. Sovereigns cannot stand still, sir; the moment their bellies are full (their ambition ceases), they and the countries they govern retrograde. No sovereign in India, sir, that has any regard for himself or his country, can with safety sit down and say that his belly is full (that he has no further ambition of conquest): he must go on to the last."*

*   The Rajah's reasoning was drawn from the practice in Oude, of seizing upon the possessions of weaker neighbours, by means of gangs of robbers. The man who does this, becomes the slave of his gangs, as the imperial robber, who seizes upon smaller states by means of his victorious armies, becomes their slave, and, ultimately, their victim, The history of India is nothing more than the biography of such men, and the Rajah has read no other.

The poor belted attendant of Chotee Sing was confounded with the logic and eloquence of the old Rajah, and said nothing more; and Chotee Sing himself kept quietly behind on his horse, with his ears well wrapped up in warm cloth, as the morning was very cold, and he was not well. He looked very grave, and evidently thought the Rajah had outlived his understanding. But the fact is that the Rajah has, by his influence at Court, taken all the lands held by his two elder nephews, Rughbur Sing and Ramadeen, and made them over to their youngest brother, Maun Sing, whom he has adopted, made his heir, and the head of the family. He has, in consequence, for the present a strong fellow-feeling with Lonee Sing; and, in all this oration at least, "his wishes were father to his thoughts."

The sharpest retort that I remember ever having had myself was given to me by a sturdy and honest old landholder of the middle class, whom I had known for a quarter of a century on the bank of the Nerbudda, in 1843. During the insurrection in the Saugor and Nerbudda territories, which commenced in 1842, I was sent down by the Governor-General Lord Ellenborough to ascertain if possible the causes which had led to it. I conversed freely with the landholders, and people of all classes in the valley, who had been plundered by the landed aristocracy of the jungles on the borders, and had one afternoon some fifty in my tent seated on the carpet. After a good deal of talk about the depredations of the jungle barons upon the people of the cultivated plains, and remonstrance at the want of support on their part to the Government officers, I said to Umrao Sing, one of the most sturdy and honest among them, "Why did you withhold from the local officers the information which you must have had of the movements and positions of the rebels and their followers, who were laying the country waste? In no part of India have the farmers and cultivators been more favoured in light assessments and protection to life and property; but there are some men who never can be satisfied; give them what you will, they will always be craving after more."—"True, sir," said Umrao Sing, looking me steadily in the face, and with the greatest possible gravity, "there are some people who never can be satisfied, give them what you will. Give them the whole of Hindoostan, and they will go off to Kabul to take more!"

There was a pause, during which all looked very grave, for they thought that the old man had exceeded the bounds of the privilege he had long enjoyed of expressing his thoughts freely to European gentlemen; and Umrao Sing continued: "The fact is, sir, that after you had, by good government, made us all happy and prosperous, and proud to display the wealth we had acquired on our persons, and in our houses and villages, you withdrew all your troops from among us, and left us a prey to the wild barons of the hills and jungles on our borders, whose families had risen to wealth, distinction, and large landed possessions under former misrule and disorder, and who are always longing for the return of such disorders, that they may have some chance of recovering the consequence and influence which they have lost under a settled and strong Government: they saw that your troops had been taken off for distant conquests, and heard of nothing but defeats and disasters, and readily persuaded themselves that your rule was at an end; for what could men, born and bred in the jungles, know of your resources to retrieve such disasters?

"After the Mahratta war, in 1817, you prohibited the people of your newly-acquired districts from carrying arms, not dreaming that the only persons who would obey or regard your order were the peaceful landholders and peasantry of the plains, who were satisfied with your Government, and anxious for its duration, but exposed to the envy and hatred of the Gond and Lodhee chiefs, who occupied the hills and jungles on their borders.

"When they came down upon us, you had no means left to protect us; and having no longer any arms or any experience of the use of them, after a quarter of a century of peace, we were unable to defend our villages, our houses, or our families; if we attempted to defend them, we and our families were killed; if we did not, we were robbed and threatened with death, if we gave you information to their prejudice. We saw that they could carry their threats into execution, for your local officers had not the means to protect us from their vengeance, and we suffered in silence; but you must not infer from this that we were tired of your rule, or pleased with their depredations; all here can testify that we longed for the return of your strength and their downfal. It is true, however," added he, "that the new European officers placed over us did not treat us with the same courtesy and consideration as the old ones, or seem to entertain the same kindly feeling towards us; and our communion with them was less free and cordial."

All approved of my old friend's speech, and declared that he had given expression to the thoughts and feelings of all present, and of all the people of the plains, who lived happily under our rule, and prayed earnestly for its duration. The portion of the estate of Mitholee, held by Lonee Sing, now contains the sites of six hundred and four villages, about one-half of which are occupied; four hundred and eighty-four of these lie in the Mahomdee district, and one hundred and twenty in that of Khyrabad. The number and names of the villages are still kept up in the accounts.

February 5, 1850.—Kurrunpoor Mirtaha, ten miles over a plain of fine muteear soil, scantily cultivated, but bearing excellent spring crops where it is so. Not far from our last camp at Gokurnath, we entered a belt of jungle three miles wide, consisting chiefly of stunted, knotty, and crooked sakhoo trees, with underwood and rank chopper grass. This belt of jungle is the same we passed through, as above described, between

Poknapoor and Gokurnath. It runs from the great forest to the north, a long way down south-east, into the Khyrabad district. From this belt to our present ground, six miles, the road passes over a fine plain, nine-tenths of which is covered with this grass, but studded with mango-groves and fine single trees. The forest runs along to the north of our road—which lay east—from one to three miles distant, and looked very like a continued mango-grove. The level plain of rich soil extends up through the forest to the foot of the hills, and is all the way capable of the finest cultivation. Here and there the soil runs into light doomuteea; and in some few parts even into bhoor, in proportion as the sand abounds; but generally the soil is the fine muteear, and very fertile. The whole plain is said to have been in cultivation thirty years ago, when Hakeem Mehndee held the contract; but the tillage has been falling off ever since, under the bad or oppressive management of successive contractors.

The estate through which we have been passing is called Bharwara, and contains the sites of nine hundred and eighty-nine villages, about one-tenth of which are now occupied. The landholders are all of the Ahbun Rajpoot tribe; but a great part of them have become Musulmans. They live together, however, though of different creeds, in tolerable harmony; and eat together on occasions of ceremony, though not from the same dishes. No member of the tribe ever forfeited his inheritance by changing his creed. Nor did any one of them, I believe, ever change his creed, except to retain his inheritance, liberty, or life, threatened by despotic and unscrupulous rulers. They dine on the same floor, but there is a line marked off to separate those of the party who are Hindoos from those who are Musulmans. The Musulmans have Mahommedan names, and the Hindoos Hindoo names; but both still go by the common patronymic name of Ahbuns. The Musulmans marry into Musulman families, and the Hindoos into Hindoo families of the highest castes, Chouhans, Rathores, Rykwars, Janwars, &c. Of course all the children are of the same religion and caste as their parents. They tell me that the conversion of their ancestors was effected by force, under a prince or chief called "Kala Pahar." This must have been Mahommed Firmally, alias Kala Pahar—to whom his uncle Bheilole, King of Delhi, left the district of Bahraetch as a separate inheritance a short time before his death, which took place A.D. 1488. This conversion seems to have had the effect of doing away with the murder of female infants in the Ahbun families who are still Hindoos; for they could not get the Musulman portion of the tribe to associate with them if they continued it.

The estate of Bharwara is divided into four parts, Hydrabad, Hurunpoor, Aleegunge, and Sekunderabad. Each division is subdivided into parts, each held by a separate branch of the family; and the subdivision of these parts is still going on, as the heads of the several branches of the family die, and leave more than one son. The present head of the Ahbun family is Mahommed Hussan Khan, a Musulman, who resides in his fort in the village of Julalpoor, near the road over which we passed. The small fort is concealed within, and protected by a nice bamboo-fence that grows round it. He holds twelve villages rent free, as nankar, and pays revenue for all the rest that compose his share of the great estate. The heads of families who hold the other shares enjoy in the same manner one or more villages rent free, as nankar. These are all well cultivated, and contain a great many cultivators of the best classes, such as Koormees, Lodhies, and Kachies.

We passed through one of them, Kamole, and I had a good deal of talk with the people, who were engaged in pressing out the juice of sugar-cane. They told me that the juice was excellent, and that the syrup made from it was carried to the district of Shajehanpoor, in the British territory, to be made into sugar. Mahommed Hussan Khan came up, as I was talking with the people, and joined in the conversation. All seemed to be delighted with the opportunity of entering so freely into conversation with a British Resident who understood farming, and seemed to take so much interest in their pursuits. I congratulated the people on being able to keep so many of their houses well covered with grass-choppers; but they told me, "that it was with infinite difficulty they could keep them, or anything else they had, from the grasp of the local authorities and the troops and camp-followers who attended them, and desolated the country like a flock of locusts; that they are not only plundered but taxed by them—first, the sipahees take their choppers, beams, and rafters off their houses—then the people in charge of artillery bullocks and other cattle take all their stores of bhoosa, straw, &c., and threaten to turn the cattle loose on their fields, if not paid a gratuity—the people who have to collect fuel for the camp (bildars) take all their stores of wood, and doors and windows also, if not paid for their redemption—then the people in charge of elephants and camels threaten to denude of their leaves and small branches all the peepul, burgut, and other trees most sacred and dear to them, near their homes, unless paid for their forbearance; and—though last, not least—men, women, and children are seized, not only to carry the plunder and other burthens gratis for sipahees and servants of all kinds and grades, and camp-followers, but to be robbed of their clothes, and made to pay ransoms to get back, while all the plough-bullocks are put in requisition to draw the guns which the King's bullocks are unable to draw themselves. In short, that the approach of King's servants is dreaded as one of the greatest calamities that can befal them."

I should here mention, that all the Telinga regiments, fourteen in number, are allowed tents and hackeries to carry them. The way in which the bullocks of such carts are provided with fodder has been already mentioned; but no tents or conveyance of any kind are allowed for the Nujeeb corps, thirty-two in number. Whenever they move (and they are almost always moving), they seize whatever conveyance and shelter they require from the people of the country around. Each battalion, even in its ordinary incomplete state, requires four hundred or five hundred porters, besides carts, bullocks, horses, ponies, &c. Men, women, and children, of all classes, are seized, and made to carry the baggage, arms, accoutrements, and cages of pet birds, belonging to the officers and sipahees of these corps. They are stripped of their clothes, confined, and starved from the time they are seized; and as it is difficult to catch people to relieve them along the road, they are commonly taken on two or three stages. If they run away, they forfeit all their clothes which remain in the hands of the sipahees; and a great many die along the road of fatigue, hunger, and exposure to the sun. Numerous cruel instances of this have been urged by me on the notice of the King, but without any good effect. The line of march of one of these corps is like the road to the temple of Juggurnaut! When the corps is about to move, detachments are sent out to seize conveyance of all kinds; and for one cart required and taken, fifty are seized, and released for a donation in proportion to their value, the respectability of the proprietors, and the necessity for their employment at home at the time. The sums thus extorted by detachments they share with their officers, or they would never be again sent on such lucrative service.

It appears that in this part of Oude the people have not for many years suffered so much from the depredations of the refractory landholders as in other parts; and that the desolate state of the district arises chiefly from the other three great evils that afflict Oude—the rack-renting of the contractors; the divisions they create and foster among landholders; and the depredations of the troops and camp-followers who attend them. But the estate has become much subdivided, and the shareholders from this cause, and the oppression of the contractors, have become poor and weak; and the neighbouring landholders of the Janwar and other Rajpoot tribes have taken advantage of their weakness to seize upon a great many of their best villages. Out of Kurumpoor, within the last nine years, Anorud Sing, of Oel, a Janwar Rajpoot, in collusion with local authorities, has taken twelve; and Umrao Sing, of Mahewa, of the same tribe, has taken eighteen, making twenty villages from the Kurumpoor division. These landholders reside in the Khyrabad district, which adjoins that of Mahomdee, near our present camp.

The people everywhere praise the climate—they appear robust and energetic, and no sickness prevails, though many of the villages are very near the forest. The land on which the forest stands contains, in the ruins of well-built towns and fortresses, unquestionable signs of having once been well cultivated and thickly peopled: and it would soon become so again under good government. There is nothing in the soil to produce sickness; and, I believe, the same soil prevails up through the forest to the hills. Sickness would, no doubt, prevail for some years, till the underwood and all the putrid leaves should be removed. The water that stagnates over them, and percolates through the soil into the wells, from which the people drink, and the exhalations which arise from them and taint the air, confined by the dense mass of forest trees, underwood, and high grass, are, I believe, the chief cause of the diseases which prevail in this belt of jungle.

It is however remarkable, that there are two unhealthy seasons in the year in this forest—one at the latter end of the rains in August, September, and October, and the other before the rains begin to fall in the latter part of April, the whole of May, and part of June. The diseases in the latter are, I believe, more commonly fatal than they are in the former; and are considered by the people to arise solely from the poisonous quality of the water, which is often found in wells to be covered with a thin crust of petrolium. Diseases of the same character prevail at the same two seasons in the jungles, above the sources of the Nerbudda and Sohun rivers, and are ascribed by the people to the same causes—those which take place after the rains, to bad air; and those which take place immediately before the rains, after the cold and dry seasons, to bad water. The same petrolium, or liquid bitumen, is found floating on the spring waters in the hot season, when the most fatal diseases break out in the jungles, about the sources of the Nerbudda and Sohun, as in the Oude Tarae; and, in both places, the natives appear to me to be right in attributing them to the water; but whether the poisonous quality of the water be imparted to it by bitumen from below, or by the putrid leaves of the forest trees from above, is uncertain; the people drink from the bituminous spring waters at this season, as well as from stagnant pools in the beds of small rivers, which have ceased to flow during part of the Cold, and the whole of the hot, season. These pools become filled with the leaves of the forest trees which hang over them.

The bitumen, in all the jungles to which I refer, arises, I believe, from the coal measures, pressed down by the overlying masses of sandstone strata, common to both the Himmalaya chain of mountains over the Tarae forest, and the Vendeya and Sathpoor ranges of hills at the sources of the Nerbudda and Sohun rivers. It is, however, possible that the water of these stagnant pools, tainted by the putrid leaves, may impart its poison through the medium of the air in exhalations; and I have known European officers, who were never conscious of having drunk either of the waters above described, take the fever (owl) in the month of May in the Tarae, and in a few hours become raving mad. These tainted waters may possibly act in both ways—directly, and through the medium of the air.

While on the subject of the causes or sources of disease, I may mention two which do not appear to me to have been sufficiently considered and provided against in India. First, when a new cantonment is formed and occupied in haste, during or after a campaign, terraces are formed of the new earth dug up on the spot to elevate the dwellings of officers and soldiers from the ground, which may possibly become flooded in the rains; and over the piles of fresh earth officers commonly form wooden floors for their rooms to secure them from the damp, new earth. Between this earth and the wooden floor a small space of a foot or two is commonly left. The new earth, thus thrown up from places that may not have been dug or ploughed for ages, absorbs rapidly the oxygen from the air above, and gives out carbonic acid, nitrogen and hydrogen gases, which render the air above unfit for men to breathe. This noxious air accumulates in the space below the wooden floor, and, passing through the crevices, is breathed by the officers and soldiers as they sleep.

Between the two campaigns against Nepal in 1814 and 1815, the brigade in which my regiment served formed such a cantonment at

Nathpoor, on the right bank of the river Coosee. The land which these cantonments occupied had been covered with a fine sward on which cattle grazed for ages, and was exceedingly rich in decayed vegetable and animal matter. The place had been long remarked for its salubrity by the indigo-planters and merchants of all kinds who resided there; and on the ground which my regiment occupied there was a fine pucka-house, which the officer commanding the brigade and some of his staff occupied. In the rains the whole plain, being very flat, was often covered with water, and thousands of cattle grazed upon it during the cold and hot seasons. The officers all built small bungalows for themselves on the plan above described; and the medical officers all thought that they had, in doing so, taken all possible precautions. The men were provided with huts, as much as possible on the same plan. These dwellings were all ready before the rains set in, and officers and soldiers were in the finest state of health and spirits.

In the middle and latter part of the rains, officers and men began to suffer from a violent fever, which soon rendered the European officers and soldiers delirious, and prostrated the native officers and sipahees; so that three hundred of my own regiment, consisting of about seven hundred, were obliged to be sent to their homes on sick leave. The greater number of those who remained continued to suffer, and a great many died. Of about ten European officers present with my regiment, seven had the fever, and five died of it, almost all in a state of delirium. I was myself one of the two who survived, and I was for many days delirious.

Of the medical officers of the brigade, the only one, I believe, who escaped the fever was Adam Napier, who, with his wife and children, occupied apartments in the brigadier's large pucka-house. Not a person who resided in that house was attacked by the fever. There was another pucka-house a little way from the cantonments, close to the bank of the river, occupied by an indigo-planter, a Mr. Ross. No one in that house suffered. The fever was confined to those who occupied the houses and huts which I have described. All the brigade suffered much, but my regiment, then the first battalion of the 12th Regiment, and now the 12th Regiment, suffered most; and it was stationed on the soil which had remained longest unturned and untilled on what had been considered a park round the pucka-house, in which the brigadier resided. I believe that I am right in attributing this sickness exclusively to the circumstances which I have mentioned; and I am afraid that, during the thirty-five years that have since elapsed, similar circumstances have continued to produce similar results. I am myself persuaded, that had the sward remained unbroken, and the houses and huts been raised upon it, over wooden platforms placed upon it, to secure officers and men from the damp ground, there would have been little or no sickness in that brigade.

The second of the two causes or sources of disease, to which I refer, is the insufficient room which is allowed for the accommodation of our European troops in India. Within the room assigned for the non-commissioned officers and soldiers, they soon exhaust the atmosphere around of its oxygen or vital air, while they expire or exhale carbonic acid, nitrogen and hydrogen gases, which render it altogether unfit to sustain animal life; and death or disease must soon overtake those who inhale or inspire it.

I may illustrate this by a fact within my own observation. In 1817, a flank battalion of six hundred European soldiers was formed at Allahabad, where I then was with my regiment to escort the Governor-General the Marquess of Hastings. With these six hundred soldiers there were thirty-two European officers. The soldiers and non-commissioned officers were put into the barracks in the fort, where they had not sufficient room. The commissioned officers resided in bungalows in the cantonments, or in tents on the open plain. The men were effectually prevented from exposing themselves to the sun, and from indulging in any kind of intemperance, and every possible care was taken of them. The commissioned officers lived as they liked, denied themselves no indulgence, and were driving about all day, and every day, in sun and rain, to visit each other and their friends. A fever, similar to that above described, broke out among the soldiers and non-commissioned officers in the fort, and great numbers died. Of the six hundred, only sixteen escaped the fever. When too late, they were removed from the fort into tents on the plain. From that day the deaths diminished, and the sick began to recover. Of the thirty-two commissioned officers, only one, I think, was ever sick at all, and his sickness was of a kind altogether different; and, it is impossible to resist the conclusion, that the non-commissioned officers and soldiers got their disease from want of sufficient room, and, consequently, of sufficient pure air to breathe. Subsequent experience has, I believe, tended to confirm the conclusion; and, I may safely say, that more European soldiers have died from a disregard of it, than from all the wars that we have had within the thirty-three years that have since elapsed. The cause is still in operation, and continues to produce the same fatal results, and will continue to do so till we change the system of accommodating our European troops in India.

The buildings in which they are lodged should all have thatched or tiled roofs, through which the hot and impure air, which has been already breathed, may pass, and be replaced within by the pure air of the atmosphere around, instead of roofs of pucka-masonry which confine this air to be breathed over again by the people within; and double or quadruple the space now allowed to each man should be given. At the cost now incurred in providing them with this insufficient room, under roofs of pucka-masonry, they could be provided with four times the space, under roofs of thatch and tiles, which would be so much more safe and suitable.

The state of the Bharwara district may be illustrated by that of one of its four divisions or mahals, Alleegunge. In the last year of Hakeem Mehudee's role (1818), this division was assessed at one hundred and thirty-eight thousand rupees, with the full consent of the people, who were all thriving and happy. The assessment was, indeed, made by the heads of the principal Ahbun families of the district, with Mahommed Hussan Khan as chief assessor. One hundred and thirty-two thousand were collected, and six thousand were remitted in consequence of a partial failure of the crops. Last year, by force and violence, the landholders of this division were made to agree to an assessment upon the lands in tillage of ten thousand and five hundred rupees, of which not six thousand can be collected. The other three divisions are in the same state. Not one-tenth of the land is in tillage, nor are one-tenth of the villages peopled. The soil is really the finest that I have seen in India; and I have seen no part of India in which so small a portion of the surface is unfit for tillage. The moisture rises to the surface just as it is required; and a tolerable crop is got by a poor man who cannot afford to keep a plough, and merely burns down the grass and digs the surface with his spade, or pickaxe, before he sows the seed. Generally, however, the tillage, in the portion cultivated, is very good. The surface is ploughed and cross-ploughed from six to twenty, or even thirty, times in the season; and the harrow and roller are often applied till every clod is pulverized to dust.

The test of first-rate preparation for the seed is that a ghurra, or earthen pitcher, full of water, let fall upon the field from a man's head, shall not break. The clods in the muteear soil are so pulverised only in the fields that are to be irrigated, or to the surface of which moisture rises from below as the weather becomes warm. The people say that it does so rise when required in land even a good way from the forest, and that the clods are, in consequence, not necessary to retain it. This is the only part of India in which I have known the people take ratoon, or second crops of sugar-cane from the same roots; and the farmers and cultivators tell me that the second crop is almost as good as the first. The fields in tillage are well supplied with manure, which is very abundant where so large a portion of the surface is waste; and affords such fine pasture. They are also well watered, for the water is near the surface, and in the tight muteear soil a kutcha well, or well without masonry, will stand good for twenty seasons. To make pucka-wells, or wells lined with burnt bricks and cement, would be costly. Each well of this kind costs about one hundred rupees. The kutcha-wells, which are lined with nothing, or with thick ropes of twigs and straw, cost only from five to ten rupees. The people tell me that oppression and poverty have made them less fastidious than they were formerly; that formerly it was considered disgraceful to plough with buffaloes, or to use them in carts, but they are now in common use for both purposes; that vast numbers of the Kunojee Brahmins and others, who could not formerly drive their own ploughs, drive them now; and that all will in time condescend to do so, as the penalties of higher payments with and for daughters in marriage cease to be exacted from men whose necessities have become so pressing.

March 6, 1850. **—Halted at Kurunpoor, where the gentlemen of my camp shot some floricans, hares, partridges, and a porcupine along the bank of the small river Ole, which flows along from north-west to south-east within three miles of Kurunpoor.

March 7, 1850.—Teekur, twelve miles. The road, for three miles, lay through grass jungle to the border of the Khyrabad district, whence the plain is covered with cultivation, well studded with trees, clusters of bamboos, and well peopled with villages, all indicating better management. A great many fields are reduced to the fine dust above described to receive the sugar-cane, which is planted in February. The soil is muteear, but has in many parts become impaired by over-cropping. The people told me that the crops were not so rich as they ought to be, from the want of manure, which is much felt here, where there is so little pasture for cattle. The wheat has almost everywhere received an orange tint from the geerwa, or blight, which covers the leaves, but, happily, has not as yet settled upon the stalks to feed on the sap. This blight, the cultivators say, arises from the late and heavy rain they have had, and the easterly wind that prevailed for a few days. The geerwa is a red fungus, which, when it adheres to the stems, thrusts its roots through the pores of the epidermis and robs the grain of the sap as it ascends. When easterly winds and sultry weather prevail, the pores of the epidermis appear to be more opened and exposed to the inroads of these fungi than at other times. If the wind continue westerly for a fortnight more, little injury may be sustained; but should easterly winds and sultry weather prevail, the greater part may be lost. "We cultivators and landholders," said Bukhtawur Sing, "are always in dread of something, and can never feel quite easy: if little rain falls, we complain of the want of more; if a good deal comes down, we are in dread of this blight, and never dare to congratulate ourselves on the prospect of good returns." To the justice and wisdom of this observation all assented.*

*   Westerly winds and cold weather prevailed and the blight did little apparent injury to the crops; but the wheat crops, generally, over Oude and the adjoining districts, was shrivelled and deficient in substance. It had "run to stalk" from the excess of rain.

The landholders of this purgunnah are chiefly Janwar Rajpoots. Kymara, a fine village, through which we passed, about five miles from Kurunpoor, is the residence of the present head of this family, Rajah Ajeet Sing. He has a small fort close by, in which he is now preparing to defend himself against the King's forces. The poor old man came out with all his village community to meet and talk with me, in the hope that I might interpose to protect him. He is weak in mind and body, has no son, and, having lately lost his only brother and declared heir to the estate, his cousins and more distant relations are scrambling for the inheritance. The usual means of violence, collusion, and intrigue have been had recourse to. The estate is in the Huzoor Tuhseel, and not under the jurisdiction of the contractor of Khyrabad. The old man seemed care-worn and very wretched, and told me that the contractor, whom I should meet at Teekur, had only yesterday received orders from Court to use all his means to oust him from possession, and make over the estate to his cousin, Jodha Sing, who had lately left him in consequence of a dispute, after having, since the death of his brother, aided him in the management of the estate; that he had always paid his revenues to the King punctually, and last year he owed a balance of only one hundred and sixty rupees, when Anrod Sing, his distant relative, wanted him to declare his younger brother, Dirj Bijee Sing, his heir to the estate, in lieu of Jodha Sing.

This he refused to do, and Anrod Sing came, with a force of two thousand armed men, supported by a detachment from Captain Barlow's regiment, and laid siege to his fort, on the pretence that he was required to give security for the more punctual payment of the revenue. To defend himself, he was obliged to call in the aid of his clan and neighbours, and expend all that he had or could borrow, and, at last, constrained to accept Anrod Sing's security, for no merchants would lend money to a poor man in a state of siege. Anrod Sing had now gone off to Lucknow, and bribed the person in charge of the Huzoor Tuhseel, Gholam Ruza Khan, one of the most corrupt men in the corrupt Court of Lucknow, to get an order issued by the Minister to have him turned out, and the estate made over to Jhoda Sing, from whom he would soon get it on pretence of accumulated balances, and make it over, in perpetuity, to his brother, Dirj Bijee Sing. In this attempt, the old man said, a good many lives must be lost and crops destroyed, for his friends would not let him fall without a struggle.*

* The old man has been attacked and turned out with the loss of some lives, in spite of the Resident's remonstrance, and the estate has been made over to Jodha Sing, on the security for the payment of the revenue of Anrod Sing. Jodha Sing is, naturally, of weak intellect; and Anrod Sing will soon have him turned out as an incompetent defaulter, and get the estate for himself, or for his younger brother. Luckily Anrod Sing and Lonee Sing, of Mitholee, are at daggers-drawn about some villages, which Anrod Sing has seized, and to which Lonee Sing thinks he has a better right. Their dread of each other will be useful to the Government and the people.

As soon as we left the poor old man, Bukhtawur Sing said, "This, sir, is the way in which Government officers manage to control and subdue these sturdy Rajpoot landholders. While they remain united, as in the Bangur district, they can do nothing with them, and let them keep their estates on their own terms; but the moment a quarrel takes place between them they take advantage of it: they adopt the cause of the strongest, and support him in his aggressions upon the other members of his family or clan till all become weak by division and disorder, and submit. Forty or fifty years ago, sir, when I used to move about the country on circuit with Saadut Allee Khan, the then sovereign, as I now move with you, there were many Rajpoot landholders in Oude stronger than any that defy the Government now; but they dared not then hold their heads so high as they do now. The local officers employed by him were men of ability, experience, and character, totally unlike those now employed. Each had a wing of one of the Honourable Company's regiments and some good guns with him, and was ready and able to enforce his master's orders and the payment of his just demands; but, since his death, the local officers have been falling off in character and strength, while the Rajpoot landholders have risen in pride and power. The aid of the British troops has, by degrees, been altogether withdrawn, and the landholders of this class despise the Oude Government, and many of them resist its troops whenever they attempt to enforce the payment of even its most moderate demands. The revenues of the State fall off as the armed bands of these landholders increase, and families who, in his time, kept up only fifty armed men, have now five hundred, or even a thousand or two thousand, and spend what they owe to Government in maintaining them. To pay such bands they withhold the just demands of the State, rob their weaker neighbours of their possessions, and plunder travellers on the highway, and men of substance, wherever they can find them.

"When Saadut Allee made over one-half of his dominions to the British Government in 1801, he was bound to reduce his military force and rely altogether upon the support of your Government. He did so; but the force he retained, though small, was good; and while that support was afforded things went on well—he was a wise man, and made the most of the means he had. Since that time, sir, the Oude force has been increased four-fold, as your aid has been withdrawn; but the whole is not equal to the fourth part which served under Saadut Allee. You see how insignificant it everywhere is, and how much it is despised even by the third-class Rajpoot landholders. You see, also, how they everywhere prey upon the people, and are dreaded and detested by them: the only estates free from their inroads are those under the 'Huzoor Tuhseel,' into which the Amils and their disorderly hosts dare not enter. If the landholders could be made to feel that they would not be permitted to seize other men's possessions, nor other men to seize theirs, as long as they obeyed the Government and paid its just dues, they would disband these armed followers, and the King might soon reduce his. He will never make them worth anything; there are too many worthless, but influential persons about the Court, interested in keeping up all kinds of abuses, to permit this. These abuses are the chief source of their incomes: they rob the officers and sipahees, and even the draft-bullocks; and you everywhere see how the poor animals are starved by them."

Within a mile of the camp I met the Nazim, Hoseyn Allee Khan, who told me that Rajah Goorbuksh Sing, of Ramnuggur Dhumeree, had fulfilled all the engagements entered into before me at Byramghat, on the Ghagra, on the 6th of December, and was no longer opposed to the Government; and that the only large landholder in his district who remained so at present was Seobuksh Sing, of Kateysura, a strong fort, mounted with seven guns, near the road over which I am to pass the day after tomorrow, between Oel and Lahurpoor. As he came up on his little elephant along the road, I saw half-a-dozen of his men, mounted on camels, trotting along through a fine field of wheat, now in ear, with as much unconcern as if they had been upon a fine sward to which they could do no harm. I saw one of my people in advance make a sign to them, on which they made for the road as fast as they could. I asked the Nazim how he could permit such trespass. He told me, "That he did not see them, and unless his eye was always upon them he could not prevent their doing mischief, for they were the King's servants, who never seemed happy unless they were trespassing upon some of his Majesty's subjects."

Nothing, certainly, seems to delight them so much as the trespasses of all kinds which they do commit upon them.

March 8, 1850.—Oel, five miles, over a plain of the same fine muteear soil, beautifully cultivated and studded with trees, intermixed with numerous clusters of the graceful bamboo. A great-grandson of the monster Nadir Shah, of Persia, Ruza Kolee Khan, who commands a battalion in the King of Oude's service, rode by me, and I asked him whether he ever saw such a cultivated country in Persia. "Never," said he: "Persia is a hilly country, and there is no tillage like this in any part of it. I left Persia, with my father, twenty-two years ago, when I was twenty-two years of age, and I have still a very distinct recollection of what it was then. There is no country in the world, sir," said the Nazim, "like Hindoostan, when it enjoys the blessings of a good government. The purgunnah of Kheree, in which we now are, is all held by the heads of three families of Janwar Rajpoots: Rajah Ajub Sing, of Kymara; Anrod Sing, of Oel; and Umrao Sing, of Mahewa. There are only sixty-six villages of Khalsa, or Crown lands left, yielding twenty-one thousand rupees a-year. The rest have been all absorbed by the heads of these Rajpoot families.

	Villages.	Jumma.
Kymara	82	13,486 0 0
Oel	170	54,790 0 0
Mahewa	70	20,835 0 0
	322	89,111 0 0
Khalsa	66	21,881 0 0
	388	1,10,992 0 0

"These heads of families have each a fort, surrounded by a strong fence of bamboos, and mounted with good guns; and the King cannot get so large a revenue from them as he did thirty years ago, in the time of Hakeem Mehndee, though their lands are as well tilled now as they were then, and yield more rent to their holders. They spend it all in keeping up large armed bands to resist the Government; but they certainly take care of their cultivators and tenants of all kinds, and no man dares molest them.

"But," said Bukhtawur Sing, "this beautiful scene would all be changed were they encouraged or permitted to contend with each other for the possession of the lands. I yesterday saw a great number of the merchants of Kymara following the Resident's camp; and, on asking them why, they told me that the order from Court obtained by Gholam Ruza for you (the Nazim) to assist the Oel chief, Anrod Sing, in despoiling Rajah Ajub Sing of his estate, had driven out all who had no fields of corn or other local ties to detain them, and had anything to lose by remaining. The chief and his retainers were repairing their fort, and preparing to fight for their possessions to the last; and if you take your disorderly force against them according to orders, the crops now in the ground will be all destroyed, and the numerous fields now prepared to receive sugar-cane and the autumn seed will be left waste: they will make reprisals upon Oel; others of their clan will join in the strife; and this district will be what that of Bharwara, which we have just left, now is. The merchants are in the right, sir, to make off: no property in such a scene is ever safe. There is no property, sir, like that in the Honourable Company's paper: it is the only property that we can enjoy in peace. You feel no anxiety about it. It doubles itself in fifteen or sixteen years; and you go on from generation to generation enjoying your five per cent., and neither fearing nor annoying anybody."

The two villages of Oel and Dhukwa adjoin each other, and form a large town; but the dwelling-houses have a wretched appearance, consisting of naked mud walls, with but a few more grass-choppers than are usually found upon them in Oude towns. There is a good-looking temple, dedicated to Mahadeo, in the centre of the town, and the houses are close upon the ditch of the fort, which has its bamboo-fence inside its ditch and outer mud walls. I have written to the Durbar to recommend that the order for the attack upon Rajah Ajub Sing be countermanded, and more pacific measures adopted for the settlement of the claims of the Exchequer and Anrod Sing upon poor old Ajub Sing.

The Kanoongoes of this place tell me that the dispute has arisen from a desire, on the part of the old man's wife, to set aside the just claim of Jodha Sing, the old man's nephew, to the inheritance, in favour of a lad whom she has adopted and brought up, by name Teeka Sing, in whose name the estate is now managed by a servant; that Jodha Sing is the rightful heir, and managed the estate well for his uncle, after the death of his brother, till lately, when his aunt persuaded his uncle to break with him, which he did with reluctance; that Jodha Sing now lives in retirement at his village of Barkerwa; that Anrod Sing's design upon the inheritance for his younger brother, Dirj Bijee Sing, is unjust; and that he is, in consequence, obliged to prosecute it on the pretence of recovering money due, and supporting the claim of Jodha Sing, and in collusion with the officers of Government; that Gholam Ruza, who has charge of the Huzoor Tuhseel, is ready to adopt the cause of any one who will pay him; and that Anrod Sing is now at Lucknow paying his court to him, and getting these iniquitous orders issued.

Oel was transferred to the Huzoor Tuhseel in 1834, Kymara in 1836, and Mahewa in 1839. These Rajpoot landholders do not often seize upon the lands of a relative at once, but get them by degrees by fraud and collusion with Government officers, so that they may share the odium with them. They instigate these officers to demand more than the lands can pay; offer the enhanced rate, and get the lands at once; or get a mortgage, run up the account, and foreclose by their aid. They no sooner get the estate than they reduce the Government demand, by collusion or violence, to less than what the former proprietor had paid.

March 9, 1850.—Lahurpoor, twelve miles, over a plain of doomuteea soil, well studded with groves and single trees, but not so fully cultivated the last half way as the first. For the first halfway the road lies through the estate of Anrod Sing, of Oel; but for the last it runs through that of Seobuksh Sing, a Gour Rajpoot, who has a fort near the town of Kuteysura, five miles from Lahurpoor, and seven from Oel. It is of mud, and has a ditch all round, and a bamboo-fence inside the outer walls. It is of great extent, but not formidable against well-provided troops. The greater part of the houses in the town are in ruins, and Seobuksh has the reputation of being a reckless and improvident landholder. He is said not only to take from his tenants higher rates of rent than he ought, but to extort from them very often a *property tax*, highly and capriciously rated. This is what the people call the *bhalmansae*, of which they have a very great abhorrence. "You are a *bhala manus*" (a gentleman, or man of substance), he says to his tenant, "and must have property worth at least a thousand rupees. I want money sadly, and must have one-fifth: give me two hundred rupees." This is what the people call "*bhalmansae*," or rating a man according to his substance; and to say that a landlord or governor does this, is to say that he is a reckless oppressor, who has no regard to obligations or to consequences.

There are manifest signs of the present landholder, Seobuksh Sing, being of this character; but others, not less manifest, of his grandfather having been a better man, in the fine groves which surround Lahurpoor, and the villages between this place and Kuteysura, all of which are included in his estate. These groves were, for the most part, planted during the life of his grandfather by men of substance, who were left free to-dispose of their property as they thought best.

All the native gentlemen who rode with me remarked on the beauty of the approach to Lahurpoor, in which a rich carpet of spring crops covers the surface up to the groves, and extends along under the trees which have been recently planted. There are many young groves about the place, planted by men who have acquired property by trade, and by the savings out of the salaries and perquisites of office at Lahurpoor, which is the residence of the Nazim, or local governor, during several months in the year; and the landlord, Seobuksh, cannot venture to exact his *property-tax* from them. The air and water are much praised, and the general good health of the troops, civil establishments, and residents of all classes, show that the climate must be good. The position, too, is well chosen with reference to the districts, and the character of the people under the control of the governor of the Khyrabad district.

The estate of Seobuksh is very extensive. The soil is all good and the plain level, so that every part of it is capable of tillage. Rutun Sing, the father of Seobuksh, is said to have been a greater rack-renter, rebel, and robber than his son is, and together they have injured the estate a good deal, and reduced it from a rent-roll of one hundred thousand to one of forty. Its rent-roll is now estimated in the public accounts at 54,640, out of which is deducted a *nankar* of 17,587, leaving a Government demand of only 37,053. This he can't pay; and he has shut himself up sullenly in his mud fort, where the Nazim dares not attack him. He is levying contributions from the surrounding villages, but has not yet plundered or burnt down any. He was lately in prison, for two years; but released on the security of Rajah Lonee Sing, of Mitholee, whose wife is his wife's sister. He, however, says that he was pledged to produce him when required, not before the *present Nazim*, but his *predecessor*, and that he is no longer bound by this pledge. This reasoning would, of course, have no weight with the Government authorities, nor would it be had recourse to were Lonee Sing less strong. Each has a strong fort and a band of steady men. The Nazim has not the means to attack Seobuksh, and dares not attack Lonee Sing, as his estate of Pyla is in the "Huzoor Tuhseel," and under the protection of Court favourites, who are well paid by him.

Lonee Sing's estate of Mitholee is in the Mahomdee district, and under the jurisdiction of the Amil; and it is only the portion, consisting of one hundred and four recently-acquired villages, which he holds in the Pyla estate, in the Khyrabad district, that has been made over to the Huzoor

Tuhseel.* He offered an increased rate for these villages to the then Amil, Bhowood Dowlah, in the year A.D. 1840. It was accepted, and he attacked, plundered, and murdered a good many of the old proprietors, and established such a dread among them, that he now manages them with little difficulty. Basdeo held fourteen of these villages under mortgage, and sixteen more under lease. He had his brother, maternal uncle, and a servant killed by Lonee Sing, and is now reduced to beggary. Lonee Sing took the lease in March, 1840, and commenced this attack in May.

* Anrod Sing holds twenty-eight villages in the Pyla estate, acquired in the same way as those held by Lonee Sing.

The Nazim had with him, of infantry, 1. Futteh Aesh Nujeebs. 2. Wuzeree, ditto. 3. Zuffur, Mobaruk Telinga. 4. Futteh Jung ditto; Ruza Kolee Khan. 5. Captain Barlow's ditto. Eleven guns. But, being unable to get any duty from the three regiments first named, he offered to dispense with the two first, on condition that the command of the third should be placed at his disposal for his son or nephew.

This request was complied with; and, on paying a fee of five thousand rupees, he got the dress of investiture, and offered it to Lieutenant Orr, a very gallant officer, the second in command of Captain Barlow's corps, as the only way to render the corps so efficient as he required it to be. The Durbar took away the two regiments; but, as soon as they heard that Lieutenant Orr was to command the third, they appointed Fidda Hoseyn, brother of the ruffian Mahommed Hoseyn, who had held the district of Mahomdee, and done so much mischief to it. Fidda Hoseyn, of course, paid a high sum for the command to be exacted from his subordinates, or the people of the district in which it might be employed; and the regiment has remained worse than useless. Of the eleven guns, five are useless on the ground, and without bullocks. The bullocks for the other six are present, but too weak to draw anything. They had had no grain for many years; but within the last month they have had one-half seer each per day out of the one seer and half paid for by Government.

There is no ammunition, stores, or anything else for the guns, and the best of the carriages are liable to fall to pieces with the first discharge. They are not allowed to repair them, but must send them in to get them changed for others when useless. The Durbar knows that if they allow the local officers to charge for the repair of guns, heavy charges will be made, and no gun ever repaired; and the local officers know that if they send in a gun to be repaired at Lucknow, they will get in exchange one *painted* to look well, but so flimsily done up that it will go to pieces the first or second time it is fired.

Captain Barlow's corps is a good one, and the men are finer than any that I have seen in our own infantry regiments, though they get only five rupees a-month each, while ours get seven. They prefer this rate under European officers in the Oude service, to the seven rupees a-month which sipahees get in ours, though they have no pension establishment or extra allowance while marching. They feel sure that their European commandants will secure them their pay sooner or later; they escape many of the harassing duties to which our sipahees are liable; they have leave to visit their homes one month in twelve; they never have to march out of Oude to distant stations, situated in bad climates; they get fuel and fodder, and often food, for nothing; their baggage is always carried for them at the public cost. But to secure them their pay, arms, accoutrements, clothing, &c., the commandant must be always about the Court himself, or have an *ambassador* of some influence there at great cost. Captain Barlow is almost all his time at Court, as much from choice as expediency, drawing all his allowances and emoluments of all kinds, while his second in command performs his regimental duties for him. The other officers like this, because they know that the corps could not possibly be kept in the state it is without it. Captain Barlow has lately obtained three thousand rupees for the repair of his six gun-carriages, tumbrils, &c., that is, five hundred for each. They had not been repaired for ten years; hardly any of the others have been repaired for the last twenty or thirty years.

The Nazim of this district of Khyrabad has taken the farm of it for one year at nine lacs of rupees, that is one lac and a half less than the rate at which it was taken by his predecessor last year. He tells me, that he was obliged, to enter into engagements to pay in gratuities fifty thousand to the minister, of which he has as yet paid only five thousand; twenty-five thousand to the Dewan, Balkishun, and seven thousand to Gholam Ruza, who has charge of the Huzoor Tuhseel—that he was obliged to engage to pay four hundred rupees a-month, in salaries, to men named by the Dewan, who do no duty, and never show their faces to him; and similar sums to the creatures of the minister and others—that he was obliged to pay gratuities to a vast number of understrappers at Court—that he was not made aware of the amount of these gratuities, &c., till he had received his dress of investiture, and had merely promised to pay what his predecessor had paid—that when about to set out, the memorandum of what his predecessor had paid was put into his hand, and it was then too late to remonstrate or draw back. There may be some exaggeration in the rate of the gratuities demanded; but that he has to pay them to the persons named I have no doubt whatever, because; all men in charge of districts have to pay them to those persons, whether they hold the districts in contract, or in trust.

The Zuffer Mobaruk regiment, with its commandant, Fidda Hoseyn, is now across the Ghagra in charge of Dhorehra, an estate in the forest belonging to Rajah Arjun Sing, who has absconded in consequence of having been ruined by the rapacity of a native collector last year; and they are diligently employed in plundering all the people who remain. The estate paid 2,75,000 a-year till these outrages began; and it cannot now pay fifty thousand. Arjun Sing and Seobuksh Sing, of Kuteysura, are the only refractory landholders in the Khyrabad district at present.

March 10, 1850.—Halted at Lahurpoor. There is good ground for large civil and military establishments to the south of the town, about a mile out, on the left of the road leading to Khyrabad. It is a fine open plain of light soil. New pucka-wells would be required; and some low ground, near the south and north, would also require to be drained, as water lies in it during the rains. There is excellent ground nearer the town on the same side, but the mango-groves are thick and numerous, and would impede the circulation of air. The owners would, moreover be soon robbed of them were a cantonment, or civil station, established among or very near to them. The town and site of any cantonment, or civil station, should be taken from the Kuteysura estate, and due compensation made to the holder, Seobuksh. The town is a poor one; and the people are keeping their houses uncovered, and removing their property under the apprehension that Seobuksh will attack and plunder the place. All the merchants and respectable landholders, over the districts bordering on the Tarae forest, through which we have passed, declare, that all the colonies of Budukh dacoits, who had, for many generations, up to 1842, been located in this forest, have entirely disappeared. Not a family of them can now be found anywhere in Oude. Six or eight hundred of their brave and active men used to sally forth every year, and carry their depredations into Bengal, Bebar and all the districts of the north-west provinces. Their suppression has been a great benefit conferred upon the people of India by the British Government.

March 11, 1850.—Kusreyla, ten miles, over a plain of excellent muteear soil scantily cultivated, but studded with fine trees, single and in groves. Kusreyla is among the three hundred villages which have been lately taken in mortgage from the proprietors, and in lease from Government, by Monowur-od Dowlah, the nephew and heir of the late Hakeem Mehndee. He is inviting and locating in these villages many cultivators of the best classes; and they will all soon be in a fine state of tillage. No soil can be finer, and no acre of it is incapable of bearing fine crops. The old proprietors and lessees, to whom he had lent money on mortgage, have persuaded him to foreclose, that they may come under so substantial and kind a landholder. They prefer holding the sub-lease under such a man, to holding the lease directly under Government, subject to the jurisdiction of the Nazim. Monowur-od Dowlah pays forty thousand rupees a-year for the whole to Government, and has had the whole transferred to the Huzoor Tuhseel.

The Nazim of Khyrabad rode by my side during this morning's march, and at my request he described the mutiny which took place in two of the regiments that attended him in the siege of Bhitolee, just before I crossed the Ghagra at Byramghat. These were the Futteh Aesh, and the Wuzeeree. Their commandants are Allee Hoseyn, a creature of one of the singers, Kootab Allee; and Mahommed Akhbur, a creature of the minister's. They were earnestly urged by the minister and Nazim to join their regiments for the short time they would be on this important service, but in vain; nothing could induce them to quit the Court. All the corps mentioned above, as attending the Nazim, were present, and the siege had begun when, on the 17th of November, some shopkeepers in camp, having been robbed during the night by some thieves, shut up their shops, and prepared to leave the camp in a body. The siege could not go on if the traders all left the place; and he sent a messenger to call the principal men that he might talk to them. They refused to move, and the messenger, finding that they were ready to set out, seized one of them by the waist-hand, and when he resisted, struck him on the head with a stick, and said he would make him go to his master. The man called out to some sipahees of the Wuzeeree regiment, who were near, to rescue him. They did so: the messenger struggled to hold his grasp, but was dragged off and beaten. He returned the blows; the sipahees drew their swords: he seized one of the swords and ran off towards his master's tent, waiving it over his head, to defend himself, followed by some of the sipahees. The others ran back to the grove in which their regiment and the Futteh Aesh were bivouaced; both regiments seized their arms and ran towards the Nazim's tents; and when they got within two hundred yards, commenced firing upon them.

The Nazim had with him only a few of his own armed servants. They seized their arms, and begged permission to return the fire, but were restrained till the regiment came near, and two tomandars, or officers, who stood by the Nazim, were shot down, one dead; and the other disabled. His men could be restrained no longer, and they shot down two of the foremost of the assailants. The Nazim then sent off to Lieutenant Orr, who was exercising his corps with blank cartridge on the parade; and, supposing that one of these regiments was doing the same thing near the Nazim's tents, he paid no attention to them. He and his brother, the Adjutant, ran forward, and entreated the two regiments to cease firing; and the Nazim sent out Syud Seoraj-od Deen (the commandant of the Bhurmar regiment, stationed in the adjoining district of Ramnugger Dhumeree, who had just come to him on a visit), with the Koran in his hand, to do the same. The remonstrances of both were in vain. They continued to fire upon the Nazim, and Lieutenant Orr went off to bring up his regiment, which stood ready to move on the parade. Alarmed at this, the two regiments ran off to their grove, and the firing ceased.

During all this time, the other two regiments, the Zuffer Mobaruk and Futteh Jung, stood looking on as indifferent spectators; and afterwards took great credit to themselves for not joining in this attempt to blow up the viceroy, who was obliged, the next day, to go to their camp and apologize humbly for his men having presumed to return their fire, which he declared that they had done without his orders! On his doing this, they consented to forego their claim to have the unhappy messenger sent to their camp to be *executed*; and to remain with him during the siege. As to taking any part in the siege and assault on the fort, that was altogether out of their line. Ruza Kolee Khan, the commandant of the Futteh Jung, was at Lucknow during this mutiny, but he joined a few days after. Lieutenant Orr gave me the same narrative of the affair at the dinner-table last night; and said, that he and his brother had a very narrow escape—that his regiment would have destroyed all the mutineers had they been present; and he left them on the parade lest he might not be able to restrain them in such a scene. Even this mutiny of the two regiments could not tempt their commandants to leave Court, where they are still enjoying the favour of their patrons, the minister and the singers, and a large share of the pay and perquisites of their officers and sipahees, though the regiments have been sent off to the two disturbed districts of Sundela and Salone.

They dare not face the most contemptible enemy, but they spare not the weak and inoffensive of any class, age, or sex. A respectable landholder, in presenting a petition, complaining of the outrages committed upon his village and peasantry, said a few days ago—"The oppression of these revenue collectors, and their disorderly troops, is intolerable, sir—they plunder all who cannot resist them, but cannot lift their arms, or draw their breath freely in the presence of armed robbers and rebels—it is a proverb, sir, that *insects* prey upon soft *wood*; and these men prey only upon the peaceful and industrious, who are unable to defend themselves." The Nazim tells me, that the lamentations of the poor people, plundered and maltreated, were incessant and distressing during the whole time these two corps were with him; and that he could exercise no control whatever over them, protected as they were, in all their iniquities, by the Court favour their two commandants enjoyed at Lucknow.*

* Kootab Allee was one of the singers who were soon after banished from Oude in disgrace. But all the influence they exercised over the King has been concentrated in the hands of the two singers who remained, Mosahib Allee and Anees-od Dowla. All are despicable *domes*; but the two, who now govern the King, are much worse characters than any of those who were banished.

I asked Bukhtawur Sing, before the Nazim overtook us this morning, why it was, that these governors always took so many troops with them when they moved from place to place, merely to settle accounts and inspect the crops. "Some of them," said he, "take all the troops they can muster, to show that they are great men; but, for the most part, they are afraid to move without them. They, and the greater part of the landholders, consider each other as natural and irreconcilable enemies; and a good many of those, who hold the largest estates, are at all times in open resistance against the Government. They have their Vakeels with the contractors when they are not so, and spies when they are. They know all his movements, and would waylay and carry him off if not surrounded with a strong body of soldiers, for he is always moving over the country, with every part of which they are well acquainted. Besides, under the present system of allowing them to forage or plunder for themselves, it is ruinous to any place to leave them in it for even a few days—no man, within several miles, would preserve shelter for his family, or food for his cattle, during the hot and rainy months—he is obliged to take them about with him to distribute, as equally as he can, the terrible burthen of maintaining them. Now that the sugar-cane is ripe, not one cane would be preserved in any field within five miles of any place where the Nazim kept his troops for ten days."

March 12, 1850.—Seetapoor, nine miles over a plain of muteear soil, the greater part of which is light, and yields but scanty crops without manure, which is very scarce. Immediately about the station and villages, where manure is available, the crops are good. The wind continues westerly, the sky is clear, and the blight does not seem to increase.

The 2nd Regiment of Oude Local Infantry is stationed at Seetapoor, but it has no guns or cavalry of any kind. Formerly there was a corps of the Honourable Company's Native Infantry here, with two guns and a detail of artillery. The sipahees of this corps, and of the 1st Oude Local Infantry, at Sultanpoor, are somewhat inferior in appearance to those of our own native infantry regiments, and still more so to the Oude corps under Captains Barlow, Magness, and Bunbury. They receive five rupees eight annas a-month pay, and batta, or extra allowance, when marching; and the same pay as our own sipahees of the line (seven rupees a-month) when serving with them. But the commandants cannot get recruits equal to those that enlist in our regiments of the line, or those that enlist in the corps of the officers above named. They have not the rest and the licence of the one, while they have the same drill and discipline, without the same rate of pay as the other. They have now the privilege of petitioning through the Resident like our sipahees of the line, and that of the pension establishment, while Barlow's, Bunbury's, and Magness's corps have neither. They have none but internal duties—they are hardly ever sent out to aid the King's local authorities, and do not escort treasure even for their own pay. It is sent to them by drafts from Lucknow on the local collectors of the district in which they are cantoned; and the money required for the Resident's Treasury—a great portion of which passes through the Seetapoor cantonments—is escorted by our infantry regiments of the line, stationed at Lucknow, merely because a General Order exists that no irregular corps shall be employed on such duties while any regular corps near has a relief of guards present. The corps of regular infantry at Shajehanpoor escorts the treasure six marches to Seetapoor, where it is relieved by a detachment from one of the regular corps at Lucknow, six marches distant.

The native officers and sipahees of these two corps have leave of absence to visit their families just as often and for just as long periods as those of the corps under the three above-named officers—that is, for one month out of twelve. The native officers and sipahees of these three corps are not, however, so much drilled or restrained as those of the two Oude local corps, in which no man dares to help himself occasionally to the roofs of houses and the produce of fields or gardens; nor to take presents from local authorities, as they are hardly ever sent out to assist them. The native officers and sipahees of the very best of the King of Oude's corps do all this more or less; and they become, in consequence, more attached to their officers and the service. Moreover, the commandants of the two corps of Oude local infantry never become *mediators* between large landholders and local governors as those of the King of Oude's corps so often do; nor are any landed estates ever assigned to them for the liquidation of their arrears of pay, and confided to their management. So highly do the native officers of these three Oude *Komukee* corps appreciate all the privileges and perquisites they enjoy, when out on duty under district officers, that they consider short periods of guard duty in the city, where they have none of them, as serious punishments.

The drainage about Seetapoor is into the small river Surain, which flows along on the west boundary, and is excellent; and the lands in and about the station are at all times dry. The soil, too, is good; and the place, on the whole, is well adapted for the cantonment of a much larger force.

March 13, 1850.—Khyrabad, east nine miles, over a plain of doomuteea soil with much oosur. A little outlay and labour seem, however, to make this oosur produce good crops. On entering the town on the west side, we passed over a good stone bridge over this little stream, the Surain; and to the east of the town is another over the still smaller stream of the Gond. Khyrabad is not so well drained as Seetapoor, nor would it be so well adapted for a large cantonment. It is considered to be less healthy. There is an avenue of good trees all the way from Seetapoor to Khyrabad, a distance of six miles, planted by Hakeem Mehndee. Our camp being to the eastern extremity of the town, renders the distance nine miles.

Yesterday at Seetapoor I had a visit from Monowur-od Dowla, late prime minister, and Moomtaz-od Dowla, grandson to the late King, Mahommed Allee Shah, on their way out to the Tarae forest to join Kindoo Rao, the brother of the Byza Bae, of Gwalior, in pursuit of tigers. This morning on the road, old Bukhtawur Sing, after a sigh, said: "I presented a nazur to the prince, Moomtaz-od Dowla, sir; he is the grandson of a King, and the victim of the folly and crime of shooting a monkey! His father, Asgur Allee Khan, was the eldest son of Mahommed Allee Shah, and elder brother of Amjud Allee Shah, the father of the present King. He was fond of his gun, and one day a monkey, of the red and short-tailed kind, came and sat upon one of his out-offices. He sent for his gun, and shot it dead with a ball. The very next day, sir, he had a severe attack of fever, which carried him off in three days. During this time he frequently called out in terror, 'Save me from that monkey! save me from that monkey!'—pointing to the part of the room in which he *saw him*. The monkey killed Asgur Allee Khan, sir; and no man ever escapes death or misery who wilfully kills one. Moomtaz-od Dowla might, sir, have been now King of Oude had his father not shot that monkey."

"But I thought," said I, "it was the *hanoomaun*, or long-tailed monkey, that was held sacred by the Hindoos?"—"Sir," said Bukhtawur Sing, "both are alike sacred.* Nuseer-od Deen Hyder, the predecessor of Mahommed Allee Shah, went one day shooting in the dilkhoosha park. Several of the long-tailed monkeys came and sat upon a mango-tree near him. He could not resist the temptation, and shot several of them, one after another, with ball. He returned to the palace; but had not been home more than three hours, when he and his favourite wife, the Kooduseea Begum,** had a fierce quarrel, in which both became insane; she was so enraged that she took poison forthwith, and, in her agony, actually spit up her liver, which had been torn to pieces by the force of the poison! The King could not stand the horrible sight, and ran off and hid himself in the race-stand, near which you fell and broke your thigh-bone in April last; there he remained shut up till she died. He had had warning, sir, for a few months after his accession to the throne; I attended him and his minister, Aga Meer, on a visit to the garden, called padshah baag, on the opposite side of the river: he had a gun with him, and, seeing a monkey on a tree, he ordered the prime minister to try his hand at it. I told Aga Meer that evil would certainly befall him or his house if he shot the animal, and begged his Majesty not to assist upon the minister's doing it. Both laughed at what they thought my folly; the minister shot the monkey; and in a few days he was out of office and in a prison. One way or other, sir, a man who wilfully destroys a monkey is sure to be punished."

*   That Asgur Allee Khan, the eldest son of the King, Mahommed Allee Shah, did shoot the monkey, got a fever a few days after, and died of it, are facts well known at Lucknow. That he often mentioned the monkey during his delirium, is generally believed; and that his death was the consequence of his shooting that animal is the opinion of all the Hindoo, and a great part of the Musulman, population. His death, while his father lived, deprived his son, Moomtaz-od Dowla, of the throne.

** The Kooduseea Begum had been introduced into the palace as waiting-woman to Mulika Zumanee, whom she soon superseded in the King's affections, which she retained till her death. She was married to the King on the 17th December, 1831, and died on the 21st of August 1834.

At Khyrabad there is a handsome set of buildings, consisting of a mausoleum over his father, a mosque, an *imambara*, and a *kudum rusool*, or shrine with the print of the prophet's foot, erected by Mucka Durzee, a tailor in the service of the King, who made a large fortune out of his master's favours, and who still lives, and provides for their repair and suitable endowment. These buildings are, like all others of the same kind, infested by a host of professional religious mendicants of both sexes and all ages, who make the air resound with their clamours for alms. Not only are such buildings so infested, but all the towns around them. I could not help observing to the native gentlemen who attended me, "that when men planted groves and avenues, and built reservoirs, bridges, caravansaries, and wells, they did not give rise to any such sources of annoyance to travellers; that they enjoyed the water, shade, and accommodation, without cost or vexation, and went on their way blessing the donor." "That," said an old Rusaldar, "is certainly taking a new and just view of the case; but still it is a surprising thing to see a man in this humble sphere of life raising and maintaining so splendid a pile of buildings."*

* Mucka the tailor, to whom these buildings belong, is the person mentioned in the account of the death of the King, Nuseer-od Deen Hyder, and the confinement of Ghalib Jung.

The town of Khyrabad has still a good many inhabitants; but the number is fast decreasing. It was the residence of the families of a good many public officers in our service and that of Oude; and the local authorities of the district used to reside here. They do so no longer; and the families of public officers have almost all gone to reside at other places. Life and property have become exceedingly insecure, and attacks by gang-robbers so frequent that no man thinks his house and family safe for a single night. Government officers are entirely occupied in the collection of revenue, and they disregard altogether the sufferings and risks to which the people of towns are exposed. The ground around the place is low, and the climate is inferior to that of Seetapoor. Salt and saltpetre are 'made from the soil immediately round the town.

I have mentioned that Moomtaz-od Dowla might now have been King of Oude had his father not died before his father. The Mohammedan law excludes for ever the children of any person who dies before the person to whom he or she is the next heir from all right in the inheritance. Under the operation of this law, the sons of the eldest son of the reigning King are excluded from the succession if he dies before his father, and the crown devolves on the second son, or on the brother of the King, if he leaves no other son. The sons of all the sons who die, while their father lives, are *mahjoob-ol-irs*, that is, excluded from inheritance. In the same manner, if the next brother of the King dies before him, his sons are excluded from the succession, which devolves on the third brother, and so on through all the brothers. For instance, on the death, without any recognised issue, of Nuseer-od Been Hyder, son of Ghazee-od Deen, he was succeeded on the throne by Mahommed Allee Shah, the third brother of Ghazee-od Deen, though four sons of the second brother, Shums-od Dowla, still lived. On the death of Mahommed Allee Shah, he was succeeded by his second son, Amjud Allee Shah, though Moomtaz-od Dowla, the son of his eldest son, Asgur Allee Khan, still lived. Shums-od Dowla died before his elder brother, Ghazee-od Deen; and Asgur Allee Khan before his father, Mahommed Allee Shah: and the sons of both became, in consequence, *mahjoob-ol-irs*, excluded from succession. The same rule guides the succession among the Delhi sovereigns. This exclusion extends to all kinds of property, as well as to sovereignty.

Moomtaz-od Dowla is married to Zeenut-on Nissa, the daughter of Mulika Zumanee, one of the consorts of Nuseer-od Deen Hyder, late King of Oude; and he has, I fear, more cause to regret his union with her than his exclusion from the throne. Zeenut-on Nissa enjoys a pension of ten thousand rupees a-month, in her own right, under the guarantee of the British Government. I may here, as an episode not devoid of interest, give a brief account of her mother, who, for some years, during the reign of Nuseer-od Deen Hyder, presided over the palace at Lucknow. Before I do so I may mention that the King, Nuseer-od Deen Hyder, had been married to a grand-daughter of the Emperor of Delhi, a very beautiful young woman, of exemplary character, who still survives, and retains the respect of the royal family and people of Lucknow. Finding the Court too profligate for her, she retired into private life soon after the marriage, and has remained there ever since upon a small stipend from the King.

Mulika Zumanee, queen of the age, was a daughter of a Hindoo of the Koormee caste, who borrowed from his neighbour, Futteh Morad, the sum of sixty rupees, to purchase cloth. He soon after died, leaving a widow, and a daughter named Dolaree, then five years of age. They were both seized and confined for the debt by Futteh Morad; but, on the mother's consenting to leave her daughter in bondage for the debt, she was released. Futteh Morad's sister, Kuramut-on Nissa, adopted Dolaree, who was a prepossessing child, and brought her up as her daughter; but finding, as she grew up, that she was too intimate with Roostum, the son by a former husband of her brother's second wife, she insisted on their being married, and they were so. Futteh Morad soon after died, and his first wife turned the second, with her first son, Roostum, and his wife, Dolaree, and the two sons which she had borne to Futteh Morad—Futteh Allee Khan and Warus Allee Khân—out of her house. They went to Futteh Morad's aunt, Bebee Mulatee, a learned woman, who resided as governess in the house of Nawab Mohubbet Khan, at Roostumnugger, near Lucknow, and taught his daughters to read the Koran. Finding Dolaree to be not the most faithful of wives to Roostum, she would not admit them into the Nawab's house, but she assisted them with food and raiment; and Roostum entered the service—as a groom—of a trooper in the King's cavalry, called Abas Kolee Beg. Dolaree had given birth to a boy, who was named Mahommed Allee; and she now gave birth to a daughter; but she had cohabited with a blacksmith and an elephant-driver in the neighbourhood, and it became a much "vexed question" whether

473

the son and daughter resembled most Roostum, the blacksmith, or the elephant-driver; all, however, were agreed upon the point of Dolaree's backslidings. Mahommed Allee, *alias* Kywan Ja, was three years of age, and the daughter, *Zeenut-on Nissa*, one year and half, when some belted attendants from the palace came to Roostumnugger in search of a wet-nurse for the young prince, Moona Jan, who had been born the night before; and Bebee Mulatee, whose reputation for learning had readied the royal family, sent off Dolaree as one of the candidates for employment. Her appearance pleased the queen, the Padshah Begum, the quality of her milk was pronounced by the royal physicians to be first rate, and she was chosen, as wet-nurse for the new-born prince.

Moona Jan's father (then heir-apparent to the throne of Oude) no sooner saw Dolaree than, to the astonishment of the Queen and her Court, he fell desperately in love with her, though she seemed very plain and very vulgar to all other eyes; and he could neither repose himself, nor permit anybody else in the palace to repose, till he obtained the King's and Queen's consent to his making her his wife, which he did in 1826. She soon acquired an entire ascendancy over his weak mind, and, anxious to surround herself in her exalted station by people on whom she could entirely rely, she invited the learned Bebee Mulatee and her daughter, Jumeel-on Nissa, and her son, Kasim Beg, to the palace, and placed them in high and confidential posts. She invited at the same time Futteh Allee and Warus Allee, the sons of Futteh Morad by his second wife; and persuaded the King that they were all people of high lineage, who had been reduced, by unmerited misfortunes, to accept employments so humble. All were raised to the rank of Nawabs, and placed in situations of high trust and emoluments. Kuramut-on Nissa, too, the sister of Futteh Morad, was invited; but when Dolaree's husband—the humble Roostum—ventured to approach the Court, he was seized and imprisoned in a fort in the Bangur district till the death of Nuseer-od Deen, when he was released. He came to Lucknow, but died soon after.

Soon after the death of Ghazee-od Deen had placed the heir-apparent, her husband, on the throne, 20th of October, 1827, she fortified herself still further by high alliances: and her son, Mahommed Allee, was affianced to the daughter of Rokun-od Dowla, brother of the late King; and her daughter, Zeenut-on Nissa, to Moomtaz-od Dowla, the prince of whom I am writing. These two marriages were celebrated at a cost of about thirty lacs of rupees; Dolaree was declared the first consort of the King, under the title of "Mulika Zamanee," queen of the age, and received an estate in land yielding six lacs of rupees a-year for pin-money. Not satisfied with this, she prevailed upon the King to declare her son, Mahommed Allee, *alias* Kywan Ja, to be his *own and eldest son*, and heir-apparent to the throne; and to demand his recognition as such from the British Government, through its representative, the Resident. His Majesty, with great solemnity, assured the Resident, on many occasions during November and December, 1827, *that Kywan Ja was his eldest son*; and told him that had he not been so, his uncle would never have consented to bestow his daughter upon him in marriage, nor should he himself have consented to expend twenty lacs of rupees in the ceremonies. The Resident told him that the universal impression at Lucknow was, that the boy was three years of age when his mother was first introduced to his Majesty. But this had no effect; and, to remove all further doubts and discussions on the subject, he wrote a letter himself to the Governor-General, earnestly protesting that Kywan Ja was his *eldest son and heir-apparent to the throne*; and as such he was sent from Lucknow to Cawnpoor to meet and escort over Lord Combermere in December, 1827.

On the birth of Moonna Jan, the then King, Ghazee-od Deen Hyder, declared to the Resident that the boy was not his grandson, and that his son, Nuseer-od Deen, pretended that he was his son merely to please his imperious mother, the Padshah Begum, and to annoy his father, with whom they were both on bad terms. Ghazee-od Deen had, however, before his death declared that he believed Moonna Jan to be his grandson.* In February, 1832, the King, Nuseer-od Deen Hyder, first through the minister, and then in person, assured the Resident that neither of the boys was his son, and requested that he would report the same to his Government, and assure the Governor-General "that both reports, as to these boys being sons of his, were false, and arose from the same cause, *bribery* and *ambition*, that Mulika Zumanee had paid many lacs of rupees to influential people about him to persuade him to call her son his, and declare him heir-apparent to the throne; and that Fazl Allee and Sookcheyn had done the same to induce others to persuade him to acknowledge Moonna Jan to be his son. But, said his Majesty, I know positively that he is not my son, and my father knew the same."

* I believe that Ghazee-od Deen's first repudiation of Moonna Jan arose entirely from a desire to revenge himself upon his termagant wife, whose furious temper left him no peace. She was, from his birth, very fond of the boy; and to question his legitimacy was to wound her in her tenderest point. This was the "raw" which her husband established, and which his son and successor afterwards worked upon.

The wary minister then, to clench the matter, remarked that his Majesty had mentioned to him that he had ceased to cohabit with Moonna Jan's mother for twenty-four months before the boy was born; and the King assured the Resident that this was quite true. Hakeem Mehndee was as anxious as Aga Meer had been to keep the King estranged from his imperious mother, and the only sure way was to make him persist in repudiating the boy or postponing his claim to the succession.

Mulika Zumanee's influence over the king had, however, been eclipsed, first, by Miss Walters, Mokuddera Ouleea, whose history has already been given; secondly, by the beautiful Taj Mahal; and, thirdly, by the Kuduseea Begum. She entered the palace as a waiting-woman to Mulika Zumanee, and, on the 17th of December, 1831, the King married her; and from that day till her death, on the 21st of August, 1834, she reigned supreme in the palace and in the King's affections.

On the King's paying a visit of ceremony to Mulika Zumanee one evening, he asked for water, and it was brought to him in a gold cup, on a silver tray, by the Kuduseea Begum, then one of the women in waiting. Her face was partially unveiled; and the King, after drinking, threw the last few drops from the cup over her veil in play. In return, she threw the few drops that had been spilled on the salver upon the King's robe, or vest. He pretended to be angry, and asked her, with a frown, how she could dare to besprinkle her sovereign; she replied—"When children play together there is no distinction between the prince and the peasant." The King was charmed with her half-veiled beauty and spirit, and he paid a second visit the next day, and again asked for water. He did the same as the first day, and she returned the compliment in the same way. He came a third time and asked for water, but Mulika Zumanee had become alarmed, and it was presented by another and less dangerous person. A few days after, however, the Queen was constrained to allow her fair attendant to attend the King, and receive from him formal proposals of marriage, which she accepted.

She was handsome and generous; but there was no discrimination in her bounty, and she is said to have received from the King nearly two millions of money out of the reserved treasury for pin-money alone. Of this she saved forty-four lacs of rupees. The King never touched this money, and it formed, in a separate apartment, the greater part of the seventy lacs found in his reserved treasury on his death, out of the ten krores or ten millions sterling, which he found there when he ascended the throne in 1827.

She is said to have been the only one of his wives who ever had any real affection for the King. She was haughty and imperious in her temper; and the only female, who had any influence over her, was a Mogulanee, who taught her to read and write. She assisted her mistress very diligently in spending her pin-money, and made the fortunes of sundry of her relations. Altercations between the Kuduseea Begum and the King were not uncommon; but, on the 21st of August, 1834, the King became unusually excited, and told her that he had raised her from bondage to the throne, and could as easily cast her back into the same vile condition.

Her proud spirit could not brook this, and she instantly swallowed arsenic. The King relented, and every remedy was tried, but in vain. The King watched over her agonies till she was about to expire, when he fled in a frantic state and took refuge in the apartments of the race-stand, about three miles from the palace, till the funeral ceremonies were over. It is said, that in her anxiety to give birth to an heir to the throne, she got the husband, from whom she had been divorced, smuggled into her apartments in the palace in a female dress more than once; and that this was reported to the King, and became the real cause of the dispute.

The Mogulanee attendant, who had accumulated twenty lacs of rupees, was seized and commanded to disgorge. She offered five lacs to Court favourites on condition that they saw her safely over the river Ganges into British territory. The most grave of them were commissioned to wait upon his Majesty, and entreat him most earnestly to banish her forthwith from his territories, as she was known, in the first place, to be one of the most *potent sorceresses* in India; and, in the next, to have been exceedingly attached to her late mistress: that they had strong grounds to believe that it was her intention to send his Majesty's spirit after hers, that they might be united in the next world us they had been in this. The King got angry, and said, that he had no dread of sorceresses, and would make the old lady disgorge her twenty lacs. That very night, however, in his sleep, he saw the Kuduseea Begum enter his room, approach his bed, look upon him with a countenance still more kind and bright than in life, and then return slowly with her face still towards him, and beckoning him with her hand to follow! As soon as he awoke he became greatly agitated and alarmed, and ordered the old sorceress to be sent forthwith across the Ganges to Cawnpoor. She paid her five lacs, and took off about fifteen; but what became of her afterwards I have not heard.

One of the first cases that I had to decide, after taking charge of my office, was that of a claim to five Government notes of twenty thousand rupees each, left by Sultan Mahal, one of the late King, Amjud Allee Shah's, widows. The claimants were the reigning King, and the mother, brother, and sister of the deceased widow. She was the daughter of a greengrocer, and, in February 1846, at the age of sixteen, she went to the palace with vegetables. The King saw and fell in love with her; and she forthwith became one of his wives, under the name of "Sultan Mahal." In November, 1846, the King invested eighteen lacs and thirty thousand rupees in Government notes as a provision for his wives and other female relations. The notes were to be made out in their names respectively; and the interest was to be paid to them and their heirs. Of this sum, Sultan Mahal was to have one hundred thousand; and, on the 21st of November, she drew the interest, in anticipation, up to the 30th of December of that year. The five notes for twenty thousand each, in her name, were received in the Resident's Treasury on the 20th of April, 1847. On the 28th of August, she sent an application for the Notes to the Resident, but died the next day. The King, her husband, had died on the 18th February, 1847.

Nine days after, on the 6th of September, the new King, Wajid Allee Shah, sent an application to have these five notes transferred to one of his own wives; urging, that, as his father and the Sultan Mahal had both died, he alone ought to be considered as the heir. It was decided, that the mother, sister, and brother were the rightful heirs to the Sultan Mahal; and the amount was distributed among them according to Mahommedan law. The question was, however, submitted to Government at his Majesty's request; and the decision of the Resident was upheld on the ground that the notes were in the lady's name, and she had actually drawn interest on them; and, as she died intestate, they became the property of her heirs.

By a deed of engagement with the British Government, dated the 1st of March, 1820, the King contributed to the five per cent loan the sum of sixty-two lacs and forty thousand rupees, the interest of which, at five per cent, our Government pledged itself to pay, in perpetuity, to four females of the King's family. To Mulika Zumanee, ten thousand a-month; to her daughter, Zeenut-on Nissa, four thousand; to Mokuddera Ouleea (Miss Walters), six thousand; and to Taj Mahal, six thousand: total, twenty-six thousand rupees a-month. On the death of Mulika Zamanee, which took place on the 22nd December, 1843, her daughter succeeded to her pension of six thousand a-month.

The other portion of her pension—four thousand rupees a-month—went to her grandson, Wuzeer Mirza, the son of Kywan Ja, who had died on the 16th of May, 1838, before his mother.* Of this four thousand a-month, one thousand are given to Zeenut-on Nissa for the boy's subsistence and education, and three thousand a-month are invested in Government securities, to be paid to him when he comes of age. But, besides the six thousand rupees a-month which she inherits from her mother, Zeenut-on Nissa enjoys the pension of four thousand rupees a-month, which was assigned to her by the King in the same deed; so that she now draws eleven thousand rupees a-month, independent of her husband's income.** By this deed the stipends are to descend to the heirs of the pensioners, if they have any; and if they have none, they can bequeath their pensions to whom they please. Should they have no heirs, and leave no will, the stipends are to go to the moojtahids and moojawurs, or presiding priests of the shrine of kurbala, in Turkish Arabia, for distribution among the needy pilgrims.

* Wuzeer Mirza is not the son of Rokun-od Dowla's daughter. Kywan Ja's marriage with that lady was never consummated.

** She takes after her mother, and makes her worthy husband very miserable. She is ill-tempered, haughty, and profligate.

An European lady, who visited the zunana of the King, Nuseer-od Deen Hyder, on the anniversary of his coronation, on the 18th of October, 1828, writes thus to a female friend:—"But the present King's wives were superbly dressed, and looked like creatures of the Arabian Tales. Indeed, one (Taj Mahal) was so beautiful, that I could think of nothing but Lalla Rookh in her bridal attire. I never saw any one so lovely, either black or white. Her features were perfect, and such eyes and eyelashes I never, beheld before. She is the favourite Queen at present, and has only been married a month or two, her age, about fourteen; and such a little creature, with the smallest hands and feet, and the most timid, modest look imaginable. You would have been charmed with her, she was so graceful and fawn-like. Her dress was of gold and scarlet brocade, and her hair was literally strewed with pearls, which hung down upon her neck in long single strings, terminating in large pearls, which mixed with and hung as low as her hair, which was curled on each side her head in long ringlets, like Charles the Second's beauties. On her forehead she wore a small gold circlet, from which depended and hung, half way down, large pearls interspersed with emeralds. Above this was a paradise plume, from which strings of pearls were carried over the head, as we turn our hair. Her earrings were immense gold rings, with pearls and emeralds suspended all round in large strings, the pearls increasing in size. She had a nose ring also with large round pearls and emeralds; and her necklaces, &c., were too numerous to be described. She wore long sleeves, open at the elbow; and her dress was a full petticoat with a tight body attached, and open only at the throat. She had several persons to bear her train when she walked; and her women stood behind her couch to arrange her head-dress, when, in moving, her pearls got entangled in the immense robe of scarlet and gold she had thrown around her. This beautiful creature is the envy of all the other wives, and the favourite at present of both the King and his mother, both of whom have given her titles—See *Mrs. Park's Wandering*, vol. i., page 87. Taj Mahal still lives and enjoys a pension of six thousand rupees a-month, under the guarantee of the British Government. She became very profligate after the King's death; and after she had given birth to one child, it was deemed necessary to place a guard over her to prevent her dishonouring the memory of the King, her husband, any further by giving birth to more."

Of Miss Walters, alias Mokuddera Ouleea, the same lady writes:— "The other newly-made Queen is nearly European, but not a whit fairer than Taj Mahal. She is, in my opinion, plain; but she is considered by the native ladies very handsome, and she was the King's favourite before he saw Taj Mahal. She was more splendidly dressed than even Taj Mahal. Her head-dress was a coronet of diamonds, with a fine crescent and plume of the same. She is the daughter of a European merchant, and is accomplished for an inhabitant of a zunana, as she writes and speaks Persian fluently, as well as Hindoostanee; and it is said that she is teaching the King English, though when we spoke to her in English, she said she had forgotten it, and could not reply. She was, I fancy, afraid of the Queen Dowager, as she evidently understood us; and when asked if she liked being in the zunana, she shook her head and looked quite melancholy. Jealousy of the new favourite, however, appeared to be the cause of her discontent, as, though they sat on the same couch, they never addressed each other."

Of Mulika Zumanee, the same lady says:—"The mother of the King's children, Mulika Zumanee, did not visit us at the Queen Dowager's; but we went to see her at her own palace. She is, after all, the person of the most political consequence, being the mother of the heir-apparent; and she has great power over her royal husband, whose ears she boxes occasionally."

CHAPTER IV.

Nuseer-od Deen Hyder's death—His repudiation of his son, Moonna Jan, leads to the succession of his uncle, Nuseer-od Dowlah—Contest for the succession between these two persons—The Resident supports the uncle; and the Padshah Begum supports the son—The ministers supposed to have poisoned the King—Made to disgorge their ill-gotten wealth by his successor—Obligations of the treaty of 1801, by which Oude was divided into two equal shares—One transferred to the British Government, one reserved by Oude—Estimated value of each at the time of treaty—Present value of each—The sovereign often warned that unless he governs as he ought, the British Government cannot support him, but must interpose and take the administration upon itself—All such warnings have been utterly disregarded—No security to life or property in any part of Oude—Fifty years of experience has proved, that we cannot make the government of Oude fulfil its duties to its people—The alternative left appears to be to take the management upon ourselves, and give the surplus revenue to the sovereign and royal family of Oude—Probable effects of such a change on the feelings and interests of the people of Oude.

When in February, 1832, the King, Nuseer-od Deen Hyder, assured the Resident that Moonna Jan was not his son. Lord William Bentinck was Governor-General of India. A more thoroughly honest man never, I believe, presided over the government of any country. The question of right to succession was long maturely and most anxiously considered,

483

after these repeated and formal repudiations on the part of the King, Nuseer-od Deen Hyder; and Government would willingly have deferred a final decision on so important a question longer, but it was deemed unsafe any longer from the debauched habits of the King, the chance of his sudden death, and the risk of a tumult in such a city, to leave the representative of the paramount power unprepared to proclaim its will in favour of the rightful heir, the moment that a demise took place. Under these considerations, instructions were sent to the Resident, on the 15th of December, 1833, in case of the King's death without a son, or pregnant consort, to declare the eldest surviving brother of the late King, Ghazee-od Deen Hyder, heir to the throne, and have him placed upon it. According to the law already noticed (which applies as well to sovereignty as to property) the sons of Shums-od Dowlah, the second son of Saadut Allee Khan, who had died shortly before his eldest and reigning brother, Ghazee-od Deen, were excluded from all claims to the succession, and the right devolved upon the third son of Saadut Allee, Nuseer-od Dowlah. Ghazee-od Deen had only one son, the reigning sovereign, Nuseer-od Deen Hyder.

This prince had impaired his constitution by drinking and other vicious indulgences, in which he had been encouraged in early life by his designing or inconsiderate adoptive mother, the Padshah Begum; but for some time before his death, he used frequently to declare to his most intimate companions that he felt sure he should die of poison, and that at no distant period. He for some time before his death had a small well in the palace, over which he kept his own lock and key; and he kept the same over the jar, in which he drew the water from it for his own drinking. The keys were suspended by a gold chain around his neck. The persons who gave him his drink, except when taking it out of English sealed bottles, were two sisters, Dhuneea and Dulwee. The latter and youngest is now the wife of Wasee Allee Khan. The eldest, Dhuneea, still resides at Lucknow. The general impression at Lucknow and over all Oude was, that the British Government would, take upon itself the management of the country on the death, without issue, of Nuseer-od Deen Hyder; and the King himself latterly seemed rather pleased than otherwise at the thought that he should be the last of the Oude kings. He had repudiated his own son, and was unwilling that any other member of the family should fill his place. The minister and the other public officers and Court favourites, who had made large fortunes, wished it, as it was understood by some, that by such a measure they would be secured from all scrutiny into their accounts, and enabled to keep securely all that they had accumulated.

About half-past eleven, on the night of the 7th July, 1837, the Durbar Wakeel, Gholam Yaheea,* came to the Resident and reported that the King had been taken suddenly ill, and appeared to be either dead or in a dying state, from the symptoms described to him by his Majesty's attendants. The Resident, Colonel Low, ordered his two Assistants, Captains Paton and Shakespear, the Head Moonshee and Head Clerk, to be in attendance, and wrote to request the Brigadier, commanding the troops in Oude, to hold one thousand men in readiness to march to the Residency at a moment's notice. The Residency is situated in the city near the Furra Buksh Palace, in which the King resided. The Resident intended that five companies of this force should be sent in advance of the main body and guns, for the purpose of placing, sentries over the palace gates, treasuries, and other places containing valuables within the walls. But this intention was not unfortunately made known to the Brigadier. Captain Magness, who commanded a corps of infantry with six guns, and a squadron of horse, had been ordered by the minister at half-past eight o'clock, to proceed with them to a place near the southern entrance of the palace, and there to wait for further instructions, and he did so. This was three hours before the minister made any report to the Resident of the King's illness, and Captain Magness was told by the people in attendance that the King was either dead or dying.

* Gholam Yaheea Khan was the maternal uncle of Shurf-od Dowlah, who was, afterwards, some time minister under Mahommed Allee Shah.

Having given these orders, the Resident proceeded to the palace, attended by Captain Paton, the first Assistant, and Dr. Stevenson, the Residency Surgeon. They found the King lying dead upon his bed, but his body was still warm, and Dr. Stevenson opened a vein in one arm. Blood flowed freely from it, but no other sign of life could be discovered. His features were placid and betrayed no sign of his having suffered any pain; and the servants in attendance declared that the only sign of suffering they had heard or seen was a slight shriek, to which the King gave utterance before he expired; that after that shriek he neither moved, spoke, nor showed any sign whatever of life. His Majesty had been unwell for three weeks, but no one had any apprehension of danger from his symptoms. He had called for some sherbet a short time before his death, and it was given to him by Dhuneea, the eldest of the two sisters.

The Resident took with him a guard of sipahees from his escort, and Captain Paton distributed them as double sentries at the inner doors of the palace, and outside the chief buildings and store-rooms, with orders to allow no one but the ministers and treasurers to pass. Captain Madness had placed one sentry before at each of these places, and he now added a second, making a party of four sipahees at each post. Captain Paton at the same time, in conjunction with the officers of the Court, placed seals on all the jewels and other valuables belonging to the King and his establishments; and as the night was very dark, placed torch-bearers at all places where they appeared to be required.

Having made these arrangements the Resident returned with Dr. Stevenson to the Residency, leaving Captain Paton at the palace; and wrote to the Brigadier to request that he would send off the five companies in advance to the palace direct, and bring down all his disposable troops, including artillery, to the city. The distance from the palace to the cantonments, round by the old stone bridge, was about four miles and half. The iron bridge, which shortens the distance by a mile and half, had not then been thrown over the Goomtee river, which flows between them. The Resident then had drawn up, for the consent of the new king, a Persian paper, declaring that he was prepared to sign any new treaty for the better government of the country that the British Government might think proper to propose to him.

It was now one o'clock in the morning of the 8th of July, and Captain Shakespear, attended by the Meer Moonshee, Iltufat Hoseyn, and the Durbar Wakeel, proceeded to the house of the new sovereign, Nuseer-od Dowlah, who then resided where the present King now resides, a distance of about a mile from the Residency. The visit was altogether unexpected; and, as the new sovereign had been for some time ill, some delay took place in arranging for the reception of the mission. After explaining the object of his visit. Captain Shakespear presented the paper, which the King perused with great attention, and then signed without hesitation. Captain Shakespear returned with it to the Resident, who repaired again to the palace, and sent Captain Paton, the first Assistant, to the Residency, to proceed thence with Captain Shakespear and the Durbar Wakeel, to the house of the new sovereign, and escort him to the palace, where he would be in readiness to receive him. He arrived about three o'clock in the morning, and being infirm from age, and exceedingly reduced from recent illness, he was, after a short conversation with the Resident, left in a small adjoining room, to repose for a few hours preparatory to his being placed on the throne and crowned in due form. His eldest surviving son, afterwards Amjud Allee Shah, his sons, the present King, Wajid Allee Shah, and Mirza Jawad Khan, the King's foster brother, Hummeed-od Dowlah, and his confidential servant, Rufeek-od Dowla, were left in the room with him; and the Resident and his Assistants sat in the verandah facing the river Goomtee, which flows under the walls, conversing on the ceremonies to be observed at the approaching coronation, and the persons to be invited to assist at it, when they were suddenly interrupted by the intelligence that the Padshah Begum, the adoptive mother of the late King, with a large armed force, and the young pretender, Moonna Jan, were coming on to seize upon the throne, and might soon be expected at the principal entrance to the palace to the north-west.

When the Resident was about to proceed to the palace, the first time about midnight, he was assured by the minister, Roshun-od Dowla, that every possible precaution had been taken by him to prevent the Padshah Begum from attempting any such enterprise, or from leaving her residence with the young pretender; that he had placed strong bodies of troops in every street or road by which she could come. But, to make more sure, and prevent her leaving her residence at the Almas gardens, five miles from the palace, the Resident sent off one of his chobdars, Khoda Buksh, with two troopers and a verbal message, enjoining her to remain quietly at her palace. These men found her with her equipage in the midst of a large mass of armed followers, ready to set out for the palace. They delivered their message from the Resident, but were sent back with her Wakeel, Mirza Allee, to request that she might be permitted to look upon the dead body of the late King, since she had not been permitted to see him for so long a period before his death. But they reached the Resident with this message, only ten minutes before the Begum's troops were thundering for admittance at the gate. The Resident gave the chobdar a note for the officer in command of the five companies, supposed to be in advance on their way down from cantonments; but before he could get with this note five hundred yards from the palace, he met the Begum and her disorderly band filling the road and pressing on as fast as they could. Unable to proceed, he returned to the palace with all haste, and gave the Resident the first notice of their near approach. Captain Magness had placed two of his six guns at each of the three entrances to the south and west, but was now ordered to collect all, and proceed to the north-western entrance, towards which the Begum was advancing. Before he could get to that entrance she had passed in, and he returned to the south-western entrance for further orders.

On passing the mausoleum of Asuf-od Dowlah, where the Kotwal or head police officer of the city resided, she summoned him, with all his available police, to attend his sovereign to the throne of his ancestors. He promised obedience, but, with all his police, stood aloof, thinking that her side might not be the safe one to take in such an emergency. A little further on she passed Hussun Bagh, the residence of the chief consort of the late King and niece of the emperor of Delhi, and summoned and brought her on, to give some countenance to her audacious enterprise. The Resident admonished the minister for his negligence and falsehood in the assurance he had given him; and directed Rajah Bukhtawur Sing, with his squadron of one hundred and fifty horse, and Mozuffer-od Dowlah, the father of Ajum-od Dowlah, and Khadim Hoseyn, the son-in-law of Sobhan Allee Khan, the deputy minister, with all the armed men they could muster, to arrest the progress of the pretender; but nothing whatever was done, and the excited mass came on, and augmented as it came in noise and numbers. All whom the Resident sent to check them, out of fear or favour, avoided collision, and sought safety either in their homes or among the pretender's bands.

Captain Paton, as soon as he heard the pretender's' men approach, rushed to the gate to the north-west, towards which the throng was approaching rapidly. He had only four belted attendants with him, and the gate was guarded only by a small party of useless sipahees, under the control of three or four black slaves. By the time he had roused the sleepy guard and closed the gates, the pretender's armed mass came up, and with foul abuse, imprecations, and with threats of instant death to all who opposed them, demanded admittance. Captain Paton told them, that the Resident had been directed by the British Government to place Nuseer-od Dowlah, the uncle of the late King, on the throne as the rightful heir; that he was now in the palace, and all who opposed him would be treated as rebels; that the gates were all closed by order of the Resident, and all who attempted to force them would be put to death. All was in vain. They told him with fury that the Padshah Begum, and the son of the late King, and rightful heir to the throne, were among them, and must be instantly admitted. Captain Paton despatched a messenger to the Resident to say, that he could hold the gate no longer without troops: but before he could get a reply, the insurgents brought up an elephant to force in the gate with his head. The first failed in the attempt, and drew back with a frightful roar. A second, urged on by a furious driver, broke in the gate, one-half fell with a crash to the ground, and the elephant plunged in after it. Captain Paton was standing with his back against this half, and must have been killed; but Mukun, one of his chuprassies, seeing the gate giving way, caught him by the arm and dragged him behind the other half. The other three chuprassies ran off in a fright and hid themselves. Two of them were Surubdawun Sing and Juggurnath, two brothers, who will be mentioned elsewhere in this diary.*

*   See Juggurnath chuprassie in Chapter V., Vol. II.

The furious and confused mass rushed in through the half-opened gate, and beat Captain Paton to the ground with their bludgeons, the hilts of their swords, and the butt-ends of their muskets. Mukun, chuprassie, his only remaining attendant, was beaten down at the same time and severely bruised, but he soon got up, covered with blood, made his way out through the crowd, and ran to meet the five companies of the 35th Regiment, then not far distant, under Colonel Monteath. As soon as he heard from Mukun the state in which he had left his master, he sent on a party of thirty sipahees under Captain Cowley, with orders to make all possible haste to the rescue. They arrived in time to save his life from the fury of the assailants, but found him insensible from his wounds.

In a few minutes every court-yard within the palace walls was filled with the armed and disorderly mass. The Resident, Captain Shakespear, and their few attendants, tried to stop them by every impediment they could throw in their way, but in vain. The assailants rushed past or over them, brandishing their swords and firelocks, with loud shoutings and flaming torches, and soon filled all the apartments of the palace, save those occupied by the ladies and their female attendants, and the dead body of the late King. The Resident and his Assistant, and the Meer Moonshee, were soon separated from the new sovereign and his small party, who lay for some time concealed in the small room in which he had been left to repose, while they were confined to the northern verandah overlooking the river, and the long room leading into it. The armed and furious throng filled all the other rooms of the palace, the court-yard, eighty yards long, leading to the baraduree (or summer-house) and all the four great halls of that building, in one of which the throne stood.

The Resident felt that he was helpless in his present position, and unable to do anything whatever to prevent the temporary triumph of the insurgents, and the consequent tumult, pillage, and loss of life that must follow; and that it would be better to try any change than to remain in that helpless state. He thought that he might, if he could once reach the Begum, be able to persuade her of the impossibility of her ultimately succeeding in her attempt to keep the pretender on the throne; and if not, that it would be of advantage to get so much nearer to the place where the British troops most soon arrive, and be drawn up in a garden to the south of the baraduree, and to gain time for their arrival by a personal and open conference with the Begum, during which he thought her followers would not be likely to proceed to violence against his person, and those of his attendants. He therefore persuaded one of the rebel sentries placed over him to apprize the Begum that he wished to speak to her. She sent to him Mirza Allee, one of her Wakeels; and with him Captain Shakespear, and the Meer Moonshee, he forced his way through the dense crowd, and got safely into the baraduree.

They found all the four halls, small apartments, and verandahs, leading into them, filled with armed men in a state of great excitement, and in the act of placing the pretender, Moonna Jan, on the throne. The Begum sat in a covered palankeen at the foot of the throne; and as the Resident entered, the band struck up "*God save the King,*" answered by a salute of blunderbusses within, and a double royal salute from the guns in the "*jullooknana*," or northern court-yard of the palace through which the Begun had passed in. Other guns, which had been collected in the confusion to salute somebody (though those who commanded and served them knew not whom), continued the salute through the streets without.

A party of dancing-girls, belonging to the late King, or brought up by the Begum, began to dance and sing as loud as they could at the end of the long hall in front of the throne, at the same time that the crowd within and without shouted their congratulations at the top of their voices, and every man who had a sword, spear, musket, or matchlock, flourished it in the air amidst a thousand torches. A scene more strange and wild it would be difficult to conceive.

In the midst of all this the Resident and his Assistants remained cool under all kinds of foul abuse and threats from a multitude so excited, that they seemed more like demons than human beings, and resolved to force them to commit some act or make use of some expression that might seem to justify their murder. They fired muskets close to their ears, pointed others loaded and cocked close to their breasts and faces, flourished swords close to their noses, called them all kinds of opprobrious names, but all in vain. The Resident, in the midst of all this confusion, pointed out to the Begum the impossibility of her ultimately succeeding in her attempt to secure the throne for the pretender, since he was acting under the orders of his Government, who had declared the right to be another's; and if he and all his Assistants were killed, his Government would soon send others to carry out their orders. "I am," she said, "in my right place, and so is the young King, my grandson, and so are you. Why do you talk to me or to anybody else of leaving the throne and the baraduree?" But some of her furious followers, afraid that she might yield, seized him by his neckcloth, dragged him towards the throne, on which the boy sat, and commanded him to present his offerings of congratulation on the threat of instant death. They had, they said, placed him on the throne of his ancestors by order of the Begum, and would maintain him there. Had he or either of his Assistants lost their temper or presence of mind, and attempted to resent any of the affronts offered to them, they must have been all instantly put to death, and a general massacre of all their supposed adherents, and the pillage of the palace and city, would have followed.

The Begum's Wakeel, Mirza Allee, seeing the life of the Resident and those of his Assistants and attendants in such imminent peril, since he so resolutely refused to give any sign whatever of recognition to the pretender, and aware of the consequences that would inevitably follow their murder, seized him by the arm, and in a loud voice shouted out that it was the Begum's order that he should conduct him out into the garden to the south. He pushed on with him through the crowd, followed by all his small party, and with great difficulty and danger they at last reached the garden, where Colonel Monteath had just brought in and drawn up his five companies in a line facing the baraduree. Finding the entrance to the north-west occupied by the Begum's party. Colonel Monteath marched along the street to the west of the palace, and entered the baraduree garden by the south-west gate. As the Resident went out. Colonel Roberts, who commanded a brigade in the Oude service, went in, and presented to the pretender his offering of gold mohurs, and then went off and hid himself, to wait the result of the contest. Captain Magness drew up his men and guns on the left of Colonel Monteath's, and was told to prepare for action. He told the Resident that he did not feel quite sure of his men in such a crisis, and the line of British sipahees was made to cover his rear, to secure them. The King and minister had commanded him to act precisely as directed by the Resident, and he himself knew this to be his only safe course, but the hearts of his men were with Moonna Jan and the Begum.

The Begum, as soon as the Resident left her, deeming all safe, went over to the female apartments, where her adopted son, the late king, lay dead; and after gazing for a minute upon his corpse, returned to the foot of the throne, on which the pretender had now been seated for more than three hours. It was manifest that nothing but force could now remove the boy and his supporters, but the Begum tried to gain more time in the hope of support from a popular insurrection from without, which might take off the British troops from the garden; and she sent evasive messages to the Resident by her wakeels, urging him to come once more to her, since it was impossible for her to make her way to him without danger of collision between the troops of the two States. He refused to put himself again in her power, and commanded her to come down with the boy to him and surrender; and promised that if she did so, and directed all her armed followers to quit the palace and city of Lucknow, all that had passed should be forgiven, and the large pension of fifteen thousand rupees a-month, promised by the late King, secured to her for life. All was in vain, and the Begum was gaining her object. Robberies of State property in the eastern and more retired parts of the palace-buildings had commenced. Gold, jewels, shawls, &c., to a large amount were being carried off. Much of such property lay about in places not guarded by Captain Paton in the morning, or known to the minister, or other respectable servants of the State, all holding out temptation to pillage. Acts of plunder and ill-treatment to unoffending and respectable persons in the city were every moment reported, and six or eight houses had been already pillaged, and attempts had been made on others by small parties, who were every moment increasing in numbers and ferocity.

Several parties of the King's troops had openly deserted their posts and joined the pretender's followers in the baraduree, and dense masses of armed men were crowding in upon the British troops, whose officer became anxious, and urged the Resident to action, lest they should no longer have room to use their arms. At one time these armed crowds got within two yards of the British front; and on Colonel Monteath's telling them to retire a few paces and leave him a clear front, they did so in a sullen and insolent manner, and one of them actually attempted to seize one of the sipahees by his whiskers, and an affray was with difficulty prevented.

Mostufa Khan, Kundaharee, who had command of a regiment of a thousand horse in the late King's service, was with many others commanded by the Begum to attend the young King on the throne; and he did so some time after Brigadier Johnstone reached the garden, in front of the baraduree, though he knew that Nuseer-od Dowlah had been declared the rightful heir to the throne, and was actually in the palace. He said that "he was the servant of the throne; that the young King was actually seated upon it, and that he would support him there, happen what might." He presented his offerings of gold to the young King, and was forthwith appointed to supersede all the other wakeels in the Begum's negotiations with the Resident. He merely repeated what the other wakeels had said, urging the Resident to go up to the Begum, since she could not come down to him. The Resident repeated to him what he had told the Begum herself, and taking out his watch, told him that unless his orders were obeyed in less than one-quarter of an hour, the guns should open upon the throne-room; that when once they opened, neither she nor her followers could expect favour, or even mercy; and unless he, Mostapha Khan, separated himself from her party, he should be hung as a traitor if taken alive.

Owing to the height of some houses and walls about the left part of the position of the British troops, the guns could not be conveniently brought to bear upon the south-western corner of the baraduree and throne-room, and two of the guns had to be taken round by a road one-third of a mile, to be placed in a better position. On seeing this the crowd shouted out, "The cravens are already running away!" and became more insolent and furious than ever.

The minister and Durbar Wakeel had been swept away by the crowd, who rushed into the palace, and separated from the Resident and his party, and as they passed through the balcony overlooking the river, the wakeel threw off his turban, and leaped over from a height of about twenty feet. The ground was soft, but he sprained both his ankles. He was taken up by some boatmen, who had put-to near the bank, and concealed in their boat till the affair was over. The new sovereign remained still unnoticed, and apparently unknown, having long led a secluded life; but his son, grandsons, and the rest of his attendants were at last discovered, very roughly treated by the insurgents, and would, it is said, have been put to death, had not Rajah Bukhtawur Sing and some others, who thought it safe to be on friendly terms with the ruffians, persuaded them that they would be useful hostages in case of a reverse. The minister had had all his clothes, save his trousers, torn from him, and his arms and legs pinioned preparatory to execution, and the princes had been treated with little more ceremony. All had given themselves up for lost.

The Begum remained firm to her purpose, her hopes from without increasing with the increasing noise, tumult, and reports of pillage in the city. The quarter of an hour had passed, and the Resident, turning to the Brigadier, told him, that the work was now in his hands, just an hour and twenty minutes after he had brought his troops into the garden. The guns from the British, and Captain Magness' parks opened at the same instant upon the throne-room and the other halls of the baraduree with grape; and after six or seven rounds, a party of the 35th Regiment, under Major Marshall, was ordered to storm the halls. With muskets loaded and bayonets fixed they rushed first through a narrow covered passage; then up a steep flight of steps, and then into the throne-room, firing upon the affrighted crowd as they advanced, and following them up with the bayonet as they rushed out over the two flights of steps on the north side, and through the courtyard which separates the baraduree from the palace. Other parties of sipahees ascended at the same time over ladders collected at the suggestion of Doctor Stevenson, and placed on the southern front of the baraduree; and the halls were soon cleared of the insurgents, who left from forty to fifty men killed and wounded on the floors of the four halls.* In this assault Mostufa Khan, Kundaharee, was killed. Moonna Jan was found concealed in a small recess under the throne, and the Begum in a small adjoining room, to which she had been carried as soon as the guns opened. They were taken into custody, and sent to the Residency, with Imam Buksh, a bihishtee, or water-carrier, a notorious villain, who had been her chief instigator in all this affair, and appointed Commander-in-Chief to the young King. Many who had been wounded got out of the halls, and some even reached their homes, but the killed and wounded are supposed to have amounted altogether to about one hundred and twenty. The Begum and the boy were accommodated in the Residency, and their *Commander-in-Chief* was made over to the King's Courts for trial. He is still in prison at Lucknow. No one was killed on our side, but three or four of our sipahees were wounded in the assault.

* As they entered the hall at the end opposite the throne, they saw their own figures reflected in the large mirror, which stands behind the throne; and, taking them to be their enemy preparing to charge, they poured their first volley into the mirror, by which many lives were saved at the expense of the glass.

The Delhi princess, the chief consort of the deceased King, a modest, beautiful, and amiable young woman, who had been forced to join the Begum, in order to give some countenance to the daring enterprise, was, as soon as the guns opened, carried by her two female attendants in her litter to a small side-room, facing the palace at the east end of the throne-room. One of these females had her arm shattered by grape shot, but the other tied some clothes together, and let the princess and her wounded attendant down from a height of about twenty-four feet into a court-yard, whence they were conveyed to her palace by some of her attendants, and all three escaped. The sipahees occupied both of the flights of steps in the northern face of the baraduree. She was afraid, to trust herself to them, and saw no other way of escape than that described.

It was nine o'clock before the palace could be cleared of the insurgents; and the Resident was very anxious that the new Sovereign should be crowned, as soon and as publicly as possible, in order to restore tranquillity to the city, which had become greatly disturbed from the number of loose and desperate characters that always abound in it, and are at all times ready to make the most of any tumult that may arise from whatever cause. The new Sovereign had become greatly agitated and alarmed at the danger to which he and his family had been so long exposed, and at the fearful scene which they witnessed at the close; and the Resident exerted himself to soothe and prepare him for the long and tedious ceremonies of the coronation, while the killed and wounded were being removed and the throne-room and the other halls of the baraduree cleaned out and properly arranged and furnished. When all was ready the Resident conducted him from the palace through the court-yard to the baraduree, accompanied by the brigadier and all the principal officers of the British force and the Court, seated him on the throne, placed the crown on his head, under a royal salute, repeated from every battery in the city, and proclaimed him King of Oude, in presence of all the aristocracy and principal persons of Lucknow, who had flocked to the place on hearing that the danger had passed away.

From the time that the Resident discovered that the King was dead, till the arrival of the five companies under Colonel Monteath, the whole of the British force in this vast city, containing a population of nearly a million persons, amounted to only two companies and a half of sipahees under native officers. One of the companies guarded the Resident's Treasury, one constituted the honorary guard of the Resident, and the half company guarded the gaol. A part of the honorary guard, with as many sipahees as could be safely spared from the Treasury and gaol, were taken by Captain Paton to the palace, and distributed as already mentioned. They all stood nobly to their posts during the long and trying scene, and no attempt was made to concentrate them for the purpose of arresting the tumultuous advance of the Begum's forces. Collectively they would have been too few for the purpose, and it was deemed unsafe to remove them from their respective charges at such a time. The Resident relied upon the minister's repeated assurances that he had taken all necessary precautions to prevent her approach; upon the two companies, called the Khas companies, under the command of Mujd-od Dowlah; and the squadron of one hundred and fifty horse, under Rajah Bukhtawur Sing, whom he had himself ordered to guard the passage by which they entered. Of all these men not one was employed for the purpose. They and their Commanders all stood aloof, and left the British soldiers to their fate.

The minister was a fool, under the tutelage of his deputy, Sobhan Allee Khan, a great knave, who disappeared as soon as he heard that the Begum was approaching with his son-in-law, Khadim Hoseyn. Mozuffer Allee Khan, a person in high office and confidence under the late King, did the same. The minister and the Durbar Wakeel were the only officers of the State of Oude who stood by the new King and the British Resident. The minister afterwards declared that a strong detachment of troops had been placed outside the gate through which the Begum ultimately forced her way, as well as at the other passages leading to the palace and baraduree; and Captain Shakespear, on his way to the new Sovereign, ascertained that guards had actually been posted outside all the other gates leading to the palace and baraduree. From this, the supineness and seeming apathy of many of the palace guards and servants, and the perversion of the orders sent by him before and during the tumult, the minister concluded that there must have been many about him interested in promoting the enterprise of the Begum; and that the approach to the gate through which she forced her way must have been purposely left unguarded. There is now little doubt, that from the time that it became known, that the contest was between Moonna Jan and Nuseer-od Dowlah, a person but little known except as a prudent and parsimonious old man, a large portion not only of the civil and military establishments, but of the population of the city, felt anxious for the success of the Begum's enterprise; for both had, under the harsh treatment of the last two sovereigns, become objects of sympathy.

A good many of the members of the royal family, who were brought up from childhood with the deceased King, Nuseer-od Deen Hyder, and near his person to the last, declare that Moonna Jan was his son; but that the King was ashamed and afraid to acknowledge him after he had so frequently and so formally declared to the British Government that he was not his son, and that he had ceased to cohabit with the boy's mother for two years before his birth. But all such persons admit that Moonna Jan was a boy of ungovernable temper, and the worst possible dispositions; and that he must soon have forfeited the crown by his cruelty, bigotry, and injustice, had he been placed upon it by the British Government. I saw him in January 1838, at Chunar, and a more unpromising boy I have rarely seen.

The ministry dreaded being called to account for their malversations as much from the Begum, on account of their successful efforts to keep the King alienated from her and his son, as from Nuseer-od Dowlah, on account of his parsimony, prudence, and great experience in business during the reign of his able father, Saadut Allee Khan. But they would have a better chance of escape from the Begum and the boy than from the vigilant old man, who afterwards made them all disgorge their ill-gotten wealth; and, in consequence, they made no effort to obstruct her enterprise. The military and civil establishments were all in favour of the boy, who would probably be as regardless of their number and discipline as his father had been, while the old man would assuredly reduce the one, and endeavour, by rigorous measures, to improve the other. Hardly any one at Lucknow at present doubts that the minister and his associates caused the King to be poisoned, and employed Duljeet and the two sisters; Dhunneea and Dulwee, for the purpose, in expectation that the British Government would take upon itself the Oude administration, as the only possible means of improving it.

The respectable and peaceable portion of the city, though their sympathies were with the boy, had too much in property, and the honour of their families, at stake to aid in any movement in his favour, since it would involve a tumult, and for a time, at least, insure the supremacy of the mob. Their security and that of their families depended upon the success of the British troops; and they were all prepared to acquiesce in any cause which the British Government might adopt for the sake of order. They would rather that it should adopt that of the Begum and the boy than that of Nuseer-od Dowlah; but in either case were resolved to remain neuter, and let the representative of the British Government take his own course.

It is a fact not unworthy of remark, that more than three millions sterling, or three crores of rupees, in our Government securities, are held by persons who reside and spend the interest arising from them in the city of Lucknow; and that the fall in their value in exchange during the times that we have been engaged in our most serious wars has been less in Lucknow than in Calcutta, the capital of British India; so much greater assurance do the people feel of our resources being always equal to our exigencies. At such times the merchants of Lucknow commission their agents in Calcutta to purchase up Government securities at the rate to which they fall in Calcutta, for sale at Lucknow, where they seldom fall at all. About three crores and half of rupees, or three millions and half sterling, have been at different times contributed to our loans by the sovereigns of Oude as a provision for the different members of their respective families and dependents; and the interest is now paid to them and their descendants, at the rates which prevailed at the time of the several loans (four, five, and six per cent.) to the amount of fourteen lacs thirty-five thousand and four hundred and ten rupees a-year.

The Begum's haughty and violent temper, and inveterate disposition to meddle in public affairs, were the real cause of her continual disquietude and ultimate disgrace and ruin. The minister of the day dreaded the ascendancy of so imperious and furious a character, should she ever become reconciled to the King. During the whole reign of Ghazee-od Deen, her husband, from the 12th of July 1814, to the 20th of October 1827, her own frequent ebullitions, which often disfigured the King's robes and vests, and left even the hair on his head and chin unsafe, and Aga Meer's sagacious suggestions, satisfied him that his own personal safety and peace of mind, and the welfare of the State, depended upon his keeping as much as possible aloof from her. He was fond of his son, Nuseer-od Deen Hyder, but during his minority he always took the part of his adoptive mother, the Padshah Begum; and, in consequence, remained almost as much as she was alienated from the King, his father. His natural mother died soon after his birth; and people suspected that the Padshah Begum had her put to death that she might have no rival in his affections; and she had an entire ascendancy over him, acquired by every species of enervating indulgences; and he remained all his life utterly without character, ignorant of the rudiments of public affairs, and altogether incapable of taking any useful part in them.

She retained this ascendancy over him for some time after he became King, first from habit and affection, and latterly from the fears with which she continued to inspire him, that she could, by her disclosures, whenever she pleased, prevail upon the British Government to set him aside in favour of some other member of the royal family, as the Buhoo Begum of Fyzabad had set aside Wuzeer Allee. She made him dismiss his father's minister, Aga Meer, with disgrace, and confer the seals on Fuzl Allee, the nephew of her favourite waiting-woman, Fyzon Nissa; but when the shrewd and sagacious Hakeem Mehndee became minister three years after, he soon persuaded the young King, that all fears of his adoptive mother's disclosures or wishes were idle, and that nothing which she could do or say would induce the British Government to disturb his possession of the sovereignty of Oude. He is said to have been the first person who ventured to hint to him the murder of his natural mother by the Padshah Begum; and he was, or pretended to be, violently shocked and grieved. He then built a splendid tomb or cenotaph for her; and endowed it with the means for maintaining pious men to read the Koran in it, and attendants of all kinds to keep it in a condition suitable for the mother of a King. He shuddered, or pretended to shudder, at the mention of the name of the Padshah Begum, as the most atrocious of murderesses. The minister of the day always made it a point to bring the reigning favourite of the seraglio over to his views, by giving her a due share of the profits and patronage of his office; and it was for this reason, that the high-born chief consort, whose influence over the King could not be so purchased, was soon made to retire from the palace, and, ever after, to live separated from her husband.

The Padshah Begum had only one child, a daughter, who was united in marriage to Mehndee Allee Khan, by whom she had three children, Mohsen-od Dowlah, who was married to the daughter of Nuseer-od

Dowlah, the new King; and two daughters who were married to Mirza Abool Kasim, and Mirza Aboo Torab. They lost their mother while yet children, and the Padshah Begum brought them up and became much attached to them. They had all from childhood been brought up with Nuseer-od Deen, and were all much attached to him and to each other. The ministers, fearing that this attachment might possibly lead to a reconciliation between the King and his adoptive mother, and to their ruin, left him and her no peace till, to save them, she forbade them her house, and sent the girls to their husbands, and the boy to his father-in-law, Nuseer-od Dowlah, whose succession to the throne of Oude has been here described. All objects of mutual interest and affection were in this manner carefully excluded from attendance on either, till they showed themselves to be entirely subservient to the minister of the day.*

* The mother always declared, and her two daughters and son all declare, Moonna Jan to have been the son of Nuseer-od Deen, and exactly like him in person, voice, and temper. But he was indulged by the Padshah Begum in such habits of atrocious cruelties to other children, that he soon became detested by all around him but herself and the boy's natural mother, Afzul-mahal.

Thus alienated from her son, all her affections were transferred to her grandson, Moonna Jan, and there is too much reason to believe, that in both cases she purposely did her best to prevent their ever becoming men of business, in order that she might have the guidance of public affairs in her own hands when they should be called to the throne.

The Resident accommodated the Begum, the boy, and her two female attendants in apartments at the Residency, and had a guard placed over them. The new King told him, "that the Begum was the most wicked and unscrupulous woman he had ever known, and that he could expect no peace at Lucknow while she remained." He promised to consult his Government as to her disposal, and on returning to the Residency he increased that guard to two companies of Native Infantry, and all remained quiet when he made his report to Government on the 9th. But towards the close of that day, the city became again agitated. Reports prevailed, that Government was to be consulted as to whether they preferred the rights of Moonna Jan to the throne or those of Nuseer-od Dowlah; that the Begum's adherents were ready at her call to fall upon the Resident and his party, and put them all to death, or to attack the apartments in which she was confined, rescue her and the boy from prison, and place him again on the throne. The Court favourites of the late King, and all the public military and civil establishments in the city, dreaded the rigid economy and strict supervision of the new King, who had conducted the duties of the ministry for some time, under his able and vigilant father, Saadut Allee Khan; and all that numerous class who benefit by the lavish expenditure of a thoughtless and profligate Court were equally anxious to have the Government in the hands of an extravagant woman and thoughtless boy, and ready to join and incur some risk in supporting their cause.

Under all these circumstances the Resident determined to send the Begum and her boy out of Oude as soon as possible. At midnight on the 11th, a detachment of three companies of Infantry, under Major Lane of the 2nd Regiment, marched from Cawnpore and arrived at Newulgunge, midway to Lucknow, a distance of twenty-two miles, in the morning of the 12th, with one troop of cavalry. Another troop proceeded to Onow, the first stage from Cawnpore, and a third to Rahmutgunge, the second stage, to relieve the first on their return. At each of these stages, relays of sixty palankeen-bearers and six torch-bearers were placed by the Post-Master at Cawnpore. As the bridge over the Ganges at Cawnpore had been washed away by the flood, a company of Native Infantry was placed on the Oude side of that river, to hold boats in readiness, and assist in escorting over the party when they came. About the same time, at midnight, the Begum, her boy, and two of her female attendants were placed in palankeens and sent off from the Residency under the escort of a regiment of Infantry, and a detail of artillery, attended by the Second Assistant, Captain Shakespear.

They marched without resting through one of the hottest days of the year, and the party reached Cawnpore in safety about half-past nine o'clock in the evening of the 12th, and were securely lodged in apartments prepared for them at the custom-house. So well had things been arranged between the Resident and Brigadier commanding the troops in Oude, and the Major-General commanding the Division at Cawnpore, that very few persons at Lucknow knew that the Begum and her party had left the Residency when she passed the Ganges at Cawnpore. The three companies under Major Lane, who had marched twenty-two miles in the morning, kept pace with the palankeens all the way back, making a march of forty-four miles, between midnight of the 11th, and half-past nine in the evening of the 12th, in so hot a day.

The Begum and Moonna Jan were sent off with their attendants to the fort of Chunar, where they were lodged as state prisoners. As it became safe, the restrictions to which they were at first subjected became by degrees relaxed, and they were permitted to enjoy all the freedom and comforts compatible with their safe keeping. Both died at Chunar, Moonna Jan some time before the Begum. He left three sons by two slave-girls at Chunar, and they still reside there, supported by a small stipend of three hundred rupees a-month from the Oude Government, under the protection of the commandant of the garrison, and the guardianship of Afzul mahal, the mother of the late Moonna Jan.

All these circumstances, as they occurred, were reported by the Resident to the Government of India, who took time to deliberate, and did not reply till the 19th of July 1837, when they signified their approval of all that the Resident had done, with the exception of the written declaration to which he had obtained the consent and signature of the new King. They did not think that it would be considered dignified or becoming the paramount power, to exact such a declaration, binding himself to absolute submission, from the sovereign of a country so much under their control, on ascending a throne to which he was called as of right; and were of opinion that his character as a prudent man of business, well trained to public affairs, during the time he acted as minister under his father, rendered such a declaration unnecessary. It was therefore annulled; and the Governor-General, Lord Auckland, addressed a letter to his Majesty expressing, in kind terms, his congratulations on his accession to the throne, and his hopes of a better administration of the Government of Oude under his auspicious guidance. This letter, despatched by express, the Resident received on the 25th of July.

The Resident concluded, on good grounds, that the Government deemed a new and more stringent treaty indispensable for the better government of the country, and that advantage should be taken of the occasion to prepare the new King for it. Government desired, that the negotiations for a new treaty should be based "upon reason and right, and not upon demand and submission." Had the declaration been allowed to stand good, there would have been *right* as well as *reason* in the treaty of 1837, which was soon after concluded.

The Resident intimated the receipt of these letters to the King, and on the 28th, he waited on his Majesty, to present the Governor-General's letter. He found him sitting up in his bed in a small apartment in the baraduree, in his dishabille, having spent a restless night from rheumatic pains; but he was cheerful and in good spirits, and requested the Resident to present his respectful compliments to the Governor-General, and grateful thanks for his consideration and congratulations. All his relations, the chief officers of the Government, and other persons of distinction about the Court, were assembled to hear the letters read, and make their offerings on this recognition of his authority by the paramount power. "The King assured the Resident, that the arrival of this recognition, and its public announcement, would greatly strengthen his hands in the exercise of public duties, for during the last few days bad reports had been industriously circulated by evil-disposed persons to the effect, that the delay in the recognition of his succession to the throne by the paramount power in India, had arisen from discussions between the members of the Government in Calcutta, as to the amount of money to be taken on the occasion from the new King, as the price of his sudden elevation; and that no letter was to be presented by the

Resident until the money was paid, or security given for its punctual payment; that the Governor-General himself wanted *two crores* of rupees, but some members of the Government would be satisfied with *a crore and half* each, and others even with *one crore* each, provided that these sums were paid forthwith." In relating this story, which the Resident had heard from many others within the last few days, the King observed, "that he was too well acquainted with the character for honour and justice of the Honourable Company's Government, to give the slightest credit to such scandal, the more especially since no demand of the kind had been made on the accession of either of the last two Kings, who were known to be rich, while he was equally well known to be poor; but that nothing but the arrival of this despatch confirming him on the throne, could convince many, even well-disposed persons, of the utter groundlessness of such wicked rumours; that many poor but respectable persons, who had been weak enough to believe such rumours, would feel much relieved when they heard the salutes which were now being fired, for they had apprehended, that they might be severe sufferers by being compelled to contribute their own property, in order to enable him to make up the *peshkush*, or tribute, required by the British Government, since the late King had squandered the ten crores, which he found in the treasury on the death of his father."

It is certain, that a great portion of the population of Lucknow expected that some such demand would be made by the British Government from the new sovereign, since his right to the throne could be disputed, not only by Moonna Jan, the supposed son of the late King, but by the undoubted sons of Shums-od Dowlah, the elder brother of the present King, whose rights were barred only by that peculiar feature of the Mahommedan law elsewhere adverted to in this Diary. Every day of delay, in promulgating the final orders of the Supreme Government, tended to add to this number; and by the time that these final orders came, by far the greater portion of the city were of the same opinion. The fears of the people tended to add to their numbers, and give strength to the opinion, for all knew, that there was but little left in the reserved treasury, that the expenses greatly exceeded the annual revenue, and that the troops and establishments were all greatly in arrear; and all believed that a general contribution would have to be levied to meet the demand when it came.*

* Nuseer-od Dowlah reigned under the title of Mahommed Allee Shah, from the 8th of July, 1837, to the 16th of May, 1842. Nuseer-od Deen Hyder, his predecessor, had reigned from the 20th of October, 1827, to the 7th of July, 1837. He, Nuseer-od Deen, found in the treasury, when he ascended the throne, ten crores of rupees, or ten millions sterling. He left in the treasury, when he died, only seventy lacs of rupees, including the fifty-three lacs left by the Koduseea Begum. Mahommed Allee Shah left in the treasury thirty-five lacs of rupees, one hundred and twenty-four thousand gold mohurs, and twenty-four lacs in our Government securities. Amjud Allee Shah reigned from the 16th of May, 1842, to the 13th of February, 1847; and left in the treasury ninety-two lacs of rupees, one hundred and twenty-four thousand gold mohurs, and the twenty-four lacs in our Government securities. His son, Wajid Allee Shah, has reigned from the 13th of February, 1847.

The assertion, on the part of the late King, that he had ceased to cohabit with Afzul mahal, the mother of Moonna Jan, for two years, or even for six months before his birth, is now known to have been utterly false, and known at the time to be so by his mother, the Padshah Begum; with whom they both lived. Afzul-mahal, though of humble birth and pretensions, maintained a fair reputation among those who knew her best in a profligate palace, and has continued to maintain the same up to the present day in adversity. In prison and up to the hour of her death, which took place some time after that of Moonna Jan himself, the old Begum declared that she had seen the boy born, and had never lost sight of him; and that the story of his not being the son of Nuseer-od Deen, was got up to prevent her ever becoming reconciled to the King through the means of his son; and her extraordinary affection for him never diminished while he lived. When she retired from the palace of Nuseer-od Deen to her new residence of Almas Bagh, she kept fast hold of the boy, and would never let him out of her sight till they entered the prison at Chunar, when they were obliged to occupy separate apartments. Up to his death she watched over him with the tenderest care; and always declared to the European officers placed over her, that the boy's father and mother always resided with her up to the time of his birth. The boy was remarkably like Nuseer-od Deen in form and features, as well as in temper and disposition.

Afzul-mahal was a person of great good sense and prudence, and in all things trusted by the old Begum, who before her death executed a formal will, leaving to her the charge of Moonna Jan's three children, and all the establishments; and since the death of the old lady she has executed the trust conscientiously, and with great economy; and with much difficulty managed to maintain all in respectability upon the small stipend of three hundred rupees a-month, allowed for their support by the King of Oude. In this, she has been very much impeded and annoyed by the two slave-girls, the mothers of Moonna Jan's children, who have been always striving to get this stipend into their own hands, that they may share it with their paramours. At the death of the old lady most of her female companions and attendants refused to return to Lucknow, and remained at Chunar with Afzul-mahal and the children; and all have to be subsisted out of this small stipend. The slave-girls urge, that they might have had separate pensions, had they obeyed the orders to return to Lucknow on the death of the Begum, and that they ought not now to share in the stipend of the children. Five or six of the females were ladies of rank, and one of them, who died lately, was a widow of Saadut Allee Khan.

This pension may be discontinued when the boys become of age, or appropriated by them and their mothers for their own exclusive use, and the Government of Oude should be required to assign pensions for life to Afzul mahal, and the other females who are now supported from it.

The salary of the prime minister, during the five years that Roshun-od Dowlah held the office, was twenty-five thousand rupees a-month, or three lacs a-year, and over and above this, he had five per cent. upon the actual revenue, which made above six lacs a-year. His son, as Commander-in-Chief, drew five thousand rupees a-month, though he did no duty—his first wife drew five thousand rupees a-month, and his second wife drew three thousand rupees a-month, total eighty-eight thousand rupees a-month, or ten lacs and fifty-six thousand rupees a-year. These were the avowed allowances which the family received from the public treasury. The perquisites of office gave them some five lacs of rupees a-year more, making full fifteen lacs a-year.

Roshun-od Dowlah held office for only three months, under the new sovereign, Mahommed Allee Shah. He was then superseded by Hakeem Mahndee, thrown into prison, and made to pay twenty lacs to the treasury, and two lacs in gratuities to Court favourites. After paying these sums, he was permitted to go and reside at Cawnpore; but his houses in the city, valued at three lacs, were afterwards confiscated by the present King, on the ground of unpaid balances. He took into keeping Dulwee, the younger of the two sisters; but she was afterwards seduced away from him by one of his creatures, a consummate knave, Wasee Allee, whose wife she now is. Dhunneea, the eldest sister, is still residing at Lucknow. Roshun-od Dowlah's first wife took off with her more than three lacs of rupees in our Government securities, and his son, the Commander-in-Chief, took off eight lacs of rupees in the same securities. Roshun-od Dowlah carried off a large sum himself. She and his son afterwards left him, and now reside in comfort upon the interest of these securities at Futtehgur, while he lives at Cawnpore in poor circumstances.

Sobhan Allee, his deputy, was made to pay to the treasury seven lacs of rupees, and in gratuities to court favourites five lacs more. Roshun-od Dowlah was one of the principal members of the old aristocracy of Lucknow, and connected remotely with the royal family; and he got off more easily in consequence, compared with his means, than his deputy, who had no such advantages, and was known to have been the minister's guide in all things, though he would never consent to hold any ostensible and responsible office.

Duljeet, a creature of Roshun-od Dowlah's, and prime favourite of the late King, carried off, while the King lay dead, money and jewels to the value of one lac of rupees, and concealed them in a vault at Constantia. His associates, not satisfied with what he gave them, betrayed him. The money and jewels were discovered and brought back, and he was made to pay another lac of rupees to the treasury as a fine. Dhunneea, the eldest of the two sisters, was made to disgorge two lacs of rupees. Many other favourites of the late King were fined in the same way.

The King had, in the case of Ghalib Jung, already described in this Diary, declared his resolution of looking more closely into his accounts in future, and punishing all transgressors in the same way; and Roshun-od Dowlah often expressed to the Resident his apprehensions that his turn to suffer must soon come. Sobhan Allee Khan had much stronger grounds to fear, since he had made himself utterly detested by the people generally, and had neither friends nor connexions in the royal family or aristocracy of Lucknow. Under the strong and general impression that the British Government was determined to interpose, and take upon itself the administration of the country, and that the King himself wished the independent sovereignty of Oude to terminate with his reign, they most earnestly desired his early death as their only chance of escape. The British Government would not, they knew, make them refund any of their ill-gotten wealth without full judicial proof of their peculations, and this proof they knew could never be obtained. Indeed they were satisfied that our Government, aware of the difficulty of finding such proof, and occupied in forming and working a new system, would not trouble themselves to seek for it; and that they should all be left to reside where they chose, and enjoy freely the fruits of their malversation.

The Resident had kept the instructions of the 15th of December, 1832, from the supreme Government, a profound secret, lest they might lead to intrigue and disturbance, and, above all, to the poisoning of many innocent persons who might be considered to have a claim of right to the throne; and all were surprised and confounded when it was announced that the paramount power had already decided in favour of Nuseer-od Dowlah, whose claims had never been thought of by the people, or apprehended by the ministers. The instant they heard this decision, they dreaded the scrutiny of the sagacious and parsimonious old man, and the enmity of the favourites by whom he had been surrounded in private life. These men, whom they had, in their pride and power, despised and insulted, would now have their revenge; and they wished for the success of the old woman and the boy, from whom they might have a better chance of escape, till they could get their wealth and their families out of the country.

I may here mention a similar repudiation of a supposed eldest son by the late King. Mostafa Allee was brought up in the palace as his eldest son, and on all occasions treated as such. Mahommed Allee Shah, the late King's father, was always very fond of him, but shortly before his death he became angry with him for some outrages committed in the palace, and put him under restraint. The young man requested the late King, his supposed father, to mediate with his grandfather for his release. He refused to do so, and the young man drew his sword, and threatened to kill him. He was kept under more strict restraint till the grandfather died, and his father ascended the throne, on the 16th of May, 1842. The King then requested the Resident to assure the Governor-General that Mostafa Allee was not his son—that he was a year and a-half old when his mother entered the palace. The Resident reported accordingly on the 26th of that month. The Governor-General required the statement to be made under the King's own sign and seal, and it was transmitted on the 6th of June, 1842. The present King was then declared heir-apparent to the throne, and Mostafa Allee has ever since been in strict confinement under him. The general impression, however, is that he was the eldest son of the late King, and repudiated solely on account of his violent temper and turbulent conduct. That he was treated as such during the life of Mahommed Allee Shah, and that the late King dared not repudiate him while his father lived, is certain.

By the treaty of 1801 we bound ourselves to defend the territories of the sovereign of Oude from all foreign and domestic enemies; and to defray the cost of maintaining the troops required for this purpose, and paying some pensions at Furruckabad and Benares, the sovereign of Oude ceded to our Government the under-mentioned districts, then yielding the revenues specified opposite their respective names.*

Districts ceded by Oude to the British Government by the treaty of 1801.

Etawa, Korah, Kurra		55,48,577	11 9
Rehur and others		5,33,374	0 6
Furruckabad		4,50,001	0 6
Khyreegurh, and Kunchunpore		2,10,001	0 0
Azimgurh, Mounal, and Benjun		6,95,624	7 6
Goruckpore	5,09,853 8 0		
Botwul	40,001 0 0	5,49,854	8 0
Allahabad and others		9,34,963	1 3
Bareilly, Moradabad, Bijnore, Budown, Pilibheet, and Shahjehanpore		43,13,457	11 3
Nawabgunge, Rehlee, &c.		1,19,242	12 0
Mohowl and others, with exception of Jaulluk Arwu		1,68,378	4 0
	Total	1,35,23,474	8 3
	Deduct		
Nawabgunge	1,19,242 12 0		
Khyreegurh	2,10,001 0 0	3,29,243	12 0
	Total	1,31,94,230	12 3
	Add		
Handeea or Kewae		1,52,905	0 0
	Total	1,33,47,135	12 3

Present Revenues of the Territories we hold from Oude under the treaty of 1801, according to the Revised Statistical Return of the Districts of the North-West Provinces for 1846-47, prepared in 1848, A.D.

	Land Revenue 1846-47.	Abkaree for 1846-47.	Stamp for 1846-47.	Total for 1846-47.
Rohilcund	64,44,341	2,47,854	2,04,576	68,96,771
Allahabad, including Handeea alias Kewae	21,29,551	1,41,409	61,802	23,32,762
Furruckabad	13,57,544	88,061	49,698	14,95,303
Mynpooree	12,33,901	24,822	20,484	12,79,207
Etawa	12,80,596	19,647	10,355	13,10,598
Goruckpore	20,80,296	2,10,045	96,549	23,86,890
Azimgurh, including Mahoul	14,89,887	81,257	53,925	16,25,069
Cawnpore	21,51,155	1,26,155	57,406	23,34,700
Futtehpore	14,25,431	60,370	21,063	15,06,864
Total	1,95,92,686	9,99,620	5,75,858	2,11,68,164

** The lands are the same with the exception of Khyreegurh, Nawabgunge ceded since, and Handeea received; but the names are altered.

Khyreegurh and Kunchunpore were re-ceded to the Oude sovereign in the treaty of the 11th of May, 1816, with the Turae lands, taken from Nepaul, between Khyreegurh and Goruckpore, in liquidation of the loan of one crore of rupees. In the same treaty, Handeea (*alias* Kewae) was ceded by Oude to the British Government, in lieu of Nawabgunge, which was made over to the Oude sovereign by the British Government. Handeea, or Kewae, now in the Allahabad district, yielded land revenue, for 1846-47, rupees one lac, fifty-two thousand, and nine hundred and five.

The British Government retained the power to station the British troops in such parts of the Oude territories as might appear to it most expedient; and the Oude sovereign bound himself to dismiss all his troops, save four battalions of infantry, one battalion of Nujeebs and Mewaties, two thousand horsemen, and three hundred golundages, or artillerymen, with such numbers of armed peons as might be deemed necessary for the purpose of collecting the revenue, and a few horsemen and nujeebs to attend the persons of the amils. It is declared that the territories ceded, being in lieu of all former subsidies and of all expenses on account of the Honourable Company's defensive establishments with his Excellency the sovereign of Oude, no demand whatever shall be made upon his territory on account of expenses which the Honourable Company may incur by assembling forces to repel the attack, or menaced attack, of a foreign enemy; on account of the detachment attached to his person; on account of troops which may be occasionally furnished for suppressing rebellions or disorders in his territories; on account of any future charge of military stations; or on account of failures in the resources of the ceded districts, arising from unfavourable seasons, the calamities of war, or any other cause whatever.

The Honourable Company guarantees to him and to his heirs and successors, the possession of the territories which remain to him after the above cessions, together with the exercise of his and their authority within the said dominions; and the sovereign of Oude engages to establish, in his reserved dominions, such a system of administration, to be carried into effect by his own officers, as shall be conducive to the prosperity of his subjects, and calculated to secure the lives and property of the inhabitants; and to advise with, and act in conformity to the counsel of, the officers of the British Government.

In the time of Asuf-od Dowlah, who died on the 21st September, 1797, the military force of Oude amounted to eighty thousand men of all arms, and in the direct pay of Government. Saadut Allee Khan, his brother and successor, on the conclusion of the above treaty, and the transfer of half his territory, reduced the number to thirty thousand.

Relying entirely upon the efficiency of British troops to defend him against external and internal enemies, and to suppress rebellion and disorder, he laboured assiduously to reduce his expenditure within the income arising from the reserved half of his dominions. He resumed almost all the rent-free lands which had been granted with a lavish hand by his predecessor, and paid off and discharged all superfluous civil and military establishments, and, by his prudence and economy, he so reduced his expenditure within the income, that on his death on the 12th of July, 1814, he left fourteen millions sterling, or fourteen crores of rupees, in a treasury which he found empty when he entered upon the government in 1797. In this sum were included the confiscations of the estates of some favourites of his predecessors, Asuf-od Dowlah and Wuzeer Allee, who had grown rich upon bribery and frauds of all kinds. He never confiscated the estates of any good and faithful servants, who left lawful heirs to their property.

He had been freely aided by British troops, according to the stipulations of the treaty of 1801; but the British Government had been made sensible, on several occasions, of the difficulty of fulfilling its engagements with the sovereign with a due regard to the rights and interests of his subjects. Saadnt Allee Khan was a man of great general ability, had mixed much in the society of British officers in different parts of India, had been well trained to habits of business, understood thoroughly the character, institutions, and requirements of his people, and, above all, was a sound judge of the relative merits and capacities of the men from whom he had to select his officers, and a vigilant supervisor of their actions. This discernment and discrimination of character, and vigilant supervision, served him through life; and the men who served him ably and honestly always felt confident in his protection and support. He had a thorough knowledge of the rights and duties of his officers and subjects, and a strong will to secure the one and enforce the other. To do so he knew that he must, with a strong hand, keep down the large landed aristocracy, who were then, as they are now, very prone to grasp at the possessions of their weaker neighbours, either by force or in collusion with local authorities. In attempting this with the aid of British troops, some acts of oppression were, no doubt, committed; and, as the sympathies of British officers were more with the landed aristocracy, while his were more with the humbler classes of landholders and cultivators who required to be protected from them, frequent misunderstandings arose, acts of just severity were made to appear to be acts of wanton oppression, and such as were really oppressive were exaggerated into unheard-of atrocities.

Our relations with the state of Oude, from the treaty of 1801 to the death of Saadut Allee, were conducted by able men; but they had a very difficult task to perform in conducting them to the satisfaction of both parties to that treaty; and when the Government devolved upon less able and well-disposed sovereigns, ministers, and public officers, our Government and its representative became less and less willing to comply with their requisitions for the aid of British troops in the collection of the revenue, and the suppression of rebellion and disorder. Our Government demanded, that the British Resident should be fully informed of the cause which led to the resistance complained of to legitimate authority; and be fully satisfied of the justice and necessity of such aid before he afforded it; and the sovereigns of Oude admitted the justice of this demand on the part of the paramount power. But the Resident could never hear fully and fairly both sides of the question, and the officers commanding the troops were seldom disposed to do so; and neither was competent to pass a sound judgment upon the justice and necessity of complying with the requisitions made for the aid of the British troops.

But when, under an imbecile and debauched sovereign, like Ghazee-od Deen, and an unscrupulous minister, creatures and favourites began to share so largely in the revenues of the country, this sort of scrutiny on the part of the Resident and officers commanding troops, employed in aid of the King's officers, became exceedingly distasteful; and the minister gradually increased the military force of Oude at his disposal, that he might do without it. During the last few years of Ghazee-od Deen's reign, the Oude forces of all arms amounted to about sixty thousand men. During the first few years of his successor's, Nuseer-od Deen's, reign, these forces were augmented by the ministers for the sake of the profit and patronage they gave them; and in the year 1837, the forces of all arms, paid from the treasury, amounted to more than sixty thousand men. A memorandum given to the British Resident by the minister on the 8th of April 1837, showed the men of all descriptions, belonging to the Oude army, to amount to sixty-seven thousand nine hundred and fifty-six. The artillery, cavalry, and infantry, composing what they call the regular army, amounted to twenty thousand, all badly paid, clothed, armed, accoutred, and disciplined; and for the most part placed under idle, incompetent, and corrupt commanders. The rest were nujeebs employed in the provinces under local officers of the revenue and police, and obliged to provide their own clothes, arms, accoutrements, and ammunition. They were altogether without discipline.

Government, on the 26th November, 1824, informs the Resident, "that our troops are to be actively and energetically employed in the Oude territory in cases of real internal commotion and disorder." And again on the 22nd of July, 1825; Government condemns the Resident for his disregard of the orders of the 26th of November, 1824, regarding the employment of British troops in Oude, and states, "that it is sincerely disposed to maintain the rights of the King of Oude to the fullest extent, as guaranteed to him by the treaty with his father, on the 20th of November, 1801; but observes, that upon the maturest consideration of articles 3rd, 5th, and 6th of that treaty, and of Lord Wellesley's memorandum in 1802, of the final results of discussions between him and Saadut Allee, whilst Government admits that, according to article the 3rd of the treaty, we were bound to defend his Majesty's present territories 'against all foreign and domestic enemies,' and that, in pursuance of the 4th article, the Company's troops are to be employed, without expense to his Majesty, not only 'to repel the attack, or menaced attack, of a foreign enemy,' but also for suppressing rebellion and disorder in his Majesty's territories; and that, in a strict adherence to the 6th article, the King of Oude is entitled to exercise complete sovereign authority within his own dominions, by a system of administration conducive to the prosperity of his subjects, to be carried into effect by his own officers, with the advice and counsel of the officers of the British Government (in conformity to which his Majesty is expressly engaged to act); yet the Governor-General in council considered it to be indispensable and inherent in the nature of our obligations, under the treaty referred to, that whenever the King of Oude requires the aid of British troops, to quell any disturbance, or to enforce any demand for revenue or otherwise, the British Government is clearly entitled, as well as morally obliged, to satisfy itself by whatever means it may deem necessary, that the aid of its troops is required in support of right and justice, and not to effectuate injustice and extortion.

"This principle, which has often been declared and acted upon daring successive Governments, must still be firmly asserted, and resolutely adhered to; and the Resident must consider it to be a positive and indispensable obligation of his public duty, to refuse the aid of British troops until he shall have satisfied himself, on good and sufficient grounds (to be reported in each case as soon as practicable, and when the exigency of the case may admit of it, before the troops are actually employed), that they are not to be employed but in support of just and legitimate demands."

On the 13th of July, 1827, Government, in reply to the Resident's letter of the 30th May idem, expresses "its surprise that, under the circumstances therein stated, he should have suffered so long a period to elapse without adopting the most active and decided measures against a subject of Oude, whose conduct is that of a public robber and rebel against the authority of his Government; and whom the King has plainly stated that he is unable to reduce to subjection without the aid of British troops."

On the 20th of January, 1831, the Governor-General, Lord William Bentinck, held a conference with the King of Oude, and told his Majesty, in presence of his minister, that the state of things in Oude, and maladministration in all departments, were such as to warrant and require the authoritative interference of the British Government for their correction; that he declined to make himself a party to the nomination of the minister, or to have it understood that the measure was a joint resolution of the two governments, so that both should be responsible for its success in effecting reformation; that the act was his Majesty's own, and the responsibility must be his; that his Lordship hoped that a better system would be established by his minister's agency, but if he failed, and the same abuses and misrule continued, the King must be prepared to abide the consequences; that the Governor-General intended to make a strong representation to the authorities in England on the state of misrule prevailing, and to solicit their sanction to the adoption of specific measures, even to the length of assuming the direct administration of the country, if the evils were not corrected in the interim.

In the letter from Government dated the 25th of August, 1831, referring to this advice, the Resident is told that by treaty we are bound to give the aid of troops to quell internal resistance, as well as to keep off external enemies, but by the same treaty the Oude Government is bound to establish a good system of administration, and to conform to our advice in this respect; that, finding it impossible to procure the establishment of such an improved system, and seeing that our troops were liable to be made the instruments of violence, and vindictive and party proceedings, it was determined to withhold the aid of troops except after investigation into the cause which might lead to the application for them; that, by recent orders from the Court of Directors, the Government would be authorised in withholding them altogether, in the hope that the necessities of the Oude Government might compel a reform such as we might deem satisfactory; that matters had not, however, been brought to such an issue, for the Oude Government having been deprived of the services of British troops to execute its purposes, has entertained a body stated at sixty thousand men, cavalry, infantry, and artillery, whereof forty-five thousand are stationed in the interior for the special purpose of reducing refractory zumeendars without British aid. Government urges the necessity of reducing this number, and states that if British troops be employed to enforce submission, it seems impossible to avoid becoming parties to the terms of submission, and guarantees of their observance afterwards on both sides, in which case we should become mixed up in every detail of the administration; it is therefore required that each case shall be investigated and submitted for the specific orders of the Governor-General.

On the 15th of August, 1832, the Governor-General addressed a letter to his Majesty, the King of Oude, in the last sentence of which he says, "I do not use this strong language of remonstrance without manifest necessity. On former occasions the language of expostulation has been frequently used towards you with reference to the abuses of your Government, and as yet nothing serious has befallen you. I beseech you, however, not to suffer yourself to be deceived into a false security. I might adduce sufficient proof that such security would be fallacious, but I am unwilling to wound your Majesty's feelings, while the sincere friendship which I entertain for you prevents my withholding from you that advice which I deem essential to the preservation of your own dignity, and the prosperity of your kingdom."

The Resident is told that the allusion in the concluding sentence of his Lordship's letter refers to Mysore; that the King had probably heard of our actual assumption of the government of that country, and the Resident must avail himself of this topic to impress upon-his mind the consequences which a similar state of things may entail upon himself.

On the 11th of September, 1837, a subsidiary-treaty was concluded with the new sovereign, Mahommed Allee Shah, on the ground that though a larger force was kept up by the King of Oude than was authorised by the treaty of 1801, still it was found inadequate to the duties that devolved upon it, and it was therefore expedient to relax the restrictions as to the amount of military force to be maintained by the King of Oude, on condition that an adequate portion of the increased forces should be placed under British discipline and control. It was stipulated accordingly that the King might employ such a military establishment as he might deem necessary for the government of his dominion: that it should consist of not less than two regiments of cavalry, five of infantry, and two companies of artillery; that the Government of Oude should fix the sum of sixteen lacs of rupees a-year for the expenses of the force, including their pay, arms, equipments, public buildings, &c.; that the expenditure on account of this force of all descriptions should never exceed sixteen lacs; that the organization of this force should not commence till eighteen months after the 1st of September, 1837; that the King should take into his service an efficient number of British officers for the due discipline and efficiency of this force; that this force should be fixed at such stations in Oude as might seem to both Governments, from time to time, to be best, and employed on all occasions on which its services might be deemed necessary by the King of Oude, with the concurrence of the Resident, but not in the ordinary collections of the revenue; that the King should exert himself, in concert with the Resident, to remedy the existing defects in his administration; and should he neglect to attend to the advice and counsel of the British Government, or its representative, and should gross and systematic oppression, anarchy, and misrule, at any time hereafter prevail within the Oude territories, such as seriously to endanger the public tranquillity, the British Government would have the right to appoint its own officers to the management of all portions of the Oude territory in which such misrule might have occurred for so long a period as it might deem necessary, the surplus receipts in such case, after defraying all charges, to be paid into the King's treasury, and a true and faithful account rendered to his Majesty of the receipts and expenditure of the territories so assumed; that should the Governor-General of India in Council be compelled to resort to the exercise of this authority, he would endeavour, as far as possible, to maintain (with such improvements as they might admit of) the native institutions and forms of administration within the assumed territories, so as to facilitate the restoration of those territories to the sovereign of Oude when the proper period of such restoration should arrive.

This treaty was ratified by the Governor-General in Council on the 18th of September, 1837, but the Honourable the Court of Directors, with that anxious regard for strict justice which, after long and varied experience, I have always found to characterise their views and orders, disapproved of that part of the above treaty which imposed on the Oude state the expense of the auxiliary force; and on the 8th of July, 1839, the King was informed, amidst great rejoicings, that he was relieved from this burthen of sixteen lacs of rupees a-year, which the British Government took upon itself. Only part of this auxiliary force had been raised when these orders came, and only two regiments of infantry out of that part were retained, one stationed at Soltanpore, and the other at Seetapore.

Up to 1835, the British forces in Oude amounted to two companies of artillery, with fourteen guns, and six regiments of infantry. Early in that year (1835), four guns, with a proportion of artillerymen, and one regiment of Native Infantry, were withdrawn, leaving the British force in Oude one company and a-half of artillery, with ten guns, and five regiments of Native Infantry. In 1837, when two infantry regiments of the auxiliary force had been raised, four guns more, with a detail of artillery, and two regiments more of Native Infantry were withdrawn from the two stations of Soltanpore and Seetapore, leaving the force paid by the British Government one company of artillery, with six guns, stationed at Lucknow, three regiments of Native Infantry at Lucknow, one regiment of the Oude auxiliary force stationed at Soltanpore, and the other at Seetapore. There had been artillery and guns at Pertabgur, Soltanpore, Secrora and Seetapore, and a regiment of regular cavalry at Pertabgur. In 1815 this regiment of cavalry was withdrawn for the Nepaul war, and subsequently it was retained for the Mahratta war. It was sent back to Pertabgur in 1820, but finally withdrawn in 1821. The British Government now maintains no cavalry in any part of the King of Oude's dominions, and no artillery or guns at any place but Lucknow.*

* There is a small detachment of thirty sowars from an irregular corps attached to the Resident.

In fairness there should be guns at Seetapore and Soltanpore, and a corps of regular or irregular cavalry at Lucknow, or some other more convenient station. The stations of Secrora and Pertabgur were done away with by general orders 28th January, 1835, when one regiment of Native Infantry was withdrawn altogether from Oude, and one added to the two theretofore stationed at Lucknow. In consequence of these arrangements, the British force in Oude is much less than it was when the treaty of the 11th of September, 1837, was made, and assuredly less than it should be with a due regard to our engagements and the Oude requirements. Our Government instead of taking upon itself the additional burthen of sixteen lacs of rupees a-year to render the Oude Government more efficient, has relieved itself of a good deal of that which it bore before the new treaty was entered into, and this is certainly not what the Court of Directors contemplated, or the Oude Government expected.

Our exigencies became great with the Affghan war, and have continued to be so from those wars which grew out of it with Gwalior, Scinde, and the Punjab; but they have all now passed away, and those of our humble ally should be no longer forgotten or disregarded. Though we seldom give him the use of troops in support of the authority of his local officers, still the prestige of having them at hand, in support of a just cause, is unquestionably of great advantage to him and to his people, and this advantage we cannot withhold from him with a due regard to the obligations of solemn treaties.

But in considering the rights which the sovereign of Oude has acquired by solemn treaties to our support, we must not forget those which the five millions of people subject to his rule have acquired by the same treaties to the protection of our Government, and it is a grave question, that must soon be solved, whether we can any longer support the present sovereign and system of government in Oude, without subjecting ourselves to the reproach of shamefully neglecting the duties we owe to these millions.

The present King ascended the throne on the death of his father, on the 13th of February, 1847. In a letter dated the 24th of July of that year, the Resident is told "that it will be his Majesty's duty to establish such an administration, to be carried out by his own officers, as shall insure the prosperity of the people; that any neglect of this essential principle will be an infringement of treaty; and that the Governor-General must, in the performance of his duty, require the King to fulfil his obligations to his subjects—that his Majesty must understand that, as a sovereign, he has duties to perform to, as well as claims to exact from, the people committed to his care."

In the month of November in that year, the Governor-General. Lord Hardinge, visited Lucknow; and in a conference held with the King, he caused a memorandum which he had drawn up for the occasion to be read and carefully explained to his Majesty. It stated, "that in all our engagements the utmost care had always been taken, not only to uphold the authority of native rulers, but also to secure the just rights of the people subject to their rule; that the same principle is maintained in the treaty of 1801 with Oude, in the sixth paragraph of which the engagement is entered into 'for the establishment of such a system of government as shall be conducive to the prosperity of the King's subjects, and calculated to secure to them their lives and properties;' that in the memorandum of 1802, signed by the Governor-General, the King engages to establish judicial tribunals for the free and pure administration of justice to all his subjects; and that it is recorded in the sovereign's own hand in that document, 'let the Company's officers assist in enforcing obedience to these tribunals;' that it is, therefore, evident that in all these stipulations the same principle prevailed—namely, that while we engage to maintain the prince in the full exercise of his powers, we also provide for the protection of his people.

"That, in the more recent treaty of 1837, it is stated that the solemn and paramount obligation provided by treaty for the prosperity of his Majesty's subjects, and the security of the lives and property of the inhabitants, has been notoriously neglected by several successive rulers in Oude, thereby exposing the British Government to the reproach of having imperfectly fulfilled its obligations towards the Oude people; that his Lordship alludes to the treaty of 1837, as confirming the original treaty of 1801, and not only giving the British Government the right to interfere, but declaring it to be the intention of the Government to interfere, if necessary, for the purpose of securing good government in Oude; that the King can, therefore, have no doubt that the Governor-General is not only justified, but bound by his duty, to take care that the stipulations provided by treaty shall be fairly and substantially carried into effect; that if the Governor-General permits the continuation of any flagrant system of mismanagement which by treaty he is empowered to correct, he becomes the participator in abuses which it is his duty to redress; and in this case no ruler of Oude can expect the Governor-General to incur a responsibility so repugnant to the principles of the British Government, and so odious to the feelings of the British people.

"That, in the discussion of this important subject, advice and remonstrance have been frequently tried, and have failed; that the Governor-General hopes that the King will exercise a sounder judgment than those who have preceded him, and that he will not be compelled to exchange friendly advice for imperative and absolute interference; that when the Governor-General, Lord William Bentinck, had a conference with the former King, Nuseer-od Deen Hyder, on this subject, on the 20th of January, 1831, he deemed it right frankly to inform him that if the warning which he then gave was disregarded by his Majesty, it was his intention to submit to the home authorities his advice that the British Government should assume the direct management of the Oude dominions; that the Honourable the Court of Directors coincided in his Lordship's views and, in order that no doubt may remain on the King's mind as to the sentiments of the home authorities on this point, he, Lord Hardinge, here inserts an extract from the despatch of that Court, for his information; that it is as follows:—'We have, after the most serious consideration, come to the determination of granting to you the discretionary power which you have requested, from us for placing the Oude territories under the direct management of officers of the British Government; and you are hereby empowered, if no real and satisfactory improvement shall have taken place in the administration of that country, and if your Government shall still adhere to the opinion expressed in the minute of the Governor-General, to carry the proposed measure into effect, at such period and in such manner as shall appear to you most desirable;' that this resolution was communicated to the Resident and to the King, and advantage was taken of it to press upon his Majesty the necessity of an immediate reform of his administration; that the above extract will enable the King to form a clear judgment of the position in which the sovereigns of Oude are placed by treaty; that the Governor-General is required, when gross and systematic abuses prevail, to apply such a remedy as the exigency of the case may appear to require—that he has no option in the performance of that duty.

"That by wisely taking timely measures for the reformation of abuses, as one of the first acts of his reign, his Majesty will, with honour to his own character, rescue his people from their present miserable condition; but if he procrastinates he will incur the risk of forcing the British Government to interfere, by assuming the government of Oude; that the former course would redound to his Majesty's credit and dignity, while the latter would give the British Government concern in the case of a prince whom, as our ally, we sincerely desire to honour and uphold; that for these reasons, and on account of the King's inexperience, the Governor-General is not disposed to act immediately on the power vested in him by the Honourable Court's despatch above quoted, still less is he disposed to hold him responsible for the misrule of his predecessors, nor does he expect that so inveterate a system of misgovernment can suddenly be eradicated; that the resolution, and the preliminary measures 'to effect this purpose,' can and ought at once to be adopted by the King; that if his Majesty cordially enters into the plan suggested by the Governor-General for the improvement of his administration, he may have the satisfaction, within the period specified of two years, of checking and eradicating the worst abuses, and, at the same time, of maintaining his own sovereignty and the native institutions of his kingdom unimpaired; but if he does not, if he takes a vacillating course, and fail by refusing to act on the Governor-General's advice, he is aware of the other alternative and of the consequences. It must, then, be manifest to the whole world that, whatever may happen, the King has received a friendly and timely warning."

On the 24th of December in that year, 1847, Government, in reply to the Resident's letter of the 30th November, states that it does not consider the King's reply in any respect satisfactory; that the Resident is to remind his Majesty that under paragraph the 23rd of the memorandum read out to him by the Governor-General's direction, the Resident has been required to submit periodical reports of the state of his dominions, and that his Majesty must be fully aware of the responsibility he incurs if he neglects, during the interval allowed him, to introduce the requisite reforms in his administration.

More than two years have elapsed since this caution was given, and the King has done nothing to improve his administration, abstained from no personal indulgence, given no attention whatever to public affairs. He had before that time tried to imitate his father, attend a little to public affairs, and see occasionally the members of the royal family and aristocracy, at least of the city, and heads of departments; but the effort was painful, and soon ceased altogether to be made. He had from boyhood mixed in no other society than that in which he now mixes exclusively, and he will never submit to the restraints of any other. The King has utterly disregarded alike the Governor-General's advice and admonitions, the duties and responsibilities of his high office, and the sufferings of the many millions subject to his rule. His time and attention are devoted entirely to the pursuit of personal gratifications; he associates with none but such as those who contribute to such gratifications—women, singers, and eunuchs; and he never, I believe, reads or hears read any petition from his suffering subjects, any report from his local officers civil or military, or presidents of his fiscal and judicial courts, or functionaries of any hind. He seems to take no interest whatever in public affairs, and to care nothing whatever about them.

The King had natural capacity equal to that of any of those who have preceded him in the sovereignty of Oude since the death of Saadut Allee in 1814, but he is the only one who has systematically declined to devote any of that capacity, or any of his time, to the conduct of public affairs; to see and occasionally commune with the heads of departments, the members of the royal family, and native gentlemen of the capital; to read or have read to him the reports of his local functionaries, and petitions or redress of wrongs from his suffering subjects.*

* This systematic disregard of his high duties and responsibilities still continues to be manifested by the King of Oude; and is observed, with feelings of indignation and abhorrence, by his well-disposed subjects of all classes and grades, who are thereby left to the mercy of men without any feeling of security in their tenure of office, any scruples of conscience, or feelings of humanity, or of honour. So inveterate is the system of misgovernment—so deeply are all those, now employed in the administration, interested in maintaining its worst abuses—and so fruitless is it to expect the King to remove them, or employ better men, or to be ever able to inspire any men, whom he may appoint, with a disposition to serve him more honestly, and to respect the rights of others, or consider the reputation and permanent interests of their own master, that the impression has become strong and general, that our Government can no longer support the present Government of Oude, without seriously neglecting its duty towards the people.—1851, W. H. S.

In the reports of the Resident on the state of affairs in Oude, and the replies of Government, much importance has been always attached to the change from the contract, or *ijara* system, to that of the *amanee*, or trust management system; and since the time of Lord Hardinge's visit many more districts have been put under the latter system; but this has not tended, in the smallest degree, to the benefit of the people of these districts. The same abuses prevail under the one system as under the other. The troops employed in the districts under the one are the same as those employed in the districts under the other, and they prey just as much upon the people. There is the same system of rack-rent in the one as in the other, and the same uncertainty in the rate of the Government demand. The manager under the *amanut* system demands the same secret gratuities and *nuzuranas* for himself and his patrons at Court from the landholders, as the contractor; and if they refuse to pay them they are besieged, attacked, and cut up, and their estates desolated in the same manner. The *amanut* manager knows that his tenure of office depends as much upon the amount which he pays to his sovereign, and to his patrons at Court, as that of the contractor, and he exacts and extorts as much as he can in the same manner. Unless he pays his patrons the same he knows that he shall soon be removed, or driven to resign by the want of means to enforce the payment of the revenues justly due.

The objections which are urged against the employment of British troops in support of the authority of revenue contractors, are equally applicable to their employment in support of that of amanee managers. Their employment is just as liable to abuse under the one as under the other. It is not a whit easier to ascertain whether a demand for balance of revenue from, or a charge of contumacy against, a landholder is just or unjust in the one than in the other. In neither is the demand set forth in public documents understood by either party to be the real demand. Both parties are equally interested in preventing a portion of the *real* demand from appearing in the public accounts; and the quarrel is almost always about the rate of this concealed portion—the collector trying to augment, and the landlord trying to reduce it.

In a letter to the Resident, dated the 29th of March, 1823, Government observes: "As some palliation of the mischief of our forces being constantly employed in what might be too often termed the cause of injustice and extortion, the Government in 1811 distinctly declared our right of previously investigating, and of arbitrating the demands which its troops might be called upon to support as also its resolution to exercise that right on all future occasions. The execution of the important duty in question seems to be almost invariably delegated by the Resident to the officers commanding at the different stations, who, after receiving general powers to attend to the requisitions of the amils, become the sole judges of the individual cases, in which aid is to be afforded or withheld; and the discretion again unavoidably descends from them, in many instances, to the officers commanding parties detached from the main body. It is obvious that an inquiry of this description can afford but a partial check to, and a feeble security against, injustice and oppression where specific engagements rarely exist, and where the point at issue is frequently the demand for augmenting rates of revenue, founded on alleged assets sufficient to meet that increase.

"Neither is the aid thus afforded at all effectual for the purposes of the Government of Oude, whether present or future, as is clear from the annual repetition of the same scenes of resistance and compulsion. As fast as disorders are suppressed in one quarter they spring up in another. Forts that are this year dismantled are restored again the next; the compulsion exercised upon particular individuals in one season has no effect in producing more regularity on their parts, or on that of others in the ensuing season, until the same process has been again gone through; whilst the contempt and odium attaching to a system of collecting the revenues, by the habitual intervention of the troops of another State, infallibly tend to aggravate the evil, by destroying all remains of confidence in his Majesty, or respect for his authority."

The aid of British troops in the collection of the revenues of Oude has long ceased to be afforded; but when they have been afforded for the suppression of leaders of atrocious bands of robbers, who preyed upon the people, and seized upon the lands of their weaker neighbours, and they have been driven from their forts and strongholds, the privilege of building them up again, or re-occupying and garrisoning them with the same bands of robbers, to be employed in the same way, is purchased from the local authorities, or the patrons of these leaders at Court, during the same or the succeeding season. The same things continue to be done every season where no British troops are employed. Such privileges are purchased with as much facility as those for the supply of essence or spices in the palace; unless the Resident should interpose authoritatively to prevent it, which he very rarely does. Indeed it is seldom that a Resident knows or cares anything about the matter.

I may say generally, that in Oude the larger landholders do not pay more than one-third of their net rents to the Government, while some of them do not pay one-fifth or one-tenth. In the half of the territory made over to us in 1801, the great landholders who still retain their estates pay to our Government at least two-thirds of their net rents. In Oude these great landholders have, at present, about two hundred and fifty mud forts, mounting about five hundred guns, and containing on an average four hundred armed men, or a total of one hundred thousand, trained and maintained to fight against other, or against the Government authorities; and to pillage the peaceful and industrious around whenever so employed. In the half of the territory ceded to us in 1801, this class of armed retainers has disappeared altogether. Hence from the Oude half we have some fifty thousand native officers and sipahees in our native army, while from our half we have not perhaps five thousand.

One thing is clear, that we cannot restore to the Oude Government the territory we acquired from it by the treaty of 1801, and the people who occupy it; and that we cannot withdraw our support from that Government altogether without doing so. It is no less clear that all our efforts to make the Government of Oude, under the support which we are bound by that treaty to give it, fulfil the duties to its people to which it was pledged by that treaty, have failed during the fifty years that have elapsed since it was made.

The only alternative left, appears to be for the paramount power to take upon itself the administration, and give to the sovereign, the royal family, and its stipendiary dependents, all the surplus revenues in pensions, opening as much as possible all employments in the civil administration to the educated classes of Oude. The military and police establishments would consist almost exclusively of Oude men. Under such a system more of these classes would be employed than at present, for few of the officers employed in the administration are of these classes—the greater part of them are adventurers from all parts of India, without character or education. The number of such officers would be multiplied fourfold, and the means of paying them would be taken from the favourites and parasites of the Court who now do nothing but mischief.

Such a change would be popular among the members of the royal family itself, who now get their pensions after long intervals—often after two and even three years, and with shameful reductions in behalf of those favourites and parasites whom they detest and despise, but whom the minister, for his own personal purposes, is obliged to conciliate by such perquisites. It would be popular among the educated classes, as opening to them offices now filled by knaves and vagabonds from all parts of India, It would be no less so to the well-disposed portion of the agricultural classes, who would be sure of protection to life, property, and character, without the expensive trains of armed followers which they now keep up. But to secure this, we should require to provide them with a more simple system of civil judicature than that which we have at work in our old territories.

The change would be popular, with few exceptions, among all the mercantile and manufacturing classes. It would give vast employment to all the labouring classes throughout the country, in the construction of good roads, bridges, wells, tanks, temples, suraes, military and civil buildings, and other public works; but above all, in that of private dwellings, and other edifices for use and ornament, in which all men would be proud to lay out their wealth to perpetuate their names, when secured in the possession by an honest and efficient Government; but more especially those who would be no longer able to employ their means in maintaining armed bands, to resist the local authorities and disturb the peace of the country. On the whole, I think that at least nine-tenths of the people of Oude would hail the change as a great blessing; always providing, that our system of administration should be rendered as simple as possible to meet the wants and wishes of a simple people.

Though the Resident has never been able to secure any substantial and permanent improvement in the administration, he often interposes successfully in individual cases, to relieve suffering, and secure redress for wrongs; and the people see that he interferes in no others. Their only regret is, that he does not interpose more often, and that his efforts, when he does, should be so often thwarted or disregarded. The British character is, in consequence, respected in the remotest village and jungle in Oude; and there is, I believe, no part of India where an European officer is received, among the people of all classes, with more kindness and courtesy than in Oude. There is, certainly, no city or town in any other native State in India where he is treated in the crowded streets with more respect. This must of course be accounted for in great measure from the greater part of the members of the royal family, and the relatives and dependents of the several persons who have held the highest offices of the State since 1814, either receiving their incomes from the British Government in treaty pensions, or in interest on our Government securities, or being guaranteed in those which they receive from the Oude Government by ours. A great many of the families of the middle classes depend entirely upon the interest which they receive from us on our Government securities. There is, indeed, hardly a respectable family in Lucknow that is not more or less dependent upon our Government for protection, and proud to have it considered that they are so. The works and institutions which would soon be created out of revenues, now absorbed by worthless Court favourites, would soon embellish the face of the country, improve the character, condition, and habits of the people, stimulate their industry in agriculture, manufactures, and commerce; and render our connection with the Oude Government honourable to our name in the estimation of all India.

CHAPTER V.

Baree-Biswa district—Force with the Nazim, Lal Bahader—Town of Peernuggur—Dacoitee by Lal and Dhokul Partuks—Gangs of robbers easily formed out of the loose characters which abound in Oude—The lands tilled in spite of all disorders—Delta between the Chouka and Ghagra rivers—Seed sown and produce yielded on land—Rent and stock—Nawab Allee, the holder of the Mahmoodabad estate—Mode of augmenting his estate—Insecurity of marriage processions—Belt of jungle, fourteen miles west from the Lucknow cantonments—Gungabuksh Rawat—His attack on Dewa—The family inveterate robbers—Bhurs, once a civilized and ruling people in Oude—Extirpated systematically in the fourteenth century—Depredations of Passees—Infanticide—How maintained—Want of influential middle class of merchants and manufacturers—Suttee—Troops with the Amil—Seizure of a marriage procession by Imambuksh, a gang leader—Perquisites and allowances of Passee watchmen over corn-fields—Their fidelity to trusts—Ahbun Sing, of Kyampoor, murders his father—Rajah Singjoo of Soorujpoor—Seodeen, another leader of the same tribe—Principal gang-leaders of the Dureeabad Rodowlee district—Jugurnath Chuprassie—Bhooree Khan—How these gangs escape punishment—Twenty-four belts of jungle preserved by landholders always, or occasionally, refractory in Oude—Cover eight hundred and eighty-six square miles of good land—How such atrocious characters find followers, and landholders of high degree to screen, shelter, and aid them.

February 14, 1850.—Peernuggur, ten miles south-east, over a plain of the same soil, but with more than the usual proportion of oosur. Trees and groves as usual, but not quite so fine or numerous. The Nazim of Khyrabad took leave of me on his boundary as we crossed it about midway, and entered the district of "Baree Biswa," which is held in farm by Lal Bahader,* a Hindoo, who there met us. This fiscal officer has under him the "Jafiree," and "Tagfore" Regiments of nujeebs, and eight pieces of cannon. The commandants of both corps are in attendance at Court, and one of them, Imdad Hoseyn, never leaves it. The other does condescend sometimes to come out to look at his regiment when *not on service*. The draft-bullocks for the guns have, the Nazim tells me, had a little grain within the last month, but still not more than a quarter of the amount for which the King is charged. Peernuggur is now a place of little note upon the banks of the little river Sae, which here flows under a bridge built by Asuf-od Dowlah some sixty years ago.

* This man was in prison at Lucknow as a defaulter, but made his escape in October, 1851, by drugging the sentry placed over him, and got safe into British territory.

Gang-robberies are here as frequent as in Khyrabad, and the respectable inhabitants are going off in the same manner. One which took place in July last year is characteristic of the state of society in Oude, and may be mentioned here. Twelve sipahees of the 59th Regiment Native Infantry, then stationed at Bareilly, lodged here for the night, in a surae, on their way home on furlough. Dal Partuk, a Brahmin by caste, and a man of strength and resolution, resided here and cultivated a small patch of land. He had two pair of bullocks, which used to be continually trespassing upon other men's fields and gardens, and embroiling him with the people, till one night they disappeared. Dal Partuk called upon his neighbours, who had suffered from their trespasses, to restore them or pay the value, and threatened to rob, plunder, and burn down the town if they did not.

A great number of pausees reside in and around the town, and he knew that he could collect a gang of them for any enterprise of this sort at the shortest notice. The people were not disposed to pay the value of his lost bullocks, and they could not be found. While he was meditating his revenge, his relation, Dhokul Partuk, was by a trifling accident driven to take the field as a robber. An oil-vender, a female, from a neighbouring village, had presumed to come to Peernuggur, and offer oil for sale. The oil-venders of the town, dreading the consequences of such competition, went forthwith to the little garrison and prayed for *protection*. One of the sipahees went off to the silversmith to whom the oil-vender had sold twopence-worth of oil, and, finding the oil-vender still with him, proceeded at once to seize both, and take them off to the garrison as criminals. Dhokul Partuk, who lived close by, and had his sword by his side, went up and remonstrated with the sipahee, who, taking him to be another silversmith, struck him across the face with his stick. Dhokul drew his sword, and made a cut at the sipahee, which would have severed his head from his body had he not fallen backwards. As it was, he got a severe cut in the chest, and ran off to his companions. Dhokul went out of the town with his drawn sword, and no one dared to pursue him. At night he returned, took off his family to a distant village, became a leader of a band of pausee bowmen, and invited his kinsman, Dal Partuk, to follow his example.

Together, they made an attack at night upon the town, and burnt down one quarter of the houses. Dal Partuk offered to come to terms and live in the town again, if the people would pay the value of his lost bullocks, and give him a small income of five rupees a-month. This they refused to do, and the plunder and burning went on. At last they made this attack upon the party in the surae, which happened to be so full that several of the sipahees and others were cooking outside the walls. None of the travellers had arms to defend themselves, and those inside closed the doors as soon as they heard the alarm. The pausees, with their bows and arrows, killed two of the sipahees who were outside, and while the gang was trying to force open the doors of the surae, the people of the town, headed by a party of eight pausee bowmen of their own, attacked and drove them back. These bowmen followed the gang for some distance, and killed several of them with their arrows. The sipahees who escaped proceeded in all haste to the Resident, and the Frontier Police has since succeeded in arresting several of the gang; but the two leaders have hitherto been screened by Goorbuksh Sing and other great landholders in their interest. The eight pausees who exerted themselves so successfully in defence of the town and surae were expecting an attack from the pausees of a neighbouring village, and ready for action when the alarm was given.

These parties of pausee bowmen have each under their charge a certain number of villages, whose crops and other property they are pledged to defend for the payment of a certain sum, or a certain portion of land rent-free. In one of these, under the Peernuggur party, three bullocks had been stolen by the pausees of a neighbouring town. They were traced to them, and, as they would neither restore them nor pay their value, the Peernuggur party attacked them one night in their sleep, and killed the leader and four of his followers, to deter others of the tribe from trespassing on property under their charge. They expect, they told us, to be attacked in return some night, and are obliged to be always prepared, but have not the slightest apprehension of ever being called to account for such things by the officers of Government. Nor would Dal and Dhokul Partuk have any such apprehension, had not the Resident taken up the question of the murder of the Honourable Company's sipahees as an international one. After plundering and burning down a dozen villages, and murdering a score or two of people, they would have come back and reoccupied their houses in the town without any fear of being molested or *questioned* by Government officers. Nor would the people of the town object to their residing among them again, provided they pledged themselves to abstain in future from molesting them. Goorbuksh Sing, only a few days ago, offered the contractor, Hoseyn Allee, the sum of five thousand, rupees if he would satisfy the Resident that Dal Partuk had nothing whatever to do with the Peernuggur dacoitee, and thereby induce him to discontinue the pursuit.*

* Dhokul Partuk and Dal Partuk were at last secured. Dhokul died in the king's gaol, but Dal Partuk is still in prison under trial.

The people of towns and villages, having no protection whatever from the Government, are obliged to keep up, at their own cost, this police of pausee bowmen, who are bound only to protect those who pay them. As their families increase beyond the means derived from this, their only legitimate employment, their members thieve in the neighbouring or distant villages, rob on the highroads, or join the gangs of those who are robbers by profession, or take the trade in consequence of disputes and misunderstandings with Government authorities or their neighbours. In Oude—and indeed in all other parts of India, under a Government so weak and indifferent to the sufferings of its subjects—all men who consider arms to be their proper profession think themselves justified in using them to extort the means of subsistence from those who have property when they have none, and can no longer find what they consider to be suitable employment. All Rajpoots are of this class, and the greater part of the landholders in Oude are Rajpoots. But a great part of the Mahommedan rural population are of the same class, and no small portion of the Brahmin inhabitants, like the two Partuks above named, consider arms to be their proper profession; and all find the ready means of forming gangs of robbers out of these pausee bowmen and the many loose characters to whom the disorders of the country give rise.

A great many of the officers and sipahees of the King's nujeeb and other regiments are every month discharged for mutiny, insubordination, abuse of authority, or neglect of duty, or merely to make room for men more subservient to Court favourites, or because they cannot or will not pay the demanded gratuity to a new and useless commandant appointed by Court favour. The plunder of villages has been the daily occupation of these men during the whole period of their service, and they become the worst of this class of loose characters, ready to join any band of freebooters. Such bands are always sure to find a patron among the landholders ready to receive and protect them, for a due share of their booty, against any force that the King's officers may send after them; and, if they prefer it as less costly, they can always find a manager of a district ready to do the same, on condition that they abstain from plundering within his jurisdiction. The greater part of the land is, however, cultivated, and well cultivated under all this confusion and consequent insecurity. Tillage is the one thing needful to all, and the persons from whom trespasses on the crops are most apprehended are the reckless and disorderly trains of Government officials.

February 16, 1850.—Biswa, eighteen miles east, over a plain of excellent soil, partly doomut, but chiefly mutteear, well studded with trees and groves, scantily cultivated for the half of the way, but fully and beautifully for the second half. The wheat beginning to change colour as it approaches maturity, and waving in the gentle morning breeze; intervening fields covered with mixed crops of peas, gram, ulsee, teora, surson, mustard, all in flower, and glittering like so many rich parterres; patches here and there of the dark-green *arahur* and yellow sugar-cane rising in bold relief; mango-groves, majestic single trees, and clusters of the graceful bamboo studding the whole surface, and closing the distant horizon in one seemingly-continued line of fence—the eye never tires of such a scene, but would like now and then to rest upon some architectural work of ornament or utility to aid the imagination in peopling it.

The road for the last six miles passes through the estate of Nawab Allee, a Mahommedan landholder, who is a strong man and a good manager and paymaster. His rent-roll is about four hundred thousand rupees a-year, and he pays Government about one hundred and fifty thousand. His hereditary possession was a small one, and his estate has grown to the present size in the usual way. He has lent money in mortgage and foreclosed; he has given security for revenue due to Government by other landholders, who have failed to pay, and had their estates made over to him; he has given security for the appearance, when called for, of others, and, on their failing to appear (perchance at his own instigation), had their lands made over to him by the Government authorities, on condition of making good the Government demand upon them; he has offered a higher rate of revenue for lands than present holders could make them yield, and, after getting possession, brought the demand down to a low rate in collusion with Government officers. Some three-fourths of the magnificent estate which he now holds he has obtained in these and other ways by fraud, violence, or collusion within the last few years. He is too powerful and wealthy to admit of any one's getting his lands out of his hands after they have once passed into them, no matter how.

The Chowka river flows from the forest towards the Ghagra, about ten miles to the east from Biswa, and I am told that the richest sheet of cultivation in Oude is within the delta formed by these two rivers.* At the apex of this delta stands the fort of Bhitolee, which I have often mentioned as belonging to Rajah Goorbuksh Sing, and being under siege by the contractor of the Khyrabad district when we passed the Ghagra in December. Biswa is a large town, well situated on a good soil and open plain, and its vicinity would be well suited for a cantonment or seat for civil establishments. Much of the cloth called sullum used to be made here for export to Europe, but the demand has ceased, and with it the manufacture.

* This delta contains the following noble estates; 1, Dhorehra; 2, Eesanuggur; 3, Chehlary; 4, Rampore; 5, Bhitolee; 6, Mullahpore; 7, Seonta; 8, Nigaseen; and 9, Bhera Jugdeopore. The Turae forest forms the base of this delta, and the estates of Dhorehra, Eesanuggur, and Bhera Jugdeopore lie along its border. They have been much injured by the King's troops within the last three years. Bhitolee is at the apex.

February 17 *and* 18, 1850.—Detained at Biswa by rain.

February 19, 1850.—Yesterday evening came to Kaharpore, ten miles, over a plain of the same fine soil, mutteear of the best quality, running here and there into doomutteea and even bhoor. Cultivation good, and the plain covered with rich spring crops, except where the ground is being prepared to receive the autumn seed in June next. It is considered good husbandry to-plough, cross-plough, and prepare the lands thus early. The spring crops are considered to be more promising than they have been at any other season for the last twenty years. The farmers and cultivators calculate upon an average return of ten and twelve fold, and say that, in other parts of Oude where the lands are richer, there will be one of fifteen or twenty of wheat, gram, &c. The pucka-beega, two thousand seven hundred and fifty-six square yards, requires one maund of seed of forty seers, of eighty rupees of the King's and Company's coinage the seer.* The country, as usual, studded with trees, single, and in clusters and groves, intermingled with bamboos, which are, however, for the most part, of the smaller or hill kind.

* The pucka-beega in Oude is about the same as that which prevails over our North-Western Provinces, two thousand seven hundred and fifty-six and a quarter square yards, or something more than one-half of our English statute acre, which is four thousand eight hundred and forty square yards. This pucka-beega takes of seed-wheat one maund, or eighty pounds; and yields on an average, under good tillage, eight returns of the seed, or eight maunds, or six hundred and forty pounds, which, at one rupee the maund, yields eight rupees, or sixteen shillings. The stock required in Oude in irrigated lands is about twenty rupees the pucka-beega. The rent on an average two rupees. In England an acre, on an average, requires two and three-quarter bushels of seed wheat, or one hundred and seventy-six pounds, or two maunds and sixteen seers, and yields twenty-four bushels, or one thousand five hundred and thirty-six pounds. This at forty shillings the quarter (512 lbs.) would yield six pounds sterling. The stock required in England is estimated at ten pounds Sterling per acre, or ten times the annual rent. It is difficult to estimate the rate of rent on land in England, since the reputed owner is said to be "only the ninth and last recipient of rent."

On reaching camp, I met, for the first time, the great landholder, Nawab Allee, of Mahmoodabad. In appearance, he is a quiet gentlemanly man, of middle age and stature. He keeps his lands in the finest possible state of tillage, however objectionable the means by which he acquires them. His family have held the estates of Mahmoodabad and Belehree for many generations as zumeendars, or proprietors; but they have augmented them greatly, absorbing into them the estates of their weaker neighbours.*

* Akram Allee and Muzhur Allee inherited the estate in two divisions. Akram Allee got Mahmoodabad, and had two sons, Surufraz Allee, who died without issue, before his father; and Mosahib Allee, who succeeded to the estate, but died without issue. Muzhur Allee got the estate of Belehree, and had two sons, Abud Allee, and Nawab Allee. Abud Allee succeeded to the estate of Belehree, and Nawab Allee to that of Mahmoodabad by adoption.

Akram Allee held Mahmoodabad, and was succeeded in the possession by his son, Mosahib Allee, who died about forty years ago, leaving the estate to his widow, who held it for twenty-eight years up to A.D. 1838, when she died. She had, the year before, adopted her nephew, Nawab Allee, and he succeeded to the estate. The Belehree estate is held by his elder brother, Abud Allee, who is augmenting it in the same way, but not at the same rate. I may mention a few recent cases, as illustrative of the manner in which such things are done in Oude.

Mithun Sing, of an ancient Rajpoot family, held the estate of Semree, which had been held by his ancestors for many centuries. It consisted of twelve fine villages, paid to Government 4000 rupees a year, and yielded him a rent roll of 20,000. Nawab Allee coveted very much this estate, which bordered on his own. Three years ago, he instigated the Nazim to demand an increase of 5000 rupees a-year from the estate; and at the same time invited Mithun Sing to his house, and persuaded him to resist the demand, to the last. He took to the jungles, and in the contest between him and the Nazim all the crops of the season were destroyed, and all the cultivators driven from the lands. When the season of tillage returned in June, and Mithun Sing had been reduced to the last stage of poverty, Nawab Allee consented to become the mediator, got a lease from the Chuckladar for Mithun Sing at 4500 rupees a-year, and stood surety for the punctual payment of the demand. Poor Mithun Sing could pay nothing, and Nawab Allee got possession of the estate in liquidation of the balance due to him; and assigned to Mithun Sing five hundred pucka-beegas of land for his subsistence. He still resides on the estate, and supports his family by the tillage of these few beegas.

Amdhun Chowdheree held a share in the estate of Biswa, consisting of sixty-five villages; paying to Government 12,000 rupees a-year, and yielding a rent-roll of 65,000. His elder brother's widow resided on the estate, supported by Amdhun, who managed its affairs for the family. Nawab Allee got up a quarrel between her and her brother-in-law; and she assumed the right to authorize Nawab Allee to seize upon the whole estate. Amdhun appealed to his clan, but Nawab Allee, in collusion with the Nazim, was too strong for him, and got possession by taking a strong force, and driving out all who presumed to resist him. The estate had been held by the family for many centuries.

Mohun Sing held the estate of Mundhuna, which had been in his family for many generations. He was, by the usual process, five years ago, constrained to accept the security of Nawab Allee for the punctual payment of the revenue; and his estate was absorbed in the usual way, the year after. He is now, like a boa-constrictor, swallowing up Chowdheree Pertab Sing, who holds a large share in the hereditary estate of Biswa, which has been in the possession of the family for a great many generations. This share consisted of thirty-six villages, and paid a revenue to Government of fourteen thousand. Last year, Nawab Allee instigated the Nazim to demand ten thousand more. The Nazim, to prevent all disputes, assigned the twenty-four thousand to Mirza Hoseyn Beg, the commandant of a troop of cavalry, employed under him, in liquidation of their arrears of pay. The commandant gave him a receipt for the amount, which the Nazim sent to the treasury, and got credit for the amount in his accounts. But poor Pertab Sing could not pay, and was imprisoned by the cavalry, who kept possession of his person, and took upon them the collection of his rents. Nawab Allee came in and paid what was due; and gave security for the punctual payment of the revenue for the ensuing year. The estate was made over to him; and he put on score after score of *dustuk* bearers, who soon reduced Pertab Sing to utter beggary. Ten thousand rupees were due to Nawab Allee, and he had nothing left to sell; and under such circumstances no man else would lend him anything.

The dustuk bearers are servants of the creditor, who are sent to attend the debtor, extort from him their wages and subsistence, and see that he does not move, eat, or drink till he pays them. During this time the creditor saves all the wages of these attendants; and they commonly exact double wages from the debtor, so that he is soon reduced to terms. In this stage we found the poor Chowdheree on reaching Biswa. I had him released, and so admonished Nawab Allee, that he has some little chance of saving his estate.

Bisram Sing held the estate of Kooa Danda, which had been in the possession of his family of Ahbun Rajpoots for many centuries. It consisted of thirty-five villages, paid a revenue of six thousand rupees a-year, and yielded a rent-roll of eighteen thousand and five hundred. Nawab Allee coveted it as being on his border, and in good order. As soon as his friend; Allee Buksh, was appointed Nazim of the district, he prevailed upon him to report to the Durbar that Bisram Sing was a refractory subject, and plunderer; and to request permission to put him down by force of arms. This was in 1844, while Bisram Sing was living quietly on his estate. On receiving the order, which came as a matter of course, the Nazim united his force with that of Nawab Allee, and attacked the house of Bisram Sing, which had only twenty-two men to defend it against two thousand. Six of the twenty-two were killed, eight wounded, and eight only escaped; and Nawab Allee took possession of the estate.

Bisram Sing was at Lucknow at the time, trying to rebut the false charges of the Nazim; but his influence was unhappily too strong for him, and he got no redress. Soon after Nirput Sing, a sipahee in the 9th Regiment Native Infantry, presented a petition to the Resident, stating that he was the brother of Bisram Sing, and equally interested in the estate; and a special officer, Busharut Allee, was ordered by the Durbar to investigate and decide the case. He decided in favour of Nirput, the sipahee, and Bisram Sing. Another special officer was sent out to restore Bisram to possession. Nawab Allee then pleaded the non-existence of any relationship between Nirput and Bisram; and a third special officer has been sent out to ascertain this fact.

Belehree, held by Abud Allee, consists of forty villages, pays a revenue of twelve thousand rupees a-year, and yields a rent-roll of forty thousand. Abud Allee holds also the estate of Pyntee, in the same district, consisting of eighty villages, paying a revenue of thirty-five thousand, and yielding a rent-roll of one hundred and forty thousand. It had been held by his relative Kazim Allee, who was succeeded in the possession by Nizam Allee, the husband of his only daughter. Nizam Allee was in A.D. 1841 killed by a servant, who was cut down and killed in return by his attendants. Nizam Allee's widow held till 1843, when she made over the estate to Abud Allee, by whom she is supported.

Nawab Allee has always money at command to purchase influence at Court when required; and he has also a brave and well-armed force, with which to aid the governor of the district, when he makes it worth his while to do so, in crushing a refractory landholder. These are the sources of his power, and he is not at all scrupulous in the use of it—it is not the fashion to be so in Oude.

February 20th, 1850.—Came on sixteen miles to Futtehpore, in the estate of Nawab Allee, passing Mahmoodabad half way. Near that place we passed through a grove of mango and other trees called the "Lak Peree," or the grove of a hundred thousand trees planted by his ancestors forty years ago. The soil is the same, the country level, studded with the same rich foliage, and covered with the same fine crops. As we were passing through his estate, and were to encamp in it again to-day, Nawab Allee attended me on horseback; and I endeavoured to impress upon him and the Nazim the necessity of respecting the rights of others, and more particularly those of the old Chowdheree Pertab Sing. "Why is it," I asked, "that this beautiful scene is not embellished by any architectural beauties? Sheikh Sadee, the poet, so deservedly beloved by you all, old and young, Hindoos and Mahommedans, says, 'The man who leaves behind him in any place, a bridge, a well, a church, or a caravansera, never dies.' Here not even a respectable dwelling-house is to be seen, much less a bridge, a church, or a caravansera." "Here, sir," said old Bukhtawur, "men must always be ready for a run to the jungles. Unless they are so, they can preserve nothing from the grasp of the contractors of the present day, who have no respect for property or person—for their own character, or for that of their sovereign. The moment that a man runs to save himself, family, and property, they rob and pull down his house, and those of all connected with him. When a man has nothing but mud walls, with invisible mud covers, they give him no anxiety; he knows that he can build them up again in a few days, or even a few hours, when he comes back from the jungles; and he cares little about what is done to them during his absence. Had he an expensive house of burnt brick and mortar, he could never feel quite free. He might be tempted to defend it, and lose some valuable lives; or he might be obliged to submit to unjust terms. Were he to lay out his money in expensive mosques, temples, and tombs, they would restrain him in the same way; and he is content to live without them, and have his loins always girded for fight or flight."

"True," said Nawab Allee, "very true; we can plant groves and make wells, but we cannot venture to erect costly buildings of any kind. You saw the Nazim of Khyrabad, only a few days ago, bringing all his troops down upon Rampore, because the landlord, Goman Sing, would not consent to the increase he demanded of ten thousand, upon seventeen thousand rupees a-year, which he had hitherto paid. Goman Sing took to the jungles; and in ten days his fine crops would all have been destroyed, and his houses levelled with the ground, had you not interposed, and admonished both. The one at last consented to take, and the other to pay an increase of five thousand. Only three years ago, Goman Sing's father was killed by the Nazim in a similar struggle; and landholders must always be prepared for them."

February 21st, 1850.—Bureearpore, ten miles south-east, over a plain of the same fine soil, well cultivated, and carpeted with the same fine crops and rich foliage. Midway we entered the district of Ramnuggur Dhumeree, held by Rajah Gorbuksh Sing under the security of Seoraj-od Deen, the person who attempted in vain to arrest the charge of the two regiments upon the Khyrabad Nazim by holding up the *sacred Koran* over his head. He met me on his boundary, and Nawab Allee and the Nazim of Baree Biswa took their leave. Nawab Allee's brother, Abud Allee, came to pay his respects to me yesterday evening. He is a respectable person in appearance, and a man of good sense. The landscape was, I think, on the whole richer than any other that I have seen in Oude; but I am told that it is still richer at a distance from the road, where the poppy is grown in abundance, and opium of the best quality made.*

* Opium sells in Oude at from three to eight rupees the seer, according to its quality. In our neighbouring districts it sells at fourteen rupees the seer, in the shops licensed by Government. Government, in our districts, get opium from the cultivators and manufacturers at three rupees and half the seer. The temptation to smuggle is great, but the risk is great also, for the police in our districts is vigilant in this matter.

Still lamenting the want of all architectural ornament to the scene, and signs of manufacturing and commercial industry, to show that people had property, and were able to display and enjoy it, and gradations of rank, I asked whether people invested their wealth in the loans of our Government. "Sir," said Bukhtawur Sing, "the people who reside in the country know nothing about your Government paper; it is only the people of the capital that hold it or understand its value. The landholders and peasantry would never be able to keep it in safety, or understand when and how to draw the interest."

"Do they spend more in marriage and other ceremonies than the people of other parts of India, or do they make greater displays on such occasions?"

"Quite the reverse, sir," said Seoraj-od Deen; "they dare not make any display at all. Only the other day, Gunga Buksh, the refractory landholder of Kasimgunge, attacked a marriage-procession in the village of—, carried off the bridegroom, and imprisoned him till he paid the large random demanded from him. In February last year Imam Buksh Behraleen, of Oseyree, having quarrelled with the Amil, attacked and carried off a whole marriage party to the jungles. They gave up all the property they had, and offered to sign bonds for more, to be paid by their friends for their ransom; but he told them that money would not do; that their families were people of influence, and must make the King's officers restore him to his estate upon his own terms, or he would keep them till they all died. They exerted themselves, and Imam Buksh got back his estate upon his own terms; but he still continues to rob and plunder. These crimes are to them diversions from which there is no making them desist."

"There are a dozen gang leaders of this class at present in the belt of jungle which extends westward from our right up to within fourteen miles of the Lucknow cantonments; and the plunder of villages, murder of travellers, and carrying off of brides and bridegrooms from marriage processions, are things of every-day occurrence. There are also in these parts a number of pansee bowmen, who not only join in the enterprises of such gangs as in other districts, but form gangs of their own, under leaders of their own caste, to rob travellers and plunder villages.

"Gunga Buksh of Kasimgunge has his fort in this belt of jungle, and he and his friends and relations take good care that no man cuts any of it down, or cultivates the land. With the gangs which he and his relatives keep up in this jungle, he has driven out the greater part of the Syud proprietors of the surrounding villages, and taken possession of their lands. After driving out the King's troops from the town of Dewa, and exacting ransoms from many of the inhabitants, whom he seized and carried off in several attacks, he, in October last, brought down upon it all the ruffians he could collect, killed no less than twenty-nine persons—chiefly Syuds and land proprietors—and took possession of the town and estate. The chief proprietor, Bakur Allee, was killed among the rest; and Gunga Buksh burnt his body, and suspended his head to a post in his own village of Luseya. He dug down his house and those of all his relations who had been killed with him, and now holds quiet possession of his estate."

This was all true. The Resident, on the application of Haffiz-od Deen, a native judicial officer of Moradabad district—one of the family which had lost so many members in this atrocious attack—urged strongly on the Durbar the necessity of punishing Gunga Buksh and his gang. The Ghunghor Regiment of Infantry, with a squadron of cavalry, and six guns, was sent out in October 1849, for the purpose, under a native officer. On the force moving out, the friends of Gunga Buksh at Court caused the commandant to be sent for on some pretext or other; and he has been detained at the capital ever since. The force has, in consequence, remained idle, and Gunga Buksh has been left quietly to enjoy the, fruits of his enterprise. The Amil having no troops to support his authority, or even to defend his person in such a position, has also remained at Court. No revenue has been collected, and the people are left altogether exposed to the depredations of these merciless robbers. The belt of jungle is nine miles long and four miles wide; and the west end of it is within only fourteen miles of the Lucknow cantonments, where we have three regiments of infantry, and a company of artillery.

February 22nd, 1850.—A brief history of the rise of this family may tend to illustrate the state of things in Oude. Khumma Rawut, of the pansee tribe, the great-grandfather of this Gunga Buksh, served Kazee Mahommed, the great-grandfather of this Bakur Allee, as a village watchman, for many years up to his death. He had some influence over his master, and making the most of this and of the clan feeling which subsisted among the pansees of the district, he was able to command the services of a formidable gang when the old Kazee died. He left a young family, and Khumma got possession of five or six villages out of the estate which the old Kazee left to his sons. The sons were too weak to resist the pansees, and when Khumma died he left them to his five sons:—1. Kundee Sing; 2. Bukhta Sing; 3. Alum Sing; 4. Lalsahae; 5. Misree Sing. As the family increased in numbers it has gone on adding to its possessions in the same manner, by attacking and plundering villages, murdering or driving off the old proprietors of the lands, and taking possession of them for themselves. Each branch of the family, as it separates from the parent stock, builds for itself a fort in one or other of the villages which belong to its share of the acquired lands. In this fort the head of each branch of the family resides with his armed followers, and sallies forth to plunder the country and acquire new possessions. In small enterprises each branch acts by itself; in larger ones two or more branches unite, and divide the lands and booty they acquire by amicable arrangement.

They seize all the respectable persons whom they find in the villages which they attack and plunder, keep them in prison, and inflict all manner of tortures upon them, till they have paid, or pledged themselves to pay, all that they have or can borrow from their friends, as their ransom. If they refuse to pay, or to pledge themselves to pay the sum demanded, they murder them. If they pay part, and pledge themselves to pay the rest within a certain time, they are released; and if they fail to fulfil their engagements, they and their families are murdered in a second attack. After the last attack above described upon Dewa, Gunga Buksh seized seven fine villages belonging to the family of Bakur Allee Khan, which they had held for many generations. He, Gunga Buksh, now holds no less than twenty-seven villages, all seized in the same manner, after the plunder and murder of their old proprietors. The whole of this family, descendants of Khumma Rawut, hold no less than two hundred villages and hamlets, all taken in the same manner from the old proprietors, with the acquiescence or connivance of the local authorities, who were either too weak or too corrupt to punish them, and restore the villages to their proper owners.*

* Kundee Sing had two sons, 1. Cheytun Sing; 2. Ajeet Sing. Cheytun Sing had two sons, 1. Sophul Sing; 2. Thakurpurshad. Sophul Sing had two sons, 1. Keerut Sing; 2. Jote Sing. Ajeet Sing had two sons, 1. Bhugwunt Sing; 2. Rutun Sing. Thakur Purshad, Bhugwunt Sing, and Rutun Sing, reside in a fort which they have built in Bhetae, four miles from Dewa, in the north-west border of the belt of jungle. They hold forty villages, besides hamlets, which they have taken from the old proprietors of the Dewa and Korsee estates. Thakur Purshad has another fort called Buldeogur, near that of Atursae, two coss south of Dewa; and Bhugwunt Sing has the small fort of Munmutpore, close to Bhetae. Bukta Sing had only one son, Bisram Sing, who had only one son, Gunga Buksh, who built the fort of Kasimgunge, on the north-eastern border of the same belt of jungle, two miles south of Dewa, and on the death of his father, he went to reside in it with his family and gang. He holds twenty-seven fine villages, with hamlets. Twenty of these he seized upon from six to twelve years ago; and the other seven he got after the attack upon Dewa, in October last. He has also a fort called Atursae, two coss south from Dewa; a mile west from Buldeogur. Alum Sing's descendants have remained peaceable cultivators of the soil in Dewa, and are, consequently, of too little note for a place in the genealogical table of the family.

Lalsahae had three sons, 1. Dheer Sing; 2. Bustee Sing; 3. Gokul Sing, all dead. Dheer Sing had two sons, Omed Sing and Jowahir Sing. Omed Sing had three sons, Dirgpaul Sing, Maheput Sing, and Gungadhur, who was murdered by Thakur Pershad, his cousin. Jowahir Sing had one son, Priteepaul Sing. Bustee Sing had two sons, Girwur Sing and Soulee Sing. Girwur Sing had two sons, Dhokul Sing and Shunker Sing. This branch of the family hold the forts of Ramgura and Paharpore, on the border of the jungle six miles south-west from Dewa, and twelve villages besides hamlets taken in the same manner from the old proprietors. Gokul Sing had two sons, Dulloo Sing and Soophul Sing. Dulloo Sing has one son. They reside with the families of Dheer Sing and Bustee Sing.

Misree Sing, the fifth son of Khumma, had three sons, 1. Boneead Sing; 2. Dureeao Sing; 3. name forgotten—all three are dead. Bonead

Sing had two sons, 1. Anoop Sing; 2. Goorbuksh Sing. Dureeao Sing had two sons, 1. Anokee Sing; 2. name forgotten. The third son of Misree Sing had three sons, 1. Mulung Sing; 2. Anunt Sing; 3. name forgotten— all three still live.

This branch of the family resides in Satarpore, one mile west from Kasimgunge, in this belt of Jungle, and two miles from Dewa, in a fortified house built by them. They have got a small fort, called Pouree, near this place. They form part of Gunga Buksh's gang, and share with him in the booty acquired.]

To record all the atrocities committed by the different members of this family in the process of absorbing the estates of their neighbours, and the property of men of substance in the countries around, would be a tedious and unprofitable task; and I shall content myself with mentioning a few that are most prominent in the recollection of the people of the district. About ten years ago, Gunga Buksh and his gang attacked the house of Lalla Shunker Lal, a respectable merchant of Dewa, plundered it, killed the tutor of his three sons, and carried them and their father off to his fort, where he tortured them till they paid him a ransom of nine thousand rupees. On their release they left Dewa, and have ever since resided in Lucknow. Two years after they attacked the village of Saleempore, two miles east from Dewa, killed Nyam Allee, the zumeendar, and seized upon his estate. About six years ago Munnoo, the son of Gunga Buksh, with a gang of near two thousand men, attacked the King's force in the town of Dewa, killed four sipahees, two artillery-men, and two troopers, and plundered the place. About six months ago this gang attacked the house of Ewuz Mahommed, in Dewa, plundered it, levelled it with the ground, and took off all the timbers to their fort of Kasimgunge. Soon after he made the attack in which he killed twenty-nine persons in Dewa, as above described.

Thakur Purshad, about fourteen years ago, attacked the village of Molookpore, two miles east from Dewa, plundered it, took possession of the land, seized and carried off the proprietor, Sheikh Khoda Buksh, and put him to death in his fort of Bhetae. Three years after he attacked the house of Gholam Mostafa, in Dewa, killed him, and seized upon all the lands he held. Three years ago he attacked the house of Janoo, a shopkeeper, plundered it, and confined and tortured him till he paid a ransom of two hundred and fifty rupees. Three months after he seized and carried off to his fort Roopun, another shopkeeper, and confined and tortured him till he paid a ransom of three hundred rupees. Last year he seized and took off Jhow Dhobee from Dewa, and extorted forty rupees from him. Six months ago he attacked a marriage-procession in Dewa, plundered it, took off the bridegroom, Omed Allee, and confined and tortured him till he paid eleven hundred and fifteen rupees. These men all levy black mail from the country around; and it is those only who cannot or will not pay it, or whose lands they intend to appropriate, that they attack. They created the jungle above described, of nine miles long by four wide, for their own evil purposes, and preserve it with so much vigilance, that no man dares to cut a stick, graze a bullock, or browse a camel in it without their special sanction; indeed, they are so much dreaded, that no man or woman beyond their own family or followers dares enter the jungle.

Omed Sing, fifteen years ago, invited to his house the four proprietors of the village of Owree, Gholam Kadir, Allee Buksh, Durvesh Allee, and Moiz-od Deen, residents of Dewa, and put them to death because they could not, by torture, be made to transfer their lands to him. He then seized their village, and built the fort of Rumgura Paharpore upon it. Omed Sing, Jowahir Sing, Dhokul Sing, and Soophul Sing all reside in this fort with the son of Dulloo Sing. This family of pansees, or, as they call themselves, Rawuts, form at present one of the most formidable gangs of robbers in Oude, and one of the most difficult to put down from their union and inveterate habit of plunder. They can always, at short notice and little cost, collect bands of hundreds of the same tribe and habit to join them in plunder and resistance to lawful authority.

On the 25th of February, 1838, Rajah Dursun Sing, then in charge of the district, wrote to the Durbar to say, "that Gunga Buksh of Dewa was the worst robber in the district, would pay no revenue, and instigated others to withhold theirs; that numerous complaints had been made against him to the Durbar by the people, and that he had been urged by Government to do his best to punish him; that he had long tried all he could to do so, but had not sufficient troops; that his evil deeds increased, however, so much, that he at last determined to run all risks, and on the 27th of that month, on Friday, he left Amaneegunge, and marched forty-eight miles without resting; and on Saturday, before daybreak, reached the fort of Kasimgunge, and invested it on all sides; that he found the fort large and strong, and surrounded with dense jungle; that he had only three guns with him, but, as the enemy were taken by surprise, he took all their outworks one after another; that the besieged got a crowd of their adherents to attack his force in the rear on Saturday night, that they might get off in the confusion, but his troops were ready to intercept them at all points; and, in attempting to cut his way through, Gunga Baksh was seized with all his followers, but the women and children were permitted to go their way; that a good many of the enemy had been killed, and he, Dursun Sing, had had one golundaz and five sipahees killed and ten persons wounded."

The King sent Dursun Sing a dress of honour with the title of Rajah on the 3rd of March, 1838, and ordered him to have the fort levelled with the ground. Dursun Sing, in reply, states that he had men employed in pulling down the fort; and, in reply to an order to send in a list of the property taken from the besieged, he states, on the 12th of March, 1838, that none whatever had been secured. Gunga Buksh soon bribed his way out of prison at Lucknow, returned to Kasimgunge, rebuilt his fort, and made it stronger than ever; and continued to plunder the country, and increase his landed possessions by the murder of the old proprietors. He became enlisted into the tribe of Rajpoots, and his sister was married to the Powar Rajah of *Etonda*, seven coss north from Lucknow. Jode

Sing, the present Rajah of that place, is her son; and he is associated with Gunga Buksh in his depredations. *Sahuj Ram*, of Pokhura, of the Ametheea tribe of Rajpoots, in the Hydergurh purgunna, on the right bank of the Goomtee river, married a daughter of Gunga Buksh's, and has a strong fort, called Raunee, thirty miles east from Lucknow. He is said to have been present at the murder of the twenty-nine persons at Dewa in October last, and to have had with him four hundred armed men and two guns. He and all his followers are notorious and inveterate robbers, like Gunga Buksh himself. The descendants of Khumma, the village watchman, have already built ten forts upon the lands which they have seized, and there are no less than seventy of these forts or strongholds within a circuit of ninety miles round Bhetae and Khasimgunge, the centre being not more than eighteen miles from the Lucknow cantonments.

The Minister having informed the Resident that, without some aid from British troops, it was impossible for him to put down or punish these atrocious murderers and robbers, who had so many mud-forts well garrisoned by their gangs, he, on the 26th of March, 1850, ordered a wing of the 2nd Battalion of Oude Local Infantry under Captain Boileau to join the force, consisting of, 1. A wing of the 2nd Oude Local Infantry; 2. Captain Barlow's regiment, with two nine-pounders and one eight-inch howitzer; 3. Nawab Allee's auxiliaries, two thousand men and three small guns; 4. Sufshikum Khan, the Amil of the district, with one thousand men and five guns; 5. Seoraj-od Deen, the Amil of Ramnuggur, with one hundred and fifty men and two guns; 6. Ghalib Jung, with one thousand foot soldiers, forty camel jinjals (tumbooraks), seven guns, and one hundred troopers, in an attack upon Kasimgunge. The different parts of this force had been so disposed as to concentrate upon and invest the fort at daybreak on the morning of that day. The surprise was complete.

Shells were thrown into the fort from Captain Barlow's guns, but Captain Boileau did not consider the force sufficient to take the fort and secure, the garrison, and wrote to request a reinforcement. The distance from Kasimgunge to the cantonments was twenty miles. A wing of the

10th Regiment Native Infantry, with two guns, was sent off under Captain Wilson; but the garrison had evacuated the fort and fled on the night of the 26th, and the wing was ordered to proceed direct to the fort of Bhetae, four miles nearer to the cantonments, which was to be invested by the same force on the morning of the 28th.

Captain Wilson had with him Lieutenant Elderton, as adjutant of the wing, and Ensigns Trenchard and Wish, with a native officer in charge of the two guns. They reached Bhetae at 7 A.M., were joined by the Bhetae force at 8 A.M., and the two forts of Bhetae and Munmutpore were forthwith invested. Munmutpore stood about three hundred yards to the west of Bhetae; and both forts were held by Thakur Purshad and Bhugwunt Sing, members of the same family of pansee robbers, and their gangs. Captain Wilson was the chief in command; and he, with his own and Captain Boileau's wing, took up his position on the north side of Bhetae, and placed Captain Barlow on the west side of Munmutpore. There was a deep dry ditch all round outside the outer wall, and a thick fence of bamboos inside. Between this fence and the citadel in both forts was a still deeper ditch. Between the fence of bamboos and the inner ditch was a small intricate passage, intersected by huts and trenches.

The wall of the citadel was about twenty feet high, and the upper part formed a parapet eight feet high, filled with loopholes for matchlocks. Between Bhetae and Munmutpore, midway, was a large bastion filled with matchlock-men, to keep open the communication and prevent an enemy from taking up any position between the two forts. The investing force was distributed all round, with orders to attack the nearest and weakest points as soon as Captain Wilson should commence his upon the main point, the northern face.

On the afternoon of the 29th, about half-past three, a small party of the garrison came out of the gate on the northern face, and appeared disposed to attack Captain Wilson's two nine-pounders, and a third gun, which had all three been advanced on to within a short distance of the gate. During this time Captain Barlow was throwing shells into both forts from his position to the west of Munmutpore. The subahdar-major had command of the advanced party in charge of Captain Wilson's three guns. He charged and drove back into the fort the small party which threatened his guns, and Captain Wilson hastily assembled all his and Captain Boileau's force, and followed to support the subahdar-major. Finding his officers and men all excited and anxious to push on into the fort, Captain Wilson unfortunately yielded to the impulse, and entered the outer gate with one of his two nine-pounders, in the hope of taking the place by a *coup-de-main*.

The garrison all retired into the citadel as he entered, and kept up a distressing fire upon the assailants as they went along the narrow passage between the bamboo fence and the ditch in search of a way into the citadel. Several rounds were fired from the gun, in the hope of making a breach in the wall, but the balls penetrated and lodged midway in the wall, without bringing down any part of it; and musketry was altogether useless against a thick parapet with loopholes, so slender on the outside and so wide within. The huts, which might have sheltered officers and men, were set fire to by accident, and tended to increase the confusion. The entrance to the citadel was over a narrow mud causeway, which the garrison had not had time to remove; but it was hidden from the assailants by a projection which they could not attain, and the men began to fall fast before the fire from the loopholes of the parapet.

On hearing the firing on Captain Wilson's side, the officers commanding the troops on the other three sides, commenced their attack on the nearest and seemingly weakest points, as before directed. Captain Barlow lost some men in an unsuccessful attempt to enter the fort of Munmutpore on the west side; but the auxiliary force of Nawab Allee effected an entrance on the east side of that fort. They were, however, arrested by the second ditch within, in the same manner as Captain Wilson's force had been, and a good many men were shot down in the same manner, in attempting to get over it. The force under Sufshikum Khan, on the east side of Bhetae, effected an entrance, but was arrested by the second ditch in the same manner, and lost many men. The enemy in Bhetae had eleven men killed and nineteen wounded, a good many of them from the shells thrown in by Captain Barlow. The loss of the enemy in Munmutpore was never ascertained.

After Captain Wilson had been engaged within the wall about three-quarters of an hour, and the ammunition of the gun had become exhausted. Lieutenant Elderton, who had behaved with great gallantry during the whole scene, and was standing in advance with Captain Boileau, received a shot in the neck, and fell dead by his side. Having lost so many men and officers in fruitless efforts to penetrate into the citadel, and seeing no prospect of carrying the place by remaining longer under the fire from the parapet, Captains Wilson and Boileau drew off their parties; but the bullocks which drew the gun had been all killed or wounded, and they were obliged to leave it behind with the bodies of the killed. The men attempted to draw off the gun; but so many were shot down from above that it was deemed prudent to abandon it. About midnight both garrisons vacated the forts, and retired unmolested through the jungle to the eastward, where Ghalib Jung's troops had been posted. There is good ground to believe that he connived at their escape, and purposely held back from the attack as a traitor in connivance with some influential persons in the Durbar.

The 10th Native Infantry had one European officer, Lieutenant Elderton, ten sipahees, and one calashee, killed; five native officers and twenty-two privates, wounded.

The 2nd Oude Local Infantry, six sipahees, and one calashee, killed; and seven native officers and thirteen privates, wounded.

The artillery had one native officer and nine privates wounded.

This reverse arose from the commandant's yielding to the impetuosity of his officers and sipahees, and attempting to take by a rush a strong fort whose defences he had never examined and knew nothing whatever about, as he had never before seen any place of the kind, or had one described to him. He and all his men had courage in abundance, but they wanted prudence.

Gunga Buksh and his son, Runjeet Sing, were afterwards taken, convicted before the highest tribunal in Oude, of the murder of the twenty-seven persons in Dewa, in October, 1849, and executed on the 18th of September, 1850. Thakur Purshad and his cousin, Bhugwunt Sing, remained at large, and at the head of their gang of robbers continued to plunder the country, and levy blackmail from landholders and village communities till the 1st of February 1851, though pressed by a force of one thousand infantry, fifty troopers, and some ten guns. On the morning of that day, Captain Hearsey, commanding a detachment of the Oude Frontier Police, who had been ordered to co-operate with this force in putting down this gang, took advantage of a dense fog, fell upon them, and with the loss of one non-commissioned officer killed, and three non-commissioned officers and three sipahees wounded, killed one of the chief leaders, Bhugwunt Sing, and twenty-two of their followers, wounded many more, and took eight prisoners, among them the son of the leader Bhugwunt Sing. The other two leaders, Thakur Purshad and Keerut Sing, were bathing at the time in the river Goomtee, and escaped by swimming across.

Rajah Bukhtawur Sing declares, that the taking of daughters from families of this caste by Rajpoots is one of the punishments inflicted upon them for the murder of their own. They will not condescend to give daughters in marriage to such persons; and they take daughters from them merely to get their money, and assistance on emergency in resisting the Government, and murdering and plundering its subjects.

This part of Oude, comprising the districts of Dureeabad Rudowlee, Ramnuggur Dhumeree, Dewa Jahangeerabad, Jugdispoor, and Hydergur, has more mud forts than any other, though they abound in all parts; and the greater part of them are garrisoned in the same way by gangs of robbers. It is worth remarking, that the children in the villages hereabout play at fortification as a favourite amusement, each striving to excel the others in the ingenuity of his defences. They all seem to feel that they must some day have to take a part in defending such places against the King's troops; and their parents seem to encourage the feeling. The real mud forts are concealed from sight in beautiful clusters of bamboos or other evergreen jungle, so that the passer-by can see nothing of them. Some of them are exceedingly strong, against troops unprovided with mortars and shells. The garrison is easily shelled out by a small force, or starved out by a large one; but one should never attempt to breach them with round shot, or take them by an escalade or a rush.

It is still more worthy of remark, that these great landholders, who have recently acquired their possessions by the plunder and murder of their weaker neighbours, and who continue their system of pillage, in order to acquire the means to maintain their gangs, and add to these possessions, are those who are most favoured at Court, and most conciliated by the local rulers; because they are more able and more willing than others to pay for the favours of the one, and set at defiance the authority of the other. They often get their estates transferred from the jurisdiction of the local governors to that of the person in charge of the Hozoor Tuhseel at Lucknow. Almost all the estates of this family of Rawuts have been so transferred.

Local governors cannot help seeing or hearing of the atrocities they commit, and feeling some *sympathy* with the sufferers; or at least some apprehension, that they may lose revenue by their murder, and the absorption of their estate; but the officer in charge of the Hozoor Tuhseel sees or hears little of what they do, and cares nothing about the sufferers as long as their despoilers pay him liberally. If the local governor reports their atrocities to Government, this person represents it as arising solely from enmity; and describes the sufferers as lawless characters, whom it is meritorious to punish. If the Court attempts to punish or coerce such characters, he gives them information, and does all he can to frustrate the attempt. If they are taken and imprisoned, he soon gets them released; and if their forts and strongholds have been taken and pulled down, he sells them the privilege of rebuilding or repairing them. It is exceedingly difficult at all times, and often altogether impossible, to get one of these robber landholders punished, or effectually put down, so many and so formidable are the obstacles thrown in the way by the Court favourite, who has charge of the Hozoor Tuhseel, and their other friends at the capital. Those who suffer from their crimes have seldom any chance of redress. Having lost their all, they are no longer in a condition to pay for it; and without payment nothing can be got from the Court of Lucknow.

February 23, 1850.—Badoosura, ten miles south-east over a plain covered with rich crops and fine foliage; soil muteear generally, but in some parts doomut; tillage excellent. Passed over some more sites of Bhur towns. The Oude territory abounds with these sites, but nothing seems to be known of the history of the people to whom they belonged. They seem to have been systematically extirpated by the Mahommedan conquerors in the early part of the fourteenth century. All their towns seem to have been built of burnt brick, while none of the towns of the present day are so. There are numerous wells still in use, which were formed by them of the finest burnt brick and cement; and the people tell me that others of the same kind are frequently discovered in ploughing over fields. I have heard of no arms, coins, or utensils peculiar to them having been discovered, though copper sunuds, or deeds of grant from the Rajahs of Kunoje, to other people in Oude, six hundred years ago, have been found. The Bhurs must have formed town and village communities in this country at a very remote period, and have been a civilized people, though they have not left a name, date, or legend inscribed upon any monument. Brick ruins of forts, houses, and wells, are the only relics to be found of these people. Some few of the caste are still found in the humblest grade of society as cultivators, police officers, &c., in Oude and other districts north of the Ganges. Up to the end of the thirteenth century their sovereignty certainly extended over what are now called the Byswara and Banoda districts; and Sultanpore, under some other name, appears to have been their capital. It was taken and destroyed early in the fourteenth century by Allah-od Deen, Sultan of Delhi, or by one of his generals, and named Sultanpore. Chandour was another great town of these Bhurs. I am not aware of any temples having been found to indicate their creed.*

* The Bhur Goojurs must, I conclude, have been of the same race.

The landholders, who have become leaders of gang-robbers, are more numerous here than in any other part of Oude that I have seen, save Bangur: but they are not here, as there, so strongly federated. The Amil is so weak, that, in despair, he connives at their atrocities and usurpations as the only means of collecting the Government revenue, and filling his own pockets. The pausee bowmen are here much more formidable than they are even in Bangur. There they thieve, and join the gangs of the refractory landholders; but here they have powerful leaders of their own tribe, and form formidable independent gangs. They sometimes attack and plunder villages, and spare neither age nor sex. They have some small strongholds in which they assemble from different villages over pitchers of spirits, made from the fruit of the mhowa tree, and purchased for them by their leaders; and, having determined upon what villages to attack, proceed at once to work before they get sober. Every town and village through which we pass has suffered more or less from their atrocities, and the people are in a continual state of dread.

In 1843, the pausees, who resided in the village of Chindwara, in the Dewa district, ran off to avoid being held responsible for the robbery of a merchant in the neighbourhood. They were pacified and brought back; but the landholder was sorely pressed by the Government collector to pay up his balance of revenue, and he, in turn, pressed the pausees to pay up the balances due by them for rents. They ran off again, but their families were retained by the landholder. The pausees gathered together all of their clan that they could muster from the surrounding villages, attacked the landholder's house, killed his mother, wife, four of his nephews, the wife of one of his nephews, two of the King's sipahees who attempted to defend them, and several of the landholder, Yakoob Husun's, servants, and plundered him of everything he had. The landlord himself happened to be absent on business, and was the only one of the family who escaped. In all twenty-nine persons were murdered by the pausees on that occasion. They were all permitted to come back and settle in the village, as if nothing had happened; the village was made over to another, and Yakoob Husun has ever since been supplicating in vain for redress at the King's gate.

About three miles from Badoosura, we passed from the Ramnuggur district into that of Dureeabad Rodowlee; but the above description is applicable to both, though in a somewhat less degree to Ramnuggur than to Dureeabad. It is equally applicable to the Dewa district, which we left on our right yesterday, midway between our road and Lucknow. There Gunga Buksh Chowdheree and his relatives have large gangs engaged in plundering towns, and seizing upon the lands of their weaker and more scrupulous neighbours. In the Dureeabad district, the leaders of gangs are chiefly of the Behraleea tribe of Rajpoots, so called after the district of Behralee, in which they reside.

I this morning asked Nowsing, a landholder of the Rykwar Rajpoot clan, who came to me, in sorrow, to demand redress for grievous wrongs, whether he did not think that all the evils they suffered arose from murdering their female infants. "No, sir, I do not." "But the greater part of the Rajpoot families do still murder them, do they not?" "Yes, sir, they still destroy them; and we believe that the father who preserves a daughter will never live to see her suitably married, or that the family into which she does marry will perish or be ruined." "Do you recollect any instances of this?" "Yes, sir, my uncle, Dureeao, preserved a daughter, but died before he could see her married; and my father was obliged to go to the cost of getting her married into a Chouhan family at Mynpooree, in the British territory. My grandfather, Nathoo, and his brother, Rughonath, preserved each a daughter, and married them into the same Chouhan families of Mynpooree. These families all became ruined; and their lands were sold by auction; and the three women returned upon us, one having two sons and a daughter, and another two sons. We maintained them for some years with difficulty, but this year, seeing the disorder that prevailed around us, they all went back to the families of their husbands. It is the general belief among us, sir, that those who preserve their daughters never prosper, and that the families into which we marry them are equally unfortunate."

"Then you think that it is a duty imposed upon you from above to destroy your infant daughters, and that the neglect and disregard of that duty bring misfortunes upon you?" "We think it must be so, sir, with regard to our own families or clan."

I am satisfied that these notions were honestly expressed, however strange they may appear to others. Habit has brutalized them, or rendered them worse than brutes in regard to their female offspring. They derive profit, or save expense and some mortification, by destroying them, and readily believe anything that can tend to excuse the atrocity to themselves or to others. The facility with which men and women persuade themselves of a religious sanction for what they wish to do, however cruel and iniquitous, is not, unhappily, peculiar to any class or to any creed. These Rajpoots know that the crime is detestable, not only to the few Christians they meet, but to all Mahommedans, and to every other class of Hindoos among whom they live and move. But the Rajpoots, among whom alone this crime prevails, are the dominant class in Oude; and they can disregard the feelings and opinions of the people around them with impunity. The greater part of the land is held by them, and in the greater part of the towns and villages their authority is paramount.

Industry is confined almost exclusively to agriculture. They have neither merchants nor manufacturers to form, or aid in forming, a respectable and influential middle class; and the public officers of the state they look upon as their natural and irreconcileable enemies. When the aristocracy of Europe buried their daughters alive in nunneries, the state of society was much the same as it now is in Oude. The King has prohibited both infanticide and suttee. The latter being essentially a public exhibition, the local authorities have continued, in great measure, to put down; but the former was certainly never more common than it is at present, for the Rajpoot landholders were never before more strong and numerous. That suttees were formerly very numerous in Oude is manifest from the numerous suttee tombs we see in the vicinity of every town and almost every village; but the Rajpoots never felt much interested in them; they were not necessary either to their pride or purse.*

* Suttee, infanticide, suicide, the maiming of any one, or making any one an eunuch, were all prohibited by the King of Oude, on the 15th of May, 1833, as reported to Government by the Resident on the 6th November, 1834. These prohibitions were reported to the Resident, by the King, on the 14th of June, 1833.

February 24th, 1850.—Dureeabad, ten miles south-east, over a plain of good soil—doomut and mutteear—covered with the same rich crops and fine foliage. There is at present no other district in Oude abounding so much in gang robbery and other crime as this of Dureeabad Rodoulee, in which the Amil, Girdhara Sing, is notoriously conniving at these crimes from a consciousness of utter inability to contend with the landholders who commit them, or employ men to commit them. Yet he has at his disposal a force that ought to be sufficient to keep in order a district five times as large. He has the Jannissar battalion of nujeebs, under Seetla Buksh at present; the Zoolfukar Sufderee battalion of nujeebs, under Bhow-od Dowlah, who never leaves Court; and the Judeed, or new regiment, consisting of a thousand men. He has nine guns, and a squadron of horse. Of the guns, five are on the ground, utterly useless; four will bear firing a few rounds. For these four he has bullocks, but they are not yet in condition. Of the seer and half of corn, drawn for each bullock per diem, only half a seer is given. Of the corps, more than one-half of the men are at Lucknow, in attendance upon Court favourites; and of the half present not one-third are fit for the work of soldiers.

The Amil rode by my side, and I asked him about the case of the marriage-procession. "Sir," said he, "what you heard from Seoraj-od Deen is all true. Imam Buksh had a strong fort in his estate of Ouseyree, five miles to our right, where he had a formidable gang, that committed numerous dacoitees and highway robberies in the country around. I was ordered to attack him with all my force. He got intimation, and assembled his friends to the number of five thousand. I had not half the number. We fought till he lost seventy men, and I had thirty killed and fifteen wounded. He then fled to the jungles, and I levelled his fort with the ground. He continued, however, to plunder, and at last seized the bridegroom and all the marriage party, and took them to his bivouac in the jungles. The family was very respectable, and made application to me, and I was obliged to restore him to his estate, where he has lived ever since in peace. I attacked him in November 1848, and he took off the marriage party in February following." "But," said a poor hackery driver, who was running along by my side, and had yesterday presented me a petition, "you forgot to get back my two carts and bullocks which he still keeps, and uses for his own purpose, though I have been importuning you ever since." "And what did he do to you when he got you into the jungles?" "He tied up and flogged all who seemed respectable, and worth something—such as merchants and shopkeepers—and poked them with red-hot ramrods till they paid all they could get, and promised to use all the influence and wealth of their families to force the Amil to restore him to his estate on his own terms." "And were the parties married after their release?" "Yes, sir, we were released in April, after the Amil had been made to consent to his terms; and they were married in May; but I could not get back my two carts." "And on what terms did you restore this Imam Buksh to his estate?" "I granted him a lease, sir," said the Amil, "at the same rate of five thousand rupees a-year which he had paid before."*

* This Imam Buksh, in April, 1850, went in disguise to the annual fair held at Bahraetch, in honour of the old saint. He was recognized by some of Captain Bunbury's soldiers, who attempted to seize him. He was armed with sword, spear, and shield, and defended himself as long as he could. Seeing no chance of escape, he plunged both sword and spear into his own belly, and died, though Captain Bunbury came up, had his wounds sewn up, and did all he could to save him.

Stopping to talk with the peasantry of a village who had come out to the roadside to pay their respects and see the procession, I asked them how, amidst such crimes and disorders, they could preserve their crops so well. "Sir," said they, "we find it very difficult and expensive to do so, and shall find it still more so when the crops are cut and stacked, or have been threshed and stored; then these gangs of robbers have it all their own way, and burn and plunder all over the country; we are obliged to spend all we have in maintaining watchmen for our fields." "But the pausee bowmen have an allowance for this duty, have they not?" "Yes, sir, they have all an allowance. Every cultivator, when he cuts his crop, leaves a certain portion standing for the pausee who has guarded it, and this we call his *Bisar*. Over and above this he has a portion of land from the proprietor or holder of the village, which he tills himself or gets tilled by others." "And they are strong and faithful watchmen, are they not?" "Yes, sir, they are; and though they will thieve and join gangs of robbers in any enterprise, they will never betray their trust. They consider it a *point of honour* not to trespass on fields or property under the guardianship of members of their own class with whom they are on good terms, or to suffer any persons whatever to trespass on what is under their own care. The money which we send to the treasuries is commonly intrusted to pausees, and their fidelity and courage may be relied upon. The gang robbers do little injury to our fields while the crops are green, for they take animals of hardly any kind with them in their enterprises; and having to move to and from their points of attack as quickly as possible, they could carry little of our crops with them; they are, too, afraid of the arrows of the pausee bowmen at night, if they venture to trespass upon our fields." "And are these pausee bowmen paid at the rate you mention all over the country?" "No, sir; they are in some parts paid in what is called the beega arhaeya, or two seers and half of grain from every beega. From a pucka beega they get pucka two and half seers; and from a kutcha beega, a kutcha two and half seers."* "Your crops, my friends, are finer than I have ever before seen them in Oude." "Yes, sir, they are very fine; but how we shall gather them God only knows, with such gangs of desperate robbers all around us. The alarm is sounded every night, and we have no rest. The Government authorities are too weak to protect us, or too indifferent to our sufferings; and we cannot afford to provide the means to protect ourselves."

* The kutcha measure bears the same relation to the pucka in weight as in land measurement.

As we went on, I asked the Amil what had become of Ahburun Sing, of Kyampore, the landholder who murdered his father to get possession of his estate, as mentioned in the early part of this Diary. "Ahburun Sing, sir, is still in possession of his estate of Kyampore, and manages it exceedingly well." "I thought he had taken to the jungles with his gang, like the rest of his class after such a crime, in order to reduce you to terms?" "It was his father, sir, Aman Sing, that was doing this. He was the terror of the country; neither road nor village was safe from him. He murdered many people, and plundered and burnt down many villages; and all my efforts to put him down were vain. At last I came to an understanding with his eldest son, who remained at home in the management of the estate, and was on bad terms with his father. He had confidential persons always about his father for his own safety; and when he was one night off his guard, he went at the head of a small band of resolute men, and seized him. He kept him in prison for six months, and told me that while so much plunder was going on around, he did not feel secure of keeping his father a single night; that many of his old followers wanted him back as their leader, and would certainly rescue him if he was not disposed of; that he could not put him to death, lest he should be detested by his clan as a parricide; but if I would make a feigned attack on the fort, he would kill him, and make it appear that he had lost his life in the defence of it. I moved with all the force I had against the fort, discharged many guns against the walls, made a feigned attempt at escalade; and in the midst of the confusion *Aman Sing was killed.* As soon as this was done, I returned with my force; the son remained in possession of the estate, and all the surrounding country was delighted to hear that so atrocious a character had been got rid of."

This was all true, and the Amil did not seem to think that any one who listened to him could suppose that he had done anything dishonourable in all this: he seemed to think that all must feel as he did, seeing his utter inability to cope with these baronial robbers in any other way, and the evils they every day inflicted upon the people. This Aman Sing was the most formidable of these robbers in this district, and the high road from Lucknow to Fyzabad was for some time closed by his gang. Of those whom he robbed, he used to murder all who appeared likely to be able to get a hearing at Court or at the Residency.

The Behraleea Rajpoots, of the Soorujpore Behreyla purgunna, are now the most formidable and inveterate robbers and plunderers in the district. The Rajah of this estate, Singjoo, was for some years the most formidable robber in Oude. He had taken a dislike to the family of a sipahee of the Governor-General's bodyguard; and, in an evil hour, he buried the sipahee's father, and some members of his family, alive. Strong remonstrances were made through the Resident, and Man Sing, the son of Dursan Sing, who has been already mentioned in this diary, had orders to seize him. In March, 1845, he made a march of forty miles at the head of five hundred active and brave men; and, on the night of the 20th of that month, reached the gate of the fort of Soorujpore, broke it open, entered, killed and wounded fifty of the Rajah's men, and lost five of his own.

The Rajah escaped and took shelter in the fort of Goura. After taking possession of the fort, eight guns, and some elephants, and releasing two hundred unhappy prisoners, Man Sing followed the Rajah to Goura, where he was joined by Captain Magness and his corps. The gate of this fort was giving way before Man Sing's pickaxemen, when Singjoo surrendered. He was taken to Lucknow, and there died in gaol. The village, in which his father had been buried alive, Hukkamee, was given to the sipahee, and is still held by the family;* but they are a good deal worried in the possession by the widow of the old Rajah, who still lives at Soorujpore, and would be as formidable as her late husband was if she could.

* In the interval, during which Singjoo held this village, he had added to its boundaries a good deal of land belonging to himself and others, under the impression that he was secure in the hereditary possession. The sipahee's family seized upon all these lands, while they paid Government only the old rate of revenue. The widow of Singjoo has been ever since trying to recover them, in the usual way, by night attacks, and a good many lives have been lost on both sides, but most on the side of the sipahee's family. December 4th, 1851.

Seodeen, another leader of the same tribe, had been seized in the same manner by Man Sing's father, Dursun Sing, in October, 1830; and soon after three of his nephews were seized, and all four died in gaol at Lucknow; but Chunda and Indul, the brothers of these three men, are still among the most formidable robbers of the district. Hardly a night passes without their plundering some village or other, though Chunda continues to hold his estate, which yields 2250 rupees a-year, under the security of Seetla Buksh, the commandant of the Jannissaree battalion, for the payment of four hundred and fifty rupees a-year. The other robbers of the Dureeabad Rodowlee district, most formidable, are—

1. Imambuksh, above described, as having seized the marriage party. In October last he attacked the town of Syud Mahomedpore, killed three of the Syud proprietors, and plundered it of all he could find. In the interval between his being driven out of his stronghold and restored, he attacked and plundered no less than twelve villages, in the same purgunna of Bussooree Mowae. In one of them, Myrmow,

belonging to Ameer Chowdheree, he killed no less than twelve of the inhabitants. He still keeps up his gang, and plunders, though restored to his estate on his own terms.*

* The death of this robber, Imam Buksh, has been already described in a note.

2. Junuck Sing, Behraleea, and his brother, Jeskurun, only twenty days ago, attacked, plundered, and burnt down the town of Meeangunge, through which we passed this morning, and carried off all the inhabitants from whom they thought they could extort any ransom. Only two days ago, they attacked and plundered the village of Bhojpore, belonging to Soorujbulee Canoongo, one of the most respectable men in the district; and cut off the hands of six persons, one of whom died from loss of blood. The next day they attacked and plundered Gorawa, a village belonging to the same person, and burnt it down. Two of the inhabitants were severely wounded, and many bullocks perished in the flames. Within the last year they have taken off more than two thousand head of cattle from the purgunna of Soorujpore Behreyla, in which these villages are situated. Their chief associates in the crimes they commit every day are Chunda and Indul, their clansmen above named.

3. Daood Khan, zumeendar of Sundona, in Mowae Bussooree. He has murdered several of his co-sharers in the estate, and taken their lands—frightened out others, and taken theirs, and at the head of his band of ruffians he robs on the highway, and plunders villages.

4. Benee Sing Kana, Rajpoot of Deeh, in the Mohlara purgunna. He is blind of one eye, and has a small but formidable gang. In November, 1850, the native collector of Mohlara, sent a detachment of one hundred men, accompanied by Seonath Sing, a co-sharer of Benee Sing, in the village of Deeh, and Oree Sing, a sipahee, in Captain Orr's Frontier Police, to attack his small gang in their stronghold at Atgowa, in the Rodowlee purgunna. They reached the place at the dawn of day, and forthwith commenced the attack. Benee Sing and

his men made a stoat defence. Rajah Man Sing came up, and great numbers of the armed peasantry joined in the attack. They took the place about nine o'clock; but Benee Sing, with fourteen of his stoutest men, defended his house as a citadel till morning, when the house was set fire to by the assailants. One of the fourteen was burnt and disabled, when Benee Sing and the remaining thirteen rushed out, sword in hand, to sell their lives as dearly as possible. Benee Sing and twelve of the thirteen were killed; and the thirteenth at last threw down his arms, and called for quarter. He got it, and was saved. Six of his men had before been killed in defending the place. Man Sing had three men wounded and one killed; three more of the assailants were killed, and seven wounded. The head of the "one-eyed robber" was sent in to the king, and was received with much joy.

5. Jeskurun Behraleea, zumeendar of Kiteya, in Soorujpore.
6. Rughbur Behraleea, of Kiteya, an associate of Imam Buksh and Chunda. Four months ago his gang seized two carts laden with valuable property belonging to Seodeen subahdar, of the Honourable Company's service. Through the interposition of the Resident they were restored fifteen days ago.
7. Jugurnath *Chuprassee*, a bhala soltan Rajpoot. This is one of the most formidable of the leaders of banditti in this and the adjoining district of Jugdeespore. He and his elder brother, Surubdowun Sing, were chuprassees on the establishment of Captain Paton, when he was the First Assistant at Lucknow, and had charge of the Post-office, in addition to his other duties. A post-office runner was one night robbed on the road, and Jugurnath was sent out to inquire into the circumstances. The Amil of the district gave him a large bribe to misrepresent the case to his master; and as he refused to share this bribe with his fellow-servants, they made known his manifold transgressions to Captain Paton, who forthwith dismissed him. Surubdowun Sing was soon after dismissed for some other offence, and they both retired to their estate of Oskamow, in the Jugdeespore district.

This estate comprised fifteen villages. They obtained the leases of these villages by degrees, through the influence which their position at the Residency gave them. As soon as they got the lease of a village, they proceeded to turn out all the old proprietors and cultivators, in order the better to secure possession in perpetuity; and those among them of the military class, fought "to the death," to retain or recover possession of their rights. To defend what they had iniquitously acquired, Jugurnath and his brothers collected together bands of the most desperate ruffians in the country, and located them in the several villages, so as to be able to concentrate and support each other at a concerted signal. The ousted proprietors attacked only those who presumed to reside in or cultivate the lands of which they had been robbed; but Jugurnath and his brethren were less scrupulous; and as they could afford to pay such bands in no other way, they gave them free licence to plunder all the villages around, and all travellers on the highway. Their position and influence at the Residency enabled them to deter the local authorities from exposing their iniquities; and they went on till all the villages became waste, and converted into dens of robbers.

They were, in all, six brothers, and they found their new trade so profitable and exciting, that they all became leaders of banditti, by profession, long before the dismissal of the two brothers from the Residency, though no one, I believe, ventured to prefer charges against them to the Resident or the Durbar. Soon after their dismissal, however, Jugurnath one night attacked and murdered his eldest brother, Surubdowun Sing, in order to get the whole estate to himself, and put his widow and daughter into prison. His other four brothers became alarmed, separated from him, and set up each his separate gang. But Jugurnath contrived soon after, in a dark night, to shoot the third brother, Himmut, dead, with one ball through the chest. Purmode Sing, the youngest brother, was soon after shot dead by some villager, whose cattle he was driving off in a night attack. Bhugwunt Sing the fourth, and Byjonath, still survive, and have gangs of their own, afraid to trust themselves with Jugurnath, who has built two forts, Oskamow and Futtehpore, in the Jugdeespore district, and a third in two small villages, which he has lately seized upon and made waste, in the Rodowlee district, in order that he may have a stronghold to fly to when pressed by the governors of other districts.

They pay no rent or revenue to Government for any of the villages they hold. The king's officers are afraid to demand any from them. They have plundered a great many villages, and are every month plundering others. They have murdered a great many persons of both sexes and all ages, and tortured more into paying ransoms in proportion to their supposed means. Jugurnath is still the terror of the surrounding country, and a reward of five hundred rupees has been offered for his apprehension.*

* See note to Chapter VI., Vol. II., on the capture of Maheput Sing. A reward of one thousand rupees has since been offered for Jugurnath's arrest. See in Chapter IV., Vol. II:, an account of his desertion of his master, Captain Paton. He is still at large, and plundering. December 4th, 1851.

8. Moorut Sing, of *Kiteya*, which has eleven small villages depending upon it, all occupied by Rajpoot robbers. Nowgowa, in Mohlara, in Rodowlee, on the left bank of the Goomtee river, twenty miles below Lucknow, has, in the same manner, twelve villages depending upon it, all occupied by Rajpoots, who rob, or shelter robbers, when pursued from the east. On the opposite bank is the village of Kholee, in the Hydergurh purgunna, held by Surfraz Chowdheree, and occupied by Brahmans and Musulmans, who shelter robbers in the same way. When they are pressed in Nowgowa they take shelter in Kholee, and when pressed in Kholee they take shelter in Nowgowa. All the robbers above named find shelter in these villages when pursued, and share their plunder with the inhabitants.

8. Bhooree Khan. The great-grandfather of Bhooree Khan, Rostam Khan. was the leader of a large gang of Musulman freebooters. The estate of Deogon, containing thirty-seven villages, belonged to a family of Bys Rajpoots. Rostam Khan and his gang seized upon them all, and turned out the Rajpoot proprietors, and by force made three of them

Musulmans, Kanhur, Bhooree, Geesee; and all their descendants are of the same creed.

Imam Buksh, the father of Bhoree Khan, built a fort in Deogon, which the *family* still held. In 1829, Rajah Dursun Sing took the mortgage of the estate for twenty-eight thousand one hundred and ten rupees, to enable Imam Buksh to liquidate a balance of revenue due to Government. When the time of payment came, in 1832, Imam Buksh could pay nothing; and he transferred the estate to Dursun Sing, on a deed of sale or bynama. He continued to manage the estate for Dursun Sing in farm; but, falling in balance, he was put into confinement, where he remained till he died, three years after, in the year 1842. Bhooree Khan was then a boy, but he continued to receive the usual perquisites from the estate while Dursan Sing held it. In the year 1846, the governor of the district, Wajid Allee Khan, took the estate from Dursun Sing's family, and made it over to Bhooree Khan for a present of five thousand rupees. He ceased to pay the Government demand, collected a gang, and became a leader of banditti. He plundered all the people around, and all travellers on the road, seized and confined all who seemed likely to be able to pay ransom, and tortured and maimed them till they did pay; and those who could not or would not pay, he put to cruel deaths. The thirty-six villages on his estate became deserted by all save his followers, and those whom he could make subservient to his purposes, as robbers and murderers.

Ousan Opudeea resided at the village of Etapore, in the estate of Deogon, and possessed and cultivated lands in that and other villages around, for which he paid an annual rent of five hundred and ninety-nine rupees. In 1846, Bhooree Khan demanded from Ousan an increase of one hundred and fifty rupees, which he paid. The year after 1847, he demanded a further increase of the same amount, which he paid. He was then summoned to appear before Bhooree Khan, and was on his way when told that he would be seized with all his family, and tortured. He, in consequence, took his family to the village of Patkhoree. Bhooree Khan followed with a gang of several hundred men, and two guns, attacked, plundered, and burnt down his house, and fifteen bullocks and buffaloes perished in the flames. One hundred and fifty head of cattle belonging to the village were taken off by the gang. Dwarka, one of Ousan's sons, was killed in defending the house; and the other two, Davey, aged sixteen, and Seochurun, aged seventeen, were seized, bound, and taken off to the jungle, with Ramdeen, Ousan's nephew, and many others of the respectable inhabitants of the village. After exacting a ransom from all the rest, he let them go; but retained the two sons of Ousan, and demanded twelve hundred rupees for their ransom. Ousan had lost all his property in the attack, and could raise no more than seven hundred rupees among his relatives and friends. This would not satisfy Bhooree Khan, who, after torturing and starving the boys for twelve months, and taking the seven hundred rupees, took them to the jungle of Gaemow, with fetters on their legs, and bamboo collars round their necks. He there had them tied to trees, and after firing at them as targets, for some time, with bows and arrows, he had them cut to pieces with swords, and then seized upon all the lands which their father held.

In 1848, Bhooree Khan attacked and plundered the house of Peer Khan, in Khanseepoor in Deogon, and bound and carried him off with his two brothers, Ameer Khan and Jehangeer Khan. He had them beaten with sticks, and caused small iron spikes to be driven up under their nails, and their eyelids to be sewn up with needle and thread, and their beards to be burned, till he extorted from them a ransom of eight hundred rupees.

While they were thus confined and being tortured, they saw four travellers brought in by the gang, and tortured and beaten to death, because they could not pay the ransom demanded from them.

Bhoree Khan, in this month of August 1848, attacked the house of Sirdar Khan, an invalid naek of the 36th Regiment of Bengal Native Infantry, and, after robbing it, burnt it to the ground, and bound and carried off to his fort in Deogon, Sirdar Khan himself and his three sons, Khoda Buksh, Allah Buksh, and Allee Buksh; the first fourteen years of age, the second eight, and the third seven years. He tortured all three, and demanded a ransom of nineteen hundred rupees. This sum was borrowed and paid by Jehangeer Khan, the brother of the naek, and the naek was released. Bhooree Khan would not, however, release either of the sons till he got five hundred rupees more; but Sirdar Khan was unable to procure this further sum, and, in April 1849, Bhooree Khan had two of the boys, Khoda Buksh and Alla Buksh, tied to trees and shot to death with arrows, for the amusement of his gang. They were then hacked with swords, and their bodies were thrown into a ditch, whence he would not permit their friends to remove them for burial. Sirdar Khan became for a time deranged on hearing of the sufferings of his sons, and wandered about the country. Bhooree Khan, with his gang, again attacked the village, and burned it all down, and drove off all the cattle, including all that Sirdar Khan possessed. He recovered, and changed his residence to the village of Deokalee. Bhooree Khan still retained the third son, Allee Buksh, alias Pulleen, and he is still in prison.*

* The Resident effected the release of the third son, Allee Buksh, in January, 1851, through the aid of Captain Orr, of the Frontier Police.

Sirdar Khan's ancestors were the Rajpoot proprietors of the estate of Deogon, and were forcibly converted to Mahommedanism by Bhooree Khan's ancestors when they seized upon the estate. Sirdar Khan cultivated eighteen beegahs of land in the village of Salteemow, in Deogon, for which he had long paid thirty-six rupees a year rent. Bhooree Khan demanded sixty-five a-year before the attack, and this sum Sirdar Khan paid, but it had no effect in softening the robber leader.

In the year 1847, soon after he took possession of the estate, Bhooree Khan sent a gang under the command of his cousin, Mungul Khan, to attack the house of Dulla, the most opulent and respectable merchant of the district, who resided in the town of Mukdoompore. Dulla had two sons, Nychint and Pursun Sing. After plundering the house, the gang seized Dulla, his son Nychint, Golbay the son of Pursun Sing, and

Ajoodheea the son of Nychint. Pursun Sing, the other son of the old merchant, had gone off to the Governor of the district, Rajah Incha Sing. to adjust his annual accounts. The females of the family got out through the back-door of the female apartments, and escaped to the village of Etwara, in the Jugdeespore district, where they had a residence. All the valuables had been buried in a pit in the house, some ten feet deep, and the females had no time to take them up.

The old man, his son Nychint, and his two sons, were sent off to Bhooree Khan, who, on learning that the valuables had not been found, came with fifty more armed men, accompanied by Baboo Mudar Buksh, the tallookdar of Silha in Jugdispore, his own agent Muheput, and a Brahmin prisoner named Cheyn, who knew Dulla, and the wealth he possessed. He brought with him the merchant's son Nychint, and commanded him to point out the place in which the valuables lay concealed. He would not do so, and Bhooree Khan then drove four tent-pins into the ground in the courtyard, placed Nychint on his face, and tied his hands and feet to these pegs. He then had him burnt into the bones with red-hot ramrods, but the young man still persisted in his refusal. He had then oil boiled in a large brass pot which they found in the house, and poured it over him till all the skin of his body came off. He became insensible for a time, and when he recovered his senses he pointed out the spot. Gold and silver ornaments and clothes of great value, and brass utensils belonging to the family, or held as pledges for money due to the old man, were taken up, with one hundred and fifty matchlocks and the same number of swords. They found also many pits, containing several thousand maunds of grain. The valuables, and as much of the grain as he could find carriage for, Bhooree Khan and his gang carried off, and the rest of the grain he gave to any one who would take it. The value of the whole plunder was estimated at one hundred and fifty thousand rupees.

Nychint was unbound, but died that night, and the body was made over to the Brahmin, Cheyn, who had now become a Mussulman. He took it to the jungle, where he had it burnt with the usual ceremonies.

Bhooree Khan still detained Ajodheea, the son of Nychint, and Golbay, the son of Pursun Sing, and demanded a further ransom for them, but he released Dulla, who came home and died of grief and of the tortures inflicted upon him in less than a month after. Cheyn, Dabey Sookul, and Forsut, all Brahmins of Mukdoompoor, were witnesses to the tortures inflicted upon Nychint, and to the plunder of the house. He kept Dulla's grandsons for a year more, with occasional tortures, but the surviving son, Pursun Sing, had nothing more to give, and no one would give or lend him anything. Golbay, his son, at last contrived to get a letter conveyed to him, stating that he was now less carefully guarded than he had been; that he and his cousin, Ajodheea, were sent to take their meals with a bearer, who lived in a hamlet on the border of the jungle, where they were guarded by only four pausee bowmen, and if his father could come with fifty armed men, and surprise them at a certain hour, he might rescue them. He assembled fifty men from surrounding villages, and at the appointed time, before daybreak, he surprised the guard, and rescued his son and nephew.

Gunga Purshad, son of Chob Sing, canoongo of Silha, in Deogon, left the place when Bhooree Khan took to plundering, and went off, in 1847, with his family to reside at Budulgur, a village held by Allee Buksh, a mile distant. A month after he had settled in that place, Bhooree Khan came with his gang, surrounded his house at night, plundered it, and seized and took off his brother, Bhowanee Purshad, two younger brothers, and his, Gunga Purshad's, daughter and son, with Gowree Lall and Gunesh Purshad, his relations, who had come on a visit to congratulate him on the prudence of his change of residence. Gunga Purshad was absent at the time on business. All the prisoners were taken to the jungles and tortured with red-hot iron ramrods, and put into heavy fetters. He demanded a ransom of nine hundred and fifty rupees for all. Gunga Purshad sold all he had except some cows and bullocks, and collected four hundred rupees, and his relation's clubbed together and raised one hundred more. The five hundred were sent to Bhooree Khan, and he took them and released all but Bhowanee Purshad. His two younger brothers collected the cows and bullocks, and went with them to Mukdoompoor, in the hope of being allowed to till their lands; but Bhooree Khan and his gang came, seized and sold all the cows and bullocks they had saved, plundered them of everything, and took their lands from them. They all fled once more, and went to reside at Putgowa. At Mukdoompoor, Bhowanee Purshad had Bhowanee Purshad flogged so severely that he fell down insensible, and he then had red-hot iron spikes thrust into his eyes, and a few days after he died in confinement of his sufferings. The value of the property taken from the family, besides the five hundred rupees' ransom, was one thousand rupees. He, about the same time, seized and carried off from Mukdoompoor Gunga Sookul, a Brahmin, tortured him to death, and threw his body into the river.

About the same time, August 1847, he seized and carried off Cheyn, a Brahmin of Mukdoompoor, son of Bhowanee Buksh. He had come to him to pay the year's rent for the lands he held in that village. After paying his own rents and those of others who were afraid to put themselves into Bhooree Khan's power, and had sent by Cheyn all that was due, he demanded from him a ransom of four hundred rupees. He could give no more, and was put under a guard and tortured in the usual way. As he persisted in declaring his inability to pay more, a necklace of cow's bones was put round his neck, and one of the bones was thrust into his mouth, and the blood of a cow was thrown over him, from which he became for ever an outcast from his religion. He expected to be put to death, but a friend conveyed to him the sum of ten rupees, which he gave to the robbers employed to torture him, and they spared his life. His son had taken shelter in the village of Pallee, whence he sent a pausee bowman, named Bhowaneedeen, to inquire after *him*, and offered him ninety rupees if he would rescue his father. The pausee pledged himself to Bhooree Khan to pay the money punctually, and Cheyn was released. But Bhooree Khan had cut down all the crops upon the lands, and taken them away, and cut down also the five mango-trees which stood upon his land and had been planted by his ancestors. During his confinement, Cheyn saw Bhooree Khan torture and murder many men, and dishonour many respectable women, whom he had seized in the same way.

In the same month, August 1847, Bhooree Khan seized Sudhae, the son of Tubbur Khan, of Salteemow, in Deogon, and his (Sudhae's) two sons, Surufraz and Meerun Buksh, and took them to the jungle. Sadhae had paid him the eighty rupees rent due for the land he tilled, but Bhooree Khan demanded one hundred rupees more; and when he could not pay he made him over to the Jumogdar, to whom he had become pledged for the payment of a certain sum. The Jumogdar had him beaten till he saw that nothing could be beaten out of him, when he let him go to save the cost of keeping him. Bhooree Khan became very angry, and, with his gang, attacked and plundered the house of Sudhae's brother, Badul Khan, in Salteemow, with whom Sudhae lived. The two brothers and their families expected this attack, and escaped unhurt, and fled, but they lost all their property.

Bhooree Khan then ordered one of his followers, Mirdae, to take Surufraz to a tank outside the village and cut off his nose. He took out at the same time Bukhtawur, a Brahmin, and cut off his nose first. Mirdae then ordered a Chumar, of Deogon, to cut off the nose of Surafraz, and standing over him with a sword, told him to cut it off deep into the bone. Surufraz prayed hard for mercy, first to Bhooree Khan and then to Mirdae; but his prayers were equally disregarded by both. The Chumar cut off his nose with a rude instrument into the bone, and with it-all his upper lip. He was then let go; but he fell down, after going a little distance, from pain and the loss of blood, and was there found by his uncle, Badul Khan, who had gone in search of him. He was taken home, but died the same night. His brother, Meerun Buksh, was soon after released for a ransom of fifty rupees.

Golzar Khan, sipahee of the Dull Regiment, in the King of Oude's service, tilled some lands in the village of Mukdoompore, for which he paid rent to Bhooree Khan. In 1847 he first extorted from him double the rent agreed upon, then seized all the crops, and plundered his house, and lastly seized the sipahee's sister, and had her forcibly married to his servant and relative, Mungul Khan.

In 1846 Bhooree Khan attacked the house of Allah Buksh of Gaemow, in Deogon, plundered it, killed his brother, Meerun Buksh, cut off the hands of his relative, Peer Buksh, and wounded three other relatives who happened at the time to be on a visit with his family. The articles of property that were taken off by Bhooree Khan and his gang consisted of five horses and mares, fifteen matchlocks, four maunds of brass utensils, three hundred and twenty-five maunds of grain, five swords, four boxes of clothes, fifteen cows and bullocks, five hundred and forty rupees in money. The houses of all the rest of the village community were plundered in the same manner. They cut down all the mango and mhowa trees belonging to the family, as well as all those belonging to other people of the village.

In 1847 he attacked the house of Akber Khan, in the village of Kanderpore, in Deogon; and after plundering it, he bound and carried off his son, Rumzam, a lad of fifteen years of age; and the year after, 1848, he again attacked his house, and seized and took off his brother, Wuzeer Khan. He has them still in confinement under torture, because Akber Khan cannot get the sum demanded for their ransom; and all applications for their release to the Government authorities have been disregarded.*

* The Resident could not effect the release of these two persons, the son and brother of Akber Khan, till January, 1851.

In the month of August, 1848, Pransook, a Rajpoot, and Lullut Sing, his cousin, of Booboopore, in Rodowlee, went to purchase a supply of bhoosa for their cattle to Mukdoompore, in the Deogon estate, and were there seized by Aman Sing, an agent of Bhooree Khan, who pretended that they had given shelter to some of the cultivators who had fled from Deogon, and demanded their surrender. They protested that they had never seen any such cultivators, and knew nothing whatever about them. They were bound and taken off to Deogon to Bhooree Khan, who had them both put into the stocks. After having been in the stocks for five days, they were again taken to Bhooree Khan, who ordered them to produce the cultivators, or pay a ransom of one hundred and five rupees. They were then taken back to prison, and confined for eighteen days more; and having no food supplied them, they were obliged to sell all the clothes they wore to procure a scanty supply.

To frighten them, Bhooree Khan one day ordered his followers to make outcasts in their presence of two respectable men whom he had in prison, Deena Sing, a Chowan Rajpoot of Jooreeum, and a Brahmin of Poorwa, a small hamlet near Deogon, while he sat on the roof of his house to look on. One of his Musulman followers forced open Deena Sing's mouth, and spit into it; and the others tied the bones of a neelgae round the neck of the Brahmin, by which both of them were deprived of their caste. They then told Pransook and Lullut Sin that they would be served in the same manner unless they paid the ransom demanded. They became alarmed, and sent to their friends to request them earnestly to borrow all they could, and send it for their ransom. Their cousin, Sheobuksh Sing Jemadar, an invalid pensioner from the 2nd Regiment of Bengal Native Infantry, collected one hundred and eighteen rupees, and sent them. Bhooree Khan took one hundred and five for himself, and his servants took thirteen, and they were released; but they were made to swear on the tomb of the saint Shah Sender that they would not complain of the treatment they had received, and had their swords and shields taken from them. They had been confined twenty-seven days.

In 1846 Davey Sookul, a Brahmin, cultivated land in Mukdoompore, for which he paid an annual rent of seventy-one rupees. In consequence of murders and robberies perpetrated by Bhooree Khan and his gang, he went off with his family to reside at Budulgur, under the protection of Rajah Allee Buksh, a mile distant. He had witnessed the murder of Bhowanee Purshad and the torture of many other persons. One morning his brother, Gunga Purshad, returned to Mukdoompore to gather some mangoes from trees there planted by their ancestors. He was there seized by Bhooree Khan and his gang, who were lying in wait for him. They demanded a ransom of three hundred rupees, which Davey Sookul could not raise. He kept Gunga Purshad in prison for four months, and had him tortured every day. Finding that the money was not forthcoming, Bhooree Khan had a firebrand thrust into one of his eyes, and then had him flogged with bunches of sticks till he died. Khoda Buksh, of Kurteepore, one of the followers of Bhooree Khan, went and reported this to his brother and widow, who wept over the tale of his sufferings. His brother, Boodhoo Sookul, a sipahee of the 45th Regiment, presented a petition to the Resident, describing these atrocities, and praying redress, but none was afforded.

Bukhtawur, son of Kaushee, a Brahmin, tilled lands in Deogon, for which he paid an annual rent of sixty-eight rupees. In 1847 Bhooree Khan demanded double that sum; and when he could not pay, he seized and sold all the stock on the land, and seized and took off to the jungles Bukhtawur and his two brothers, Heeralall and Jankee, and seized upon all their lands, and all the property they had to the value of five hundred rupees. He kept them in prison for six months, and then had Bukhtawur's nose cut off by a Chumar, because he could not pay him the ransom demanded. The nose of Surufraz was cut off at the same time, as above described, and he died in consequence. Bukhtawur's two brothers made their escape three months afterwards.

In 1848 he attacked the house of Choupae Tewaree, a Brahmin of Ottergow, and after plundering it he took off the son of Choupae, then thirteen years of age, and his, the son's, wife, and his young son and his wife, and tortured all, till Choupae borrowed and begged all he could, and paid the ransom demanded.

Purotee Aheer tilled sixteen beegahs of land in Deogon, for which he paid an annual rent of thirty-two rupees a-year. As soon as Bhooree Khan got the estate from Maun Sing, in November, 1846, he demanded double the sum, and exacted it. He, in 1848, demanded two hundred and fifty, seized Purotee, sold all his cows and bullocks, sixteen in number, and other property, and then released him. Purotee then sent off secretly all his family to Duheepore, two miles distant; but Bhooree Khan sent off his servants, Bundheen and Bugolal pausees, to trace them. They seized his two daughters, one fourteen and the other ten years of age, and his son Nihal's wife, and his son, then only four years of age. Bhooree Khan ravished the two girls, and then released them, with Nahal's wife and her little son. Purotee saw the noses of Bukhtawar and Surafraz cut off while he was in confinement, and saw Bhooree Khan put them on a plate, which he placed in a recess in the wall. It was in March, 1848, when he went to pray that his daughters might be released after they had been ravished. The family went to reside in the village of Mohlee, in Khundara, but have all been turned out of their caste in consequence of the dishonour of his daughters.

In the same year he attacked the house of Foorsut Aheer of Dehpal ka Poorwa, made him prisoner, and tortured him till he paid eight hundred rupees. After this he made his escape; but Bhooree Khan seized and sold all his bullocks, cows, and buffaloes, and stores of grain.

In 1845 Bhoore Khan and his gang attacked the house of Buldee Sing, subahdar in the Honourable Company's service, in the village of Ghurwae, and, after plundering him of all the property they could find, they seized him and his wife, and took them to the jungles, where they tortured them till they gave all they could borrow or beg to the amount of many thousand rupees.

About the same time he seized and carried off Eesuree Purshad, a Brahmin, who had fled from Palpore, in Deogon, and gone for shelter to the Bazaar of Ottergow; and after cutting off his nose, he put him on an ass with a young pig tied to his neck, and paraded him through the bazaar, with a drummer before him, to render him an outcast.

In the same year, 1848, he seized Rampurshad Tewaree, and his son Runghoor, cultivators of Deogon, and demanded from them four times the rent due for the land they tilled; and when they could not pay, be sold all their cattle, grain, and other property, and had iron spikes driven up under their nails. Unable to extort money by this means, he caused Sotun Bhurbhoonja, or grain-parcher, to—in his father's face, and then released him.

In 1848 he demanded from Junga Salor, a cultivator of Bhudalmow, in Deogon, double rent for the land he tilled; and when he could not pay, seized and took off his wife, and cohabited with her four or five days, and then made some of the followers do the same before he released her.

In the same year, 1848, he and his gang attacked the village of Byrampore, in the Kisnee purgunna, and seized Omrow Sing, a Bys Rajpoot, and Boodhea, a Goojur, and all the respectable inhabitants they could get hold of, with their families. After torturing the rest for eight days, and extorting from them all they could pay, he let them go; but detained Omrow Sing, and had him flogged every day till he reduced him to a dying state, when he let him go. He was taken off to his home; but he died as soon as he entered the house and saw his family. The wife of Boodheea, the Goojur, he confined and violated. Bukhtawur deposes that he saw all this while he was in confinement.

He, in 1848, seized and carried off to his stronghold Kaseeram, a Brahmin, of Deogon, and cut off his nose, and tortured him with hot irons till he got from him all that he and his relations could be made to pay, and then let him go.

In the same year and month be attacked and plundered the village of Puttee, in the Jugdeespore purgunna, carried off all the shopkeepers of the place, and tortured them till they paid him altogether three thousand rupees.

In the same year he attacked the village of Koteea, in the Rodowlee district, carried off one of the shopkeepers, and drove iron pins up under his nails till he paid a ransom of one hundred and fifty rupees. He drove off and sold all the cattle of the village.

In the same year he attacked and plundered the village of Budulgur, in the Jugdeespore purgunna, in the same way.

In the same year he attacked and plundered the village of Khorasa, in Rodowlee, carried off Sopae, the Putwaree, with his mother and wife, and tortured them till they paid a ransom of two hundred rupees. He murdered about the same time the son of Buksh Khan, the holder of the village of Gaepore, and two members of the family of Poorae, a carpenter of Almasgunge, in Deogon.

After plundering the house of Sungum Doobee, a respectable Brahmin of Mukdoompore, he seized him and his nephew, took them off to his fort, and, because they could not pay the ransom he demanded, he caused melting lead to be poured into their ears and noses till they died. About the same time he, with his own hands, for some slight offence, cut the throat of his table-attendant, Kbyratee, of Kunhurpore.

About the same time he seized two travellers; and, because they could not pay the ransom demanded, he suspended one of them to a tree in the village of Sathnee, on the bank of the Goomtee river, and the other to a tree in the village of Mukdoompore. He had their arms first broken with bludgeons, and then their feet cut off, and at last they were beaten over the head till they died.

> Bhooree Khan, in March, 1850, went with a gang of three hundred men to assist Gunga Buksh and his family in the defence of Kasimgunge and Bhetae; but he was too late. On his way back, in the beginning of April, he left his gang in a grove, six miles from Lucknow, and entered the city alone in a disguise to visit a celebrated dancing-girl of his acquaintance, named Bunnee. He had been with her two days, and on the 15th of April he went to see the magnificent tomb of Mahommed Allee Shah, of which he had heard much. While sauntering about this place he was recognised by three or four persons belonging to another dancing-girl of his acquaintance, named the Chhotee Gohur, or "little Gem," whom he had formerly visited. They seized him. As soon as Bunnee heard of this she sent ten or twelve of her own men, and rescued him from the followers of the "Little Gem." They took him to Bunnee, who made a virtue of necessity, and went off with him forthwith

to the Minister, who rewarded her with a pair of shawls, and made suitable presents to her followers.

It is said that he was pointed out to the followers of the "Chhotee Gohur" by Peer Khan, of Khanseepore, in Deogon, whom Bhooree Khan had some time before plundered and tortured for a ransom, as already stated. Bhooree Khan was sentenced to transportation beyond seas for life, and sent off in October, 1851.

After reading such narratives, an Englishman will naturally ask what are the means by which such atrocious gangs are enabled to escape the hands of justice. He will recollect the history of the MIDDLE AGES, and think of strong baronial castles, rugged hills, deep ravines, and endless black forests. They have no such things in Oude.* The whole country is a level plain, intersected by rivers, which, with one exception, flow near the surface, and have either no ravines at all, or very small ones. The little river Goomtee winds exceedingly, and cuts into the soil in some places to the depth of fifty feet. In such places there are deep ravines; and the landholders along the border improve these natural difficulties by planting and preserving trees and underwood in which to hide themselves and their followers when in arms against their Government. Any man who cuts a stick in these jungles, or takes his camels or cattle into them to browse or graze without the previous sanction of the landholder, does so at the peril of his life. But landholders in the open plains and on the banks of rivers, without any ravines at all, have the same jungles.

* The Terae forest, which borders Oude to the north, is too unhealthy to be occupied by any but those who have been born and bred in it. The gangs I am treating of are composed of men born and bred in the plains, and they cannot live in the Terae forest.

In the midst of this jungle, the landholders have generally one or more mud forts surrounded by a ditch and a dense fence of living bamboos, through which cannon-shot cannot penetrate, and man can enter only by narrow and intricate pathways. They are always too green to be set fire to; and being within range of the matchlocks from the parapet, they cannot be cut down by a besieging force. Out of such places the garrison can be easily driven by shells thrown over such fences, but an Oude force has seldom either the means or the skill for such purposes. When driven out by shells or any other means, the garrison retires at night, with little risk, through the bamboo fence and surrounding jungle and brushwood, by paths known only to themselves. They are never provided with the means of subsistence for a long siege; and when the Oude forces sent against them are not prepared with the means to shell them out, they sit down quietly, and starve or weary them out. This is commonly a very long process, for the force is seldom large enough to surround the place at a safe distance from the walls and bamboo fence, so as to prevent all access to provision of all kinds, which the garrison is sure to get from their friends and allies in the neighbourhood, the garrison generally having the sympathy of all the large landholders around, and the besieging force being generally considered the common and irreconcilable enemy of all.

As soon as the garrison escapes, it goes systematically and diligently to work in plundering indiscriminately all the village communities over the most fertile parts of the surrounding country, which do not belong to baronial proprietors like themselves till it has made the Government authorities agree to its terms, or reduced the country to a waste. The leaders of the gang may sometimes condescend to quicken the process by appropriating a portion of their plunder to bribing some influential person at Court, who gets an injunction issued to the local authorities to make some arrangement for terminating the pillage and consequent loss of revenue, or he will be superseded or forfeit his contract. The rebel then returns with his followers, repairs all the mischief done to his fort, improves its defences, and stipulates for a remission of his revenue for a year or more, on account of the injury sustained by his crops or granaries. The unlucky Amil, whose zeal and energy have caused the necessity for this reduction, is probably thrown into gaol till "he pays the uttermost farthing," or bribes influential persons at Court to get him released on the ground of his poverty.

I may here mention the jungles in Oude which have been created and are still preserved by landholders, almost solely for the above purposes. They are all upon the finest soil, and in the finest climate; and the lands they occupy might almost all be immediately brought into tillage, and studded by numerous happy village communities.

I may, however, before I begin to describe them, mention the fact that many influential persons at Court, as well as the landholders themselves, are opposed to such a salutary measure. If brought under tillage and occupied by happy village communities, all the revenue would or might flow in legitimate channels into the King's treasury; whereas in their present state they manage to fill their own purses by gratuities from the refractory landholders who occupy them, or from the local authorities, who require permission from Court to coerce them into obedience. Of these gratuities such a salutary measure would deprive them; and it is, in consequence, exceedingly difficult to get a jungle cut down, however near it may be to the city where wood is so dear, and has to be brought from jungles five or ten times the distance.

In the Sultanpore District.

1st.—The Jungle of Paperghat, about one hundred miles south-east from Lucknow, on the bank of the Goomtee river, ten miles long, and three wide, or thirty square miles.

In this jungle Dirgpaul Sing, tallookdar of Nanneemow, has a fort; and Rostum Sing, tallookdar of Dera, has another.

2nd.—The Dostpore Jungle, one hundred and twenty miles south-east from Lucknow, on the bank of the Mujhoee river, twelve, miles long, and three broad, or thirty-six square miles.

3rd.—The Khapra Dehee Jungle, one hundred miles south-east from Lucknow, on the plain, about ten miles long, and six miles broad, or sixty square miles.

4th.—The Jugdeespore Jungle, on the bank of the Goomtee river, fifty miles south-east from Lucknow, sixteen miles long, and three miles broad, forty-eight square miles.

Allee Buksh Khan, tallookdar, has the fort of Tanda in this jungle, on the bank of the Kandoo rivulet, which flows through it into the Goomtee. The fort of Bechoogur in this jungle is held by another tallookdar.

5th.—Gurh Ameytee, seventy miles from Lucknow, south-east, on the bank of the Sae river, nine miles long and three broad, or twenty seven square miles.

Rajah Madhoe Sing has a fort in this jungle, and is one of the very worst, but most plausible men in Oude.

6th.—Daoodpoor Jungle, seventy miles south-east from Lucknow, on the plain, four miles long and three broad, or twelve square miles.

The Beebee or Lady Sagura has her fort and residence in this jungle.

7th.—Duleeppore Jungle, one hundred and ten miles east from Lucknow, on the bank of the Sae river, ten miles long, and three miles wide, thirty square miles.

Seetla Buksh, who is always in rebellion, has a fort in this jungle.

8th.—The Matona Jungle, fifty miles south-east from Lucknow, on the bank of the Goomtee river, twelve miles long and three wide—square miles, thirty-six.

Allee Buksh Khan, a notoriously refractory tallookdar, has a fort in this jungle.

In the Uldeemow District.

9th.—Mugurdhee Jungle, one hundred and forty miles east from Lucknow, on the bank of Ghogra river, eight miles long and three broad—square miles, twenty-four.

10th.—Putona Jungle, one hundred and twenty miles east from Lucknow, on the bank of the Tonus river, eight miles long and four miles broad—square miles, thirty-two.

11th.—Mudungur Jungle, one hundred and twenty miles east from Lucknow, on the bank of the Tonus river, six miles long, and three miles broad—square miles, eighteen.

Amreys Sing and Odreys Sing, sons of Surubdowun Sing (who was killed by the King's troops thirty years ago), hold the fort of Mudungur in this jungle.

12th.—Bundeepore Jungle, east from Lucknow one hundred and forty miles, on the plain, seven miles long and one broad—seven square miles.

13th.—Chunderdeeh, south-east from Lucknow one hundred and ten miles, on the bank of the Goomtee river, seven miles long, and three miles wide—square miles, twenty-one.

In the Dureeabad District.

14th.—Soorujpore Behreyla Jungle, east from Lucknow forty miles, on the bank of the Kuleeanee river, sixteen miles long, and four miles broad—square miles, sixty-four.

Chundee Sing has a fort in this jungle, and the family have been robbers for several generations. The widow of the late notorious robber, Rajah Singjoo, the head of the family, has a still stronger one.

15th.—Guneshpore Jungle, sixty miles south-east from Lucknow, on the bank of the Goomtee river, six miles long and two broad—twelve square miles.

Maheput Sing, an atrocious robber, holds his fort of Bhowaneegur in this jungle.

In the Dewa Jahangeerabad District.

16th.—The Kasimgunge and Bhetae Jungle, eighteen miles north-east from Lucknow, sixteen miles long, and four miles wide—square miles, sixty-four, on the bank of the little river Reyt.

Gunga Buksh holds the forts of Kasimgunge and Atursae in this jungle; Thakur Purshad those of Bhetae and Buldeogur; and Bhugwunt Sing that of Munmutpore. Other members of the same family hold those of Ramgura Paharpore. The whole family are hereditary and inveterate robbers.

In the Bangur District.

17th.—Tundeeawun Jungle, on the plain, west from Lucknow, seventy-two miles, twelve miles long and six broad—square miles, seventy-two.

In the Salone District.

18th.—The Naen Jungle, eighty miles south from Lucknow, on the bank of the Sae river, sixteen miles long and three wide—square miles, forty-eight.

Jugurnath Buksh, the tallookdar, holds the fort of Jankeebund, in this jungle; and others are held in the same jungle by members of his family.

19th.—The Kutaree Jungle, on the bank of the Kandoo river, south-east from Lucknow sixty miles, eight miles long and three broad—square miles, twenty-four.

Surnam Sing, the tallookdar, has a fort in this jungle.

In the Byswara District.

20th.—The Sunkurpore Jungle, south of Lucknow seventy miles, on the plain, ten miles long and three wide—square miles, thirty.

Benee Madhoe, the tallookdar, has three forts in this jungle.

In the Hydergur District.

21st.—The Kolee Jungle, fifty miles south-east from Lucknow, on the bank of the Goomtee river, three miles long and one and a half wide—square miles, four and a half.

The rebels and robbers in this jungle trust to the natural defences of the ravines and jungles.

22nd.—Kurseea Kuraea Jungle, south-east from Lucknow fifty miles, on the bank of the Goomtee river, three miles long and one wide—square miles, three.

The landholders trust in the same way to natural defences.

In the Khyrabad and Mahomdee Districts.

23rd.—Gokurnath Jungle, north-west from Lucknow one hundred miles, extending out from the Terae forest, and running south-east in a belt thirty miles long and five wide—square miles, one hundred and fifty.

Husun Rajah, the tallookdar of Julalpore, has a fort in this jungle. Sheobuksh Sing, the tallookdar of Lahurpore, holds here the fort of Katesura; and Omrow Sing, the tallookdar of Oel, holds two forts in this jungle.

In the Baree and Muchreyta Districts.

24th.—The Suraen Jungle, north-west from Lucknow thirty-four miles, along the banks of the Suraen river, twelve miles long and three miles wide—square miles, thirty-six.

In this jungle Jowahir Sing holds the fort of Basae Deeh; Khorrum Sing, that of Seogur; Thakur Rutun Sing, that of Jyrampore. They are all landholders of the Baree district, and their forts are on the *north* bank of the Saraen river. Juswunt Sing holds the fort of Dhorhara; Dul Sing, that of Gundhoreea; Rutun Sing holds two forts, Alogee and Pupnamow.—

They are all landholders of the Muchreyta district, and their four forts are on the *south* bank of the Saraen river.

This gives twenty-four belts of jungle beyond the Terae forest, and in the fine climate of Oude, covering a space of eight hundred and eighty-six square miles, at a rough computation.* In these jungles the landholders find shooting, fishing, and security for themselves and families, grazing ground for their horses and cattle, and fuel and grass for their followers; and they can hardly understand how landholders of the same rank, in other countries, can contrive to live happily without them. The man who, by violence, fraud, and collusion, absorbs the estates of his weaker neighbours, and creates a large one for himself, in any part of Oude, however richly cultivated and thickly peopled, provides himself with one or two mud forts, and turns the country around them into a jungle, which he considers to be indispensable as well to his comfort as to his security.

* The surface of the Oude territory, including the Terae forest, is supposed to contain twenty-three thousand seven hundred and thirty-nine square miles. The Terae forest includes, perhaps, from four to five thousand miles; but within that space there is a great deal of land well tilled and peopled.

The atrocities described in the above narrative were committed by Bhooree Khan, in the process of converting his estate of Dewa into a jungle, and building strongholds for his gang as it increased and became more and more formidable. Having converted Deogon into a jungle, and built his strongholds, he would, by the usual process of violence, fraud, and collusion with local authorities, have absorbed the small surrounding estates of his weaker neighbours, and formed a very large one for himself. The same process, no doubt, went on in England successively under the Saxons, Danes, and Normans; and in every country in Europe, under successive invaders and conquerors, or as long as the baronial proprietors of the soil were too strong to be coerced by their Sovereign as they are in Oude.

An Englishman may further ask how it is that a wretch guilty of such cruelties to men who never wronged him, to innocent and unoffending females and children, can find, in a society where slavery is unknown, men to assist him in inflicting them, and landholders of high rank and large possessions to screen and shelter him when pursued by his Government. He must, for the solution of this question, also go back to the MIDDLE AGES, in England and the other nations of Europe, when the baronial proprietors of the soil, too strong for their sovereigns, committed the same cruelties, found the same willing instruments in their retainers, and members of the same class of landed proprietors, to screen, shelter, and encourage them in their iniquities.

They acquiesce in the atrocities committed by one who is in armed resistance to the Government to-day, and aid him in his enterprises openly or secretly, because they know that they may be in the same condition, and require the same aid from him to-morrow—that the more sturdy the resistance made by one, the less likely will the Government officers be to rouse the resistance of others. They do not sympathise with those who suffer from his depredations, or aid the Government officers in protecting them, because they know that they could not support the means required to enable them to contend successfully with their Sovereign, and reduce him to terms, without plundering and occasionally murdering the innocent of all ages and both sexes, and that they may have to raise the same means in a similar contest to-morrow. They are satisfied, therefore, if they can save their own tenants from pillage and slaughter. They find, moreover, that the sufferings of others enable them to get cultivators and useful tenants of all kinds upon their own estates, on more easy terms, and to induce the smaller allodial or khalsa proprietors around, to yield up their lands to them, and become their tenants with less difficulty. It was in the same manner that the great feudal barons aggrandised themselves in England, and all the other countries of Europe, in the MIDDLE AGES.

In Oude all these great landholders look upon the Sovereign and his officers—except when they happen to be in collusion with them for the purpose of robbing or coercing others—as their natural enemies, and will never trust themselves in their power without undoubted pledges of personal security. The great feudal tenants of the Crown in England, and the other nations of Europe, did the same, except when they were in collusion with them for the purpose of robbing others of their rights; or fought under their banners for the purpose of robbing or destroying the subjects and servants of some other Sovereign whom he chose to call his enemy.

Only one of these sources of union between the Sovereign and his great landholders is in operation in Oude. Some of them are every year in collusion with the governors of districts for the purpose of coercing and robbing others; but the Sovereign can never unite them under his banners for the purpose of invading and plundering any other country, and thereby securing for himself and them present *glory*, wealth, and high-sounding titles, and the admiration and applause of future generations. The strong arm of the British Government is interposed between them and all surrounding countries; and there is no safety-valve for their unquiet spirits in foreign conquests. They can no longer do as Ram did two thousand seven hundred years ago—lead an army from Ajodheea to Ceylone. They must either give up fighting, or fight among themselves, as they appear to have been doing ever since Ram's time; and there are at present no signs of a disposition to send out another "Sakya Guntama" from Lucknow, or Kapila vastee to preach peace and good-will to "all the nations of the earth." They would much rather send out fifty thousand more brave soldiers to fight "all the nations of the east," under the banners of the Honourable East India Company.

An English statesman may further ask how it is that so much disorder can prevail in a small territory like Oude without the gangs, to which it must give rise, passing over the border to depredate upon the bordering districts of its neighbours. The conterminous districts on three sides belong to the British Government, and that on the fourth or north belongs to Nepaul. The leaders of these gangs know, that if the British

Government chose to interpose and aid the Oude Government with its troops, it could crush them in a few days; and that it would do so if they ventured to rob and murder within its territory. They know, also, that it would do the same if they ventured to cross the northern border, and rob and murder within the Nepaul territory. They therefore confine their depredations to the Oude territory, seeing that, as long as they do so, the British Government remains quiet.

CHAPTER VI.

Adventures of Maheput Sing of Bhowaneepoor—Advantages of a good road from Lucknow to Fyzabad—Excellent condition of the artillery bullocks with the Frontier Police—Get all that Government allows for them—Bred in the Tarae—Dacoits of Soorujpoor Bareyla—The Amil connives at all their depredations, and thrives in consequence—The Amil of the adjoining districts does not, and ruined in consequence—His weakness—Seetaram, a capitalist—His account of a singular *Suttee*—Bukhtawar Sing's notions of *Suttee*, and of the reason why Rajpoot widows seldom become *Suttees*—Why local authorities carry about prisoners with them—Condition of prisoners—No taxes on mango-trees—Cow-dung cheaper than wood for fuel—Shrine of "Shaikh Salar" at Sutrik—Bridge over the small river Rete—Recollection of the ascent of a balloon at Lucknow—End of the pilgrimage.

Poorae Chowdheree, of Kuchohee, held a share in the lands of the village of Bhanpoor in Radowlee. He mortgaged it in 1830, to a co-sharer, who transferred the mortgage to *Meherban Sing*, of Guneshpoor. Poorae disliked the arrangement, and made all the cultivators desert the village of Bhanpoor, and leave the lands waste. Meherban attacked the village of Kuchohee in consequence, killed Porae, and seized upon all the lands of Bhanpoor for himself. Rajah Ram, one of the ousted co-sharers in these lands, attacked and killed Meherban in 1832, and seized upon all the lands of Bhanpoor.

After the death of his first wife, Meherban had attacked the house of Bhowanee Sing, Rajpoot, of Teur, carried off his daughter, who had been affianced to another, and forcibly made her his wife. By her he had one daughter and one son, named *Maheput Sing*, who now inherited from his father a fifteenth part of one of the six and half shares into which the lands of Guneshpoor were divided. He, by degrees, murdered, or drove out of the village, all his co-sharers, save Gunbha Sing and Chungha Sing, joint proprietors of a small part of one of the shares, known by the name of the Kunnee Puttee. From the year 1843, Maheput Sing became a robber by profession, and the leader of a formidable gang; and in three years, by a long series of successful enterprises, he acquired the means of converting his residence, on the border of the town of Guneshpoor, into a strong fort, among the deep ravines of the Goomtee river. This fort he called *Bhowaneegur*, after Bhowanee, the patroness of the trade of murder and robbery, which he had adopted.

I shall now mention, more circumstantially, a few of the many atrocities committed by him and his gang, during the last few years of his career, as illustrative of the state of society in Oude. Bulbhudder Sing, a subadar of the 45th Regiment of Bengal Native Infantry, resided at Rampoor Sobeha, in the Dureeabad district. By degrees he purchased thirteen-sixteenths of the lands of these two small villages, which adjoin each other, out of the savings from his pay, and those of his nephew, Mugun Sing, havildar of the 43rd Regiment Bengal Native Infantry. On his being transferred to the invalid establishment, the subadar resided with his family in Rampoor, and in May, 1846, his nephew, Mugun Sing, came home on furlough to visit him. Gujraj, an associate of Maheput Sing's, held the other three-sixteenths of the lands of these two villages; and by the murder of the subadar and all his family, he thought he should be able to secure for himself the possession of the whole estate in perpetuity. The family consisted of the subadar and his wife,—Mugun Sing, the son of his deceased brother, Man Sing, and his wife; and his son Bijonath and his wife,—Dwarka Sing, son of Ojagur Sing, another deceased brother of the subadar,—Mahta Deen, the son of Chundun Sing, another deceased brother of the subadar, and his wife and young son, Surubjeet Sing, seven years of age,—Kulotee Sing, son of Gobrae, another deceased brother of the subadar,—Bag Sing, a relative,—Bechun Sing, a servant,—Seo Deen, the gardener,—Jeeawun Sing, the barber, and the widow of Salwunt Sing, another son of Mugun Sing, havildar.

When the family were all assembled, Maheput Sing, with Gujraj and other associates, and a gang of one hundred and fifty armed followers, proceeded to the village at midnight, and carefully reconnoitred the premises. It was, after consultation, determined to defer the attack till daybreak, as the subadar and his nephews were known to be brave and well-armed men, who kept watch till towards morning, and would make a desperate resistance, unless taken by surprise. They remained concealed within the enclosure of Gujraj's house, till just before daylight, when they quietly surrounded the subadar's house. As day dawned the subadar got up, opened the door and walked out, as usual, to breathe the fresh air, thinking all safe. He was immediately shot down, and on Mugun Sing's rushing out to assist his uncle, he received a shot in the eye, and fell dead on his body. The robbers then rushed in, cut down Jeeawun, the barber, while attempting to shut the door, and wounded Kulotee Sing,* Bag Sing, and others of the party. Finding that they could no longer stand against the numbers, rushing in at the doors and windows, the defenders climbed from the inside to the flat roof of the house, over the apartments of the men, fired down upon the robbers, who were still inside, and shot one of them. The robbers, finding they could not otherwise dislodge them, set fire to that part of the house, and the men were obliged to leap off to save themselves. In doing this, Bag Sing hurt his spine, and Seo Deen sprained his ankle, and both lay where they fell, pretending to be dead, till night. The others all went off in search of succour.

*   Kulotee Sing was murdered, a few days afterwards, by Maheput and Gujraj, as he was superintending the cultivation of his lands.

The robbers found the boy, Surubjeet, lying sick on his bed, attended by his mother. They seized him and dashed his head against the ground;

and when he still showed signs of life, Gujraj cut him to pieces with his sword. They then seized and stripped the females naked, and sprinkled boiling oil over their bodies, till they pointed out all the property concealed in the house. Seventeen hundred rupees were found buried in the floor; and the rest of the property in clothes, gold and silver ornaments, and brass utensils, amounted to about ten thousand rupees.

About noon, while the robbers were still in the house, the Amil of Mohlara came with a large force and one gun, and surrounded them; but stood at a safe distance, whence he kept up for some time a fire from his gun and his matchlocks, which had no effect whatever. The robbers fired in return from the house, merely to show that they were not to be frightened from their booty in that way. This went on till after dark in the evening, when the robbers all retired to the jungles with their booty, unmolested by the Amil.

Byjonath, who had brought the Amil to the spot, urged him on as much as he could to save the property and females, and avenge the death of those who had fallen, and he killed one man and seized another, the son of one of the leaders; but he was obliged to give him up to the Amil as an hostage, for the recovery of the property, and a witness to the robbery. The Amil kept him for six months, and then let him go on the largest ransom he could get for him from his father. The circumstances were all represented, through the Resident, to the Durbar, and redress prayed for, but none was ever obtained.*

* When the Resident visited this place, in his tour, in January, 1850, Dwarka Sing and other members of the family described all the circumstances of this attack, and they were taken down; and have been confirmed since by a judicial investigation.

In May 1846, Maheput attacked the house of Seobuksh, a gardener, and after plundering it, he seized and carried off to the jungle the gardener's brother, Puroutee, and tortured him to death with hot irons, because he could not raise the sum demanded for his ransom.

In August 1847, Maheput Sing and his gang attacked the house of Meherban Tewaree, subadar of the Gwalior Contingent, in the village of Hareehurpoor, in the district of Rodowlee. It was about ten at night, and the whole family were asleep. The subadar lay on his cot below, near the door, his brother, Angud Tewaree, slept on the upper story. Some placed ladders and entered the upper story through a window; Maheput, with others, broke open the door, near which the subadar slept below. The brother got a sword-cut in the hand, and called out from the upper story as loud as he could for help; but their neighbours were all too much alarmed to come to their aid. Maheput seized and bound the subadar with his own waistband, and commanded his brother to come down, saying, that he need not call for help, as the villagers all knew him too well to molest him; and if he did not come down instantly he would set fire to the house. Seeing no chance of help, he came down, and was bound with his own waistband in the same manner. When the subadar remonstrated against this treatment, Maheput struck him over the face. They then plundered the house of all the property it contained, to the value of six hundred and fifty rupees; and took the subadar and his brother to the jungles; and, in the morning, demanded a ransom of one thousand rupees. At last they came down to four hundred rupees and the horse, which the subadar kept for his own riding. The subadar consented, and his brother was released to get the money and horse. He borrowed the money and sent it with the horse through Bhowanee Deen Tewaree, landholder of Ladeeka Poorwa, and the subadar was released. He presented three petitions, through the Resident, and orders were sent from the Durbar to the local authorities, Hurdut Sing and Monna Lal, but they were both in league with the robbers, and tried to get the subadar made away with, to save further trouble, and he sought security with his regiment.*

* Meherban Tewaree, subadar, was present, as a witness at the subsequent trial of Maheput and Gujraj, who were sentenced to transportation beyond seas for life.

In January 1847, Maheput and his gang attacked the village of Bahapoor, in the Rodowlee district; and after plundering all the houses, seized and carried off among others Seetul, the spirit-dealer, and the two sons of Reehta, the widow of Bhosoo, one twenty-two years of age, and the other eighteen. They tortured them with red-hot irons, and tied bamboos round their necks every day for fifteen days. Maheput then shot the eldest son, and cut his body to pieces with his sword. The younger son, at night, made his escape while they were asleep, and returned to tell the tale of his brother's murder to his mother. Seetul, the Kalwar, got his uncle to lend him twenty-eight rupees, for which he was released.

In April 1847, Maheput Sing and his gang attacked the house of Ramoutar, Brahmin, of the Brahmin village of Guneshpoor, in Rodowlee; plundered it of properly valued at one hundred rupees, and then bound Ramoutar, his father and two sons, and took them off to the jungles; and there tortured them all for seven days. He then had the two boys, one nine years old and the other five, suspended to a tree and flogged; and Ramoutar himself tied to a thorny tree and beaten till the blood flowed down and drenched his waistband, because he could pay nothing, and would not sign a bond to pay two thousand rupees. His sufferings and the sight of those of his two sons made him at last sign one for one thousand rupees. He was flogged again till his friends brought four hundred out of the thousand, and Cheyt Sing, Thakoor, a respectable landholder of Koleea, in Rodowlee, consented to give security for the payment of two hundred and forty-two rupees more. Ramoutar and his family were then released, after they had been confined and tortured for thirty-six days, and they went off and resided at Bookcheyna in Khundasa. A year after his house was there attacked by Maheput Sing and his gang, and plundered of all it contained; and his brother Seetul, and his youngest son were seized and taken off to his fort at Bhowaneegur, and there tortured and starved for six months. Ramoutar then borrowed one hundred and sixty rupees, and obtained the release of his brother Seetul, and a year after he was able to raise forty-seven rupees more, with which he ransomed his son.

In May 1847, Maheput Sing attacked the house of Seolal Tewaree of Torsompoor, in Rodowlee, at midnight; and after plundering it and stripping his mother and wife, and the wife of his brother, Jurbundun Sing, of all the clothes and ornaments they had, he bound and carried off to the jungle the two brothers, Seolal and Jurbundun. They were flogged, and had hot irons applied to their bodies every day for twenty days, and had only a little flour to eat and water to drink, once in three days. After twenty days they contrived to make their escape one dark and stormy night, and got home; but three days after he again attacked their house and burnt it to the ground, with all they possessed. He, at the same time, burnt down the house of their uncle, in the same village, and that of one of their ploughmen; and two cows and one bullock were burnt to death in the flames.

In July 1847, Maheput Sing and his gang attacked the house of Chubbee Lal, Brahmin, in the village of Bunnee, in the Rodowlee district, and after plundering it of property to the value of five hundred rupees, he bound and took the old Brahmin off to the jungles, and demanded from him a ransom of eight thousand rupees. This sum the old man could not pay, and he was flogged with thorns, and had red-hot irons applied to his body every day. Maheput then sent a letter to the old man's son, Dwarka, desiring him to send the eight thousand rupees if he wished his father to live. The house having been plundered, the family had nothing left, and could persuade no one to lend them. On receiving a reply to this effect, Maheput had the old man's body plastered all over with moist gunpowder, and made him stand in the sun till it was dry. He then set fire to the powder, and the poor man was burnt all over. He then cut off both his hands at the wrists, and his nose, and sent them to his family, and in this condition be afterwards sent the poor man to his home upon a cot. The son met his father at the door, but the old man died as soon as his son had embraced him.

Maheput carried off Pem, the son of Teeka, at the same time, and tortured him till his family paid the ransom demanded. He was witness to the tortures of the old Brahmin.

In August 1847, Maheput and his gang attacked the house of Bichook, a Brahmin, in the village of Torsompoor, in Rodowlee, at midnight, while he was sleeping, and bound and carried him off to the jungle. The next day, when he was about to have him tortured for a ransom, one of his followers interceded for him, and he was released. But a month after, Maheput and his gang again attacked his house, and after plundering it of all it contained, they burnt it to the ground. Bichook had run off on hearing their approach, and he escaped to Syudpoor.

In November, 1846, Maheput Sing attacked the house of Sook Allee, in Guneshpoor, at midnight, with a gang of one hundred men; and, after plundering it of all the property it contained, to the amount of four hundred rupees, he burnt it to the ground, and bound and carried off Sook Allee to the house of his friend, Byjonath Bilwar, a landholder in the village of Kholee, eight miles distant. He there demanded a ransom of five hundred rupees; and on his declaring that he neither had nor could borrow such a sum, he had him tortured with hot irons, and flogged in the usual way. He kept him for two months at Kholee, and then took him to Tukra, in the Soorajpoor purgunnah, where he kept him for another month, torturing, and giving him half a meal every other day. At the end of three months, Akber Sing and Bhowanee Deen, Rajpoot landholders of Odemow, contrived to borrow two hundred rupees for Sook Allee, and he was released on the payment of this sum. The marks of the hot irons, applied to his body by Maheput Sing, with his own hands, are still visible, and will remain so as long as he lives.*

* I saw these marks on the sufferer.

About the same time—the latter end of 1846—Maheput Sing sent to Sheik Sobratee, of the same place, a message through a pausee, named Bhowanee Deen, demanding twenty-five rupees. This sum was sent; but six weeks had not elapsed, before Sheik Sobratee received another demand for the same amount, through the same person. He had no money, but promised to send the sum in ten days. At midnight, on the fourth day after this, Maheput and his gang attacked his house, and plundered it of all they could find, female ornaments, and clothes, and brass utensils. Sobratee was that night sleeping at the house of his friend Peree, the wood-dealer, in the same town. Maheput tried to make his mother and wife point out where he was, by torturing them, but they either would not or could not do so. After some search, however, they discovered him, and bound and took him off, with handcuffs, and an iron collar round his neck, to the Kurseea jungle, in the Hydergur pergunnah. His son, a boy, had escaped. After torturing him in the usual way for eight days, they sent a message to his mother by Maheput's servant, Salar, to say, that unless she sent a ransom of five hundred rupees, her son's nose and hands should be cut off and sent to her as those of *Chubbee Lal*, Brahmin, of Bunnee, had been. She prevailed upon Baroonath Gotum to lend the money; and Maheput sent Sobratee to him, accompanied by one of his armed retainers, with orders to make him over to the Gotum, if he pledged himself in due form to pay. He did so, and Sobratee was made over to him, and the next day sent home to his wife and mother. Some months after, however, when he had completed his fort of Bhowneegur, Maheput sent to demand two hundred rupees more from Sobratee, and when he found he could not pay, he had his house pulled, down, and took away all the materials to his fort. What he did not require he caused to be burnt. He got from Sobratee, in ransom and plunder, more than three thousand rupees; and he has been ever since reduced to great poverty and distress.

In November 1847, Maheput Sing and his gang seized and carried off Khosal, a confectioner, of Talgon, in Rodowlee, who had gone to his sister at Buhapoor, near Guneshpoor, to attend a marriage—took him to the jungle, and tortured and starved him in the usual way for five weeks. He had him burnt with red-hot irons, flogged and ducked in a tank every day, and demanded a ransom of two hundred rupees. At last, his brother, Davey Deen, borrowed thirty-three rupees from Rambuksh, a merchant of Odermow, and offered to pay it for his ransom. Maheput sent Khosal, with his agent, Bhowanee Deen, to Rambuksh, and he released him on getting the money. He still bears on his body the marks of the stripes and burnings.*

* These marks I have seen.

In December 1847, Maheput and his gang attacked the house of Motee Lal Misser, a Brahmin, in the village of—, and after robbing it of all that it contained, he seized and carried off his nephew, Ram Deen, a boy of seven years of age, and tortured him for a month in the jungle. He then cut off his left ear and the forefinger of his right hand, and sent them to the uncle in a letter, stating, that if he did not send him one thousand rupees, he would send the boy's head in the same manner. The boy's father had died, and his uncle, with great difficulty, prevailed upon his friends and neighbours to lend him two hundred and twenty rupees, which he sent to Maheput, and his nephew was released. The boy declares to me that Maheput cut off his ear and finger with his own hands.*

* This boy was present, as a witness, at the trial of Maheput.

In June 1848, Forsut Pandee, of Resalpandee-ka-Poorwa, in Rodowlee, accompanied Girwar Sing, a Rajpoot of Bowra, in Rodowlee, to Guneshpoor, on some business. They were smoking and talking together at the house of Mungul Sing, Thakoor, a large landholder of that place, when five of Maheput's armed men came up, and told Forsut Pandee to attend them to their master. Girwar Sing remonstrated and declared that his honour had been pledged for Forsut Pandee's personal safety. Mungul Sing, Thakoor, however, told him, that he must offer no opposition, as they seized all travellers who came that way, and it was dangerous to oppose them. He was taken to Maheput Sing, in his fort at Bhowaneegur, situated half a mile from Guneshpoor. Maheput told him that he had heard of his having a good flint gun, and a shawl in his house, and that he must have them. Forsut Pandee swore on the Ganges that he had no such things. He then had him tied up to a tree and flogged him with his own hands with thorny bushes, the scars of which are still visible. He then demanded a ransom of three hundred rupees, and had him flogged and tortured every day for a month, while he gave him to eat only half a pound of flour every two or three days. The prisoner's brother, Bhoree Pandee, sold all the clothes and ornaments of his family, utensils, and furniture, and their hereditary mango and mhowa grove, and raised two hundred and six rupees, which he sent to Maheput, through Baldan Sing, a landholder of Bharatpoor, two miles from Guneshpoor. On the receipt of this Forsut Pandee was released.

In October 1848, Maheput Sing sent ten of his gang to seize a cultivator, by name Khosal, who was engaged in cultivating his land in a hamlet, one mile south of the town of Syudpoor. They seized and bound him and took him off to their leader, Maheput, who had him tortured for a month in the usual way. He had him tied up to a ladder and flogged. He had red-hot irons applied to different parts of his body—he put dry combustibles on the open palms of his hands and set fire to them, so that he has lost the use of his fingers for life. For the whole month he gave him only ten pounds of flour to eat; but his friends contrived to convey a little more to him occasionally, which he ate by stealth. He was reduced, by hunger and torture, to the last stage, when his family, by the sale of all they had in the world, and the compassion of their friends, raised the sum of one hundred and twenty-six rupees, which they sent to Maheput, by Thakoor Persaud, a landholder of the village of Somba, and obtained his release. The tortures have rendered him a cripple, and the family are reduced to a state of great wretchedness.*

* This man was a witness at the trial of Maheput, and I saw the signs of his sufferings.

The village of Guneshpoor yielded a revenue to Government of twenty-one thousand rupees a-year, and was divided into six and half shares each, held by a different person. One belonged to Omrow Sing, Rajpoot, the father of Hunmunt Sing, a corporal in the 44th Regiment Bengal Native Infantry, and descended to Omrow Sing's eldest son, Davey

Sing. One share was held, jointly, by Maheput Sing and Chotee Sing, when, in October 1848, Maheput assembled a gang of about two hundred men, and attacked the house of Davey Sing, while his brother Hunmunt Sing was at home on recruiting service. There were in the house the corporal and his three brothers, and all mounted, with their friends, to the top of the house, with their swords and spears, but without fire-arms. The robbers, unable to ascend from the outside, broke open the doors, but the brothers descended and defended the passage so resolutely, that the gang was obliged to retire and watch for a better opportunity.

Three months after, in January 1849, Maheput attacked the house again, with a gang of five hundred men and good scaling-ladders. Some ascended to the top on the ladders, while others broke open the doors and forced their way in. The brothers and the other male members of the family defended themselves resolutely. One of the brothers, Esuree Sing, his uncle, Runjeet Sing, sipahee of the 11th Regiment Bengal Native Infantry, his cousin, Beetul Sing, sipahee of the 8th Regiment Bombay Native Infantry, were all killed, and hacked to pieces by Maheput and his gang. No person came to the assistance of the family, and the robbers retired with their booty, consisting of five hundred and ten rupees in money, four muskets, and four swords, and twelve hundred maunds of corn, and all the clothes, ornaments, and utensils that could be found. They burnt down the house, and dispossessed the family of their share in the estate, and plundered all the cultivators. Davey Sine the eldest brother, went to reside at Bhanpoor, in the neighbourhood. While he was engaged in cutting a field of pulse, in the morning, about seven o'clock, in the month of March following, Maheput Sing, with a gang of two hundred men, attacked his house, killed his two brothers, Gordut and Hurdut Sing, and their servant, Omed, and shot down his nephew, Gorbuksh Sing. Ramsahae, the nephew of Maheput Sing, ran up to despatch him with his sword, but Gorbuksh rose, cut him down, and killed him with his sword before he himself expired.

The corporal, Hunmunt Sing, of the 44th Native Infantry, described all these things in several petitions to the Resident, and prayed redress, but no redress was ever obtained. Saligram and other relatives of the corporal had been plundered and wounded by Maheput Sing and his gang, and he describes many other atrocities committed by the same gang. His petition of the 27th September 1849, was sent to the King by the Resident, who was told, that the Amil of the district of Dureeabad, Girdhara Lal, had been ordered to seize Maheput Sing and his gang. This Amil was always in league with them.

In December 1847, Maheput Sing and his gang attacked the house of a female, named Arganee, the widow of Sheik Rozae, in the village of Pertab Pahae. It was midnight, and she was sleeping with her two grandchildren, the sons of her son, who was a sipahee in the 66th Regiment of Bengal Native Infantry. They bound her hands: and leaving her young grandchildren alone, took her off to the jungle eight miles distant. There Maheput demanded from her the seven hundred rupees which she was said to have accumulated; and when she pleaded poverty, and said that the sipahee's pay was their only means of subsistence, he had her stripped naked and flogged in the usual way. For a month he had her stripped and flogged in the same manner every day. She then signed a bond to pay one hundred rupees on a certain day, and was released. She sold all she had, and borrowed all she could, and on the fourth day sent him fifty, and the other fifty on the fifteenth day; but he afterwards had the poor widow's house pulled down and all the wood-work carried to his fort of Bhowaneegur.

In April 1849, Maheput Sing and his gang attacked the house of Seodeen Misser, sipahee of the 63rd Regiment Bengal Native Infantry; and after plundering it, seized and carried off to the jungle his brother and that brother's two sons—one seven years of age and the other five— and his sister. He sold the two boys as slaves for two hundred rupees to a person named Davey Sookul, of Guneshpoor; and tortured the brother and sister till the sipahee and his friends sold all they had in the world for their ransom, when he released them.

In the month of May 1849, Maheput Sing and his gang at midnight attacked the house of Eseree Sing, a Rajpoot of the Chouhan tribe, in the village of Salpoor, in Dureeabad; and after stripping his mother and all the other females of the family of their clothes and ornaments, plundering the house of all it contained, rupees, twenty-five in money, two handsome matchlocks, two swords, two spears, and two shields, and brass utensils, weighing one hundred and sixty pounds, he bound Eseree Sing himself, and took him off with his sister, four years of age, and his daughter, only three, to a jungle, four miles distant. He there released Eseree Sing himself, but took on the girls, and made over his daughter to Akber, one of his followers, and his sister to Bechoo, another of his gang, to be united to them in marriage. It was at their instigation, and for that purpose chiefly, that he made the attack.*

* Akber and Bechoo are now in prison, with Maheput, at Lucknow.

In August 1849, Maheput and his gang attacked the houses of Seetul, Gorbuksh, and Sook Lal, Brahmins, of Guneshpoor; and after plundering them, he carried off Gorbuksh and his son, Ram Deen, and Bhowanee, the son of Seetul, and Sook Lal, and murdered them. He carried off and tortured, in a shocking manner, Benee, of the same place, till he paid a ransom; and Ongud, son of Khunmun, an invalid Khalasie, of the 26th Regiment Native Infantry.

In September 1849, Maheput attacked and plundered the house of Ongud Sing, sipahee of the 24th Regiment Bengal Native Infantry, and confined the sipahee for some time. His petition was sent to the King on the 11th November 1849.

On the 15th of December 1849, Monowur Khan, havildar of the 62nd Regiment Bengal Native Infantry, complained that Maheput Sing had seized him as he was walking on the high road, and extorted eleven rupees from him. His petition was sent to the King, with a request, that all local authorities might be urged to aid in his arrest; and orders were again sent to the Frontier Police.

On the 24th December 1849, Madho Sing, sipahee of the 11th Regiment Bengal Native Infantry, complained that Maheput Sing had attacked and plundered his house twice, burnt it down, and cut down all the trees which the family had planted for generations, and turned them all out of the village—that in the second attack he had murdered his daughter, a girl of only nine years of age. His petition was sent to the King, who, on the 13th of February 1850, replied that he had proclaimed Maheput as a robber and murderer, and offered a reward of three thousand rupees for his arrest.

On the 16th of March 1850, Goverdhun complained, that Maheput had attacked and plundered his house, and carried off his father to the jungles, and extorted from him a ransom of one hundred and ten rupees. His petition was sent to the King, who, on the 27th March, replied, that he had given frequent and urgent orders for the arrest of Maheput Sing.

Gunga Deen, a trooper of the Governor-General's body-guard, complained to the Resident, on the 9th of August 1844, that Maheput Sing had attacked and killed with his own hand his agent, Thakoor Sing, while he was taking seven hundred and seventy-four rupees to the revenue-collector. On the 11th of September 1849, he again complained to the Resident, that Maheput Sing had plundered Bhurteemow and other villages, in Dureeabad, of property to the value of six thousand seven hundred and fifty-nine rupees, and murdered five men, besides Thakoor Sing, his servant, and had committed numerous robberies in other villages during the year 1848. Among them one in Bhurteemow, in which he killed Ramjeet and four other men—that he had soon after committed a robbery in which no less than twenty-two persons were killed and wounded, and property to the value of two thousand rupees was carried off. The King was frequently pressed most earnestly to arrest this atrocious robber; and on the 9th of December 1849, the Frontier Police was, at the Kings request, directed to do all in their power to seize him.

In July 1847, Maheput Sing and his gang attacked the house of Mungul Sookul, a corporal of the 24th Regiment of Bengal Native Infantry, at midnight, robbed it of property to the value of five hundred rupees, and so rent the ears of his little son, by the violence with which he tore the gold rings from them, that the boy was not likely to live. The commanding officer of the regiment sent the corporal's petition for redress, through the Resident, to the Durbar; and orders were sent to the local authorities to afford it, but they were unable or unwilling to do anything.

Gunga Aheer, of Buroulee, in the district of Rodowlee, had been for three years a sipahee in the 48th Regiment of Bengal Native Infantry, under the name of Mata Deen. Continued sickness rendered him unfit for duty, and he obtained his discharge, and came home to his family. In March 1850, having been long without employment, and reduced, with his family, to great distress, he went to his relation, Ramdhun, of the Intelligence Department, in the service of the King of Oude, and then; on duty at Dureeabad, with the Amil. A reward of three thousand rupees having been offered by the King for the arrest of Maheput Sing, the Amil ordered Ramdhun to try his best to trace him out, and he took Gunga Aheer with him to assist, on a promise of securing for him good service if they succeeded. They went to a jungle, about two miles from Guneshpoor, and near the foot of Bhowaneegur. While they were resting at a temple in the jungle, sacred to Davey, Maheput came up, with twenty followers, to offer sacrifice; and as soon as they recognized the Harkara, Ramdhun, they seized both, and took them off in the evening to a jungle, four miles distant. In the hope of frightening Maheput, the Harkara pretended to be in the service of the Resident at Lucknow; but as the reward for his arrest had been offered on the requisition of the Resident, on the application of injured sipahees of the British army, this did not avail him. Their hands were tied behind their backs, and as soon as it became dark, they took Ramdhun off to a distance of twenty paces from where Maheput Sing sat, and made him stand in a circle of men with drawn swords. One man advanced, and at one cut with his sword, severed his right arm from his body, and it fell to the ground. Another cut into the side, under the stump, while a third cut him across the left side of the neck with a back cut, he all the time calling out for mercy, but in vain. On receiving the cut across the neck he fell dead, and the body was flung into the river Goomtee. Maheput sat looking on without saying a word.

They then amused themselves for some time by flogging Gunga Aheer with thorn bushes, while he in agony cried for mercy. The next day, by Maheput's orders, they laid him upon a bed of thorns and beat him again, while he screamed from pain, and they laughed at his cries. One of the followers told Maheput, that they had been cautioned by the outlaw, Jugurnath, the chuprassie, not to murder Ramdhun and his companion, or the English would some day avenge them; but he laughed and said that spies must be punished, to deter others from pursuing them. One of his followers then sat on Gunga's chest while another held his arms, and a third his legs, while a fourth cut off his nose, and one of his hands at the wrist, and the fingers of the other hand. He became senseless, and Maheput and his followers all left him in this state. In the evening a servant of Seochurn Chowdheree, of Bhowaneepoor, on his way to the jungle, saw him and reported his condition to his master, who sent people and had him taken to him on a litter. He had his wounds dressed by a village surgeon, and the next day sent him home to his wife and mother. The landlord of the village reported the case to Captain Orr, of the Frontier Police, at Fyzabad, who had Gunga taken off to the hospital at Lucknow, where he remained under the care of the Residency surgeon till he recovered. This poor man had to support his mother, wife, and daughter by his labour. His mother came in with him, and attended him in hospital, while his wife and child remained at their village.

While in hospital recovering, Maheput Sing was brought before him, by the Frontier Police, to be recognized. As soon as he saw him all the terrible scene of Ramdhun's murder and his own torture came so vividly before him, that he trembled from head to foot, like a man in an ague fit, and was for some time unable to speak. At last, when he saw the fetters on Maheput's legs, and the handcuffs on his wrists, and armed Government servants around him, he recovered his senses; and by degrees, recorded what he had witnessed and suffered at his hands.

On the 25th March 1850, Rajah Maun Sing, under orders from the Durbar, with all the force he could muster, invested the fort of Bhowaneegur, while the force under Captains Weston, Thomas, Bunbury, and Magness, attacked the three forts belonging to Rajah Prethee Put, of Paska. Maheput Sing left the fort on the 27th, with eleven followers, to collect reinforcements and harass the besiegers, and the garrison was commanded by his nephew.

On the 28th, Maun Sing had three men killed and several wounded, from the fire of the garrison, and wrote for reinforcements to Captain Weston, who was at Dureeabad, twelve miles distant. As soon as he got the letter, he mounted his horse, and leaving the force to follow, rode with his Assistant, Captain Orr, to the place, which is half a mile from Guneshpoor south, and two hundred yards from the left bank of the Goomtee river north. They were attended by a few sowars, under Seo Sing, and they reached the place before daybreak, on the 29th; and as soon as day appeared, proceeded with Captain Magness, who had galloped on in advance of his regiment to reconnoitre the fort, and were fired upon by the garrison wherever they were seen. Maun Sing's people had retired after the loss of a few men, to the distance of a mile, and lay scattered over the jungle.

The Infantry came up before sunset, and the guns before it grew dark, and all were placed in position, and a fire opened upon the fort till it grew too dark to point the guns. The garrison soon after attempted to escape by the west side, and were fired upon by the parties posted on that quarter. Captain Weston, hearing the fire, collected all the men he could, and getting with difficulty into the fort, found it empty. In the attempt to cut their way through, the garrison had two men killed and fifteen wounded and taken, and five managed to escape, under cover of the night, into the thick jungle. Bikhai, one of the most atrocious of Maheput's followers, was killed; but he killed two of the besiegers, and wounded two more before he fell. Akber Sing, the most atrocious of all the gang, had his arm taken off by a cannon-shot, and was seized. Maheput's nephew, the commandant of the garrison, was taken, with one of Maheput's secretaries and advisers.

Of Maun Sing's party, four were killed and thirteen wounded, and Captain Magness had one havildar severely wounded. The fort was levelled, and the jungle around cut down. The force then proceeded and took possession of the forts of Futtehpoor, Oskamow, Sorrea, Dyeepoor, and Etonja, all belonging to Jugurnath Chuprassie, another leader of banditti of that district They were only a few miles distant from Bhowaneegur, and were deserted by his gangs on their seeing a British force and hearing the guns open upon Bhowaneegur. Two hundred head of stolen cattle were found in the forts of Jugurnath, and restored to their proper owners. Parties were sent in pursuit of Maheput Sing, and two of his followers were secured; but he himself escaped for the time. The forts were all destroyed. Captain Orr, the Assistant Superintendent, in charge of the Frontier Police at Fyzabad, had been long in pursuit of Maheput Sing, and his parties, knowing all his haunts and associates, gave him no rest. His subadar, Seetul Sing, became acquainted with Prethee Paul, tallookdar of Ramnuggur, who had been deprived of his estate for defalcation, and become associated with Maheput Sing. The subadar persuaded this landholder that it would be to his advantage to aid in the arrest of so atrocious a robber and murderer; and when Maheput next came to him to seek some repose from his pursuers, and consult about future plans, he sent intimation to Seetul Sing, whose detachment of sipahees was at no great distance. On receiving the intimation, the subadar marched forthwith, and reached the place at the dawn of day, on the morning of the 1st of July 1850. Maheput Sing had just left the house to perform his ablutions, but on seeing them, he suspected their designs and re-entered the house. The subadar's party saw him, immediately surrounded the house, and demanded his surrender, Maheput Sing begged Prethee Paul to join him in defending the house or cutting their way through; but Prethee Paul told him that he had ruined himself by his atrocities, and must now submit to his fate, since he could not involve himself and all his family in ruin merely to assist him. Prethee Paul then took him by the arm, brought him out, and made him over to Seetul Sing, who had threatened to set fire to the house, forthwith unless he did so. He was then secured and taken off, well guarded, and in all possible haste, to Captain Orr, lest his gang might collect and attempt a rescue. Captain Orr sent him off, under a strong guard and well fettered, to Lucknow, to Captain Weston, the Superintendent of the Frontier Police.

Prethee Paul, the tallookdar, for the good service, got back his estate from the Oude sovereign, and an addition of five hundred rupees a-year to his nankar or personal allowance. Gunga Aheer is now a pensioner on the Residency fund, and his family has been provided for. Maheput Sing and his associate Gujraj were sentenced to transportation beyond seas, and sent off in October 1851.

It is remarked by the people, that few of these baronial robbers ever die natural deaths—that they either kill each other, or are killed sooner or later by the servants of Government. More atrocious crimes than those which they every month commit it is difficult to conceive. In the Bangor district, through which we passed last month, this class of landholders are certainly as strong and as much disposed to withhold the just dues of Government, and to resist its officers and troops, as they are here, but they do not plunder and burn down each other's villages, and murder and rob each other's tenants so often as they do here. The coalition has introduced among them a kind of *balance of power*, which makes them respect each other's rights, and the rights of each other's tenants, for the chiefs are dependent upon the attachment and fidelity of their respective tenants. The above list contains only a part of the leaders of gangs, by which the districts of Dureeabad, Rodowlee, Sidhore, Pertabgunge, Deva, and Jehangeerabad, are infested. We have seen no manufacture of any exportable commodity in Oude, nor have we seen traffic on any road in Oude, save that leading from Cawnpore to Lucknow.

In consequence of some bad seasons, a good deal of the grain required at the Capital, and in the districts to the north-east, comes from Cawnpore over this road. Were the road from Fyzabad to Lucknow good and safe, a good deal of land produce would, in ordinary seasons, come over it from the Goruckpoor district, and those intervening between Lucknow and Fyzabad. It would, however, be useless to make the road till the gangs which infest it are put down. A good and secure road from Lucknow through Sultanpoor to Benares, would be of still greater advantage.

February 25, 1850.—Halted at Dureeabad. I here saw the draft-bullocks attached to the guns, with Captain Orr's companies of Frontier Police. They are of the best kind, and in excellent condition. They have the same allowance of a seer and half of grain a-day, which is drawn for every bullock attached to his Majesty's artillery. The difference is that they get all that is paid for in their name, while the others get one-third; and really got none when on detached duty till lately. On Fridays, Captain Orr's bullocks get only half; and this is, I believe, the rule with all the others that get any at all. His bullocks are bred in the Nanpara, Nigasun, Dhorehra, and other districts in the Oude Tarae, and are of an excellent quality for work. They cost from 40 to 75 rupees a-pair. In these districts of the Tarae forest, the cows are allowed to go almost wild in large grass preserves, where they are defended from tigers; and the calves are taken from them, when a year old, to be taken care of at home, till sold for the dairy or for work. Captain Orr's bullocks have no grazing-ground, nor are they sent out at all to graze—they get nothing but bhoosa (chaff) and corn. Of bhoosa they get as much as they can eat, when on detached duty, as they take it from the peasantry without payment; but when at Lucknow, they are limited to a very small quantity, as Government has to pay for it. On the 15th of May, 1833, the King prohibited any one from taking bhoosa without paying for it, either for private or public cattle; and directed that bhoosa, for all the Artillery bullocks, should be purchased at the harvests, and charged for in the public accounts; but the order was disregarded like that against the murder of female children.

February 26, 1850—Sidhore, sixteen miles, W.S.W. The country, a plain, covered as usual with spring crops and fine foliage; but intersected midway by the little river Kuleeanee, which causes undulations on each side. The soil chiefly doomut and light, but fertile. It abounds more in white ants than such light soil generally does. We passed through the estate of Soorujpoor Behreylee, in which so many of the baronial robbers above described reside, and through many villages beyond it, which they had lately robbed and burnt down, as far as such villages can be burnt. The mud-walls and coverings are as good as bomb-proofs against the fire, to which they are always exposed from these robbers. Only twenty days ago, Chundee Behraleea and his party attacked the village of Siswae, through which we passed a few miles from this—plundered it, and killed three persons, and six others perished in the flames. They served several others in the neighbourhood in the same manner; and have, within the same time, attacked and plundered the town of Sidhore itself several times.

The boundary which separates the Dureeabad from the Sidhore district we passed some four miles back; and the greater part of the villages lately attacked are situated in the latter, which is under a separate Amil, Aga Ahmud, who is, in consequence, unable to collect his revenue. The Amil of Dureeabad, Girdhara Sing,* on the contrary, acquiesces in all the atrocities committed by these robbers, and is, in consequence, able to collect his revenue, and secure the favour of the Court. Some of the villages of the estate, held by the widow of Singjoo, late Rajah of Soorujpoor, are under the jurisdiction of the Sidhore Amil; and, as she would pay no revenue, the Amil took a force a few days ago to her twelve villages of Sonowlee, within the Dureeabad district, and seized and carried off some three hundred of her tenants, men, women, and children, as hostages for the payment of the balance due, and confined them pell-mell, in a fort. The clamour of the rest of the population as

I passed was terrible, all declaring that they had paid their rents to the *Ranee*, and that she alone ought to be held responsible. She, however, resided at Soorujpoor, within the jurisdiction, and under the protection of the Amil of Dureeabad.

* Girdhara Sing's patron is Chundee Sahaee, the minister's deputy, whose influence is paramount at present.

The Behraleea gangs have lately plundered the five villages of Sadutpoor, Luloopoor, Bilkhundee, and Subahpoor, belonging to Soorujbulee, the head Canoongo, or Chowdheree of Dureeabad, who had never offended them. Both the Amils were with me for the latter part of the road; and the dispute between them ran very high. It was clear, however, that Girdhara Sing was strong in his league with the robbers, and conscious of being able to maintain his ground at Court; and Aga Ahmud was weak in his efforts to put them down, and conscious of his being unable much longer to pay what was required, and keep his post. He has with him two Companies of Nujeebs and two of Telingas, and eight guns. The guns are useless and without ammunition, or stores of any kind; and the Nujeebs and Telingas cannot be depended upon. The best pay master has certainly the best chance. It is humiliating and distressing to see a whole people suffering such wrongs as are every day inflicted upon the village communities and town's people of Dureeabad, Rodowlee, Sidhore, and Dewa, by these merciless freebooters; and impossible not to feel indignant at a Government that regards them with so much indifference.*

* Poor Aga Ahmud was put into gaol, for defalcation, at the end of the season; but Girdhara Sing was received with great favour by the Court. The government of the district, for the next season, was confirmed, and the usual dress of honour was conferred upon him, but the Resident deemed it to be his duty to interpose and insist upon his not being sent out. The government of the district was, in consequence, taken from him, and made over to Rajah Maun Sing.

A respectable young agricultural capitalist from Biswa, Seetaram, rode along by my side this morning, and I asked him, "over whom these suttee tombs, near Biswa, and other towns were for the most part raised."—"Sir," said he, "they are chiefly over the widows of Brahmins, bankers, merchants, Hindoo public officers, tradesmen, and shopkeepers." "Are there many such tombs in Oude, over the widows of Rajpoot landholders?"—"I have not seen any, sir, and have rarely heard of the widow of a Rajpoot landholder burning herself." "No, sir," said Bukhtawar Sing, "how should such women be worthy to become suttees? They dare not become suttees, sir, with the murder of so many innocent children on their heads. Sir, we Brahmins and other respectable Hindoos feel honoured in having daughters; and never feel secure of a happy life hereafter till we see them respectably married. This, sir, is a duty the Deity demands from us, and the neglect of which we do not believe he can ever excuse. When the bridegroom comes sir, to fetch our daughter, the priest reads over the marriage-service, and the parents of the girl wash her feet and those of her bridegroom; and, as they sit together after the ceremonies, put into her arms a tray of gold and silver jewels, and rich clothes, such as their condition in life enables them to provide; and then invoke the blessing of God upon their union; and then, and not till then, do they feel that they have done their duty to their child. What can men and women, who murder their daughters as soon as they are born, ever hope for in this life or in a future state? What can widows, conscious of such crimes, expect from ascending the funeral pile, with the bodies of their deceased husbands who have caused them to commit such crimes?" "And you think that there really is merit in such sacrifices on the part of widows, who have done their duties in this life?"—"Assuredly I do, sir; if there were none, why should God render them go insensible to the pain of burning? I have seen many widows burn themselves in my time, and watched them from the time they first declared their intention to their death; and they all seemed to me to feel nothing whatever from the flames: nothing, sir, but support from above could sustain them through such trials. Depend upon it, sir, that no widow of a Rajpoot murderer of his own offspring would ever be so supported; they knew very well that they would not be so; and, therefore, very wisely never ventured to expose themselves to the trial: faithful wives and good mothers only could so venture. The Rajpoots, sir, and their wives were pleased at the prohibition, because others could no longer do what they dared not do!" "What do you think, Seetarum?"—"I think, sir, that this crime of infanticide had its origin solely in family pride, which will make people do almost anything. These proud Rajpoots did not like to put it into any man's power to call them *salahs* or *sussoors*,* (brothers-in-law or fathers-in-law).

*   These are terms of abuse all over India. To call a man sussoor or salah, in abuse, is to say to him, I have dishonoured your daughter or your sister!

"I remember an instance of a woman burning herself at Lasoora, six miles from Biswa, when I was fifteen years of age, and I am now twenty-five. She certainly seemed to suffer no pain. One forenoon she told her husband that in a former birth she had promised him that when he should be born a *maha brahman* at Biswa, she would unite herself in marriage to him, and live with him as his wife for twelve years; that these twelve years had now expired, and that she had that night received intimation from Heaven that her real husband, *Rajah Kirpah Shunker*, of Muthura, had died without having been married in this birth; that she was in reality his wife, and had already burnt herself five times with his body, and would now mix her ashes with his for the sixth time, and he must forthwith send her to the village of Lasoora, where she would become a suttee. The husband was astounded, for they had always lived together on the best possible terms, and out of the four children they had had two still survived. He and all their relations did all they could to dissuade her, but she disregarded them, and ran off to the Sewala (temple) in Biswa, which was built by my father. Thence she sent a Brahmin, by name Gokurn, to call me and my elder brother, Morlee Munohur, then seventeen years of age. We went, and she told us that she had been our mother in a former birth, and wished to see us once more before she died; she blessed us, and prayed that we might have each five sons, and then told us to arrange for her funeral pile at Lasoora, as all her former five suttees had been performed at that place.

"We thought she was delirious, and no one supposed that she would really burn herself. She, however, left the temple and proceeded towards Lasoora on foot, followed by a party of women and children, and by her husband, who continued to implore her to return home with him. He had a litter with him to take her, but she would not listen to him or to any one else. We reached Lasoora about an hour and a half before sunset, and she ordered the people to collect a large pile of wood for her, and told them that she would light it with a flame from her own mouth. They seemed to regard her as an inspired person, and did so. She mounted the pile, and it soon took fire, how I know not! Many people said they saw the flame come from her mouth, and all seemed to believe that it did so. The flames ascended, for it was in the month of March, and the wood was dry, and she seemed to be quite happy as she sat in the midst of them, and was burnt to death. Her husband told us, that she had lost one son some years before, and another only four days before she burnt herself, and that she had been much afflicted at his death. Whether there really had been such a person as Rajah Kirpah Shunker, no one ever thought it necessary to inquire. Her suttee tomb still stands at Lasoora among many others. Our mother was alive, though our father had been dead many years, and she used to say that the poor woman must have become deranged at the death of her child. The people all believed that she told the truth, and the husband was obliged to yield, though he seemed much afflicted. Her two sons still live, and reside at Biswa." *

* Moorlee Monowur, a very respectable agricultural capitalist, tells me, that all that his younger brother, Seetaram, told me, about the suttee, if strictly true, and can be proved by a reference to the poor woman's husband and sons, who still survive, and to the people of Bilwa and Lasoora.

I asked the Amil, "How he fed, clothed, and lodged his prisoners?" He said, "We always take them with us in our marches, secured in stocks or fetters. We cannot leave them behind, because we have no gaols or other places to keep them in, and require all our troops to move with us. As to food and clothing, they are obliged to provide themselves, or get their families or friends to provide them, for Government will not let us charge anything for their subsistence and clothing in the accounts."

"I understand that you and all other public servants who have charge of prisoners not only make them provide themselves with food and clothing, but make them pay for lamp-oil, whether they have a lamp burning at night or not?"—"When they require a lamp they must of course pay for it, sir; prisoners are always a source of much anxiety to us, for if we send them to Lucknow, they are almost sure to be let out soon, on occasions of thanksgiving, or on payment of gratuities, and enabled to punish all who have assisted us in the arrest; and with hosts of robbers around us, we are always in danger of an attempt to rescue them, which may cost us many lives." "If the gaol darogahs at Lucknow had not the power to sell his prisoners, sir," said Bukhtawar Sing, "how should he be able to pay so much as he does for his place? He is obliged to pay five hundred rupees or more for his place, and is not sure of holding it a month after he has bought it, so many are the candidates for a place so profitable!" "But he gets a share of the subsistence money, paid for the prisoners from the Treasury, does he not?"—"Yes, sir; of the four pice a-day paid for them by the King, he takes two, and sends them to beg through the city for what more they require." "If they get more than what he thinks they require from the public or their friends, he takes the surplus from them, I am told?"—"It is very true, sir, I believe. Fellows, sir, who have no substantial friends, and cannot and will not beg, soon sink under this scanty supply of food."

February 27, 1850—Sutrick, sixteen miles west, over a plain of muteear soil, tolerably well cultivated, and very well studded with trees of the finest kinds, single, in clusters and in groves. The mango-trees are in blossom, and promise well. The trees are said to bear only one season out of three, but some bear in one season, and others in another, so that the market is always supplied, though in some seasons more abundantly than in others. A cloudy sky and easterly wind, while the trees are in blossom, are said to be very injurious. A large landholder told me that they never took a tax upon any of the trees, not even the mhowa-trees, but the owner could not, except upon particular occasions, dispose of one to be cut down, without the permission of the zumeendar upon whose lands it stood. He might cut down one without his permission for building or repairing his house, or for fuel, on any occasion of marriage in his family, but not otherwise. A good many fine trees were, he said, destroyed by the local officers of Government. Having no tents, they collected the roofs of houses from a neighbouring village in hot or bad weather, cut away the branches to make rafters, and left the trunks as pillars to support the roofs, and under this treatment they soon died. He told me that cow-dung was cheaper for fuel than wood in this district, and consequently more commonly used in cooking; but that they gathered cow-dung for fuel only during four months in the year, November, December, January, and February; all that fell during the other eight months was religiously left, or stored for manure. In the pits in which they stored it, they often threw some of the inferior green crops of autumn, such as kodo and kotkee; but the manure most esteemed among them was *pigs' dung*—this, he said, was commonly stored and sold by those who kept pigs. The best muteear and doomut soils, which prevail in this district, are rented at two rupees a kutcha beegah, without reference to the crop which the cultivator might take from them; and they yielded, under good tillage, from ten to fifteen returns of the seed in wheat, barley, gram, &c. There are two and half or three kutcha beegahs in a pucka beegah; and a pucka beegah is from 2750 to 2760 square yards.

Sutrick is celebrated for the shrine of Shouk Salar, alias *Borda Baba*, the father of Syud Salar, whose shrine is at Bahraetch. This person, it is said, was the husband of the sister of Mahmood, of Ghuznee. He is supposed to have died a natural death at this place, while leading the armies of his sovereign against the Hindoos. His son had royal blood in his veins, and his shrine is held to be the most sacred of the two. A large fair is held here in March, on the same days that this fair takes place at Bahraetch. All our Hindoo camp followers paid as much reverence to the shrine as they passed as the Mahommedans. It is a place without trade or manufactures; but a good many respectable Mahommedan families reside in it, and have built several small but neat mosques of burnt bricks. There is little thoroughfare in the wretched road that passes through it.

The Hindoos worship any sign of manifested might or power, though exerted against themselves, as they consider all might and power to be conferred by the Deity for some useful purpose, however much that purpose may be concealed from us. "These invaders, however merciless and destructive to the Hindoo race, say they must have been sent on their mission by God for some great and useful purpose, or they could not possibly have succeeded as they did: had their proceedings not been sanctioned by Him, he could at any moment have destroyed them all, or have interposed to arrest their progress." These, however, are the speculations of only the thinking portion. At the bottom of the respect shown to such Mahommedan shrines, by the mass of Hindoos, there is always a strong ground-work of *hope* or *fear*: the soul or spirit of the savage old man, who had been so well supported on earth, must still, they think, have some influence at the Court of Heaven to secure them good or work them evil, and they invoke or propitiate him accordingly. They would do the same to the tomb of Alexander, Jungez Khan, Tymour, or Nadir Shah, without any perplexing inquiries as to their creed or liturgy.

February 28, 1850.—Chinahut, eleven miles west, over a plain intersected by several small streams, the largest of which is the Rete, near Sutrick. There is a good deal of kunkur-lime in the ground over which we have passed today; but the tillage is good where the land is at all level, and the crops are fine. The plain is cut up here and there by some ravines, but they are small and shallow, and render but a small portion of the surface unfit for tillage. The banks of the small streams are, for the most part, cultivated up to the water's edge.

We passed the Rete over a nice bridge, built by Rajah Bukhtawar Sing twenty-five years ago, at a cost of twenty-five thousand rupees, out of his own purse. He told me that one morning, in the rains, he came to the bank of this river, on his way to Lucknow from Jeytpoor, a town which we passed yesterday, and found it so swollen that he was obliged to purchase some large earthen jars, and form a raft upon them to take over himself and followers. While preparing his raft, which took a whole day, he heard that from five to ten persons were drowned, in attempting to cross this little river, every year, and that people were often detained upon the bank for four or five days together. He resolved to save people from all this evil; and as soon as he got home set about building this bridge, and got it ready before the next rains. It is a substantial work, with three good arches. About two miles on this side of the bridge he pointed out to me the single tree, near a mango-grove, where some eighteen or twenty years ago he overtook a large balloon, which the King, Nuseer-od Deen Hyder, had got made in the Dilkosha Park at Lucknow. It was made, he tells me, by a tall and slender young English gentleman, who visited Lucknow, with his uncle, for the special purpose of constructing and ascending in this machine. "When it was all ready, sir, the young man got into a small boat that was suspended under it, taking with him a gun and some artificial fish. We asked him what he intended to do with a gun in the clouds; and he told us, that in the sky he was in danger of meeting large birds that might hurt the balloon, and the gun was necessary to frighten them off. As the balloon began to ascend the old gentleman's eyes filled with tears, and I asked him why. He told me, that this young man's father had fallen into the sea, and been drowned; and he was always afraid, when the son went up, that he might never see him alive again.

"The King was sitting at the window in the upper story of the Dilkosha house, with some English gentlemen, when the balloon passed up close by, and the gentleman took off his hat and bowed gracefully as he passed, at which the King seemed much pleased. I commanded a regiment of Dragoons, and the King told me to take a party of my boldest and best-mounted men and follow the balloon. I selected seventeen, and we were all ready in our saddles. The balloon went straight up, and we lost sight of the man and the boat in which he sat. The machine, though it was sixty feet long, including boat and all, and twelve feet wide, seemed at last to be no larger than a small water-jug. Below we had no wind, but we soon saw the balloon driven by an upper current to the eastward, along the Fyzabad road. We followed as fast as the horses could carry us, crossed the Goomtee river over the old stone bridge, and passed many travellers on the road staring at the extraordinary machine, for they had heard nothing about it, and we had no time to tell them. When we had gone about seventeen miles, the balloon began to descend. It was in the month of March, and the weather was hot, and I had lost three horses before it came to the ground. The young man then began to let go his fish, and they came fluttering down, while the oil-cloths about the balloon made a noise like the growling of a wild beast. Seeing the enormous machine going at this rate, followed by us at full speed, the people along the road, who are always numerous in the morning, became so panic-struck that a great many fell down senseless upon their faces, and some of them could not be got to rise for some hours afterwards.

"We were not far from it when it approached the ground, and swept along on the border of this grove, on our left. Fortunately for the young man, it did not strike any trees. He was dressed all in black, and a very tall, handsome young man he was. As soon as he found himself near enough to the ground, he jumped out, holding one rope in his hand, and tried to stop the balloon, calling out to the people on the road, as loud as he could, *puckaro, puckaro!*—seize, seize! We were then within two hundred yards of it, and at full speed; and, instead of helping the young man, the people on the road, thinking the order was to seize them, fell down flat on their faces, unable to look upon the balloon, or utter a word. They all thought that it was some terrible demon from above come to seize and devour them. When we had headed it a little, we all sprang from our saddles, joined the young man at the ropes, and lashed them round anything we could find, as we were being dragged along. The young man took out his penknife, and gave the balloon a gash in the side, to let out the *smoke* that inflated it, and it collapsed and stopped. The first thing, sir, that the young man did was to call for fire, take a cigar from his waistcoat pocket, and begin to smoke, while we went to the assistance of the panic-struck travellers, many of whom were still lying senseless on the ground. We got water, and threw it in their faces; and when they were able to sit up, we mounted the young man upon one of our horses, and took him back slowly to Lucknow. He told me that it was so very cold above, that it gave him a severe headache, and that he found a cigar a good thing to remove it. The King was very glad when we brought him back, and he gave him several thousand rupees over and above the cost of making the balloon, and providing him and his uncle during their stay. They soon after left Lucknow for Lahore, and what became of them I know not."

Passing a Mahommedan village, I asked some of the landholders, who walked along by the side of my elephant, to talk of their grievances, whether they ever used pigs' dung for manure. They seemed very much surprised and shocked, and asked how I could suppose that Mahommedans could use such a thing. "Come," said Bukhtawar Sing, "do not attempt to deceive the Resident. He has been all over India, and knows very well that Mahommedans do not keep or eat pigs; but he knows, also, that there is no good cultivator in Oude who does not use the dung of pigs for manure; and you know that there is no other manure, save' pigeons' dung, that is so good." "We often purchase *manure* from those who prepare it," said the landholders, "and do not ask questions about what it may be composed of; but the greater part of the manure we use is the cow-dung which falls in the season of the rains, and is stored exclusively for that purpose. In the dry months, sir, the dung of cows, bullocks, buffaloes, &c., is gathered, formed into cakes, and stacked for fuel; but in the rains it is all thrown into pits and stored for manure."

Chinahut is the point from which we set out on the 2nd of December, and here I was met by the prime minister, Nawab Allee Nakee Khan, and the chancellor of the exchequer, Maharajah Balkrishun, to whom I explained my views as to the measures which ought to be adopted to save the peaceful and industrious portion of his Majesty's subjects from the evils which now so grievously oppress them.

Here closes my pilgrimage of three months in Oude; and I can safely say that I have learnt more of the state of the country, and the condition and requirements of the people, than I could possibly have learnt in a long life passed exclusively at the capital of Lucknow. Any general remarks that I may have to make on what I have seen and heard during the pilgrimage I must defer to a future period.

At four in the afternoon, I left Chinahut, and returned to Lucknow. At the old race-stand, about three miles from the Residency, I was met by the heir-apparent, and drove with him, in his carriage, to the Furra Buksh Palace, where we alighted for a few minutes, to go through the usual tedious ceremonies of an Oriental Court. On the way we were met by Mr. Hamilton, the chaplain, and his lady. Dr. and Mrs. Bell, and Captain Bird, the First Assistant, and his brother and guest. After the ceremony, I took leave of the Prince, and reached the Resident at six o'clock. My wife and children had left me at Peernuggur, to return, for medical advice, to the Residency, where I had the happiness to find them well, and glad to see me. Having broken my left thigh hone, near the hip joint, in a fall from my horse, in April, 1849, I was unable to mount a horse during the tour, and went in a tonjohn the first half of the stage, and on an elephant the last half, that I might see as much as possible of the country over which we were passing. The pace of a good elephant is about that of a good walker, and I had generally some of the landholders and cultivators riding or walking by my side to talk with.

END OF THE TOUR.

PRIVATE CORRESPONDENCE

RELATING TO THE ANNEXATION OF THE KINGDOM OF OUDE TO BRITISH INDIA.

Camp, Nawabgunge, 5th December, 1849.

My Dear Bird,

I had heard from Mahomed Khan what you mention regarding the imposition practised on the King by the singers; but from his having conferred a khilaut on the knaves, they supposed that he had, as usual, pardoned all. If you have grounds to believe that the King is prepared to punish them, or to acquiesce in their punishment, pray ask an audience and ascertain his Majesty's wishes. When we last went, I was in hopes that he would tell me that he wished to be relieved of their presence, and did all I could to encourage him to do so. If the King wishes to have them removed, encourage him to give immediate orders to the minister to confine them; and offer any assistance that may be required to take them across the Ganges, or put them into safe custody. When it is done, it must be done promptly.

As to the Taj Mahal, I went on an order by Richmond, "that the King should put a Mahaldarnee upon her if he wished." I was told that such was Richmond's order, and I give mine in consequence. I will refer to the Dufter for his order. But you must at once insist upon all sipahees being withdrawn from her house. This order was given by me and should be enforced by you. I said that the Mahaldarnee might remain, but it must be alone, without sipahees, &c.

On emergency, act of course on your own discretion I only wish that the King may be induced to consent to the removal of all the singers, and meddling eunuchs also.

Yours sincerely,
(Signed) W. H. SLEEMAN.

To Captain Bird,
First Assistant.

Sadik Allee should be secured, and punished with the rest.

(Signed) W. H. SLEEMAN.

* * * * *

Camp, Bahraetch, 10th December, 1849.

My Dear Bird,

The conduct of the singers which exasperated the King had no reference to public matters with which he was pledged not to permit them to interfere; and my only request was, that you should offer your aid in removing them should his Majesty indicate any wish for it. The King said he would himself punish them for their conduct by banishment across the Ganges, and he must be left to do so: it was not from any demand made by us, but from resentment for a personal affront, or an affront to his understanding. We cannot call upon the King to do what he said he would do under such circumstances, but must leave it to himself. The removal of two out of a dozen fellows of this description will be of no use—their places will soon be filled by others. Any attempt on your part to supply their places by better men will only tend to indispose the King towards them; and it is no part of our duty to dictate to his Majesty with whom he shall associate in his private hours.

I have had abundant proof that, to reduce the influence of the present favourites, has no tendency to throw the power into better hands—no authority of any kind taken from them has, by the minister, been confided to better men; the creatures of one are not a whit better than the creatures of the other. If his Majesty were to rouse himself, and apply his own mind to business, we might hope for some good, and I see little chance of this.

You are not to order that the King fulfil his promise, because, as I have said, it was no pledge made on the requisition of our Government on the Resident. If he does not fulfil it, it is only one proof more added to a hundred of his exceeding weakness. There are at least a dozen worse men now influencing all that the King and minister do than Kotab Alee and Gholam Ruza. The last order given regarding Taj Mahal by me was, that she should admit a Mahaldarnee from the King, but that no sipahees should be forced upon her. I wrote to the King to this effect, and my order must be enforced. I am told by the moonshee, that when the King expressed a wish to have such guardians upon many, Richmond replied that he might have one upon Taj Mahal, who had given such proof of profligacy. It was not a judicial decision, to be referred to as a guide under all circumstances, but a mere arrangement which might any day require to be altered. Taj Mahal is so profligate and insolent a woman, that if she refuses to obey my order, and receive the King's Mahaldarnee, I shall withdraw the Residents.

After what the Governor-General had told the King in November, 1847, regarding what our Government would feel itself bound to do, unless his Majesty conducted the duties of a sovereign better than he had hitherto done; and after the experience we have since had of his entire neglect of those duties, you should not, I think, have said what you mention having said to him, that our Government had no wish to deprive him of one iota of the power he had. It was a declaration not called for by the circumstances, or necessary on the occasion, and should have been avoided, as it is calculated to impair the impression of his responsibility for the exercise of his power. No sovereign ever showed a greater disregard for the duties and responsibilities of his high office than he has done hitherto, and as our Government holds itself answerable to the people of Oude for a better administration, he should not be encouraged in the notion that he may always show the same disregard with impunity—that is, continue to retain every iota of his power whether he exercised it properly or not. No man, I believe, ever felt more anxious for the welfare of the King, his family, and country, than I do; but unless he exercises his fearful power better, I should be glad, for the sake of all, to see the whole, or part of it, in better hands.

The minister has his Motroussil with me, and I have daily communications of what is done or proposed to be done, and you may be sure that I lose no occasion of admonition. I did not mention anything you said regarding your interview with the King in your letter to Mahomed Khan; but in a few hours after your letter came he got the whole from the minister, and reported it to me. He wants us to undertake the work of turning out the King's favourites, that he may get all the power they lose, without offending his master by any appearance of moving in the matter.

We go hence to-morrow; hope to be at Gonda on the 14th, and Fyzabad on the 18th. I have requested the post-master to send all our letters to Fyzabad by the regular dawk from Thursday next, the 13th. From Fyzabad I will arrange for their coming to my camp.

Yours sincerely,
(Signed) W. H. SLEEMAN.

To Captain Bird,
&c. &c.

* * * * *

Camp, Ghunghole, 12th December, 1849.

My Dear Bird,

I got your letter of the 9th instant last night, at our last ground. In what you have done, you have not, I think, acted discreetly. You asked me whether, in any case of emergency, you should act on your discretion, and I told you in reply that you might do so; but surely, whether the King should have a dozen singers or only ten could not be considered one of such pressing emergency as not to admit of your waiting for instructions from me, or, at least, for a reply to your letter. The King has told you truly, that the matter in which the offenders had transgressed had reference to his house, and not to his Government or ours. This is a distinction which you appear to have lost sight of from the first. If I demand reparation from another for wrong or insults suffered from his servants, and he promises to punish them by dismissal from his service but afterwards relents and detains them, I consider it due to myself and my character to insist upon the fulfilment of his promise; but if I voluntarily visit any friend who has at last become sensible of the impositions of his servants which had long been manifest to all his neighbours, with a view to encourage him in his laudable resolution to dismiss them from his service, and to offer my aid in effecting the object should he require it, and he promises me not to swerve from it, but afterwards relents and retains the impostors, I pity his weakness, but I do not consider it due to myself, or to my character, to insist upon his fulfilling his promise. By considering two cases so very distinct, the same, you have placed yourself in a disagreeable situation, for I cannot support you; that is, I can neither demand that the requisitions made by you be complied with, nor can I tell the King that I approve of them. Had you waited for my reply, which was sent off from Bahraetch on the 10th, you would have saved yourself all this annoyance and mortification. It has arisen from an overweening confidence in your personal influence over his Majesty; the fact is, I believe that no European gentleman ever has had or ever will have any personal influence over him, and I very much doubt whether any real native gentleman will ever have any. He never has felt any pleasure in their society, and I fear never will. He has hitherto felt easy only in the society of such persons as those with whom he now exclusively associates, and to hope that he will ever feel easy with persons of a better class is vain. I am perfectly satisfied, in spite of the oath he has taken in the name of his God, and on the head of his minister, that he made to you the promise you mention; and I am no less satisfied that the minister wished for the removal of the singers, provided it should be effected through us without his appearing to his master to move in the matter, and that he wished their removal solely with a view to acquire for himself the authority they had possessed. You should not have any more audiences with the King without previous reference to me; nothing is likely to occur to require it.

Yours sincerely,
(Signed) W. H. SLEEMAN.

To Captain Bird,
&c. &c.

* * * * *

Camp, Fyzabad, 18th December, 1819.

My Dear Bird,

I send you the letter which you wish to refer to. As you quote my first letter, pray let me see it. I kept no copy, but have a distinct recollection of what I intended to say in it regarding this affair of the singers. It shall be sent back to you. The term "indiscreet" had reference only to your second visit, and demand from the King of the fulfilment of his promise. I had no fault whatever to find with your first visit. The term "private" must have had reference, not to the promise or to the person to whom it was made, but to the offence with which the singers stood charged. It was an affront offered to the King's understanding that he took affront at, and whether he had made a promise to resent it as such to me, or to you could make no difference. If he did not fulfil it, we should pity this further instance of his weakness, but could have no right to insist upon his doing so. Even had the offence been an interference in public affairs, and breach of the King's engagements, I should not have demanded their banishment without a reference to the Governor-General, because the delay of waiting for instructions involved no danger or serious inconvenience; that is, I should not have demanded it when the King was so strongly opposed to it. I must distinctly deny that you demanded the King's fulfilment of his promise in conformity to any instructions received from me, or in accordance with my views of what was right or expedient in this matter. Your second visit and demand were neither in conformity to the one nor in accordance with the other. You must have put a construction upon what I wrote which it cannot fairly bear. By "requisitions" I mean your requirements that the two men should be banished by the King, according to his promise. No notice has been made to me of your visit by the Court, and I have therefore had no occasion to say anything whatever about it in my communications to the Court, nor shall I have any I suppose. In your letter of the 4th instant, you say, with regard to the Taj Mahal's case, "Not knowing whether you do or do not wish me to act in any sudden emergency during your absence, I suppose, therefore, that had you had any such wish you would have instructed me on the subject." In reply, I requested that you would so act on your own discretion in any such sudden case of emergency.

Yours sincerely,
(Signed) W. H. SLEEMAN.

To Captain Bird,
&c. &c.

* * * * *

Camp, Mahomdee, 2nd February, 1850.

My Dear Sir Erskine,

Had it not been too late for you to join my camp conveniently, I should have asked you to run out and see a little of the country and people of Oude, after you had seen so much of those of the Honourable Company's dominions. A few years of tolerable government would make it the finest country in India, for there is no part of India with so many advantages from nature. I have seen no soil finer; the whole plain of which it is composed is capable of tillage; it is everywhere intersected by rivers, flowing from the snowy chain of the Himmalaya, which keep the moisture near the surface at all times, without cutting up any of the land on their borders into deep ravines; it is studded with the finest groves and single trees, as much as the lover of the picturesque could wish; it has the boldest and most industrious peasantry in India, and a landed aristocracy too strong for the weak and wretched Government; it is, for the most part, well cultivated; yet with all this, one feels, in travelling over it, as if he was moving among a people suffering under incurable physical diseases, from the atrocious crimes every day perpetrated with impunity, and the numbers of suffering and innocent people who approach him, in the hope of redress, and are sent away in despair.

I think your conclusion regarding the source of the signs you saw of beneficial interference in the north-west provinces a fair one. A Lieutenant-Governor is able to see all parts of the country under his charge every year, or nearly all; and while he is sufficiently "monarch of all he surveys" to feel an interest in, and to provide for the general good, he has a sufficient knowledge of the internal management of particular districts to control the proceedings of the local officers. He is also well seconded in a very efficient Board of Revenue. But I must not indulge in these matters any further, till I have the pleasure of meeting you where we can talk freely about them.

I trust that all at Lucknow will be conducted to your satisfaction and that of Mrs. Erskine. I have this morning received a note from Mr. Erskine, who left you, it appears, before the little heir-apparent returned your visit. I expect to complete my tour and return to Lucknow on the 20th, when I shall have seen all that I required to see, to understand the working of the existing system, and the probable effects of any suggested changes.

With kind regards to Mrs. Erskine,

Believe me,
Yours very sincerely,
(Signed) W. H. SLEEMAN.

To Sir Erskine Perry.

P.S.—I must not omit to thank you for the expression of your favourable opinion of the "Rambles." There is one thing of which I can assure you, that the conversations mentioned in it are genuine, and give the real thoughts and opinions of the people on the subjects they embrace.

W. H. S.

* * * * *

Lucknow, 26th April, 1850.

My Dear Elliot,

I did not send Weston's letters with the other papers, because they were not written in an official form. He was the senior officer with the force, and had authority from the Durbar to call upon all local, civil, and military authorities to co-operate in the work; but he did not take upon himself the command, or write in official form. He inspired all with harmony and energy, and brought the whole strength of the little force to bear upon the right points at the right time.

The head of Prethee Put of Paska was cut off by Captain Magness's sipahees after his death, to be sent to the King as a trophy, but Captain Weston would not let it come in. The body was offered to his family and friends for interment, but none of the family or tribe (Kolhun's Rajpoots) would have anything to do with the funeral ceremonies of a man who had murdered his eldest brother and the head of his tribe. The body was, with the head, put into a sheet, taken to the river Ghagra, and committed to the stream, to flow to the Ganges, as the best interment for a Hindoo. These sipahees knew nothing of the man's history; but the people who saw the affair from the Dhundee Fort mentioned that the body was thrown into the river at the precise place where he had thrown in that of his eldest brother, after murdering him in the boat with his own hands, as stated in the extract from my Diary; and all believe that this retribution arises from an interposition from above. The eldest son of the murdered brother will, I hope, be put into possession of the estate.

The Governor-General may like to peruse these letters, and I send them. They give, perhaps, a fuller and better account of what was done, and the manner in which it was done, than more studied compositions, in an official form, would have given.

Yours sincerely,
(Signed) W. H. SLEEMAN.

To Sir H. M. Elliot, K.C.B.

* * * * *

Lucknow, 8th July, 1850.

My Dear Sir James,

I feel that my Indian career, which has now lasted forty years, must be drawing to a close, and I am anxious for the settlement in life of my only son, now between seventeen and eighteen years of age. Having no personal claims upon any member of the Home Government of India, I solicit the insertion of his name on his Grace the Duke of Wellington's list of candidates for a commission in the Dragoons; and he is now preparing for his examination under the care of Mr. Yeatman, at Westow Hill, Norwood, Surrey, near London. But he is ambitious to obtain an appointment to Bengal, where his father has served so long, and may, possibly, have friends and recollections that might be useful to him in the early part of his career. It falls to the lot of few to have the opportunities that I have had to carry out the benevolent views of Government in measures of great and general benefit to the people, and to secure their gratitude and affection to their rulers. All the measures which I have been employed to carry out have tended to display the benevolent solicitude of the Government of India for the welfare of the people committed to its charge; the object of all has been the greater security of life and property throughout the country, the greater confidence of the people in the wisdom and efficiency of our rule, and their greater feeling of interest in this stability. These measures, as far as they have been confided to my care, have all succeeded; but, as I have stated (p. 79) in a printed report, a copy of which will be sent to you, they have neither flattered the vainglory of any particular nation, nor enlisted on their side the self-love of any influential class or powerful individual, and they have, in consequence, been attended with little *éclat*. They have, however, tended to secure to the Government the gratitude and affection of the people of India, and are measures of which that Government may justly feel proud. The stability of our Government in India must depend less upon our military victories than upon the confidence and affection with which our civil and political administration may inspire the great mass of the people. The general belief is, that our object is their substantial good, and that we are instruments in the hands of Divine Providence to effect that object. In our military glory they can feel no sympathy, and in our territorial acquisitions little interest; but they can and do appreciate every measure which tends to improve the security of life, property, and industry through the land—to restore the bond of good feeling between the Government and governed, where it has for a time been severed or impaired by accident—to provide the people with works tending to improve their comfort and convenience—to mitigate sufferings from calamities of season, and to encourage all to exert themselves honestly in their proper sphere. In carrying out the views of Government in such measures, and such only, has my life in India been spent; and for doing so to the best of my humble ability I have, I believe, done much to make its rule revered throughout India. It is by such measures that the respect and confidence of the great mass of the people have been secured, so as to enable Europeans, male and female, to pass from one end of the country to the other with the assurance, not only that they will suffer no personal injury, but no mark of disrespect. Should anything occur to deprive us of this confidence and respect among the great mass of the people, the recollection of our victories, and assurance of our superior military organization will avail us but little; and it is as one who has zealously and successfully aided Government in securing them, that I now venture to address you, in the hope that you will—if you can do so consistently with your public duties and pledges to others—open to my son the same career of usefulness by conferring upon him a nomination to the civil service of India. He is now five months above seventeen years of age; and by the time he is eighteen, he will, I hope, under Mr. Yeatman's judicious care, be able to pass his examination for Haileybury, should he, through your means, obtain this the utmost object of his ambition. Over and above the desire to follow his father's footsteps in India, he is anxious to avoid the necessity of encroaching so much upon the small means I have to provide for his four sisters, by entering so expensive a branch of the public service as the Dragoons. I know the great nature of the favour I ask from you. It is the first favour that I have ever asked from any member of the Home Government of India; and I solicit it from you solely on the ground of service rendered to the Government and people of India. I am told that I must address my application to an individual; and I address it to you, under the impression that you are the member with whom such ground is likely to meet with most consideration;—not that I think any member of the Honourable Court would disregard it; for I believe, after long and varied experience in public affairs, and much thought and reading, that no body intrusted with the Government of a distant possession ever performed their duties with more earnest solicitude for its welfare than the Court of Directors of the Honourable East India Company; but because your public career has inspired me with more confidence than that of any other member of the Court as now constituted. If you cannot grant me the favour I ask, you will, I know, pardon the liberty I have taken in asking it.

And believe me, with great respect,
Yours faithfully,
(Signed) W. H. SLEEMAN.

To Sir James Weir Hogg, Bart.

* * * * *

Lucknow, 20th September, 1850.

My Dear Sir Charles,

The papers give us reason to hope that it is your intention to visit Lucknow on your way down from the hills, and if you can make it convenient to come, I shall be rejoiced to have the opportunity of showing you all that is worth seeing, and be able to afford all who come with you, ladies and gentlemen, accommodation.

The only road to Lucknow for carriages is from Cawnpore, and if you come that way, I will have carriages sent for you. If you come by any other road, I will have elephants sent to whatever place you may mention, and tents if required. It has been usual, when the Commander-in-chief visits Lucknow, for Government to intimate the intention to the King through the Resident in Oude, that preparation may be made for his reception in due form.

I mention this that you may make known your wish or intention to the Governor-General, in time for me to prepare the King and his Court.

From Cawnpore to this is only a drive of six hours, the distance being fifty miles, and the road good. All officers, &c., will be glad to have an opportunity of paying their respects to their distinguished Chief.

Believe me,
Yours very faithfully,
(Signed) W. H. SLEEMAN.

To his Excellency
Sir Charles Napier, G.C.B.,
&c. &c. &c.

* * * * *

Lucknow, 7th November, 1850.

My Dear Allan,

In the "Englishman" of the 28th, and the "Hurkara" of the 29th, there are some strictures on Oude affairs. The editors of both papers are, I believe, sturdy, honest men; but their correspondents are not acquainted with the merits of the particular case referred to, or with Oude affairs generally. I vouch for the truth of everything stated in the enclosed paper, and shall feel obliged if you will give it to the one most likely, in your opinion, to make a fair use of it. There can be no harm in putting an editor in possession of the real truth in a question involving not only individual but national honour; for he must be anxious to make his paper the vehicle of truth on all such questions.

I do not like to address either of the editors, because Government expect all their servants will abstain from doing so in their own vindication, and will leave their honour in their keeping. I have done so since 1843, and should now do so were I alone concerned in this affair. You may mention my name as authority for what is stated, but pray let it be mentioned confidentially. Government has been informed of the truth, and it is well that the public should be so.

Yours sincerely,
(Signed) W. H. SLEEMAN
To J. Allan, Esq.

* * * * *

Lucknow, 17th November, 1850.

My Dear Sir James,

I thank you for your very kind letter of the 7th ultimo: my son is preparing for his examination, and expects his commission in some regiment of cavalry very soon. He has not only become reconciled to it, but would, I believe, now prefer remaining at home as a cavalry officer to coming to India in any capacity. As I have only one son, and he has four sisters to look after, I should be unwilling to have him sent out to India as a cadet, were he anxious to be so. A good regiment is an excellent school for a young man, but no school could be worse than a bad regiment; and among so many, there must always be some bad. I have seen some of the sons of my old friends utterly ruined in character and constitution by being posted to such regiments when too young to think for themselves. I feel, however, as grateful to you for your very kind offer as I should be, were I to avail myself of it.

If I return to England, I shall take advantage of the earliest opportunity to pay my respects and become personally acquainted with you; but I have no intention to leave India as long as I feel that I can perform efficiently the duties intrusted to me.

I had a few days ago, in referring to Government an important question that must some day come before you, occasion to mention an important and interesting fact. During the last collision with the Seiks, I found that the Government securities kept up their value here, while in Calcutta they fell a good deal; and the merchants here employed agents in Calcutta to purchase largely for sale here. Paper to the value of more than three millions sterling, or three crores of rupees, is held by people residing in the city of Lucknow, and the people had never the slightest doubt that we should be ultimately triumphant. The question was whether heirs and executors of persons domiciled here and leaving property in Government securities, should apply to Her Majesty's Supreme Court in Calcutta, for probates to wills and letters of administration, or whether an act should be passed to render the decision of the highest Court at Lucknow, countersigned, by the Resident, as valid as the certificate of a judge in our own provinces, as far as such property in Government securities might be concerned. A provision of this sort had been omitted in Act 20 of 1841, which was considered applicable to all British India, of which the kingdom of Oude was held to form a part.

We have now a fair prospect of long peace, during which I hope our finances will improve. The lavish life-pensions granted after wars in Central and Southern India will be lapsing with the death of the present incumbents, many of whom are becoming old and infirm, and our means of transit and irrigation will increase with the new works which are being formed, and we shall always have it in our power to augment our revenue from indirect taxation, as wealth and industry increase.

Believe me, My Dear Sir James,
Very faithfully and obligedly yours, (Signed) W. H. SLEEMAN.

To Sir James Weir Hogg, Bart.

* * * * *

Lucknow, 2nd March, 1851.

My Lord,

The mail of the 24th January has just come in, and I find my only son Henry Arthur gazetted for the 16th Dragoons. He told me by the last mail that he was to be so if he passed his examination on the 10th of that month, which he hoped to do; but I deferred writing to thank you for your kind exertions in his behalf till his name should appear in the "Gazette." I pray your Lordship to accept my most grateful acknowledgments for this act of kindness, added as it has been to the many others which I have received at your hands. It is not the less valuable that it is the only favour I have received from England since I left it more than forty years ago, though, I believe, few have done more to benefit the people of its eastern dominions, and to secure for it their esteem and affection.

I trust that my son will never do anything to make your Lordship regret the favour conferred upon me and him on this occasion. He is, I believe, in disposition, manners, and education a little gentleman; and in time he will, I hope, become a good officer.

If I might take the liberty, I would pray your Lordship to offer, in such terms as may appear to you suitable, my grateful acknowledgments for the consideration I have received, to his Grace the Duke of Wellington, and to Lord Fitzroy Somerset. My London Agents, Messrs. Denay, Clark, and Co., of Austin Friars, have been instructed to pay for my son's commission and outfit, and to provide him with the funds indispensably necessary in addition to his pay.

We shall now look with much interest to the Parliamentary discussions on Indian affairs, for we must expect some important changes on the renewal of the Charter. Whatever these changes may be for the home or local Government, I trust the benefit of the people of India will be considered the main point, and not the triumph of a party. The statesman who shall link India more closely with New Zealand will be a benefactor to both England and India, and that colony also. It might, with advantage to itself, take those children of Indian officers who cannot find employment of any kind in India, and ought not to be thrown back upon the mother-country. With this view, it might be useful to transfer our orphan institutions to that island, to direct that way our invalid and pensioned officers, who, while subsisting upon their pensions or stipends, would be able to establish their children in a climate suitable to the preservation of their race, which that of India certainly is not.

India is at present tranquil, and likely to remain so. We have no native chiefs, or combination of native chiefs, to create uneasiness; and if we continue to satisfy the great body of the people that we are anxious, to the best of our ability, to promote their happiness and welfare, and are the most impartial arbitrators that they could have, we shall have nothing to fear. The moment that this mass is impressed with the belief that we wish to govern India only for ourselves, or as the French govern Algiers, from that moment we must lose our vantage ground and decline. We may war against the native chiefs of India, but we cannot war against the people—we need not fear what may be called political dangers, but we must guard carefully against those of a social character which would unite against us the members of all classes and all creeds.

But I must no longer indulge in speculations of this sort, in which you can now feel little interest amidst the important changes which are now taking place in the institutions and relations of European nations. With grateful recollections of kindness received, and great respect,

I remain,
Your Lordship's obedient servant,
(Signed) W. H. SLEEMAN.

To the Right Hon.
the Earl of Ellenborough.

P.S.—Since writing the above, I have received your Lordship's letter of the 18th of January, and have been much gratified with the favourable opinion you entertain of the commandant and officers. It is the best assurance I could have of my boy being safe. Nothing could be more auspicious than the opening of the lad's career, and I trust he will profit by the advantage.

* * * * *

Lucknow, 18th March, 1851.

My Dear Sir Erskine,

I have read over with much interest the two small works you have done me the favour to send me, the one on Buddhism, and the other on Law Reform; but I have not ventured upon the Seventh Report of the Board of Education yet, because I have had a good deal to do and think about; and a good deal of it is in small print, very trying for my eyes, which are none of the strongest. I shall, however, soon read it.

I concur in all your views about the necessity of throwing overboard the whole system of special pleading, and have been amused with Sir J. P. Grant's horror of your proposed innovations. It is not less than that which he expressed at the little Macaulay Code, intended to blow up the whole pyramid raised by "the wisdom of our ancestors," in which so many illustrious characters he entombed. He was, indeed, as you say, "a great *laudator temporis acti*;" but the number of those like him at all times in England and its distant possessions is fearful. One likes to look to America in this as in all things tending to advancement; but there the "damned spot" stares us in the face, blights our hopes, and crushes our sympathies—hideous slavery—hideous alike in the recollection of the past, the contemplation of the present, and the anticipation of the future. I wish two things—1. That you would write a work on the subject less "sketchy and perfunctory," as you call it, so that any one not versed in English law and procedure might be able to understand it and appreciate it thoroughly. 2nd. That you would, when relieved from your present office, come out as our law member of council, to press your views on our Government with effect. With these law reforms, as with railroads, there were less impediments in India than in England; but there is one thing that I would observe. In our own Indian Courts our judges would—for a time at least—want the aid of honest *masters* to condense and report upon cases under trial. Such men would be made in time; and in considering such things, we must recollect that almost the only persons in India who can send agents into all parts of it, with a perfect assurance of honest dealing, are the native merchants and bankers. But I won't dwell on this subject. I can't find amongst the numerous Buddhists here, one who knows anything about "Kapila vasta," which you place near to Lucknow. I should like to visit the birth-place of a man who did so much for mankind as Sakeen Gantama.

He would hardly have done as I have, placed my only son in the 16th Lancers. However, I may console myself, for he may be in it a long time without doing much mischief, for I do hope that the people of the nations of modern Europe are too strong and too wise to let their sovereigns and ministers play such fantastic tricks as they were "wont to play," when George the 3rd, and Edward the 3rd, and Henry the 5th were kings. Property, good sense, and good business have greatly increased and spread, and are every day producing good fruits.

Believe me,
Yours very trusting,
(Signed) W. H. SLEEMAN.

To Sir Erskine Perry,
&c. &c.

* * * * *

Lucknow, 31st March, 1851.

My Dear Sir,

I grieve to say that I can do nothing whatever for the son of my late friend Colonel Ouseley, and have been obliged to write to him to that effect, as to many other sons of old and valued friends whom I should be glad to aid if I could.

Tens of thousands of the most happy families I have seen in India owe all they have to the able and judicious management of the late Colonel Ouseley when in the civil charge of the districts of Houshengabad and Baitool, in the Saugor territories; and no man's memory is more dear to the people of those districts than his now is. The family of a man who had done so much to make his government beloved and respected over so large a field should never want if I could prevent it; but I have no situations whatever in my gift, nor have I any influence over any persons who have such situations to bestow.

> Believe me,
> Yours truly,
> (Signed) W. H. SLEEMAN.

To Captain Harrington.

* * * * *

Lucknow, 24th November 1851.

My Lord,

Lucknow affairs are now in a state to require the assumption of the entire management of the country; and the principal question for your Lordship's consideration is, whether this shall be done by a new treaty or by simple proclamation. Treaties not only justify but enjoin the measure; our pledges to the people demand it; and all India are, I believe, satisfied of its justice, provided we leave the revenues for the maintenance of the royal family in suitable dignity, and for the benefit of the people.

We may disencumber our Government of the pay of two regiments of Oude Local Infantry, and incorporate them with the Oude force to be raised, and of that of the officers of the residency, altogether about two lacs and a-half of rupees; and when things are settled down a little, the brigade now here—of three infantry regiments and a company of artillery, costing some four lacs more—may be dispensed with, perhaps.

If I may be permitted to give an opinion as to the best mode of the two, I should say proclamation, as the more dignified.

I have prepared all the information I believe your Lordship will require, and am ready to wait upon you with it when and where it may seem most convenient.

The treasury is exhausted, and fifty lacs are required to pay the stipendiaries of the royal family and establishments; and assuredly all the members of that family, save the King's own household, are wishing for some great measure to place them under the guarantee of the British Government. The people all now wish for it, at least all the well-disposed, for there is not a man of integrity or humanity left in any office. The King's understanding has become altogether emasculated; and though he would not willingly do harm to any one, he is unable to protect any one. He would now, I believe, willingly get rid of his minister; and, having exhausted the treasury, the minister would not much dislike to get rid of him. I shall do my best to prevent his being released from the responsibility of his misdoings till I meet your Lordship. I should like, if possible, to meet your Lordship where there is likely to be the least crowd of expectants and parade to take up your time and distract your attention. If at Cawnpore, I hope you will permit me to have my camp on the Oude side of the river, with a tent in your camp for business during the day. With your Lordship's commands to attend, it will be desirable to have an order to make over my treasury to the First Assistant, to prevent delay. Should you desire any memoranda to be sent, they shall be forwarded as soon as ordered. If any further public report upon the state of Oude affairs appears to be required, I must pray your Lordship to let me know as soon as convenient. I shall not propose any native gentlemen for the higher offices; but it will be necessary to have a great many in the subordinate ones, to show that your Lordship wishes to open employment in all branches of the new administration to educated native gentlemen.

> I remain,
> Your Lordship's obedient servant,
> (Signed) W. H. SLEEMAN.

> To the Most Noble
> The Marquis of Dalhousie,
> Governor-General,
> &c. &c. &c.

* * * * *

Lucknow, 18th March, 1852.

My Lord,

I was favoured with your Lordship's letter of the 24th ultimo in due course, and did not reply immediately as I had stated, or was about to state, in a public form, all that seemed to be required about Captain Bird and Dr. Bell. Dr. Bell had apologised for indiscretions in conversation, but denied ever having authorised Mr. Brandon to make use of his name; and pretended utter ignorance of the intrigues which he was carrying on at the time that he was doing his utmost to convey wrong impressions to the Durbar. I feel grateful for the support your Lordship has given me. I cared nothing about the intrigues of these very silly men while under the impression that it was your intention to interpose effectually for the benefit of the people of Oude, because the new arrangements would have rendered them harmless; but when I found that you could not do so at present, it became necessary, for my own dignity and that of the Government, to do my best to put a stop to them. Most assuredly Captain Bird had been trying hard to persuade the King and his minister that our Government could not interfere, and that all the threats of the Governor-General would continue to be what they had hitherto been, and might be disregarded.

I find that your Lordship has departed slightly from your original plan in regard to Burmah, by sending a detachment to make a demonstration upon Rangoon and Martaban. There is no calculating upon the result of such a demonstration in dealing with a Government so imbecile, and so ignorant of our resources. The places are too far from the capital, and the war party may succeed in persuading the King that in this demonstration we put forth all our strength. I can appreciate your motive—the wish to avoid, if possible, a war of annexation, which a war upon any scale must be. We should have to make use of a vast number of suffering people, whom we could not abandon to the mercy of the old Government.

In the last war our great difficulties were the want of quick transit for troops and stores by sea, the want of carriage cattle, and sickness. These three impediments will not now beset us. Our own districts on the coast will supply land-carriage, steam-vessels will carry our troops and stores, and subsequent experience will enable us to avoid sources of endemial diseases. I have no map of the country; but some letters in the papers about the Busseya river interested me much. Our strong point is steam; and the discovery of a river which would enable us to use it in getting in strength to the rear or flank would be of immense advantage. There must be healthy districts; indeed Burmah generally must be a healthy country, or the population would not be so strong and intelligent as they are known to be. In religious feeling they are less opposed to us than any other people not Buddhists. Indeed, from the people we should have nothing to fear; and the army must be insignificant in numbers as well as equipments. I am very glad to find that so able and well-trained a statesman as Fox Maule has been put at the head of the Board of Control; and trust that your Lordship will remain at our head till the Burmah affair is thoroughly settled.

The little affair of the Moplars, on the Malabar coast, may grow into a very big one unless skilfully managed. A brother of the Conollys is the magistrate, I believe. We can learn nothing of the cause of the strong feeling of discontent that prevails among this fanatical people. No such strong feeling can exist in India without some "canker-worm" to embitter the lives and unite the sympathies of large classes against their rulers or local governors, and make them think that they cannot shake it off without rebelling and becoming martyrs. I must pray your Lordship to excuse this long rambling letter, and

> Believe me, with great respect,
> Your obedient servant,
> (Signed) W. H. SLEEMAN.

> To the Most Noble
> The Marquis of Dalhousie,
> Calcutta.

* * * * *

Lucknow, 4th April, 1852.

My Dear Sir James,

Your present of the cadetship for her son made the poor widow's heart glad, and I doubt not that she has written to express her grateful feelings. The young man will, I hope, prove himself deserving of the favour you have conferred upon him so gracefully. The Court has called for a copy of my Diary of the tour I made through Oude soon after I took charge of my office; and I have sent off two copies, one for Government and the other for the Court. I purchased a small press and type for the purpose of printing it in my own house, that no one but myself and the compositor might see it. I will send home two copies for yourself and the chairman as soon as they can be bound in Calcutta. The Diary contains a faithful picture of Oude, its Government, and people, I believe. I have printed only a few copies, and they will not be distributed till I learn that the Court consider them unobjectionable. In spirit they will be found so. I intend, if I can find time, to give the history of the reigning family in a third volume. My general views on Oude affairs have been given in my letters to Government, which will, I conclude, be before the Court. A ruler so utterly regardless of his high duties and responsibilities, and of the sufferings of the people under his rule, as the present King, I have never seen; nor have I ever seen ministers so incompetent and so unworthy as those whom he employs in the conduct of his affairs. We have threatened so often to interpose for the benefit of the poor people, without doing anything, that they have lost all hope, and the profligate and unprincipled Government have lost all fear. The untoward war with Burmah prevents our present Governor-General from doing what he and I believe the Honourable Court both wish. We certainly ought not any longer to incur the odium of supporting such a Government in its iniquities, pledged as we are by treaties to protect the people from them. I do not apprehend any serious change in the constitution of the Court of Directors in the new charter. No ministers would hazard such a change in the present state of Europe. The Court is India's only safeguard. No foreign possession was ever so governed for itself as India has been, and this all foreigners with whom I have conversed, admit. The Governor-General of the Netherlands India was with me lately on his way home. He is a first-rate statesman, and he declared to me that he was impressed and delighted to see a country so governed, and apparently so sensible of the benefits conferred upon it by our paternal rule. He will tell you the same thing if you ever meet him. His name is Rochasson. The people appreciate the value of the Court of Directors, and no act, as far as it is known to them, has tended more to strengthen their confidence in it than that which has brought retribution on the great sinner in Scinde, Allee Murad. No punishment was ever more just or merited. Scinde, however, is too remote for the people in general to feel much interest in its affairs or families. Our weak points in the last Burmese war were:—1. The want of transport for troops and stores; 2. The want of carriage by land, for arms and stores; 3. Sickness. All these things have been remedied, and the war, when begun in earnest, can last but a short time. We know more of the country and shall avoid the sources of endemial disease; our steam provides for the rapid transport of troops and stores; and draft-cattle will be supplied from our own districts on the coast. Where our Government has no representative as Resident or Consul, all Europeans should be told that they remain entirely on their own responsibility. Unless this is done, the Governments must be eternally in collision. If war be carried on in earnest, it must be one of annexation: we must make use of persons whom we cannot abandon to the mercy of the Burmese Government. We have nothing to fear from the people: they have no religious feeling against us, being all Buddhists; and they have seen too much of the benefits conferred by us on the territories taken during the last war to have any dead of our dominion. Lord Dalhousie has, I believe, been most anxious to avoid a war—it has been forced upon him.

Believe me,
Yours very faithfully,
(Signed) W. H. SLEEMAN.

To Sir James W. Hogg,
Deputy Chairman,
India House.

* * * * *

Lucknow, 6th April, 1842.

My Dear Mr. Halliday,

We are all wrong here in the Martinière institution, and you have now an admirable opportunity of setting all right and doing an infinite deal of good with little trouble. I know how little you have of time and attention to devote to such things, and conclude that Mr. Devereux cannot have much more, and you may feel assured that I shall do all in my power to assist you. We are here attempting to give the education of gentlemen to beggar-boys, who must always depend upon their daily work for their daily bread. The senior boys are in despair, for they find that they have learnt hardly anything to fit them for the only employments open to them, and this tends to discourage the younger ones. The Roorkee Civil Engineering School seems to have been eminently successful, and a fine field is open to all who are taught in it. We shall no doubt have a similar field open in Oude when Government interposes in behalf of the suffering people, and we might prepare for it by converting the Martinière into a similar school or college. The committee has just expressed to you a hope that Mr. Crank, the officiating principal, may be able to pass an examination in the native languages. This hope can never be realised; and if he does I shall have to record my opinion that he is otherwise unfitted. The power of nominating a principal rests entirely with the trustees; and if you concur in my views you might at once prepare for the change by getting a man from England or elsewhere, such as Mr. Maclagan, the late superintendent of the Roorkee school, fitted to teach civil engineering in all its branches. You have the command of funds to provide him with assistants of all kinds; and we have accommodations and funds to raise more, and provide machinery, books, &c. The thing might be set going at once, after you send a competent man to superintend it; and the work will be honourable to our Government and ourselves, and of vast benefit to the boys brought up at this Martinière, and to their parents and families. If you think favourably of the proposed change, and will direct the committee to take it into consideration, I will do my best to make it respond cordially to your call; or if you direct the measure to be adopted at once, I will see that it is worked out as it should be. Mr. Crank has a good knowledge of mathematics and mechanics, and will make a good second under a good first; but he would be quite unfit for a first. Mr. Maclagan intended going home, via Bombay, as soon as relieved by Captain Oldfield, and has embarked by this time. He might be written to, to send out a competent person and the required machinery. Constantia is admirably adapted for such an establishment; the river Goomtee flows close under it; the grounds are ample, open, and level, and the climate fine. It would interest the whole of the Oude aristocracy, and induce them to send their sons there for instruction. It would be gratifying to the Judges of the Supreme Court to know that the funds available were devoted to a purpose so highly useful; and you would carry home with you the agreeable recollection of having engrafted so useful a branch upon the almost useless old trunk of the Martinière.

Yours very truly,
(Signed) W. H. SLEEMAN.

To F. J. Halliday, Esq.
Secretary to Government,
Calcutta.

Mr. Maclagan is a Lieutenant of Engineers, and lives in Edinburgh.

* * * * *

Lucknow. 10th April, 1852.

My Lord,

In September 1848, I took the liberty to mention to your Lordship my fears that the system of annexing and absorbing native States—so popular with our Indian service, and so much advocated by a certain class of writers in public journals—might some day render us too visibly dependent upon our native army; that they might see it, and that accidents might occur to unite them, or too great a portion of them, in some desperate act. My only anxiety about Burmah arises from the same fears. Our native army has been too much *petted* of late; and they are liable to get into their heads the notion that we want them more than they want us. Had the 38th been at first ordered to march to Aracan, they would, in all probability, have begged their European officers to pray Government to permit them to go by water.

We committed a great mistake in not long ago making all new levies general service corps; and we have committed one not less grave in restricting the admissions into our corps to high-caste men: and encouraging the promotion of high-caste men to the prejudice of men equally deserving but of lower caste. The Brahmins in regiments have too much influence, and they are at the bottom of all the mischief that occurs. The Rajpoots are too numerous, because they are under the influence of the Brahmins, and feel too strong from their numbers.

We require stronger and braver men than the Madras Presidency can afford, with all their readiness for general service. The time may not be distant when England will have to call upon India for troops to serve in Egypt; and the troops from Madras, or even from Bombay, will not do against Europeans. Men from Northern or Western India will be required, and, in order to be prepared, it would be well to have all new corps—should new corps be required—composed of men from the Punjaub or the Himmalayah chain, and ready for any service. Into such corps none but Seiks, Juts, Goojurs, Gwalas, Mussulmans, and Hillmen should be enlisted. Too much importance is attached to height, merely that corps may look well on parade. Much more work can be got out of moderate sized than tall men in India. The tall men in regiments always fail first in actual service—they are fit only for display at reviews and on parades: always supposing that the moderate-sized men are taken from Western and Northern India, where alone they have the strength and courage required.

No recruit should henceforward be taken except on condition of general service; and by-and-by the option may be given to all sipahees, of a certain standing or period of service, to put their names down for general service, or retire. This could not, of course, be done at present. No commanding officer can say, at present, what his regiment will do if called upon to aid the Government in any way not *specified in their bond*. They have too commonly favourites, who persuade them, for their own selfish purposes, that their regiments will do anything to meet their wishes, at the very time that these regiments are watching for an occasion to disgrace these favourites by refusal. I have known many occasions of this. None but general service corps or volunteers should be sent to Burmah from Bengal during this campaign, or we shall hazard a disaster. There are, I believe, several that your Lordship has not yet called upon. They should be at hand as soon as possible, and their present places supplied by others. In the mean time, corps of Punjaubies and Hillmen should be raised for general service. Not only can no commanding officer say what his corps will do under circumstances in which their religion or prejudices may afford a pretext for disobedience, but no officers can say how far their regiments sympathise with the recusant: or discontented, corps, and are prepared to join them.

In case it should ever be proposed to make all corps general service corps, in the way I mention, a donation would, of course, be offered to all who declined of a month's pay for every year of past service, or of something of that kind. A maximum might be fixed of four, five, or six months. It would not cost much, for but few would go. I must pray your Lordship to excuse the liberty I take in obtruding my notions on this subject, but it really is one of vital importance in the present state of affairs in India, as well as in Europe.

With great respect, I remain, &c.,
(Signed) W. H. SLEEMAN.

To the Moat Noble
The Marquis of Dalhousie, K.T.
Governor-General of India,
Calcutta.

Memorandum.

In the year 1832 or 1833 the want of bamboos of large size, for yokes for artillery bullocks, was much felt at Saugor and the stations of that division; and the commissariat officer was authorised to form a bamboo grove, to be watered by the commissariat cattle, in order to supply the deficiency for the future. Forty beegas, or about twenty acres of land, were assigned for the purpose, and Government went to the expense of forming twelve pucka-wells, as the bamboos were planted upon the black cotton-soil of Central India, in which kutcha-wells do not stand. The first outlay was, therefore, greater than usual, being three thousand rupees. The establishment kept up consisted of one gardener, at five rupees a month, and two assistants at three rupees each. The bamboos were watered by the artillery bullocks and commissariat servants.

In a few years the bamboos became independent of irrigation, and no outlay has since been incurred upon them. The bamboos are now between forty and fifty feet high, and between four and five inches in diameter. They are used by the commissariat and ordnance departments at Saugor, but are not, I believe, required for yokes for the artillery bullocks.

There is a grove of sesum trees near the Lucknow cantonments formed in the same way, but with little or no outlay in irrigation. The trees were planted, and all the cost incurred has been in the people employed to protect them from trespass. In a dryer climate they might require irrigation for a few years. Groves of saul, *alias* sukhoo trees, might be formed in the same manner in the vicinity of all stations where there are artillery bullocks; and the bullocks themselves would benefit by being employed in the irrigation. The establishments kept up for the bullocks would be able to do all the work required.

The complement of bullocks for a battery of 6 guns, 6 waggons, and 2 store carts, is 106. The number yoked to each gun and waggon is 61, [transcriber's note, should be 6], and to each cart 4, leaving a surplus of 26 for accidents. There would, therefore, be always a sufficient number of bullocks available for the irrigation of such groves where such a battery is kept up. These bullocks are taken care of by 4 sirdars and 59 drivers; and an European sergeant of artillery is appointed as bullock-sergeant to each battery, to superintend the feeding, cleaning, &c. &c. The officer on duty sees the bullocks occasionally, and the commanding officer sometimes. Such groves might be left to the care of the commandant of artillery at small stations, and to the commissariat officer at large ones.

At every large station there might be a grove of sesum, one of sakhoo, and one of bamboos, each covering a hundred acres; and at all stations with a battery, three groves of the same kind, covering each twenty acres or more. For the convenience of carriage by water, such groves might be formed chiefly in the vicinity of rivers, or in that of the places where the timber is most likely to be required; but no battery should be without such groves. The men and bullocks would both benefit by the employment such groves would give them. The men, to interest them, might each have a small garden within the grove which he assists in watering.

Such groves would tend to improve the salubrity of the stations where they are formed, and become agreeable and healthful promenades for officers and soldiers. In most stations, kutcha-wells, formed at a cost of from 20 to 50 rupees, would suffice for watering such groves. They might be lined, like those of the peasantry, by twisted cables of straw and twigs; and the men who attend the bullocks might be usefully employed in weaving them, as all should learn to make fascines and gabions. Willows should be planted near all the wells, to supply twigs for making the cables for lining the wells, and the manure of the artillery draft-bullocks should be appropriated to the groves.

[Submitted to the Governor-General through the Private Secretary, in March, 1852, with reference to a conversation which I had with his Lordship in his camp.]

* * * * *

Lucknow, 23rd August, 1852.

My Lord,

Permit me to offer my congratulations, not only on the success which has hitherto attended your Lordship's arrangements in Burmah, but on the very favourable impression which that success has made upon the Sovereign and people of England. It has enabled you to show that the war is not with the people of Burmah, but with a haughty, insolent, and incompetent Government, with whom that people has no longer any sympathy; and that, should circumstances render the annexation of any portion of its territory necessary, the people of that portion would consider the measure a blessing, and be well pleased to live in harmony under the efficient protection of the new rule.

They are not in any way opposed to us from either religions or political feelings, for they seem to consider Christianity as a branch only of their own great system of Buddhism, which includes almost half of the human race; and they are evidently weary of the political institutions under which they now live, and which have ceased to afford them protection of any kind. In the annexation of Pegu—should it be forced upon your Lordship—there would be nothing revolting to the feelings of its people or to those of the people of England; on the contrary, both would be satisfied, after the disposition the people of Pegu have manifested towards us, that the measure was alike necessary to their security and to the honour and interest of our Government.

Nor do I think that there would be any ground to apprehend that the resources of the territory taken would not, after a time, be sufficient to defray the costs of the establishments required to retain and govern it. Among the people of Pegu we should find men able and willing to serve us faithfully and efficiently in both our civil and military establishments, and the drain for the maintenance of foreigners would not be large. I have heard the mental and physical powers of the men of Pegu spoken of in the highest terms by persons who have spent the greater part of their lives among them; and a country which produces such men cannot be generally insalubrious. This early demonstration has enabled your Lordship to ascertain and expose the determination of the Government of Ava not to grant the redress justly demanded for wrongs suffered, so as to enlist on our side the sympathy of all civilized nations, and at the same time to discover the real weakness of the enemy and the facilities offered to us, in their fine rivers, for the use of our strong arm—the steam navy. Not a single "untoward event" has yet occurred to dispirit our troops, or give confidence to the enemy, or to prejudice the people of Burmah against us: and there certainly is nothing in this war to make us apprehend "that our political difficulties will begin when our military successes are complete." It is not displeasing to perceive the strong tendency to an early onward move, while your Lordship has so prudent a leader in General Godwin to restrain it within due bounds.

I remain, &c.,
(Signed) W. H. SLEEMAN.

To the Most Noble
The Marquis of Dalhousie, K.T.
Governor-General of India.
Calcutta.

* * * * *

Lucknow, September, 1852.

My Lord,

The longer the present King reigns, the more unfit he becomes to reign, and the more the administration and the country deteriorate. The

State must have become bankrupt long ere this, but the King, and the knaves by whom he is governed, have discontinued paying the stipends of all the members of the royal family, save those of his own father's family, for the last three years; and many of them are reduced to extreme distress, and without the hope of ever getting their stipends again unless our Government interferes. The females of the palaces of former sovereigns ventured to clamour for their subsistence, and they were, without shame or mercy, driven into the streets to starve, beg, or earn their bread by their labour. This deters all from complaining, and they are in a state of utter dismay. No part of the people of Oude are more anxious for the interposition of our Government than the members of the royal family; for there is really no portion more helpless and oppressed: none of them can ever approach the King, who is surrounded exclusively by eunuchs, fiddlers, and poetasters worse than either; and the minister and his creatures, who are worse than all. They appropriate at least one-half of the revenues of the country to themselves, and employ nothing but knaves of the very worst kind in all the branches of the administration. The King is a crazy imbecile, who is led about by these people like a child, and made to do whatever they wish him to do, and to give whatever orders may best suit their private interests. At present, the most powerful of the favourites are Decanut od Doula and Husseen od Doula, two eunuchs; Anees od Doula and Mosahib od Doula, two fiddlers; two poetasters, and the minister and his creatures. The minister could not stand a moment without the eunuchs, fiddlers, and poets, and he is obliged to acquiesce in all the orders given by the King for their benefit. The fiddlers have control over the administration of civil justice; the eunuchs over that of criminal justice, public buildings, &c. The minister has the land revenue; and all are making enormous fortunes. The present King ought not certainly to reign: he has wilfully forfeited all right to do so; but to set him aside in favour of his eldest, or indeed any other son, would give no security whatever for any permanent good government A well-selected regency would, no doubt, be a vast improvement upon the present system; but no people would invest their capital in useful works, manufactures, and trades, with the prospect of being handed over a few years hence to a prince brought up precisely in the same manner the present King was, and as all his sons will be. What the people want, and most earnestly pray for is, that our Government should take upon itself the responsibility of governing them well and permanently. All classes, save the knaves, who now surround and govern the King, earnestly pray for this—the educated classes, because they would then have a chance of respectable employment, which none of them now have; the middle classes, because they find no protection or encouragement, and no hope that their children will be permitted to inherit the property they may leave, not invested in our Government securities; and the humbler classes, because they are now abandoned to the merciless rapacity of the starving troops, and other public establishments, and of the landholders, driven or invited into rebellion by the present state of misrule. There is not, I believe, another Government in India so entirely opposed to the best interest's and most earnest wishes of the people as that of Oude now is; at least I have never seen or read of one. People of all classes have become utterly weary of it. The people have the finest feelings towards our Government and character. I know no part of India, save the valley of the Nurbuddah, where the feeling towards us is better. All, from the highest to the lowest, would, at this time, hail the advent of our administration with joy; and the rest of India, to whom Oude misrule is well known, would acquiesce in the conviction, that it had become imperative for the protection of the people. With steamers to Fyzabad, and a railroad from that place to Cawnpore, through Lucknow, the Nepaul people would be for ever quieted, with half of the force we now keep up to look after them; and the N. W. Provinces become more closely united to Bengal, to the vast advantage of both. I mentioned that we should require a considerable loan to begin with; but I think that an issue of paper money, receivable in Oude in revenue, and payable to public establishments in Oude, might safely be made to cover all the outlay required to pay off odd establishments and commence the new work. Little money goes out of Oude, and the increased circulating medium, required for the new public works and new establishments, would soon absorb all the paper issued. It might be issued at little or no cost by the financial department of the new administration. Though everybody knows that the King has become crazy and imbecile, it would be difficult to get judicial proof that he is so, where the life and property of every one are at his mercy and that of the knaves who now govern him. His every-day doings sufficiently manifest it. There is not the slightest ground for hope that he will ever be any other than what he now is, or that his children will be better. There are too many interested in depriving them of all capacity for a part in public affairs that they may retain the reins in their own hands when the children come of age to admit of their ever becoming better than their father is. I have not lately made the reports which Lord Hardinge directed the Resident to make periodically, but shall be prepared to resume them whenever your Lordship may direct. I suspended them on account of hostilities with Burmah. I have printed eighteen copies of the establishments, as they are and were last year, and as I proposed for the new system. I shall not let any one have a copy till your Lordship permits it, and they are all at your disposal if required. This, and the "Substantive Code," are the only papers connected with Oude, except the Diary that I have had printed, or shall have printed, unless ordered by you.

> I remain, with great respect,
> Your Lordship's obedient servant,
> (Signed) W. H. SLEEMAN.

P.S.—I believe that it is your Lordship's wish that the whole of the revenues of Oude should be expended for the benefit of the royal family and people of Oude, and that the British Government should disclaim any wish to derive any pecuniary advantages from assuming to itself the administration.

(Signed) W. H. SLEEMAN.

To the Most Noble
The Marquis of Dalhousie, K.T.
Governor-General,
&c. &c. &c.

* * * * *

Lucknow, 21st September, 1852.

My Dear Sir,

I will reply to the queries contained in your letter of the 16th instant to the best of my recollection. I was in Calcutta in January, 1838, when the late Dyce Sombre was there, and about to embark for England. I had seen a good deal of him at Sirdhanah, in March 1836, soon after the Begum Sumroo's death, and he afterwards spent a short time with me at Mussoorie, and consulted me a good deal on the subject of a dispute with his father.

Colonel James Skinner and Dr. Drener were, I believe, executors to his will. Colonel Skinner was at Delhi, and Dr. Drener had either gone home or was going, I forget which, and Dyce Sombre asked me to consent to become one of his trustees, for the conduct of his affairs in this country. I consented, and I think the circumstance was inserted in a codicil or memorandum added to his will or deed; but my recollection on this point is not distinct.

I had, however, nothing to do with the conduct of his affairs in this country until the death of Colonel James Skinner, which took place in December, 1841, when Mr. Reghilini, the overseer or agent at Sirdhanah, got my sanction to the outlay for establishments, &c. At this time I corresponded with Dyce Sombre, and continued to do so until his affairs were thrown into Chancery. I then sought a lawyer's opinion as to my proper course, and refused to give Mr. Reghilini any further orders. The opinion was, "that my only safe course was to do nothing whatever in the conduct of his affairs;" and I never afterwards did anything. I never heard of any Colonel Sheerman, and his name may have been inserted by mistake for mine; but I was then (1838) only a major, and was not promoted until 1843. I never heard of any desire on the part of Dyce Sombre, or the Begum Sumroo, to found a college other than as an appendage to the Sirdhanah church, nor of his having given the residue of his property for the purpose; at least, I have no recollection of having heard of such desire. I always hoped, and expected, until I heard of his marriage, that he would return and reside at Sirdhanah.

Dyce Sombre always spoke to me of Mrs. Troup and Mrs. Soloroli as his sisters: he regarded them alike as such, and so did the Begum Sumroo. I always understood them to be the children of the same mother; but the question was never mooted before me, and I have always heard that Mrs. Troup was very like Dyce Sombre in appearance, and that Mrs. Soloroli was not so.

Mr. Reghilini, who is, I believe, still at Sirdhanah, may know whether a Colonel Sheerman was appointed executor or not. Dr. Drener must know. The notes which passed between me and Dyce Sombre, after he left India, were on the ordinary topics of the day, and were destroyed as soon as read. I have none of them to refer to, nor would they furnish any confirmation on the matter in question if I had.

Believe me, yours, very truly,
(Signed) W. H. SLEEMAN.

Charles Prinsep, Esq.,
Barrister-at-Law,
Calcutta.

To Messrs. Molloy, Mackintosh, and Poe, Calcutta.

Dear Sirs,

In reply to your letter of the 16th instant, I enclose the copy of a letter addressed by me on the 21st ultimo to Mr. Charles Prinsep, in reply to similar queries. To what I stated in that letter I can add but little.

Dyce Sombre always spoke to me of Mrs. Soloroli and Mrs. Troup as his sisters, and of the former as the eldest of the two; and Mrs. Troup spoke of Mrs. Soloroli as her eldest sister. They were always treated by the Begum Sumroo as his sisters; and when Dyce Sombre went to England I think he left the same provision for both in addition to what they had received from the Begum.

I was introduced to Mrs. Troup by her husband as an old friend on my way back from Mussoorie in November, 1837, but I did not see Mrs. Soloroli, though she and her husband were at the same place, Sirdhanah, at that time. They both lived under the curtain, secluded from the sight of men, after the Hindoostanee fashion, as long as they remained in India, I think; and I was introduced to Mrs. Troup as a friend of the family, whom all might require to consult. Her husband only was present during the interview. Dyce Sombre had left the place for Calcutta. I never heard a doubt expressed of their being sisters by the same mother and father till the new will came under discussion at the end of last year.

I may refer you to pages 378 and 396 of the second volume of a work by me, entitled "Rambles and Recollections," in which you will find it mentioned that the grandmother of Dyce Sombre died insane at Sirdhanah in 1838. She must have been insane for more than forty years up to her death. Her son Zuffer Yab Khan was a man of weak intellect, and he was the father of Dyce Sombre's mother, of whom I know nothing whatever.

Dyce Sombre, showed no symptoms of derangement of mind while I knew him; but he inherited from his grandmother a predisposition to insanity, which I apprehended might become developed by any very strong feelings of excitement; and I urged him to return and settle at Sirdhanah, when he had seen all he wished to see in Europe.

He saw a good deal of English society in India, and understood well the freedom which English wives enjoy in general society; but I doubted whether he could ever thoroughly shake off his early predilections for keeping them secluded. It would, I thought, be always to him a source of deep humiliation to see his wife mix with other men in the manner in which English married ladies are accustomed to do. Since his affairs were put into Chancery I have always felt persuaded that this must have been the principal "exciting cause" acting upon the predisposition derived from his grandmother, which led to it. I have never had the slightest doubt that he suffered under an aberration of mind upon this point, though he never mentioned the subject in any of his short letters to me from England, nor did he in any of them show signs of such aberration.

Believe me, yours, faithfully,
(Signed) W. H. SLEEMAN.

26th October, 1852.

* * * * *

Lucknow, 28th October, 1852.

My Dear Sir James,

Your letter of the 6th ultimo reached me by the last mail, and I trust we shall see your hopes of an early renewal of the Charter with few alterations realised. I entirely concur with you in opinion that the power of recall is indispensable to the due authority of the Court; and was much surprised to find Maddock opposed to it. Many thinking men at home have been of opinion that the Ministers would secure for the Queen the nomination of a certain number to the Direction, on the ground that many of the best men from India are deterred from becoming candidates by the time and pledges required in the canvass. The late elections, however, seem to have come in time to increase the Jealousy of ministerial influence, and prevent such a measure.

Hostilities with Burmah have prevented my making public periodical reports to Government about Oude affairs since I submitted my Diary. I took the liberty to send, through my London agents copy to yourself and the Deputy Chairman. Things have not improved since it was written. The King is as regardless of his high duties and responsibilities as ever: he is, indeed, an imbecile in the hands of a few fiddlers, eunuchs, and poetasters, and the minister, who is no better than they are, and obliged to provide for all these men out of the revenues and patronage of the country, and sundry women about the Court, also, to secure their influence in his favour.

The King contrives to get the stipends of those immediately about him, and of his mother, brothers, and sisters, paid out of the revenues; but is indifferent about those of his more distant relatives, and hardly any of them have had any stipends for the last two and even three years. Those who happen not to have a little Company's paper given to them by former Sovereigns, or pensions guaranteed by our Government and paid out of our Treasury, are starving, and pray for the day when our Government may interpose in the administration. The expenditure is much above the income, and the reserved treasury is exhausted; but the King has his jewels and some personal property in Government notes, derived from his father and grandmothers. He thinks himself the best of kings and the best of poets, and nothing will induce him willingly to alter his course or make room for a better ruler or better system.

If our Government interpose, it must not be by negotiation and treaty, but authoritatively on the ground of existing treaties and obligations to the people of Oude. The treaty of 1837 gives our Government ample authority to take the whole administration on ourselves, in order to secure what we have often pledged ourselves to secure to the people; but if we do this we must, in order to stand well with the rest of India, honestly and distinctly disclaim all interested motives, and appropriate the whole of the revenues for the benefit of the people and royal family of Oude. If we do this, all India will think us right, for the sufferings of the people of Oude, under the present system, have been long notorious throughout India; and so have our repeated pledges to relieve the people from these sufferings, unless the system should be altered. Fifty years of sad experience have shown to us and to all India, that this system is incapable of improvement under the present dynasty; and that the only alternative is for the paramount power to take the administration upon itself.

Under the treaty of 1801, we took one-half of the territory of Oude, and that half yields to us above two crores of rupees; though, when taken, it was estimated at one hundred and thirty-three lacs. The half retained by the Oude Sovereign was estimated at the same; but it now yields to the Sovereign only one crore. The rest is absorbed by the knaves employed in the administration and their patrons at Court. All that is now so absorbed would come to the Treasury under us, and be employed in the maintenance of efficient establishments, and the construction of useful public works; and we should have ample means for providing for all the members of the royal family of Oude.

We should derive substantial benefit from the measure, without in any degree violating our declaration of disinterestedness. We now maintain five regiments of Infantry, and a company of Artillery, at a cost of from five to six lacs a-year. We maintain the Residency and all its establishments at a cost of more than one lac of rupees a-year. All these would become fairly chargeable to the Oude revenues under the new administration; and we might dispense with half the military forces now kept up at Cawnpore and Dinapore on the Ganges, as the military force in Oude would relieve us from all apprehension as to Nepaul.

Oude would be covered with a network of fine macadamised roads, over which the produce of Oude and our own districts would pass freely to the benefit of the people of both; and we should soon have the river Ghagra, from near Patna on the Ganges, to Fyzabad in Oude, navigable for steamers: with a railroad from Fyzabad, through Lucknow to Cawnpore, to the great benefit of the North-West Provinces and those of Bengal.

Were we to take advantage of the occasion to *annex* or *confiscate* Oude, or any part of it, our good name in India would inevitably suffer; and that good name is more valuable to us than a dozen of Oudes. We are now looked up to throughout India as the only impartial arbitrators that the people generally have ever had, or can ever hope to have without us; and from the time we cease to be so looked up to, we must begin to sink. We suffered from our conduct in Scinde; but that was a country distant and little known, and linked to the rest of India by few ties of sympathy. Our Conduct towards it was preceded by wars and convulsions around, and in its annexation there was nothing manifestly deliberate. It will be otherwise with Oude. Here the giant's strength is manifest, and we cannot "use it like a giant" without suffering in the estimation of all India. Annexation or confiscation are not compatible with our relations with this little dependent state. We must show ourselves to be high-minded, and above taking advantage of its prostrate weakness, by appropriating its revenues exclusively to the benefit of the people and royal family of Oude. We should soon make it the finest garden in India, with the people happy, prosperous, and attached to our rule and character.

We have at least forty thousand men from Oude in the armies of the three Residencies, all now, rightly or wrongly, cursing the oppressive Government under which their families live at their homes. These families would come under our rule and spread our good name as widely as they now spread the bad one of their present ruler. Soldiers with a higher sense of military honour, and duty to *their salt*, do not exist, I believe, in any country. To have them bound to us by closer ties than they are at present, would of itself be an important benefit.

I can add little to what I have said in the latter end of the fourth chapter of my Diary (from p. 187*, vol. ii.), on the subject of our relations with the Government of Oude; and of our rights and duties arising out of those relations. The diaries political, which I send every week or fortnight to the Government of India, are formed out of the reports made every day to the Durbar, by their local or departmental authorities. The Residency News-writer has the privilege of hearing these reports read as they come in; and though the reports of many important events are concealed from him, they may generally be relied upon as far as they go. The picture they give of affairs is bad enough, though not so bad as they deserve.

There are so many worthless and profligate people about the Court, interested in smothering any signs of common sense and good feeling on the part of the heir apparent to the throne, in order to maintain their ascendancy over him as he grows up, that he has not the slightest chance of becoming fit to take any part in the conduct of public affairs when he comes of age. The present King has three or four sons, all very young, but it is utterly impossible for any one of them to become a man of business; and it would be folly to expect any one of them to make a better Sovereign than their father. He is now only twenty-eight or twenty-nine years of age; but his understanding has become quite emasculated by over-indulgencies of all kinds. He may live long, but his habits have become too inveterate to admit of his ever becoming better than he now is or fit to be intrusted with the government of a country.

I shall recommend that all establishments, military, civil, and fiscal, be kept entirely separate from those of our own Government, that there may be no mistake as to the disinterestedness of our intentions towards Oude. The military establishments being like Scindiah's contingent, in the Gwalior state, or the Hydrabad contingent in the Nizam's. I estimate the present expenditure at, civil and fiscal establishments, and stipendiaries, 38 lacs. Military and police, 55. King's household, 30. Total, 123 lacs. Establishments required for an efficient administration—civil and fiscal—at 22 lacs. Military, 26 lacs. Families and dependents of former Sovereigns, 12 lacs. Household of the Sovereign, his sons, brothers, and sisters, 15 lacs. Total, 75 lacs.

This would leave an abundant store for public works, military stores, contingent charges, pension establishments for the civil and military officers employed under us, &c. To pay off all the present heavy arrears of stipends, salaries, to provide arms, ammunition, and stores, and to commence upon all the public works, our Government would have either to give or guarantee a loan; or to sanction the issue of a certain amount of paper money, to circulate exclusively in Oude, by making it receivable in the Oude Treasuries in taxes.

The revenues would be at once greatly increased, by our taking for the treasury all that is now intercepted and appropriated by public officers and Court favourites for their own private purposes, by our making the great landholders pay a due portion of their assets to the state, and by our securing the safe transit of raw produce and manufactured goods to their proper markets.

By adopting a simple system of administration, to meet the wishes of a simple people, we should secure the goodwill of all classes of society in Oude; and no class would be more pleased with the change than the members of the royal family themselves, who depend upon their stipends for their subsistence, and despair of ever again receiving them under the present Sovereign and system.

I hope a happy termination of the present war with Burmah will soon leave Lord Dalhousie free to devote his attention to Oude affairs. As far as I am consulted, I shall advocate, as strongly as may be compatible with my position, the measures above described, because I think they will be found best calculated to benefit the people of Oude, to meet the wishes of the home Government, and to sustain his Lordship's own reputation, and that of the nation which he represents throughout our Eastern empire.

You are aware of some of the difficulties that I have had to contend with, in carrying out important measures beneficial to the people, and honourable to the Government of India; but in no situation in life have I ever had to struggle with so many as here, in pursuing an honest and steady course of policy, calculated to secure the respect of all classes for the Government which I represent. Such a scene of intrigue, corruption, depravity, neglect of duty, and abuse of authority, I have never before been placed in, and hope never again to undergo; and I have had to contend with bitter hostility where I had the best right to expect support. I have never yet failed in the performance of any duty that Government has intrusted to me, and, under Providence, I hope that I shall ultimately succeed in the performance of that which I have committed to me here.

Lucknow is an overgrown city, surrounding an overgrown Court, which has, for the last half century, exhausted all the resources of this fine country; and so alienated the feelings of the great body of the people that they, and the Sovereign, and his officers, look upon each other as irreconcileable enemies. Between the city, the pampered Court and its functionaries, and the people of the country beyond, there is not the slightest feeling of sympathy; and if our troops were withdrawn from the vicinity of Lucknow, the landholders and sturdy peasantry of the country would, in a few days, rush in and plunder and destroy it as a source of nothing but intolerable evil to them.

Though I have written a long letter, I may have omitted many things which you wished me to notice. In that case I must rely upon your letting me know; and in the mean time, I shall continue to write whenever I have anything to communicate that is likely to interest you.

Believe me, dear Sir James,
Yours very faithfully,
W. H. SLEEMAN.

To Sir James Weir Hogg, Bart.
&c. &c. &c.

P.S. By treaty, we are bound to keep up a certain force near the capital for the protection of the Sovereign; and we should be obliged, till things were quite settled under the new system, to retain the brigade we now have of our regular troops in the cantonments, which are three miles from the city.

W. H. SLEEMAN.

* * * * *

Lucknow, 20th November, 1852.

My Dear Sir James,

To be prepared for accidents, I deem it right to send a duplicate of the letter which I sent to you by the last mail, addressed to the care of my London agents, Messrs. Denny and Clark, Austin Friars. I have nothing new or interesting to communicate from Oude. The Burmese war seems likely to divert the Governor-General's attention from Oude and Hydrabad affairs for some time to come; and the death of the Duke of Wellington, and probable changes in the ministry at home, may prevent him from venturing upon any important change in the Oude administration when that war closes.

The war is an "untoward event," arising from a very small cause; and it should prevent our ever guaranteeing British subjects in countries where we have no accredited agents to conduct our relations with the Government. All such subjects, and all the subjects of our European and American allies, should in future be made to understand that they enter such countries entirely upon their own responsibility. Without some such precaution we must always be liable to be involved in war with bordering countries by adventurers of one land or another; and as war is almost always followed by annexation or confiscation, our Indian empire, like that of the Romans, must soon sink from its own weight. The people will think that we are perpetually seeking pretexts for war in order to get new territories, and the general or universal impression will be dangerous.

When the public press of England abuse those who have to conduct the present war for delay, they do not sufficiently consider our ignorance of the state of the rivers and of the military resources of the country in which it was to be carried on when we entered upon it. We did not know that the rivers were navigable, nor did we know how they were defended; nor did we know what forces Burmah could muster, nor how they were distributed. It was not intended to commence the war till after the rains, when it would be safe to move troops over the country; for it was not reasonable to suppose that the Government of the country could be so haughty and insolent without military force to support its pretensions, and we have often had sad experience of the danger of underrating the power of an enemy. The object of the earlier movement was merely to secure some points of support, at which to concentrate our forces as they came up, and not to advance at once on the capital or into the country at a season when no troops could move by land.

Our strong arm was, no doubt, the steam flotilla; but it would have been madness in us, with our ignorance of the rivers and resources of the country, to have calculated upon conquering Ava by steamers alone. With what we now know, people may safely say that General Godwin has failed to make all the use he might of the flotilla, as Lord Gough failed to make all the use he might of his "strong arm," the artillery, in the battles of the Punjaub; but Lord Gough was not ignorant of the country in which he had to operate, nor of the resources of the country he had to contend with. According to previous calculations, the war ought not to have begun till this month. The earlier movement has, however, been of great advantage—it has taught us what the rivers and resources of the country are; and, what is of still more importance, what the people and their feelings towards their Government and ours are. It is manifest that they fully appreciate the value of the protection which the people, under our rule, enjoy; and that they have neither religious nor political feelings of hostility towards us; and that the people of Pegu, at least, would hail the establishment of our rule as a blessing.

You were so kind as to express a wish to see my son. He is now with his regiment, the 16th Lancers, in Ireland, and has lately obtained his

Lieutenancy. He will be twenty years of age in January. I will make known to him your kind wish, and doubt not that he will pay his respects when he visits London.

> Believe me, My Dear Sir James,
> Yours very faithfully,
> W. H. SLEEMAN.

> To Sir James Weir Hogg, Bart,
> &c. &c. &c.

P.S.—In page 217, line 4, vol. i., of my Diary, the printer has put "months" for weeks. Pray do me the favour to have this corrected.—W. H. S.

* * * * *

My Lord,

Your Lordship's wishes in regard to the papers on Oude affairs shall be strictly attended to. They are locked up in my box, and no one shall see them. I had no wish to print any but those I mentioned in my last letter, and they are locked up with the others, which I have not looked at since I left your Lordship's camp; the Diary, excepted.

Things in Oude are just as they were; and the King's ambition seems to be limited to the reputation of being the best drum-beater, dancer, and poet of the day. He is utterly unfit to reign; but he is himself persuaded that no man can be more fit than he is for anything, and he will never willingly consent to make over the reins of Government to any one. It would be impossible to *persuade* him to abdicate even in favour of his own son, much less to resign his sovereignty in perpetuity. If our Government interpose, it must be by the exercise of a right derived from the existing relations between the two Governments, or from our position as the paramount power in India.

Of this your Lordship will have to consider and decide when your mind is relieved from Burmese affairs, which appear to be drawing very *quietly* to a close. I shall not write publicly about Oude affairs generally till I have your Lordship's commands to do so. The Diary will continue to be transmitted regularly; but the Periodical General Report will be suspended.

Mr. Bushe remained a few days at Lucknow. He has since seen Agra, Bhurtpoor, and other places, and is now on his way back to Calcutta, well pleased with his tour.

With great respect,
Your Lordship's obedient Servant,
W. H. SLEEMAN.

To the Most Noble
The Marquis of Dalhousie, K.T.,
Governor-General of India.

* * * * *

Lucknow, 2nd January, 1853.

My Dear Sir James,

I enclose two sets of Tables of Errata for the Diary, and must pray you to do me the favour to have one set put into the two volumes of the copy you have, and the other sent to the Deputy-Chairman for insertion in his copy. I did not take the liberty to send a copy to the President of the Board of Control, but if you think I should do so, I will.

The King of Oude is becoming more and more imbecile and crazy, and his servants continue more and more to abuse their power and neglect their duty. The King, every day manifests his utter unfitness to reign, in some new shape. He, on several occasions during the Mohurrum ceremonies which took place lately, went along the streets beating a drum tied round his neck, to the great scandal of his family and the amusement of his people. The members of his family have not been paid their stipends for from two to three years, and many of them have been reduced to the necessity of selling their clothes to purchase food. All classes, save the knaves who surround him, and profit by his folly, are become disgusted with and tired of him.

I do not interfere, except to protect our pledges and guarantees; and to conduct the current duties of the Residency in such a manner as to secure the respect of all classes for the Government which I represent. While the present King reigns, or has anything whatever to do with the Government, no interference could produce any substantial and permanent reform. The minister is a weak man and a great knave; but he has an influence over his master, obtained by being entirely subservient to his vices and follies, to the sacrifice of his own honour; and by praising all that he does, however degrading to him as a man and a sovereign.

Though the King pays no attention whatever to public affairs or to business of any kind, and aims at nothing but the reputation of being the best dancer, best versifier, and best drummer in his dominions, it would be impossible to persuade him that any man was ever more fit to reign than he is. Nothing would ever induce him willingly to abdicate even in favour of his own son, much less to make him willingly abdicate in perpetuity in favour of our Government, or make over the conduct of the administration to our Government. If, therefore, our Government does interfere, it must be in the exercise of a right arising out of the existing relations between the two States, or out of our position as the paramount power in India. These relations, under the Treaty of 1837, give our Government the *right* to take upon itself the administration, under present circumstances; and, indeed, imposes, upon our Government the *duty* of taking it: but, as I have already stated, neither these relations nor our position, as the paramount power, gives us any right to *annex* or to *confiscate* the territory of Oude. We may have a right to take territory from the Nizam of Hyderabad in payment for the money he owes us; but

Oude owes us no money, and we have no right to take territory from her. We have only the right to interpose to secure for the suffering people that better Government which their Sovereign pledged himself to secure for them, but has failed to secure.

The Burmese war still prevents the Governor-General from devoting his attention to Oude and Hyderabad. In the last war we did not march our armies to the capital because we were not prepared to supply a new Government for the one which we should thereby destroy; and insurrection and civil war must have followed. Our conduct in that was wise and benevolent. When we moved our armies to Rangoon this time, we upset one Government without providing the people with another. The Governor-General could not provide for the Civil Government, because he could not know that the Government of Ava would force us to keep possession of any portion of its dominions; and taking upon ourselves the civil administration would compromise the people, should he have to give them up again to their old rulers. The consequence has been great suffering to a people who hailed us as deliverers. The folly of supposing that any country can be taken by steamers on their rivers alone has now become sufficiently manifest. The Governor-General has however, adopted the best possible measures for securing ultimate good government to Pegu. It would have been more easily effected had they been taken earlier, but this circumstance prevented.

There is a school in India, happily not yet much patronised by the Home Government nor by the Governor-General, but always struggling with more or less success for ascendancy. It is characterised by impatience at the existence of any native State, and its strong and often insane advocacy of their absorption—by honest means, if possible—but still, their absorption. There is no pretext, however weak, that is not sufficient, in their estimation, for the purpose; and no war, however cruel, that is not justifiable, if it has only this object in view. If you know George Clerk or Mr. Robertson, both formerly Governors of our North-West Provinces, they will describe to you the school I mean. They, I believe, with me, strongly deprecate the doctrines of this school as more injurious to India and to our interest in it, than those of any other school that has ever existed in India. Mr. George Campbell is one of the disciples of this school.—See the 4th chapter of his "Modern India." The "Friend of India" is another, and all those whom that paper lauds most are also disciples of the same school. The Court of Directors will have to watch these doctrines carefully; and I wish you would speak to George Clerk and Mr. Robertson about them. They are both men of large views and sound judgment.

> Believe me, My Dear Sir James,
> Yours sincerely,
> (Signed) W. H. SLEEMAN.

> To Sir James Weir Hogg,
> &c. &c. &c.

* * * * *

Lucknow, 12th January, 1853.

My Dear Sir James,

I wrote to you on the 23rd October, 20th November, and the 2nd of this month; I mention this lest any of my letters miscarry; of the first letter I sent a duplicate on the 2nd, but I shall not send duplicates of the last two, or of this. I now write chiefly to call your attention to a rabid article in the "Friend of India," of the 6th of this month, written by Mr. Marshman, when about to proceed to England, to become, it is said, one of the writers in the London "Times." Of coarse, he will be engaged to write the Indian articles; and you will find him advocating the doctrines of the school mentioned in my last letter of the 2nd of this month. I consider their doctrines to be prejudicial to the stability of our rule in India, and to the welfare of the people, which depends on it.

The Court of Directors is our only safeguard against these Machiavellian doctrines; and it may be rendered too powerless to stem them by the new arrangements for the Government of India. The objects which they propose for attainment—religion, commerce, &c.—are plausible; and the false logic by which they attempt to justify the means required to attain them, however base, unjust, and cruel, is no less so. I was asked by Dr. Duff, the editor of the "Calcutta Review," before he went home to write some articles for that journal, to expose the fallacies, and to counteract the influences of the doctrines of this school; but I have for many years ceased to contribute to the periodical papers, and have felt bound by my position not to write for them. Few old officers of experience, with my feelings and opinions on this subject, now remain in India; and the influence of this school is too great over the rising generation, whose hopes and aspirations they tend so much to encourage. Mr. Elphinstone, Mr. Robertson, and George Clerk will be able to explain their danger to you. India must look to the Court of Directors alone for safety against them, and they will require the exertion of all its wisdom and strength.

Mr. Robertson will be able to tell you that, when I was sent to Bundelcund, in 1842, the feelings of the people of that province were so strongly against us, under the operation of the doctrines of this school, that no European officer could venture, with safety, beyond the boundary of a cantonment of British troops; and their servants were obliged to disguise themselves in order to pass from one cantonment to another. In a brief period, I created a feeling entirely different, and made the character of British officers respected and beloved. In the Gwalior territories the same result was obtained by the same means. However impulsive on other occasions, Lord Ellenborough behaved magnanimously after his victories over the Gwalior troops; but in sparing the State, he acted, I believe, against the feelings of his Council, amongst whom the doctrines of the absorbing, annexing, and confiscating schools prevailed; and the "Friend of India" condemned him, though the invasion was never justified, except on the ground of expediency. Had I, on these occasions, adopted the doctrines of the absorbing school, I might have become one of the most popular and influential men in India; but I should, at the same time, have rendered our rule and character odious to the people of India, and so far have injured our permanent interest in the country. I mention all this merely to show that my opposition to the doctrines of this school is not new, nor in theory only, but of long standing and practice, as far as my influence has extended. I deem them to be dangerous to our rule in India, and prejudicial to the best interests of the country. The people see that these annexations and confiscations go on, and that rewards and honorary distinctions are given for them, and for the victories which lead to them, and for little else; and they are too apt to infer that they are systematic, and encouraged, and prescribed from home. The native States I consider to be breakwaters, and when they are all swept away, we shall be left to the mercy of our native army, which may not always be sufficiently under our control. Such a feeling as that which pervaded Bundelcund and Gwalior in 1842 and 1843, must, sooner or later, pervade all India, if these doctrines are carried out to their full extent; and our rule could not, probably, exist under it. With regard to Oude, I can only say that the King pursues the same course, and every day shows that he is unfit to reign. He has not the slightest regard for the duties or responsibilities of his high position; and the people, and even the members of his own family, feel humiliated at his misconduct, and grow weary of his reign. The greater part of these members have not received their stipends for from two to three years, and they despair of ever receiving them as long as he reigns. He is neither tyrannical nor cruel, but altogether incapable of devoting any of his time or attention to business of any kind, but spends the whole of his time with women, eunuchs, fiddlers, and other parasites. Should he be set aside, as he deserves to be, three courses are open: 1. To appoint a regency during the minority of the heir-apparent, who is now about eleven years of age, to govern with the advice of the Resident; 2. To manage the country by European agency during the regency, or in perpetuity, leaving the surplus revenue to the royal family;

3. To confiscate and annex the country, and pension the royal family. The first plan was prescribed by Lord Hardinge, in case of accident to the King; the second is what was done at Nagpore, with so much advantage, by Sir Richard Jenkins in 1817; the third is what the absorbing school would advocate, but I should most deprecate. It would be most profitable for us, in a pecuniary point of view, but most injurious, I think, in a political one. It would tend to accelerate the crisis which the doctrines of that school must, sooner or later, bring upon us. Which course the Governor-General may prefer I know not.

Believe me,
My Dear Sir James,
Yours very faithfully
(Signed) W. H. SLEEMAN

To Sir James Weir Hogg, Bart.,
&c. &c. &c.

* * * * *

Lucknow, 12th January, 1853.

My Dear Sir,

I shall send you by this mail a copy of my Diary under cover, addressed, as you suggest, to Mr. Secretary Melvill. It is coarsely bound, as I could find no good binder here. I printed eighteen copies, and have sent one to Government, in Calcutta, for itself, and one for the Court of Directors; one to the Governor-General, and one each to the Chairman and Deputy-Chairman. I have also sent one to a brother, and one to each of my five children. All to whom I have sent it of my family have been enjoined to consider it as private and confidential, and they will do so. Government may publish any portion of it they please. A memorandum of errata has been added to the copy to be sent to you.

Over and above what you justly observe as to the cultivation and population not being much diminished, and the State not having incurred any public debt, I may mention the fact noticed, I believe, somewhere in the Diary, that the landed aristocracy of the half of Oude, reserved in 1801, has been better preserved than that of the half made over to us. Had they not combined generally against the Government, they would all have been crushed ere this, as ours have been. This makes me mention a school of too much influence in India, of whose doctrines I have a great abhorrence. They are best expounded by the so-called "Friend of India," in the last number of which (6th January, 1851) there is a rabid article on the subject worthy of your perusal, and that of all men interested in the welfare of India and the stability of our rule over it. It is in the true Machiavellian spirit, which justifies, or would persuade the world to justify, every means, however base, dishonest, and cruel, required to attain any object which they have persuaded themselves to be desirable for ourselves. This school is impatient at the existence of any native principality in India, however related to or dependent upon us. Mr. George Campbell is a disciple of this school, almost as rabid as the "Friend of India," as you will see in the fourth chapter of his book on "Modern India." If Mr. Marshman is to write the Indian articles for the "Times," as reports give out, you will see these doctrines advocated in that influential journal. The Court of Directors is the only safeguard of India, and of our stability in it, against those doctrine which, in my opinion, tend strongly to the injury of both; and its power may be rendered too powerless to shun them.

Believe me,
My Dear Sir,
Yours sincerely,
(Signed) W. H. SLEEMAN.

To Colonel Sykes,

Director Hon. East India Company,
London.

P.S.—I have felt much interested in the geology of Central and Southern India; and if you have seen any satisfactory account of the origin of the stratum which caps the basaltic plateau, shall feel obliged if you will point it out to me.

* * * * *

Lucknow, 24th April, 1853.

My Dear Sir,

By the last mail I received from a friend in London two articles, whose merits had been much canvassed at the clubs, one from the London "Times," of the 9th February, and the other from the "Daily News," a Manchester paper. The "Times" article must have been written by Mr. J. Marshman, or one of the most rabid members of the school of which he is the great organ, and whose chief characteristic is impatience at the existence of any native territorial chief or great landholder in India. The other article is a reply to it, and generally supposed to have been written by Sir George Clerk. I feel quite sure that it was written either by him or by Mr. T. C. Robertson, who preceded him in the government of our North-West Provinces. The article from the "Times" has been noticed in most of the Indian papers—the "Friend of India," April 7th, 1853, and the "Englishman," 15th April. But I have not seen that in the "Daily News" noticed in any Indian papers, though admirably written. I intended to send it to you, but have mislaid it. I think you can advocate the cause it adopts more consistently, more powerfully, and more wisely than any other editor now in India. I hope you will do so; for I consider the doctrines of the "Times" disgraceful to our morality, and dangerous to the stability of our rule. As I consider the welfare of the people of India to depend upon the stability of our rule, I am very anxious to see the fallacies of the atrocious doctrines which endanger it ably exposed. In no publication are these fallacies more obvious or more numerous than in Mr. George Campbell's "Modern India," chapter fourth, with, perhaps, the exception of the "Friend of India." With the "Friend," the theory of confiscation and annexation has become a disease, and he cannot praise or even tolerate any public officer or statesman who is not known to be a convert to the doctrines of this school.

I forget the date of the "Daily News" in which Sir George Clerk's article appeared, but it was immediately after the article appeared in the London "Times" of the 9th February. I hope you will give the article a prominent place in your paper, for it really deserves to be printed in letters of gold. Though I feel that the character of our nation, and our safety in India, are compromised by the open avowal of such atrocious doctrines in our leading journals, still the orders against officers in political employ writing in the papers are so strict, that I dare not attempt to expose the fallacies on which they are based, or express the indignation which they excite in me, in any public paper. To my superiors, and in the discharge of my public duties, I shall never cease to express my abhorrence of such doctrines, for I look upon them as worse than any that Machiavelli ever wrote.

Believe me,
Yours very sincerely,
(Signed) W. H. SLEEMAN.

To G. Buist, Esq.

P.S.—Of course, this note will be considered as confidential.

(Signed) W. H. S.

* * * * *

Lucknow, 24th April, 1853.
Dear Sir,

An article in your paper of the 15th instant, on the subject of the international law of India, has interested and pleased me much. It has reference to an article in the London "Times" of the 9th February last; and I write to invite your attention to an article which appeared in the "Daily News," a Manchester paper, in reply to it, written by Sir G. Clerk, lately Governor of Bombay. Both these articles have been much discussed at the London clubs, and the morality of the "Daily News" article has been very favourably contrasted with that of the article in the "Times." The article in the "Times" is supposed to have been penned by Mr. J. Marshman himself, or by one of the most rabid members of the school whose Machiavellian doctrine he advocates.

These doctrines are considered by some of our wisest statesmen to be as dangerous to the stability of our rule in India as they are disgraceful to our morality; and as these statesmen consider the well-being of the people of India to depend upon that stability, they are always glad to see their fallacies exposed and their iniquities indignantly denounced by the moat able and steady of our public journalists. I hope you will be able to find the able article in the "Daily News" to which I refer, and consent to give it a prominent place in the "Englishman." It was sent to me by a friend in London, but I have, unfortunately, mislaid it. This note will, of course, be considered as confidential.

Yours sincerely,
W. H. SLEEMAN.

To W. C. Harry, Esq.

* * * * *

Lucknow, 5th June, 1853.

My Lord,

I have read with great interest in the English journals your Lordship's able Minute on the Burmese war, and am glad that it has been published, as it cannot fail to disabuse the public mind at home, and bring about a reaction in the feeling of the people excited by some very unfair articles in the London "Times." I attributed these articles to the Napiers, who, however talented, are almost always wrong-headed.

I am persuaded that the new Sovereign will acquiesce in your possession of Pegu, and that he would not have ceded it by treaty under any circumstances. The old Sovereign might have done it, though at great risk, but the new Sovereign could not dare to do it.

Our own history affords us instances enough of powerful ministers anxious, for the public good, to get rid of conquered, but expensive and useless possessions, but deterred from proposing the measure by the dread of popular odium, which ambitious and factious rivals are always ready to excite.

There is one argument against the advance which I do not think that your Lordship has urged with the force of the rest. While the new Sovereign remains undisturbed in the rest of his dominions he will maintain his authority over them, and do his best to prevent our new frontier from being disturbed, knowing that we can advance to his capital and punish him if he does not. But, were he to be driven from his capital, all the rest of his dominions would soon fall into a state of anarchy, and our frontiers would soon be disturbed by leaders of disorderly bands, anxious to carve out principalities for themselves, and having no other means than plunder to maintain their followers. For the acts of such men we could hold no one responsible, after we had driven their Sovereign from his capital to the hills and jungles; and half a century might elapse before order could be restored. In the mean time, wealth would be growing up within our border to invite their aggression, while they would become poorer and poorer from disorders, and more and more anxious to seize upon it.

With regard to an advance upon Amarapoora, it will not be difficult after the rains, if circumstances render it necessary. The Madras cattle are much better for hard work and all climates than those of Bengal, and sufficient could be collected for the occasion by sea. Your Lordship's reasons for not trusting to steamers alone are unanswerable, and it seems impossible for a land and river force to act jointly. In this, we almost realize the contest between the winds and the moschettoes before the court of the genii in the Arabian tale: when the winds appeared, the moschettoes could not, and when they appeared, the winds could not. For the prestige of our own name in the rest of India, to advance to the capital and then give the rest of the country to the Sovereign might, perhaps, be the best; but for the security of our new acquisition, and that of the people of the rest of Burmah, it would certainly be better to stay where we are. The benefits of our rule might, by degrees, be imparted to that of the rest of Burmah. The Government would be obliged to treat their people better than they have done in order to keep them.

Here everything still is what I have described it to be so often; that is, as bad as it can be. The King is the same, and the officers and favourites whom he employs are the same. I shall not write public reports on the state of affairs till I learn that your Lordship wishes it, which will be, I conclude, when you have carried out your arrangements in Burmah.

The terrible war of races in China, to which I have been looking forward for some years, seems to be coming slowly on. I wrote to Sir H. M. Elliot about it some two or three years ago, and recommended him to write a better life than we have of Jungez Khan, in order to show what the Tartars now really are. When he led his swarms of them over China, Central Asia, and a great part of Europe, they worshipped the god of war; they now worship the god of peace: but there are millions of Lamas in Tartary who would change their crosiers for the sword at the call of a kindred genius, and are now impatient to do so, and prophesying his advent, just at the time that the rebels threaten the capital of China and the extinction of the Tartar dynasty. That dynasty will throw itself upon Tartary, and a new one will be raised by the successful leader.

> Your Lordship's faithful and obedient servant,
> (Signed) W. H. SLEEMAN.

> To the Most Noble
> The Marquis of Dalhousie, K.T.,
> Governor-General.

* * * * *

Lucknow, 24th June, 1853.

Dear Sir,

Your letter of the 20th instant perplexes me a good deal. I have no place in my own office to offer you, and I never recommended any one for employment to the King. You cannot, according to rules laid down for our guidance, act as an advocate in any case before the Resident or his assistants. All landholders in Oude, except the few whose estates are included in what is called the Hozoor Tuhseel, transact their business through the Amils, Chuckladars, and Nazims of districts, and have nothing to do directly with the Durbar at Lucknow. Having nothing to do with their affairs, I cannot have anything to say with the employment by them of wakeels, or advocates. They, the landholders, generally employ native wakeels, who are willing to bear a good deal of ill-treatment on the part of Durbar officials for the sake of very small salaries. Your situation as a wakeel on their part would be ill remunerated and exceedingly humiliating.

If the son of Ghalib Jung has offered to introduce you to the minister, and to assist in getting employment for you at Lucknow, he must, I think, do so in the hope of being able to make use of you in some intrigue; for those only who can aid in such intrigues are fostered and paid at

Lucknow. Honest men can get nothing, and find no employment about the Court. If you secure employment about the Court, I cannot hold any communication with you. I should compromise myself by doing so. In your situation, I would rather be a section writer in Calcutta, or at Agra, than hold any employment in the Oude Durbar that you can get by honest means. One of the tasks imposed on you would be, I conclude, to praise bad persons and things, and abuse good, in the newspapers. This, of course, you would not do, and you would be punished accordingly. I strongly advise you to have nothing to do with Oude at present.

Yours very truly,
(Signed) W. H. SLEEMAN.

To G. Norton, Esq.,
Azimgurh.

* * * * *

Lucknow, 11th August, 1853.

My Dear Sir,

Your brother, the late Lieut.-Colonel Ouseley, was a valued friend of mine. Before his appointment as Governor-General's Agent of the south-eastern frontier districts, he had for many years held the civil charge of different districts in the Sangor and Nerbudda territories. I had for many years the civil charge of districts bordering on those under his charge, and abundant opportunity of seeing how much he had made himself beloved, and the character of his Government respected, by the manner in which he conducted the duties confided to him.

When I became Commissioner over those territories in 1844, I passed through the districts which had so long been under his charge, and I can honestly say that I have never known a man who had made himself more beloved and revered by the people. Thousands of happy families were proud to acknowledge that they owed all their happiness to the careful and liberal revision of the settlement of the land-revenue made by him, in which he had provided for the interests of the higher and middle classes connected with the land, while he secured the rights of the humblest.

I visited at the same time the districts of those territories which bordered upon his then charge of the south-east frontier, and communed with many people from that quarter. They all spoke of him as beloved and respected by all classes as much in his then charge as he had been in his old one. In a country where it is the duty of every Englishman to make the character of his Government and his nation respected and beloved, one cannot but feel proud to hear a countryman and fellow-labourer spoken of by tens of thousands of respectable, contented, and happy people as your brother was and still is. I know no part of India where the people of all classes and all grades are so attached to our character and our Government as that of the Saugor and Nerbudda territories, and I believe that no man did more to establish that fine feeling than your brother.

Your brother's temper was warm, and he was not always happy in putting his thoughts and feelings to paper. Hence arose occasional misunderstandings with his official superiors. But while those superiors were men who could understand and appreciate his noble nature, such occasional misunderstandings never led to serious consequences. In the bitterness of his anguish, after his removal from the south-east frontier, he wrote to me; and it was most painful to me to feel that I was not in a position, or in circumstances, to advocate his cause, and describe the value of such a man as the representative of the Government and the national character among a wild and half-civilized people like those over whom he had been placed. I think it was on the representation of the late Mr. Launcelot Wilkinson, one of the most able and estimable members of the India Civil Service, that he was sent to the south-east frontier. He had seen his value in the Saugor and Nerbudda districts while he was political agent at Bhopaul, which bordered on the districts under your brother's charge.

It has been to me a source of much regret that I have not had it in my power to aid his son in getting employment in India.

Believe me,
Yours very truly,
(Signed) W. H. SLEEMAN.

To Major Ouseley, &c. &c.

* * * * *

Lucknow, 14th September, 1853.

Dear Sir,

The King of Oude will certainly not assist you to get up a newspaper at Lucknow; and you will certainly be disappointed if you come in expectation of such assistance from him. If you can get into his service in any other capacity, I am not aware of any objections to it, but as I have already told you and many others, I cannot recommend any one for employment under him. The humiliations to which honest and respectable Christians have to submit in his service, from the jealousies of influential persons about the Durbar, are such as few can or ought to submit to; and I certainly would not advise any one to enter such a service. Under whatever pledge or whatever influence they might enter it, their tenure of office and their pay would be altogether precarious, and the Resident would be unable to assist them in retaining the one or recovering the other.

Yours faithfully,
(Signed) W. H. SLEEMAN.

To G. Norton, Esq.

P.S.—The King of Oude and his family are in no danger from the British Government, on whose good faith they repose. I only wish that his honest and industrious subjects were as safe from the officers whom he employs in all branches of the administration, and from whom they are nowhere safe I fear.

(Signed) W. H. SLEEMAN.

* * * * *

Lucknow, 27th September, 1853.

My Dear James,

Under the circumstances you mention, I see but one course open to you; and that is, to recommend to the Government of Bombay to do as Lord William Bentinck did in the Bengal Presidency under similar circumstances, appoint a special Commissioner for the trial of offenders under Acts XX.[*sic*] of 1836, and XXIV. of 1843; or for the revision of trials under these Acts, conducted by Sessions' Judges.

The first would be the best if feasible; but the second would do, since the Sessions' Judges seem now to be disposed to give their aid to Government in putting down the evil, and the Sudder Judges do not. Formerly, I believe, the Sudder Judges were so disposed, and the Sessions Judges not. In my reply to the Government of Bombay, you will see reference made to Lord William's appointment of Mr. Stockwell as special Commissioner. He was at the time Commissioner of the Allahabad division, and the work was imposed upon him in addition to his other duties.

If the Bombay Government does not think it has authority to appoint such a special Commission, they may apply to the Legislative Council to pass an Act authorising the Government of every Presidency to appoint such a Commission when circumstances may render it necessary.

This will be better and safer than to frame and enforce new rules of evidence for the guidance of existing Judicial Courts. The one would be for a special emergency, and temporary; and Government would not be very averse to it; but the other they certainly would not venture upon, particularly at this time. A great fuss would be made about it here and at home; and lawyers are too influential in both places.

You can show that there is no alternative—that this system of crime must be left to prosper in the Bombay Presidency, where alone it now prevails, or such a Commission must be appointed; and as the Acts and the machinery for giving effect to them have succeeded in putting it down in all the rest, it would be hard to leave the people of Bombay exposed to all the evils arising from the want of such a special Commission. Such Commissions have been adopted to relieve the people from the hardships of the resumption laws, which affected but a small portion of the community; and you hope it would not be considered unreasonable in you to propose one for the relief of the whole community; for the life and property of no family will be safe an hour, if these classes of offenders by hereditary profession are assured that they may carry on their trade with impunity, as they must be if your agency be withdrawn, and all the prisoners be released.

If you make a forcible representation to the Bombay Government in this strong case, they will adopt the measure if they have the power, or ask the power from the supreme Government; and I think the supreme Government will give it. I would say a special Commission for the trial of commitments under XXX. of 1836, and XXIV. of 1843, or a special Commission for the revision of trials under these Acts, as may seem best to Government; but you can say that you think the first would answer the purpose best in the Bombay Presidency. You may offer to run down to Bombay and submit your views to the Government in Council if required. They would not think it necessary, but would be pleased with the offer. Where men are committed on the general charge, it has always been thought necessary to show that the gang committed a murder or a robbery, though it is not so to show what part the prisoners took in them. If your assistant has not done this, he has failed in a material point. He should be very cautious in dealing with whole classes. The fault of our Bombay assistants has always been a disposition to make offenders of whole classes, when only some of the members are so.

You must make your best of the present case—show the necessity of the remedy clearly, and urge it respectfully without pretending to find fault with the Judges; merely say that their interpretation of the laws of evidence laid down for their guidance, however conscientious, forms an insurmountable obstacle to the conviction of offenders by hereditary profession, whose system has been founded upon the experience of their ancestors in the most successful modes of defeating these laws, and the technicalities of ordinary Judicial Courts. This is, I think, all that I can say on the subject at present. The Moncktons leave us this evening, and Amelie intends to set out for the hills on the 6th proximo.

Yours affectionately,
(Signed) W. H. SLEEMAN.

To Captain J. Sleeman.

* * * * *

Lucknow, 28th September, 1853.

My Dear James,

On further consideration, I think that you should say nothing about the second proposal of a special Commissioner to revise the trials of offenders tried by Sessions Judges. You should suggest the first proposal of a special Commissioner to try all prisoners committed for trial under Acts XXX. of 1836, and XXIV. of 1843, and perhaps also XI. of 1841. See my Printed Report, page 357.

You may mention that such Commissioner should be required to submit his sentences for the consideration and final orders of Government, as all political officers did till March, 1835; or merely for the information of Government, as political officers did after that time.

On the 23rd of March, 1835, the Secretary to the Government of India forwarded to the Resident of Lucknow, for his guidance, the copy of a letter addressed on that date to the Agent of the Governor-General in the Saugor and Nerbudda territories, requesting that he would carry into execution his sentences on Thugs, and not make any reference to Government for confirmation, but merely submit to Government abstract statements of sentences; but desiring that the sanction of the King of Oude should be required before any capital sentence was carried into effect. No capital sentence was from that time passed. As all prisoners will be tried on the general charge, no capital sentence will ever be passed by the special Commissioner, and the Bombay Government may be disposed to give him the same orders. But the Governor in Council at Bombay will be the best judge of that.

Lord Falkland may possibly be deterred by apprehensions that late events may have altered the tone of feeling at home towards him; but I am persuaded that he would be glad to carry this measure into effect. I will send you a copy of the Government letter to the Resident here; and you may get from the agent's office a copy of that sent on the same date to him, though you may not readily find that office under the new arrangements. You will, I think, have a strong case, and I wish you success in it.

Yours affectionately,
(Signed) W. H. SLEEMAN.

To Captain Jas. Sleeman.

* * * * *

Lucknow, 4th November, 1853.

My Dear Malcolm,

I should recommend for the Baee a money stipend for life of five thousand rupees a-month, with the understanding that if she adopted a child she would have to provide for him out of her savings from this stipend, and out of her private property. All the Rajah's private property, save what he may will away to others, will of course be left to her, to be disposed of as she may think fit. But this stipend should be independent of those to be continued to the stipendiaries of the Rajah. There are several who have nothing else to depend on but the stipends which they now receive from the Rajah; and it must be borne in mind that they have no longer Bajee Rao, Benaek Rao, the Jhansi and Saugor chief, to go to. This will be the last of the Brahmin dynasties founded in that part of the world by the Peshwas. Our Government should therefore be liberal in taking possession of the estate as an escheat.

The Mahratta language in accounts should at once be done away with; but out of the revenues of the estate, Government should found a good school for English and Hindoo, and Persian; and, above all, for a very good hospital and dispensary, under well educated and tried surgeons, native and European, capable of throwing out branches.

All the public officers of the Rajah should have stipends or employment, or both, in proportion to their period of service and respectability. If they take employment the stipends should be deducted from their salaries while in office, as in our own service.

In the case of the Baee Regent at Saugor, we continued a small part of her pension to her adopted son,—one thousand rupees a-month,— to enable him to provide for her non-pensioned dependents. We took the management long before her death, and left her only a private lady, with a large pension of, I think, eight thousand rupees a-month; besides pensions—too large—to the family of her manager, Benaek Rao: this will be unnecessary at Jhansi. All the large hereditary landholders of the Jhansi estate should have liberal settlements at fixed rates. They are all from the landed aristocracy of Bundelcund, and should be treated with consideration. The first settlement of the land revenue should be very moderate. The lands will lose the most valuable market for their produce in the breaking up of the Court and establishment of the Rajah at the capital, and yield less money, &c., than before. This must be borne in mind.

You may freely use these my views as you think best on the Jhansi question.

As to the management, I should make as little changes possible, till the final orders arrive from the Court of Directors, that you may have nothing to undo of what you have done. I would leave the management to Ellis, under your supervision, and interfere only on references in special cases, except, of course, on emergency. I know not what the system is to be, or what system the Governor-General has recommended, except that there is to be one head, as in Rajpootana; and that all correspondence with Government is to go through that head, In this state of the matter I know not what to suggest or say.

Yours sincerely,
(Signed) W. H. SLEEMAN.

To Major Malcolm,
&c. &c.

* * * * *

Lucknow, 11th November, 1853.

My Lord,

I feel grateful for your Lordship's letter of the 27th ult., but cannot say that I have any hope of discovering the instruments employed, or the employer, in the late affair. The whole power of the Government is in the hands of men who are deeply interested in concealing the truth, and making it appear that no attempt was really made. The minister has, by his intrigues, put himself so much in the power of the knave whom I suspect, that he dares not do anything to offend him. The man could at once ruin him by his exposures if he chose, and he would do so if he found it necessary for his own security. The man is biding his time, as he has often done with former ministers; and the time would have come ere this had not the King, to save himself, married one of the minister's pretty daughters.

The King's chief consort; was the niece of the minister, and her son is the heir-apparent; so that it was her interest, and that of her uncle, the minister, to get rid of the King as soon as possible. She is a profligate woman, and the King's mother is supposed to have given him a hint of his danger. He took a liking to one of the daughters, and married her, in order to make it the minister's interest to keep him alive as long as possible. He now contrives to make the King believe that neither his life nor reign can be in any danger as long as he is in his present position.

The night after this affair took place, a sipahee of the 35th Native Infantry, standing sentry at one end of the house, fell asleep while he was leaning with his right wrist on the muzzle of his musket. The musket went off; the ball passed through his wrist, grazed a large beam above him, struck against a stone in the roof of the portico, and fell down flattened by the side of the sentry, as he lay insensible and bleeding on the ground below. The wrist was sahttered,[*sic*] and several of the arteries cut through. He bled profusely, and when taken up he talked incoherently, declaring that some man had fired at him from behind the railing, twenty paces off. I have seen similar cases of incoherency, arising from a similar cause. As soon as day appeared the ball was found, and its marks on the beam and stone above showed the real state of the case. His right knee was probably leaning on the lock of the musket when he fell asleep. I have made no public or official report of this circumstance to Government.

I have now before me a curious instance of the difficulty of getting at the truth when it is the interest of the minister and others about this

Court to prevent it. A wanton attack was made in April last by about one hundred armed men, led by one of the King's collectors, on a native British subject coming from Cawnpore to visit a brother in Oude. The man himself received a wound, from which he some days afterwards died at Cawnpore; two of his attendants were killed, and twenty thousand rupees were taken from him. I have investigated the case myself, with the aid of my assistant, Captain Hayes, and with the attendance of an assessor on the part of the King. The case is a very clear one, but they have produced about thirty witnesses to swear that no man of the poor merchant's party was hurt; and that, instead of being attacked, he invaded the Oude territory with more than one hundred armed followers, and wantonly attacked the King's party of only fifteen unoffending men, while engaged in the discharge of their duty in collecting the revenue. I have translated the depositions with the prospect of having ultimately to submit the case to Government, unless the King consents to punish the offenders and afford redress. The assessor, an old man, bewildered by the conflicting testimony, and anxious to escape from all responsibility, slept soundly through the greater part of the inquiry, which has been a very tedious one.

I remain, your Lordship's
Most obedient and humble servant,
(Signed) W. H. SLEEMAN.

To the Most Noble
the Governor-General of India.

* * * * *

Lucknow, 28th December, 1853.

My Dear Mr. Colvin,

I was glad to see your handwriting again, and to find that time had made so little alteration in it. Oude affairs are, as you suppose, much as they used to be, save that the King is now persuaded by his minister and favourite that, had his predecessors had men and women about them so wise as they are, they never would have acted as if they believed that the Government of India ever really intended to carry into effect the penalty of misgovernment, so often threatened. Our Government has cried "wolf" so often that no one now listens to it. The King is an utter imbecile, from over-indulgences of all kinds; and the knaves whom he employs in his administration contrive to persuade him that the preservation of his life and throne depends entirely upon their vigilance and his doing nothing. Had I come here when the treasury was full, and Naseer-od Doon Hyder was anxious to spend his money in the manner best calculated to do good and please our Government, I might have covered Oude with useful public works, and much do I regret that I came here to throw away some of the best years of my life among such a set of knaves and fools as I have to deal with.

I think you will do much good in your present charge in the subject to which you refer. In the matter of discourtesy to the native gentry, I can only say that Robert Martin Bird insulted them whenever he had the opportunity of doing so; and that Mr. Thomason was too apt to imitate him in this as in other things. Of course their example was followed by too many of their followers and admirers; but, like you, I have been delighted to see a great many of the elder members of the civil service, in spite of these bad examples, treat the native gentry with all possible courtesy, and show them that they had their sympathy as long as they deserved it by their conduct.

It has always struck me that Mr. Thomason, in his system, did all he could to discourage the growth of a middle and upper class upon the land—the only kind of property on which a good upper and middle class could be sustained in the present state of society in India. His village republics and the Ryutwar system of Sir Thomas Munro had precisely the same tendency to subdivide minutely property in land, and reduce all landholders to the common level of impoverishment. The only difference was that the impoverished tenants in the North-Western Provinces were supposed to manage their own affairs, while those at Madras had them managed by a very mischievous class of native public officers. He (Mr. Thomason) would have forced his village republics upon any new country or jungle that came under his charge, and thereby rendered improvement impossible. I would have introduced into all such new countries a system of paternal government in imitation of our Government of India itself, which would have rendered improvement certain, and the growth of a middle and higher class no less so. He would have put the whole under our judicial courts, and thereby have created a middle class of pettifogging attorneys to swallow up all the surplus produce of the land. I would have kept the whole of the land in the hands of our fiscal courts, by making it all leasehold property, and maintaining the law of primogeniture in all estates of villages. Mr. Thomason, I am told, systematically set aside all the landed aristocracy of the country as a set of middlemen, superfluous and mischievous.

The only part of our India in which I have seen a middle and higher class maintained upon the land is the moderately-settled districts of the Saugor and Nerbudda territories; and there is no part of India where our Government and character are so much beloved and respected. You have sent Mr. Read to that part; and if he be bigoted to Mr. Thomason's system, he will upset all this, and, in my opinion, lay the foundation of much evil. We found a system of paternal government in every village, and maintained and improved it. They were all little principalities; and by the printed rules of the Sudder Board of Revenue, which are very good, all the sub-tenants were effectually secured in their rights.

In making a tour through Oude in the end of 1849 and beginning of 1850 I had a good deal of talk with the people. Many of them had sojourned in our territories in seasons of disturbance. The general impression was that they would be glad to see the country taken under British management, provided we could dispense with our tedious procedure in civil cases. They all had a very unfavourable impression of our civil courts, and of the cost and delay of the procedure. Mills and Harrington, to whom the duty, which was to have devolved on you, has been confided, may do much good, and I hope will, for there really is nothing in our system which calls so much for remedy. I am persuaded that, if it were to be put to the vote among the people of Oude, ninety-nine in a hundred would rather remain as they are, without any feeling of security in life or property, than have our system introduced in its present complicated state; but that ninety-nine in a hundred would rather have our Government than live as they do, if a more simple system, which they could understand, were promised at the same time.

In 1801, when the Oude territory was divided, and half taken by us and half left to Oude, the landed aristocracy of each were about equal. Now hardly a family of this class remains in our half, while in Oude it remains unimpaired. Everybody in Oude believes those families to have been systematically crushed. If by-and-by we can get the people to take an interest in our railroads, and outlays upon other great public works, it will tend to create the middle class upon which I set so much value, and to give that feeling of interest in the stability of our rule which we so much require. We shall then have objects of common interest to talk and think about, and become more united with them in feeling.

Maddock is in Ceylon, but intends to return by the steamer which is to leave Calcutta on the 5th proximo. His speculations there have been failures. Had he looked after his estates there instead of joining the effete party of the Derbyites he might have done well. He has made great mistakes, and he now suffers for them. His support of Lord Torrington was his first.

Believe me,
Yours very sincerely,
(Signed) W. H. SLEEMAN.

To Mr. Colvin.

* * * * *

Lucknow, 5th March, 1854.

My Dear Low,

I have to-day written to Government a letter, which you will of course see, on the subject of a proposal made to me by Mr. B. Government will, I have no doubt, consider the reason assigned by me for refusing to permit him to send an European agent to Lucknow, ostensibly to collect debts, sufficient; but whether it will consent to adopt my suggestion, and empower the Resident to assure the King that it will not again consent to permit Mr. B. to return and reside at Lucknow, after he has been twice expelled for his misdeeds, I know not. One thing is certain, that his residence at Cawnpore, under the assurance from the minister that he shall come back and be made wealthy if he can aid in getting rid of the Resident, is very mischievous.

B., Wasee Allee, and the Minister, succeeded in persuading the King that Shurfod Dowla, and all the most respectable members of the Lucknow aristocracy, had signed a memorial to the Government of India, praying that it would set aside the present King as an incompetent fool, and put Mostafa Alee on the throne in his place. All this was reported by me to Government on the 2nd of March, 1853.

The seals were all forged or filched here at Lucknow, but the papers were written in Calcutta, under the agency, I believe, of Synd Jan, Sir H. E.'s moonshee, from Bilgram, where his family have long enjoyed an estate rent-free, for the aid he has given to the minister in his intrigues. I have never been able to remove this delusion from the mind of the imbecile King; and it is the "*raw*" on which these knaves have been ever since acting; for it enables the minister to persuade him that his vigilance alone preserves his life and crown.

The minister is aware that I know all this, and may some day be able to show the King how he has been deluded and befooled by him; and he would give all he is worth to get rid of me in any way. He would give any sums to B. and his other agents to bribe editors to write against me; but the only editors who have yielded have been those of the "Mofussilite," before Mr. C. took the management. Mr. B. complains at Cawnpore, that he gave Mr. L. a large sum to do his dirty work at home; but that he did nothing for it. This is not unlikely. That the minister and Wasee Alee got up the attempt at the Residency, either to make away with me, or to alarm me into going away, I am persuaded; but to get judicial proof of it I shall not attempt. It would be vain here, where the minister has all the revenues of the State to work with.

All the native gentlemen whose seals were forged to this document, look to me for protection; and they have been ever since in a state of great alarm. It was to keep up this alarm that they tried to turn Shurfod Dowla out of Oude. I had rarely seen him before that time; and I have only seen him once since he went to the cantonments; and then only for five minutes during my walk in the garden, to talk about Mulki Jahan's affairs. They punish any one who ventures to approach the King; and they would ruin any one who ventured to approach the Resident if they could, lest he might open the eyes of the King to the iniquities they commit. The troops are starved, and almost all the old members of the royal family, who had no Government paper or guarantees, have been already starved or driven out. Oude has never before been afflicted by a Sovereign so utterly imbecile and regardless of his duties and the sufferings of his people; nor has there ever been a minister so utterly regardless of his own reputation and that of his master. He bribes with money, power, and patronage, every one who has access to the King, to sound his praise in prose or verse; and the King is persuaded that his life and throne depend upon his abstaining altogether, from interfering in the conduct of affairs.

When I was in the Governor-Generals camp at Futtehgur, M. H., the son of S. A. K., came there armed, I knew, with four lacs of rupees. He was an old acquaintance of E.'s, and he (E.) told me that he had asked for an interview, and asked me whether he ought to consent to see him. I told him that, if he did see him, he must make up his mind to the man's persuading the King that he had given him the greater part of the money, though the man himself kept all that he did not give to his moonshee. He refused to see the man; but he has ever since been with Mr. L. at Allahabad, intriguing with his people to chouse men out of their ancient possessions; or with the Oude people, to keep up the *raw* they have established on the King's mind. The King, by over-indulgence, has reduced his intellect below the standard of that of a boy of five years of age. It is painful to talk to a man with a mind so utterly emasculated.

Our Government would be fully authorized at any time to enforce the penalty prescribed in your treaty of 1837, and it incurs great odium and obloquy for not enforcing it. But Lord D. has, no doubt, solid reasons for not taking such responsibility upon himself at this time. I do all I can to save the people, and the people are sensible of what I do, and grateful for it; for the Resident is the only person they can look up to with any hope. If Government can comply with my wish to have the King assured that it will not permit Mr. B. to return and reside at Lucknow again, it will be of great use to me and to the people, for the hopes held out to him are like a premium offered for my head, or for my ruin; and one never feels very comfortable under such offers, at any time or in any country. The reckless lies which this man gets adventurers at Cawnpore to write for him, and careless or corrupt editors to publish, are apt to stagger those who do not know the vile character of the individual, or the true nature of the facts referred to.

I am glad you saw W. He is a man of high character and first-rate ability, and has abundance of sagacity and energy. I miss him very much. He will be a credit to his regiment if engaged on active service.

Yours sincerely,
(Signed) W. H. SLEEMAN.

To Colonel Low, C.B.

P.S.—I shall say nothing in this of your domestic bereavement, though I have felt much for you.

W. H. S.

In my public letter, I have referred to that of the Marquess of W. to L., when he was Resident. Do refer to it Page 388, Vol. 1., "Despatches."

* * * * *

Lucknow, 1st June, 1854.

My Dear Low,

In my letter of the 10th of November, 1853, I solicited permission to retain Weston with me for reasons stated therein. In reply, I was told, in Mr. Dalrymple's letter of the 2nd of December, "that the Governor-General in Council had every wish to consult my views, but, for the present at least, his Lordship in Council thinks that Lieutenant Weston must in fairness be required to join his regiment, like other officers."

I am so very anxious to have his services again in the office he filled, that I have to-day ventured, in a public letter to the Foreign Secretary, to request that he will submit my wishes to the Governor-General in Council, should they deem the state of affairs in Burmah at present to be such as to admit of his being withdrawn from his regiment I have said, in my public letter, that should any exigency arise he could, of course, quickly join his regiment on service again.

If you can give me any assistance in obtaining his services, I shall feel very much indebted to you, for I have that confidence in his abilities and high-mindedness which I cannot feel in those of his *locum tenens*; and I am very anxious to keep things in good train here till the end of the cold weather, when I must go on leave to recruit. I am really in a very difficult position here, not with regard to the King, for he has, I believe, entire confidence in me; but he has become so entangled with his minister, that he is afraid of him; and the minister would give all he has (and he has all the revenues of the country) to get me out of the way.

I carried the Government orders regarding Shurfod Dowla into effect, and he is now, with his family, quiet and safe. The King behaved very well, and resisted all the attempts of the minister to persuade him to remonstrate. I am to-day to submit Shurfod Dowla's letter of grateful thanks to Government. I hope Government will not write to him in reply, as this might mortify and vex the King, since he is not written to by the Governor-General.

I think I told you of the *raw* the minister, Wasee Alee and Co., had established on the King's mind—the belief that a party of the members of the royal family and native gentlemen at Lucknow had been trying to persuade Government to set him aside, and put his reputed brother, Mostafa Alee, on the throne. Whenever they want to make the King angry with any one, they tell him that he is a leader in this cabal. But the King is, by degrees, growing out of this folly. There never was on the throne, I believe, a man more inoffensive at heart than he is; and he is quite sensible of my anxious desire to advise him rightly, and see justice done in all cases. But I am a sad stumbling-block to the minister and the other bad and incompetent officers employed in the administration.

If you wish it, I will be more circumstantial about Weston's *locum tenens*, Lieut. B., of the 1st Cavalry. For his own repute, and that of the Government, I think the less he has to do with the political department the better. He would be better in a military staff appointment than a political one.

> Yours sincerely,
> (Signed) W. H. SLEEMAN.

> To the Hon. Colonel Low, C.B.

* * * * *

Lucknow, 11th September, 1854.

My Lord,

The post which this morning brought me your Lordship's letter of the 6th instant brought me also one from Bombay, which I enclose for your Lordship's perusal. Should you think it worth while, Colonel Outram will be able to sift the matter to which it refers. I have long been aware of the intrigue, and have taken care to let the King know that I am so; but as I knew, at the same time, that the object was merely to get money out of him, and to strengthen his confidence in his minister, which had begun to give way, I did not think it necessary to trouble your Lordship with any reference on the subject. I knew that letters had been forged as from the King of Persia to the King of Oude, proposing to divide Hindoostan between them, and I thought it to be my duty to tell him so, in order to warn him; but, as he denied ever having received such letters, I told him that I should take the word of a King, and say no more about it. He is certainly not of sound mind, and things must, ere long, come to a crisis. His mind may have been of an average kind when he was young, but it has long become emasculated by over-indulgence; and the minister and his minions can make him believe or do what they please. They know that it cannot last long, and they have agents in Bombay and Calcutta to assist them in fleecing the King of money on all manner of false pretences.

The minister, a consummate knave, and one of the most incompetent men of business that I have ever known, has all the revenues and patronage of the country to distribute among those who have access to the King exclusively—they are poets, fiddlers, eunuchs, and profligate women; and every one of them holds, directly or indirectly, some court or other, fiscal, criminal, or civil, through which to fleece the people. Anything so detestable as the Government I have nowhere witnessed, and a man less competent to govern them than the King I have never known.

Had your Lordship left the choice of a successor to me, I should have pointed out Colonel Outram; and I feel very much rejoiced that he has been selected for the office, and I hope he will come as soon as possible. There are many honest men at Lucknow, and a finer peasantry no country can boast. But no honest man can obtain or retain office under Government with the present minister and heads of departments.

But where the whole revenues of a fine country are available to suborn witnesses to prove the King to be a *Solomon*, no Resident would be able to find judicial proof of his being a fool; but that he is so I have had abundance of, to me, satisfactory evidence ever since I have been here. It must soon, however, become clear, without the Resident's efforts to make it so. Where the Government of India is so solemnly pledged to see justice done to the people of a country, it cannot fairly permit them to be reigned over much longer by so incompetent a Sovereign. Proofs enough of bad government and neglected duties were given in my Diary; and a picture more true was, I believe, never drawn of any country. The duty of remedying the evils, and carrying out your Lordship's views in Oude, whatever they may be, must now devolve on another.

No one of my present assistants knows anything whatever about Oude, its Government, or its people; and Colonel Outram will, therefore, labour under great disadvantages. I hope, therefore, that your Lordship will pardon the liberty I take in suggesting that he be allowed the aid of Captain Weston. He went over the whole of Oude with me, and knows almost all who have made themselves prominent for good or for evil within the last five years. I know that, as soon as I go, some of the most atrocious villains whom I have kept out of office will try to purchase their way back; and there is no man too bad for the minister, provided he pays for his restoration.—The murderer of the banker, mentioned in my Diary, vol. i., p. 131, and the murderer of thousands mentioned in the same volume. Captain Weston is high minded, sagacious, energetic, hard-working, conciliatory and, to Colonel Outram, his services in the new charge would be invaluable.

I have the honour to remain,
Your Lordship's faithful and obedient servant,
(Signed) W. H. SLEEMAN.

To the Most Noble
The Marquis of Dalhousie, K.T.
Governor-General.

THE END.

BIBLIOBAZAAR

The essential book market!

Did you know that you can get any of our titles in large print?

Did you know that we have an ever-growing collection of books in many languages?

**Order online:
www.bibliobazaar.com**

Find all of your favorite classic books!

Stay up to date with the latest government reports!

At BiblioBazaar, we aim to make knowledge more accessible by making thousands of titles available to you- *quickly and affordably*.

Contact us:
BiblioBazaar
PO Box 21206
Charleston, SC 29413